AF412355

# Goethe Yearbook

Goethe Yearbook

# Goethe Yearbook

Publications of the Goethe Society
of North America

Edited by
Patricia Anne Simpson
(University of Nebraska-Lincoln)
and
Birgit Tautz
(Bowdoin College)

With Sean Franzel
Book Review Editor
(University of Missouri-Columbia)

Volume XXVIII

 CAMDEN HOUSE

Manuscripts for consideration by the *Goethe Yearbook* should be directed to
Patricia Anne Simpson (psimpson4@unl.edu) at the Department of
Modern Languages and Literatures, 1111 Oldfather Hall,
University of Nebraska-Lincoln, NE 68588-0315
or
Birgit Tautz (btautz@bowdoin.edu) at the Department of German,
Bowdoin College, 7700 College Station, Brunswick, ME 04011-8477

Books for review should be sent to Sean Franzel (franzels@missouri.edu)
at the Department of German and Russian Studies, University of
Missouri-Columbia, 451 Strickland Hall, Columbia, MO 65211-4170

Additional information on the Goethe Society of North America can be found
on the World Wide Web at https://www.goethesociety.org



First published 2021 by
Camden House

Camden House is an imprint of Boydell & Brewer Inc.
668 Mt. Hope Ave., Rochester, NY 14620, USA
and of Boydell & Brewer Limited
P.O. Box 9, Woodbridge, Suffolk, IP12 3DF, UK
www.boydellandbrewer.com

ISSN: 0734-3329
ISBN-13: 978-1-64014-095-0

Set in Garamond Book and Garamond Ultra type
and printed on acid-free paper.
Manufactured and bound for maximum durability.
Printed in the United States of America.

Designed and typeset by Mizpah Publishing Services Private Limited.

# Contents

## Forum: (New) Directions in Eighteenth-Century German Studies

## Book Reviews

PATRICIA ANNE SIMPSON AND BIRGIT TAUTZ

# Editors' Preface

VIRTUALLY EVERY ASPECT of our professional and political lives has changed dramatically over the past year, and the compilation and production of this volume is no exception. The Covid-19 pandemic hit hard just as we were fielding readers' reports, granting extensions, and embracing the arrival of late submissions. For these and other reasons, we are especially grateful for the support and enthusiasm of our colleagues—contributors, readers, and Camden House editors. Without the collective effort, we would not have been able to produce such a robust volume.

The pandemic also affected planning processes beyond this issue of the *Goethe Yearbook*, as the Atkins Goethe Conference, organized around the theme "Goethe's Things," had to be postponed until 2021. Despite the challenges, Volume 28 presents a wide spectrum of scholarly interventions into eighteenth-century Goethe and German studies from established and emerging scholars across multiple disciplines. Every article breaks new ground on the German literary landscape around 1800 by presenting original research in a global context, widening the lens on conventional approaches, or revisiting and revising theoretical frameworks. Sheila Dickson's engagement with K. P. Moritz speaks to an ever-abiding interest in the writer, while Martin Wagner casts new light on vice and variation in eighteenth-century comedy. Karin Schutjer's reading of *Xenien* pushes the refresh button on the reading of well-worn texts. Invoking the scope of Atkins Conferences past, Daniel Purdy's substantive piece on relationships between eighteenth-century Nanjing and Weimar takes us back to persistent "reorientations" around Goethe. Contributions by Matthew Feminella on masks, Anna Christine Spafford on embarrassment in *Die Wahlverwandtschaften*, and Carrie Collenberg-González on the daisy oracle in *Faust* each illuminate new perspectives on canonical genres and texts through their innovative approaches.

Several articles take us beyond the realm of the textual. With a focus on magic and music, Hans Lind reconsiders the *Zauberflöte* in the late eighteenth century. From the realm of Goethe as a collector and creator, Lesley Fulton elaborates on the Hemsterhuis gem collection and its possible impact on aesthetics. Monika Nenon applies media theory to eighteenth-century adaptations of novels. Ilinca Iurescu previews—albeit unintentionally—the focus of the 2021 Atkins Conference in Chicago with her richly suggestive and substantive submission on "paper thinking" and pedagogy in the nineteenth century. Elisabeth Krimmer reads Napoleon through the lens of

Goethe and Caroline de la Motte Fouqué, casting new light on the emperor's image. Robert Kelz's extensive chronicle of German classical ideas and Goethe as icon in interwar Latin America takes us into the twentieth century in the first of a two-part series on Goethe Years. Continuing with the impact of German-language culture on the last century, Ethan Blass's article features the resonances between Goethe's "Erlkönig" and Hitchcock's cinema. We are proud to again present exciting research and to discuss position papers on new directions and trends in the Forum for Volume 28, which focuses on "(New) Directions in Eighteenth-Century German Studies." Covering considerable territory, contributions by Stephanie M. Hilger, Eleoma Bodammer, Mary-Helen Dupree, Peter Höyng, Obenewaa Oduro-Opuni, Matthew H. Birkhold, Brent Petersen, and Bridget Swanson remove borders from the discipline and invite new perspectives from medical humanities and disability studies to decoloniality, the law, and the environment. We round out the volume with the book review section and take a moment to pause and appreciate the scholarship that lends such vibrancy to our profession.

The scope of research on Goethe, his contemporaries, and his legacies is impressive as is the always remarkable and increasing diversity of contributors; colleagues at all ranks and from either side of the Atlantic submitted their work, which we are privileged to feature here.

*University of Nebraska-Lincoln*
*Bowdoin College*

SHEILA DICKSON

# Eclectic Dichotomies in K. P. Moritz's Aesthetic, Pedagogical, and Therapeutic Worlds

**Abstract:** Karl Philipp Moritz's highly abstract aesthetic theories of the sublime and of artistic autonomy, the honest, pragmatic self-reflection in his autobiographical novel *Anton Reiser*, and his pioneering edited collection of psychological case histories in the *Magazin zur Erfahrungsseelenkunde* approach concepts such as perfection, harmony, and balance through dichotomies such as objectivity/subjectivity, creation/destruction, health/illness, and beauty/desolation. For this reason, Moritz focused on self-development and on perfecting and creating beauty as dynamic processes rather than goals, as negative dialectics that remove that which is expedient in order to uncover what is innate. Moritz wished to understand the function of beauty on the psyche in order to make it useful to mankind and to highlight the value of each human being; however, he simultaneously recognized, was on occasion overwhelmed by, and, in essence, acknowledged the pernicious dissension of human existence. The aim of this essay is to demonstrate how this so-called outsider figure, who still struggles to be accepted into the canon, engaged creatively with the new anthropological worldview—which itself eclectically brought together aesthetics, philosophy, pedagogy, and (avant la lettre) psychology—and contributed substantially to the debate.

**Keywords:** Karl Philipp Moritz, aesthetic theory, psychological case histories, autobiography, pedagogy, perfection as process

KARL PHILIPP MORITZ's publications range from pedagogical and stylistic tracts to prose, drama, and poetry, from travelogues to classical scholarship, from aesthetic theory to psychological and therapeutic case studies. While Moritz's interest in these various topics changed over the course of his life, he did not compartmentalize them, and it can be argued that each informed the other.[1] However, rather than postulating a resulting consensus or consistency, what follows will highlight a series of dichotomies in Moritz's work; what seem like contradictions in fact illustrate the complexity and interdisciplinarity of his thought.

I will principally refer to the novel *Anton Reiser*, as Moritz's most successful work of literature; to the journal *Magazin zur Erfahrungsseelenkunde*

(Journal of Empirical Psychology), as his pathbreaking editing venture in the emerging area of empirical psychology and to which he also contributed as an author; and to his aesthetic writings, as the most directly influential of his works on a range of illustrious contemporaries representing both Weimar classicism and Romanticism. Even a fairly cursory overview highlights many links between these works: Moritz's novel has been interpreted as a narrative of illness or a medical case history; the journal includes contributions on education, discussions of narrative style, and responses to literature and art, as well as psychological case histories; and the essays on aesthetics reframe positions on literature, art, psychology, pedagogy, and therapy in highly abstract terms. They all include important theoretical, self-reflective statements that illustrate Moritz's self-understanding, aims, and objectives and thus allow us to judge his diverse output by his own standards, to consider how the different areas impact on each other, and to acknowledge the equivocality of each part as well as the whole.

In order to appreciate Moritz's contribution to debates on aesthetics, pedagogy, and psychology, it is necessary in each case to first establish his engagement with the ideas of his contemporaries. The introduction to *Anton Reiser* makes reference to Friedrich Blankenburg's influential theory of the novel in its comments on learning about oneself (psychology) and teaching others (pedagogy):

> **Blankenburg:** Wenn der Dichter nicht das Verdienst hat, daß er das *Innere* des Menschen aufklärt, und ihn sich selber kennen lehrt: so hat er gerade—gar keins.[2]

> If the poet does not have the merit of illuminating the *inner self* of man and teaching him to know himself, then he really has—none at all.

> **Moritz:** [das Buch soll] vorzüglich die *innere* Geschichte des Menschen schildern ... [es soll] vorzüglich in pädagogischer Rücksicht ... den Blick der Seele in sich selber schärfen ... die Aufmerksamkeit des Menschen mehr auf den Menschen selbst ... heften, und ihm sein individuelles Daseyn wichtiger , , , machen.[3]

> [the book's main purpose] is to describe man's internal history ... [it is intended] especially from an educational viewpoint , , , to give the soul a sharper insight into itself ... to direct man's attention to man himself and to make him attach more importance to his individual existence.

Blankenburg's ideas had pointed firmly in the direction of the *Bildungsroman*: "Der Dichter soll die Empfindungen *bilden*; er soll es uns lehren, was werth sey, geschätzt und geachtet, so wie gehaßt und verabscheuet zu werden. Er soll unsre Empfindungen nicht irre leiten; sondern uns Gelegenheit verschaffen, sie an würdigen Gegenständen zu üben" (Blankenburg 435; The poet should *educate* emotions; he should teach us what is worthy of being valued and respected along with what should be hated and despised. He must not lead our emotions astray, rather, he should provide us with the opportunity to practice them on worthy objects, emphasis in original). In order to do this, according to Blankenburg, "wird ein Geist erfordert, der das Ganze zu übersehen vermag" (Blankenburg 62; a mind is required that is able to oversee the whole). Leaving aside Blankenburg's terminology—he is referring to the author and not to the twentieth-century textual construct of the narrator[4]—it can be said that his theory posits what would now be termed a heterodiegetic or third-person narrator as the only possible narrative perspective since only this can supply an overview of characters' development and motivation and bring all strands together in a harmonious conclusion. However, when Moritz, in the introduction to *Anton Reiser*, highlights his aim as illuminating the inner life history of man, he immediately follows this with the proviso: "Freylich ist dieß nun keine so leichte Sache, daß gerade jeder Versuch darinn glücken muß—aber wenigstens wird doch vorzüglich in pädagogischer Rücksicht, das Bestreben nicht ganz unnütz seyn, die Aufmerksamkeit des Menschen mehr auf den Menschen selbst zu heften, und ihm sein individuelles Daseyn wichtiger zu machen" (Moritz, *Reiser*, 10; This of course is no easy matter, and not every attempt can succeed—but at least, and especially from an educational viewpoint, it can never be entirely useless to try to direct man's attention to man himself, and to make him attach more importance to his individual existence, 3).

Moritz asserts that the writer cannot always (perhaps can never totally) succeed, but that it is never useless to try. His text does not include Blankenburg's prescriptive modal verb *sollen* (should). Furthermore, a comparison of the other verbs used—Blankenburg: kennenlernen, lehren, lernen (get to know, teach, learn) versus Moritz: nicht ganz unnütz, wichtiger machen (never entirely useless, attach more importance)—demonstrates that Moritz is less dogmatic and more discriminating in his aspirations. He highlights the importance of the seemingly insignificant in the context of the whole: "Wer den Lauf der menschlichen Dinge kennt, und weiß, wie dasjenige oft im Fortgange des Lebens sehr wichtig werden kann, was anfänglich klein und unbedeutend schien, der wird sich an die anscheinende Geringfügigkeit mancher Umstände, die hier erzählt werden, nicht stossen" (Moritz, *Reiser*, 10; Anyone who is familiar with the course of human affairs, and knows how something that initially seemed small and insignificant can often become very important as life advances, will not mind the apparent triviality of many of the circumstances that are here related, 3). In his judgment, it is only by means of the process of focusing on all aspects of the inner life history—trivial as well as weighty—that the mind can gain greater insight into itself.[5]

Moritz's choice of words also indicates that the knowledge and insight achieved through this process is accorded less weight than the act of engagement. He identifies a comparative increase in importance ("wichtiger") and a process of getting better at looking ("den Blick schärfen"). Whereas the superlative form would indicate completion, Moritz's use of the comparative indicates an ongoing development, in which there is always more to be done.[6] He also adds another dimension to this endeavor that points in a different direction to Blankenburg's focus on educating and perfecting of humans ("die Vervollkommung des Menschen"[7]): by making humans more self-aware, they will learn to attach more importance to their individual existence. The call for the appreciation of the value of the individual human being is a crusade that informed all of Moritz's work.

The author's theoretical aims in the introduction are put into practice in the novel that follows. In *Anton Reiser*, Moritz the novelist and closet autobiographer, the literary anthropologist and social critic, creates a heterodiegetic narrator à la Blankenburg who can distance himself and comment on Anton's childhood experiences, giving detailed descriptions of inner and outer factors that contribute to his character's development. However, Moritz's "Geist …, der das Ganze zu übersehen vermag" (a mind able to oversee the whole) departs markedly from that prescribed by Blankenburg. Rather than following the development of the protagonist, the novel presents a series of episodes with substantial repetition in the kind of experiences described; the character Anton is shown to be unable to learn from his mistakes, his mental health issues are far from resolved, and the ending is abrupt and in no way harmonious: "—Die Sp … che Truppe war also nun eine zerstreuete Heerde" (Moritz, *Reiser,* 425; Speich's troupe, therefore, was now a scattered flock, 351).

The analytical gaze of the heterodiegetic narrative situation aspires to and indeed claims to rise above this fragmentation and lack of development. The distanced narrative voice observes and analyses as objectively as the "kalter Beobachter" (cold observer) described with reference to the parallel project of *Magazin zur Erfahrungsseelenkunde*[8] and presents itself as the voice of health reporting on illness: but the account is autobiographical, not fictional. The commentary in volume 1 of the ongoing critical edition of Moritz's work supplies detailed and authoritative information on the author's biography that ties in with almost every circumstance and incident in the novel, thus enabling the reader to raise questions of narrative (un)reliability on factual and interpretative levels. If Moritz had employed the perspective of a homodiegetic, first-person narrator telling the story of his own childhood, the narrative voice would clearly not have had the same status or authority. Yet if we accept that Moritz is telling his own story, the reporting figure he has created must be considered an unreliable narrator.[9] As with any unreliable narrator, the reader is challenged to question the status of the information given: to analyze what is being described and to conjecture as to what is not being described. Moreover, the types of information this figure comments on—such as childhood memories and play-acting—resemble greatly those forms of behaviors that Moritz was identifying as most problematic in terms of authenticity and reliability as part of his deliberations for the *Magazin* (Moritz, "Vorschlag," 492, 496–99). And those he does not mention here—dysfunctional relationships with close family and authority figures that range from neglect to traumatic humiliation—are at least equally problematic. The narrative voice repeatedly exposes what it labels as Anton's pretense, self-deception, and expediency, alongside its damning criticism of the appalling behavior of those in positions of responsibility toward him. Once the reader is aware of the narrative situation, however, any definitive judgments on the protagonist must remain equivocal. If we understand Anton and/or Moritz better having read the novel, it is through analyzing the narrative voice as much as the character. Readers cannot or at least should not build on the narrator's interpretations, they can only take on the role of "kalter Beobachter" (cold observer) themselves, while being simultaneously confronted with the difficulties of doing so, and compare individual insights, looking for patterns and trying to identify that which seems disingenuous or manipulative on the part of the character and/or the narrator.

Clearly, there is no "worthy" character, no harmonious ending that Blankenburg would recognize in Moritz's novel. Inner and outer factors crush the individual and there is an almost exclusive focus on deviance and mental health disorders, in particular narcissism, masochism, and depression. In light of this, the novel has been called an anti-*Bildungsroman*, that is, the opposite of Blankenburg's theory of "Bildung" (education) and "Vervollkommnung des Menschen" (perfecting of man). But if we interpret Moritz's work in terms of his stated aim of "die innere Geschichte des Menschen schildern" (to describe man's internal history) and "die Aufmerksamkeit des Menschen mehr auf den Menschen selbst . . . heften" (to direct man's attention to man himself), coupled with his proviso that this can rarely if ever succeed but is always worth trying, then a strong argument could be made that he has achieved this and perhaps even surpassed his own expectations. *Anton Reiser* does indeed provide fascinating insight into the inner life history of the main character: insight that is not necessarily reliable but that is genuine if we accept that it derives from a painstaking engagement through the medium of literature with different stages in the development of one individual by one individual: the author Moritz. Moreover, his character Anton does on occasion manage to transcend his personal misery through perceiving it as part of mankind's history of suffering.[10] In these moments, he can rise above the subjectivity of his self-absorption to gain enough distance, if not objectivity, to appreciate his value as a human being and experience a sense of self-worth otherwise denied him. Whereas Blankenburg conceived insight into the inner self of the individual in a novel as synonymous with educating and perfecting the individual and as encouraging the reader to undergo the same process, Moritz's novel is much more open and complex, raising questions about the nature of the insight gained and about who has learned or can learn from it, and provoking further debate on health and illness, objectivity and subjectivity as relative premises in themselves and as complements rather than antitheses.

*Anton Reiser* does not exclusively devote itself to mental health issues, and another important strand to the novel is Anton's relationship with the creative arts and his ambitions to become an actor. In the same way that Anton fails to overcome debilitating personality traits due to a lack of self-insight, he is clearly also a failed artist, for much the same reason. His attempts to use art as an escape from unpleasant realities go against Moritz's understanding of artistic creation and reception as expressed in his aesthetic writings, in which he responds to contemporary positions held by Charles Batteux, Friedrich Blankenburg, and Moses Mendelssohn, for whom the purpose of art was to evoke pleasure in the recipient. Moritz rejected this and argued that the purpose of art lies in itself: art for art's sake.[11] He described the artist's craft in similar terms to those he used to define his own aim for the novel *Anton Reiser*, namely "[die Natur] in ihrer geheimen Werkstatt . . . belauschen" (eavesdropping on nature in her secret workshop) and "in das Innere der Wesen [dringen]" (penetrating into the inner world of all beings).[12]

And indeed, although the novel does reveal Anton as a damaged individual and an ineffective artist, *Anton Reiser* is successful as a work of art in so far as it gives form and expression to the destructive experiences and pain experienced by the individual; its achievement goes far beyond the dilettantism of a mediocre artist. The novel is successful aesthetically *because* it remains unfinished, fragmentary, and unsettling. As the product of an ongoing process of self-engagement, it highlights the character's merit and his value as a human being; he is worthy in a sense similar to Goethe's protagonist Werther, who, in spite of his failure, is worth more than his peers.[13] At the same time, however, Anton is clearly a very negative character; both his inner and outer life histories reflect destructiveness and desolation through the medium of the beautiful and creative work of literature.

Moritz's aesthetic writings illustrate these principles in theoretical terms. In the essay "In wie fern Kunstwerke beschrieben werden können" (The Extent to Which Works of Art Can Be Described), he cites the story of Philomene as an example of how "[das] verborgne Schöne findet allenthalben statt, und dient der häßlichsten Oberfläche sehr oft zur Unterlage" (hidden beauty can be found everywhere and often serves as a base for the ugliest surface).[14] The narrative of Philomene's terrible fate, in the form of her tapestry, is the clearest and most beautiful expression of what cannot be expressed in words (both literally, as Philomene has been forcibly silenced, and figuratively, as such horror cannot be adequately described), and the aesthetic representation of this moment by the actor or the visual artist is "die vollkommenste Erklärung der Vollkommenheit, die im Innern der Natur verborgen, unter tausend Gestalten lauscht, und mehr oder weniger sich unserm Blick entzieht" (the most perfect explanation of the perfection that is hidden within nature, eavesdropping from underneath a thousand forms and more or less hidden from view).[15] In a letter to Goethe, Moritz praised in similar terms how, in *Tasso*, "das Qualenvollste und Drückendste der menschlichen Verhältnisse in die mildeste Erscheinung sich vollendet" (the most distressing and oppressive human affairs become perfect in the most benign vision).[16] Moritz saw the negative and the destructive as an integral part of art, just as it is always part of the inner (and outer) life of man: "Tod und Zerstöhrung selbst verlieren sich in den Begriff der *ewig bildenden Nachahmung des über die Bildung selbst erhabnen Schönen*, dem nicht anders als, durch *immerwährend sich verjüngendes Dasein*, nachgeahmt werden kann" (Moritz, "Nachahmung," 57; Even death and destruction lose themselves in the concept of the *eternally developing imitation of a beauty that itself transcends development*, which can be imitated in no other way than through *constantly rejuvenating existence*, emphasis in original). This is far removed from the negativity and naive rectitude expressed in Blankenburg's admonition not to lead the reader's emotions astray: directing emotions in purely salutary directions renders, by definition, any insight into the individual's inner life history fragmentary and one-sided. Moreover, Blankenburg's understanding of aesthetic pleasure remains firmly attached to a beneficial process of learning and perfecting:

> Der Dichter soll in seinen Lesern, . . . Vorstellungen und Empfindungen erzeugen, die die Vervollkommung des Menschen und seine Bestimmung befördern

können. Vorstellungen, die uns angenehm beschäftigen, indem sie uns denken lehren; und Empfindungen, die zugleich lehrreich sind, indem sie uns vergnügen, das ist [sic] solche, wie wir sie nach Anlage unsrer Natur und vermöge unsrer Bestimmung haben müssen. (Blankenburg 252)

The poet should generate ideas and emotions in his reader that can promote the perfecting of man and his destiny. Ideas that occupy us pleasantly by teaching us to think; and emotions that are simultaneously instructive in that they entertain us, that is, those that we ought to have according to the disposition of our nature and by virtue of our destiny.

If *Bildung* for Moritz cannot be understood in terms of Blankenburg's *Bildungsroman*, the constant oscillation between creation and destruction he posits—indicated by the adverbs "ewig" (eternally) and "immerwährend" (perpetually)—that facilitates change and development is highly reminiscent of Herder's ideas.[17] Rather than simply overcoming the negative and inadequate in art, Moritz defines the process of perfecting and creating aesthetic beauty as itself continually developing, creating, and destructing in a vigorous dynamic of "Thatkraft" (energy) or "thätige Kraft" (Moritz, "Nachahmung," 32–33; active force). Only in this way can the subjective attain a higher status—that of the *"über die Bildung selbst erhabnen Schönen"* (Moritz, "Nachahmung," 57, *a beauty that itself transcends development*, emphasis in original)—a status that could be understood as objectivity but one that can only be transient[18] and one that encompasses both creation and destruction.

The reception of the work of art is conceived in parallel terms to its creation. In order to achieve even this fleeting appreciation of visual art or literature as beautiful and complete in itself, the viewer or reader must locate what Moritz termed the "Mittelpunkt" (central point) or "Brennpunkt" (focus).[19] In keeping with his dynamic theories of production, this centrifuge is not fixed or static; it is perpetually forming and reforming and it can only be a single, ephemeral point in time. Moritz described this aesthetic experience in terms of yearning rather than closure: "ein Vorgefühl von jener grossen Harmonie, in welche Bildung und Zerstöhrung einst Hand in Hand, hinüber gehn" (Moritz, "Nachahmung," 55; a presentiment of that great harmony into which development and destruction, originally hand in hand, will pass).[20] It is these principles that *Anton Reiser* follows through the unreliable narrative situation described above: any insight to be gained for the individual—whether character, narrator, author, or reader—that might enable them to rise above the terrible life experience described is a process of engagement with unreliable sources and can therefore only be fallible, partial, and momentary.

Moritz's understanding of art as an ongoing process was perhaps most revolutionary in that it does not involve a positive act of creating the beautiful; rather, it is a negative act of destroying, of paring away and leaving out what detracts from it: "Der Dichter schneidet die Fäden ab, wodurch die Begebenheiten eine Neigung außer sich bekommen könnten, er läßt dasjenige weg, was in eine andere Sphäre von Begebenheiten eingreift" (the poet cuts away the threads which could give events a propensity beyond themselves, he leaves out whatever impinges upon another sphere of events).[21] In his essay "Über die bildende Nachahmung des Schönen" Moritz goes so far as to say that in order to identify what is beautiful we have to work out what is *not* beautiful: "Nun kann aber nur die Vorstellung von dem, was das Schöne *nicht zu seyn braucht*, um schön zu seyn, und was als überflüssig davon betrachtet werden muß, uns auf einen nicht unrichtigen Begriff des Schönen führen" (Moritz, "Nachahmung," 25; Now it is only the conception of that which the beautiful *does not have to be* in order to be beautiful, and which has to be considered as superfluous to this, that can lead us to a concept of the beautiful that is not inaccurate, emphasis in original). His use of the adjective "überflüssig" (superfluous) expresses how beauty is created through expunction. This is also a stated aim for *Anton Reiser*. In the introduction Moritz eschews all irrelevancy: the work as a whole is focused completely on one individual, Anton: "Auch wird man in einem Buche, welches vorzüglich die innere Geschichte des Menschen schildern soll, keine große Mannigfaltigkeit der Charaktere erwarten: denn es soll die vorstellende Kraft nicht vertheilen, sondern sie zusammendrängen und den Blick der Seele in sich selber schärfen" (Moritz, *Reiser*, 10; Nor will any great variety of characters be expected from a book whose main purpose is to describe man's internal history: for it is intended not to disperse the imaginative faculty, but to concentrate it, and to give the soul a sharper insight into itself, 3).

As argued above in the comparison between Blankenburg's theory of the novel and Moritz's stated aims for *Anton Reiser*, Moritz's ideal was an ongoing act of self-engagement and engagement with others to gain insight into the inner life history of man, to achieve a greater awareness of and to cultivate every individual's personal worth, moving toward (but never achieving) perfection. Although not a pedagogical novel in Blankenburg's one-dimensional sense, Moritz identifies its purpose as teaching mankind about themselves. The processes of learning and teaching were of profound significance for Moritz, himself a teacher with knowledge of and practical experience with contemporary developments in this area. With Rousseau's natural education and Basedow's (purported) lack of coercion as his sounding boards, Moritz's pedagogy aimed to make the value per se of each individual visible and to permit each one to flourish and develop.[22] In his novel *Andreas Hartknopf*, he illustrates this process using the analogy of visual art: "Jeder Stein des Anstoßes, den er weggeräumt hat, [ist] Gewinn für das Ganze . . . ein einziger ausgetilgter Fleck aus diesem großen Gemählde es der Vollkommenheit näher bringt, als der zierlichste Rahmen, worinnen es eingefaßt wird" (every infelicity that he has removed benefits the whole . . . a single stain that is eradicated from this great painting brings it closer to perfection than the most delicate frame in which it is set).[23]

Once again, Moritz's use of the comparative "näher" (closer) is important, as it indicates process not completion, and his choice of the verb "wegräumen" (remove) describes the already familiar negative dialectic of clearing away pretense and expediency to uncover innate beauty. Moritz repeatedly criticized using a person as a tool or machine. In his essay "Vorbereitung des Edlern durch das Unedlere / Einheit—Mehrheit—menschliche Kraft" (Preparation of the More Noble by the Less Noble / Unity—Plurality—Human Strength), he argued that no one should ever be seen merely as useful ("nützlich"), criticizing the utilitarianism he observed in society:

Der Mensch muß es wieder empfinden lernen, daß er um sein selbst willen da ist ... Der einzelne Mensch muß schlechterdings niemals als ein bloß *nützliches* sondern zugleich als ein *edles* Wesen betrachtet werden, das seinen eigenthümlichen Werth in sich selbst hat ... Der Staat kann eine Weile seine Arme, seine Hände brauchen, daß sie wie ein untergeordnetes Rad in diese Maschine eingreifen—aber der Geist des Menschen kann durch nichts untergeordnet werden, er ist ein in sich selbst vollendetes Ganze.[24]

Human beings must relearn the feeling that they exist for their own sake. An individual human being must absolutely never be seen as a merely *useful* object, but simultaneously as a *noble* being which has its own particular value in itself. The state can use his arms and hands for a while, so that he plays his part as a subservient cog in this machine—but the spirit of a human being cannot be made subservient, it is complete in itself.

This principle is, for Moritz, true of all men, including the poorest, the mentally ill and the deformed, all of whom can learn, and all of whom are deserving: "Ich stelle mich auf die unterste Stufe, worauf mich der Zufall versetzen konnte, und gebe keinen von meinen Anspruechen auf die Rechte der Menschheit auf. ... Man sollte auch den geringsten Individuis nur ihre Wichtigkeit erst begreiflich machen" (I place myself on the lowest level that I could find myself by chance and give up none of my claims to the rights of humanity. ... Even the meanest individual ought to be made to understand his importance).[25] The individual, as a noble creation of nature, is "ein in sich vollendetes Ganze" (a whole, complete in itself), in same way as a work of art must be.[26] For Moritz this concept always refers to intrinsic value, not perfection; it is a process, not a state, encompassing both creation and destruction, and according the subject(ive) a level of objectivity.

At the same time as he was writing the novel *Anton Reiser*, Moritz was editing his pathbreaking *Magazin zur Erfahrungsseelenkunde*. As the title states and Moritz reaffirms in the first volume, the aim is to gain knowledge of the mind through empirical observation and in this he aligns himself with the medical theories of his friend and physician Marcus Herz.[27] For Moritz, this enterprise is predicated in the same way as his literary work and aesthetic writings upon the value and worthiness of the individual as subject matter and he emphatically rejects generalization at this stage.[28] The only way to advance understanding in mental illness, as prescribed in the "Vorschlag," is detailed ongoing engagement with "den jedesmaligen Zustand des Kranken ..., die innere Natur und Beschaffenheit der Krankheit selbst" (Moritz, "Vorschlag," 487; the condition of the ill person at each point, the inner nature and character of the illness itself). Through the nature of the case study, however, the individual will produce insight into the general.[29]

Both the empirical approach and the focus on the individual reflect contemporary developments in medicine, of which Herz was very much part, including a new kind of treatment of mental illness called moral management, or moral treatment, from the French *traitement moral*. It involved the practitioner getting to know each patient well in order to work out a personal therapy regime in which he acted as a model of healthy and pious living and used his authority to promote good behavior.[30] Moral management reflected Enlightenment optimism that a mentally ill person could be cured through a pedagogical process of being taught to behave rationally. This could only be achieved through controlling the emotions, it was argued, and from mid-eighteenth century onwards this was understood as an aesthetic process by philosophical doctors such as Johann Christian Bolten, who argued "die philosophische Pathologie ist die Lehre von denen Affecten, deren aesthetischer Theil lehret, wie man die Gemüthesbewegungen erregen, unterdrücken, und in seiner Gewalt haben soll" (philosophical pathology is the doctrine of the emotions and the aesthetic part teaches how to excite, suppress and control the passions).[31] and that "man mus also die Aesthetick inne haben, um psychologische Curen verrichten zu lernen" (one must have a command of aesthetics in order to learn how to carry out psychological cures).[32] In order to be considered cured, those exposed to moral management had to show that they could act rationally, or at least be able to play this role. Moritz's Anton is very adept at playing roles, but he undergoes no "psychologische Cur" (psychological cure), and the novel narrates his ongoing struggles with controlling his emotions. This model of self-restraint as cure was criticized as early as the beginning of the nineteenth century however,[33] and the view is still held that the successes of moral management lay in the genuine personal engagement between practitioner and patient, the former recognizing the worthiness of the latter, and the latter gaining a sense of self-worth.

While Moritz rejected premature theorizing and systematization, his statement of intent in the "Vorschlag" contains his intentions and expectations for the journal, and he collates initial hypotheses as early as Volume 1, then in the *Revisionen* (reviews) from Volume 4, and in particular in his responses to Karl Friedrich Pockels' editorship in Volumes 7 and 8. The aim of collecting accounts is initially identified as facilitating a therapeutic learning process: a community of self- and mutual help through better understanding of mental states: "Was war es als *wechselseitige Mittheilung von Erfahrungen*, wodurch man endlich eine Heilkunde für den Körper fand, und warum fand man noch keine für die Seele?" (Moritz, *Magazin*, 1.1:114; What was it if not *mutual exchange of experiences* that led eventually to finding ways to cure the body, and why have we not found any for the mind?, emphasis in original). However, Moritz expresses this aim in a typically circumspect way through his use of the comparative form, and his terminology of perfecting rather than healing echoes both his pedagogical and aesthetic principles:

> Welch ein wichtiges Werk für die Menschheit könte dieses werden! das wäre noch der einzige Weg, wie das menschliche Geschlecht durch sich selber mit sich selber bekanter werden, und sich zu einem höhern Grade der Vollkommenheit empor schwingen könte, so wie ein einzelner Mensch durch Erkenntniß seiner selbst vollkomner wird. (Moritz, "Vorschlag," 489–99)

> What an important task for humanity this could become! It would be the only way for the human race to become better acquainted with itself and rise upwards to a higher level of perfection, in the same way as an individual person becomes more perfect through self-knowledge.

In a review of the project seven years on, Moritz distances himself more clearly from the utilitarian focus that "healing" might imply and reiterates the importance of rendering the mind more noble and beautiful and adding value to life:

> Und gesetzt auch, daß aus [dieser Erforschung unsers Wesens, diesem Rückblick auf uns selber] sich für das eigentliche Leben kein unmittelbarer Nutzen zeigte, so würde doch dieser Gesichtspunkt immer dazu dienen, den Kreis des menschlichen Denkens überhaupt zu veredeln, und zu verschönern, und allen übrigen Dingen im Leben mehr Interesse, und Würde zu geben. (Moritz, *Magazin*, 8.1:2)

> And even assuming that this investigation of our being, this self-reflection, produces no immediate usefulness in real life, this perspective would still serve to ennoble and to beautify the sphere of human thought in general and to give all other things in life more interest and value.

As in the preface to *Anton Reiser*, Moritz is very reticent in making claims about what he believes can be attained by means of exploring our inner life history.[34] While he is quite clear that only a "kalter Beobachter" (cold observer) can hope to see "wie die ersten Keime von den Handlungen des Menschen sich im Innersten seiner Seele entwickeln" (Moritz, "Vorschlag," 492–93; how the first beginnings of a person's actions develop in the depths of his mind), he devotes a substantial part of this introductory essay to detailing the many ways in which self-observation can be distorted. And with respect to the development of "die ersten Keime" (the first beginnings), he admits "dies bemerken wir nur so selten bei uns selber, geschweige den bei andern" (Moritz, "Vorschlag," 493; we so seldom notice these in ourselves, never mind in others). However, Moritz is equally clear that the act of creating an archive of attempts to illuminate inner life histories must be a useful exercise in itself, and one that makes each story more valuable. On this basis, the *Magazin* is constructed from dichotomies similar to those underpinning *Anton Reiser.* The veneer of health reporting on illness, hidden subjectivity behind surface objectivity, is replayed in the *Magazin* through a large number of contributors struggling to engage with their own inner life history or that of others. The authenticity of sources is often undermined in the text itself or important information is missing.[35] There are further examples of homodiegetic narrators telling stories as heterodiegetic narrators and other heterodiegetic narrators trying to conceal their personal involvement in events. To reiterate the point made above with reference to *Anton Reiser*, as with any unreliable narrator, the reader is challenged to question the status of the information given: to analyze what is being described and to conjecture as to what is not being described. Readers of the *Magazin* cannot or at least should not build on the narrators' interpretations; they can only take on the role of "kalter Beobachter" (cold observer) themselves, while being simultaneously confronted with the difficulties of doing so, and compare individual insights, looking for patterns to try to identify that which seems disingenuous or manipulative on the part of the character and/or the narrator.

The novel *Anton Reiser* focuses on one individual's inner life history; the *Magazin zur Erfahrungsseelenkunde* records a multitude of different cases by many different, often unidentified authors over 10 volumes. Those whose psychology is explored range from the poorest and most vulnerable members of society to eminent figures such as Moses Mendelssohn, Marcus Herz, and J. J. Spalding. Although individual contributors do make value judgments according to class, this does not represent Moritz's philosophy that each individual has equal value: one of the aspects of coeditor Karl Friedrich Pockels's editorial policy that enraged Moritz when he was in Italy was the patronizing attitude toward superstitious beliefs held by individuals from lower classes. While it is difficult to make general statements on so many disparate inner life histories, it is striking that abnormal psychology is so often equated with an inability or refusal to communicate. Spalding loses the ability to talk, Herz describes a period of delirium, others hide themselves away from society, usually due to paranoid fears of danger. In a contribution dealing with kleptomania, in addition to stealing money, the individual's aberrant behavior involves persistent begging for leftover food—even fighting with a dog over a bone—and hiding amongst his unsavory hoard:

> Dieser Vorrathswinkel, welchen er immer wieder anfüllt, wenn er auch noch so oft ausgeleert und gereinigt wird, gleicht einem wahren Saustalle. Verschimmelte Brodrinden, Zucker, faule Knochen, stinkendes Fleisch, Speck, Wurst, Butter, Wein und Kaffee unter einander gegossen. Neigen von Bier und Suppe, Kuchen, Arzeneien liegen da in größter Unordnung unter einander, und er ist nie glücklicher, als wenn er in diesem stinkenden Winkel stundenlang einsam seine Zeit verträumen kann. (Moritz, *Magazin*, 5.1:23)

> This hidden store, which he keeps filling up again no matter how often it is emptied and cleaned, resembles a veritable pigsty. Moldy breadcrusts, sugar, rotten bones, stinking meat, bacon, sausage, butter, wine and coffee poured together, dregs of beer and soup, cake, medicines lie there all together in the greatest muddle, and he is never happier than when he can dream away the time for hours on end, alone in this stinking hideout.

In another example, the weaver Schönfeld, is convinced he has located hidden treasure, which is rejected as a fantasy· by everyone around him (Moritz, *Magazin*, 1.1:21–24). Such cases often create a sense of uncertainty not present, for example, in stories of the stereotypical raving madman. If a person does not communicate, makes fantastic claims, or conceals what might be significant, what that person is really thinking and experiencing are only matters for conjecture. Thus, the question as to whether that person should in fact be diagnosed as mentally ill at all is open to interpretation. If we approach the description of Schönfeld's fixed idea that he has found treasure as a medical case history, we can interpret his assertion as true (it is very well hidden) or false (it only exists in his imagination) and declare the weaver sane or mad. If we approach the same report as a *story*, the weaver Schönfeld's treasure could be metaphorically understood as that which is covered up, buried, or otherwise hidden in the mind—conceivably the creative potential of the imagination, which a fanciful person could easily interpret as a precious, valuable, and beautiful treasure, and a prosaic person might just as readily dismiss as fantasy. If we construe the kleptomaniac's symptoms in a similarly figurative way, his clearly distasteful cache might represent the toxic dross that makes up the damaged or aberrant psyche.

Motifs of buried gold and jewels representing the treasures of the imagination or the unconscious would later be exploited extensively by the Romantics, but Moritz was already writing in very similar terms: "unser denkendes Wesen sollte es … wagen, in seine eigenen Tiefen herabzusteigen, und dem edelsten Metalle da nachzuspähen, wo es so selten gesucht wird" (Moritz, *Magazin*, 7.3:10; our thinking self should dare to descend into its own depths and search for the most precious metals where they are so seldom looked for). The opposite, rationalistic view that such beliefs are expressions of madness was a standpoint often presented as a counterpoint in Romantic narrative, creating ambiguity or, in the best tales, sustained ambivalence, whereby it is made impossible for the reader to decide. This rationalistic view is also frequently expressed in the *Magazin zur Erfahrungsseelenkunde*, although never by Moritz.

Moritz's conception of the "edelsten Metalle" (most precious metals) also reiterates his belief that the most difficult thing for an individual to achieve is knowledge of the inner depths of the thinking self. From the unpalatable to the repulsive, each inner life history contains debris alongside every jewel, some of which is not even recognized and much of which is difficult to confront never mind express, such as addictions or mad fantasies or the mental scars caused by harrowing experiences (*viz*. Anton Reiser). Consequently, Moritz's proposals for psychological therapy expressed in his contributions to the *Magazin* are based on the same negative dialectic of clearing and paring away what is disingenuous, manipulative, traumatic, and dysfunctional, and on the same dynamic interaction between creation and destruction facilitating change and development that characterize his pedagogy and aesthetics. The oft-quoted conclusion in the final volume of the *Magazin zur Erfahrungsseelenkunde* that enough material has been gathered was penned by Salomon Maimon (Moritz, *Magazin*, 10.3:2). Moritz believed that the process could never be finished and, as was the case with his novel *Anton Reiser*, his ambition for the *Magazin* was successfully achieved *because* it remains fragmentary, unfinished, and inconclusive.[36]

Many of the contradictions and ambiguities in Moritz's work: the focus on dynamic process rather than on completion, the importance afforded the unconscious, and within this, the interest in illness and aberrant psychology, all point forward to Romantic preoccupations.[37] His influence on Goethe and Schiller's development of Weimar classicism, in particular Schiller's *Spieltrieb* (play drive), in which all utilitarianism and pretense are discarded, is already well established. In fact, writers aligned to both classicism and Romanticism dipped into the archive of Moritz's insights, much as subsequent psychologists dipped into the *Magazin* throughout the nineteenth century, helping themselves to the particular morsels they found appealing. Because of the rich and diverse range of his work, this still happens today; however, by focusing on the contradictions and ambiguities themselves, it is possible to do justice to the depth and congruity of Moritz's work as well as to its breadth and heterogeneity. Only in this way can its significance be adequately captured.

*University of Glasgow*

# NOTES

1. See, for example, Hans-Joachin Schrimpf, "Karl Philipp Moritz," in *Deutsche Dichter des 18. Jahrhunderts. Ihr Leben und Werk* ed. Benno von Wiese (Berlin: Erich Schmidt, 1977) 881–910, here 899; Lothar Müller, "Karl Phillip Moritz," in *Deutsche Dichter. Leben und Werke deutschsprachiger Autoren*, ed. Gunther E. Grimm and Frank Rainer Max (Stuttgart: Reclam, 1988–89) 242–49, here 247–48; Helmut Pfotenhauer, "Karl Philipp Moritz: Erfahrungsseelenkunde als Literatur," *in Literarische Anthropologie: Selbstbiographien und ihre Geschichte—am Leitfaden des Leibes* (Stuttgart: Metzler, 1987) 93–115, here 107–8.

2. Friedrich von Blankenburg, *Versuch über den Roman* (Leipzig: Liegnitz, 1774), Faksimiledruck, ed. Eberhard Lämmert (Stuttgart: Metzler, 1965) 356, emphasis in original. All translations from German in this article are my own, except those from *Anton Reiser*. Subsequent references to Blankenburg's work will be made parenthetically in the text.

3. Karl Philipp Moritz, *Sämtliche Werke*, ed. Anneliese Klingenberg, Albert Meier, Conrad Wiedemann, and Christof Wingertszahn, vol. 1, *Anton Reiser*, ed. Christof Wingertszahn (Tübingen: Max Niemeyer, 2006) 10, emphasis in original. Karl Philipp Moritz, *Anton Reiser: A Psychological Novel*, trans. Ritchie Robertson (London: Penguin, 1997), 3. Subsequent references to this source and to its English translation will be made parenthetically in the text as *Reiser*. The espousal of Pope's all-embracing maxim "the proper study of mankind is *Man*" is also evident in Blankenburg and Moritz's programmes: Alexander Pope, *An Essay on Man: Being the First Book of Ethic Epistles* (London: John Wright, 1734) epistle 2, line 2.

4. Mediation as the defining characteristic of narrative was posited by Plato, but modern debate on this issue is associated with Käte Friedemann, *Die Rolle des Erzählers in der Epik* (Leipzig: Haessel, 1910) and Franz Stanzel, *Die typischen Erzählsituationen im Roman. Dargestellt an "Tom Jones," "Moby-Dick," "The Ambassadors," "Ulysses," u. a.* (Vienna: Braumüller, 1955).

5. On the "Gewebe" (mesh) of memories from childhood to the present that constructs individuality, see Richard P. Apgar, "Moritz's veil: Observation, the Rupture of Individuality, and *Magazin zur Erfahrungsseelenkunde*," *Goethe Yearbook* 27 (2020): 47–62, here 50–53.

6. See Apgar 54 on the fragmentation of the individual and of knowledge.

7. For examples see Blankenburg 13, 252, 354, 432.

8. Karl Philipp Moritz, "Vorschlag zu einem Magazin einer Erfarungs-Seelenkunde" (Proposal for a Magazine of Empirical Psychology), *Deutsches Museum* 1 (1782): 485–503, here 495. Subsequent references to this essay will be made parenthetically in the text as "Vorschlag."

9. See Wayne C. Booth, *The Rhetoric of Fiction* (Chicago: U of Chicago P, 1961; 2nd ed., 1983) and Marcus Amit, *Self-Deception in Literature and Philosophy* (Trier: Wissenschaftlicher Verlag Trier, 2007).

10. For example when he reads Hamlet's soliloquy: "er dachte sich nicht mehr allein, wenn er sich gequält, gedrückt, und eingeengt fühlte; er fing an, dieß als das allgemeine Looß der Menschheit zu betrachten" (Moritz, *Reiser*, 227; he no longer imagined himself alone when he felt tormented, crushed, and constricted; he began to regard this as the universal lot of humanity, 186).

11. See Karl Philipp Moritz, "Nachwort," in *Schriften zur Ästhetik*, ed. Christof Wingertszahn (Ditzingen: Reclam, 2018) 123-98, here 129-38, and Cristina Fossaluzza, *Subjektiver Antisubjektivismus. Karl Philipp Moritz als Diagnostiker seiner Zeit* (Hannover: Wehrhahn, 2006) 189, 194, 206.

12. Karl Philipp Moritz, "Über die bildende Nachahmung des Schönen" (On the Formative Imitation of Beauty), in Karl Philipp Moritz, *Schriften zur Ästhetik* 16-57, here 30. Subsequent references to this essay will be made parenthetically in the text as "Nachahmung."

13. Moritz was greatly influenced by *Werther*, see Elliott Schreiber, *The Topography of Modernity. Karl Philipp Moritz and the Space of Autonomy* (Ithaca, NY: Cornell UP and Cornell Library, 2012) 19-23.

14. Karl Philipp Moritz, "In wie fern Kunstwerke beschrieben werden können," in Karl Philipp Moritz, *Schriften zur Ästhetik* 58-72, here 61.

15. Moritz, "In wie fern Kunstwerke," 61.

16. Letter to Johann Wolfgang von Goethe, Berlin, June 6, 1789. Karl Philipp Moritz, *Schriften zur Ästhetik und Poetik*, ed. Hans Joachim Schrimpf (Tübingen: Niemeyer, 1962) 326.

17. See Moritz, "Nachwort," 169.

18. See Schreiber 18. On the transience of this moment, see Mattias Pirholt, "Disinterested Love: Ethics and Aesthetics in Karl Philipp Moritz's 'Versuch einer Vereinigung aller schönen Künste und Wissenschaften unter dem Begriff des in sich selbst Vollendeten,'" *Goethe Yearbook* 27 (2020): 63-81, here 73.

19. See Schreiber 22-33. Also of relevance here is Moritz's excursus "Gesichtspunkt" (point of view), in ΓΝΩΘΙ ΣΑΥΤΟΝ *oder Magazin zur Erfahrungsseelenkunde, herausgegeben von Karl Philipp Moritz, Karl Friedrich Pockels und Salomon Maimon* 4, no. 2 (1786): 16-23 (ed. Sheila Dickson and Christof Wingertszahn, https://www.mze.gla.ac.uk/). Subsequent references to this journal will be made parenthetically as *Magazin*, followed by volume.issue:page number.

20. See also Schreiber 32-33.

21. Karl Philipp Moritz, "Die metaphysische Schönheitslinie," in Karl Philipp Moritz, *Die große Loge oder der Freimaurer mit Wage und Senkblei* (Berlin: Ernst Felisch, 1793) 169-84, here 174.

22. On Moritz's engagement with the pedagogical ideas of his contemporaries see Schreiber 63-101.

23. Karl Philipp Moritz, *Andreas Hartknopf. Eine Allegorie* (Berlin: Johann Friedrich Unger, 1786) 89-90.

24. Karl Philipp Moritz, "Was giebt es Edleres und Schöneres in der ganzen Natur," in *Sämtliche Werke*, ed. Anneliese Klingenberg, Albert Meier, Conrad Wiedemann and Christof Wingertszahn, vol. 11, *Denkwürdigkeiten*, ed. Claudia Stockinger (Tübingen: Max Niemeyer, 2013) 13-19, here 16-17, emphasis in original.

25. Karl Philipp Moritz, "Das Edelste in der Natur," in Karl Philipp Moritz, *Die große Loge* 74-88, here 82; Moritz, "Vorschlag," 497.

26. The artist creates "eine eigne Welt …, worin gar nichts Einzelnes mehr statt findet, sondern jedes Ding in seiner Art ein fuer sich bestehendes Ganze ist" (Moritz, "Nachahmung," 31; his own world, in which no individual thing happens any longer, but rather every thing is a complete entity of its kind that exits for itself).

27. Moritz, "Vorschlag," 497; Moritz, *Magazin* 1.1:33.

28. "Was ist unsre ganze Moral, wenn sie nicht von Individuis abstrahirt ist?" (Moritz, "Vorschlag," 487; What is all our morality if it is not abstracted from the individual?).

29. See Sheila Dickson, "'Unerhörte Begebenheiten' in Karl Philipp Moritz's 'Journal of Empirical Psychology' (1783-1793)," *Pacific Coast Philology* 48, no. 1 (2013): 1-24, here 3.

30. See Sheila Dickson, "Der aufgeklärte Einsiedler im *Magazin zur Erfahrungsseelenkunde*. Ein Krankheitsbild in der Spätaufklärung und in der Romantik," in *Einsamkeit und Pilgerschaft. Figurationen und Inszenierungen in der Romantik*, ed. Antje Arnold, Walter Pape and Norbert Wichard (Berlin: De Gruyter, 2018) 221-34, here 221-22.

31. Johann Christian Bolten, *Gedancken von psychologischen Curen* (Thoughts on psychological cures) (Halle: Carl Hermann Hemmerde, 1751) 62. See Robert Leventhal, "Die Fallgeschichte zwischen Ästhetik und Therapeutik," in *"Fakta, und kein moralisches Geschwätz." Zu den Fallgeschichten im "Magazin zur Erfahrungsseelenkunde" (1783-1793)*, ed. Sheila Dickson, Stefan Goldmann, and Christof Wingertszahn (Göttingen: Wallstein, 2011) 65-83, here 69-72.

32. Leventhal 59-60.

33. Heinz Schott und Rainer Tölle, *Geschichte der Psychiatrie. Krankheitslehren, Irrwege, Behandlungsformen* (Munich: Beck, 2006) 254. These principles were condemned vociferously in twentieth century by Foucault as a more sophisticated method of torture than the traditional chains and whips (Michel Foucault, *History of Madness*, ed. Jean Khalfa, trans. Jonathan Murphy and Jean Khalfa [London: Routledge, 2006] 484-85).

34. One of Moritz's later contributions to the journal is an essay on "Selbsttäuschung" (self-deception) (Moritz, *Magazin* 7.3:45-47).

35. See, for example *Magazin* 3.1:40; *Magazin* 3.2:121, 126. On this point see Dickson, "Unerhörte Begebenheiten" 13-14.

36. Moritz poses the rhetorical question in his "Vorschlag": "Aber wie sol ein solches Werk jemals vollendet werden?" (Moritz, "Vorschlag," 491; But how could such a task ever be completed?).

37. See also Pirholt 73.

MARTIN WAGNER

# *Sturm und Drang* Comedy and the Enlightenment Tradition

**Abstract:** Breaking with the traditional view of *Sturm und Drang* comedy as a radically new beginning in the history of the comic genre, this article highlights important continuities that define German comedy from the Enlightenment through *Sturm und Drang*. More precisely, this article traces the variations on the central theme of vice that extend from the Enlightenment poetics of Johann Christoph Gottsched to *Sturm und Drang* plays by Lenz and Wagner. At the center of the analysis are the comedies *Das Testament* (1745) by Luise Gottsched, *Minna von Barnhelm* (1767) by Gotthold Ephraim Lessing, and *Der Hofmeister* (1774) by J. M. R. Lenz, as well as the drama *Die Reue nach der That* (1775) by Heinrich Leopold Wagner. Through these readings, *Sturm und Drang*'s innovations become legible as the continuation of a well-established tradition of variations on a stable theme—a perspective that revises our understanding of the history of German comedy and that bears broader implications for the periodization of eighteenth-century German literature.

**Keywords:** comedy, Enlightenment, *Sturm und Drang*, German literary history, genre studies, variation, vice

IN HER 2018 STUDY *Zeitenwandel als Familiendrama. Genre und Politik im deutschsprachigen Theater des 18. Jahrhunderts* (Historical Change as Family Drama: Genre and Politics in Eighteenth-Century German-Language Theater), Romana Weiershausen retraces the remarkably slow and continuous transition from the heroic tragedy to the modern bourgeois tragedy in the middle decades of the eighteenth century. Contrary to what older scholarship had suggested, these genres were, for much of that time, experienced as coexisting possibilities of writing, and their respective relevance was based on this simultaneity. The present article presents a similar thesis with respect to eighteenth-century German comedy. Concretely, I shed light on the continuities of German comedy from its Enlightenment origins in the poetics of Johann Christoph Gottsched through *Sturm und Drang*. This proposed argument significantly revises our view, especially of *Sturm und Drang* comedy, which, by and large, still tends to be seen as a radical new beginning. Classical (and otherwise still very instructive) studies of Enlightenment comedy—including Horst Steinmetz's *Die Komödie der*

*Aufklärung* (1966; Enlightenment Comedy), Rüdiger van den Boom's *Die Bedienten und das Herr-Diener Verhältnis in der deutschen Komödie der Aufklärung* (1979; Domestics and the Lord-Servant Relationship in German Enlightenment Comedy), and Eckehard Catholy's *Das deutsche Lustspiel von Aufklärung bis Romantik* (1982; German Comedy from Enlightenment to Romanticism)—usually end rather abruptly with Lessing's *Minna von Barnhelm* (1767).[1] This, however, is an unlikely endpoint, given the fact that Lessing's comedy is prominently mentioned in a strikingly positive way in the first *Sturm und Drang* comedy, Lenz's *Der Hofmeister* (1774; *The Tutor*).[2] But, even in newer scholarship, including the very recent *Lenz-Handbuch* (2017; Lenz Handbook), we are still presented with the view that Lenz thinks comedy anew.[3]

These established readings of *Sturm und Drang* comedy are generally out of touch with the now dominant understanding of *Sturm und Drang*, which sees in this episode of German literary history no longer a direct and complete rupture with the Enlightenment, but instead a self-critical outgrowth of the Enlightenment. Matthias Luserke-Jaqui, one of the leading *Sturm und Drang* scholars of the past decades, sums this newer view up in the following terms: "Gerade die Gleichzeitigkeit von Weiterentwicklung auf der einen und radikaler Infragestellung aufgeklärter Positionen auf der anderen Seite charakterisiert den Sturm und Drang." (*Sturm und Drang* is characterized especially by the simultaneity of a further development of Enlightenment ideas, on the one hand, and a radical questioning of these ideas on the other.)[4] While the dialectics of continuity and rupture have been fruitfully applied to the explicit politics of *Sturm und Drang* (concerning questions of individual autonomy and of morality, for instance[5]), they have hardly been tested with respect to formal and generic characteristics of *Sturm und Drang*. The present article addresses this gap in the scholarship by focusing on comedy—the most important dramatic genre for at least one of *Sturm und Drang*'s protagonists, J. M. R. Lenz (1751–92).

To the extent that critics have stressed continuities in eighteenth-century comedy, it is largely by reference to the old comic character of the *Hanswurst* or *Harlekin*, which—despite famously being banned from the German stage by Johann Christoph Gottsched and his associated theater practitioners in the 1730s[6]—retained, under its various guises, a presence in German comedies all the way from Luise Gottsched through Johann Elias Schlegel, G. E. Lessing, J. M. R. Lenz, and beyond.[7] What I propose in this article, by contrast, is viewing *Sturm und Drang* comedy as deeply embedded in a play of variations on the topic of vice, which has a longstanding tradition in Enlightenment comedy. The ridiculing portrayal of vice for pedagogical purposes is what Gottsched introduced as the central element (and essential justification) of comedy in his *Critische Dichtkunst* (Critical Poetics)—and much of the history of German comedy in the following decades can be read as guided by the attempt to find ever-new variations on that theme.[8] Indeed, it might be worthwhile to read these variations as, to some extent, just that: playful variations on a theme. In this case, German comedy, like the medieval *Minnesang*, could be interpreted as a form of *Variationskunst* (art of variation), with its main interest for contemporary audiences (who, in both cases, were well acquainted with the genre) deriving not only from the specific content of individual plays but also from the way in which writers found ever new ways of reassembling works based on the very limited defining formal elements of the genre.[9]

It is true, of course, that the concept of vice is heavily engrained in the intellectual and religious fabric of the eighteenth century and that variations on this concept bear important cultural implications. As Wolfgang Martens has shown in his seminal study of German Enlightenment moral weeklies, vice was, at this time, newly conceptualized as being situated in the individual's agency rather than in a superior evil force to which men and women succumb.[10] Like the moral weeklies, Gottschedian comedy participated in the establishment of this new, secularized notion of vice. However, the present article pays relatively little attention to this and other important cultural dynamics that may help to explain the variations on the comic paradigm. This is a deliberately reductive reading, meant to sharpen our awareness of playful variation as *another* crucial motor of literary history. Polemically reducing the differences of German comedy to a continuous play on a stable theme—without introducing a clear timeline of before and after—allows us to view eighteenth-century comedy as a synchronous field of playful variations in which the weighty and complex discussions regarding the essence of vice are less crucial.

All that being said, and at the risk of a performative contradiction, the following discussion nevertheless adheres to a relatively conventional timeline, moving from Gottsched's poetological treatise *Critische Dichtkunst* (first edition, 1729; fourth edition cited here, 1751) through Enlightenment comic productions of the 1740s and 1760s by Luise Gottsched (*Das Testament* [The Testament], 1745) and Gotthold Ephraim Lessing (*Minna von Barnhelm*, 1767), and ending with a discussion of two *Sturm und Drang* plays by J. M. R. Lenz (*Der Hofmeister*, [The Tutor], 1774) and Leopold Wagner (*Die Reue nach der That* [The Remorse after the Deed], 1775). The conventional chronological sequence, however, is used here not so much to suggest development, but simply as a means of organization. Finally, it should be emphasized that the goal of the following readings is not an exhaustive interpretation, but merely a brief spotlight on the range of variations that the Enlightenment comic paradigm underwent in the course of the eighteenth century.

## Comedy and Vice in Johann Christoph Gottsched's *Critische Dichtkunst*

In reading Johann Christoph Gottsched's theory of comedy in his *Critische Dichtkunst*, one of the things that stands out most is the extent to which comedy is constructed as a mirror image of tragedy. Be it in terms of its purpose (instruction), plot structure (distinguishing between simple and complex comedies as those without or with peripeteia), in terms of organization (bound to the three unities of place, time, and action), in terms of the structure of acts and scenes, or in terms of probability as a key category, Gottsched demands that comedy fulfill very much the same elements expected of tragedy. As has been noted, this construction of comedy as a mirror image of tragedy serves as an important means of "ennobling" (in more than one sense) the dramatic genre suited for the representation of the middle class—i.e., comedy (tragedy, in Gottsched's conservative poetics, is reserved for the representation of the fate of the high nobility).[11]

It is largely according to three aspects that comedy nevertheless is different from tragedy in Gottsched's view. First (and as just mentioned), comedy focuses on middle-class characters, including, notably, the characters of lower nobility: "ordentliche Bürger, oder doch Leute von mäßigem Stande, dergleichen auch wohl zur Noth Baronen, Marquis und Grafen"[12] (respectable members of the bourgeoise or, in any case, of moderate social standing, including, if necessary, barons, marquis, and counts). Second, comedy is distinguished by its style. In contrast to the elevated register of tragedy, comedy, as a middle-class genre, is written in common language—Gottsched prescribes "eine ganz natürliche Schreibart"[13] (a completely natural style). Finally, and perhaps most importantly, comedy is distinguished, according to Gottsched, by its content. Tragedy, in Gottsched's view, focuses on "harte und unvermuthete Unglücksfälle"[14] (severe and unexpected misfortune) of noble men and women to prepare the audience for their own misery.[15] By contrast, comedy, Gottsched argues in a somewhat liberal invocation of Aristotle's authority,[16] is the imitation of a vicious or immoral (*lasterhafte*) action that is so laughable that it has the potential both to entertain the audience and to instruct it to abstain from such vice: "Die Komödie ist nichts als eine Nachahmung einer lasterhaften Handlung, die durch ihr lächerliches Wesen den Zuschauer belustigen, aber auch zugleich belehren kann."[17] (Comedy is nothing but the imitation of a vicious act that can, on account of its laughable nature, amuse but simultaneously also instruct the spectator.)

The main contention of this article is that while the first two mentioned characteristics of comedy—its focus on the middle class and its natural language—were essentially undermined in the dramatic practice of the following decades, the prescribed focus on laughable vice remained surprisingly robustly intact. Indeed, as playwrights sought comic effects through exaggeration, they rarely obeyed the prescribed limitation to a natural idiom (and tragic playwrights simultaneously approached in their works a more natural register than envisioned by Gottsched). Moreover, and as is well-known, the so-called *Ständeklausel* (estates clause), which limited tragedy to the fates of gods and kings, and comedy to the middle class, was one of the most prominent victims of eighteenth-century literary innovation. The focus on laughable vice, by contrast, experienced no such radical critique. This is not to say that the depiction of vice remained static over the course of the century. However, more importantly than commonly stated, much of eighteenth-century comedy can be read as a game of variations on this very theme of laughable vice—and this game already begins in the works of Gottsched's wife, Luise Gottsched. A brief discussion of *Das Testament* (1745), traditionally seen as the only original comedy by Luise Gottsched (i.e., not based on a French or other model),[18] serves here to remind us of her creative appropriation of her husband's poetological framework.

# Luise Gottsched and the Art of Variation

To be sure, in Eckehard Catholy's seminal study of German Enlightenment comedy, the work of Luise Gottsched is introduced as a mere illustration of her husband's dramatic prescriptions. Catholy positions the chapter on "die Gottschedin" directly after the chapter on her husband's critical work, and he entitles it "Luise Gottsched: Das Lustspiel als Exempel der Lustpieltheorie"[19] (Luise Gottsched: Comedy as an Example of the Theory of Comedy). There are certainly some good reasons for describing Luise Gottsched's comedies, including *Das Testament* (1745), as an illustration of a preexisting poetic framework. Johann Christoph Gottsched himself included *Das Testament* in the sixth volume of his edition of exemplary works, *Die deutsche Schaubühne*, and he adorned it with great praise in the volume's preface.[20] Luise Gottsched's classically built five-act comedy *Das Testament*, which observes all three unities, corresponds very clearly to Gottsched's general dramatic poetics. And the play also largely adheres to Gottsched's more specific demands for comedy (more on that below). And yet, even according to Catholy's own account (and in striking tension to the chapter heading he chooses), Luise Gottsched's work is characterized as much by mere implementation as by interesting variations on the foundational set of rules. The significance of these variations, relatively modest though they might appear, can hardly be overstated, because what they ultimately imply is that there is no clearly identifiable rupture between the production of comedies in Gottschedian terms and a departure from these prescriptions. Instead, there is a continuum of playful variations on the Gottschedian paradigm of comedy that begins already with Luise Gottsched herself and that extends to *Sturm und Drang* works by J. M. R. Lenz and Heinrich Leopold Wagner.

Luise Gottsched's *Das Testament* focuses on the vice of selfishness. "Eigennutz" is the word she uses for this vice at very strategic points of the play, both at the outset (in the second scene) and then again at the end of the play[21]—a structure that continues to shape comedy, as we shall see, all the way through Lenz's *Der Hofmeister*. Along the lines of Gottsched's poetics, selfishness is, moreover, shown to be a ridiculously unlikable trait. It is embodied in two siblings—a young man and a young woman—who ruthlessly pursue their aunt's inheritance. The aunt, in turn, engages a false doctor who, in a typically comic double-play, pretends to support the siblings' plots only to give them the opportunity to reveal the depth of their vices. Eventually, the nephew and niece are exposed and the aunt reprimands them for their bad behavior. The two siblings appear to show signs of remorse and subtly signal betterment (the niece silently kisses the aunt's hand and the nephew bows equally silently; neither of the two speaks a single word at the end).

While all of this corresponds directly enough to J. C. Gottsched's poetics, there are nevertheless important beginnings of variation to be seen. First, the play supplements the focus on one laughable vice (selfishness) with a passing treatment of a series of additional vices—a process against which J. C. Gottsched appears to caution playwrights (Catholy identifies these other vices as dishonesty, levity, megalomania, and indolence[22]). More importantly, the vicious characters are not altogether laughable; instead, the comedy also invites the audience to laugh *with* the vicious characters about their carefree witticisms and likably silly humor. When the depraved nephew is reprimanded by his sisters, for instance, he jokingly addresses them as "meine gnädige Herren Fräulein"[23] (roughly: "milord women"). Such light-heartedness is completely in line with the vice of levity that Catholy associates with the nephew, but if the audience chuckles here at the nephew's remark, it is likely not because it recognizes levity as a laughable vice, but simply because it finds the unusual and paradoxical form of address (mildly) amusing. In scenes like this, the old character of the fool, who invites us to laugh *with* him, shines through the new Gottschedian character, *about* whom we ought to laugh, and in whose behavior we should recognize the ridiculousness of vice.[24] In some sense, however, the precise nature of these variations is almost less important than the fact that there are variations to begin with. What matters here is that German Enlightenment comedy has, from the outset, begun a play of variations on Gottsched's poetological paradigm.

## Lessing's *Minna von Barnhelm*: The Vice of a Virtuous Man

In the decades following Luise Gottsched's play, a complex series of further and more far-reaching variations on the Gottschedian paradigm of a satirical portrayal of vice emerge—notably in Christian Fürchtegott Gellert's sentimental comedy, which supplements (but not replaces) the focus on vice with a parallel focus on virtuous behavior (see, for instance, Gellert's 1747 comedy *Die zärtlichen Schwestern* [The Affectionate Sisters]).

Even more so than Gellert's comedies, however, Lessings's 1767 comedy *Minna von Barnhelm oder das Soldatenglück: Ein Lustspiel verfertiget im Jahre 1763* (Minna von Barnhelm, Or the Soldiers' Fortune: A Comedy Written in the Year 1763) is conventionally seen as an endpoint of German Enlightenment comedy. As mentioned above, Horst Steinmetz's classic study of the genre ends its discussion with this play. In Steinmetz's reading, *Minna von Barnhelm* still starts out as a conventional Enlightenment comedy by presenting a leading character, the officer Major von Tellheim, whose folly will be revealed and cured over the course of the play. But, as the play continues, the focus on Tellheim as a stereotyped bearer of a certain folly or vice dissipates. Instead, Lessing's interest, according to Steinmetz, consists in portraying Tellheim as a multifaceted, individualized character.[25] What, for Steinmetz, determines the rupture with Enlightenment satirical comedy is that "es sich bei Tellheim nicht mehr um einen Charaktertyp, um die Personifizierung einer bestimmten menschlichen Schwäche handelt, sondern um eine mehrschichtige Person, um einen *Charakter*"[26] (in Tellheim, we do not encounter a character type or the personification of a given human weakness any longer, but a multifaceted person, a *character*).

Steinmetz's interpretation, in a way, complements Goethe's famous remarks in *Dichtung und Wahrheit* (*Poetry and Truth*), where Goethe also emphasizes the extraordinary innovation that this play inaugurated. In contrast to Steinmetz, however, Goethe does not primarily see the novelty of *Minna von Barnhelm* in the process of individualization; rather, he seems to think of the separated lovers, Minna and Tellheim, as typified representatives of their respective home states, Saxony and Prussia, which had been enemies in the Seven Years' War, the culmination of which provides the temporal setting of the play.[27] Indeed, Goethe stresses Lessing's pronounced reference to contemporary social and political reality, which is already emphasized in the play's unusual subtitle, which refers to the year in which the play was written. Goethe writes of Lessing's comedy: "Es ist die erste, aus dem bedeutenden Leben gegriffene Theaterproduktion, von spezifischem temporären Gehalt, die deswegen auch eine nie zu berechnende Wirkung tat" (FA 14:307; This is the first theater production based on important historical events of specific relevance for the present and, for that reason, it also had an incalculable effect).[28]

However, although Steinmetz, Goethe, and others certainly highlight important innovative aspects of Lessing's play, their interpretations potentially take away from an awareness of the continuities that bind Lessing's play to the tradition of German Enlightenment comedy. Far more interestingly, what one can discover in *Minna von Barnhelm* is a strikingly new variation of the established paradigm of comedy as a genre focused on laughable vice. Specifically, Lessing's playful variation here—which, incidentally, is not clearly present in his earlier comedies, *Die Juden* (The Jews) or *Der Freigeist* (The Libertine; both 1749)—focuses on a character in whom vice and virtue remain indistinguishable.[29] In an important line from this play, which is revealing both in terms of Tellheim's character and this play's larger poetological discourse, Minna declares Tellheim to be a man of all virtues: "Er spricht von keiner [Tugend]; denn ihm fehlt keine."[30] (He does not talk about any [virtue] because he does not lack any.) Other characters in the play issue similar statements—for instance, Minna's uncle, who assures Tellheim of the highest esteem he has for him.[31] To be sure, Minna's hyperbolic statement is repeatedly qualified over the course of the play—beginning, in fact, with an immediate correction by Minna herself, in which she accuses Tellheim, half in jest, of being a squanderer (*Verschwender*[32]). More importantly, later on, after praising Tellheim as an "ehrlichen, edlen Mann"[33] (honest, noble man), Minna accuses him of "bloß ein wenig zu viel Stolz"[34] (just a little too much pride). But, by and large, Lessing focuses his comedy on the paradoxical premise of the vice of a flawless man.[35]

Lessing's comedy goes through all the motions of a comedy, including the well-established play-within-the-play, which is supposed to reveal to the main characters their own vices so that they can better themselves. But, importantly, in *Minna von Barnhelm*, this play-within-the-play does not lead anywhere. If Tellheim and Minna are, in the end, happily reunited, it is not because either had to change their behavior (as flawless characters, they do not have to change), but because of a happy turn in external circumstance. While Tellheim initially refuses to reunite with Minna because he does not want to burden her as a now poor and dishonorably dismissed officer, he eventually overcomes his reservations after the Prussian king reinstates his honor and

fortune. Although Tellheim's virtuous, albeit all-too-stubborn, refusal to burden Minna (even when she does not perceive the burden) certainly approximates a traditionally comic vice to be cured, the play leaves it very much
open as to whether this behavior constitutes a vice indeed—and it certainly
does not require Tellheim to change his behavior in order for the play to
arrive at a happy ending.[36]

Lessing's paradoxical focus on the vice of a flawless man is quite
remarkable, and it matches, incidentally, Lessing's critical assertions in his
*Hamburgische Dramaturgie* (*Hamburg Dramaturgy*, chapter 28), written
around the same time, in which he posits the possibility of laughing about a
character whom one also esteems. Aside from all the other important innovations mentioned by Goethe, Steinmetz, and others, this alone is enough to
secure Lessing's comedy a place in literary history. And yet it is important
to recall that Lessing's playful innovation is not completely unprecedented.
Already in Johann Elias Schlegel's 1847 comedy *Die stumme Schönheit*
(Silent Beauty), characters are allowed to live on with their vices happily ever
after.[37] Moreover, Lessing does not cause a complete paradigm change—for,
as well shall see, *Sturm und Drang* writers continued to produce new variations on the central theme of comedy as a genre concerned with revealing
laughable vice.

## Vice between Individual and Institution: Lenz's *Der Hofmeister*

That *Sturm und Drang* did indeed continue in the footsteps of Enlightenment
comedy becomes clear if one considers the work of J. M. R. Lenz, the most
important theorist and writer of *Sturm und Drang* comedies. To be sure,
Lenz's comedies, with their rather serious social and political subject matter,
appear to completely overturn what it is that we understand comedy to be,
and they confront us with the question of why Lenz characterized his three
most well-known plays as comedies to begin with. *Der Hofmeister* (1774),
*Der neue Menoza* (1775; *The New Menoza*), and *Die Soldaten* (1776; *The
Soldiers*) are all labeled as "Komödie."[38] Although it is not usually discussed
in this context, it is nevertheless significant that Lenz chose the Greek-based
term *Komödie*, instead of the Germanic term *Lustspiel*.[39] Almost the entire
German Enlightenment tradition before him preferred the term *Lustspiel*,
Prominent plays by Luise Gottsched (for instance, *Das Testament*, which
is even more emphatically defined as "ein deutsches Lustspiel" [a German
comedy]), Gellert (*Die zärtlichen Schwestern*), Johann Elias Schlegel (*Die
stumme Schönheit*), and Lessing (*Die Juden, Der Freigeist, Minna von
Barnhelm*) appeared under this genre designation.[40] Lenz's consistent
choice of the term *Komödie*, which departs from the German dramatic tradition of the previous decades, already tentatively signals a rupture in the tradition—or, perhaps, a new return to the genre's origins. When Lenz calls his
plays "Komödien," in other words, he willfully places them both within *and*
outside of the tradition of the genre that his German audience would have
been accustomed to.

Setting the question of the lexical valences of *Lustspiel* and *Komödie* aside, general answers to the question of why Lenz called his plays "comedies" can be found in his theoretical writings, notably in *Anmerkungen übers Theater* (1774, Comments on Theater) and in the review of his own play, *Der neue Menoza* (the review appeared in 1775, the same year in which the play was published). Both texts appear to rethink the divide between comedy and tragedy, placing them on a foundation entirely different from the one established by Gottsched almost half a century earlier.

Famously, in *Anmerkungen übers Theater*, Lenz distinguishes between tragedy and comedy based on the relative importance of character and action. Whereas in tragedy, character prevails over action, in comedy, action prevails over character: "Die Hauptempfindung in der Komödie ist immer die Begebenheit, die Hauptempfindung in der Tragödie ist die Person, die Schöpfer ihrer Begebenheiten." (Lenz, *Werke* 2:668; The principal sentiment of comedy is always the event, while the principal sentiment of tragedy is the person, the creator of the events.[41]) This definition does indeed help explain why Lenz called his plays comedies—notably in *Der Hofmeister*, where the main character appears almost completely subjected to his environment and to the actions that this environment engenders.

In "Rezension des neuen Menoza, von dem Verfasser selbst aufgesetzt" ("Review of *The New Menoza*, Written by the Author Himself") Lenz introduces another fundamental distinction between comedy and tragedy by emphasizing the nature of the audience to which the respective genres cater. Defending himself against the accusation that his play *Der neue Menoza* is too serious for a comedy, Lenz explains that he understands comedy not to be defined by laughter, but by addressing the general public: "Ich nenne durchaus Komödie nicht eine Vorstellung die bloß Lachen erregt, sondern eine Vorstellung die für jedermann ist. Tragödie ist nur für den ernshaftern Teil des Publikums." (Lenz, *Werke* 2:703; I certainly don't call comedy a performance that arouses merely laughter, but a performance that is for everyone. Tragedy is only for the more serious part of the audience [....], Lenz, *Works* 294.)

Both of Lenz's distinctions between comedy and tragedy provide helpful context to explain the meaning of genre in Lenz's own plays, and neither of them easily maps onto the definition of comedy as focused on laughable vice, which Gottsched emphasized. Both in light *of Anmergkungen übers Theater* and in light of "Rezension des neuen Menoza," it appears justified to say that Lenz reconceived the very notion of comedy.[42]

And yet the relationship between Lenz's comic production and the German Enlightenment tradition is much more complicated than the notes above suggest, and it is certainly insufficiently described in terms of a mere rupture. The explicit and—at least on the surface—very positive reference to Lessing's *Minna von Barnhelm* in Lenz's *Der Hofmeister*, already alluded to above, is a first indicator of this complex relationship. It occurs in one of the many digressive genre scenes of the play (act 2, scene 3), focusing, in this case, on the everyday student life in Halle, Saxony. What the students discuss in this scene, aside from the cost and condition of their accommodations, is the arrival of Karl Theophilus Döbbelin's (historical) theater troupe, which, we are told, has come to Halle to perform Lessing's *Minna von*

*Barnhelm*—news that triggers great enthusiasm among the students. While one should distinguish here between the opinions expressed by some of the play's characters versus the opinions presumably held by the author, the students' enthusiasm surrounding Lessing's comedy can likely be interpreted as genuinely reflective of the esteem in which the young *Sturm und Drang* student generation held Lessing's still fairly recent comedy.

Lenz, however, does much to complicate this relatively straightforward affirmative nod to the Enlightenment playwright. As it turns out, one of the students, Pätus, is in such financial straits that he has no appropriate coat to wear to the theatre. All he has left is a wolfskin coat that is quite unsuitable for the hot summer weather. As luck would have it, the theater troupe arrives during the "dog days" of summer ("Hundstage," Lenz, *Werke* 1:66)—in more than one sense: while the heatwave is raging, ten raging dogs are also roaming the town of Halle. Nevertheless, as we are later told in a crudely comic scene featuring a group of young women acquainted with the students, Pätus is so desperate to see the play that he does eventually venture out in his wolfskin coat to see the play. But, as he makes his way to the theater, three of the raging dogs start chasing him, attracted, apparently, by his coat. The young woman who describes the chase (her traditionally comic descriptive name is Jungfer Knicks [literally, Miss Curtsey]) casts it as hilarious entertainment. Indeed, she claims that the scene is so amusing that she no longer wishes to attend the theater, for: "ich würde da doch nicht soviel zu lachen kriegen" (Lenz, *Werke* 1:67; I wouldn't have as much to laugh at there, Lenz, *Works* 45).

Jungfer Knicks's account strangely complicates Lenz's initially simple and affirmative reference to Lessing's play. In some sense, it appears that Lenz uses the episode as a means to emphasize how he is outdoing the social realism that Lessing's comedy, with its precise dating and its focus on money (and especially the lack thereof), is known for. Lenz's characters are so poor that they cannot even make it to the theater to watch Lessing's comedy about money problems. But, in another sense, Lenz also turns the social and psychological realism of Lessing's comedy into a farcical, grotesquely comic scene of the student in a wolfskin coat being chased by raging dogs. According to that reading, Lenz appears to use this scene to polemically reactivate an older tradition of crude onstage humor that the previous two generations of playwrights had tentatively—albeit never completely—banned from the German stage.

However one reads Lenz's complex reference to Lessing, it is clear that Lenz does much to deeply embed his play within the German comic tradition. But, rather than placing his comedy simply and squarely within this tradition, in some way or another, the episode surrounding the wolfskin coat serves to capture not only the still-current enthusiasm for Lessing but also some critical distance. Nevertheless, Lenz does seek to position his play in ways that make it meaningful from the viewpoint of this tradition.

Moreover (and more importantly), beyond this intertextual play with Lessing's comedy, Lenz's *Der Hofmeister* reads in many ways as just another play in a long series of creative, liberal appropriations of the Gottschedian paradigm of laughable vice. Already the title, *Der Hofmeister*, which references at once the main hero and the main laughable "vice," is structurally parallel to the Molière-like comedy that Gottsched had in mind when he developed his poetics. Compare Molière's most famous comedies: *Tartuffe ou L'Imposteur* (1664; *Tartuffe, or The Hypocrite*), *Le Misanthrope* (1666; *The Misanthrope*), or *L'Avare* (1668; *The Miser*). And, in rather traditional ways, Lenz explicitly marks, in both the opening and closing scenes of the play, the folly of tutoring as the central point of his comedy.[43]

The important difference to earlier plays—whether Molière's or those of the German tradition—is, of course, that the titular tutor represents not so much an individual vice (nor an individual's vice), such as avarice, greed, bigotry, or hypochondria, but a profession and a social institution.[44] Indeed, as the famous opening scene makes clear, Läuffer, the tutor of the play, is more or less pushed into this profession as his only career option (however, the play repeatedly calls into question exactly how inescapable the pressure to become a tutor really is, most notably by the school principal and privy councilor, Herr von Berg [Lenz, *Werke* 1:54-60; Lenz, *Works* 36-40]). The play's subtitle already broadens the focus from the individual tutor ("Der Hofmeister") to the general social institution of private education ("Vorteile der Privaterziehung"; Advantages of Private Education). This shift of concentration from the individual to the underlying social structures as an explanation for the dramatic behavior on stage marks an important innovation both in German intellectual history and in German drama, and thus foreshadows the work of Lenz's avid readers Georg Büchner and Bertolt Brecht in subsequent centuries.

If the Gottschedian paradigm consists in secularizing vice by making it the product of an individual's misbehavior rather than a diabolic influence in the world, Lenz's comic practice introduces another shift by tentatively characterizing vice as the responsibility of social structures and institutions. At the same time, however, and in contrast to those influenced by Lenz in the following centuries, Lenz still marks this social critique as analogous to or as a variation of the focus on individual laughable vice heralded by German Enlightenment comedy. Moreover, as important as Lenz's innovation is, his shift in focus to social and political problems had been prefigured in the comedies of playwrights of the previous generation. Notably, Lessing's *Die Juden* (1749), with its critique of anti-Judaism, has long been recognized for including broader social and ideological problems into the genre of comedy.[45] And one might even wish to reconsider whether the strong dichotomy between the focus on individuals' vices and the focus on underlying social problems really holds. To the extent that comedy has a longstanding affinity with money, as Daniel Fulda has most recently demonstrated, broader economic and social questions are always nearby—even if they are not explicitly discussed or at the center of attention. A play like Luise Gottsched's *Das Testament* already embeds its moral tale of *Eigennutz* in a broader social and economic narrative about property, inheritance, and labor. The point here, to be sure, is not to deny the existing differences between Lenz (or *Sturm und Drang* more broadly) and the Enlightenment, but to make them legible as existing on a continuum of variations that preclude the identification of an unambiguous rupture.

# The Tragic Turn of Comic Vice:
# Wagner's *Die Reue nach der That*

The fact that *Sturm und Drang* did indeed still adhere to the paradigm of German Enlightenment comedy (by continuing the tradition of its variations) is perhaps even better illustrated by Heinrich Leopold Wagner's *Die Reue nach der That* (1775). Wagner's play is not explicitly a comedy; rather, Wagner labeled it a "Schauspiel," and recent scholarship has also described it as a *Bürgerliches Trauerspiel* (bourgeois tragedy).[46] Despite these competing genre designations, however, *Die Reue nach der That* remains clearly recognizable as connected to the comic tradition. Indeed, the play presents an interesting case study for how the mixing of genres (of comedy and tragedy) as a hallmark of *Sturm und Drang* aesthetics emerges from a longstanding tradition of variations on the comic paradigm. My contention is that Wagner's play begins in many ways as a traditional comedy—even more so, in fact, than Lenz's *Hofmeister*, which was published one year earlier.[47] Following the Gottschedian prescriptions very closely, *Die Reue nach der That* focuses on one specific vice—namely, class arrogance—and displays this vice as a laughable aberration in the ridiculous figure of the widowed (and half impoverished) Justizrätinn Lange, who desperately clings to her standing as a member of the (lower) nobility.[48] Insisting on her superiority as a member of the nobility, she does all she can to prevent her son, the young civil servant Assessor Langen, from marrying Fridericke, the daughter of the emperor's coachman.

To the extent that the focus here is on a love story complicated by a class conflict between the nobility and the middle class, the designation of the play as a bourgeois tragedy does make sense (even though it is already rather untypical, in that it focuses more on the plight of the young nobleman than on that of the middle-class daughter). Nevertheless, because of the portrayal of the ridiculous Justizräthinn, who is characterized largely by one single vice, I argue that the play presents itself to the reader and spectator as a comedy. And, again, aligning with the genre expectations, the Justizräthinn does, in the end, recognize her misbehavior and agrees to the marriage of her son and Fridericke.

What Wagner does to present a new variation of the traditional paradigm is at once exceedingly simple and profoundly far-reaching. As the title of the play already indicates, the turn to the better occurs too late—and this is precisely what, rather surprisingly, makes the traditional comedy flip over into the realm of tragedy in the end. By the time the Justizräthinn changes her behavior, the desperate Fridericke has already poisoned herself, which, in turn, leads Assessor Langen to commit suicide as well (the legacy of both Shakespeare's *Romeo and Juliet* and Lessing's *Miß Sara Sampson* is palpable here). To be sure, to the extent that the play evokes, from the outset, the paradigm of bourgeois tragedy, this ending does fit rather unproblematically. Indeed, one might be tempted to call the entire play a bourgeois tragedy and describe its comic elements simply as a typical feature of bourgeois tragedy's general indebtedness to the comic genre.[49] However, interpreting this play as a bourgeois tragedy, I argue, is really only convincing retrospectively because of the play's ending. And this "tragic" ending is little else than the result of just another variation in the comic paradigm of depicting a laughable vice. The play stages a laughable vice turning into something much more serious (and this constitutes the important variation)—but this more serious ending does not change the fact that the play still proceeds from the theme of a recognizably laughable vice.

The goal in all of this here, to repeat this crucial point in closing, is certainly not to flatten the dynamic development of literary history by downplaying the many important innovations that the middle decades of the eighteenth century brought about. What this article however seeks to achieve, is to illustrate how *Sturm und Drang* is much more clearly situated in the tradition of Enlightenment comedy than scholars normally suggest. More precisely, *Sturm und Drang* remained indebted not so much to a fixed form of literary representation (namely comedy), but to a long and dynamic tradition of variations on this form. As I suggested at the outset of this article, this reading of *Sturm und Drang* as continuing the German Enlightenment comic tradition fits very well into the general view of *Sturm und Drang* suggested by scholars of the last few decades. Currently, the dominant idea is that *Sturm und Drang* is best understood not as a rupture with Enlightenment ideas but as an internal critique of the Enlightenment. As the present article aims to demonstrate in its analysis of comedy, this view, which is usually applied only to the explicit politics of *Sturm und Drang*, can very likely be extended to *Sturm und Drang*'s treatment of formal and generic traditions as well.

*University of Calgary*

## NOTES

1. The stark rupture between the discussion of Enlightenment and *Sturm und Drang* comedy in Catholy's study was already criticized upon its first publication in 1982 (see Wulf Koepke, review of *Das deutsche Lustspiel von der Aufklärung bis zur Romantik*, by Eckehard Catholy, *German Studies Review* 7, no. 2 [1984]: 345–46; here 345). Some recent studies depart from this assumed rupture by studying comedy in ways that extend from Enlightenment through Romanticism; see, for instance, Tom Kindt, *Literatur und Komik. Zur Theorie literarischer Komik und zur deutschen Komödie im 18. Jahrhundert* (Berlin: Akademie Verlag, 2011); and Joel Lande, *Persistence of Folly: On the Origins of German Dramatic Literature* (Ithaca, NY: Cornell UP, 2018).

2. This positive highlighting of Lessing's comedy in Lenz's 1774 play thus parallels the well-known reference to Lessing's tragedy *Emilia Galotti* in Goethe's *Die Leiden des jungen Werthers*, published in the same year.

3. Julia Freytag, "Dramen und Dramenfragmente," in *J. M. R. Lenz-Handbuch*, ed. Julia Freytag and Hans-Gerd Winter (Berlin: De Gruyter, 2017) 47–127, here 47.

4. Matthias Luserke-Jaqui, "Zur Wissenschaftsgeschichte des Sturm und Drang," in *Handbuch Sturm und Drang*, ed. Matthias Luserke-Jaqui (Berlin: De Gruyter, 2017) 8–28, here 20.

5. See Luserke 20–24. Unless otherwise noted all translations are my own.

6. Eckehard Catholy, *Das deutsche Lustspiel. Von der Aufklärung bis zur Romantik* (Stuttgart: Kohlhammer, 1982) 11–12.

7. See, most recently and most extensively, Lande, *The Persistence of Folly*.

8. The emphasis on Gottsched's poetics in this article is not meant to denigrate the importance of other influences from beyond the German-speaking realm on the development of German comedy. What is important for the present purposes, however, is that these other influences did not lead to a complete break with the Gottschedian paradigm in eighteenth-century German comedy.

9. For a discussion of Minnesang as *Variationskunst*, see Günther Schweikle, *Minnesang* (Stuttgart: Metzler, 1995) 196.

10. Wolfgang Martens, *Die Botschaft der Tugend. Die Aufklärung im Spiegel der deutschen Moralischen Wochenschriften* (Stuttgart: Metzler, 1968) 234–35.

11. Catholy 12.

12. Johann Christoph Gottsched, *Versuch einer critischen Dichtkunst. Vierte sehr vermehrte Auflage* (Leipzig: Bernhard Christoph Breitkopf, 1751) 647.

13. J. C. Gottsched, *Versuch* 652. Gottsched allows either prose or verse, as long as the comedy retains "die gemeinsten Redensarten" (Gottsched, *Versuch*, 652; the most common idiom).

14. J. C. Gottsched, *Versuch*, 606.

15. J. C. Gottsched, *Versuch*, 606.

16. Gottsched here is apparently thinking of Artistotle's *Poetics* (1449a):"Comedy, as we said, is mimesis of baser but not wholly vicious characters: rather the laughable is one category of the shameful. For the laughable comprises any fault or mark of shame which involves no pain or destruction: most obviously, the laughable mask is something ugly and twisted, but not painfully." (Aristotle, *Poetics*, ed. Stephen Halliwell (Boston: Harvard University Press, 1999) 45. In Gottsched's poetics, these lines from Aristotle are silently combined with the Horatian insistence in *Ars Poetica* that the purpose of literature is to either entertain or instruct—or to do both at the same time.

17. J. C. Gottsched, *Versuch*, 643.

18. Catholy 30.

19. J. C. Gottsched, *Versuch*, 645; Catholy 20.

20. Johann Christoph Gottsched, "Vorrede," in *Der deutschen Schaubühne nach den Regeln und Mustern der Alten, sechster und letzter Theil*, ed. Johann Christoph Gottsched (Leipzig: Bernhard Christoph Breitkopf, 1745) [15-26], here [20].

21. Luise Gottsched, *Das Testament*, in *Der deutschen Schaubühne nach den Regeln und Mustern der Alten, sechster und letzter Theil*, ed. Johann Christoph Gottsched (Leipzig: Bernhard Christoph Breitkopf, 1745) 81–204, here 94, 204.

22. Catholy 31.

23. Luise Gottsched 193.

24. For the distinction between "laughing with" and "laughing about," see Catholy 20–40.

25. Newer studies appear to echo Steinmetz's reading of the play; see, for instance, Monika Fick, *Lessing-Handbuch. Leben—Werk—Wirkung* (Stuttgart: Metzler, 2000) 251–52.

26. Horst Steinmetz, *Die Komödie der Aufklärung* (Stuttgart: Metzler, 1966) 64.

27. Johann Wolfgang Goethe, *Faust*, in *Sämtliche Werke. Briefe, Tagebücher und Gespräche*, hrsg. Friedmar Apel et al., 40 Bde. (Frankfurt a/M: Deutscher Klassiker Verlag, 1985–2013). Hereafter abbreviated as FA and cited parenthetically.

28. More recent interpretations have further underscored Lessing's new emphasis on the portrayal of social reality in *Minna von Barnhelm* (see, notably, Benjamin Bennett, "The Generic Constant in Lessing's Development of a Comedy of Institutions and Alienation," *The German Quarterly* 56, no. 2 (1983): 231–42.

29. In my emphasis on the indistinction between vice and virtue in the play, I find myself in agreement with K. F. Hilliard's recent interpretation of the play. K. F. Hilliard, "Lessing's Comedies," in *Lessing and the German Enlightenment*, ed. Ritchie Robertson (Oxford: Voltaire Foundation, 2013) 159–77, here 173–77.

30. Gotthold Ephraim Lessing, *Minna von Barnhelm oder das Soldatenglück. Ein Lustspiel verfertiget im Jahre 1763*, ed. Jürgen Hein (Stuttgart: Reclam, 2003) 24.

31. Lessing, *Minna*, 105.

32. Lessing, *Minna*, 24.

33. Lessing, *Minna*, 64.

34. Lessing, *Minna*, 64.

35. It might be argued that Lessing's sincere character Tellheim is less a figure of comedy than of bourgeois tragedy (and there is, to be sure, some affinity between the two genres in Lessing's oeuvre). At least if one takes the indistinction between vice and virtue as the measure, the titular character from *Miß Sara Sampson* (1755) would certainly appear similar to Tellheim. But this abstract parallel should not blind us to the marked distinction between these two characters—and thus between the two genres from which they emerge. Virtuous though she may prove herself to be, Sara is burdened by a consciousness of vicious behavior that makes her a significantly graver character than Tellheim.

36. Benjamin Bennett goes so far as to say that Tellheim's refusal to marry is perfectly justified: society would indeed have judged Minna for marrying a poor and dishonored former officer (Bennett 232).

37. On this feature of Schlegel's comedy, see Catholy 38.

38. In the case of *Die Soldaten* alone, Lenz wanted to change the label from "Komödie" to "Schauspiel." In a letter to Johann Georg Zimmermann, Lenz explains: "Es [die Bezeichnung der Komödie] könnte außer der Seltsamkeit noch den Schaden haben, daß ein ganzer Stand, der mir ehrwürdig ist, dadurch ein gewisses Lächerliche, das nur den verdorbenen Sitten einiger Individuen desselben zugedacht war, auf sich bezöge" (Despite being strange, the designation of the play as a comedy could also have the adverse effect that an entire class that I admire would appear ridiculous, even though I intended to portray only a few individuals from this class in this manner). J. M. R. Lenz, *Werke und Briefe in drei Bänden*, ed. Sigrid Damm (Frankfurt a/M: Insel, 1897), vol. 3, 395. Further references to this edition are cited parenthetically in the text as "*Werke*." Lenz's request, however, came too late to be reflected in the printed edition of this play.

39. Paradoxically, perhaps, Lenz called his early adaptations of Plautus *Lustspiele nach dem Plautus* ("Lustspiele" in the Style of Plautus).

40. The interesting exception to this is Johann Christoph Gottsched, who, in his *Critische Dichtkunst*, uses both terms interchangeably: his chapter on comedy is called "Von Komödien oder Lustspielen" (J. C. Gottsched, *Versuch*, 631).

41. J. M. R. Lenz, *Selected Works: Plays, Stories, Essays, and Poems*, ed. Martin Wagner and Ellwood Wiggins (Rochester, NY: Camden House, 2019) 282. Further references are given parenthetically in the text as "*Works.*"

42. Freytag 47.

43. Famously, the final words of the play read: "Wenigstens, mein süßer Junge, werde ich dich nie durch Hofmeister erziehen lassen." (Lenz, *Werke* 1:123; At least, my sweet boy, I shall never have you educated by tutors. Lenz, *Works* 89.)

44. The extent to which Lenz's critique aims at social structures rather than individual moral behavior has been controversially discussed. For a skeptical view of Lenz as a social critic, see David Hill, "Das Politische in *Die Soldaten*" *Orbis Litterarum* 43, no. 3 (1988): 299–315.

45. Steinecke 61; more recently, Fick 62.

46. Lisa Wille, "*Die Reue nach der That*" in *Handbuch Sturm und Drang*, ed. Matthias Luserke-Jaqui (Berlin: De Gruyter, 2017) 386–92; here 391.

47. Incidentally, this clearer adherence to the traditional paradigm might also explain why, in contrast to Lenz's plays, *Die Reue nach der That* had relatively robust success in German theaters of the time, having at least four distinct productions between 1775 and 1781 (Wille 386). For my discussion of *Die Reue nach der That* as emerging from the tradition of German Enlightenment comedy, I am indebted to Gaby Pailer, who developed a related thesis at the roundtable "Radical and Moderate *Sturm und Drang*" at the 2020 conference of the Modern Language Association.

48. Like Lenz's play, albeit less radically, *Die Reue nach der That* transgresses a number of other rules set out by Gottsched for the writing of drama, notably the three unities.

49. The less elevated style of bourgeois tragedy and its focus on the middle class are perhaps the most obvious ways in which bourgeois tragedy approximates comedy. Moreover, Lessing's paradigm-setting *Miß Sara Sampson* also includes in the figure of the innkeeper a typically laughable and vicious comic character. Indeed, the untrustworthy innkeeper of *Miß Sara Sampson* appears to be a direct precursor of the innkeeper in Lessing's comedy *Minna von Barnhelm*. More generally, the *comédie larmoyante* (tearful comedy) as produced by Gellert in Germany in the 1740s is seen as a precursor to the bourgeois tragedy developed by Lessing in the following decade. See, Helga Stipland, "Bourgeois Tragedy," in *Encyclopedia of German Literature*, ed. Matthias Konzett (New York: Routledge, 2000).

KARIN SCHUTJER

# Heaven Help Us! Journals! Calendars!: Goethe and Schiller's *Xenien* as Circulatory Intervention

**Abstract:** In their *Xenien* project, Goethe and Schiller weaponized the classical epigrammatic distich on behalf of their own vision of a public sphere. In response to an oversaturated market in journals and in the context of falling subscription numbers for their own journal *Die Horen*, they published hundreds of epigrams attacking rival journals and authors. Taking a cue from new formalist approaches, this article analyzes the specific structural and rhetorical affordances of the distich and the broader formal strategies the authors deploy in this cultural intervention. The generic resources of the epigram are deployed to disrupt a commercial circulation generated by second-rate journals and their networks of "Philistine" writers and critics, to deconstruct false paradigms and overblown conceptions, to parody the overaccelerated or excessively sluggish pace of cultural production and exchange, and to expose those forces bent on overturning established social or political hierarchies. At the same time, the epigrams aim to set in motion a more rhythmic circulation that aligns with natural processes and classical antecedents, is shaped by the reciprocal exchange characterizing Goethe and Schiller's own friendship, gives rise to more elastic and internally differentiated conceptions of the whole, and ultimately sustains rather than overturns societal structures.

**Keywords:** Schiller, *Die Horen*, *Xenien*, distich, epigram, formalism, journal, public sphere

*Das deutsche Reich.*

Deutschland? aber wo liegt es? Ich weiß das Land nicht zu finden
Wo das gelehrte beginnt, hört das politische auf. (222)[1]

*The German Empire.*

Germany? But where is it? I don't know where to find that land.
Where the land of letters begins, the political one ends.

"DAS DEUTSCHE REICH" may be the best-known couplet from Goethe and Schiller's *Xenien* (*The Xenia*), their collection of 414 epigrams lampooning their contemporaries, and published in Schiller's *Musenal-manach für das Jahr 1797* (Muses' Almanac for the Year 1797). This particular epigram is often quoted as a pithy rebuke to the nationalist stirrings of the era. The first line already deals the blow: the "Deutschland" appealed to by an unnamed other (or others) simply does not exist. But the second line demands a little more consideration: why must the political Germany end where the land of letters begins? Evoked here, I argue, is in fact a bitter contest between two journals that represent competing bids, learned and political, to define "das deutsche Reich." Schiller's own pet project, the explicitly apolitical journal *Die Horen* (The Horae), constituted by a "Gesellschaft bekannter Gelehrten" (June 13, 1794; society of well-known men of letters) is implicitly pitted against a bête noir of the *Xenien*, Johann Friedrich Reichardt's overtly political journal *Deutschland* (Germany).[2]

Reichhardt's presumptuous journal titles (prior to *Deutschland*, he launched the journal *Frankreich* [*France*][3]) are explicitly mocked in another epigram:

*Nur Zeitschriften.*
*Frankreich* faßt er mit einer, das arme *Deutschland* gewaltig
    Mit der andern, doch sind beyde papieren und leicht! (251)


*Only Journals.*
*France* he seizes with one, poor *Germany* mightily
    With the other, but both are papery and light!

Here the *"Frankreich"* and *"Deutschland"* that Reichardt presumes to commandeer, titan-like, turn out to be paper-thin constructs. The currency in weak or fraudulent constructs or *forms* is the broader target of the *Xenien*. Ultimately at stake in the battles staged by the *Xenien* is the opportunity to define an overarching and inclusive social form—the German public sphere—through a new or renewed cultural circulation.

To be clear, my analysis relies on a promiscuous use of the term "form" that can refer to constructs as disparate as *Deutschland*, the distich, the literary market, or truth.[4] In doing so, I take cues from Caroline Levine, whose expansive definition of form encompasses not only aesthetic practices and patterns but also sociopolitical structures. For Levine's account of the portability of forms across domains—whether aesthetic, social, economic, political, or scientific—aligns well with the broader morphological assumptions informing Schiller and Goethe's thought in this era, where an aesthetic form indeed has the capacity to reflect, participate in, advance, or resist, broader social, political, natural, and even cosmological forms. In drawing out the specific features of the epigrammatic distich that serve Goethe and Schiller's broader cultural agenda, I am helped by Levine's discourse of "affordances," the latent properties and potentialities of forms. Furthermore, in my discussion below, I borrow Levine's taxonomy of overlapping and mutually interacting forms—networks, wholes, rhythms, and hierarchies—to describe the multiple schemes and configurations through which the *Xenien* do their cultural work.[5]

Drawing on these conceptual resources, then, I show how Goethe and Schiller deploy the epigram to disrupt the circulation they see generated by commercial networks of second-rate journals and "Philistine" writers and critics, a circulation that trades in false paradigms or overblown conceptions and wholes, that is too accelerated or too sluggish in its rhythm, too crassly commercial, or bent on overturning established social or political hierarchies. They aim to substitute a circulation modeled on natural processes, one that takes off from their own emerging friendship and extends to an elite network of contemporary and historical authors, that leads to more elastic conceptions of the whole and produces a social dynamism with a more even-paced rhythm, that sustains rather than overturns societal hierarchies, and ultimately forges a new, ever-broadening audience for their own cultural program, as embodied by their faltering journal *Die Horen*. The classical distich, as I will portray, turns out to offer a wealth of affordances for such offensive and defensive maneuvers.[6]

## The Vision for *Die Horen*

But first we return to the aspirations and failings of *Die Horen*, which set the stage for the *Xenien* project. Schiller's conception for *Die Horen* emerged against the backdrop of a saturated market in literary journals, with as many as five hundred titles in the mid-1790s.[7] *Die Horen* thus had to create a network of authors and readers expansive enough to overcome that extreme market fragmentation. In the invitation extended to Goethe and others, Schiller proposes joining forces to consolidate this large but disparate public:

> Treten nun die vorzüglichsten Schriftsteller der Nation in eine literarische Assoziation zusammen, so vereinigen sie eben dadurch das vorher geteilt gewesene Publikum, und das Werk, an welchem alle Anteil nehmen, wird die ganze lesende Welt zu seinem Publikum haben. (NA 22:104)

> When the most excellent authors of the nation assemble into a literary association, they thereby unite the previously divided public, and the work in which they all share will have the entire reading world as its audience.

Schiller projects this expansive "lesende Welt" through his eventual list of contributors in the journal's "Ankündigung" (Announcement). In addition to the half dozen authors centered in Weimar and Jena, the outposts reach as far as Breslau (Wroclaw) and Mietau (Jelgava, Latvia) to the east and northeast; Hamburg and Amsterdam to the north and northwest; and Colmar, Switzerland, and Rome to the southwest and south (NA 22:108–9). The journal promises to overcome borders in other respects: it promises to bring together the scholarly and poetic (*schöne*) worlds through the "Aufhebung der Scheidewand" (lifting of the partition) separating them (NA 22:107) and to reconcile scholarly and nonscholarly worlds by only allowing content at the intersection of their interests (NA 22:103). By banning all political material, *Die Horen* will overcome narrow partisan allegiances and unite a politically divided world (NA 22:106).

Perhaps the most important network forged by *Die Horen* was the Goethe-Schiller dyad. Their correspondence commences in the summer of 1794 when Schiller invites Goethe to collaborate on the journal. While Schiller remained the editor, and Goethe a member of the governing committee, the journal took on the character of a joint project, referred to as "uns[ere] Unternehmung" (our undertaking) by Schiller (September 29, 1794).[8] Indeed, the journal became not just the occasion and the vehicle of their collaboration but also its theoretical manifesto. In an early letter, Schiller casts his new relationship as an encounter of speculative (Schillerian) and intuitive (Goethean) spirit.

> Beim ersten Anblicke zwar scheint es, als könnte es keine größeren Opposita geben, als den speculativen Geist, der von der Einheit, und den intuitiven, der von der Mannigfaltigkeit ausgeht. Sucht aber der erste mit keuschem und treuem Sinn die Erfahrung, und sucht der letzte mit selbstthätiger freier Denkkraft das Gesetz, so kann es gar nicht fehlen, daß nicht beide einander auf halbem Wege begegnen werden. (August 23, 1794)

> At first look, it may appear as if there could be no greater oppositions than the speculative spirit, which assumes unity, and the intuitive one, which assumes multiplicity. But if the former seeks experience with a chaste and faithful sense, and the latter seeks the law with self-acting, free mental powers, then it cannot fail that they will both meet each other halfway.

Schiller posits here a reciprocal exchange between oppositional terms like unity and diversity, law and experience, even, implicitly, masculine (*selbsttäthig, frei*) and feminine (*keusch, treu*) principles. This friendship paradigm expands into full-blown models of human culture in his essays "Über die ästhetische Erziehung des Menschen in einer Reihe von Briefen" ("On the Aesthetic Education of Man in a Series of Letters") and "Über naïve und sentimentalische Dichtung" ("Naive and Sentimental Poetry"), both published in *Die Horen.*

In its classicizing stance, *Die Horen* also endorses steady rhythms and hierarchy over the accelerated pace and tumultuous upheavals of the Revolutionary era, citing the fear and tension caused by "das nahe Geräusch des Kriegs" (the nearby sound of war), "der Anblick der Zeitbegebenheiten" (the view of contemporary events), and "de[r] allverfolgende[ ] Dämon der Staatskritik" (NA 22:106; the all-pursuing daemon of criticism directed against the state). Instead, the journal takes its name from the ancient goddesses who encircle the world as escorts of Venus, and evokes the rhythms of the natural order: "die welterhaltende Ordnung, aus der alles Gute fließt, und die in dem gleichförmigen Rhythmus des Sonnenlaufs ihr treffendstes Sinnbild findet" (NA 22:107; The world-sustaining order from which all good flows and which finds its most fitting symbol in the steady rhythm of the sun's course). This elevated, orbital imagery also reflects the pervasive hierarchical stance of the journal, its "allgemeines und höheres Interesse an dem, was *rein menschlich* und über allen Einfluß der Zeiten erhaben ist" (NA 22:106, emphasis in original; universal and higher interest in that which is *purely human* and elevated above all epochal influence).

Ultimately, *Die Horen* aspires to illuminate new aesthetic and conceptual "wholes," such as truth and beauty. For both Goethe and Schiller, these arc won through reciprocity and mediation. Schiller's aesthetic "play drive" involves a chiastic exchange of characteristics between sense and thought, much like the dynamics of his friendship with Goethe. If beauty emerges through mediation, it serves further, according to *Die Horen-Ankündigung*, as a "Vermittlerin der Wahrheit" (NA 22:107; mediator of truth). The closest equivalent to Schiller's aesthetic play drive in Goethe's thought is perhaps *Bildung*. In his essay "Literarischer Sanskulottismus" (Literary Sanscullotism) also published in *Die Horen*, Goethe laments the lack of a productive middle space in Germany, the absence of "ein Mittelpunkt gesellschaftlicher Lebensbildung" (a centerpoint of formative societal processes), where authors could convene to develop themselves with a common sense of purpose (FA 1.18: 321). Like Schiller's conception of the aesthetic, Goethe's ideal of *Bildung* involves exchange and mutual determination by internal and external forces. For both authors, the outcome of these processes is conceived as an ideal social domain, but not one to be conflated with a political state. The result of the play drive is the "Reich des schönen Scheins" (empire of beautiful semblance), where true (rather than mere political) equality is achieved, even if such an empire rarely exists in reality (NA 20:411). For Goethe, as he will write a few years later: "Wo wir uns *bilden*, da ist unser Vaterland" (FA 1.6: 888, emphasis added; Where we *educate* ourselves, there is our fatherland).

## The Decline of *Die Horen* and the Rise of the *Xenien*

Despite the lofty rhetoric, *Die Horen* was of course very much a commercial enterprise and economic lifeline for Schiller in particular.[9] For example, in negotiating with Cotta for a higher than contractual honorarium for Goethe, Schiller characterized his new friend in blatantly commercial terms, as "eine zu kostbare Acquisition, als daß man ihn nicht um welchen Preis es auch sey, erkaufen sollte" (a too precious acquisition than that one ought not to purchase him at whatever price).[10] Goethe's glee in the frenzied initial reaction to the journal hardly comports with the smooth and orderly motion promised in the journal's announcement: "Im Weimarischen Publico rumoren die Horen gewaltig . . . man ist eigentlich nur *dahinter her*, man reißt sich die Stücke aus den Händen" (March 18, 1795; In the Weimar public the Horae are rumbling mightily .. people are after them, they tear the issues from each other's hands). While Schiller was concerned to offer a prestige commodity, which, through typography, format, and high quality paper, would stand out favorably among the "Haufen der Journale" (December 22, 1794; piles of journals), he was also soon willing to compromise on the quality of content for the sake of sales, acquiescing sarcastically: "gerade so, wie unsere Werten Leser es lieben" (September 18, 1795; just so, the way our esteemed readers love it).

Even so the commercial enterprise soon began to falter. While numbers in the first year (1795) were strong, with around 1800 subscriptions and additional sales resulting in a total print run of 2500 copies, the first inklings of trouble ahead were already emerging by September of that year.[11] The second-year subscription number declined to around 1500, and then fell further in the third year to around 1000, well under the break-even threshold of 1300, causing the journal to fold.[12]

Meanwhile, as concerns about numbers rose, Schiller and Goethe became increasingly riled by negative reviews of *Die Horen* in other journals. Goethe takes a particularly combative tone and begins to contemplate revenge, "zu überlegen wäre es, ob man nicht vor Ende des Jahrs sich über einiges erklärte und unter die Autoren und Rezensenten Hoffnung und Furcht verbreitetete" (September 16, 1795; it's worth considering, whether before the year's end one might not make some declarations and spread hope and fear among the authors and reviewers). Not long afterward, he suggests they collect, hold court, and burn the negative commentary in a bundle (October 28, 1795). Finally, in late December, his retaliatory intent assumed concrete form, modeled on Martial's *Xenia:*

> Den Einfall, auf alle Zeitschriften Epigramme, jedes in einem einzigen Disticho, zu machen, wie die Xenia des Martials sind, der mir dieser Tage gekommen ist, müssen wir kultivieren und eine solche Sammlung in Ihren Musenalmanach des nächsten Jahres bringen. (December 23, 1795)

> We must cultivate the idea that came to me recently of making epigrams for all journals, each in a single distich, like Martials Xenia, and bring out such a collection in your Muses' Almanac for next year.

Schiller was quickly sold: "Der Gedanke mit den Xenien ist prächtig und muß ausgeführt werden" (December 29, 1795; The idea with the Xenia is splendid and must be carried out) and suggested expanding their attacks to include individual works.

Even as Goethe and Schiller widened their scope, the new year brought them a new focus for their aggression that exemplified all of their grievances: Johann Friedrich Reichardt launched his journal *Deutschland* with a disparaging review of *Die Horen* in its inaugural issue. The gist of Reichardt's critique was that *Die Horen*'s apolitical posture—its pledge to maintain silence concerning the popular obsessions of the day—was pure pretense. With reference to the negative portrayal of Republican sympathies in *Unterhaltungen deutscher Ausgewanderten* (*Conversations of German Refugees*), one of the works featured in *Die Horen*, he inquires whether it indeed reflects an honest silence about contemporary political matters: "Heißt das nicht vielmehr, die wichtigen Gegenstände mit dictatorischem Uebermuthe aburtheilen?" (Doesn't that really mean passing judgment on important matters with dictatorial arrogance?)[13]

Reichardt, who composed many musical settings for Goethe's works, had in fact long enjoyed a friendship with the poet. But Goethe had recently distanced himself, just as Reichardt was suffering the loss of royal patronage because of his political beliefs. Schiller knew Reichardt, but never liked him.[14] Now, Reichardt's journal seemed to compete with *Die Horen* in the role of forging public life, but with reference to a "Deutschland" that Goethe and Schiller abjured. Reichardt writes:

> Deutschland hat viele Zeitschriften, vielleicht mehr als für den guten Geschmack an ächt belehrender Lektüre zu wünschen sein möchte; aber es hat keine, die sich so recht eigentlich mit Deutschland beschäftigten, und auf wahren Gemeinsinn, der uns guten Deutschen mehr als alles andere fehlt, abzweckten."[15]

> Germany has many journals, perhaps more than are desirable with regard to good taste in genuinely instructive reading material, but it has none that were actually occupied with Germany and were aimed at a true public spirit, which we good Germans are missing more than anything else.

With this journal, Reichardt had, according to Schiller, invaded their rightful territory; "er [machte] uns auf unserem legitimen Boden den Krieg" (February 5, 1796; he [made] war with us on our legitimate ground). Goethe and Schiller's reaction was furious. In one letter, after characterizing Reichardt as an insect, Schiller proclaims "Wir sollen es zu Tode hetzen" (October 16, 1796; We should hound it to death). In the end, a substantial portion of the *Xenien* output was directed against Reichardt.[16] (As a target of the *Xenien*, Reichardt was rivaled only by a much older foe of Goethe's, who was also responsible for a negative review of *Die Horen*, the pedantic champion of the Enlightenment, Friedrich Nicolai.)

While *Die Horen* may have provided the initial opportunity for collaboration, the Goethe-Schiller alliance was cemented through their shared defensive outrage at its lack of success, and through their revenge project the *Xenien*. Eibl asserts that given the profound differences between the two men, they perhaps needed "diese[r] gemeinsame[ ] Aggressions-Rausch[ ]" (this shared, aggression-fueled rush) to forge them together emotionally (FA 1:1 1162). Since the authors left their names off their individual contributions and combined their work into one collection, the *Xenien* can be seen, according to Ammon, as "die erste wirkliche literarische Koproduktion Schillers und Goethes" (the first true literary coproduction of Schiller and Goethe).[17]

In any case, the *Xenien* would bring the commercial success that eluded *Die Horen*. Schiller had already discovered that epigrams were a popular form with readers and sought to include them in *Die Horen* (September 13, 1795). The publication of hundreds of inflammatory epigrams thus had the potential to be a commercial sensation and to achieve a cultural circulation far beyond that of his high-minded journal. Schiller writes to Humboldt, "Ich zweifle ob man mit Einem Bogen Papier . . . so viele Menschen zugleich in Bewegung setzen kann, als diese Xenien setzen werden" (NA 28:155; I doubt whether so many people can be set in motion at once with a single sheet of paper . . . as these Xenien will). The gamble paid off. The *Musenalmanach für das Jahr 1797* had two additional print runs for a total of 3000 copies—well beyond what *Die Horen* had achieved in its best year.[18]

## The Martiallian Epigrammatic Distich

The often witty and insulting epigrams of the first-century Roman poet Martial might seem to be a fitting model for Goethe and Schiller's literary salvos, but the choice of his *Xenia* collection, in particular, is curious. Martial's

*Xenia* were single distichs describing gifts of food traditionally distributed on the Roman festival of Saturnalia as a gesture of hospitality; his playful epigrams could be bought and distributed in lieu of the food item they described. What, then, do these culinary gift-epigrams have to do with Goethe and Schiller's attack-distichs? Presumably, the connection between food and culture involves an implicit play on the notion of taste, or *Geschmack*. Indeed, Schiller, in particular, often refers to their literary offerings in culinary terms. He complains to Cotta of readers who prefer the "Waßersuppen in andern Journalen" (watery soup in other journals) to the "kräftige Speise in den Horen" (NA 28:39; hearty fare in The Horae). In his correspondence with Goethe, he refers to the audience—albeit sarcastically—as their guests: "Sie sehen, unsre deutschen Gäste verleugnen sich nicht, sie müssen immer wissen, *was* sie essen, wenn es ihnen recht schmecken soll" (May 15, 1795, emphasis in original; You see, our German guests don't deny their natures, they always have to know *what* they're eating if it is supposed to taste good to them). Thus, the *Xenien* project belongs to Goethe and Schiller's self-appointed task of expanding the taste of the German public.

Of course, the appeal to an ancient historical context also likely conveys a message. A possible point of reference is Karl Philipp Moritz's short discussion of the *Janusfest* (Janus festival) from his 1791 book, *Anthousa oder Roms Alterthümer* (Anthousa or Rome's Antiquities).[19] Moritz's interpretation of the Roman holiday rests on an error, according to a January 1796 essay by Karl Böttiger, but it may have been a productive one: Moritz conflates the two Roman festivals of winter, Saturnalia in December, which was the actual occasion for Martial's *Xenia* and the festival of Janus in January. He incorrectly locates the gift-giving custom at the beginning of the new year (instead of in December) and connects it symbolically to the two-faced god Janus, who looks both forward to the new year and backward to the past.[20] Moritz's mistake yields a rich interpretation of the *Xenia* tradition: the exchange of gifts looks forward to the future but also hearkens back to an ideal, more reciprocal form of human commerce: "Man versetzte sich also beim Anfange eines jeden Jahrs gleichsam in jene Unschuldswelt zurück, wo noch allgemeine Freiheit und Gleichheit, und wechselseitige Treue unter den Menschen herrschten" (With the beginning of each year, one placed oneself, as it were, back in that innocent world where universal freedom and equality, and reciprocal loyalty ruled among human beings).[21] Moritz also alludes, correctly this time, to the carnivalesque aspects of Saturnalia, imagining that the temporary social leveling during the festival might be a gesture toward an original human reciprocity and hospitality, "gesellige Vertraulichkeit unter den Menschen" (sociable intimacy among people).[22] In his evocation of an original freedom and equality rooted in classical values, Moritz's version of *Xenia* suggests a classical alternative to the upheavals of the French Revolution, one well-aligned with Goethe and Schiller's program.

But Goethe and Schiller are informed by the long and rich tradition surrounding the epigrammatic genre that extends well beyond Martial. One of the most influential eighteenth-century German theorists of the epigram was Lessing.[23] Lessing, drawing on Martial and other Latin epigrammists, sees the essence of the epigram in its bipartite character, as it proceeds from *Erwartung* (expectation) to *Aufschluss* (disclosure).[24] An epigram awakens and fosters one's curiosity toward an object, and then briefly and pointedly satisfies that curiosity, sometimes actually subverting the original expectation.[25]

Not all epigrams take the form of distichs, nor are all distichs epigrams, but, as with Lessing's model of the epigram, a distich has two parts: a line of hexameter followed by a line of pentameter. That bipartite metrical structure is subject to further segmentation, for a caesura splits both lines. In the hexameter line, the position of that divide is both rule-bound and somewhat flexible, coming most commonly within the third foot but sometimes later.[26] Two caesuras are also possible in the hexameter line but do not appear frequently. The caesura in the pentameter, on the other hand, has a definite location and form. Directly in the middle of the line are two stressed syllables right next to each other—the so-called *Hebungsprall* (elevated impact). The two-beat center means that the pentameter technically has six beats rather than five.

When Goethe proposed the *Xenien* scheme, he was no stranger to the distich. Indeed the decade after his return from Italy represents his period of experimentation with the poetic form, from the *Römische Elegien* (*Roman Elegies*), through the *Venezianische Epigramme* (*Venetian Epigrams*) and *Xenien*, and ending with "Metamorphose der Pflanzen" ("Metamorphosis of Plants"), his last major work in distichs. Schiller meanwhile wrote his first significant poem in distichs, "Der Spaziergang" (The Long Walk) in 1795. Certainly, by the time both men launched their epigram-writing spree, they had a clear sense of the affordances offered by this particular metrical form.

## Goethe and Schiller's Distichs

In a matter of just a few months in 1796, Goethe and Schiller had produced nearly one thousand distichs. By August, Schiller had arranged them into publishable form. He organized 414 of the epigrams into "ein eigenes Ganze" (its own whole), the *Xenien* cycle proper, and then selected more than 200 additional epigrams, which he refers to as "die philosophischen und rein poetischen, kurz die unschuldigen Xenien" (August 1, 1796; the philosophical and purely poetic, in short the innocent xenia), to be published in the first part of the same *Musenalmanach* under Goethe's name, his own name, or jointly under the title *Tabulae Votivae*. More than a quarter went unpublished.[27] In my analysis, while attending, in particular, to the structure of the *Xenien* cycle, I draw from all these groups, because they were indeed produced as part of one concerted endeavor under the *Xenien* rubric. Although it is quite possible to distinguish between the contributions of the two authors based on historical documentation, thematic preoccupations, as well as formal inclinations, that identification will not be my emphasis, except for those epigrams published under their separate names.[28] Rather, I aim for a broader account of what Goethe and Schiller jointly tried to set in motion.

How did Goethe and Schiller adapt the Martiallian and epigrammatic traditions for their own ends? Two programmatic epigrams published under Schiller's name in the *Musenalmanach* suggest their theory of the distich. The following, with its title "Erwartung und Erfülling" (Expectation and Fulfillment) is a clear allusion to Lessing's terms *Erwartung* and *Aufschluss*. Here Lessing's bipartite structure aligns with the hexameter and pentameter lines to present an elegantly compressed life narrative.

> *Erwartung und Erfüllung.*
> In den Ocean schifft mit tausend Masten der Jüngling,
> > Still, auf gerettetem Boot treibt in den Hafen der Greis. (111)

> *Expectation and Fulfillment.*
> Into the ocean sails with a thousand masts the youth
> > Quietly, in a salvaged boat floats into the harbor the old man.

The distich manages both parallelism and contrast: both lines end with the protagonist—first as "Jüngling" than as "Greis." But the adverbial phrases—the whither and the how—swap their places so that the wide destination "in den Ocean" is foregrounded for the youth; the humbled demeanor and dismal conveyance "still, auf gerettetem Boot" for the old man. The verbs tell the story too: the lightness of "schiffen"; the dull weight of "treiben." Thus Schiller shows off the extraordinary capacity of the couplet as a single narrative unit that can also trace a spatial circuit.

A second "metadistich"[29] addressing the genre itself flips the motion vertically to describe a jet of water.

> *Das Distichon.*
> Im Hexameter steigt des Springquells silberne Säule,
> > Im Pentameter drauf fällt sie melodisch herab. (67)

> *The Distich.*
> In hexameter the fountain-spring's silvery pillar rises
> > In the pentameter it thereupon falls melodically down.

Here too Schiller plays with lightness and heaviness—with the sibilant flow of "Sprinquells silberne Säule" in the hexameter and, in the pentameter, with the hard monosyllabic "drauf fällt" as the *Hebungsprall*, and concluding with a final gravitational thud, "herab." These examples manifest the sense of natural circulation latent in the bipartite form—whether describing the cycle of a human life or the circuit of a natural spring.

But Goethe and Schiller exploit not just the metric divide marked by the two lines, but also the further divisions imposed by the caesuras. One caesura in each line (the most typical case) yields four segments, which Goethe and Schiller combine into a whole range of constellations through various repetitions and parallel and contrastive words and structures.[30] In the example below from the collection attributed to Schiller in the *Musenalmanach*, we see Schiller's signature rhetorical device, chiasm, highlighted through this four-way segmentation:

> *Das Ehrwürdige.*
> Ehret ihr immer das *Ganze,* | ich kann nur *einzelne* achten,
> > Immer in *Einzelnen* nur || hab ich das *Ganze* erblickt. (32)

*Worthy of Honor.*
You venerate always the whole, I can respect only individuals
   Only in individuals have I beheld the whole.

As my caesura notations and added italics above demarcate, the keywords (ganz, einzeln) are neatly distributed in an ABBA pattern across the four segments. In this way, the couplet redefines the individual as the true locus of wholeness. This shift is especially clear in the contrast between the first and fourth segments. The subject shifts from the plural you ("ihr") to the individual subject ("ich"). The ways of knowing switches here too: from the opening word "Ehret," to the concluding, faintly echoing word "erblickt," the whole is first collectively, conventionally ("immer") venerated but then individually, empirically *beheld*.

Having established the basic structure, I will now outline, with help from Levine's taxonomy, how Goethe and Schiller deploy the distich to intervene in and reconstitute cultural circulation, by recasting conceptual wholes, stabilizing hierarchies, resetting rhythms, and undermining and reforming networks. These formal categories are heuristically useful but remain mere angles from which to survey the overlapping, multidimensional strategies at work in the *Xenien*.

## Wholes

"Wholes" of many varieties are at stake in many of these distichs. In a multitude of constellations, false wholes are deconstructed into disparate parts and/or new wholes are assembled. Consider for example two epigrams concerning contemporary genres that stand in immediate juxtaposition in the *Xenien* collection. The first one, regarding German comedy, provides an example of failed synthesis.

*Deutsches Lustspiel.*
Thoren hätten wir wohl, | wir hätten Fratzen die Menge,
   Leider helfen sie nur || selbst zur Comödie nichts. (232)


*The German Comic Play*
Fools we would have, we'd have grimaces aplenty,
   Unfortunately, they actually offer for comedy nothing.

The strong caesura in the hexameter line, underscored by a comma, emphatically separates two full main clauses presenting two elements of comedy—*Thoren* and *Fratzen*. The two segments align with their identical subject ("wir") and verb ("hätten") but diverge in their predicates and syntax. In the third segment (first half of the pentameter), the two comic elements—fools and grimaces—are subsumed together by the plural pronoun "sie," and yet in the last segment fail to add up. The final word "nichts" brings home the point: no whole emerges.

In the next example, concerning Goethe's Märchen,[31] the synthesis does succeed.

*Das Mährchen.*
Mehr als zwanzig Personen | sind in dem Mährchen geschäftig,
   Nun, und was machen sie denn || alle? Das Mährchen, mein Freund. (233)

*The Fairytale.*
More than twenty persons are bustling about in the fairytale,
    Now then, what are they [adding] up to? The fairytale, my friend.

The bipartite hexameter line sets "twenty persons" off against the singular "fairy tale" in which they operate. The ambiguous question in the pentameter—what *are* they up to; or what do they *add* up to?—is satisfied in the final segment: they make up the whole that is the fairy tale.

One of the most important "wholes" running through Goethe and Schiller's distich collections is the term "Wahrheit" (truth). The following example of the theme from the *Tabulae Votivae* also exploits a four-part segmentation, but here in a parallel ABAB, rather than a chiastic pattern.

*Wahrheit.*
Eine nur ist sie für alle, | doch siehet sie jeder verschieden,
    Daß es Eines doch bleibt, || macht das verschiedene wahr. (167)

*Truth.*
It is a single thing for all people, yet each person views it diversely
    That singular it nonetheless remains, makes the diverse true.

The hexameter poses a paradox: truth, which one assumes to be a unified whole, appears fragmented. Correspondingly, the terms *Eine* and *verschieden* stand polarized at either end of the first line. In the pentamer, which aims to resolve the paradox, the same two words now veer closer, seeming to center in on the *Hebungsprall* "bleibt, macht," with its suggestion that both continuity (bleiben) and action (machen) lie at the heart of a more dynamic and variegated conception of truth.

## Hierarchies

In addition to using divides between and within the hexameter and pentamer to create parallel, contrastive, and sometimes chiastic formulations, Goethe and Schiller also frequently use enjambment between the two lines to create a center around which the beginning and end of the distich pivot. Often this constellation is used to create a stabilizing middle term in hierarchical relationships or to lament the lack of such mediation.

The following two distichs, although drawn from different contexts in the *Musenalmanach*, employ this enjambement structure to address social and political hierarchies. The first belongs to a set of epigrams aimed at Reichardt, one of several that portray him, in his Revolutionary politics, as like a barking dog. The barkers, it turns out, simply hope to switch positions with the objects of their barking.

*An die Obern.*
Immer bellt man auf euch! bleibt sitzen! es wünschen die Beller
    Jene Plätze, wo man ruhig das Bellen vernimmt. (252)

*To the Higher-Ups.*
They always bark at you! Stay seated! The barkers desire
> Those places, from which one calmly hears the barking.

The enjambment executes the abrupt flip from the barkers in the hexameter to the sought-after place of the auditors in the pentameter ("Beller" / "Jene Plätze"). What this distich has in common with many others is its exposure of a missing middle. Here without meaningful mediation, the Revolutionary movement results in a simple swap. Compare, by contrast, a second distich from the group attributed to Goethe, which offers a conservative affirmation of a minister as a reconciling middle term.

*Der Minister.*
Klug und thätig und fest, bekannt mit allem, nach oben
> Und nach unten gewandt, er sey Minister und bleib's. (31)

*The Minister.*
Wise and active and steady, acquainted with all things, upward
> And downward inclined, may he be and remain the minister.

The bidirectional orientation of the minister, as expressed in the enjambment (*nach oben / nach unten*), suggests a durable seam for the society.

Far more compelling than Goethe's self-serving positioning of the minister is his vision of a middle space in the set of sixteen distichs labeled "Eisbahn" (Skating Rink) in the same collection, published later as "Winter" in his "Vier Jahreszeiten" (Four Seasons). They present, as a broader social allegory, a scene of skaters on a platform created by a frozen river, which begins to melt with the approach of spring in the final distichs. The opening distich delimits this intermediate space poised between the water-turned-ground, the sun above, and shores to the sides.

Wasser ist Körper und Boden die Welle. Das neuste Theater
> Thut, in der Sonne Glanz, zwischen den Ufern sich auf. (143)

Water is body and ground the current. The newest theater
> Unfolds in the sun's brilliance, between the shores.

The caesura late in the hexameter divides the distich into three segments, with this temporary "newest theater" dwelling in the middle of the distich, in the enjambment.

In the following distich, which similarly breaks into three syntactic and semantic segments, the middle bridging the two lines is occupied by the ice-skating learners, the teachers, and the ordinary people.

Alles gleitet unter einander, die Schüler und Meister,
> Und das gewöhnliche Volk, das in der Mitte sich hält. (144)

Everything glides intertwiningly, the pupil and master,
> And the common folk, which lingers in the middle.

Within that middle, we have a gliding interchange involving a dynamic hierarchy in the hexameter ("Schüler und Meister") and, in the pentameter, a
less mobile middle ("Volk") said to occupy the center. Described in another
distich in the set as "die kreisenden Bahnen des Lebens" (143; the circulating
paths of life), the motions of the skaters serve as an affirmative model of circulation—a circulation that is spatially and temporally conditioned, delimited
by both natural boundaries and the cycle of the seasons.

## Rhythms

Fundamental to Goethe and Schiller's critique of, and drive to reset, cultural circulation through the *Xenien*, is the issue of tempo or rhythm. Many
couplets play with meter in order to suggest a too sluggish or too frenet-
ic pace among their contemporaries. Nicolai serves as the great exemplar
of plodding pedantry. The title of the following distich refers to a passage
from Nicolai's account of a 1781 journey through Germany and Switzerland,
which stretched into twelve volumes published over thirteen years. In the
passage cited in the title of this distich, Nicolai moves, with barely a transition, from local hairstyles in Tübingen, to a certain journal published there—
*Die Horen*.[32]

> *N. Reisen XI. Band. S. 177.*
> A propos Tübingen! Dort sind Mädchen, die tragen die Zöpfe
>     Lang geflochten, auch dort giebt man die Horen heraus. (247)

> *N. Travels Volume XI. Page 177.*
> Apropos Tubingen! There are girls, they wear braids
>     Plaited long, there too they publish the Horae.

The rhythm here works to underscore the utter banality of Nicolai's observations. Goethe and Schiller's version of the German hexameter line consists
of an artful combination of dactyls and trochees, typically concluding with
a dactyl then trochee.[33] This one is heavy on dactyls, which occupy four of
the six feet and produce a repetitive galloping rhythm, i.e., "*A*-pro-pos *Tü*-bin-
gen." In the middle stands a trochee, which serves to slow down the motion
but only for an entirely trivial "Dort sind." That inconsequential emphasis is
then echoed in the *Hebungsprall* of the pentameter "dort || giebt." The only
thing connecting the girls' braids to the publisher of *Die Horen* is the location—Tübingen—indicated by the clunky adverb "dort."

   Another author associated with deficient rhythm is Goethe's scientific
rival Newton:

> *Menschlichkeiten.*
> Leidlich hat Newton gesehen, und falsch geschlossen, am Ende
>     Blieb er, ein Britte, verstockt, schloß er, bewieß er so fort. (242)

> *Human Frailties.*
> So-so did Newton see, and false conclusions he drew, in the end
>     He stayed, a Brit, stubborn, he inferred, he proved, and so on.

The accusation that Newton got stuck in his research comes to bear particularly in the pentameter where three dactyls are disrupted by commas inserted after the first stressed syllable to create a halting effect: "*Blieb* er, ein *Britte*, ver-*stockt*, || *schloß* er, be-*wieß* er so *fort.*" Meanwhile the *Hebungsprall*, "-stockt || schloß" contributes to the heavy, dragging feel of the line.

The epigrams also attack rhythms that are incessant or frenzied but amount to meaningless repetition. One distich, for example, compares Reichardt to an ostrich who constantly, clumsily paddles its foot in the sand (254). A number of couplets employ the simple repetition of words or phrases to create this sense of empty motion. The first example plays on the motto of Reichardt's earlier journal *Frankreich*: "La verité, rien que la verité, toute la verité" (The truth, nothing but the truth, all the truth).[34]

*Das Motto.*
Wahrheit sag ich euch, Wahrheit und immer Wahrheit, versteht sich:
    *Meine* Wahrheit; denn sonst ist mir auch keine bekannt. (251)

*The Motto.*
Truth I say to you, truth and always truth, it goes without saying
    *My* truth; for I am otherwise acquainted with none.

While outstripping the conventional three-part oath through a fourfold repetition of the word "Wahrheit," this distich nevertheless does not expand the province of truth. Instead of *all* the truth, it offers only *my* truth; instead of *nothing but* the truth," the penultimate word "keine" suggests there may be *no* truth there at all. A further example pillories a dull, biblically themed play by Christian Graf zu Stolberg.

*Belsatzer ein Drama.*
König Belsatzer schmaußt in dem ersten Akte, der König
    Schmaußt in dem zweyten, es schmaußt fort bis zu Ende der Fürst. (204)

*Belshazzar a Drama.*
King Belshazzar feasts in the first act, the King
    Feasts in the second, he feasts forth until the end, the ruler.

Despite the serial action indicated by the trifold repetition of "schmaußt," the synonyms with which the distich begins and ends— "König," "Fürst" —underscore an utterly static plot.

King Belsatzer's gastronomic excesses tie this distich to a number of others that thematize digestive rhythms. Some (unnamed) contemporary authors have an overhasty, foreshortened digestive tract:

*Geschwindschreiber.*
Was sie gestern gelernt, das wollen sie heute schon lehren,
    Ach! was haben die Herrn doch für ein kurzes Gedärm! (281)

*Swift Scribes.*
What they just learned yesterday they want to teach today,
    Alas! these gentlemen sure have a short bowel.

This accelerated, gluttonous writerly tempo produces a half-raw output, according to a further distich, this one alluding to Nicolai and not included in the almanac:

*Polyphem auf Reisen*
Bücher und Menschen verschluckt und ganze Provinzen der Unflat,
      Aber wie roh er sie fraß lehret das Reisegefäß. (FA 1.523/1171)

*Polyphemus on the Road.*
Books and people and whole provinces swallows up the foul one,
      But how crudely he devoured them is revealed by the travel-pot.

Another distich contemplates the readerly effects of such low-quality literary fare, warning that a recent novel by Nicolai leads to flatulence:

*Geschichte eines dicken Mannes.*
(Man sehe die Recension davon in der N. deutschen Bibliothek).
Dieses Werk ist durchaus nicht in Gesellschaft zu lesen,
      Da es, wie Recensent rühmet, die Blähungen treibt. (234)[35]

*History of a Fat Man.*
(See the review of it in the N. German Library).
This work is definitely not to be read in company,
      Since, as the reviewer boasts, it drives out gas.

These digestive metaphors clearly play into the original conceit of the *Xenien* as food gifts in the Martialian tradition, as a pair of distichs remind us:

*Martial.*
Xenien nennet ihr euch? Ihr gebt euch für Küchenpräsente?
      Ißt man denn, mit Vergunst, spanischen Pfeffer bey euch?

*Xenien.*
Nicht doch! Aber es schwächten die vielen wäßrigten Speisen
      So den Magen, daß jetzt Pfeffer und Wermuth nur hilft. (290)

*Martial.*
You call yourselves Xenia? You pretend to be culinary gifts?
      Then, allow me, do people eat Spanish pepper where you're from?

*Xenien.*
Not at all! But the many watery dishes have so weakened
      The stomach, that only pepper and wormwood now help.

The second distich recalls Schiller's complaint to Cotta quoted above about the "Wassersuppen" offered by most journals. But in place of the hearty nourishment promised in *Die Horen*, these satirical distichs deploy pungent seasonings. According to eighteenth- and nineteenth-century pharmaceutical manuals, Spanish pepper and wormwood promote vitality by stimulating dulled organs of taste and digestion (pepper), arousing appetite through bitterness (wormwood), preventing flatulence and generally aiding the digestive process (both).[36]

A further epigram asserts that verses like themselves hold the key to overcoming corporeal stoppages. Here the threatened blockage is sensory: a plugging ("zustopfen") of the ears.

> *Das Mittel.*
> Warum sagst du uns das in Versen? Die Verse sind wirksam,
> > Spricht man in Prosa zu euch, stopft ihr die Ohren euch zu. (243)

> *The Means.*
> Why do you say that to us in verses? Verses are potent,
> > If one speaks to you in prose, you plug your ears shut.

Thus, through their sharp and bitter flavor and their own prosodic features, the distichs promise to realign natural, physiological, and cultural rhythms.

## Networks

Under this final category, I consider how Goethe and Schiller deploy their epigrams in broader configurations. For their distichs not only function as potent metrical and thematic units, but they also combine into loose spatio-narrative formations that, in turn, help redefine the contours of the public sphere. The weaving of these epigrams into a plot of sorts was Schiller's innovation, but with some precedent in Goethe's "Venezianische Epigramme," published in an earlier issue of the *Musenalmanach*. In the process of this narrative tour, the distichs infiltrate and undermine existing cultural-commercial networks.

The *Xenien* cycle portrays throughout a contemporary culture driven by the exchange of empty commodities. One couplet describes the market in journals as relentless traffic bearing little of substance:

> *Currus virum miratur inanes.*
> Wie sie knallen die Peitschen! Hilf Himmel! Journale! Calender!
> > Wagen an Wagen! Wieviel Staub und wie wenig Gepäck! (260)

> *He wonders at the empty chariots of the men.*[37]
> How they crack the whips! Heaven help us! Journals! Calendars!
> > Wagon upon wagon! How much dust and how little baggage!

The dust that arises in the *Hebungsprall*—"Wieviel ‖ Staub"—suggests both the commotion and the ephemerality of the enterprise. Another distich "Der Kenner" (The Connoisseur) lampoons the craze for mass-produced Maiolica ceramics over authentic artifacts of classical culture and mocks the conviction that "Doch ein Majolica-Topf machte mich glücklich und reich" (203; Yet a Maiolica pot would make me happy and rich).[38] The Leipzig book fair serves as a hub of this deeply commodified exchange.[39] A distich entitled "Josephs II. Dictum, an die Buchhändler" (Joseph II's Dictum to the Booksellers) references the late emperor's comparison of booksellers to cheesemongers in their sheer commercialism. The *Kaiser*, it concludes, had clearly visited the Leipzig fair (270). Another couplet, "Der Glückstopf" (The Lucky Pot) sees the fair as a mere game of chance for authors: "Kommt Autoren und zieht, jeder versuche sein Glück" (200; Come, authors, and draw, let each try his luck).

This commercial pressure ultimately turns the entire intellectual realm into a flea market, or even black market, in ideas. A certain professor, for example, is deemed better suited to be a hawker in a market stall in "Verfehlter Beruf" (Missed Calling, 215).[40] An editor (Reichardt, again!) fills his journal full of material pilfered from other authors in "Sein Handgriff" (His Maneuver, 255) and "Unmögliche Vergeltung" (Impossible Requital, 255). The following two distichs suggest the way that crucial philosophical conceptions are reduced to their crass economic value. The first describes the market in metaphysics in the wake of Kant; the second advertises notions of human destiny up for sale.

> *Auction.*
> Da die Metaphysik vor kurzem unbeerbt abgieng,
> > Werden die *Dinge an sich* morgen sub hasta verkauft. (272)

> *Auction.*
> Since metaphysics recently departed without an heir,
> > The *things in themselves* will be sold off tomorrow by auction.

> *Buchhändler Anzeige.*
> Nichts ist der Menschheit so wichtig, als ihre Bestimmung zu kennen;
> > Um zwölf Groschen courant wird sie bey mir jetzt verkauft. (272)[41]

> *Booksellers' Advertisement.*
> Nothing is so important to humanity as to know human destiny;
> > For twelve silver groats I have it here for sale.

The role of the epigrams is to infiltrate and subvert this debased marketplace in order to install their own system of cultural exchange. Their circuit takes them, with many intervening excurses, from the Leipzig book fair, to the heavenly constellations, back to earth with a survey of German rivers, and finally to the underworld.[42] Each episode involves a passage through borders, what Ammon sees as instances of the "Grenzüberschreitung" (border crossing) that in his view defines the poetics of the *Xenien*.[43]

The cycle opens as the epigrams slip over the tollgate at the entrance to the city of Leipzig.

> *Xenien.*
> Distichen sind wir. Wir geben uns nicht für mehr noch für minder,
> > Sperre du immer, wir ziehn über den Schlagbaum hinweg. (199)

> *Xenia.*
> We are distichs. We don't claim to be more or less,
> > Go ahead and block the way, we'll pass over the tollgate.

This initial scene, with its border and customs procedure, sends up the travel literature craze generally and, in particular, perhaps recalls the account of entering Berlin in one of the opening features in Reichardt's *Deutschland.*[44] But here, the distichs pass right through with their light luggage—just two bags (read: two metrical lines) that have no French or anticlerical content (199).

The distichs' subsequent circuit through the heavens involves a more perilous passage:

*Litterarischer Zodiacus.*
Jetzo ihr Distichen nehmt euch zusammen, es thut sich der Thierkreis
    Grauend euch auf; mir nach Kinder! wir müssen hindurch. (215)


*Literary Zodiac.*
Pull yourselves together now, You distichs, the zodiac looms
    Dreadfully ahead; follow me, children! We've got to get through.

The "Tierkreis" that maps out the sky consists of contemporary cultural luminaries and influential editors, including, for example, Reichardt as Scorpio and Nicolai as Capricorn.[45] If the constellations in the heavens are traditionally represented as sublime and here presented as dread-inspiring, they are quickly rendered absurd by the transgressive, high-flying epigrams.

A different kind of boundary erasure occurs at the beginning of the section on German rivers.

*Rhein.*
Treu wie dem Schweitzer gebührt, bewach ich Germaniens Grenze,
    Aber der Gallier hüpft über den duldenden Strom. (223)


*Rhein.*
Loyal as befits the Swiss, I guard Germania's border,
    But the Gaul hops over the forbearing river.

As the term "Germania" hints, this distich plays with Tacitus's first-century ethnography, a key source for emerging eighteenth-century nationalist discourses. Tacitus's very first sentence asserts that the Rhein separates Germania from the Gauls and the Raeti (a tribe occupying modern-day Switzerland).[46] But in the distich, the boundary is porous: the river itself is Swiss, and a Frenchman can easily traverse it.

Finally, the winged and wraith-like epigrams are urged by the muse to cross over into the land of the dead. The muse replies to their protest that they are but monodistichs:

*Muse.*
Desto besser! Geflügelt wie ihr, dünnleibig und luftig,
    Seele mehr als Gebein, wischt ihr als Schatten hindurch. (282)


*Muse.*
So much the better! Winged as you are, thin-bodied and airy
    Soul more than body, you slide right through as shadows.

This section, inspired by Odysseus' descent, provides, according to Schiller, an occasion "die verstorbenen Autoren und hie und da auch die lebenden zu plagen" (January 31, 1796; to tease the deceased authors and also, here and there, the living ones).[47] But the impact of this border crossing is not merely satirical. The encounter with classical traditions and figures of respect such as Lessing and Shakespeare simultaneously offer models against which contemporary culture is measured and found lacking. The trip to the underworld serves to expand the web of German culture beyond the present and beyond the German-speaking world in a manner that promises reform.

As has often been remarked, the incursions of the distichs are frequently described with military metaphors.[48] For example, the following distich, directed originally against Reichardt (Goethe to Schiller, January 30, 1796) draws on a biblical episode in which Samson destroyed the crops of the Philistines by tying torches to the tales of 300 foxes (Judges 15: 4–5):

*Feindlicher Einfall.*
Fort ins Land der Philister, ihr Füchse mit brennenden Schwänzen,
    Und verderbet der Herrn reife papierene Saat. (209)


*Hostile Incursion.*
Go forth into the land of the Philistines, you foxes with burning tales,
    And spoil the gentlemen's ripe paper crop.

Yet other epigrams suggest a less scorched-earth approach. The descriptions of their mobile, narrow, winged bodies recall insects, a connection made explicit in the later appearance by *Xenien* in the "Walpurgisnachttraum" ("Walpurgis Night's Dream") in *Faust:* "Als Insekten sind wir da" (1.4303; As insects we are here). The following distich suggests the double meaning of the insect metaphor.

*Der Almanach als Bienenkorb.*
Lieblichen Honig geb' er dem Freund, doch nahet sich täppisch
    Der Philister, ums Ohr saus' ihm der stechende Schwarm! (258)


*The Almanac as Beehive.*
May it provide sweet honey to the friend, but should awkwardly approach
    The philistine, may the stinging swarm whiz around his ears.

The distichs aspire to function, then, both as defensive, stinging swarms and as networking, honey-producing pollinators.

As Goethe and Schiller aim to establish these new networks, their own collaboration forms the foundational unit. The following double-distich, which appears in the *Tabulae Votivae*, echoes the characterization of their relationship quoted from their early correspondence.

*Die Uebereinstimmung.*
Wahrheit suchen wir beyde; du aussen im Leben, ich innen
    In dem Herzen, und so findet sie jeder gewiß.
Ist das Auge gesund, so begegnet es aussen dem Schöpfer,
    Ist es das Herz, dann gewiß spiegelt es innen die Welt. (157)

*The Accord.*
Truth we both seek; you outwardly in life, I inwardly
   In the heart, and so each will certainly find it.
If the eye is healthy, then it will encounter the creator outwardly
   If the heart is healthy, then it will internally mirror the world.

Here the pursuits of the "you" and the "I" diverge in their orientations (outward and inward), employ complementary organs of knowledge (eye and heart), and ultimately converge in their results (truth). This model of the Schiller-Goethe alliance is generalized in other epigrams, where healthy antagonism, even *Feindschaft* (enmity) in the pursuit of truth provides the best way forward for the broader intellectual challenges of the era, such as the reconciliation of natural science and transcendental philosophy (244).

By analogy, moreover, even the posture of enmity in the *Xenien* project can present itself as part of a longer process of reconciliation. The following distich plays on the conceit of the whole *Xenien* collection as "gifts of hospitality" by encouraging reciprocation of those "gifts."

*Dieser Musenalmanach.*
Nun erwartet denn auch, für seine herzlichen Gaben,
   Liebe Collegen, von euch unser Calender den Dank. (264)


*This Muses' Almanac.*
Now our Calendar awaits, for its affectionate gifts,
   Dear colleagues, your thanks.

The invitation in this distich is certainly part taunt and part publicity gambit, but still alludes to a classical ideal of reciprocity and to the possibility of new, more productive networks in opposition to the crass self-interest shaping the existing public culture.[49]

## Affordances

Goethe and Schiller thus chose a remarkably supple form with which to advance and defend the program embodied by *Die Horen* and reimagine cultural circulation. In summary, the affordances of the monodistich include:

- Its segmentation, including its bipartite division into hexameter and pentameter lines, which are further subdivided through caesuras and combined through enjambment. These segments support concise narratives and cyclical motions modeled on natural processes. They undergird parallel and contrastive arrangements that enact syntheses, deconstructions, reversals, and mediations.
- Its rhythm, which, in its combination of dactyls and trochees, and other metrical features, is both fixed and flexible. Schiller and Goethe parody the disruptive or plodding rhythms they see as culturally symptomatic but otherwise seek to render their case in compelling and graceful verse rather than prose.
- Its brevity. With a length comparable to the 140 characters that later came to define Twitter, the distichs have the advantage of great

rhetorical impact and penetrative potential (whether like insects or missiles). Epigrams had already achieved popularity as a genre and secured the *Musenalmanach*'s commercial success.

- Its capacity to serve as a narrative or thematic building-block within a collaborative project. The two men together produced the raw material that Schiller then constructed into a cycle.

- Its historical meaning. Martial's model suggests an antidote to what Goethe and Schiller see as a commercialized contemporary culture: a pre-Revolutionary and nonpolitical offering of gifts. In borrowing a culinary metaphor from Martial, they promise to improve the taste and digestion of the public.

## Postlude

Schiller and Goethe's *Xenien* did indeed inspire reciprocation: the distich form they had weaponized was turned on them in hundreds of epigrams, composed by more than a dozen authors, attacking their political and cultural hypocrisy, their literary output, their personal lives, and even metrical competence. Fürchtegott Christian Fulda imagines Schiller might regret ever having armed his rivals in this way.

> S**.
> "Hätt' ich Xenien doch im Leben nimmer geschrieben!
>     Andre seh' ich nun wohl, können so gut es, wie ich."[50]

> S**.
> "If only I had never written Xenia into life!
>     Others, I see, can do it as well as I."

Two "Anti-*Xenien*" epigrams stand out for their particularly potent usurpation of Goethe and Schiller's military and circulatory rhetoric. Both employ the same metaphor to expose the true form of cultural work that the *Xenien* engage in: a *Tross*, the motley supply train, including profiteers and prostitutes, that tags along after the military. The following was published by Johann Kaspar Friedrich Manso, a frequent target of the *Xenien*:

> Guerre ouverte.
> (M.A.S. 211.)
> Offen führt man den Krieg mit rechtlichen Feinden und Streitern;
>     Aber den schmutzigen Troß necket und kneipt man, wie's kömmt.[51]

> Guerre ouverte.
> (M.A. p. 211.)
> One wages war openly with legitimate enemies and combatants;
>     But the dirty supply train one baits and nips, as the chance comes.

The second was penned but never published by Friedrich Hölderlin, who, while not in the direct line of attack, was stung by Schiller's condescending rejection of the poetry he had submitted for the *Musenalmanach*.[52]

Advocatus Diaboli.
Tief im Herzen haß ich den Troß der Despoten und Pfaffen,
    Aber noch mehr das Genie, macht es gemein sich damit.[53]


Devil's Advocate.
Deep in my heart I hate the supply train of despots and clerics,
    But even more the genius, when it joins along.

The supply-train metaphor suggests that the *Xenien* project aimed not so much for a vanguard reformation of the public sphere as for a rear-guard reinforcement of the status quo, that its governing principles were always less aesthetic autonomy than alignment with power and economic self-interest.

Perhaps the *Xenien* project did ultimately energize and expand cultural exchange and critique in a somewhat democratizing vein; perhaps it simultaneously served Goethe and Schiller's own commercial interests and helped consolidate their cultural power. Regardless of how one counts the wins and losses for Goethe and Schiller, and for the public sphere more generally, one casualty emerged from this episode to be sure: the programmatic, optimistic vision of human culture that defined the early phase of Weimar classicism in *Die Horen.*

*University of Oklahoma*

## NOTES

1. For distichs that appeared in the original collections, I quote from Friedrich Schiller, ed. *Musenalmanach für das Jahr 1797.* https://de.wikisource.org/wiki/Musen-Almanach_f%C3%BCr_das_Jahr_1797. Page numbers are given parenthetically. For distichs that were not published in those collections, as well as for other works by Goethe, I cite from the Frankfurter Ausgabe (hereafter FA), which follows a 1796 manuscript: Johann Wolfgang von Goethe, *Sämtliche Werke, Briefe, Tagebücher und Gespräche*, ed. Dieter Borkmeyer et al. 40 vols. (Frankfurt a/M: Deutscher Klassiker Verlag, 1985-1999). Works by Schiller are also cited parenthetically and refer to Friedrich Schiller, *Werke: Nationalausgabe*, eds. Julius Petersen et al. 42 vols. (Weimar: H. Böhlaus Nachfolger, 1943-), hereafter NA. Unless otherwise indicated, all translations are my own.

2. By contrast Eduard Boas suggests the target could be R. Z. Becker's *Deutsche Nationalzeitung. Goethe und Schillers Xenien-Manuskript* (Berlin: Hirsch, 1856) 87-88. Europeanlibraries. archive.org

3. The full title was *Frankreich im Jahr 179[ ], Aus den Briefen deutscher Männer in Paris.*

4. I borrow the term "promiscuous" from Jonathan Kramnick and Anahid Nersessian's defense of an eclectic and context-bound approach to literary formalism: "Promiscuity is the mark of a discipline in good enough shape to adapt its distinctive idiom to changing and specific contexts." "Form and Explanation," *Critical Inquiry* 43 (Spring 2017): 650-99, here 688.

5. Caroline Levine, *Forms: Whole, Rhythm, Hierarchy, Network* (Princeton: Princeton UP, 2015). While I borrow Levine's formalist framework because it seems a good fit for the historical context of the *Goethezeit*, Levine represents her own work as driv-

en, not by a concern for historical specificity, but rather by a sense of the contemporary political utility of formalist criticism. Thus, I embrace Levine out of an adaptive context-orientation perhaps better aligned with her critics Kramnick and Nersessian. See Levine's reply to their critique: "Still Polemicizing After All These Years," *Critical Inquiry* 44 (2017): 129–35.

6. The secondary literature on the *Xenien* is relatively sparse; lacking, in particular, is sustained attention to the project's formal dimensions in connection with its broader goals. Frieder von Ammon's 2005 book is an exception. Ammon contextualizes the *Xenien* in relationship to classical antecedents and genres and includes several exemplary close analyses of individual distichs. He sees the project governed, at every level, by a transgressive poetics "diese Poetik der Provokation, der Koproduktion, der Innovation und Hybridität, der Disproportion und Maßlosigkeit, kurz: diese *Poetik der Grenzüberschreitung*" (22). For Ammon, the project is, at its core, unclassical and opposed to the autonomous aesthetics articulated elsewhere. Frieder von Ammon, *Ungastliche Gaben, die "Xenien" Goethes und Schillers und ihre literarische Rezeption von 1796 bis in die Gegenwart*, Max Niemeyer 2005. My emphasis diverges from Ammon's in that I see the transgressive nature of the *Xenien* as only half the story: the project also aims to establish, at every level, a circulatory dynamic conceived as natural and eminently classical. Theodor Verweyen seeks the exemplary ideals underlying the satire of the *Xenien* and points to the fundamental contradictions, including between means and ends, inherent in Weimar Classicism. Theodor Verweyen, "Der andere Goethe: als Olympier im Xenienkrieg," *Euphorion*, 108, no. 2 (2014):157–93, here 193. Franz Schwarzbauer's monograph provides clear-sighted and detailed exploration of the literary, cultural-political, social, and institutional context of the *Xenien* project and thereby offers a complex image of Weimar Classicism in its evolving function. *Die Xenien. Studien zur Vorgeschichte der Weimarer Klassik* (Stuttgart: Metzler, 1992).

7. Stephan Füssel, *Schiller und seine Verleger* (Frankfurt a/M: Insel, 2005) 203.

8. Letters between Goethe and Schiller will be cited by date, all others by edition and page numbers.

9. See also Franz Schwarzbauer's two detailed chapters outlining the ambitions and failures of *Die Horen* project as the backdrop to the *Xenien* (57–68).

10. To Cotta January 9, 1795; qtd in Füssel 210–11.

11. Füssel 209; See: Schiller to Goethe September 13, 1795.

12. Füssel 212.

13. Johann Friedrich Reichardt, "Die Horen. Eine Monatschrift herausgegeben von Schiller" *Deutschland.* 1, no. 1 (1796): 55–90, here 62. Officially, the authorship and editorship were anonymous.

14. From the beginning, Schiller felt toward Reichardt "nur Mißtrauen, Verachtung, ja sogar Haß." Walter Salmen, *Johann Friedrich Reichardt. Komponist, Schriftsteller, Kapellmeister und Verwaltungsbeamter der Goethezeit* (Hildesheim: Olms, 2002) 84.

15. Johann Friedrich Reichardt, "Ankündigung" *Deutschland.* 1, no. 1 (1796): 1–6, here 1.

16. The tally varies from sixty (Verweyen 178) to seventy-six (Salmen 88).

17. Ammon 20.

18. Füssel 226.

19. Karl Philipp Moritz, *Anthousa or Roms Altertümer* (Berlin: 1791) 20–23. Digital Collections, Bavarian National Library.

20. Karl August Böttiger, "Gemahlte und geschriebene Neujahrsgeschenke der alten Römer," *Journal des Luxus und der Moden* 11, no.1 (1796): 18–25, here 18. Böttiger's article appeared after the *Xenien* project was already underway. See Goethe to Schiller January 30, 1796.

21. Moritz 21.

22. Moritz 21.

23. Also of note is Herder's essay "Anmerkungen über das griechische Epigramm" which draws out competing traditions within the genre. Johann Gottfried Herder. *Werke in zehn Bänden*, eds. Günter Arnold et al. (Frankfurt a/M: Deutscher Klassiker Verlag, 1993) 4:501–48.

24. Gotthold Ephraim Lessing, *Werke und Briefe in zwölf Bänden*, ed. Wilfried Barner et al (Frankfurt a/M: Deutscher Klassiker Verlag, 1985) 7:188. See also the discussion by Peter Hess, *Epigramm* (Stuttgart: Metzler, 1989) 47–52.

25. Lessing 7:185.

26. On conventions regarding caesuras in the hexameter and, in particular, the preference for the position after the third *Hebung* or, in a dactyl, after the first unstressed syllable following the third *Hebung*, see Erwin Arndt, *Deutsche Verslehre. Ein Abriss.* (Berlin: Volkseigener Verlag, 1968) 189 and Wolfgang Kayser, *Kleine deutsche Versschule* (Bern: Franke, 1961) 25–26.

27. Compare Verweyen 170.

28. Matthew Bell argues that the anonymous authorial approach in the *Xenien* is not just a pragmatic strategy but is rooted in principles of artistic autonomy fundamental to Weimar Classicism. "Anonymität und Autorschaft in den 'Xenien,'" *Goethe-Jahrbuch* 122 (2005): 92–106, here 97.

29. This is Ammon's term (28).

30. Compare Ammon: "Diese Zäsur verleiht dem Vers sein charakteristisches Gepräge; sie kann ihn in zwei völlig symmetrische oder zwei weitgehend asymmetrische Hälften teilen, was parallele oder chiastische Fügungen nahelegt." Ammon also emphasizes how the combination of flexibility and metric rigor makes it suitable for the representation of dynamic processes (30).

31. Eduard Boas, *Goethe und Schiller im Xenienkampf*, 2 vols. (Stuttgart: Cotta, 1851) 101.

32. See Boas 121–22.

33. See Ammon 31–32.

34. Boas 126.

35. See Schwarzbauer on how this distich distorts the original review it cites (289).

36. Wilhelm Joseph Anton Werber, *Specielle Heilmittellehre: physikalisch, chemisch, physiologisch, pathologisch, diätetisch und klinisch*, 2 vols. (Erlangen: Enke, 1859) 1:308; Theodor Husemann, *Handbuch der gesammten Arzneimittellehre*, 2 vols. (Berlin: Springer, 1875) 2:554; Johann Schroeder, *Pharmacopoeia universalis, das ist: Allgemeiner Medicinisch-Chimischer Artzney-Schatz*, 6 vols. 4th ed. (Nuremberg: Stein, 1748) 3:1086.

37. The Latin title is adapted from Book 6, line 651 of the Aeneid.

38. Directed against Friedrich Leopold Graf zu Stolberg (FA 1:1172–73).

39. Ammon 84.

40. Boas 74.

41. Refers to an ad for a new edition of *Bestimmung der Menschen* by J. J. Spalding (Boas 158).

42. Ammon also sees a return to the Leipzig book fair after the survey of rivers and before the underworld (86, 122).

43. Ammon 86, 122.

44. "Berlin. Brief eines Reisenden an seinen Freund in M." *Deutschland* 1 no. 1 (1796): 19–36, here 23–25.

45. Boas 79, 81.

46. Tacitus, *Germania*, trans. with intro and commentary by J. B. Rives (Oxford: Clarendon, 1999) 77.

47. Qtd. in Boas 179.

48. See for example Verweyen 167–68 and Ammon 32–34.

49. Cf. Ammon 144.

50. Wolfgang Stammler, ed. *Anti-Xenien* (Bonn: Marcus & Weber, 1911) 33.

51. Stammler 33. As part of the title, Manso includes the page citation in the original *Xenien* collection.

52. See Ammon's analysis of Hölderlin's distichs as response to this episode (177–86).

53. Qtd. in Ammon 180.

DANIEL L. PURDY

# Between Nanjing and Weimar:
# Goethe's Metaphysical Correspondences

**Abstract:** This article examines how Goethe places his reading about a Jesuit disputation with a Buddhist monk in seventeenth-century China within the context of German philosophical debates. Goethe immediately draws an analogy connecting Weimar debates between Kantians and idealists to the earlier Nanjing debate about Jesuit and Buddhism metaphysics. His inclination to perceive parallels between philosophy in China and Germany anticipates his later comments to Eckermann about the similarities between the Chinese and European novels that served as the basis for his pronouncements about *Weltliteratur* (world literature). A careful reading of Goethe and Schiller's letters shows that as a heretical thinker, Goethe was inclined to identify with the Buddhist dismissal of Christian theism; however, the emerging atheism controversy surrounding accusations made against Fichte's lectures at the University of Jena led him to cautiously avoid entering into yet another Enlightenment debate about religion.

**Keywords:** world literature, Chinese-German relations, Fichte's atheism controversy, Jesuit missionaries in China, analogy, similarity

ON JANUARY 3, 1798, Johann Wolfgang Goethe wrote his best friend, Friedrich Schiller, that he had just come across a curious story in an old tome describing a debate held in Nanjing, China during a banquet in 1599 involving a Jesuit missionary Matteo Ricci and an unnamed Buddhist scholar, who today is identified as the renowned abbot Xuelang Hong'en (1545–1607). The Jesuit texts refer to him as Sanhoi.[1] Goethe wrote: "Dieser Fund hat mich unglaublich amüsiert und mir eine gute Idee von dem Scharfsinn der Chineser gegeben" (This discovery amused me unbelievably and gave me a good idea of how sharp witted the Chinese are).[2] Typical for the way in which humanists combined friendship, letter writing, and intellectual labor, Goethe promised to send Schiller a handwritten copy of the passage. Three days later, Goethe followed through with his promise and went on to speculate how the Buddhist might have even more wittily turned the tables on the Jesuit Ricci. Rather than agreeing with the Jesuit arguments about the creation of the earth, Goethe takes the heterodox step of siding with the Buddhist—not a complete surprise, as he had resumed working on *Faust* the previous summer. In telling Schiller about the Chinese dinner conversation,

Goethe assigns eighteenth-century philosophical positions to each participant: the Buddhist he characterizes as "ein schaffender Idealist" (a creating
idealist), whereas the Jesuit is given the position of "ein völlig Reinholdianer"
(a complete Reinholdian), a position closer to that of Immanuel Kant (MA
8.1:484). The two writers had been sharing the latest work by J. G. Fichte
as well as a Chinese novel. For Goethe, these disparate topics suddenly con-
verged in an insight. Ever the sympathetic friend, Schiller was quick to align
himself with Goethe's interest, agreeing that the Nanjing debate could serve
as a quiet commentary on Weimar disputes.

> Das metaphysische Gespräch des Paters mit dem Chinesen hat mich sehr
> unterhalten, und es nimmt sich in der gotischen Sprache besonders wohl aus.
> Ich bin nur ungewiß, wie es in solchen Fällen manchmal geht, ob etwas recht
> Gescheites oder etwas recht Plattes hinter des Chinesen seinem Räsonnement
> steckt? … Es wäre ein Spaß, es abdrucken zu lassen mit einer leisen Anwendung
> auf unsere neuesten Philosophen. (MA 8.1:493)

> The metaphysical conversations of the father with the Chinese man enter-
> tained me very much and it comes across well in their gothic speech. I am
> just not certain, what to make of these cases, whether something intelligent
> or complete dull lies behind this Chinese reasoning. . . . It would be a laugh to
> print it with a silent reference to our newest philosophers.

China was already an established topic between the two writers. After
expressing his own uncertainty about how to interpret the Buddhist position, Schiller asks, "Wo haben Sie dies schöne Morceau gefunden?" (MA 8.1:
493; Where did you find this nice piece?) and this is where the story gets
complicated. Where did Goethe first read this story? Not in any source one
would expect.

Goethe was searching for poetic plunder in a 1670 collection of stories
about East Asia compiled by Erasmus Francisci. The tome had the long-wind-
ed title, *Neu-polirter Geschicht- Kunst- und Sitten-Spiegel ausländischer
Völcker* (Newly Polished Historical, Artistic, and Moral Mirror of Foreign
Peoples).[3] Subdivided into six volumes, this opus had been printed in
Nuremberg, a center of the seventeenth-century publishing industry. Records
show that Goethe checked out the volume from the Weimar royal library for
almost a year, between December 6, 1797, and November 10, 1798. Goethe
explains to Schiller that he is reading Francisci's compilation precisely
because it brings together so many unusual anecdotes. He was, after all, well-
versed at prowling through old collections for new inspiration. The legend
of the magician and trickster Faust had come down to him through just such
compilations. Francisci was a professional writer, born in 1627 to a noble
family in Lübeck, who renounced his title after being crippled in a horse-
riding accident. His long convalescence brought him to Nuremberg, where
he wrote many compilations for the book dealer, Johannes Endter, including an appendix for the 1674 edition, *Das ärgerliche Leben und schreckliche Ende des viel berüchtigen Ertz-Schwartzkünstlers D. Johannis Fausti*
(The Troubling Life and Horrible End of the Very Notorious Black Artist Dr.
Johannis Fausti).[4]

In typical baroque manner, Endter's edition went through six popular editions.[5] From his years of research into the Faust legend, Goethe would have well understood how popular stories of the seventeenth century would find publishers who would reissue the same material with new editorial additions.[6] The publishing history of the many *Faust* editions provides a genealogical model of how curious tales grew more complex and acquired additional characters, descriptions, locations, adventures, and connotations as they circulated within the early modern publishing industry, so that eventually later versions put forward meanings completely at odds with the original text. Baroque literature was a complex circulatory system of stories rewritten and republished, compiled, expanded, and annotated by new authors copying old ones. These tomes of stories, shocking anecdotes, and foreign histories were mined for inspiration long after their publication. By way of excusing his perusal in such dusty tomes, Goethe tells Schiller that while Francisci's compilation displays awful taste, it holds many useful stories. The scholarship on Goethe's early modern sources for *Faust* is oceanic; my goal here is to follow some of the same archival routes to understand the early modern reception of Chinese culture as it stretched into the early nineteenth century.[7] Finally, we might question how far-reaching Goethe's analogy between Weimar and Nanjing was. Was it confined to this one theological disputation, or did it reveal an underlying affinity between literati in both places? Were Weimar's poets flattering themselves with their imagined affinities with China? If so, they were hardly the first.

Nineteenth-century colonial ideology, beginning with the memoirs written about the 1793 Macartney Embassy to Peking, seeks to dismiss baroque knowledge of Asia by arguing that its categories were defined foremostly by theological concerns; however, in making this rejection, the later modernist arguments also discount the earlier attempts to draw sympathetic bonds between China and Europe. In order to understand the long history of European attitudes toward China, we need to trace out how knowledge of the Orient was transmitted across Europe and down through generations of readers. This requires us to wander into the labyrinth of baroque literature that transcribed, compiled, and revised the initial Jesuit accounts of China. If we constantly refer back just to the primary missionary reports, we will never understand how readers removed from and often critical of the Jesuits would have understood their descriptions of China. Goethe, for example, reads Matteo Ricci's report of his conversation with the Buddhist directly against the author's intention. Many Enlightenment readers did much the same. What the devout missionaries meant to convey by recounting Ricci's dialogues was not at all what Goethe, and presumably others, took from the tale. Even as he reads against Jesuit intentions, Goethe posits an affinity between Chinese and German thought without claiming a hierarchical superiority. He aligns his interest with the Buddhist position in part because the disputation provides an intellectual arena in which such choices are possible. The disputation provides a broadly applicable framework for ideas and arguments to be compared and transferred between debaters. Goethe is still operating within the logic of the scholastic disputation that presumes an intellectual parity between the two cultures—his allegiance just happens to cross over to the foreign and heretical position, one that he makes familiar by comparing it to early Weimar idealism.

Martin Mulsow describes a similar process of heretical transfer from Islam into the European radical Enlightenment. "On the one hand there was perhaps a subliminal continuity of heretical ideas in astrological, alchemical, or medical treatises, but on the other hand we need to take a simple fact into consideration: orthodoxy of one particular religion is automatically a heresy in the eyes of another. This means that those who argue especially for the truth of the doctrines of their own religion may in fact have a subversive effect on another religion."[8] For Goethe, these transfers appear directly on the page. In writing *Faust*, Goethe was clearly fascinated with the continuous tradition of heretical texts but, in the Nanjing disputation, he followed the more automatic heresy of adopting a foreign religion's belief. Completely absent from Goethe's filiations with China is the modernist presumption (typified by Hegel's history of philosophy) that Europe had superseded East Asian civilization.[9] Goethe's letter to Schiller succinctly encapsulates the long transformation whereby sympathy for China was understood first in theological terms as a shared participation in the divine truths revealed at the world's creation but which then reversed itself into a history of parallel cultures that eschewed deism in favor of the thoroughly human. Underlying both belief systems was the technological presumption that shared experiences could be transmitted across a single global space. Both Ricci and Goethe were acutely aware of how written texts communicated over great distances conditioned the recognition of identities and differences between Europe and China.

## Ricci's Arguments

The dialogue, entitled "Father Ricci debates with a Minister of the Idols," was first published for Europeans in Matteo Ricci's posthumous history of the Jesuit mission to preach Christianity in China, entitled *De Christiana Expeditione Apud Sinas*, the first edition of which was published 1615 in Augsburg.[10] The book was based on an Italian manuscript found in Matteo Ricci's desk after his death. It was then augmented and edited into a 645-page Latin volume by the Belgian priest, Nicholas Trigault. *De Christiana expeditione* was the most influential work on China in the seventeenth century. David Mungello claims the book reached more readers than any other contemporary work on China.[11] The original Latin text was translated within a decade into French, German, Spanish, Italian, and English. The German title appeared in 1617 as *Historia von der Einführung der christlichen Religion in das große Königreich China durch die Societet Jesu*.[12] Ricci also provided a Chinese account of the debate in chapter seven of *The True Meaning of The Lord in Heaven*, a work intended to offer a synthetic account of Christianity and Confucianism.[13]

Ricci's support for Confucian thought was coupled with a very clear antipathy against Buddhism, which most missionaries in East Asia perceived as idolatrous.[14] The first European reports stressed Ricci's decisive rejection of Buddhism as both idolatry and pantheism on the basis of natural reason:

Their great error, fatal to the idea of divinity, namely that God and all things material are one and the same substance, taken from the doctrine of the idol worshippers, has gradually crept into the schools of the literary class, who imagine that God is the soul of the material universe; the one mind, as it were, of a great body. After the debate at the banquet, some of the disciples of the host became frequent callers on Father Ricci and soon put aside their pantheistic ideas.[15]

While the original dialogue may have been intended to impress Nanjing literary circles, the official Jesuit circulation of the story in print was clearly intended to impress European audiences. In each dialogue, whether in Nanjing or with Europe, the Buddhist serves as the third man who is purposefully excluded from the sender-receiver communication. Whether as a rhetorical strategy or as a condition of any successful media channel, the Nanjing disputation illustrates Michel Serres's claim that, "To hold a dialogue is to suppose a third man and to seek to exclude him."[16] This principle emerges centrally in German idealism's discovery of dialectical reasoning; Fichte had already stated, "Any pair of things to distinguished must be related to a third thing."[17] If Ricci is engaging in a disputation with Buddhism, he is also specifically refraining from holding one with the Confucian literati. In a syncretic society with many religions, to distinguish between different teachings by criticizing only one of them is tantamount to seeking an accommodation with another. While many readers may have pondered the logical content of the disputation, the most important aspect of Ricci's argument with Buddhism, the pagan error that must be excluded was his two-sided appeals to Confucians within China and Catholics in Europe. As Ricci sought to draw a connection between Christianity and Confucianism, he felt obliged to block out the "noise" of Chinese idolatry, a cacophony he labeled Buddhism but which included disparate practices.

The banquet figures prominently in the early history of the Jesuit mission because it shows clearly how Ricci aligned himself with a magisterial elite by insisting on an interpretation of Confucianism that focused primarily on the early writings and that rejected later neo-Confucian syncretic appropriations of Buddhist teachings. Many historians have noted the Jesuit affinity for the polite scholarly conventions of the Confucian literati. Just as important is the story's rhetorical context. Ricci is presented within the conventions of early modern rhetoric as a subtle and understated master, capable of following long complex discussions about theological shadings as well as engaging in quick, witty one-upmanship, all in the company of the most educated men in Nanjing. Jesuits were trained in the conventions of classical rhetoric. Their flexible willingness to persuade both in speech and appearance came across in their adopting local clothing rather than holding onto European priestly vestments as a mark of difference.[18] Once he learned some Chinese, Ricci set out to translate the Latin tradition into Chinese. His first published treatise in Chinese, *On Friendship*, consisted of translated aphorisms chosen for his new audience from a sixteenth-century Latin compilation.[19] Forced to work from memory because of his limited library of European books, Ricci is known for the Chinese treatise describing his own adaptation of the memory arts first set down in print by Cicero, Quintilian, and the anonymous author of *Ad Herennium*.[20] Ricci makes a deliberate point of showing his skills in recollection by summarizing all the arguments that had been made prior to his own concluding statement, a move anyone trained in classical rhetoric would have admired: "He began by making a detailed summary, from memory, of all that had been said on the question, after which he said: 'There is no room for doubt that the God of heaven and earth must be considered as infinitely good.'"[21]

As with many debates, the stakes were more complex than the arguments presented by the two speakers—there were inevitably third and fourth parties looking on who were implicitly addressed during the disputation. For Matteo Ricci, these onlookers included the Confucian literati, whom he was trying to impress with his ability to argue in Mandarin, the Buddhists whom he was intending to refute, and Catholic readers in Europe, who were supposed to acknowledge his confrontation with idolatry. Additionally, Ricci was also offering his Confucian audience a model of Christian metaphysics without directly engaging in an interpretation of canonical Chinese texts. To the extent that the first Jesuits in China suspected that the literati were not concerned with the afterlife or God as creator, Ricci may have been elaborating this principle for his Confucian listeners while arguing with a Buddhist with the hope that they too would be persuaded. The continued reception of the debate in Nanjing can be followed through its extended circulation, its many retellings through compilers and their readers. The process entails the story's recomposition by different authors for the purposes of providing new material for the publishing industry and for the sake of reconfirming certain knowledge claims about China. The audiences and theological implications multiplied as the Nanjing disputation circulated in Europe, so that later radical Enlightenment philosophers and free-thinking poets would draw dissonant conclusions, namely that the Chinese were perfectly civilized and moral even without belief in a theistic creator and judge.

At the start of the debate, Ricci says he would like to know what his opponent thought of the creator of heaven and earth. His goal was to establish a first principle from which other conclusions could be drawn. Ricci felt that if he could demonstrate agreement that the world had been created by a single deity, then the rest of the debate would follow as he wished. Anticipating the sequence of arguments that would flow from this claim, the Buddhist does not accept this appeal to first principles as decisive: "he did not deny the existence of a moderator of heaven and earth, but at the same time he did not believe him to be a god or endowed with any particular majesty."[22] In other words, the creator was no different than anyone else seated around the table. To show how common creation was, the Jesuit text states: "He then admitted that he could create heaven and earth." The original German translation of this passage includes the marginal gloss, "Ungeschickte Sophisterey des Götzen Pfaffen" (clumsy sophistry of the idolatrous priests), which implicitly draws the connection to Socratic dialogues.

For all the warnings not to side with the Buddhist, Goethe is clearly drawn to his argument. Already in his youthful *Sturm und Drang* writings, he had extolled Promethean versions of the proposition that humans share in the ability to create the world, that the poet is a second creator, which in later, less theistic terms, one and the same with the universe. Ricci's response was to ask his opponent if he could grasp hold of a glowing stove like the one they had in front of them at the banquet, which Ricci claims flabbergasts Sanhoi. After some uproar—the Jesuit text refers to moments of heated discussion without stating exactly what was being said—Sanhoi offers an explanation of what he means by creating a universe. If an astronomer or a mathematician studies the heavens, he creates an image of the moon and the stars in his mind that he then can recall from memory. Ricci's text then has the monk state: "In other words, you have created a new sun, a new moon, and in the same way anything else can be created."[23] Goethe who so often described his own poetic creation as a process of drawing images from his storehouse of memory—a metaphor common to Roman rhetoric—would readily have identified with this line of reasoning. The image of a natural thing creates a second version of that reality. For Goethe, this was the idealist moment in the debate: that the human understanding of nature emerges only from subjective consciousness. Ricci responds by drawing a distinction between the reality of things and their representation in our minds—a move Goethe associates with Kantian epistemology. On a more general basis, Ricci and the Jesuit mission, during its long history serving the emperor, relied on astronomy as a shared intercultural form of knowledge, important to all earth-bound observers. In the context of world literature (*Weltliteratur*) and cultural comparison, astronomical observation provides a potential position of agreement. In an epistemological vein, Ricci insists that it must be obvious to everyone that there is not only a difference between a thing and its image, but also that it would be impossible to form an image of something that one had not seen—in other words, our mental representations are dependent on our perception of real natural things.

Here again, Ricci draws a distinction familiar to Kantian followers such as Reinhold. According to the Jesuit version, the debate descends into a chaotic string of arguments in which Sanhoi begins to quote mystical passages to which Ricci responds that the debate can only be carried out through appeals to natural reason and not by each side quoting their own sacred writings. Ricci's account of the debate concludes with a summary statement about the wider flaws of the Buddhist arguments, which he sees as creeping into Confucian thinking as well, namely the claim that "God and all things material are one and the same substance" so that even members of the literary class "imagine that God is the soul of the material universe, the one mind, as it were, of a great body."[24] This concluding statement tries to draw theological implications that reach far beyond the specific claims of the debate in order to make a broad criticism of pantheism. While Goethe does not refer to Ricci's summary statement in his letters, commentators (discussed below) have assumed that he would have identified strongly with just the kind of pantheism Ricci denounced. Goethe's lifetime fascination with Spinoza is well documented, and the common scholarly assumption is that he would have found nothing wrong with the principle Ricci rejects.

## **Erasmus Francisci's Retelling**

Francisci's account of Ricci's debate presented the meeting in terms familiar to European readers, namely as a rhetorical duel. Readers would have known that Jesuit schools were famous for including public debates in the curriculum. The pedagogical presumption was that students were motivated to study and prepare their arguments by their innate competitive desire to win in a forum of their peers and teachers. Even Protestants could acknowledge that Jesuits were highly skilled orators; indeed, Francesci's narrative frames the theological debate as a duel that allowed all Christians to cheer for the missionary. Buddhists are depicted as deceptive with a comical character, while the Jesuits are shown even to Protestants as honorable virtuosos defending the faith. The framework of a sociable conflict also allowed European readers to recognize a moment of identity between European aristocrats and Chinese mandarins, for any respectable duel requires both participants to share the same rank. Yet in the end, the cultural differences were most important because they made Ricci's triumph all the greater for having been managed under foreign rules.[25]

The theological details of the argument would have been familiar to European scholars, whether Protestant or Catholic, thus Ricci's critique of Buddhism would have allowed a common agreement between European denominations. His logical demonstration of the existence of a God, in heaven apart from the universe he created, was also intended for Ricci's allies among the Confucian scholars, for his entire accommodationist synthesis between Christianity and Confucianism rested on his assertion that early Confucian writings also referred to a theistic god. By demonstrating logically that a divine creator exists, Ricci was not only refuting Buddhism, he was also advocating for his own rather speculative interpretation of Confucius.

The original Jesuit text deliberately selects which heresy it addresses. Ricci specifically refrains from entering into a discussion of Buddhist writings. This reliance on reason rather than scripture in order to debate Jews and pagans can be traced back to St. Anselm's twelfth-century claim that reason alone can demonstrate God's existence. Joachim Kurtz points out that the Jesuit texts on China often stressed the superiority of European sciences in the paratext.[26] The Protestant Francisci follows a similar approach for recounting Ricci's conversation, for he frames the narration with a long paragraph explaining that Europeans have a better grasp of logical argumentation—in particular, regarding how to draw conclusions in a syllogism—than the Chinese. Natural reason is presented as a neutral, non-culturally specific mode of thinking, set in contrast to the interpretation of a region's myth and scripture. At the same time, Francesci claims that the Jesuits have a superior skill, i.e., that logical argumentation is a European trait: "The Jesuits excelled in sacred oratory: 'wisdom speaking copiously,' as Cicero defined oratory, putting eloquence and reason to serve the mysteries of the Christian faith."[27] Francesci gives the story a title, "Die ungeschickte Schluß-Künstler" (The Clumsy Concluders) and, in an appeal to European aristocratic readership, draws the direct parallel between rhetorical debate, logical reasoning, and fencing. If Francisci crosses cultural boundaries to admire how clever the Jesuits are, Goethe does the same by admiring the Chinese; he draws the exact opposite conclusion as Francisci by concluding that it is the Chinese who are more clever than the missionaries. Jesuit reports are replete with examples of Chinese cleverness, yet both Jesuits and Mandarins were known for their canniness; one reputation burnished the other. In the overlapping claims to cleverness, Goethe suggests that the Buddhist monk was perhaps the most shrewd of all, putting forward arguments that Ricci blindly believed he had refuted and therefore included in his report back to Europe but which, in the end, were the most persuasive, at least to Goethe sitting in Weimar as he pondered Spinoza and the earliest formulations of German idealism.

Francisci revises the Jesuit text so the reader seems to be examining the narrative's unfolding with detachment. He conveys the sense that the European reader is watching a distant spectacle, like a modern Olympic competition witnessed only once every four years, that draws them in emotionally only for a brief time. For early modern German readers, it was necessary to provide a context and guidelines for understanding these Chinese encounters, and inevitably foreign events were translated into familiar scenarios, sports among them—for example, a fencing match was one scenario that could be readily understood even if the motives for the fight and the combatant's utterances were unintelligible. Duels could bring in an audience that was entertained and excited by the contest, without requiring them to understand the theological expectations of the combatants. Fencing was but one useful trope that helped structure a European readership. Not only was it presumed that armed personal conflict was universal, but the fencing metaphor was easily connected to other familiar tropes in rhetoric and politics.[28] By placing the reader out of bounds, the fencing metaphor allowed for an easy appropriation of the encounter without requiring knowledge of strange languages and religions. Fencing reduced foreign encounters to a simple visual denominator.

Whereas the Jesuit narrative differentiates between different forms of Chinese thought, Francisci makes perfectly clear that the primary motive for Europeans to study foreign cultures is so that they may know themselves better. The Other is quite explicitly the mirror against which Europe defines itself, according to Francisci:

> Gott / uns sich selbsten kennen / bleibt allezeit die höchste Wissenschaft. . . .
> Zu der vollkommenen Selbst-Erkenntniß aber / befordert uns gleichwol auch
> nicht wenig die Erkenntniß andrer Menschen, wie nemlich dieselbe / in ihrer
> Weise / Gewonheit / und Bräuchen / gesittet / Hieran lernen wir / entweder
> was uns mangelt.[29]

> To know ourselves in God remains the highest form of knowledge that man
> can achieve. . . . However, to reach the highest form of self-knowledge we are
> urged to study other people as much as ourselves, as they are civilized in manner, customs, and practices. Herein we can learn what we lack.

Further translating the Jesuit text into a courtly context, Matteo Ricci's conversations are presented as a demonstration of superior skill. The theological question disproving heresy and revealing divine truth recedes in

Francisci's telling. Trigault's original narration stresses Ricci's role in giving sermons on God's law. He emphasizes Ricci's campaign against the worship of false idols, which the story will demonstrate is practiced by Buddhists not Confucian Mandarins. Trigault's interest is to further the Jesuit policy of *approachement* with the Confucian elite by writing for an ecclesiastical audience in Rome, whereas Francisci emphasizes Ricci's skill in verbal combat. As much as Francisci admires the Ricci's dexterity, he ultimately doubts the Jesuit claim that pictures of Confucius are treated with respect as a human and not as a god.[30] In other words, on the crucial question of idolatry, Francisci sides against the missionaries. For Goethe writing to Schiller, Ricci's preference for logic over scripture, however, does not appear as a universal form of humanity, rather it is quickly reduced to a particular philosophical school. Indeed, the Buddhist challenges Ricci's reliance on abstract categories by arguing that they constitute a secondary mode of creation. To postulate abstract terms for the sun, moon, and heavens amounts to their re-creation.

## Goethe's Reversal

By the time Goethe read about Matteo Ricci, European interest in China had taken on a very different tone than when the missionaries were still sending back reports about the court in Beijing. The Jesuits had been suppressed by papal decree in 1773, the China mission closed, and new ethnographic travelogues about more contemporary journeys to Peking, such as the failed British Macartney embassy, were filling the book market. Before Goethe sent his friend a copy of Francisci's report on the disputation, Schiller had already sent Goethe the first translated Chinese novel, originally published 1761 in London as *The Pleasing History* and then given a German makeover, entitled *Die angenehme Geschichte*, by Christian Gottlieb von Murr in 1766. Murr had sent Schiller a copy in 1794, which he presumably passed along to Goethe.[31] Thus, in the 1790s, Goethe and Schiller were pursuing any number of Chinese sources, driven by a clear sense of having rediscovered a culture that had been ossified into Rococo stereotypes. China was a discovery made in the library rather than on a porcelain vase. Rejecting Francisci's inclination to perceive the dinner debate as an encounter between East and West, Christianity and paganism, Goethe sees the disputation as a contest between two types of thought that have their direct parallel in Weimar as well. He characterizes his interpretation of the debate in terms of two sets of antithetical couplings, one in China, the other in Germany, thereby suggesting a set of constellations that reoccur in different times and locations.

Given how assiduously German literary historiography distinguishes between baroque literature and the classical period of autonomy aesthetics, we should pause to consider what it means for the two luminaries to read through a seventeenth-century scribe like Francisci searching for good material. In German literary history, they are the authors who define literature as a self-created reality, flowing from the internal genius of the author as a second creator. What does it mean that they have been caught poaching from an earlier, encyclopedic compilation about exotic places? Must we acknowledge that autonomy aesthetics includes literary appropriation and a mundane economics of textual circulation? Does the autonomy of the artwork presume the successful integration of external elements into a new whole and the covering up of all too obvious tracks between works, through the burning of letters and notebooks? Walter Benjamin perceives just such an "offenbares Geheimnis" (open secret) in the fact that Goethe destroyed all drafts and notes for *Die Wahlverwandtschaften* (*Elective Affinities*), thereby eliminating all trace of his procedure in writing the novel.[32]

The more unfamiliar the source, the more complex the rewriting required for a successful appropriation. Schiller refers to Francisci's style as "gothic," a term Herder used decades earlier to describe ornate courtly style, what we call baroque or rococo. Both Goethe and Schiller reassure themselves and each other that even as they read Francisci, that they can remain detached from his convoluted style. Goethe and Schiller sense that the winding confusion of archaic order needed to be renovated. In all their disavowals and complaints about the incoherent style with which old stories were collected, it becomes obvious how anxious modern writers were at mucking around in the labyrinths of seventeenth-century compilations.

Goethe shares this art of borrowing from forgotten collections with Friedrich Schiller, who, in his letter three days later, referred to the practice as searching for poetic spoils, "poetische Ausbeute" (MA 8.1:486). The language of acquisition that Goethe and Schiller use to describe the search for poetic inspiration—the borrowing of poetic images for one's own writing— contributes to the poetic atmosphere, as in the early "Harzreise im Winter" (Winter Journey in the Harz Mountains) which opens with its own image of a poet's constant search for new symbolic objects to compose:

> Dem Geier gleich,
> Der auf schweren Morgenwolken
> Mit sanftem Fittich ruhend
> Nach Beute schaut,
> Schwebe mein Lied.[33]

> Just as a raptor
> scans for prey
> upon heavy morning clouds
> with soft wings resting,
> may my song soar.

The young poet identifies himself with a bird of prey as he scans the horizon for poetic objects. In his old age, he told Eckermann much the same. Goethe's relationship to Persian and Chinese literature entails borrowing stories for the sake of his own writing—a relation of influence that he acknowledges for Shakespeare and the Bible as well:

Gehört nicht Alles, was die Vor- und Mitwelt geleistet, dem Dichter von Rechtswegen an? Warum soll er sich scheuen, Blumen zu nehmen, wo er sie findet? Nur durch Aneignung fremder Schätze entsteht ein Großes. Hab' ich nicht auch im Mephistopheles den Hiob und ein Shakespeare-Lied mir angeeignet?[34]

> Does not everything accomplished by our predecessors and contemporaries
> belong by rights to the poet? Why should he refrain from picking flowers from
> where he finds them. A great work requires the appropriation of foreign treas-
> ures. With Mephistopheles did I not take from Job and Shakespeare?

If the two poets referred to themselves ironically as marauders and magicians, we can understand these allusions on several levels: first, as a witty contradiction to the polite public discourse about artists; second, as an identification with their own critical representation of the construction of meaning in
*Faust* or *Iphigenie* as trickery or exploitation; and, third, as an acknowledgment of the fundamental intertextuality of all writing as derived from earlier
reading. Thus, classical aesthetics emerges as the appropriation of ancient
texts, i.e., as a process of rewriting already established texts:

> Bei einem *gegebenen* Stoff hingegen ist alles anders und leichter. Da werden
> Facta und Charaktere überliert und der Dichter hat nur die Belebung des Ganze
> . . . Ja, ich rate sogar zu schon bearbeiteten Gegenstände. Wie oft ist nicht
> Iphigenie gemacht, und doch sind alle verschieden; den jeder sieht und stellt
> die Sachen anders, eben nach seiner Weise.[35]

> Everything is different with already *given* material and easier. Facts and char-
> acters are then already provided and the poet has only to enliven the whole
> . . . Yes, I would advise to use objects that have already been worked upon. How
> often has Iphigenia been done and yet they are all different, for everyone sees
> and positions the situation differently, according to his own manner.

While Goethe may have lectured Eckermann, he is a little more circumspect when writing to Schiller. In the 1798 letter in which he describes
Matteo Ricci's dinner debate, Goethe refers to "we poets" as magicians
(*Taschenspieler*), who do not want anyone to see how their art is practiced.
"Wenn nuns als Dichtern, wie den Taschenspielern, daran gelegen sein mußte,
daß niemand die Art, wie ein Kunststückchen hervorgebracht wird, einsehen
dürfte, so hätten wir freilich gewonnen Spiel" (MA 8.1:484–85; If we poets,
like magicians, could manage that no one would perceive how we created a
work of art, then we would have won the game). Goethe's identification in
this passage with the most notorious early modern magicians is but a turn of
the hand away, for the tricks Mephistopheles pulls off in "Auerbachs Keller"
(Auerbach's Cellar) are labeled *Taschenspielersachen*.[36] As an example of literary magic, Goethe cites, in his letter to Schiller, the Germans' enthusiastic
reception of *Hermann und Dorothea*, an epic poem whose original source
was discovered only later in the nineteenth century. Schiller shared Goethe's
habit of roving through old chronicles and compilations for inspiration. His
ballad "Der Kampf mit dem Drachen" ("Battle with the Dragon") was based
on a tale found in Francisci collection. After Goethe praised the Jesuit com-
piler, Athanasius Kircher, Schiller was able to compose "Der Taucher" ("The
Diver") based on a tale in several Baroque compilations.[37] A key difference
between scholars and poets lies merely in their intentions as they peruse
libraries.

Goethe's reaction to reading about Matteo Ricci's disputation in Nanjing
was surprising because he readily drew a parallel to the philosophical

debates that were riling the University of Jena.[38] More remarkable still was that he aligned his own sympathies with the Buddhist position. Not only did he recognize the similarities between the epistemological quandaries in post-Kantian philosophy and Jesuit attempts to insert Christian theology into Chinese learned society, he also identified himself with a line of argumentation that from almost any European perspective was the most radical and least familiar. Goethe's parallel suggests that we might read the two pairings in opposite directions: not only does Reinhold write like a Jesuit, but Matteo Ricci could be read as compatible with Reinhold's attempt to find a universally acceptable principle that grounds Kantian philosophy. Likewise, idealism might not only reiterate Buddhist pantheism, but Buddhism may itself also be based on the principle of the absolute ego contemplating the world created by self-awareness. To the first comparison: Was Ricci's reliance on a logic outside spiritual revelation a form of transcendental reasoning? In Goethe's response to Francisci's retelling of Ricci's dinner debate, we can trace out three major philosophical approaches to Chinese thought in early modern Europe: the Jesuit accommodation that sought to recuperate early Confucianism as compatible with Christian teaching while dismissing Buddhism as idolatry, Francisci's dogmatic Christian suspicion that all Chinese belief systems, despite Jesuit assurances, amounted to pagan idol worship, and a radical Enlightenment pantheism that happily drew parallels between its own disavowal of theism and Chinese practices.

That the Nanjing debate correlated with Weimar contests also suggests a similarity between the classes of intellectuals at both sites. If the Jesuits could identify with the Chinese literati as a similar class of learned scholars ready to take on administrative assignments, Goethe could readily see himself in a similar role as the duke of Weimar's *Geheimrat* and councilor. Given that the German academic elite was characterized as mandarins by the turn of the twentieth century, there is no question that Goethe, with his combination of administrative, scientific, and poetic modes of writing, became a model for this intertwining of intellectual and state functions.[39] Goethe's last poetry cycle, "Chinesisch-Deutsche Jahres- und Tageszeiten" (Chinese-German Hours and Seasons) makes this comparison explicit. Here, Goethe assumes the voice of a Mandarin, this time clearly aligning himself with the same literati Ricci addressed in offering a synthesis between early Confucianism and Christian metaphysics—though his appeal to Chinese poet-administrators came in the moment of retiring from politics in favor of writing poetry and drinking wine in the garden, rather than as an affirmative model of state power. By abandoning the functions of running a principality, the aged Goethe nevertheless concedes that he has served like the literati for much of his life. The idealization of the Chinese administrative class with its rigorous exam structure and lack of an aristocracy had been a staple of the Enlightenment discourse. Voltaire was constantly flattering Frederick the Great that he should write poetry like the emperor of China. Goethe's last poems do not have the ruler write poetry as an ornament but as a substitution for politics. His identification follows the example of literati life depicted in Abel Remusat's translation of the Chinese romance known in English as *The Two Fair Cousins* in which court politics is abandoned in favor of writing.

Goethe's recognition of a similarity between the two disparate debates reflects the intellectual tensions and transitions of Weimar at that very particular instance. Goethe's discovery comes at a moment in Weimar and Jena when Kantian philosophy is starting to give way to a just emerging idealism, a moment that has not yet come to full existence. Walter Benjamin described how sudden insights arise in time:

> Ihre Wahrnehmung ist in jedem Fall an ein Aufblitzen gebunden. Sie huscht vorbei, ist vielleicht wiederzugewinnen, aber kann nicht eigentlich wie andere Wahrnehmungen festgehalten werden. Sie bietet sich dem Auge ebenso flüchtig, vorübergehend wie eine Gestirnkonstellation. Die Wahrnehmung von Ähnlichkeiten also scheint an ein Zeit moment gebunden.[40]

> The perception of similarity is in every case bound to a flashing up. It flits past, can possibly be won again, but cannot really be held fast as can other perception. It offers itself to the eye as a fleetingly and transitorily as a constellation of stars. The perception of similarities thus seems to be bound to a moment of time.[41]

To be sure, the inclination to draw correspondences between Europe and China was already a long-standing tradition, initiated precisely by Jesuit missionaries. However, Goethe's insight is radically different; indeed, it finds an affinity precisely where the priests would not have wanted to find one: in idealism's and Buddhism's rejection of a divine creator. The two authors had been following the emergence of Fichte's *Wissenschaftslehre (Science of Knowledge)* closely. While his lectures had already drawn a large audience, Fichte kept trying to reformulate his speculations more clearly. On February 27, 1797, Schiller writes to Goethe, recommending that he read the (first) new introduction that Fichte published (MA 8.1:318).[42] By March the two men are reading Fichte together.[43] Standing behind Goethe's correspondence with Schiller about the new metaphysical correspondence he has just found is the careful need to disguise the two thinkers' rejection of orthodox Christianity. Goethe writes diplomatically to Schiller, suggesting that they speak discretely about the similarity in person, with no paper trail. The accusations of atheism and Spinozism leveled at Christian Wolff, along with his subsequent banishment from Prussia, all because he had compared Chinese ethics to his own rationalist system, were surely familiar.[44]

A year after Goethe's discovery of the Nanjing disputation, Weimar would itself be embroiled in a scandal over whether Fichte, newly arrived at the University of Jena, had been teaching atheism. Anticipating the danger, Goethe writes in veiled analogies about his own affinity for the Buddhist monk's argument with the Catholic priest. His attention to the two-hundred-year-old theological debate, his eagerness to share his insight with Schiller, and his reticence in writing explicitly about what he saw in analogy reflects the ongoing pressure that Christian institutions placed on radical thought.

In his first letter to Schiller about the Nanjing disputation, Goethe also includes a copy of Schelling's *Ideen zu einer Philosophie der Natur (Ideas for a Philosophy of Nature)*, lending further evidence on how the aporias that frustrated the Nanjing debaters could also to be found in Weimar disagreements about the Kantian "thing in itself." Goethe was quite plausibly reading the introduction to Schelling's *Ideen* at the same time as he stumbled across Ricci's disputation in Nanjing. Schelling's ideal philosopher could well describe a Romantic conception of Buddhism:

> Die größten Geister haben, unbekümmert um die Principien ihrer Erfindungen, in ihrer eigenen Welt gelebt, und was ist der ganze Ruhm des scharfsinnigen Zweiflers gegen des Leben eines Mannes, der eine Welt in seinem Kopfe und die ganze Natur in seiner Einbildungskraft trug?[45]

> The greatest spirits have lived in their own world, undisturbed by the principles of their experience and what is the fame of the sharpest doubters compared to the life of a man that carried an entire world in his mind and all of nature in his imagination.

The opposing arguments in the debates form a constellation that allows Goethe's philosophical discourse to weave between the two settings, combining Kantian terminology with Jesuit reasoning, so that one scenario illuminates the other: "Eben so mag sich der Idealist gegen die *Dinge an sich* wehren wie er will, er stößt doch ehe er sichs versteht an die *Dinge außer ihm*, und wie mir scheint, sie kommen ihn immer beim ersten Begegnen so in die Quere wie dem Chineser die Glutpfanne" (MA 8.1:489; Just so, the idealist may ward off *things in themselves* as he will, nevertheless he will knock into *things outside of himself* before he realizes it, and in the first encounter they get in his way much like the glowing oven did for the Chinaman). Just because the idealist has a valid point that human consciousness can never know the thing in itself does not mean that things are wholly dependent on human consciousness and that they do not exert a force beyond themselves that confronts human perception, sometimes in surprising and unexpected ways. In describing the epistemological impasse in Weimar and Nanjing, Goethe prefers to avoid falling into either of the two camps but, instead, seeks to remain as long as possible in a natural state of consciousness, which Schelling claimed exists prior to philosophical inquiry, where subject and object are still inseparable.[46] Once torn out of this naive state and dropped into philosophical inquiry, Goethe suggests, a person is frustrated either by the inability to escape the internal order of things so that one can draw a connection between the empirical world with the subjective state of the mind or one cannot find an explanation for how consciousness is able to know the empirical objects outside itself. The Weimar idealist, Goethe maintains, is just as surprised by the externality of material objects as the Buddhist. In their introspective meditation of the universe, both are confronted by the painful otherness of the glowing hot pot.

The parallel Goethe draws involved the first two professors of critical (post-Kantian) philosophy at the University of Jena: Reinhold and Fichte. These types of oppositions were not unusual: Fichte himself drew a distinction between idealists, for whom "the object appears . . . as having first been created by the presentation of the intellect" (a position close to the Buddhist here) and metaphysical dogmatists for whom the object exists in nature without the aid of the intellect (far too crude to be attributed to Matteo Ricci).[47] As his argument unfolds, Fichte adds a third position—critical philosophy (in other words, Kant). Goethe's opposition is more narrowly focused and nuanced because, in writing to Schiller, he is more concerned with suggesting a correspondence between debates in Weimar and Nanjing than with summarizing the central tenets of modern European philosophy.

Buddhism and idealism seem alike because, as Fichte argues in the *Wissenschaftslehre*, empirical perceptions are knowable as facts only from a position within the self: everything that consciousness perceives as not being itself is itself the result of the self's own positing. According to Fichte, the empirical is understood within consciousness as an intuition; only a dogmatist who is captured by the causality of things would argue that empirical perceptions originate outside of self-consciousness. If we cannot know the "thing in itself," then we are left with our own intuitions of the world, which occur in consciousness, not outside of it. The *Nicht-Ich* is posited by an *absolute Ich*. Fichte points to several passages in the *Kritik der reinen Vernunft* (*Critique of Pure Reason*) that cautiously describe the self's sensation of external empirical perceptions—without declaring that they originate in some "thing in itself" that exists wholly and metaphysically by itself. Fichte argues that many of Kant's followers, and he considers Reinhold the most adept, still have a dogmatic view of the "thing in itself" as grounded outside the subject rather than recognizing that Kant himself often writes like an idealist who holds that empirical perceptions are knowable only as intuitions within consciousness, and are therefore a (somewhat dialectical) product of the self's self-positing.

Goethe takes two steps back from this debate to draw an analogy between Fichte's claim that empirical perceptions occur within consciousness rather than originating from outside of it and the Buddhist's claim that our idea of the sun is itself a (second) creation in the mind. Much as Goethe admires the Buddhist's maneuvering around Ricci's metaphysics, he also wishes the Buddhist had been able to physically demonstrate that empirical objects are solely mental images by picking up the hot pot in his hands. Like any detached yet interested spectator, Goethe enjoys the deft maneuvers of both sides; he is not rooting for any particular position. Fichte and Reinhold are themselves well aware of the public nature of their debate; indeed, they go out of their way to speak politely about each other. The two philosophers corresponded even as they held differing positions. Although they were hardly hostile to one another, Fichte had plenty of sharp words and mockery for other members of the philosophical public. Reinhold comes very close to stating that Kant's *Critique of Pure Reason* and Fichte's *Wissenschaftslehre* agree on the fundamental point that empirical facts are intelligible only because they occur within consciousness. But Reinhold sees this self as merely empirical and not transcendental. Fichte then picks up on this new difference; Reinhold almost agrees with him, but then makes a further distinction that moves the debate onward. Fichte writes generously about Reinhold in his "Second Introduction" to the *Wissenschaftslehre*, quoting the essay in which Reinhold equates and distinguishes Kant from

Fichte.[48] We can track the dialectical unfolding of Fichte and Reinhold's debate better than the Nanjing disputation, because its Jesuit representation is locked in an opposition between Christian assertions of metaphysics and Buddhist disavowals of the same.

When he equated the Jesuit reliance on logic with the Kantian arguments of Karl Leonard Reinhold, Goethe was not just being whimsical. Reinhold was born in Vienna where he attended a school with Jesuit teachers from the age of seven. In 1772, he enrolled as a novice in the Jesuit church of St. Anna but, after a year of strict monastic discipline, he was forced to leave when the Society of Jesus was suppressed. A letter written by the fifteen-year-old Reinhold to his father testifies to how stricken he felt by being forced to leave his devotional life.[49] A year later he entered the Barnabite Collegium at St. Michael, where he studied philosophy and theology. After six years, he was allowed to instruct the novices in the disciplines that comprised the philosophy curriculum: logic, metaphysics, ethics, spiritual rhetoric, mathematics, and physics.[50] By the time he was in his 20s, Reinhold had turned away from his youthful asceticism to participate in the new Enlightenment culture that had emerged in Vienna after Joseph II started introducing his progressive reforms in 1781. Reinhold joined an Enlightenment club modeled on the Free Masons that was dedicated to combatting superstition, *Schwärmerei*, and monasticism.

In 1783, with the assistance of the Leipzig professor of philosophy, Christian Friedrich Petzold, Reinhold fled Vienna and his church obligations for Protestant Saxony. When news reached Vienna that Reinhold was now teaching and studying in Leipzig, his friends advised him to move onward to Weimar, where Christoph Wieland received him generously with an offer to help edit his journal, *Der Teutscher Merkur*, following the departure of his earlier assistant, Friedrich Bertuch. While working for the *Merkur*, Reinhold began publishing letters on Kantian philosophy (1786–87), which helped make the *Critique of Pure Reason* more accessible and provided him with an appointment as the first philosophy professor at the University of Jena. Reinhold thereby inaugurated the idealist project at Jena, enabling the university to attract a succession of young thinkers—Fichte, Schelling, Hegel—along with their enthusiastic students. With his next publication, Reinhold distanced himself from the *Critique*. Following Kant's architectural model of philosophical systems, Reinhold sought to demonstrate the existence of a foundation of reason that lay below Kant's epistemological constraints on human knowledge. In the preface to his *Vorstellungsvermögen* book, Reinhold directly refers to finding philosophical principles that could be accepted by all sects; here, the reference is to schools of philosophy, yet his purposeful use of the term "sect" draws a parallel between different religions as well: "In order to consolidate the principles he seeks with all preexisting systems, he must start with propositions that no sect can challenge."[51] Reinhold may have intended to draw Protestants and Catholics together to accept these new foundations for philosophy, but Goethe recognized that this claim to a natural foundation of reason that precedes all dogmatic religion was much the same as the Jesuit's scholastic approach to disputing Asian religions.

Jörg-Peter Mittmann suggests that Reinhold's search for a fundamental principle that grounds reason is an inheritance from the work of Leibniz and Wolff; however, the position has older sources in Reinhold's scholastic training as a Jesuit.[52] Goethe's analogy between Ricci and Reinhold can be explained by this connection. Missionary work, when it is understood as the task of persuading interlocutors through philosophical demonstrations, requires a practical application of the theoretical claim that rational principles can be shared by all humans. As Wolff's lectures on Confucianism made clear to his Pietist colleagues, the trouble with this assumption for missionaries is that if all people share a basic form of rationality, which grounds their social and moral lives, then there is no need for Christian revelation.[53] In historical terms, a skeptic could have asked: Why convert other people to Christianity through logical arguments when they already have their own rational moral system? If Chinese philosophy, whether Buddhist, Confucian, or a syncretic mix is as rational as Christian metaphysics, then there would seem little need, on a strictly philosophical level, to try to convert the Chinese. This problematic became obvious as Leibniz and Wolff adapted Ricci's accommodationist interpretation of Chinese thought, thereby turning the issue into one of the most important scandals of the German Enlightenment.

The question of finding a rational principle that all sides could agree upon serves as the starting point for the Nanjing disputation as well as the succession of attempts by Jena idealists to solve Reinhold's query.[54] In other words, Sanhoi, like the idealists after Reinhold, accepts the need for finding such a basic, intercultural rational principle. The philosophical difficulties quickly emerge in the next phase of the debate, which in Goethe's constellation entails the introduction of Buddhism and philosophical idealism. While it is certainly beyond the scope of this essay to now explain how Buddhism and idealism share similarities, an entry in Goethe's diary written years later does suggest why Fichte might have seemed to Goethe to be arguing in the Buddhist manner. Like Sanhoi, Fichte seems to claim that he can create a world in his mind. Goethe says as much when he summarizes the turbulent first years of Jena's philosophy chair, during which Reinhold received the first appointment, left for a better offer, only to be replaced by Fichte, who riled up the students and defied the duke with his writing and lecturing on religion.

> After Reinhold's departure, which truly seemed a great loss for the academy, the bold, audacious step was taken to appoint Fichte in his place, who had made grand but not quite respectable statements on the most important moral and political topics. He was one of the most able persons ever, and nothing could be said against his view when taken as a whole; yet how could he keep up with the world, which, after all, he considered to be a possession of his own creation.[55]

When Goethe writes that Fichte contemplated the world to be his own self-created possession, he is alluding to both the philosopher's egoism and idealist speculation. In looking back, Goethe takes a detached view of the atheism scandal by describing Fichte's actions as "not quite respectable." Throughout the eighteenth-century, German intellectuals feared monarchical suppression whenever they publicly attacked Christianity and its institutions. Any avowal of Chinese philosophies that suggested they might be an alternative to Christian metaphysics was just as likely to confront extreme censure as simply attacking Christianity was. Goethe may have been intrigued by Sanhoi's metaphysics, but he was unlikely to let anyone other than Schiller know about that directly. Only later in life, would Goethe express his Chinese sympathies through lyric poetry, a genre that sought to avoid public conflict by adopting a voice of interior reflection.

Goethe's interest in Matteo Ricci's debate with Sanhoi and his recognition of its similarities with the philosophical debates in Jena is hardly surprising given how important such disputations were in defining the Enlightenment. The University of Jena was the latest forum in Germany's culture of debate (*Streitkultur*). While Leibniz had been a consummate diplomat throughout his career, intellectual history in the previous century had hardly been a smooth unfolding of systematic ideas. Much of the eighteenth century was filled with long stretches of quiet rumination, punctuated by explosive disagreements. The debates around Gottfried Lessing, both during and after his life, were probably its most prominent representative; however, Christian Wolff's scandalous lecture on the rationality of Confucian ethics had already shown how the Enlightenment's reception of Chinese philosophy could be turned against both Protestant and Catholic theology, in his case Pietist and Jesuit. When the aged Herder changed his mind about the Jesuits in China and published warm praise for their work, he cited the intense debates of the 1770s initiated by the Dutch writer Cornelius de Pauw, who published blanket denunciations of Jesuit writing about the Americas and Asia. Looking back on the debates between de Pauw and the Jesuits, Herder tried to find some value in the scandal by saying that even though de Pauw really was rude and ignorant, his writings were useful because they provoked comprehensive and convincing refutations from the Jesuits:"even the debates about the Chinese that de Pauw provoked brought more light to the topic through the answer that the Fathers gave them."[56] Even stupid arguments served a purpose in the long run. For example, Voltaire had a lengthy correspondence with Frederick the Great about China, motivated, in large part, by the urge to deny de Pauw's negative account. On the question of representing China, Voltaire found himself on the Jesuit's side, even though he showed little love for the order in *Candide*. Enlightenment thinkers like Herder and Voltaire still held the belief that public debates were decided by the better arguments, regardless of who made them.

This Enlightenment preference for the superior argument sometimes led to unexpected affinities. As Goethe well understood while reading about Matteo Ricci's dinner dialogue, the verbal gymnastics of religious debates often turned arguments on their head. While he claimed to avoid polemics himself, particularly concerning charges of atheism and pantheism, Goethe had a strong appreciation for watching experts attack each other in public.[57] For example, when two prominent Orientalists, Diez in Berlin and Hammer-Purgstall in Vienna, entered into a raucous debate over who better understood the Ottomans, Goethe followed the public rebuttals as part of his studies in Persian poetry. In his "Notes" on the *West-Östliche Divan* (*West-Eastern*

*Divan*) Goethe adopted Francisci's fencing metaphor when he compared their Orientalist debate to a duel in which he was a spectator was trying to learn moves from two masters (FA: 3.1:273). As Joan-Pau Rubiés points out, disputations functioned as means of transmitting knowledge from a private setting to wider and quite distant audience.[58] In public debates between skilled orators, knowledge moved through a sequence of exchanges as contradictions were exposed and then placed against each other for the sake of presenting the superior argument. These formal moves were fascinating in themselves.

The likelihood that any European would be persuaded by Sanhoi's defense of Buddhism was greatly reduced because, as every modern scholar points out, the European record presents only the Jesuit side of the story. In their critical reinterpretation of the Jesuit narrative, Goethe and Schiller speculate on the deeper significance that lay behind the Buddhist responses, meanings that were not conveyed by the Jesuit narrative but that tantalize any reader who does not believe that the Buddhist position could really be as foolish as the Jesuit story portrayed it. In their humanist mode, they attempt to find a hermeneutic or empathetic engagement with the strange Chinese figures, which for them involves imagining or projecting motives and a psychology onto the foreigner. Goethe writes that he imagines any number of different responses the monk may have made to the missionary, while Schiller, as seen above, worries "whether something smart or dull lies behind this Chinese reasoning" (MA 8.1:493). The question of what thoughts lie behind enigmatic Chinese statements weighed on Schiller particularly, for he was just at that moment rewriting Carlo Gozzi's version of *Turandot*, the now-famous opera about a beautiful Chinese princess who executes her many suitors one after the other because they cannot answer the riddles she gives them. Turandot was one of the popular representations of China that had been circulating throughout the eighteenth century. Schiller's drama would later serve as the libretto for Puccini's 1926 opera. In adapting the Italian play, Schiller worries about what could possibly have motivated such royal cruelty, a question that never arises in the Italian original where Turandot's arbitrary tyranny is simply presented as normal according to Chinese expectations. Goethe's projection and identification with the Buddhist monk show how both authors are trying to build identifications with Chinese characters. Schiller wants to get past the stock figures that characterize fairy tales and operas about despotic Asian rulers. As much as he admires Gozzi's version, he believes that modern audiences would not find Turandot to be a plausible character. Schiller writes to his friend Körner in Dresden, who also hopes to stage the play:

> Die Figuren sehen wie Marionetten aus, die am Draht bewegt werden; eine gewisse pedantische Steifigkeit herscht durch das Ganze, die überwunden werden muß. Ich habe also wirklich Gelegenheit, mir einiges Verdienst zu erwerben, und die sechs, sieben Wochen, die auf dies Geschäft gehen mögen, werden nicht verloren sein.[59]

> The figures look like marionettes controlled by a wire; the whole thing has a certain pedantic stiffness that must be overcome. I really have a chance to earn some honor and the six or seven weeks that will go into the business will not be lost.

For Schiller, the difficulty in understanding motivations lies both with Gozzi's stock characters and with the otherness of the Asian figures inherited from the original Persian tale. In order to answer his own hermeneutic concern to intuit the thoughts behind seemingly inscrutable actions, Schiller writes a monologue into the play that speaks from behind the royal façade to show Turandot explaining herself in a pseudo-feminist critique of how women are treated in Asia. Schiller has Turandot describe the subjugation of women, yet in doing so she is voicing the false consciousness of a Western anthropological critique. With her demands, she has assumed the position of the Caliph in *A Thousand and One Nights* who forces Scheherazade to tell a new tale every night, thereby reversing an established gender hierarchy. Schiller was of course not alone in wanting an Asian figure to explain their seemingly tyrannical behavior to a German theater audience. At the same moment in which he is writing *Turandot* for the Weimar theater, Schiller is also preparing a restaging of Goethe's *Iphigenie auf Tauris*, wherein Goethe projects a similar Asian inner monologue onto the Scythian king Thoas, who denounces the Greek tendency to steal treasures from barbarians, thereby gaining the sympathies of cosmopolitan (in the Kantian sense) audiences.

Goethe and Schiller were very much engaged in their own project of defining a universal humanity, in which the Jesuit hostility toward Buddhism appeared as an obstacle. For as far as they were willing to accommodate their understanding of Confucianism, the missionaries sought to establish a clear difference between Christian and Buddhist cosmology. Indeed, Goethe selects the precise point at which Ricci was least accommodating to Chinese philosophy. An enthusiast for heresies in general, he then also sides against the Jesuit, but for utterly different reasons than the pious Francisci. Since the nineteenth century, commentators on this passage in the Goethe-Schiller correspondence have speculated that the similarities between the Buddhist position and pantheism explain why Goethe would have read the story against the Jesuit side of the debate. As Woldemar von Biedermann writes: "What seemed clear to Goethe was that the Chinese position, against which Jesuit missionary Ricci was arguing, agreed with that of Spinoza, a philosophy that Goethe had long cherished and defended."[60] Spinoza has so often stood as the third term in any comparison between European pantheism and Eastern philosophy. That Goethe would compare the Buddhist position with idealism does not weaken the plausible connection to Spinoza. Schelling had written Hegel in 1795, just a few years before Goethe's encounter with the Francisci story (1798), that the poet had become a Spinozist. Schelling explains that whereas for Spinoza the world as absolute object was everything, for him it is the "I" as absolute subject.[61] As he makes clear in *Dichtung und Wahrheit* (*Poetry and Truth*), Spinoza was a profound source for Goethe's own pantheism: "Dieser Geist, der so entschieden auf mich wirkte, und der auf meine ganze Denkweise so großen Einfluß habe sollte" (FA 14:680–81; This spirit, which has so decisively changed me, and which has had an influence on my entire way of thinking).

Goethe's understanding of the divine in nature, which he attributes to Spinoza, denies the possibility of divine intervention into the world, much as the Buddhist monk rejects the supremacy Ricci attributed to God as creator: "Die Natur wirkt nach ewigen, notwendigen, dergestalt göttlichen Gesetzen, daß die Gottheit selbst daran nichts ändern könnte" (FA 14:731; Nature operates according to eternal, necessary, and therefore divine laws, so that the Deity himself could not alter anything about it). Jonathan Israel has argued that Chinese thought was often interpreted as a form of coded Spinozism; indeed, that references to Confucianism were understood as a nod toward the scandalous material metaphysics of Spinoza. Israel portrays the Enlightenment interest in China as a something of code or masquerade: "Another favourite ploy was to stress the parallels between Spinoza and Confucius, classical Chinese philosophy having, ever since Isaac Vossius, been eulogized by Temple, Bayle, Saint-Hyacinthe, Lévesque de Burigny, Wolff, and others as an entirely 'natural' philosophy based solely on reason and steeped in moral ad metaphysical truth."[62] Leibniz recognizes the possibility but understands the link as a matter of the interpreter's intentions. A believer could just as well find a theistic God. Responding to a Franciscan critique of Chinese philosophy as pantheistic, Leibniz claims that such a reading is really only a matter of how one wants to argue the point: "Father [de Sainte Marie] adds that the Chinese are like the Stoics, who pictured a material God suffused throughout the universe to animate it.... But I see nothing that prevents us from finding here a spiritual God, author of matter itself, showing His wisdom and power in brute things"[63]

Hegel also well aware of the tendency to equate Chinese philosophy with Spinoza: "Chinesische Philosophie [ist], insofern sie das Eine zugrunde legt, für dasselbe ausgegeben worden, was spater als eleatische Philosophie und als spinozistisches System erschienen sei" (Similarly the Chinese Philosophy, as adopting the One as its basis, has been alleged to be the same as at a later period appeared as Eleatic philosophy and the Spinozistic System).[64] Far from accepting the comparison as a necessary ruse for radical philosophers, Hegel considered the analogy inappropriate because to the differing material character of some metaphysical unity posited in Chinese thought and by Spinoza's *Ethics*:

> In der Vergleichung der verschiedenen Philosopheme . . . wird das übersehen, worauf es allein ankommt, nämlich die Bestimmtheit der Einheit, die man zusammen in der chinesischen, eleatischen, spinozistischen Philosophie findet, und der Unterscheid ob jene Einheit abstract oder konkret, und zwar bis zur Einheit in sich, die Geist ist, gefaßt wird.[65]

> In the same way, in that comparison of the various systems of philosophy . . . the only point of importance is overlooked, namely, the character of that Unity which is found alike in the Chinese, Eleatic, and the Spinozistic philosophy—the distinction between the recognition of that Unity as abstract and as concrete—concrete to the extent of being a unity in and by itself—a unity synonymous with Spirit. But that co-ordination proves that it gives judgment respecting philosophy, it is ignorant of that very point which constitutes the interest in philosophy.[66]

Just how slippery the comparisons between European and Chinese metaphysics were, is made clear when we recall that Goethe is drawing an analogy between undefined forms of Buddhism and a still nascent idealism. The trope coupling China with Spinoza is so well established that Biedermann and literary scholars ever since have presumed that Goethe's curiosity in Buddhism arose from his long-standing admiration for Spinozan pantheism. Clearly, the inclination to cite parallels between Confucianism and Spinoza ran counter to the Jesuit assertion that early Confucianism was compatible with Christian teachings. At stake were two approaches to Confucian writings, each grappling with the other—radical rationalism and reformed Catholicism. Chinese philosophy became the third element in this European contest, the external referent that both sides cited as proof of their own intra-European validity. Because China presented such a well-respected and ancient civilization, both philosophical camps aspired to claim Confucianism as an ally.

Goethe reverses Ricci's reversal; by attending a dinner and finding an opportunity to debate and then refute the Buddhist, Ricci has walked the thin line of hospitality. As a guest it is appropriate to engage in such a debate; in arguing with the Buddhist, Ricci demonstrates that he has acquired the skills of a Mandarin, but also deploys them against an outside monk. The strategy was presumably intended to draw a clear separation between Confucian and Buddhist links to Christianity. Francisci's text presumes and reinforces the expectation that the European reader will identify and agree with Ricci; Goethe reverses that expectation, preferring instead to side with the Buddhist, so that his reading also turns against the rules of politeness.

## Conclusion

This essay has moved backward in history from the late eighteenth to the late sixteenth century in order to outline three constellations of European reflections on China. These three pairings Goethe-Schiller—Reinhold-Idealism—Ricci-Buddhism are stretched out across four levels of textual commentary and recapitulation: the Goethe-Schiller correspondence, Erasmus Francisci's compilation, the official Jesuit history of the China mission, *De Christiana Expeditione Apud Sinas*, and Ricci's Italian manuscript. All these texts are of course embedded in oral communications that are not always repeated in writing: what was actually said over dinner in Nanjing, Ricci's instructions to Trigault, and Goethe and Schiller's frequent chats. As we fill in the space between Goethe and Matteo Ricci, we find further German-Chinese constellations.

The debate in Nanjing has its own prehistory; the Chinese disputation is a repetition of earlier divisions in which Christian metaphysics tried to incorporate another religion through the claim that both share a similar "foundation" in a monotheistic rationality. The debates varied of course, so that the theological stakes in medieval disputes with Judaism differed from those with East Asian Buddhism, yet the dialectic always sought a resolution through an ever more all-encompassing claim to a rational order that could also align itself with scriptural interpretation. These constellations became rhetorically visible over the course of theological disputations and theatrical performances that were written about and commented upon long after the initial scene had been completed. Thus, the terms of the Nanjing debate were

retold and studied for at least two-hundred years, just as the major disputations in German philosophical history resurface with renewed vigor long
after the immediate historical context has disappeared. As Goethe noted,
disputations reveal the ideas that were on everyone's mind but had not yet
found expression.

Matteo Ricci engages in a disputation with Buddhism because his primary interest is to avoid one with Confucianism. His overall strategy for establishing Christianity in China centers on finding an accommodation between
his interpretation of Confucian thought and Christianity that reiterates the
slow synthesis that medieval Christianity undertook with Plato and Aristotle.
Accommodation and synthesis are the inverse of disputation. Ricci presented himself as fighting Buddhist heresy because he needed to convince his
European audience that he had not abandoned his mission.

At every disputation, there are some onlookers who seek out a diplomatic
resolution. Goethe may have depicted disputations but he carefully avoided
becoming trapped in one. For much of his later career, Goethe maneuvered
between institutions with much the same skill and detachment that Gottfried
Leibniz had maintained a hundred years earlier as he tried to resolve the
antagonisms between Protestant and Catholic princes. For Goethe, one challenge was to evade the charge of atheism as he wrote poetry on superstitious
encounters with demons and learned reveres about Muslims.

Disputations create a tension that appears to challenge the systematic
operation of different faiths. The regularized practices of a system are open
to sudden change by the disputation, which allows the speakers to question
publicly rituals and principles that have been accepted as valid without argumentation. They provide a shock to normality. They also reveal the limits of
what can be said; they show the confines within which learned debate takes
place, the point at which state authority intervenes in academic reasoning.

The ability of disputations to reveal previously unrecognized arguments
depends upon their circulation within channels of communication available
to a wide audience. Ricci surely had many conversations with Chinese monks
and administrators, but the inclusion of the Nanjing debate in the first history of Catholic mission as a complex allegory depicting the multiple sides
of Jesuit accommodation—its confrontation with Buddhism alongside its
very particular approach to Confucianism—allowed it to move continuously
through European discussions of China as an illustration of how the three
religions intermeshed. Communication networks allowed short-lived oral
debates to assume a representative function so that commentators could mull
over what had been said in a centuries-long *l'esprit de escalier* that revised
the origin conversation as if it were a dream. Given how often these debates
were retold, we must be sensitive to the possibility that what appears to be
their original recitation is already itself a revision. Particularly in intercultural
debates, there is no clear standard as to what had been said by whom at
what point in the conversation. The more we compare the Buddhist-Jewish-
Christian-Confucian versions of historical debates, the more dependent historians become on literary interpretation. Like tragedies, intercultural disputations set mythic forces in confrontation. Rhetoric and logic contain these
forces by making them presentable to foreigners raised in another tradition,

yet at some point in the proceedings force, violence, and forgery replace persuasive appeals. Learned disputations are admired because unlike tragedies they claim to hold mythic forces at bay, yet the potential for dialogue to turn into the force and the need to choose words wisely is obvious whenever the potential for violence favors one side. In the heat of a disputation, however, participants state arguments they might not have otherwise, most notably positions that offend Christian orthodoxy.

Medieval rabbis were not the only public speakers reticent to offend Church officials. Goethe avoided attacking the Church more than it seemed appropriate for a poet, as he wrote to Schiller. Their correspondence has many passages where Goethe writes that he will elaborate his point in person; often these references to oral conversations suggest that one or the other writer did not want to commit their heretical view to paper—far better to discuss atheism or pantheism while walking through the garden together. Letters often include passages to what was said outside, suggesting a complementarity between speaking and writing. Neither discourse completely subsumes the other. Goethe's walk-and-talk strategy was particularly important in Weimar because six months after their discovery of the Nanjing disputation, Fichte would become embroiled in a scandal about his supposed avowal of atheism in print and during lectures. Goethe's detached attitude toward Fichte and his acquiescence to the duke's pressure to have Fichte removed from his professorship reflect a diplomatic aversion to being labeled an unbeliever.

Goethe and Schiller could easily have been implicated in the firestorm that fell on Fichte, for the philosopher cites both poets as allies in the essay that created the uproar; specifically, Fichte quotes Faust's pantheistic answer to Gretchen's question: "Nun sag, wie hast du's mit der Religion?" (Now say: How do you feel about religion?) in the last pages of his controversial essay, "Über den Grund unseres Glaubens an eine göttliche Weltregierung" (On the Reason for Our Belief in a Divine World Order), published later in 1798.[67] Goethe may have written and spoken with Schiller about his sympathy for the Buddhist rejection of Christian theism and Fichte may have been quite correct in bringing *Faust* in support of his own position, but Goethe was in no way inclined to follow Fichte's public self-destruction as an atheist. Even when he is discussing Milton's *Paradise Lost* Goethe cuts his own critical comments off by saying that he will save them for a later conversation when they can also discuss Reinhold's response to Fichte: "Doch mag das bis zur mündlichen Unterredung aufgehoben seyn, so wie die Reinholdischen Erklärungen über den Fichtischen Atheismus" (MA 8.1:730; However, this may be best reserved for an oral conversation, just like Reinhold's explanation of Fichte's atheism).

The "atheism controversy" was but one late manifestation of the Enlightenment practice of not attacking theism in print, but instead reserving such discussions for conversations with trusted friends. Jonathan Israel's detailed examination of the radical Enlightenment is predicated on the thesis that heterodox support for Spinoza's philosophy was widespread but unstated in any public forum. Reinhard Koselleck has shown how important it was for courtiers and intellectuals to keep their most critical beliefs hidden.[68] In the heat of battle, disputations sometimes brought out statements that would otherwise have been self-censored and which, after the fact, were almost always revised, or "walked back," in the American political parlance. Because of their formal structure, because they seemingly start with no assumptions, disputations raise the possibility that anything is possible, that the conclusion could be wholly unexpected. Yet all too often their arguments unfold in a predictable fashion, so much so that cynics might assert that their conclusion was foregone. Under these circumstances, only the very open-minded audience member could find the antithetical thread that denies the foregone conclusion to the debate. Indeed, anyone who sides with the opposing side may be condemned as a perverse heretic; thus, it behooves those listening for the counterargument to remain quiet about their conversion.

Disputations also have an inherent instability built into their origins. Many hinge on the question of what had someone actually said originally: What were the Buddhist arguments at the Nanjing supper? How fluently did Ricci speak the high language of court officials? What did Christian Wolff say in his lecture on Chinese philosophy that so offended his Pietist listeners? Did Lessing really tell Jacobi that he had accepted Spinoza's philosophy? How defiant was Fichte in his negotiations with the Weimar court? In reviewing these controversies, Goethe had an inclination toward the heretical position but a strong caution against letting his views be known beyond his most trusted friends.

My argument here is not just concerned with tracing out the historic ebb and flow of Christian—Confucian—Buddhist debates. We must also consider how it is possible for members of the audience to switch sides. What justifications do the converts accept in defiance of their own community's principles? Whether by an inversion of logical arguments or by the transfer of emotions, my study asks: How did Europeans come to identify with Chinese culture? I am interested in those who pass over to the other side, an accusation first leveled against Ricci by many European Christians for his accommodation with Confucianism, but then reiterated in a literary context by nationalists offended by Goethe's concept of world literature. Among academics in the twenty-first century, Ricci's accommodation and Goethe's world literature are accepted as the obviously superior positions, which only narrow-minded dogmatists would oppose, yet any historically grounded review would show that these cosmopolitan positions were always quite tenuous, constantly challenged, and eventually dismissed by institutions opposed to their existence.

*Pennsylvania State University*

## NOTES

1. For modern scholarly treatments of this debate, see Ronnie Po-Chia Hsia, *A Jesuit in the Forbidden City: Matteo Ricci 1552-1610* (Oxford: Oxford UP, 2010) 194-198; and Iso Kern, "Matteo Riccis Verhältnis zum Buddhismus," *Monumenta Serica*, 36 (1984-85): 65-126, here 88-94.

2. Johann Wolfgang Goethe, *Briefwechsel zwischen Schiller und Goethe in den Jahren 1794 bis 1805*, ed. Manfred Beetz (Munich: Carl Hanser, 1990) 8.1:484. All subsequent citations are given parenthetically as MA.

3. Erasmus Francisci, *Neu-polirter Geschicht- Kunst- und Sitten-Spiegel ausländischer Völcker fürnemlich Der Sineser, Japaner, Indostaner, Javaner, Malabaren, Peguaner, Siammer, . . . und theils anderer Nationen mehr* (Nürnberg: Johann Andreae Endters & Wolfgang des Jüngern Erben, 1670). The Nanjing disputation appears in Book 1, 41–60.

4. See Georg Andreas Will, *Nürnbergisches Gelehrten-Lexikon oder Beschreibung aller Nürnbergischen Gelehrten beyderley Geschlechtes*, part 1, A–G (Bürnberg: Lorenz Schüpfel, 1755; Gerhard Dünnhaupt, "Erasmus Francisci, ein Nürnberger Polyhistor des siebzehnten Jahrhunderts. Biographie und Bibliographie," *Philobiblon* 19 (1975): 272–303.

5. *Das ärgerliche Leben und schreckliche Ende des viel berüchtigren Ertz-Schwartzkünstlers D. Johannis Fausti ... und einem Anhang von den Lapponischen Wahrsager-Paucken wieauch sonst etlicehn zauberischen Geschichten* (Nuremberg: Endters, 1717).

6. Jochen Schmidt, *Goethes Faust Erster und Zweiter Teil Grundlagen-Werk-Wirkung* (Munich: Beck, 1999) 28.

7. Among German Sinologists, opinions vary on Goethe's reading of Francisci. Günther Debon considers it to be without consequence (folgenlos), while Walter Bauer sees it as a turning point in Goethe's views on China. Günther Debon, "Goethes Berührungen mit China," *Goethe Jahrbuch* (2000): 46–55, here 47. Wolfgang Bauer, "Goethe und China," *Goethe und die Tradition*, ed. Hans Reiss (Frankfurt a/M: Athenäum, 1972) 177–97, here 177–78. It seems noteworthy that in his book on Goethe and China Debon does not once mention his Kommiliton and Munich Sinology colleague Wolfgang Bauer's essay on the same topic.

8. Martin Mulsow, "Socinianism, Islam and the Radical Uses of Arabic Scholarship," *Al-Qantara* 31 (2010): 549–86, here 552.

9. The two most important passages about China appear in G. W. F. Hegel, *Vorlesungen über die Philosophie der Geschichte* (Frankfurt a/M: Suhrkamp, 1986) 142–74; and *Vorlesungen über die Geschichte der Philosophie* (Frankfurt a/M: Suhrkamp, 1986) 138–47.

10. Nicholas Trigault, *De Christiana Expeditione Apud Sinas Suscepta Ab Societate Iesu ex. P. Matthaei Riccii* (Augsburg: Christoph Mangius, 1615).

11. David Mungello, "Die Quellen für das Chinabild Leibnizens," *Studia Leibnitiana* 14, no. 2 (1982): 233–243, here 234.

12. Nicholas Trigault, *Historia von der Einführung der christlichen Religion in das große Königreich China durch die Societet Jesu* (Augsburg: Antony Hjerat, 1617).

13. Matteo Ricci, SJ, *The True Meaning of The Lord in Heaven*, trans. Douglas Lancashire and Peter Hu Kuo-chon, SJ (St. Louis: Institute of Jesuit Sources, 1985) 347.

14. Haun Saussy has shown that Ricci's arguments against Buddhists coincided with a wider debate around the imperial court about mandarins who were perceived to have abandoned Confucian teachings, "In the Workshop of Equivalences: Translation, Institutions, and Media in the Jesuit Re-formation of China," in *Great Walls of Discourse and Other Adventures in Cultural China* (Cambridge: Harvard UP, 2001) 24–29.

15. *China in the Sixteenth Century: The Journals of Matthew Ricci (1583–1610)*, trans. Louis J. Gallagher (New York: Random House, 1953) 342.

16. Michel Serres, "Platonic Dialogue," *Hermes: Literature, Science, Philosophy*, ed., Josué Harari and David Bell (Baltimore: Johns Hopkins UP, 1992) 67, quoted in Bernhard Siegert, "Cacophony or Communication? Cultural Techniques in German Media Studies," trans. Geoffrey Winthrop-Young, *Grey Room* 29 (2008) 26–47, here 33.

17. J. G. Fichte, *The Science of Knowledge*, trans. Peter Heath and John Lachs (Cambridge: Cambridge UP, 1982) 243.

18. Stephen Schloesser, "Accommodation as a Rhetorical Principle: Twenty Years after John O'Malley's The First Jesuits (1993)," *Journal of Jesuit Studies* 1 (2014): 347–72, here 358.

19. Ricci's source was Andreas Eborensis's *Sententiae et Exempla, ex probatissimis quibusque scriptoribus collecta et per locos communes digesta* (Collected Sayings and Anecdotes by the most esteemed writer digested into common places). See Ana Carolina Hosne, "Friendship among Literati: Matteo Ricci SJ (1552–1610) in Late Ming China," *Transcultural Studies* 1 (2014): 190–214.

20. Jonathan D. Spence, *The Memory Palace of Matteo Ricci* (New York: Viking, 1983).

21. Matteo Ricci, *China in the Sixteenth Century: The Journals of Matthew Ricci (1583–1610)*, trans. Louis J. Gallagher (New York: Random House, 1953) 341.

22. Ricci, *The Journals of Matthew Ricci*, 340.

23. Ricci, *The Journals of Matthew Ricci*, 340.

24. Ricci, *The Journals of Matthew Ricci*, 342.

25. Baldesar Castiglione, *The Book of the Courtier*, trans. Charles Singleton (New York: Anchor, 1959), book 2, paragraph 38, here 135. "All the courtier's behavior . . . is designed to make people marvel at him," Wayne Rebhorn, "Baldesar Castiglione, Thomas Wilson and the Courtly Body of Renaissance Rhetoric," *Rhetorica* 11 no. 3 (1993): 249.

26. Joachim Kurtz, "Framing European Technology in Seventeenth-Century China; Rhetorical Strategies in Jesuit Paratexts," *Cultures of Knowledge; Technology in Chinese History* (2011) 209.

27. Hsia, *A Jesuit in the Forbidden City*, 12.

28. Dena Goodman draws a direct parallel between the forensic pedagogy of Jesuit schools and fencing, *The Republic of Letters*, 94.

29. Erasmus Francisci, *Neu-polirter Geschicht- Kunst- und Sitten-Spiegel ausländischer Völcker fürnemlich Der Sineser, Japaner, Indostaner, Javaner, Malabaren, Peguaner, Siammer, . . . und theils anderer Nationen mehr. Welcher, in sechs Büchern, sechserley Gestalten weiset . . .* (Nürnberg: Endter, 1670), "Vorrede" (no pagination)

30. Francisci, *Neu-polirter . . . Spiegel*, 1012.

31. Schiller mentions Goethe reading a Chinese novel in a letter dated January 24, 1796. *Briefwechsel*, vol. 1, 148. Goethe's diary entry from January 12, 1796 likewise mentions the Chinese novel—at this point only one had been translated.

32. Walter Benjamin, "Goethes *Wahlverwandtschaften*" in *Gesammelte Schriften*, eds., Rolf Tiedemann and Hermann Schweppenhäuser (Frankfurt a/M: Suhrkamp, 1977) 1.1:147; and "Goethe's *Elective Affinities*," trans. Stanley Corngold in *Selected Writings* (Cambridge: Harvard UP, 1996) 1:314.

33. J. W. Goethe, "Harzreise im Winter," *Sämtliche Werke*, ed., Karl Eibl (Frankfurt a/M: Deutsche Klassiker Verlag, 1987) 1:322. All references to this edition will be given as FA.

34. Johann Wolfgang Goethe, "Gespräch 17 Dezember 1824 mit von Müller and Eckermann," in *Anhang an Goethes Werke. Abtheilung für Gespräche, 1824–1826*, ed. Woldemar Freiherr von Biedermann (Leipzig: F. W. v. Biedermann, 1890) 5:120.

35. Johann Peter Eckermann, *Gespräche mit Goethe in den letzten Jahren seines Lebens*, eds., Christoph Michel and Hans Grüters (Berlin: Deutscher Klassiker Verlag, 2011), 51–52 (September 18, 1823).

36. *Faust I*, line 2267.

37. John Edwards Fletcher, *A Study of the Life and Works of Athanasius Kircher, "Germanus incredibilis"* (Leiden: Brill, 2011) 384.

38. My interpretation differs from that of the Heidelberg Sinologist, Günter Debon, who in the end remained undecided about how to draw the parallels between Nanjing and Weimar: *China zu Gast in Weimar, 18 Studien und Streiflichter* (Heidelberg: Brigitte Guderjahn, 1994) 175.

39. Fritz K. Ringer, *The Decline of the German Mandarins; the German Academic Community, 1890–1933* (Cambridge: Harvard UP, 1969).

40. Benjamin, *Gesammelte Schriften*, 2.1:206–7. Johannes Endres, "Unähnliche Ähnlichkeit. Zu Analogie, Metapher und Verwandtschaft," *Similitudo. Konzepte der Ähnlichkeit in den Künsten*, ed., Martin Gaier, Jeanette Kohl, and Alberto Saviello (Munich: Wilhelm Fink, 2012) 27–56.

41. Benjamin, "Doctrine of the Similar," trans. Michael Jennings, *Gesammelte Schriften*, 2.2:695–96.

42. For an overview of the Weimar reactions to Fichte's additions to his lectures on the *Wissenschaftslehre*, see Johann Gottlieb Fichte, *Werke 1797–1798*, ed. Reinhard Leuth, Hans Gliwitzky, and Richard Schottky (Stuttgartt: Friedrich Frommann, 1970), 1.4:169–82.

43. Letter to J. H. Meyer, March 18, 1797. "Sodann gibt Fichte eine neue Darstellung seiner Wissenschaftslehre stückweise, in einem philosophischen Journal heraus, die wir den abends zusammen durchgehen." Goethe distances himself from speculative philosophy by writing that it represents a wrong direction for him as an artist. *Goethes Briefe*, ed. Karl Robert Mandelkow (Hamburg: Christian Wegner, 1964) 2:259–60.

44. Daniel Purdy, "Chinese Ethics within the Radical Enlightenment: Christian Wolff," *Radical Enlightenment*, ed. Carl Niekerk (Amsterdam: Ropodi, 2018) 112–30.

45. Friedrich Wilhelm Joseph Schelling, *Ideen zu einer Philosophie der Natur*, first edition (Leipzig: Breitkopf & Härtel, 1797) xvi.

46. For further elaboration on Goethe's caution, see John Noyes, "Eradicating the Orientalist: Goethe's 'Chinesisch-deutsche Jahres- und Tageszeiten,'" in *China in the German Enlightenment*, ed. Bettina Brandt and Daniel L. Purdy (Toronto: Toronto UP, 2016) 142–64, here 157–60.

47. J. G. Fichte, "First Introduction," *The Science of Knowledge*, trans. Peter Heath and John Lachs (Cambridge: Cambridge UP, 1982), 10–12.

48. Fichte, "Second Introduction," *The Science of Knowledge*, 52–53. Carl Leonhard Reinhold "Meine gegenwärtige Ueberzeugung vom Wesen der reinen Philosophie, Tra nscendentalphilosophie, Metaphysik," Auswahl vermischter Schriften (Jena: Mauke, 1797) 341–42.

49. Ernst Reinhold, *Karl Leonhard Reinhold's Leben und litterarisches Wirken* (Jena: Friedrich Frommann, 1825) 5–13.

50. Karianne J. Marx, *The Usefulness of the Kantian Philosophy: How Karl Leonhard Reinhold's Commitment to Enlightenment Influenced his Reception of Kant* (Berlin: De Gruyter 2011), 15–17.

51. Karl Leonhard Reinhold, *Versuch einer neuen Theorie des menschlichen Vorstellungsvermögens*, second edition (Prague and Jena: C. Widtmann & J. M. Mauke, 1795), 24.

52. Jörg-Peter Mittmann, *Das Prinzip der Selbstgewissheit. Fichte und die Entwicklung der nachkantischen Grundsatzphilosophie* (Bodenheim: Athenäum, 1993) 10.

53. Purdy, "Chinese Ethics," 112–30.

54. Eckhart Förster describes Fichte's attempt at finding such a first principle in *Die 25 Jahre der Philosophie. Eine systematische Rekonstruktion* (Frankfurt a/M: Klostermann, 2012) 187–88.

55. Johann Wolfgang Goethe, "Tag- und Jahres-Hefte als Ergänzung meiner sonstigen Bekenntnisse, [1749-1806]" in *Goethes Werke*, ed., Karl Redlich and Woldemar von Biedermann (Weimar: Hermann Böhlau, 1892) 35:31.

56. Quoted in Merkel, "Herder und Hegel über China," *Sinica* 17 (1942): 5–26, here 6.

57. In *Dichtung und Wahrheit*, Goethe explains his aversion to theological controversies specifically in relation to debates over Spinoza. Johann Wolfgang Goethe, *Sämtliche Werke. Briefe, Tagebücher und Gespräche*, ed. Friedmar Apel et al., 40 Vols. (Frankfurt a/M: Deutscher Klassiker-Verlag, 1985–2013) 14:728. Hereafter abbreviated as FA and cited parenthetically.

58. Joan-Pau Rubiés, "Real and Imaginary Dialogues in the Jesuit Mission of Sixteenth-century Japan," *Journal of the Economic and Social History of the Orient*, 55 (2012): 447–94.

59. Schiller letter to Körner, November 16, 1801, MA 14:291. Karl Goedeke, *Grundrisz zur Geschichte der deutschen Dicthung aus den Quellen*, vol. 2 (Hanover: L. Ehlermann, 1859) 989.

60. Woldemar Freiherrn von Biedermann, "Goethe und das Schrifttum Chinas," *Zeitschrift für vergleichende Literaturgeschichte N. F.* 7 (1894): 383–401, 888.

61. Dalia Nassar, "Spinoza in Schelling's early coneption of intellectual intuition," *Spinoza and German Idealism*, ed. Eckart Förster and Yitzhak Y. Melamed (Cambridge: Cambridge UP, 2012) 136. See also Horst Lange, "Goethe and Spinoza: A Reconsideration," *Goethe Yearbook*, 17 (2011): 12.

62. Jonathan I. Israel, *Radical Enlightenment: Philosophy and the Making of Modernity (1650–1750)* (Oxford: Oxford UP, 2001) 588.

63. Julia Ching and Willard G. Oxtoby, "Discourse on the Natural Theology of the Chinese," in *Moral Enlightenment, Leibniz and Wolff on China* (Nettetal: Steyler, 1992) 127; see also 131 for the link to Spinoza.

64. Hegel, *Vorlesungen über die Philosophie der Geschichte* in *Werke*, 90; *The Philosophy of History*, trans. J. Sibree (New York: Dover, 1956) 66.

65. Hegel, *Vorlesungen über die Philosophie der Geschichte*, 94–95.

66. Hegel, *The Philosophy of History*, 70.

67. Johann Gottlieb Fichte, "Über den Grund unseres Glaubens an eine göttliche Weltregierung," *Philosophisches Journal einer Gesellschaft Teutscher Gelehrter*, 7 no. 1 (1798): 1–20.

68. Reinhart Koselleck, *Kritik und Krise* (Frankfurt a/M: Suhrkamp, 1973) 15.

MATTHEW FEMINELLA

# Projection and Concealment: Goethe's Introduction of the Mask to the Weimar Stage

**Abstract:** Around 1800, Johann Wolfgang von Goethe conducted a series of theatrical experiments involving masks on the Weimar Stage. Such experiments were considered highly innovative at the time and were met with both praise and skepticism. This article examines the eighteenth-century European discourse on theatrical masks to contextualize the largely unprecedented nature of Goethe's use of masks. Thinkers ranging from Gotthold Ephraim Lessing and Jean-Baptiste Dubos to August Wilhelm Schlegel and Karl August Böttiger considered the unique advantages and disadvantages that masks contribute to staged performances. Each of these thinkers is forced to contend with the fact that masks necessarily conceal an actor's facial affective expressions, thereby appearing to deprive actors of a fundamental means of expressing their art. Such observations are situated in conjunction with Goethe's staging of masked performances at Weimar. Goethe's use of the mask is viewed as a means for him as a director to exert control over the bodies of actors to diminish their artistic agency. The theatrical mask is thus conceptualized as an extension of his *Rules for Actors*, a series of prescriptions for subjugating an actor's body to the aesthetic of the directorial vision.

**Keywords:** Masks, Weimar, Theater, Actors, Bodies, Affect

IN WEIMAR AROUND 1800, the date of October 24 would rarely pass by unobserved. The birthday of Anna Amalia was routinely celebrated in a variety of both public and private festivities befitting the dowager duchess' status as a generous patroness of the arts. Often a theatrical production marked the annual occasion. The tradition dates back at least to her arrival in Weimar in 1756, when Karl Theophilus Döbbelin's acting troupe performed for her seventeenth birthday. This tradition continued during Goethe's tenure at the Weimar Theater with elaborate productions such as Mozart's *The Marriage of Figaro* and Goethe's own *Palaeophron und Neoterpe*. Yet in 1801 the festivity itself overshadowed its occasion when Goethe staged the Roman dramatist Terence's *Adelphi*.[1] Terence's drama, appearing in a new translation from Friedrich Hildebrand von Einsiedel as *Die Brüder* (The Brothers), stole the show by debuting masked actors, a remarkable deviation from standard theatrical practices.[2]

History does not recall Anna Amalia's reaction to Goethe's production of *Die Brüder*. While sparing, at most, a few lines to mention the duchess' birthday, periodicals and newspapers quickly latched onto the novelty of the mask for the German stage. Descriptions rendered the play as "ein Schauspiel in Masken" (a play in masks) and "Man gab die Brüder des Terentius, und zwar in Masken" (*The Brothers* by Terence was performed, even in masks) leaving no ambiguity as to what distinguished *Die Brüder* from the conventions of the contemporary theater.[3] The fascination with the performance proved so overwhelming that the *Zeitung für die elegante Welt* (Newspaper for the Elegant World) devoted an additional article to its coverage of the event.[4]

While primarily generating a favorable reaction, Goethe's unconventional decision to utilize the mask left much room for interpretation. Given the scant precedent in the German theatrical tradition for masked performances, the author of one article on the subject asked "ob und warum Terentius gerade in Masken aufgeführt werden muß?" (whether and why Terence must now be performed in masks?).[5] This theatrical innovation poses more questions than answers, and is further complicated by Goethe's relative silence on his reasons for including the masks. The concept of the mask escapes any thorough treatment in his aesthetic writings and scarcely a word appears in his letters on the subject. Yet, as attested in his "Weimarisches Theater," the masked performance of Terence represents, for Goethe, a seminal moment in the history of the Weimar Theater, to which the little time he devotes to expounding its aesthetic objectives stands in marked contrast, leaving others to speculate on its significance.

The following elucidates Goethe's introduction of the mask onto the Weimar stage by situating it within a larger European discourse on masks and the art of acting in the late eighteenth and early nineteenth centuries. Goethe himself offers only a few insights into his justification of the theatrical mask, primarily from the 1802 essay "Weimarisches Hoftheater" (Weimar Court Theater) and the allegorical drama *Was wir bringen* (What We Bring). I supplement this with analysis of the theatrical mask from his contemporaries, such as Jean-Baptiste Dubos, Gotthold Ephraim Lessing, Karl August Böttiger, and August Wilhelm Schlegel, who discuss its purpose, merits, and potential drawbacks. In their writings, a recurring observation emerges: the capacity of the mask to nullify an actor's emotional facial expressions. While the mask can represent an unappealing obstruction for the actor wishing to display his talent for mimicry, it also ensures the integrity of the play by removing uncertainties that arise from the staging of affective expressions. By concealing the actor's face, Goethe's introduction of the mask represents an extension of corporeal discipline, as outlined in his *Regeln für Schauspieler* (*Rules for Actors*), which instrumentalizes an actor's body for onstage performance.

## The Mask: Contexts and Precedents

Goethe's lack of comprehensive pronouncements on theatrical masks has accordingly affected the scholarship on the subject. Despite the ample research examining Goethe's tenure at the Weimar Theater, surprisingly little has delved into his use of the mask.[6] The scholarship has often underrepresented the extent to which masks were used, restricting it to a series of "experiments" over an eighteen-month period from 1800 to 1802.[7] Yet Goethe's use of the mask extends beyond this period. *Palaeophron und Neoterpe*, whose private performance predated the debut of *Die Brüder* by a year, opened in 1803 with a public staging on January 1. Masks were also included in other plays by Terence in 1803—*Die Mohrin* (an adaptation of his *Eunuchus*) and *Andria*—and *Die Brüder* continued to be performed with masks at least until 1807.[8] Theatrical masks even exported themselves beyond the Duchy of Saxe-Weimar. Despite some initial skepticism as to their efficacy, *Palaeophron und Neoterpe* was successfully staged with masks in Bremen as a part of a commemoration of Schiller's death.[9] Far from merely a series of short-lived and ineffectual experiments, Goethe's introduction of the mask to the stage ignited debates in a dubious public that continued for years after the original staging of *Die Brüder*.[10]

Goethe's staging of *Die Brüder* does not, however, represent the first use of masks in the German theater. Theatergoers in Weimar would have been accustomed to seeing masked actors from performances such as Mozart's opera *Don Giovanni* or Ernst August Klingemann's 1797 intrigue drama *Die Maske* (The Mask). In productions such as these, the mask belongs to the realm of conventional props and costumes: objects of narrative consequence. In the diegetic use of the mask, both the actor's and character's face are simultaneously concealed, an act that intensifies the theatrical suspense, as both other characters and the audience eagerly await the unveiling and moment of recognition. In contrast, Goethe's staging of *Die Brüder* foregoes the diegetic mask, favoring instead its usage in antiquity, in which its stage presence exists only outside the narrative: while the actors wear masks, the characters do not. Such an approach to the mask not only stands in contrast to the notion that every mask requires an unmasking, but also entrusts its signification solely to the purview of the audience. In this shift from narrative to audience, the history of the theater provides several models for the nondiegetic mask. While the function of the theatrical mask in ancient Greece remains somewhat shrouded in mystery, there exists a strong consensus that the mask amplified the actor's visibility to a vast audience numbering in the thousands.[11] In the *commedia dell'arte* of the Italian peninsula, the mask indicates a particular canonical character, with a pointed beard and long hooked nose distinguishing Pantalone.

Although present in a variety of other cultural contexts, most notably the masquerade, Carnival season, and the death mask, the nondiegetic mask was effectively absent from the eighteenth-century German theater. While prominent in *commedia dell'arte*, the mask never established itself as a tradition in German-speaking lands. Karl August Böttiger blames the absence of the mask for the unsuccessful attempts to perform ancient plays during Gottsched's time.[12] Theatrical masks were so out of fashion by the second half of the eighteenth century that Johann George Sulzer, in his entry for "Masken" of the *Allgemeine Theorie der schönen Künste* (General Theory of the Fine Arts), dispenses with elaborating on their use in antiquity for lack of relevance, observing that only "low" forms of ballet have maintained this custom from antiquity; he instead directs interested readers to

seventeenth-century French sources.[13] The dearth of masks was not limited
to the German theatrical tradition. Writing in the early eighteenth century, Jean-Baptiste Dubos notes that the mask, with few exceptions, was no
longer used on the French stage.[14] More typically, eighteenth-century references to masks in the context of the theater were employed figuratively
to denote dissimulation and theatricality.[15] Lessing's Sir William Sampson
relies on this more common usage when he instructs his servant to read
his daughter Sara's facial expressions to understand her true feelings: "In der
kurzen Entfernung von der Tugend kann sie die Verstellung noch nicht gelernt haben, zu deren Larven nur das eingewurzelte Laster seine Zuflucht
nimmt" (In the short departure from virtue she could not have learned how
to play-act, to whose masks only deep-rooted vice resorts).[16] The absence
of the literal mask from many European theaters is conspicuously paired
with its indexical significance in marking the theatrical setting. Few symbols
so readily signify the theater as the configuration of the tragic and comic
masks, yet their practical use had long been relegated to the ornamentation
of theater walls and the covers of periodicals.

Goethe attributed great significance to his Terence experiment within
the context of the history of the Weimar Theater. Writing retrospectively
in 1802, Goethe composed a brief account of the theater, "Weimarisches
Theater" (Weimar Theater), published in the *Journal des Luxus und der
Moden* (Journal of Luxury and Fashion), in which he divided the history of
the theater into four periods:[17] The time from his appointment as intend-
ant in 1791 to the guest appearance of Iffland in 1796 constitutes the first
phase, and the renovation of the main theater hall in 1798 demarcates the
second and third phases. Goethe ascribes significant importance to the
1801 performance of Terence's *Die Brüder*, which inaugurates the fourth
and final phase of the Weimar Theater. The reasons for this staging's inclusion in Goethe's periodization are not made immediately explicit. Though
he singles out both *Die Brüder* and *Palaeophron und Neoterpe* as the kind
of masked performances that require much practice, he elaborates little on
their significance. One of the foundational principles of acting that Goethe
formulates in this essay does, however, shed light on the importance of these
masked performances. According to Goethe, the distinguished actor "müsse
seine Persönlichkeit verleugnen und dergestalt umbilden lernen, daß es
von ihm abhange, in gewissen Rollen, seine Individualität unkenntlich zu
machen" (FA 18:843; must disown his personality and learn to refashion
himself in such a way that his individuality is made unrecognizable). Praising
the ability to erase the traces of one's individuality coincides with his admiration of noted actor August Wilhelm Iffland, whose talent as an actor enabled him to figuratively mask himself. Goethe attributes Iffland's arrival with
improvements among his own acting troupe to abstract their individualities
from the performance. If the denial of the actor's off-stage self is the para-
mount objective of the art of acting, then Goethe's introduction of the mask
can be viewed as its extension. While projecting an abstracted and idealized
version of the character, the mask simultaneously conceals any individual
qualities of the actor that might interfere with the theatrical production.
Iffland's status as a master actor is proven through his ability to figuratively

mask himself, while more mediocre actors might require actual masks to achieve the same effect.

This sentiment is not unique to Goethe and was often echoed in the reception of the staging of *Die Brüder.* One article in the *Zeitung für die elegante Welt* commends the effectiveness of the masks, for "die sonst so schwer zu beseitigende Individualität des Schauspielers war hier gänzlich verschwunden" (the otherwise difficult to eliminate individuality of the actor disappeared here completely).[18] A review of the staging of *Die Brüder* for the opening of the new theater in Lauchstädt in 1802 claims that the actor Heinrich Becker held "seine ganze Persönlichkeit unter der Maske und Kleidung verborgen" (his entire personality hidden under the mask and clothing).[19] In his review of Schiller's introduction of the chorus in tragedy in 1803, Ernst August Klingemann remarks that the masks, as another theatrical custom of antiquity, "die Individualität des Schauspielers ganz verbergen, und eine ideale Erscheinung hervorführen helfen" (conceals the individuality of the actor and helps evoke an ideal appearance).[20] This theme of denying an actor's person in favor of his stage persona persistently occurs in Goethe's writings on the art of acting from this period, most notably his *Regeln für Schauspieler*, which will be addressed at the end of this article.

Goethe's most decisive pronouncement on the theatrical mask appears in his drama *Was wir bringen.* First performed only months after the debut of *Die Brüder, Was wir bringen* aims to educate the audience about the variety of theatrical genres that were utilized recently for the stage.[21] As each genre is presented allegorically, *Was wir bringen* employs the god Mercury to provide commentary on the depicted events. In the depiction of the *Maskenspiel* (masquerade), a nymph flees a masked boy and seeks refuge with Mercury. The masked boy asks Mercury to address the audience and explain his role. Mercury begins by clarifying that the boy represents the mask from ancient Rome. He then tells the boy to reveal his mask, which the god explains is a "derbe wunderliche Kunstgebild" (FA 6:296; crude and odd art object) indicative of the grotesque. When "*der Knabe die tragische Maske auf[hebt]*" (FA 6:296; *the boy lifts up the tragic mask*), Mercury provides a much more substantial explanation:

Doch dieses läßt vom Höheren und Schönen
Den allgemeinen, ernsten Abglanz ahnen.
Persönlichkeit der wohlbekannten Künstler
Ist aufgehoben, schnell erscheinet eine Schaar
Von fremden Männern, wie dem Dichter nur beliebt,
Zu mannigfaltigem Ergötzen, eurem Blick.
Daran gewöhnt euch, bitten wir nur erst im Scherz,
Denn bald wird selbst das hohe Heldenspiel,
Der alten Kunst und Würde völlig eingedenk,
Von uns Cothurn und Maske willig leihen. (FA 6:296)

However, this lets the general, serious reverberation
From the most high and beautiful be felt.
The personality of the well-known artist

Is neutralized. Quickly a group of strange men, just as the author likes it,
Appears to much captivation in your view.
To this you will grow accustomed, we ask first only in jest,
Then soon the high heroic play will,
Bearing in mind ancient art and dignity,
Freely bestow from us cothurnus and masks.

The second mask is none other than the traditional contorted tragic mask. In a moment of self-reflection on the nature of the theater, *Was wir bringen* deploys the mask diegetically to gesture to its nondiegetic future on the German stage that Goethe has in mind. Speaking to the audience, Mercury acknowledges the departure from established theatrical norms that the mask represents, which requires some patience. The "Schaar von fremden Männern," projects a vision of acting in which the performers are not encumbered by prior associations of the actor's person, but rather subject themselves completely to the role under the visage of the mask that conforms with the author's vision. The duality between the new character roles assumed in the form of the mask and the concealed identity of the actor is present in the ambiguity of the word *aufheben* (to lift *or* to nullify), whereby the boy's act of lifting up the mask ("*Der Knabe hebt die tragische Maske auf*") simultaneously nullifies the actor's individuality ("Persönlichkeit der wohlbekannten Künstler ist aufgehoben").

This passage also reveals that all masks are not created equal. While Mercury first considers the comic mask, it is evident that it only serves as a stepping stone to the more elevated mask of tragedy. Such an ambitious strategy grapples with the conventional understanding of the mask as primarily associated with comedy rather than high tragedy. The traditions of *commedia dell'arte*, the masquerade, and *Karneval* dominate the sense of frivolity that permeates the association with the mask. German theatrical discourse maintained this undertone in Goethe's day. Siegfried August Mahlmann's 1803 journal *Die Maske* illustrates this fact in its opening prologue, which presents a stylized account in verse of the search for its title and emblem.[22] After rejecting the image of a god or muse, the narrator settles on the image of the mask to best represent the journal's farcical agenda "to heal the sick world through laughter."[23] This prevailing sentiment poses severe challenges to Goethe's attempts to imbue the mask with the capacity for high forms of tragedy. In "Weimarisches Theater" Goethe provides an account for a subsequent masked performance of August Wilhelm Schegel's *Ion*, in which Goethe claims the masks of two of the characters elevated the performance into tragedy (FA 18:845). Yet in this instance, Goethe whitewashes the performance history: the debut of *Ion* is notable for driving the audience to laughter, much to Goethe's dismay.[24]

## Concealing Affect

Based on the few insights he provides, it would seem that Goethe viewed theatrical masks as a means to effectively disguise actors so that the audience concentrates more on the character being portrayed rather than their person. Such a notion would naturally come across as an affront to many actors. Actors generally strove to subjugate themselves to the demands of their character, yet their approach relied on the self-imposed rigorous control of their bodies and on-stage personas to project their character rather than on concealing themselves with a foreign overlay. In the attempt to resignify the theatrical mask to expunge traces of the actor's individuality, Goethe's innovation came into conflict with the dominant acting paradigm of his day.[25] The second half of the eighteenth century saw the rise of a new theatrical aesthetic that appealed to naturalism and stressed the erasure of the theatricality of a performance through the display of emotional expressions. At the core of this aesthetic was an actor's *Mienenspiel* or *Mimik* (facial expressions). For actors, the *Mienenspiel* was often considered the hallmark of the performance, the quality by which actors could showcase their talents. Accordingly, the face would constitute the most affective, subtle, and thereby most expressive part of the actor's body. Capable of demonstrating the greatest range of the art of acting, the face represented the critical site where an actor's skill could be assessed. Discussions of the theatrical mask, therefore, cannot be understood as distinct from the accompanying negation of the actor's affective facial expression. Goethe's contemporaries understood this fact well and thus provide a point of comparison with which we can better conceptualize his use of the mask.

Debating the appropriateness of masks for the theater harkens back to ancient Rome, where the main terms of the debate continued until Goethe's day. Cicero chided his actor friend Roscius for using masks in his performances, since they cover the most expressive part of the body.[26] Even by the eighteenth century, when the use of masks had fallen out of favor, discussions of the mask frequently addressed the issue of how they necessarily conceal affective expressions. One of the few champions of the theatrical mask in the eighteenth century was Jean-Baptiste Dubos. He notes the advantage bestowed by the masks of antiquity in the play *Amphitryon*, in which gods assume the form of other characters. This requires two sets of actors who appear identical on the stage, thus necessitating the use of masks. The major failing of Moliere's version of Plautus's *Amphitryon*, according to Dubos, is that without masks, two actors with distinct faces striving to appear identical would transgress the *vraisemblance* of the plot.[27] Dubos further claims that masks on the stages of antiquity allowed male actors to more successfully play female roles, since allegedly only a male voice could project the necessary volume in gigantic Greek amphitheaters. Yet even Dubos admits to the gross limitations of the mask for emotional expression, accepting that "masks deprived the spectators of the pleasure of seeing the passions rise, and of discerning their different symptoms on the countenance of the actor."[28] In an attempt to salvage the emotional impact of the mask, Dubos turns to the eyes, which for him constitute the most expressive part of the face. Since the mask covers the whole face except the eyes, the audience would still have access to the face's most animated feature, with "the imagination suppl[ying] what lies concealed; and when we behold the eye fired with rage, we imagine we see the rest of the countenance inflamed."[29] After his vigorous defense of masks, he concedes that they cannot match the expressive capacities of the exposed actor's face. The true justification of their use, he claims, is their ability to produce the necessary resonance to ensure that the actor's voice is heard in large amphitheaters.[30]

Dubos found few apologists for theatrical masks in his day, and by mid-century the last vestiges of the theatrical mask in France were under attack.[31] For Jean-Georges Noverre, perhaps the most eminent eighteenth-century theorist and practitioner of ballet, the notion of shrouding corporeal expressions ran counter to the naturalistic aesthetic of his time. Before his rise to prominence in the 1750s, he viewed French ballet performances as burdened by elaborate costumes that hindered free movements. For Noverre the face represents a focal point of a performance that provides meaning to all other movements of the body. Operating within the paradigm of the spontaneity and instantaneousness of affect, he observes: "it requires no time for the face to express its meaning forcibly; a flash of lightning comes from the heart, shines in the eyes and illumining every feature, heralds the conflicts of passions, and reveals, so to speak, the naked soul."[32] The mask, also a prominent feature of the ballet, effectively deprives dance of one of its primary affective signifiers by concealing expressions, replacing the range and subtlety of the human face with a cold and lifeless piece of cardboard. Noverre likely had Dubos in mind when he denounced the power of the viewer's imagination to compensate for the missing facial features concealed behind a mask.[33] Furthermore, the expressiveness and dynamism of the eyes, as Dubos claimed, produce an unnatural contrast with the mask's static essence, which cannot represent the variety and complexities of human emotions.[34] As a result, Noverre advocates "banishing the mask from dancing."[35]

As the ballet master at several European courts, Noverre's reforms reworked the landscape of dance, and the mask lost its hold on ballet. His German contemporary Gotthold Ephraim Lessing also took note in the *Hamburgische Dramaturgie* of how masks inherently nullify affective expressions. Lessing, who previously published Dubos's chapter on masks as a part of his translation of the *Critical Reflections* in the *Theatralische Bibliothek*, considered the mask in his discussions exploring the difficulties of creating affective expressions on the stage. He writes:

> Es ist dieses nicht der einzige Fall, in welchem man die Abschaffung der Masken betauern möchte. Der Schauspieler kann ohnstreitig unter der Maske mehr Contenance halten; seine Person findet weniger Gelegenheit auszubrechen; und wenn sie ja ausbricht, so werden wir diesen Ausbruch weniger gewahr.[36]

> This is not the only case, in which one might regret the elimination of the mask. The actor can indisputably maintain more composure under the mask; his person finds fewer opportunities to break out; and when it does break out, so we become less aware of this outburst.

Representative of the same shift toward affective expression on the stage as Noverre, Lessing conceptualizes facial affective display as one of the most impressive achievements for an actor. Yet producing seemingly genuine affects proved profoundly difficult, and for Lessing the question of how to produce the true appearance of affect constituted a central paradox of acting: How can actors willfully deploy affective expressions on the stage when those same expressions lie seemingly beyond intentionality? While an actor can feign affective expressions, it is difficult to produce seemingly genuine expressions such as blushing, blanching, tears and laughter. In this tongue-in-cheek moment, Lessing not so much regrets the discontinuation of the mask but rather envies the aesthetics of his ancient predecessors, whose utilization of theatrical masks obviated the need to theorize about how to stage affect. According to Lessing, the mask effectively renders obsolete two fundamental issues associated with the staging affect: there is no need to produce affect if the audience cannot view it, and there are no significant repercussions for a lingering affect that cannot be repressed when a change in scene demands it. In both cases the recalcitrance of affective expressions, both to produce and to control—one can recall the difficulty of ceasing to cry or laugh on command—is neutralized by the mask.

Distrust of the mask was not limited to those who theorized about its effect on the audience but extended also to actors themselves. Carl Reinhold, an actor who was dismissed from his position at the Weimar Theater following a quarrel, composed a polemic against Goethe's theater, "Saat von Göthe gesäet" ("Seeds Sown by Goethe"), which views masks with suspicion as an attack on the art of acting.[37] Reinhold, who was present for Goethe's mask experiments in the first few years following the turn of the century, claimed, based on the performance of Terence's *Die Brüder*, that the mask was the most memorable feature of the vast majority of the cast.[38] In opposition to the masks, he writes:

> Eben so wenig werde ich mich dabei aufhalten, die in die Sinne fallende Unzulänglichkeit der Masken für die Bühne zu erweisen, welche beinahe den größten Theil der Kunst, die Mimik, gänzlich ausschließen, sondern einen flüchtigen Ueberblick auf die Darstellung selbst werfen.[39]

> I will stop myself even so little from proving the apparent failings of masks for the stage, which nearly exclude the greatest part of art, facial expressions, and rather casts a superficial view on the performance itself.

For Reinhold, Goethe's introduction of the mask deprived actors of the ability to display the most remarkable aspect of their art: corporeal control. Control of facial expressions particularly defined the acting profession at the time, and removing this element was tantamount to depriving the status of artist to acting.[40] The mask thus instantiated a struggle between the director's and actor's artistic claims to the stage.[41]

The valorization of an actor's affective expression as represented by Noverre, Lessing, and Reinhold was not universally shared by the end of the eighteenth century. Karl August Böttiger explicitly echoes much of Dubos's sentiment in direct reference to Goethe's use of the mask. A journalist and public intellectual who specialized in archeology and classics, Böttiger reviewed the performance of *Die Brüder* in the *Journal des Luxus und der Moden*, concentrating primarily on the difficulty of reintroducing the masks of antiquity in the modern theater. Although, for Böttiger, staging classical drama without masks would effectively tear "den Köper von der Seele" (the body from the soul), he claims there exists an additional advantage of masks on the contemporary stage:"Und wenn man aufhören will, die Beweglichkeit gewisser Gesichtsmuskeln (denn die Hauptsache, Bewegung des Kopfs und der Augen bleibt auch hinter der Maske) für das höchste der Schauspielkunst im Mienenspiel zu preisen und—zu entwickeln" (and when one wants to stop praising and developing the mobility of certain facial muscles—since the most important thing, movement of the head and the eyes also remains behind the mask—for the highest of art of acting in facial expressions).[42]

While Lessing considers masks largely in terms of their practicality, fantasizing about how they would simplify his duties as dramaturge without seriously considering them, Böttiger highlights their distinct aesthetic advantages. Masks would displace the then standard eighteenth-century natural acting practices, since they limit the actor's ability to display corporeal finesse and instead create a kind of blank canvas onto which the director can inscribe any meaning desired.[43] Böttiger recalls the attitude of the audience following the performance of *Die Brüder*, in which "Mancher freute sich des neuen Mittels, den Schauspielern ihre uns nur zu sehr ansprechende Persönlichkeit zu rauben und gleichsam für jedes Stück eine ganz neue Gesellschaft von Künstlern zu erschaffen" (Many were pleased with the new means to rob actors of their too appealing personalities and at the same time to create for every play a new company of artists).[44] For Böttiger, masks are a tool for the stage that abstracts the corporeal idiosyncrasies from the art of the actor and represents the *Mienenspiel* as a danger to idealistic depiction of the performance.

August Wilhelm Schlegel recounts the use of the mask of antiquity in his *Vorlesungen über die Dramatische Kunst und Literatur* (Lectures on Dramatic Art and Literature), revealing some of the possible motivations for Goethe. Originally a series of lectures in 1808, Schlegel draws attention to the practicalities of the mask in ancient Greece that often appear in their defense; namely, that they were used (in addition to the cothurnus) to enhance the appearance of actors and render them more visible for a large body of spectators. Visual amplification likely was not a determining factor for Goethe since, in contrast to the Athenians, whose amphitheater could seat an audience of thousands, the Weimar Theater could only house a few hundred. More amenable to the aesthetic of Weimar classicism are some of the other rationales Schlegel provides. According to Schlegel, the masks of ancient Greek theater reveal their commitment to the idealism of the stage. Masks depict an ideal such as heroism, dignity, beauty, or grace in the form of a person. Subordinated to this ideal were the passionate expressions, which Schlegel derides as a kind of "Gebrauch der Maßen" (custom of the masses).[45] For Schlegel the value of the mask lies in preventing

> einen Schauspieler mit gemeinen, unedlen, auf jeden Fall mit allzu individuellen Zügen einen Apoll oder Herkules darstellen zu lassen; ja diese hätte ihnen für eine wahre Entweihung gegolten. Wie wenig vermag selbst der im Mienenspiel geübteste Schauspieler den Charakter seiner Züge zu verändern! Und dies hat doch auf den Ausdruck der Leidenschaft einen nachteiligen Einfluß, da alle Leidenschaft vom Charakter eine besondere Färbung erhält.[46]

a player with vulgar, ignoble, or strongly marked features, to represent an Apollo or a Hercules; nay, rather they would have deemed it downright profanation. How little is it in the power of the most finished actor to change the character of his features! How prejudicial must this be to the expression of passion, as all passion is tinged more or less strongly by the character.[47]

This passage instantiates the double function of the mask that informs the basic assumptions of Goethe's theatrical aesthetic: the projection of the ideal that simultaneously conceals the person of the actor. The mask fulfills its ideal representation by containing no characteristics that are particular to a single person, since to represent heroic persons or gods with the conventional and individualistic facial features of an actor would have been regarded as highly impertinent. The act of projecting an image of the ideal simultaneously conceals the body of the actor. The mask effectively renders futile the facial contortions often associated in his own time with skilled actors. The portrayal of emotional expression is further obviated.[48] Noteworthy is Schlegel's double entendre through the word *Färbung* (coloring). *Färbung* refers to the bestowing of individual characteristics for a particular role, precisely what the Greeks, according to Schlegel, were trying to avoid, as well as the change in skin coloring such as blushing and blanching associated with strong affect.[49] Ultimately for Schlegel, the theatrical masks of antiquity served as a means to subjugate an actor's performance to the governing will of the poet. He writes: "Der Schauspieler war bloß Werkzeug, und sein Verdienst bestand in der Genauigkeit, womit er seine Stelle ausfüllte, gar nicht in willkürlicher Bravur und dem Prunk besondrer Meisterschaft"[50] (The player was a mere instrument in his hands, and his merit consisted in the accuracy with which he filled his part, and by no means in arbitrary bravura, or ostentatious display of his own skill.)[51] By equating facial affective expression with an actor's autonomy, Schlegel interprets the theatrical mask as an effective means to exert control over the medium of the actor's body, thus minimizing possible uncertainty or resistance to the poet's artistic vision that could manifest in a performance.

## Masks and *Regeln für Schauspieler*

Goethe's theatrical innovation requires this contextualization in the discursive conflict between actors' facial expressions and the use of the mask. By removing concerns for affective display, the mask adheres well to Goethe's rigorous acting methodology as formulated in his *Regeln für Schauspieler*. The *Regeln* can be best described as a series of prescriptions designed to render actors amenable to the director's artistic vision.[52] Actors differ from other forms of artistic media in that, as autonomous beings, they not only have an existence independent of the stage but they can also actively challenge artistic direction. The main task of *Regeln für Schauspieler* is to outline how to train actors in such a way that their performance contains no elements associated with their person, thereby molding them into docile blank canvases onto which the demands of their roles can be more easily inscribed. *Regeln* institutes strict parameters for the theater that strive to prevent all undesirable and unintended traces of the actor's individuality from manifesting in the work of art.[53] The voice, for instance, was subject to numerous prescriptions designed to prohibit an actor's native dialect and colloquialisms from creeping into tragic speech.[54] Even the use of handkerchiefs was banned, which would otherwise remind the audience of the actor's biological necessities.

Although it was first formulated during the heyday of Goethe's masked productions,*Regeln für Schauspieler* contains no explicit references to masks. Despite this fact, the same assumptions that informed Schlegel's discussion of the aims of ancient masks run deep in the *Regeln*. Approximately one third of the prescriptions in the *Regeln* focus on directing the actor's body on the stage, emphasizing the necessity of maintaining absolute corporeal control and avoiding any impediment to movement. This is best expressed with the general principle "jeder Teil des Körpers stehe daher ganz in seiner Gewalt, so daß er jedes Glied, gemäß dem zu erzielenden Ausdruck, frei, harmonisch und mit Grazie gebrauchen könne" (FA 18:871; Therefore every part of his body should be completely under his control so that he may be able to use each limb freely, harmoniously, and gracefully in accord with the expression called for.)[55] Ensuring that actors maintain control over their bodies serves merely as a means to an end, guaranteeing that they produce no unexpected variables that would interfere with artistic direction. Yet for all the prescriptions regulating the positioning of hands, fingers, arms, elbows, chest, and torso on the stage, conspicuously absent is any thorough treatment of the face.[56] Compounding this absence is the role of emotive expressions, which is discussed only—and quite briefly—in reference to the hands. A few conclusions can be drawn from these observations. First, *Regeln für Schauspieler* is strikingly compatible with Goethe's use of masks, since prescriptions for the face are unnecessary if it is concealed. Second, by displacing emotive expressions onto other parts of the body that are easier to control, the *Regeln* is de facto masking actors by giving their faces a diminutive role.

As noted by many of his contemporaries, such decisions demonstrate Goethe's awareness of the face as the primary source for unexpected variables on an actor's body. As Lessing observed, masks essentially simplify the art of acting: if the face is concealed, then teaching actors how to blush or produce tears on command becomes unnecessary. The inanimate contours of the mask are not subject to the kinds of variability that accompany a living organism. Yet most actors in Goethe's day, such as Carl Reinhold, were eminently proud of their *Mienenspiel* precisely because facial emotive expressions were so difficult to master. An actor's lively emotional expressions, which remained the dominant aesthetic goal for most other theaters in Germany, were anathema to principles that emphasized corporeal control for the sake of the director's artistic vision. As a device in Goethe's *Schauspielkunst*, the theatrical mask therefore performs a double function whereby the repression of the actor's person is given material manifestation while at the same time externalizing the very rules that mandate corporeal control and subordination.[57] Grandiose claims about how masks help subordinate an actor's individual traits in favor of a higher ideal, as put forward in *Was wir bringen* and "Weimarisches Theater," would have constituted clear but coded language for depriving actors of their most prized artistic display. To admit this fact would have been tantamount to letting actors know that they are merely were means for his art. By not acknowledging this blatant function of the mask, Goethe effectively masks his motives. The mask functions as a kind of insurance policy for the principles that pervade *Regeln für Schauspieler*—an external intervention in case the internally policed behavior fails.

*The University of Alabama, Tuscaloosa*

## NOTES

1. *Die Brüder* was not Goethe's first performance with masks; he used this technique previously in *Palaeophron and Neoterpe*. The critical difference is that while *Palaeophron and Neoterpe* was limited to a small private audience, *Die Brüder* was the first public performance using masks. As a result, *Die Brüder* attracted significantly more interest in the world of theater.

2. Goethe is far from the first to adapt Terence for the German stage. In a certain sense, the German theatrical tradition finds its origins with Terence. According to Gottsched, excerpted manuscripts of translations for Terence's plays date back to the second half of the fifteenth century for the *Schultheater* in Zwickau. The oldest known drama in German brought to the printing press was a translation of Terence's *Eunuchus* in 1486. The remainder of his comedies were published in 1499. Whether these plays were ever performed in masks is unclear. See Johann Christoph Gottsched, *Nöthiger Vorrath zur Geschichte der deutschen Dramatischen Dichtkunst: Oder Verzeichnis aller deutschen Trauer- Lust- und Singspiele, die im Druck erschienen, von 1450 bis zur Hälfte des jetzigen Jahrhunderts gesammelt und ans Licht gestellet* (Leipzig: Teuber, 1757) 28–33.

3. "Die Brüder des Terentius: ein Schauspiel in Masken," *Zeitung für die elegante Welt*, November 12, 1801. All translations are my own unless otherwise specified.

4. The author of the article writes "Dies Ereignis hat in den Annalen des Deutschen Theaters so viel Merkwürdiges, daß man hoffen darf, die unmittelbare Folge zweier Berichte über denselben Gegenstand werde den Lesern . . . angenehm sein." "Die Brüder des Terentius: ein Schauspiel in Masken," *Zeitung für die elegante Welt*, November 12, 1801.

5. "Die Brüder des Terentius: ein Schauspiel in Masken," *Zeitung für die elegante Welt*, November 12, 1801.

6. Two works in particular are exceptions to this lacuna in recent scholarship. The first, Birgit Himmelseher's *Das Weimarer Hoftheater unter Goethes Leitung*, views the theatrical masks in Weimar as an attempt by Goethe to maintain continuity with the past after the rupture of the French Revolution. The second, Birgit Wien's *Grammatik der Schauspielkunst*, highlights how Goethe's use of the theatrical mask participated in the staging of gender norms. Wiens notes that actresses in these performances rarely appear in masks; she hypothesizes that this might have been an attempt by Goethe to recall the theaters of antiquity, which excluded women. To this observation we can add that, at least in the case of Terence's *Die Brüder*, in which female characters play such a marginal role, actresses were effectively already masked by being relegated to the background of significance. See Birgit Himmelseher, *Das Weimarer Hoftheater unter Goethes Leitung* (Berlin: de Gruyter, 2010) 60-66; Birgit

Wiens, *Grammatik der Schauspielkunst. Die Inszenierung der Geschlechter in Goethes klassischem Theater* (Tübingen: Max Niemayer, 2000) 162–65.

7. Both Walter Hinck and Willi Flemming assert that the masked performances were discontinued by 1802 with Schlegel's *Ion*. Julius Wahle provides a more complete list of masked performances extending into 1807. See Walter Hinck, *Goethe–Mann des Theaters* (Göttingen: Vandenhoeck & Ruprecht, 1982) 27; Willi Flemming, *Goethe und das Theater seiner Zeit* (Stuttgart: Kohlhammer, 1968) 169; Julius Wahle, *Das Weimarer Theater unter Goethes Leitung* (Weimar: Verlag der Goethe-Gesellschaft, 1892) 229.

8. "Ueber theatralische Darstellungen. Die Weimarsche Hof-Schauspieler-Gesellschaft in Leipzig," *Zeitung für die elegante Welt*, July 16, 1807.

9. "Schillers Todtenfeier in Bremen am 28sten Jan. 1806," *Zeitung für die elegante Welt*, February 18, 1806.

10. The appearance of these masks needs to be briefly addressed. Karl August Böttiger describes the masks as covering the forehead and nose with a beard around the chin—in one case featuring an artificial chin as well. While this would leave the mouth and parts of the cheeks uncovered, the majority of the face would have been concealed. Willi Flemming remarks that this kind of "half-mask" would have allowed some room for facial expressions. Yet, as shall be discussed in the case of Carl Reinhold, the masks used in Goethe's productions of *Die Brüder* were evidently sufficiently debilitating as to deny actors their ample emotive expression. See Karl August Böttiger, "Die Brüder des Terenz mit Masken aufgeführt; auf dem Hoftheater in Weimar," *Journal des Luxus und der Moden* (Nov. 1801) 620; Flemming, *Goethe und das Theater seiner Zeit*, 169.

11. Gregory McCart's experiments reviving the ancient mask for the modern stage are particularly illuminating for conceptualizing Goethe's innovation. Gregory McCart, "Masks in Greek and Roman Theatre," in *The Cambridge Companion to Greek and Roman Theatre* (Cambridge: Cambridge UP, 2007) 247–67.

12. Karl August Böttiger, "Die Brüder des Terenz mit Masken aufgeführt," 616.

13. Johann George Sulzer, *Allgemeine Theorie der schönen Künste in einzeln, nach alphabetischer Ordnung der Kunstwörter auf einander folgend* (Leipzig: 1775) 215.

14. Jean-Baptiste Dubos, *Critical Reflections on Poetry, Painting and Music*, vol. 3 (London: 1748) 140.

15. The figurative sense of masking is still prevalent in recent theoretical approaches to theater history. Beate Hochholdinger-Reiterer explores the use of the concept of *masquerade* from psychoanalytic discourse in conjunction with gender performativity, though she favors the term *Kostümierung* on account of its ability to connote a kind of *habitus*. See Beate Hochholdinger-Reiterer, *Kostümierung der Geschlechter. Schauspielkunst als Erfindung der Aufklärung* (Göttingen: Wallenstein, 2014) 46–49.

16. Lessing, *Werke und Briefe in zwölf Bänden*, vol. 3, ed. Conrad Wiedermann (Frankfurt a/M: Deutscher Klassiker Verlag, 1985) 468.

17. Johann Wolfgang von Goethe, "Weimarisches Theater," Frankfurter Ausgabe, vol. 18, ed. Friedmar Apel (Frankfurt a/M: Deutscher Klassiker Verlag, 1998) 842–50, here 842. Further page references to this edition appear as FA with volume and page number and will be given parenthetically in the text.

18. August von Klingemann, "Hoftheater in Weimar (Die Brüder des Terentius)," *Zeitung für die elegante Welt*, November 10, 1801.

19. "Eröffnung des neuen Schauspielhauses in Lauchstädt," *Zeitung für die elegante Welt*, July 20, 1802.

20. Klingemann, "Ueber den Chor in der Tragödie," *Zeitung für die elegante Welt*, May 14, 1803.

21. Goethe makes these objectives for *Was wir bringen* explicit in an article he published in the *Allgemeine Zeitung*. See FA 18:851.

22. It has been speculated that the title of Mahlmann's journal is a direct reference to Goethe's introduction of the mask to the Weimar stage. See *Gesang und Rede, sinniges Bewegen: Goethe als Theaterleiter*, ed. Jörn Göres. (Düsseldorf: Goethe Museum Düsseldorf, 1973) 183.

23. Siegfried August Mahlmann, *Die Maske* (1803) 6–8.

24. For an account of this dramatic incident, see Marvin Carlson, *Goethe and the Weimar Theatre* (Ithaca, NY: Cornell UP, 1978) 161–70.

25. Goethe makes it clear that he conceptualizes his theatrical aesthetic in opposition to the prevailing pretense for naturalistic acting practices, which he refers to as "ein unrichtiger Begriff von Natürlichkeit" (FA 18:843). In contrast, Dieter Borchmeyer proposes that the acting style in these early years at the Weimar Theater undoubtedly adhered to the naturalistic method. It was only after Iffland's visits in 1796 and 1798 that the antinaturalistic style more often associated with Weimar develops. See Borchmeyer, *Weimarer Klassik. Porträt einer Epoche* (Weinheim: Beltz Athenäum, 1994) 378.

26. *Actors on Acting: The Theories, Techniques, and Practices of the Great Actors, Told in Their Own Words*, eds. Toby Cole and Hellen Krich Chinoy (New York: Crown, 1970) 24.

27. Dubos, *Critical Reflections*, 145. It is a testament to the versatility of masks that they can be viewed both as necessary for theatrical verisimilitude, as with Dubos, as well as an instantiation of aesthetic autonomy, as with Goethe.

28. Dubos 148.

29. Dubos 149.

30. Dubos 150.

31. Jakob Michael Reinhold Lenz references Dubos's description of the theatrical mask in his brief satirical account of the Roman theater from *Anmerkungen übers Theater*. Lenz emphasizes the challenges to comprehension that theatrical masks would pose: "Auch würden eines so ungeheuren Parterre unruhige Zuhörer wenig Erbauung gefunden haben, wenn die Akteurs ihren Prinzessinnen zärtliche Sachen vorgelispelt und vorgeschluckt, die sie unter der Maske selbst kaum gehört." Jakob Michael Reinhold Lenz, *Werke* (Stuttgart: Reclam, 1992) 370.

32. Jean-George Noverre, *Letters on Dancing and Ballets* (Alton, Hampshire: Dance Books, 2004) 78.

33. Noverre, *Letters on Dancing and Ballets* 93.

34. Noverre 93.

35. Noverre 78.

36. Lessing, *Werke und Briefe in zwölf Bänden*, vol. 6, ed. Klaus Bohnen (Frankfurt a/M: Deutscher Klassiker Verlag, 1985) 460.

37. See Dieter Borchmeyer "Saat von Göthe gesäet . . . Die 'Regeln für Schauspieler'— Ein Theatergeschichtliches Gerücht" in *Schauspielkunst im 18. Jahrhundert* (Stuttgart: Franz Steiner, 1992) 263–67.

38. [Carl Reinhold], *Saat von Göthe gesäet dem Tage der Garben zu reifen. Ein Handbuch für Ästhetiker und junge Schauspieler* (Weimar, 1808) 139.

39. Reinhold, *Saat von Göthe gesäet*, 138.

40. The acclaimed actor Eduard Genast, son of Anton Genast, an actor from the Weimar troupe, writes of his father's experience that they created difficulties in staging of *Die Brüder*. See Eduard Genast, *Aus dem Tagebuche eines alten Schauspielers* (Leipzig: Voigt & Günther, 1862) 121.

41. Reinhold's sentiment would be echoed a few decades later by prominent mid-nineteenth-century actor and theater historian Eduard Devrient: "Freilich ging man in dem Experimente so weit, den Schauspielern die altrömischen Masken aufzudringen, also eines der wesentlichsten Elemente der modernen Kunst, den Ausdruck des Mienenspieles, durch eine archäologische Spielerei zu unterdrücken." Eduard Devrient, *Geschichte der deutschen Schauspielkunst*, vol. 3 (Leipzig: J. J. Weber, 1848) 263.

42. Karl August Böttiger, "Die Brüder des Terenz mit Masken aufgeführt," 615–16.

43. By the time of performance of *Die Brüder*, this sentiment had taken hold elsewhere in Germany. One article's reception of the performances notes that the masks would "in ihrer Darstellung aus dem platten Kopiren der Natürlichkeit heraustreten, und einen Styl gewinnen" (in their depiction would step away from the vapid imitation of nature and gain a style); nevertheless, the article remained skeptical of the performance's viability in other regions. Although generally taking a sympathetic view of the new technique, the author notices a discrepancy that leads to competing claims of the performance: while the theme of household conflict in *Die Brüder* appeals to the contemporary sentiments based on the *Natürlichkeit* of bourgeois drama, a masked performance would depart from these norms. "Die Brüder des Terentius: ein Schauspiel in Masken," *Zeitung für die elegante Welt*, November 12, 1801.

44. Böttiger, "Die Brüder des Terenz mit Masken aufgeführt," 621.

45. August Wilhelm Schlegel, *Vorlesungen über dramatische Kunst und Literatur*, vol. 1 (Leipzig: Weidmann'sche Buchhandlung, 1846) 61.

46. Schlegel, *Vorlesungen über dramatische Kunst und Literatur*, 61.

47. August Wilhelm Schlegel, *Course of Lectures on Dramatic Art and Literature* (New York: AMS, 1846) 59.

48. Schlegel is baffled in the *Vorlesungen* as to how the masked actors represented affected states in ancient Greece. He initially entertains the notion that masks could be switched between scenes, before noting its unfeasibility with any change of affect during a scene. Schlegel, *Vorlesungen über dramatische Kunst und Literatur*, 61–62.

49. Schlegel does not merely form his understanding of the theatrical mask from the ancient texts with which he was so familiar. In the *Vorlesungen* he acknowledges attending one of Goethe's productions of *Die Brüder* in Weimar. Schlegel, *Vorlesungen über dramatische Kunst und Literatur*, 241.

50. Schlegel, *Vorlesungen über dramatische Kunst und Literatur*, 64.

51. Schlegel, *Course of Lectures on Dramatic Art and Literature*, 61.

52. The rules emerged out of a series of meetings in 1803 Goethe had with two promising young actors, Pius Alexander Wolff and Karl Franz Grüner. Once Goethe was convinced of their acting potential, he began to instruct them in the conventions of his theater. Both Wolff and Grüner took notes from this conversation, which might have been at the behest of Goethe. Goethe's secretary Johann Ludwig Geist copied

these notes, with some corrections by Goethe. The Weimar librarian kept all three manuscripts until Johann Peter Eckermann formalized them in 1824. Eckermann claims he discussed the editing process with Goethe and had his permission to revise the texts; however, it is unclear to what extent Goethe was involved. Wolff's notes were later rediscovered in 1949. For a comparison of Wolff's notes with Eckermann's formalized rules, see Walter Hinck, "Der Bewegungsstil der Weimarer Bühne. Zum Problem des Allegorischen bei Goethe," in *Goethe: Neue Folge des Jahrbuchs der Goethe-Gesellschaft* 21 (1959): 94–106.

53. See Schwind, "'No Laughing!' Autonomous Art and the Body of the Actor in Goethe's Weimar" in *Theater Survey* 38, no. 2 (1997): 106.

54. While masking the face would likely divert attention to another vital organ of expression, the voice, Goethe was also heavily involved in the management of actors' speech and declamation. The extensive prescriptions written for actors' voices in the *Regeln* should be viewed as a plausible answer to an objection raised by the editor of *Die Zeitung für die elegante Welt*. "Mir scheint bei der Einführung der Masken ein Hauptzweifel nicht gehoben. Es ist gewiss, dass dadurch der ideale Charakter gewinnt und die sichtbare Individualität des Schauspielers, wenn nicht aufgehoben, doch sehr vermindert wird. Aber was spricht die innerste Eigenthümlichkeit des Menschen, sein Gemüth mehr aus, als die Stimme, in der wir gewohnt sind ihn reden zu hören? So lange diese bleibt,—und muss sie nicht?—was wird, wenigstens für die Täuschung, viel gewonnen?" Klingemann, "Ueber den Chor in der Tragödie," *Zeitung für die elegante Welt*, May 14, 1803.

55. Carlson, *Goethe and the Weimar Theatre*, 314.

56. Only mentioned once, the face needs only to be directed primarily toward the audience. FA 18:871.

ANNA CHRISTINE SPAFFORD

# Embarrassment and Individual Identity in Goethe's *Wahlverwandtschaften*

**Abstract:** Embarrassment is the central emotion in the narration of Goethe's *Elective Affinities*. As a self-reflective emotion that relies heavily on social context, frequent emphasis on embarrassment in the novel's narration points to a framework for a socially constructed individual. Ottilie's martyrdom is the result of her rejection of the plastic self necessitated by social construction. Key scenes of this analysis include the depiction of Ottilie's failures in school, her arrival at Eduard and Charlotte's estate, and the three deaths in the novel's second half. Goethe's *Elective Affinities*, therefore, should be read as an ideological sequel to *Wilhelm Meister's Apprenticeship* and a continuation of its exploration of the modern individual.

**Keywords:** *Elective Affinities*, embarrassment, modernity, social construction, individual

WILHELM MEISTERS LEHRJAHRE (*Wilhelm Meister's Apprenticeship*) is, with cause, widely held to be the epitome of the modern German novel. Its focus on the individual (Wilhelm) and fascination with progress has earned it this reputation.[1] In contrast, Goethe's last novel, *Die Wahlverwandtschaften* (*Elective Affinities*), tends to be read as a novel of social and cultural change and not as thematizing the modern individual, in spite of its almost claustrophobic focus on its set of four main characters. In this article, I argue that *Die Wahlverwandtschaften* is no less a commentary on the modern individual than *Meister*. The main difference lies in the perspective through which the individual forms a sense of self. *Meister* has a clear main character—the bumbling yet fortunate Wilhelm, who dwells on his mistakes only long enough to push through them. Wilhelm undertakes many adventures and undergoes two major career changes. He grows from an easily distracted, aspiring artist into a father and entrepreneur, only recognizing this change in himself in retrospect. While the supporting cast and surrounding scenery change around Wilhelm, his individuality remains the one constant for the reader, and the reader partakes of Wilhelm's internal journey of self-discovery through his travels, interactions, and conversations with others, most notably with the mystical *Turmgesellschaft* (Tower Society), his wards (Mignon and Felix), and his love interests (Mariane, Theresa, and Natalie).

In contrast, *Die Wahlverwandtschaften* focuses on a set cast of characters and their life on a single estate. Major plot developments unfold gradually from the relationships at the estate. There are little to no occasions for the characters' explicit self-reflection or self-discovery, despite the inclusion of excerpts from Ottilie's journal and Eduard's experiences in war, a journey that takes him far from home. Consequently, instead of a focus on the individual and his or her internal development, the reader is given a platform from which to observe the social construction of the individual. The social nature of individuality is highlighted first by the shared nature of identities of the characters, brought to us under the guise of the chemical concept of "elective affinities"; then, it is furthered throughout the novel by frequent depictions of the social emotion of embarrassment, and ultimately brought to a climax by Ottilie's refusal to accept her social role and a dynamic self.

Key to my interpretation is the prominent role that embarrassment plays in key scenes of *Die Wahlverwandtschaften*. Embarrassment, though easily dismissed as a fleeting, mildly uncomfortable emotion, highlights moments of social and individual uncertainty. Unlike shame, embarrassment usually does not directly arise from indelible aspects of identity, but from situations where social roles are uncertain or imperfectly performed. It is an emotion of self-reflection that is dependent on social circumstance. In the narrative of *Die Wahlverwandtschaften*, embarrassment signals moments where the social becomes the psychological. I will proceed by examining how themes of exchangeability and social order in the novel function to promote a concept of a socially constructed self; I then turn specifically to the function of embarrassment, elaborating on the theory behind this emotion and examining its substantial function in both the famous love quadrangle and the character of the novel's ambivalent heroine. I will argue that the prominence of embarrassment and the singularity of Ottilie's character support my claim that the self as portrayed in *Die Wahlverwandtschaften* is socially constructed. In conclusion, I hope to demonstrate that the socially constructed self of *Die Wahlverwandtschaften* is a natural continuation of the modern self-reflection of *Wilhelm Meister*.

## What's in a Name?: The Other as Part of the Self

Exchangeability, the modern nightmare most frequently expressed in socialist and Marxist works, is central to the problems of *Die Wahlverwandtschaften*.[2] In *Die Wahlverwandtschaften*, the question of human exchange value comes in the form of theoretical chemistry superimposed onto human relationships, and extends much further than the simple equation $AB + CD \rightarrow AD + CB$. The central problem posed by the chemical term "elective affinities" is one of fidelity: Can one partner be substituted for another partner that one is more chemically attracted to? This problem poses consequences to the identities of its characters, but is only the start of the novel's exploration of the individual. All four protagonists have their individuality challenged by sharing the same forename. Eduard and the captain share the name Otto, though neither goes by this name. Both female protagonists have "Otto" incorporated in their names: Charl-otte and Ott-ilie. Their names suggest that any of the four could be a placeholder for the other three.

Furthermore, social rather than familial bonds hold the group together. Ottilie and Charlotte are connected to Otto only as love interests, his/their other half/halves. Eduard/Otto and captain/Otto are old friends, while Charlotte is Ottilie's guardian, having once been close friends with her deceased mother. Eduard and Charlotte live comfortable lives, while the captain and Ottilie are financially and socially dependent on their friends' graciousness. We cannot forget, however, that Eduard and Charlotte both acquired their money by marrying wealthier spouses, only later marrying each other for love. We can easily imagine Ottilie or the captain occupying the same space of good fortune if circumstances were slightly different because Eduard and Charlotte have themselves undergone financial transformation and Ottilie, at least, is of the same class. We see two specific variables of human identity—relationship status and wealth—as potentially interchangeable between individuals. With these variables come social status, influence, and the right to love a specific partner. Moreover, as Peter Schwartz demonstrates, *Die Wahlverwandtschaften* is a novel of social change; specifically, one where class distinctions are frequently transgressed and eroded by the main characters.[3] In short, the exchange represented in the chemical equation gives the false appearance of stable identity in the face of social (ex)change—the individual components remain unchanged as the equation is written. The details of this "experiment" as it unfolds in the plot of the novel support the premise that individuals can exchange roles; however, the results challenge the assumption that the self is a static entity, unchanged by social surroundings as represented in the chemical equation so famously discussed in Chapter 4.

A further complication to individual identity exists not only in the role the individual inhabits but also in the face of the others present. This is made explicit in the novel when Eduard requires the captain's assistance to organize himself:

"Laß uns nun," sagte [der Hauptmann] zu seinem Freunde, "an das übrige gehen, an die Gutsbeschreibung, wozu schon genugsame Vorarbeit da sein muß, aus der sich nachher Pachtanschläge und anderes schon entwickeln werden. Nur *eines* laß uns festsetzen und einrichten: trenne alles, was eigentlich Geschäft ist, vom Leben! Das Geschäft verlangt Ernst und Strenge, das Leben Willkür; das Geschäft die reinste Folge, dem Leben tut eine Inkonsequenz oft not, ja sie ist liebenswürdig und erheiternd. Bist du bei dem einen sicher, so kannst du in dem andern desto freier sein, anstatt daß bei einer Vermischung das Sichre durch das Freie weggerissen und aufgehoben wird."
Eduard fühlte in diesen Vorschlägen einen leisen Vorwurf. Zwar von Natur nicht unordentlich, konnte er doch niemals dazu kommen, seine Papiere nach Fächern abzuteilen. Das, was er mit andern abzutun hatte, was bloß von ihm selbst abhing, es war nicht geschieden, so wie er auch Geschäfte und Beschäftigung, Unterhaltung und Zerstreuung nicht genugsam voneinander absonderte. Jetzt wurde es ihm leicht, da ein Freund diese Bemühung übernahm, ein zweites Ich die Sonderung bewirkte, in die das eine Ich nicht immer sich spalten mag.[4]

"Now," [the captain] said to his friend, "let us move on to our next task, the description of the property. For this, we must make a sufficient start on the work to be able to draft leases and suchlike later on. Only let us establish one principle: separate all business matters from life. Business demands earnest discipline, life demands spontaneity; business demands clear logic, but life often finds inconsistency necessary—indeed it can be desirable and entertaining. If you are sure in the one, then you can be all the freer in the other, instead of finding freedom undermining certainty and canceling it out."

Edward sensed a slight reproach in these suggestions. Though not by nature disorganized, he could never bring himself to arrange and classify his papers. He did not keep matters that had to do with other people separate from those that had to do with himself; just as he did not clearly enough distinguish between business and busyness, entertainment and diversion. Now things were made easy for him in that a friend assumed this task, a second self undertaking the separation that a single self is often reluctant to perform.[5]

Eduard has trouble separating public *Geschäft* (business), private *Beschäftigung* (business), self (*was bloß von ihm selbst abhing*—matters that had to do with himself), and others (*was er mit andern abzutun hatte*—matters that had to do with other people). Fortunately, the captain (the other male Otto) is ready to step in and help him define what goes where. The organizing mind of another individual lets Eduard know what should go where. He can maintain order and a sense of self in that he sees his own identity as a whole from which contextual Eduards splinter, so long as the task of contextualization falls to his friend, whom he internalizes as a second self (*ich*).[6] This results, however, in the dissolution of the distinctions between himself and his friend. In affecting the split of Eduard into Eduards, the captain himself becomes a part of Eduard, the second, *external* "I" through which the first "I" becomes objectified and understandable. His presence fundamentally alters Eduard's self. He becomes a part of Eduard's identity.

We see a similar mixing of selves in the "doubled adultery" that results in baby Otto. Although this child is conceived within the confines of the marital bed, his features resemble those of the captain and his eyes are almost identical to Ottilie's (226; 232). Although neither Ottilie nor the captain had a direct hand in the conception of this child, Eduard and Charlotte's extramarital affections cause their beloveds to manifest in their offspring.[7] All four "Ottos" produce a fifth, baby Otto, whose demise is caused by Ottilie's refusal to mature. Building on Jane K. Brown's psychological reading of the four "Ottos" as individual and "rational or irrational … masculine or feminine part[s of the full self],"[8] I argue that the individuals in *Die Wahlverwandtschaften* are not symbolic for different stable aspects of the self as in Freudian psychology, but rather that the characters' interconnectedness and apparent exchangeability as individuals highlights the importance of their social roles—as men/women, as figures of authority, and/or power or lack thereof—and the instability inherent in these roles because of the implied exchangeability and the fact that these roles may vary by context.

The five "Ottos" are not one and the same. They create a unity in that they are a collective, a group of individuals whose identities depend on the others within their social context. Their selves, as we see in the scene discussed above featuring Eduard and the captain, are the objective identities that each individual has of who he or she is and what role he or she plays in a given social context based on the internalization of external social knowledge. As we shall see, like Eduard, not all characters fit perfectly into their given social roles. Ultimately, *Die Wahlverwandtschaften* is the story of the creation and destruction of this collective by Ottilie, an individual who rejects the social dependence of the self.[9]

## Embarrassment, the Self, and
## *Die Wahlverwandtschaften*

The ostensible central conflict of *Die Wahlverwandtschaften* is its doubled romantic infidelity, but it is clear that this romantic transgression cannot be taken at face value. As Schwartz demonstrates, the main theme of *Die Wahlverwandtschaften* is the overwhelming social change that comes with the rise of Napoleon and the resulting loss of the totality once enjoyed by the nobility.[10] According to Christina von Braun, the famed doubled infidelity demonstrates itself in a way that is quite modern, suggesting that there are manifold ways to be a mother or father.[11] Through the figures of the captain and Ottilie, we see a complicated partial or adoptive parentage that places further pressure on parental identity because the adoptive caretakers of little Otto uncharacteristically bear physical resemblance to him, implying a biological connection where we know there is none. Friedrich Kittler more famously interprets this problem of parentage as symbolic of two ideals of pedagogy, contemporary to Goethe, that result from the privatization and secularization of the Enlightenment.[12] Kittler begins this account of the leveling (and consequently middle-class) force of education with the claim that in lust and law, all people are exchangeable.[13] Fritz Breithaupt argues that their crime is precisely this "replaceability"—Eduard and Charlotte's capacity to replace their reality with an imagined ideal.[14] All these accounts correctly measure an unsettled problem of identity in Goethe's final novel. I will argue that the novel gives us a mechanism for the mutability of identity through its use of embarrassment and emphasis on social context. The problem with the exchange of individuals in *Die Wahlverwandtschaften* is not so much that it is a crime, but that it simply does not work. Elements A and C cannot be exchanged because when they are moved they no longer remain the same.

Embarrassment plays a crucial role in *Die Wahlverwandtschaften* because of the novel's emphasis on social context. While it may be tempting to take social context for granted in a novel that, in stark contrast to *Wilhelm Meister*, remains in one place, what we are faced with in *Die Wahlverwandtschaften* is a narrative that focuses increasingly on the presence of individuals and how one appearance or exit can effect drastic change in this otherwise stable social environment. The consistency of location in

*Die Wahlverwandtschaften* showcases the power of individual presence (or absence) on a social group.

Embarrassment is highly relevant to the modern individual because it is a social emotion tightly connected to an individual's selfhood. In contrast to shame and guilt, which are tied to person-specific deeds or characteristics, embarrassment is a short-lived emotion that is specific to in-the-moment social dynamics.[15] It is a side effect of the plasticity of the human self and results when an individual in a specific social context fails to act in accordance with the role of his- or herself in that context.[16] Self and individual are not exchangeable: an individual is a person as distinguished from other people, a singularity viewed from an external, third-person perspective. The self, on the other hand, is necessarily reflexive; it is an objective identity that the individual possesses in and of itself.[17]

Embarrassment remains much less theorized than its close relatives shame and guilt.[18] Current theoretical approaches and current psychology both draw heavily on the work of the sociologist, Erving Goffman.[19] Crucial to the function of embarrassment as explained by Goffman are social expectations and the social construction of a self:

> Embarrassment has to do with unfulfilled expectations . . . things go well or badly because of what is perceived about the social identities of those present. *During interaction the individual is expected to possess certain attributes, capacities, and information which, taken together, fit together into a self that is at once coherently unified and appropriate for the occasion.* Through the expressive implications of his stream of conduct, through mere participation itself, the individual effectively projects this acceptable self into the interaction, although he may not be aware of it, and the others may not be aware of having so interpreted his conduct. *At the same time he must accept and honor the selves projected by the other participants.* The elements of a social encounter, then, consist of effectively projected claims to an acceptable self and the confirmation of the claims on the part of the others.[20]

This role-fulfilling self is not an individual's essence, but rather an internalized objectification of the individual. This self changes, then, according to social context in order to fulfill the assumed social expectations of others. Embarrassment results when those expectations are not met. Critically, embarrassment may be felt by either the one(s) whose expectations have been disappointed or the one(s) disappointing those expectations:

> When an event throws doubt upon or discredits these claims [of others onto the self], then the encounter finds itself lodged in assumptions which no longer hold. . . . At such times the individual whose self has been threatened (the individual for whom embarrassment is felt) and the individual who threatened him may both feel ashamed of what together they have brought about, sharing this sentiment just when they have reason to feel apart.[21]

Key to the understanding of embarrassment is the exposure of the individual as performer when she or he performs incorrectly. Embarrassment is particularly likely to occur in the face of unexpected social events and changing social norms.

While there is no explicit theory of embarrassment specific to the Goethezeit, it is worth noting that blushing, one type of body language closely associated with embarrassment,[22] corresponds with veracity in the works of the German *Empfindsamkeit* (sentimentality),[23] to which *Die Wahlverwandtschaften* does not belong but bears some resemblance. In a sense, embarrassment in *Die Wahlverwandtschaften* reveals the soul of the modern individual in that it reveals the ever-changing nature of the modern self.

I will argue that *Die Wahlverwandtschaften* offers a portrayal of self that closely follows Goffman's understanding of the self as role, and which, with Ottilie's death, questions the ability of any individual to maintain a stable identity on the human plane. The prevalence of embarrassment over shame and guilt emphasizes the importance of social context within the work over individualism, thus muddling efforts to definitively track causality and to form static identities. As will be seen, the characters of *Wahlverwandtschaften* perform several roles accompanied by different expectations. Some are sensitive to the fact that they (and their fellows) are actors; thus, they may exhibit more potential for embarrassment, while others exhibit less.

## I'm Mortified: Embarrassment, Avoidance, and Death

As their feelings develop, Charlotte consciously begins to avoid the captain and Eduard suppresses his desire for physical contact with Ottilie. These reactions are intended to prevent the actors from exposing deviation from their roles of husband and wife. In fact, a consistent force propelling the plot of the novel is avoidance. This attempt to escape through distance only increases as the situation evolves. When Eduard fails to free himself from his marriage to Charlotte, after having exposed his feelings to Ottilie and assuring her of their coming union, his solution is to run off to war. After baby Otto's accidental death, Ottilie tries to leave Eduard and Charlotte's estate by returning to her former finishing school. Even the captain leaves for a time, only to return as a major. Before both of their untimely deaths, first Ottilie and then Eduard hide from their companions on the estate, secluding themselves in their private rooms and avoiding social opportunities.

These relationships are ill-fated and result in the deaths of Ottilie and Eduard. Beginning with the accidental death of baby Otto, Ottilie retreats from the world and the people around her, ultimately dying of starvation because she refuses to eat. It is not guilt that kills Ottilie, but her inability to cast herself in the role of a sinner after having embraced the role of the virginal ideal.

This casting decision is made clear through Ottilie's interactions with art. After the captain leaves, he is replaced by his friend "the architect." This man, like all others, is enamored of Ottilie's beauty and childish innocence. This culminates in his casting Ottilie as the virgin mother of God in a nativity tableau. The narrator describes Ottillie as "halb verlegen" at being asked to fill this role (180; half embarrassed, 203), but an appeal to her guardian quickly overcomes modesty and Ottilie's performance moves all who see it. Her role as virgin mother is further solidified by the birth of baby Otto, for whom she becomes primary caregiver: "Durch diese sonderbare Verwandtschaft und vielleicht noch mehr durch das schöne Gefühl der Frauen geleitet, welche das Kind eines geliebten Mannes, auch von einer andern, mit zärtlicher Neigung umfangen, ward Ottilie dem heranwachsenden Geschöpf soviel als eine Mutter oder vielmehr eine andre Art von Mutter" (226; This strange connection and even more, perhaps, that happy feeling of tender affection a woman has for the child of a man she loves even when it is not her on, made Ottilie soon as good as a mother, or rather, second mother, to the growing boy, 232).

Ottilie is not put in competition with Charlotte for the position of Otto's mother; rather, her "different kind" of motherhood gives her a special status. Even when her own actions lead to Otto's accidental death, the narrator treats her as a special case. Having dropped him into the lake, Ottilie fishes the baby out and tries to coax life back into his drowned body. We are told: "Alles vergebens! Ohne Bewegung liegt das Kind in ihren Armen. . . . Knieend sinkt sie in dem Kahne nieder und hebt das erstarrte Kind mit beiden Armen über ihre unschuldige Brust, die an Weiße und leider auch an Kälte dem Marmor gleicht" (239; All in vain! Motionless the child lies in her arms. . . . Kneeling, she sinks down into the boat and lifts the lifeless infant with both arms above her innocent breast, as white, and alas, as cold as marble, too, 240). Here, with the dead baby of her rival in her hands, Ottilie remains a picture of aesthetic beauty and purity. Her innocent breast, location of the heart and its feelings, is compared to marble, a stone favored in the portrayal of deities and superhuman beauty. We are given no reason to doubt that Ottilie's intentions are in the best interest of baby Otto, but are also given to understand that this innocence belies a warmth that would have aided the child. In this sense, it is not so much Ottilie's fault that Charlotte and Eduard's child has died, but the result of a tragic flaw. While Ottilie's innocence and docility are in many ways moral and praiseworthy, circumstance has caused this trait to work against her and turn her fate for the worse.

After this event, Ottilie sensibly wants to work through her grief elsewhere. She discusses this plan with Charlotte, who reminds her that her former teacher, the headmistress's assistant, has intentions of offering her marriage. Ottilie answers:

Das Geschick ist nicht sanft mit mir verfahren . . . und wer mich liebt, hat vielleicht nicht viel Besseres zu erwarten. So gut und verständig als der Freund [der Gehülfe] ist, ebenso, hoffe ich, wird sich in ihm auch die Empfindung eines reinen Verhältnisses zu mir entwickeln; er wird in mir eine geweihte Person erblicken, die nur dadurch ein ungeheures Übel für sich und andre vielleicht aufzuwiegen vermag, wenn sie sich dem Heiligen widmet, das, uns unsichtbar umgebend, allein gegen ungeheuren zudringenden Mächte beschirmen kann. (249-50)

Fate has not been kind to me . . . and those who love me can expect to fare no better. Our friend [the schoolmaster] is kind and intelligent, and so I hope he will come to regard himself simply as a friend; he will see in me a person singled out by fate, who can atone for a monstrous calamity perhaps only by dedicating herself to all that is holy and which alone, invisibly surrounding us, can protect us from the monstrous powers that threaten us. (247)

We see here that Ottilie is firmly entrenched in a vision of herself as a "geweihte Person" (holy person). That is, she is holy, dedicated, and consecrated to a superhuman power. This connection with the holy continues into and after her death. Shortly before she dies, the narrator describes Ottilie as "das bleiche himmlische Kind" (267; the pale angelic child, 258). The word "Kind" is operative here. Ottilie dies not as a woman, not as a "kind of" mother, not as a beloved, not as a sacrifice, but as a child. She dies as a refusal of change, a refusal of growth, by refusing to eat, and is canonized by the locals.

Eduard's death has many similarities to Ottilie's. In response to her death, he retreats from the company of others, stops communicating, and obsesses over possessions that remind him of his beloved. Unlike Ottilie, he does find an outlet through alcohol and expresses his desire to be dead. Like Ottilie, his agency in his own death remains a question. Mittler simply finds him dead one day, and Charlotte happens upon Eduard's body not long thereafter:

> Charlotte stürzte herbei; ein Verdacht des Selbstmordes regte sich in ihr; sie wollte sich, sie wollte die andern einer unverzeihlichen Unvorsichtigkeit anklagen. Doch der Arzt aus natürlichen und Mittler aus sittlichen Gründen wußten sie bald vom Gegenteil zu überzeugen. Ganz deutlich war Eduard von seinem Ende überrascht worden. Er hatte, was er bisher sorgfältig zu verbergen pflegte, das ihm von Ottilien Übriggebliebene in einem stillen Augenblick vor sich aus einem Kästchen, aus einer Brieftasche ausgebreitet: eine Locke, Blumen, in glücklicher Stunde gepflückt, alle Blättchen, die sie ihm geschrieben, von jenem ersten an, das ihm seine Gattin so zufällig ahnungsreich übergeben hatte. Das alles konnte er nicht einer ungefähren Entdeckung mit Willen preisgeben. Und so lag denn auch dieses vor kurzem zu unendlicher Bewegung aufgeregte Herz in unstörbarer Ruhe; und wie er in Gedanken an die Heilige eingeschlafen war, so konnte man wohl ihn selig nennen. (273)

> Charlotte hastened in; she suspected suicide; she was about to accuse herself and them all of unforgivable negligence. But the doctor pointed out physical, and Mittler ethical reasons to convince her that this was not the case. Death had quite clearly taken Edward by surprise. He had taken a quiet moment to spread out before him objects that had belonged to Ottilie from a case and a portfolio, things he usually kept carefully hidden: a lock of hair, flowers plucked in happier times, all the notes she had sent him, starting with the very first which his wife had handed him by such ominous chance. He could not have wished to reveal all this in the event of accidental discovery. And so this heart, which had so recently been touched by infinite emotion, lay in imperturbable peace. And since he had passed away thinking of his saint, he might rightfully be called blessed. (262)

The evidence given to Charlotte and the reader to dismiss the possibility of Eduard having committed suicide is embarrassment. It is assumed that Eduard, who previously had not been held back much by propriety, could not have committed suicide because he would have never let anyone see the personal tokens of his love for Ottilie. The circumstances of Ottilie's own death are couched in a situation of social impropriety. Instead of being walked in on, like Eduard, Ottilie walks into Mittler's monologue about the

Ten Commandments at the exact moment when he begins to discuss adultery. Embarrassed and shocked, she runs away and collapses, dying shortly thereafter. Ottilie's canonization and Eduard's final description as "selig" (blessed) indicate a narratorial revolt against the religious establishment as represented by Mittler and give Ottilie's portrayal as a saintly figure double meaning: first, she has internalized the role of holy, untouchable virgin that led to not only Otto's death but also her own. Second, paradoxically, her "martyrdom" and canonization/deification point to a new religious order, a new sublime that is beyond the grasp of the likes of Mittler.

## Deviating from the Script

Brown's interpretation of Ottilie is that of a Gothic threat: she is uncanny, a water sprite, an undine out to steal the souls of men, a doppelgänger set to take Charlotte's place in life.[24] This portrayal of Ottilie as harbinger of the uncanny rings true. Her existence in the novel is unsettling, even though her demeanor is meek. Her character, through its inscrutable mix of purity and destruction, gains a kind of deep power. I argue that this power comes from embarrassment. Ottilie is unsettling because she refuses to adapt to her social context.

This possible heroine of Goethe's last novel is quite young and, more often than anything else, she is described as beautiful. As such, she is cast as a desirable, young innocent, whose modesty and shyness add to her charm. Additionally, her existence is characterized by her dependence on Charlotte and her role as competition for Charlotte's biological daughter, Luciane.

Considering that her main goal at this stage of her life ought to be to find a stable life by means of a husband, as her guardian did before her, Ottilie's main attributes, beauty and desirability, should put her in an advantageous position. But Ottilie's youth and beauty do not help her to escape from her dependence on Charlotte and Eduard, nor do they lead her to success at boarding school. Instead, even at her tender young age, Ottilie represents manifold embarrassments for her guardian well before Charlotte's spouse has fallen in love with her. In fact, despite efforts to encourage Ottilie to integrate into their community as an adult woman with a capacity for a romantic relationship, Ottilie remains a childish dependent. This incongruence with role expectations results in repeated instances of embarrassment.

First, as any good guardian might wish to do, Charlotte has previously laid plans to assist Ottilie in finding a spouse. Problematically, the plan fell through, and Charlotte ended up marrying Eduard herself, although she had thought he could not possibly be interested in her anymore. While discussing moving the dismally failing Ottilie into their home at the request of her boarding school's headmistress's assistant, Charlotte refrains from telling Eduard that she had originally planned to have him marry Ottilie: "Charlotte, so aufrichtig sie zu sprechen schien, verhehlte doch etwas. Sie hatte nämlich damals dem von Reisen zurückkehrenden Eduard Ottilien absichtlich vorgeführt, um dieser geliebten Pflegetochter eine so große Partie zuzuwenden; denn an sich selbst in bezug auf Eduard dachte sie nicht mehr" (19; But though she seemed to speak so frankly, Charlotte was concealing something. She had deliberately introduced Ottilie to Edward upon his return from his travels in order to put her beloved ward in the way of a fine match: for she had no longer thought of herself in connection with Edward, 101). Here, the narration first exposes the juxtaposition between Charlotte's roles as guardian of Ottilie and as Eduard's spouse. On the one hand, she had once very practically thought that her own former love interest, having aged well and become wealthier with time, could make a good match for her young ward. On the other hand, said former love interest had not (at that time) let go of his youthful passion towards Charlotte, and thus the maternal figure found bliss before her ward did. Although the only voiced indication of embarrassment is Charlotte's silence on the subject, the faint echo of incest should not be overlooked. This taboo does not feature strongly elsewhere in the story, but is not atypical for Goethe. In *Die Wahlverwandtschaften*, Charlotte's silence regarding her past plans is an attempt to reconcile her assumed past role as maternal guardian unrelated to Eduard with her present as his devoted, worthy wife. Ottilie therefore also functions as an ambiguous figure, having formerly been a potential spouse for Eduard (without his knowledge) and now appearing as his wife's young dependent.

Ottilie not only causes Charlotte embarrassment, but the young woman's performance at school is so abysmal that the headmistress cannot write about it herself. As her assistant reports, "Von Ottilien läßt mich unsre ehrwürdige Vorsteherin schreiben, teils weil es ihr, nach ihrer Art zu denken, peinlich wäre, dasjenige, was zu melden ist, zu melden, teils auch, weil sie selbst einer Entschuldigung bedarf, die sie lieber mir in den Mund legen mag" (45; Our honored principal has asked me to write to you about Ottilie, in part because what we have to report is, to her mind, embarrassing, and in part because she would rather have me make the apologies she owes you, 117). The assistant goes on to say that Ottilie did terribly on her exams and thus hasn't received her certificate. He describes a variety of tests and how Ottilie failed them, ultimately blaming a combination of headache and shyness for her poor results. This failure, the assistant claims, deserves an apology from the headmistress, which she would rather he offered instead. Here, we see a figure of authority whose role and self-image will not allow her to admit failure. In the assistant's attempts to explain Ottilie's failures, we see an attempt to overcome and rationalize a disparity between expectations of Ottilie's performance and the actual result. When Charlotte and the headmistress's assistant's wishes are fulfilled and Ottilie is released from the boarding school to come home to Charlotte and Eduard's, Ottilie does not cease to embarrass Charlotte. On her arrival, Ottilie greets Charlotte as a suppliant, resulting in her guardian's embarrassment: "'Wozu die Demütigung!' sagte Charlotte, die einigermaßen verlegen war und sie aufheben wollte. 'Es ist so demütig nicht gemeint,' versetzte Ottilie, die in ihrer vorigen Stellung blieb. 'Ich mag mich nur so gern jener Zeit erinnern, da ich noch nicht höher reichte als bis an Ihre Kniee und Ihrer Liebe schon so gewiß war'" (49; "Why such humility?" asked Charlotte, feeling somewhat embarrassed and trying to raise her up. "It's not meant that way," replied Ottilie, not moving from her previous position. "It's just that I so like to think of the time when I was no taller than your knee and felt so confident of your love," 120). In other words,

Charlotte expects Ottilie to greet her as an adult, but Ottilie signals a state of childishness and expresses a desire to remain a mental and emotional minority. This is especially ironic when we also take into account Charlotte's past vision of Ottilie as potential spouse for Eduard. Ottilie could have almost literally been in Charlotte's shoes for this scene but, if nothing else, her expectations of herself are woefully inadequate for such a possibility.

Thus, in the first quarter of the novel, we see Ottilie fail to meet the expectations held for her as a student and as a young noblewoman. This causes notable embarrassment in those responsible for raising her: Charlotte, the headmistress, and the assistant. At the boarding school, Ottilie is meant to play the role of a young noblewoman preparing for adult life. The headmistress's deep embarrassment makes clear that it is unacceptable for a person in Ottilie's role as young, noble student to fail at the tasks set for her. Ottilie's first interaction with Charlotte illustrates a similar inability to fulfill her part as a young noblewoman. She acts in contradiction to her adult or near-adult status, which again embarrasses the woman responsible for raising her.

Key to understanding embarrassment in *Die Wahlverwandtschaften* is the recognition that embarrassment does not simply result from one individual's failure to adhere to a single set of social mores. Rather, each individual employs his or her own variation of social norms. Ottilie is only the blushing modest angel of perfection when seen, unavailable, from a male gaze. The women around her, on the other hand, are baffled and embarrassed at her inabilities. She is debilitatingly shy, to the point where she cannot learn properly among her peers at school; she exhibits a lack of judgment and actively seeks to remain in a position of immaturity. In spite of her vulnerable position in life, Ottilie does not change her habits to suit her more powerful benefactors. Instead of becoming a full adult, she remains a child. Much like the otherworldly foundling she resembles, she destroys the lives of those who take her in. Unlike the foundling, however, she cannot be blamed for this destruction.

## Conclusion

Man hat uns die Geschichte gelehrt; ich habe nicht soviel daraus behalten, als ich wohl gewollt hätte; denn ich wußte nicht wozu ichs brauchen würde. Nur einzelne Begebenheiten sind mir sehr eindrücklich gewesen, so folgende:
Als Karl der Erste von England vor seinen sogenannten Richtern stand, fiel der goldne Knopf des Stöckchens, das er trug, herunter. Gewohnt, daß bei solchen Gelegenheiten sich alles für ihn bemühte, schien er sich umzusehen und zu erwarten, daß ihm jemand auch diesmal den kleinen Dienst erzeigen sollte. Es regte sich niemand; er bückte sich selbst, um den Knopf aufzuheben. Mir kam das so schmerzlich vor, ich weiß nicht, ob mit Recht, daß ich von jenem Augenblick an niemanden kann etwas aus den Händen fallen sehn, ohne mich darnach zu bücken. (53)

They taught us history at school; I haven't remembered as much of it as I doubtless should; for I don't know what use it might be to me. But certain incidents have remained very vividly in my mind, amongst them the following. When

Charles I of England was standing before those who presumed to be his judges, the gold knob of the stick he was carrying fell to the ground. Used to having someone help him on such occasions, he seemed to look round and expect someone to do him this small service. But no one moved; he bent down himself and picked up the knob. I was so keenly moved by this, rightly or wrongly, that from that moment on I have been unable to see anyone drop something without bending to pick it up myself. (122)

It tells us a lot about Ottilie that the main takeaway from her history courses at finishing school was to pick things up for other people to save them from embarrassment. Why does this English king inspire such sympathy from her? Why should Ottilie treat the rest of the world with social norms that apply to a seventeenth-century monarch? Ultimately, the monarch was capable and did pick up his own royal accessory. Key to this scene is that Ottilie doesn't describe the king as embarrassed or pained—only herself—because of the sudden lack of subservience from his subjects as he stood trial. What we learn here is that Ottilie is simultaneously exceedingly sensitive and blind to certain social cues. She sees herself as subordinate to the other adults around her in a way that makes her more object than subject. For this reason, whereas all others should be mortified to pick something up from the ground, she can be an exception because she does not accede to the existing social roles. This is not immediately expected or accepted by the other adults in her life, especially the people responsible for raising her (Charlotte, the schoolmistress, and her assistant), but, occasionally, Eduard and others expect Ottilie to engage in more decision-making instead of insisting on always being the immature helper. This kind of behavior is rebellious and individualistic, despite the difficulty one has in describing it as such. Ottilie engages in rebellion from the expectations of others and frequently causes embarrassment in those around her. When circumstances, her love for Eduard, and the death of Otto, conspire to compel her to act in ways unsuited to this character—in the individualistic manner of an adult (that is, to survive being the accidental cause of Otto's death and to either accept or deny Eduard's advances and plans), Ottilie rejects her reality in favor of keeping the role and sense of self she has chosen.

Andreas Grimm is correct in his interpretation of Ottilie as an egoist.[25] She clearly views herself as an exception to certain social expectations, as seen in the baffling takeaway from her history lessons. No one but Ottilie can pick up the king's golden knob, even though it is part of the story that this long-deceased man bends over to perform the task himself. Ottilie's character is forcibly servile, obstinately minor. Her insistence on maintaining minority status changes the other, older characters as well as her entire social group. Instead of influencing Ottilie to take on a more socially appropriate role (that of wife, possibly to Eduard, or of marriage-ready finishing school graduate), Charlotte and Eduard are subjected to the implosion of their relationship to each other and a loss of clear roles in this context.

In its early beginnings, *Die Wahlverwandtschaften* was conceived as part of *Wilhelm Meisters Wanderjahre (Wilhelm Meister's Journeyman Years)*.[26] With its complicated exploration of the individual/self as they relate to group dynamics, *Die Wahlverwandtschaften* truly continues the exploration of the modern individual that takes place in its predecessor, *Wilhelm Meisters Lehrjahre*. But we see the individual fragmented from a different perspective: instead of Wilhelm's internally fractured ego, Ottilie's context asks her, from an external perspective, to conform to different roles, different versions of herself. When she fails to do this, the repercussions go far beyond her own death and fundamentally alter the identities of the others involved. Where Wilhelm Meister, after looking back on his mistakes and shortcomings, accepts his new role as father of Felix and venture capitalist working with the *Turmgesellschaft*, Ottilie escapes the need for multiple selves through denial and, in doing so, destroys the social group that required her to develop this new self. Whereas Wilhelm's journey (although accompanied by multiple deaths), reads as a success, as individual growth, Ottilie's journey is a tragedy and her hyperfunction and overzealous commitment to having one role, one self, carefully foreshadows the difficulties that identity will present in the modern era—namely, the discomfort of needing to occupy a different self depending on social context.

*Die Wahlverwandschaften* presents detailed clashes between individuals, self-image, and the expectations of others. In the cases of Luciane and Eduard, self-confidence protects them from embarrassment when they transgress social norms. They often completely disregard or fail to register others' expectations of them. On the other end of the spectrum, are the captain, Charlotte, and (at the very extreme) Ottilie. The narration of *Die Wahlverwandtschaften* has a moral compass that vacillates depending on the social climate and individual disposition. The prevalence of embarrassment over guilt prevents the novel from being able to represent a strong moral position on the subject of divorce, because the issue Ottilie portrays with her death is less one of guilt than of her inability to allow for a change in her role as a pure, virginal character. In short, Ottilie literally dies of embarrassment, or kills herself with it.

As Astrida Orle Tantillo so beautifully charts in her book *Goethe's Elective Affinities and the Critics*, interpretations of Ottilie's death have been irreconcilable since its publication.[27] This lack of conclusion is facilitated by the narration of the novel, which does not take a moral stance or allocate guilt on Ottilie's behalf and which emphasizes context-specific embarrassment over morally laden shame and guilt. Even the gluttonous servant Nanny, who consumed all evidence of Ottilie's starvation, is proclaimed innocent of her mistress's death, although the circumstances of the discovery of her collusion are quite painful and embarrassing.

Throughout *Die Wahlverwandtschaften*, Ottilie is the immutable form, an unchanging ideal, that we all pretend to be when we enter a role. As such, she demonstrates the aporia that is the modern search for the self. As is demonstrated by the changing roles and attitudes of the other characters in her predicament—Eduard and his willingness to leave his marriage and join the army, Charlotte who deftly switches between her role as guardian and as competitor, and the captain, who simply shows development through gaining the rank of major—the modern individual is a figure of constant change. Ottilie withstands this need to change but she does not offer a solution to the problem. Uwe Steiner fittingly characterizes Ottilie as the genius of this novel, by the very virtue of her paradox: "Weil Genialität mithin Originalität impliziert, fordert sie zur Nachahmung auf, indem sie Nachahmung verbietet" (Because genius also implies originality, it prompts imitation in that it forbids imitation).[28]

*University of Indiana*

# NOTES

1. For two excellent examples, see Fritz Breithaupt, "Goethe and the Ego," *Goethe Yearbook* 11 (2002): 77–109 and Franco Moretti, "The World of Prose" in *The Way of the World: The* Bildungsroman *in European Culture*, trans. Albert Sbragia, 2nd ed. (New York: Verso, 2000) 129–79.

2. Taking place on a noble estate several decades before the publication of the *Communist Manifesto*, we would not necessarily expect our protagonists to be plagued by the problems akin to alienated labor. Indeed, they are not; rather, it is likely that the fears of both Marxists and the nobility of *Die Wahlverwandtschaften* are in response to the empiricism of their times. This fear response exhibits itself in our society in a still more exacerbated way today, proportional to the increased role of empiricism in modern life.

3. Peter J Schwartz, *After Jena: Goethe's Elective Affinities and the End of the Old Regime* (Lewisburg: Bucknell UP, 2010) 92–126.

4. Johann Wolfgang von Goethe, *Die Wahlverwandtschaften*, vol. 12, ed. Regine Otto (Berlin: Aufbau, 1963) 5–278, here 33–34. Further page references to this edition will be given parenthetically in the text.

5. Johann Wolfgang von Goethe, *Elective Affinities*, trans. Judith Ryan, in *The Sorrows of Young Werther, Elective Affinities, Novella*, ed. David E. Wellbery (New York: Suhrkamp, 1988) 89–262, here 110. Further page references to this edition will be given parenthetically in the text.

6. It should be noted that the German *ich* is not generally translated with the English word "self." My use of the term here is to reflect that Eduard's "zweites Ich" in the passage quoted above is his internal reflection regarding his own identity, and thereby an internalization of the knowledge he gains about himself from the captain, as opposed to the captain performing the role of a doppelgänger.

7. Friedrich A. Kittler, "Ottilie Hauptmann," *Dichter, Mutter, Kind* (Munich: Wilhelm Fink, 1991) 119–48.

8. Jane K. Brown, *Goethe's Allegories of Identity* (Philadelphia: U of Pennsylvania P, 2014) 68.

9. Mary Helen Dupree makes the point that *Meister* heavily features discussion of theatrical performance, while *Die Wahlverwandtschaften* is inundated with art forms typical of salon culture (68). These differing artistic venues parallel the two different explanations of the modern individual: the single (but split) Freudian ego set on stage to be examined, versus the temporary member of a collective, whose identity and behaviors change to meet the expectations within the solon and, upon leaving, adhere to the norms outside.

10. Schwartz, *After Jena*, 92–126.

11. Christina von Braun, "*Wahlverwandtschaften*—Ende der Blutslinie," *Schwellen-prosa (Re)Lektüren zu Goethes Wahlverwandtschaften* (Paderborn: Wilhelm Fink, 2018) 21–36, here 35.

12. Kittler 119–48.

13. Quoting Jorge Luis Borges, Kittler writes: "Alle Menschen sind im schwindelnden Augenblick des Miteinanderschlafens derselbe Mensch" (119; all people are the same person in the dizzying moment of sleeping together).

14. Fritz Breithaupt, "Culture of Images: Limitation in Goethe's *Wahlverwandtschaften*," trans. Jill Suzanne Smith *Monatshefte* 92, no. 3 (2000): 302–20, here 310.

15. This differentiation is one common among scholars in both sociology and litera-ture. See, for example, Nicole Henniger and Christine Harris, "Can Negative Social Emotions Have Positive Consequences? An Examination of Embarrassment, Shame, Guilt, Jealousy, and Envy," in *The Positive Side of Negative Emotions*, ed. W. Gerrod Parrot (New York: Guilford, 2014); Martin S. Weinberg, "Embarrassment: Its variable and invariable aspects," *Social Forces* 46, no. 3 (1968): 382–88; June Price Tangney, Rowland S. Miller, Laura Flicker, and Deborah Hill Barlow, "Are Shame, Guilt, and Embarrassment Distinct Emotions?" *Journal of Personality and Social Psychology* 70, no. 6 (1996): 1256–269; Ben Robinson, "State of Embarrassment: Kafka's 'In der Strafkolonie,'" *The Germanic Review: Literature, Culture, Theory* 90, no. 2 (2015): 101–22; and David Yau-Fai Ho, Wai Fu, and S. M. Ng, "Guilt, Shame, and Embarrassment: Revelations of Face and Self," *Culture & Psychology* 10, no. 1 (2004): 64–84.

16. Erving Goffman, "Embarrassment and Social Organization," *American Journal of Sociology* 62 (1956): 264–71.

17. Jessica L. Tracy and Richard W. Robins, "The Self in Self-Conscious Emotions: A Cog nitive Appraisal Approach," in *The Self-Conscious Emotions Theory and Research*, ed. Jessica L. Tracy, Richard W. Robins and June Price Tangney (New York: Guilford, 2007) 3–20.

18. Goffman continues to dominate theories of embarrassment. For two recent theo-ries of embarrassment, see the following, which prominently feature Goffman: Luke Purshouse, "Embarrassment: A Philosophical Analysis," *Philosophy* 76, no. 298 (2001): 515–40 and Yotam Benziman, "Embarrassment," *The Journal of Value Inquiry* 54 (2020): 77–89.

19. The following example from modern psychology does not explicitly mention Goffman. Nevertheless, the author sees embarrassment as a self-reflexive emotion that is unleashed when context-specific role expectations are not met. Rowland S. Miller, "Is Embarrassment a Blessing or a Curse?" in Tracy, Robins, and Tangney, *The Self-Conscious Emotions Theory and Research*, 245–62.

20. Goffman 268, my emphasis.

21. Goffman 268.

22. Miller, "Is Embarrassment a Blessing or a Curse?" 247–48.

23. Helmut Schneider, "Standing and Falling in Heinich von Kleist," *MLN* 115, no. 3 (2000): 502–18, here 503.

24. Brown 161–65.

25. Andreas Grimm, "'Auf das Leben bezügliche und vom Leben abgezogene Maximen': Beobachtungen zu Ottiliens Tagebuch," *Goethes Wahlverwandtschaften* (Berlin: De Gruyter, 2010) 137–48.

26. Norbert Bolz, "Die Wahlverwandtschaften," *Goethe Handbuch*, vol. 3 (Stuttgart: Metzler 1997) 152–86.

27. Astrida Orle Tantillo, *Goethe's Elective Affinities and the Critics* (Rochester, NY: Camden House, 2001).

28. Uwe C. Steiner, "'Für sich und für andre vielleicht': Ottilies Selbstsakralisierung und die Lessing-Kritik in Goethes *Wahlverwandtschaften*," in *Schwellenprosa: (Re-) Lektüren zu Goethes Wahlverwandtschaften*, ed. Hannah Dingeldein Anna-Katharina Gisbertz, Sebastian Zilles, and Justus Fetscher (Paderborn: Wilhelm Fink, 2018) 87–104. This translation is my own.

CARRIE COLLENBERG-GONZÁLEZ

# The Daisy Oracle: A New *Gretchenfrage* in Goethe's *Faust*

**Abstract:** The daisy oracle in Goethe's *Faust: Eine Tragödie* (1808) is one of the most prominent instances of flower divination in literary history and is crucial to understanding the Gretchen tragedy. By examining its origin and evolution in German literature and its role within the drama, this article argues that the daisy oracle offers critical insight into Gretchen's agency, desire, and resistance to eighteenth-century gender conventions, and poses an alternative *Gretchenfrage* that demonstrates the character's relationship to love, desire, and the divine. Gretchen, who embodies the characteristics of purity and innocence represented by the daisy, is also the agent who destroys the daisy and thus manipulates her own fate, setting the plot in motion. The coda of this paper outlines some of the most significant iterations of twentieth-century daisy oracles that borrow their form from Goethe, demonstrating the enduring resonance of the daisy oracle and its connotations and positing the daisy oracle as an allegory for the self-destructing potential of humankind's striving to manifest its own ideals and nevertheless achieve redemption.

**Keywords:** Daisy oracle, eternal feminine, *Faust*, flower divination, *Gretchenfrage*

## Introduction

IN THE "GARTEN" ("Garden") scene of Johann Wolfgang von Goethe's *Faust* (1808), Gretchen playfully plucks the petals from a daisy in what seems like nothing more than a childlike game of flower divination.[1] Couched between the scenes of "Straße" ("Street"), in which Faust and Mephistopheles plan their visit to deceive and seduce Gretchen, and "Ein Gartenhäuschen" ("A Garden Bower"), where Faust and Gretchen kiss for the first time, her seemingly innocuous consultation of the daisy oracle changes the action in the drama. Even though it appears to be Faust and Mephistopheles who plan to deceive and seduce Gretchen, it is Gretchen herself who coordinates Faust's declaration of love and thus changes the course of action in the first part of the drama that is often, and for good reason, referred to as the "Gretchen tragedy":

MARGARETE: Laßt einmal!
*(Sie pflückt eine Sternblume und zupft die Blätter ab, eins nach dem andern)*
FAUST: Was soll das? Einen Strauß?
MARGARETE: Nein, es soll nur ein Spiel.
FAUST: Wie?
MARGARETE: Geht! Ihr lacht mich aus.
*(Sie rupft und murmelt)*
FAUST: Was murmelst du?
MARGARETE *(halblaut)*: Er liebt mich—Liebt mich nicht.
FAUST: Du holdes Himmelsangesicht!
MARGARETE *(fährt fort)*: Liebt mich—Nicht—Liebt mich—Nicht—
*(das letzte Blatt ausrupfend, / mit holder Freude)*
Er liebt mich!
FAUST: Ja, mein Kind! Laß dieses Blumenwort
Dir Götterausspruch sein! Er liebt dich!
Verstehst du, was das heißt? Er liebt dich!
*(Er faßt ihre beiden Hände.)*
MARGARETE: Mich überläuft's!
FAUST: O schaudre nicht! Laß diesen Blick,
Laß diesen Händedruck dir sagen,
was unaussprechlich ist:
Sich hinzugeben ganz und eine Wonne
Zu fühlen, die ewig sein muß!
Ewig!—Ihr Ende würde Verzweiflung sein.
Nein, kein Ende! Kein Ende! *(Margarete drückt ihm die Hände, macht sich
los und läuft weg. Er steht einen Augenblick in Gedanken, dann folgt er ihr.)*


MARGARET: Let me do this!
*(She plucks a daisy and pulls out the petals one by one.)*
FAUST: A nosegay? Or what shall it be?
MARGARET: No, it's just a game.
FAUST: What?
MARGARET: Go, you will laugh at me.
*(She pulls out petals and murmurs.)*
FAUST: What do you murmur?
MARGARET *(half aloud)*: He loves me—loves me not.
FAUST: You gentle countenance of heaven!
MARGARET *(continues)*: Loves me—not—loves me—not—
*(tearing out the last leaf, in utter joy:)*
He loves me.
FAUST: Yes, my child. Let this sweet flower's word
Be as a god's word to you. He loves you.
Do you know what this means? He loves you.
*(He takes both her hands.)*
MARGARET: My skin creeps.
FAUST: Oh, shudder not! But let this glance,
And let this clasp of hands tell you
What is unspeakable:

To yield oneself entirely and feel
A rapture which must be eternal.
Eternal! For its end would be despair.
No, no end! No end! *(Margaret clasps his hands, frees herself, and runs away. He stands for a moment, lost in thought; then he follows her.)*

(3178–94)

Their hearts swell in unison the moment Gretchen pulls the last petal, which confirms that Faust must love her; they retreat to the garden bower where they kiss and make their fateful promises that determine the action of the drama. Thus, the daisy oracle in the "Garten" scene can be understood as the inciting incident of the drama—one that is central to the dramatic action of the tragedy but whose influence on the plot has been consistently underestimated.

*Das erregende Moment* (the inciting incident or exciting force) is a term Gustav Freytag uses in his elaboration of the Aristotelian theory of dramatic structure to describe the moment that initiates the rising action of a drama.[2] Freytag writes: "Der Eintritt der bewegten Handlung findet an der Stelle des Dramas statt, wo in der Seele des Helden ein Gefühl oder Wollen aufsteigt, welches die Veranlassung zu der folgenden Handlung wird, oder wo das Gegenspiel den Entschluß faßt, durch seine Hebel den Helden in Bewegung zu setzen" (The beginning of the excited action [complication] occurs at a point where, in the soul of the hero, there arises a feeling of volition which becomes the occasion of what follows; or where the counterplay resolves to use its lever to set the hero in motion).[3] For Freytag, who provides numerous examples to illustrate his theories, the inciting moment in *Faust* is when Mephistopheles crosses the threshold into Faust's study.[4] While Mephistopheles' influence on Faust no doubt changes the course of action in the play, Freytag himself acknowledges inconsistencies in form and the difficulty of wrangling *Faust* into a rigid dramatic structure. Using Freytag's definition of the inciting incident (but overriding his interpretation), the daisy oracle in Goethe's drama fulfills both of Freytag's criteria: first, both Faust and Gretchen experience powerful feelings that change the course of action; and second, Gretchen, the *Gegenspiel* (counterplay), coordinates the scene in order to set the hero in motion.

A close reading of the daisy oracle offers crucial insight into Gretchen's desire and agency and demonstrates her highly ambivalent character. With this in mind, a new *Gretchenfrage* can be posed: one that questions whether Gretchen is not a more complex character than has otherwise been assumed and one that proposes an alternative reading of the dramatic structure of the play. Establishing the centrality of the daisy oracle in *Faust* by examining its history in medieval poetry and folk rhymes contextualizes the unique version presented in Goethe's *Faust* in terms of both form, content, and resonance. The daisy oracle emerges as a site that enables Gretchen's desire and agency and relates to the larger themes of the eternal feminine and redemption in the play. The coda of this paper outlines some of the most significant iterations of twentieth-century daisy oracles that borrow their form from Goethe, demonstrating the enduring resonance of the daisy oracle and its connotations.

## The Daisy Oracle

The folklorist tradition of the daisy oracle is crucial to understanding its significance, traditional coherence, and subsequent challenges to gender conventions in *Faust*. First, it belongs to a long tradition of love oracles that exist in all European languages, it can be found in books of nursery rhymes and children's games, and it is still practiced today.[5] Second, love oracles are games usually played by children or young adults in love that allow the player to divine whether or to what degree they are loved at various stages of courtship. The game thus gives the player (usually deprived of power or agency) a space where they can articulate their desire, imagine agency, and exercise power over their future. Goethe's use is no different. The daisy oracle in *Faust* serves as a device that allows Gretchen to express her desire, assert her agency, and change her fate. However, while love oracles were well known in German culture prior to *Faust*, Goethe's unique rhetoric of the daisy oracle emphasizes its centrality in the tragedy. It marks Gretchen's agency and desire and is likely the source of the daisy oracle as we know it today: "he loves me, he loves me not. . . ."

The earliest known written reference in German to such love oracles comes from a Middle High German poem entitled "Halmorakel" (Straw Oracle, c. 1203) by Walter von der Vogelweide and describes a divination game played with a blade of grass or straw.[6] Goethe may have known Vogelweide's poem from his work in Strasbourg collecting folksongs and medieval literature with his mentor and professor Johann Gottfried Herder.[7] Although there is no clear evidence that Vogelweide's poem inspired the scene in *Faust*, there is some indication that Goethe was following similar conventions of poetic meter. Vogelweide interrupts the meter with "sie tuot, sie entuot, sie tuot, sie entuot, sie tuot!"[8] (she does, she doesn't, she does, she doesn't, she does) while Goethe uses a similar cadence: "Liebt mich – Nicht – Liebt mich – Nicht / Er liebt mich!" (Loves me – not – loves me – not / He loves me!). Goethe often deviates from the Alexandrine and Marigold meter common in *Faust*, and Albrecht Schöne notes deviations in the metrics of this scene in particular that suggest Faust's excitement in his adoption of the metrical characteristics of the preceding lines and of Gretchen's language, a topic that warrants more attention than can be granted here.[9] The game Vogelweide describes and the daisy oracle in *Faust* are similar in meter and in that they both involve plucking blades of grass or petals but Vogelweide's poem does not mention daisies specifically. Goethe's use of this meter together with a daisy in the love oracle marks a significant innovation.

Daisies are well documented in works of English literature by Geoffrey Chaucer and William Shakespeare, but the first known literary reference to a type of oracle using a daisy-like flower can be found in a fifteenth-century manuscript by Clara Hätzlerin from Augsburg. In her short text entitled "Rupfblume" (Plucking Flower) of 1471, Hätzlerin describes the symbolic language of wearing daisies:

> Whoever wears daisies [Rupfblumen, literally, "plucking-flowers"] indicates that he is in doubt whether his love truly loves him! But he who wears them

already plucked except for two remaining petals, that means he will obtain complete justice from his beloved. But he who has only one petal remaining, that means an injustice has happened to him.[10]

Hätzlerin's version indicates significant changes from Vogelweide's aforementioned poem. First, a person is playing the game with a daisy instead of a blade of grass. Second, the meaning of the petals is not determined by plucking them and letting each petal correspond to a prescribed word, but by wearing them and using the number of remaining petals to signify the meaning. Hätzlerin's text is notable as the first known account of a type of daisy oracle in literature, and one that specifies the symbolic language of daisy petals in folk culture but it does not seem to have influenced Goethe's use of the daisy oracle in *Faust* or to have had the same lasting impact.[11]

Goethe's portrayal of the daisy oracle in *Urfaust* (1772–75), *Faust: Ein Fragment* (1790), and *Faust: eine Tragödie* (1808) is nearly identical in all three versions but differs from the variations of the daisy oracle that were circulating at the turn of the nineteenth century.[12] According to examples discovered by Wolfgang Mieder in the folksong archive in Freiburg im Breisgau, the player plucks petals from a daisy and repeats the following sequences until the last petal is gone: "Er liebt mich, von Herzen, mit Schmerzen, ein klein wenig, gar nicht" (He loves me, with all his heart, with suffering, a little bit, not at all).[13] A 1777 letter from Mozart that predates Goethe's *Faust: eine Tragödie* (1808) by nearly forty years but was published just a few years after Goethe's *Urfaust* (1772–75), suggests that the rhetoric of the daisy oracle as collected by Mieder and its implications were well known, which makes Goethe's aberration in *Faust* even more remarkable. At the end of a letter to his father, Mozart writes: "und meine Schwester . . . umarme ich von Herzen, mit Schmerzen, ein wenig oder gar nicht" (and my sister, I hug with all my heart, with suffering, a little, or not at all).[14] Although Goethe does not use this language in the scene with the daisy oracle, he uses "von Herzen" five times in the play, three of which appear in the scenes directly before and after "Garten," demonstrating Goethe's familiarity with the rhyme and emphasizing his unique use of language in the daisy oracle scene.[15] After returning Faust's kiss, Gretchen herself seals the prophecy with an evocation of the well-known rhetoric drawn from the folk tradition of daisy oracles, thus making it clear that, yes, it is this well-known game that she is referring to: "Bester Mann! *von Herzen* lieb' ich dich!" (3206, emphasis added; Dear man! I love you with *all my heart*!).

Most significantly, folklore's plucking oracles extend beyond form and meter to emphasize the agency of the player of the game. In the aforementioned examples, the player of the game manipulates the number of blades of grass or petals to deliver the desired answer. As Vogelweide makes clear already in the thirteenth century, there is more to this game than just luck: as we all know, this game is played because one can always get the right answer in the end. The daisy oracle in Goethe's *Faust* functions accordingly. When Gretchen plays this game, we can assume that she is not merely the victim of chance or fate; rather, Gretchen's daisy oracle is a clear act of agency. By ensuring that the last petal lands on "Er liebt mich" (He loves me), Gretchen employs the daisy oracle to express her desire and fulfill her wishes; she manipulates the daisy oracle to elicit the answer she wants. And, while Faust's declaration of love may be expressed in a third-person register, it is convincing enough for her to lead him to the garden bower where they share their first kiss. Read in this way, Gretchen's manipulation of the otherwise well-known daisy oracle rhetoric emphasizes her agency, desire, and motivation at the most important moment of rising action.

The centrality of the daisy oracle is also evident in the nomenclature in *Faust*, and in Gretchen/Margarete's name in particular. Gretchen, whose complete name is Margarete, is so clearly connected to the daisy that she is even named after it: *"marguerite"*—French for "daisy." Other scholarship suggests plausible explanations of her names connect them to one of Goethe's first loves, the most popular names at the time, biblical names and characters, Christian dates, characters in a range of balladic literature with similar themes, the Latin and Greek word for pearl (*margarita*), and the famous public execution of Susanna Margaretha Brandt, who was tried for infanticide in Goethe's native Frankfurt.[16] The plausibility of these myriad explanations and their coexistence indicates a possibly intentional act by the author. Her name as a simultaneous site of innocence and destruction—of pearls/daisies and their connotations alongside conjoined references to lovers, saints, and child murderers—further emphasizes the nuanced role of the daisy oracle as the inciting incident of the Gretchen tragedy, the moment that realizes her character's transition from a virgin to a child murderer. The impact of the daisy oracle—like Gretchen's fate—hinges on the tension between innocence and desire in the shadow of destruction.

In many ways, the daisy's neat symbolism has supported dominant readings of Gretchen as childlike, innocent, and naive that are enabled by depictions of her by Faust and internalized by Gretchen herself. Gretchen's initiative is, however, startling when contrasted with readings of her character as simple and pious, opinions that Faust himself entertains when he concludes: "Ach, daß die Einfalt, daß die Unschuld nie / Sich selbst und ihren heilgen Wert erkennt! / Daß Demut, Niedrigkeit, die höchsten Gaben / Der liebevoll austeilenden Natur;" (3102; Oh, that the innocent and simple never / Appreciate themselves and their own worth! That meekness and humility, supreme / Among the gifts of loving, lavish nature). The daisy itself is emblematic of her character and is known to represent purity, simplicity, and innocence largely understood within a Christian context and associated with the virgin Mary and infant Christ.[17] The daisy oracle in Goethe's *Faust*, however, can be understood as a subversive and radical device that disrupts moral, religious, and gender conventions: for it is Gretchen—the ostensible embodiment of innocence herself—who destroys the neat symbolism of the daisy by pulling it apart. On the one hand, Gretchen destroys the daisy, and along with it the connotations of innocence in an act that leads to her literal deflowering, setting in motion a chain of events that constitute her tragedy. On the other hand, she eschews moral and religious convention for love and is ultimately redeemed. A closer examination of the daisy oracle demonstrates the complexity of Gretchen's character in terms of desire for *Faust* and her aspirations of upward social mobility.

# Desire

Gretchen's disavowal of moral and religious convention is located in the scene directly following the daisy oracle scene. Gretchen, who has just realized her power and agency in the destruction of the daisy and the orchestration of Faust's declaration of love, says: "Mich überläufts!" (3187) to which Faust responds, "O shaudre nicht!" (3188). The verbs *überlaufen* and *schaudern* both have complex definitions that are related to quivers of fear and pleasure but translators and readers of the German often associate these lines solely with fear, all but eliding the possibility of Gretchen's experience of desire combined with the acknowledgment of her own agency. The three most well-known English translations render her utterance "Mich überlauft's!" and his response "O shaudre nicht!" as, respectively: "My skin creeps" / "Oh, shudder not!"; "I'm afraid!" / "Read the look on my face"; and "I'm shuddering!" / "Oh, do not shudder!"[18] While these translations of *überlaufen* and *schaudern* evoke the sense of fear associated with Gretchen's potential transgression against social, religious, and gender conventions in combination with the uneasy feeling that she has around Mephistopheles, they almost universally exclude the possibility of Gretchen's carnal and intuitive desire for Faust and her projection of their future together.

If we acknowledge the possibility of Gretchen's desire, then the following connotation of *Schauder* and its relationship to *überlaufen* in the *Goethe Lexikon* might be more appropriate: "in gemildertem Sinne = heutigem "Schauer," d.i. wohltuend überrieselnde Erschütterung: Meine Augen hatten bisher auf diesen köstlichen Worten geruht, ein Sch. Überlief mich vom Kopf bis auf die Füße" (in a more mild sense = today's shiver, that is, a pleasing, overwhelming quiver: My eyes rested on these precious words, a shiver overwhelmed me from head to toe).[19] In this sense, Gretchen is, as Marlene Dietrich's character in *The Blue Angel* (1930) sings in the famous song written much later, "from head to toe in love." Like Lola Lola, Gretchen is sovereign in her desire and the stage directions indicate that Faust, like the other dusty professor we know from the film, is bewildered: "Margarete drückt ihm die Hände, macht sich los und läuft weg. Er steht einen Augenblick in Gedanken, dann folgt er ihr" (3194). Gretchen's flirtatious actions described in the stage directions that follow this moment indicate her autonomy: "Margarete springt herein, steckt sich hinter die Tür, hält die Fingerspitze an die Lippen, und guckt durch die Ritze" (3203; Margaret leaps into it, hides behind the door, puts the top of one finger to her lips, and peeks through the crack). This is a description of a woman who knows what she wants. No matter what their intentions were, there is no indication in the scene that it was Mephistopheles' magic or presence that made Gretchen invite Faust into the garden bower for a secret rendezvous. The daisy oracle is the device through which Gretchen singlehandedly becomes an agent of her own desire, whether or not she does so in the presence of a demon.

The daisy oracle also suggests a framework that explains Gretchen's desire for upward social mobility. In addition to the "von Herzen, mit Schmerzen, ein klein wenig, gar nicht" variety of daisy oracles, Mieder cites another common variation of the game in the nineteenth century that concerned the class standing of one's future spouse or job. While plucking petals (or by letting them fall), the player says: "Hirt, Wirth, Soldat, Edelmann, Bettelmann, Bauer" (Herdsman, Landlord, Soldier, Nobleman, Beggar, Peasant).[20] While it remains unclear (and unlikely) that these varieties were in circulation when Goethe wrote *Faust*, the daisy oracle's morphology provides an example of how innocent rhymes and actions can both embody and reflect the desires of rhyme sayers. While Goethe may not have known this iteration of the oracle, Gretchen's desire for upward social mobility is clearly demonstrated throughout the drama. Gretchen, who gazed at herself in the mirror while wearing the jewels that were left in her room, and who had just finished telling Faust about her arduous, precarious social situation and difficult relationship with her mother, is intrigued by her perception of Faust's social class and the life it might afford her. As the French word for "daisy," as well as the Latin and Greek word for "pearl," Gretchen's name—Margarete—suggests her desire for a better life.[21] Gretchen exceeds interpretations that might see her interest in Faust as a "a paternal 'knight in shining armor' who represents freedom, the outside world, will, agency, and desire."[22] Her intent to ensnare him indicates her autonomy as an agent of her own carnal desire as well as her aspirations of upward social mobility.

Gretchen's highly ambivalent character marks her as not only a female victim of patriarchy but also a feminist heroine. Barbara Becker-Cantarino emphasizes Goethe's patriarchal order in *Faust* in terms of Gretchen's internalization of the bourgeois male world, reductive depictions of witches and infanticide (and thus women's history), and the male appropriation of childbirth and self-sacrifice for his redemption.[23] She concludes: "Gretchen's story is complex and in its patriarchal vision depressingly perceptive of what Goethe scholars have aptly called 'the deepest drives of western civilization.'"[24] Benjamin Bennett focuses on Goethe's use of women as destabilizing factors in literature that disrupt moral order; however, he does not include Gretchen's character in this lineup.[25] Adrian del Caro sees Gretchen as a representation of an Ariadne figure caught in a labyrinth of the eternal feminine.[26] Gail K. Hart dismantles generic conventions of the bourgeois tragedy by pointing out the lack of a paternal figure in *Faust* and Gretchen's role as a leader and embodiment of the eternal feminine that pulls (*ewig heran zieht*) instead of follows.[27] Finally, Lilian R. Furst acknowledges Gretchen's desire and agency as transgressions: "Gretchen is breaking out of the ethical and social frame posited for women in the eighteenth century. By advancing a personal code of conduct and by hazarding an apologia for erotic feelings, she can be taken as an early example of a Romantic heroine."[28] Remarkably, despite their groundbreaking work on the figure of Gretchen, not one of these scholars has paid much attention to the role of the daisy oracle, which makes Gretchen's feminist moment as image and iconoclast possible and validates her complexity by acknowledging her agency and desire.[29] This reading profoundly alters the overall approach to reading *Faust* as a drama viewed through the lens of the *Gretchenfrage*.

# A New *Gretchenfrage*

Most readers familiar with the reception of *Faust* will be familiar with the established terms used in scholarly work on Gretchen, such as the "Gretchen tragedy," the idea of a play within in a play, "Das Ewig-Weibliche" (12110; the eternal feminine), the last words of salvation spoken by the Chorus Mysticus, and the so-called *Gretchenfrage*. The *Gretchenfrage* refers to the moment in Martha's garden when Gretchen asks Faust whether he believes in God (3415), a moment that is often interpreted as an example of Gretchen's naivete or piety, of her hope that Faust will feel morally indebted to protect her, of her presumed belief that love without faith is inconceivable, and of her unease in the presence of Mephistopheles.[30] Despite the significance of the *Gretchenfrage* in its confirmation of Faust's agnosticism, most readings oversimplify Gretchen's character or ignore her agency completely. Faust's answer to the *Gretchenfrage* has no impact on Gretchen's decision to willingly rendezvous with Faust that night. She gives her mother a sleeping potion from a source she suspects is highly unreliable, which leads to her mother's death, and then engages in decidedly impious and illegal acts, which lead to her pregnancy and eventually infanticide, incarceration, and death. A more apt *Gretchenfrage* comes at the end of the same scene in Martha's garden when she says "Was tu ich nicht um deinetwillen?" (3514; What would I not do for your sake?). And yet, Gretchen's character cannot be reduced to a single question. An alternative *Gretchenfrage* asks the reader to consider her as a viable and autonomous character with multifaceted concerns and desires, one that—through the daisy oracle—offers insight into the role of her complex character in a complicated play that explores what it means to be human.

Gretchen had already transgressed social norms by accepting Faust's gift of jewels and by meeting him alone, but the inciting incident of the daisy oracle seals the deal, literally with a kiss, which subsequently leads to sex, pregnancy, death, banishment, infanticide and—redemption? This last word is the hardest to reconcile when one demands a neat reading of Gretchen and the drama. How is it that Gretchen is redeemed despite her perfectly unchristian and amoral actions? With this question in mind, the daisy oracle also offers an allegorical understanding of the drama. If one takes the daisy's symbolic currency as representative of the fantasy of a moral order (innocence/Christian redemption), then Gretchen's redemption can be understood as the judgment that destroys this symbol. That is, Gretchen is as much a symbol of innocence as Christianity is simply based on good versus evil in Goethe's *Faust*. By allowing Gretchen to be redeemed despite her transgressions, Goethe establishes a moral order that is more realistic than common perceptions of Christian doctrine allow.

The daisy oracle is key to understanding the Gretchen tragedy, but it is also semantically related to the eternal feminine and the ending of *Faust II*. After the last petal divines their love, Gretchen and Faust stand together, trembling, clasping hands. Gretchen says that she is overwhelmed and Faust replies:

> "O schaudre nicht! Laß diesen Blick,
> Laß diesen Händedruck dir sagen,
> was unaussprechlich ist:
> Sich hinzugeben ganz und eine Wonne
> Zu fühlen, die ewig sein muß!
> Ewig!—Ihr Ende würde Verzweiflung sein.
> Nein, kein Ende! Kein Ende!" (3186-95)

> Oh, shudder not! But let this glance,
> And let this clasp of hands tell you
> What is unspeakable:
> To yield oneself entirely and feel
> A rapture which must be eternal.
> Eternal! For its end would be despair.
> No, no end! No end!

Gretchen's invocation of the daisy oracle is a proposition that elicits Faust's declaration of love and provides him with an enticing prelude into what a surrender to the ineffable eternal feminine might imply. Goethe returns to this sense of surrender in the final lines of *Faust II*:

> Alles Vergängliche
> Ist nur ein Gleichnis;
> Das Unzulängliche,
> Hier wird's Ereignis;
> Das Unbeschreibliche,
> Hier ist's getan;
> Das Ewig-Weibliche
> Zieht uns hinan. (12104-10)

> What is destructible
> Is but a parable;
> What fails ineluctably,
> The undeclarable,
> Here it was seen,
> Here it was action;
> The Eternal-Feminine
> Lures to perfection.

In both passages, Faust describes the ineffable (*was unaussprechlich ist* and *Das Unbeschreibliche*) in allegorical terms related to the feminine. The final passage quite literally spells out the allegorical power of the daisy oracle in the evocation of the words "Alles Vergängliche / Ist nur ein Gleichnis." (12104; What is destructible or transient is but a parable) *Alles Vergängliche* evokes established associations with mortality, flowers, innocence—and with the oracle itself—which must be destroyed in order to prophesize. As an allegory, the daisy oracle portends the destructive nature of humankind's illusory drive to manifest its own ideals.

## **Coda**

Although it is possible that Goethe's use of daisies in a love oracle was the first to have lasting impact, it is difficult to make such claims when using folk motifs that are generally known.[31] That said, the daisy oracle as we know it today (he loves me/he loves me not) was likely inspired by Goethe's use of it in *Faust* in what was to become one of the most resonant dramas in history. Many nineteenth-century etchings and representations of Gretchen pulling apart the daisy with Faust—while Mephistopheles lurks in the background—respond to the tension inherent in the scene, thus emphasizing the destructive potential of the daisy oracle in the presence of a demon or vice versa.[32] This portentous juxtaposition of innocence and annihilation has had a remarkable impact on twentieth-century depictions of the daisy oracle in Europe and the United States that seem to use both the form and signification of Goethe's example as a source.

Twentieth-century references to the daisy oracle in German culture reflect its transition from a simple game of love divination to one that expanded to allow the player to make other choices as well. Mieder notes numerous European cartoons, advertisements, and headlines in *Simplicissimus*, *Der Spiegel*, and the *Frankfurter Allgemeine Zeitung* and other sources that reference the daisy oracle's game to determine love or class, employment status, advertisement of cars, lotion, the euro, and pregnancy tests, as well as voting and election results, moral questions, and political issues like environmentalism and atomic warfare.[33] The connection to atomic warfare is particularly ominous in that it combines the tension inherent in Goethe's juxtaposition of the daisy and the devil in *Faust* with a twentieth-century politics of annihilation.

The most infamous reiteration of this tension between innocence and annihilation in the legacy of the daisy oracle is the 1964 Lyndon B. Johnson presidential campaign advertisement in the United States known as "Peace, Little Girl" or "Daisy Girl," which was used to run against Republican candidate for president Senator Barry M. Goldwater.[34] Although the ad aired only once, it had a stunning impact and is known as a seminal moment in the history of negative political television advertisements.[35] The sixty-second advertisement begins with a medium shot of a three-year-old girl in a grassy field who is plucking the petals of a daisy and counting to ten. When she gets to ten, the ambient bird sounds are replaced by the harsh male voice of a mission-control countdown. She looks up, the shot freezes, and the camera zooms in; it reaches her pupil at the same time the voice reaches zero. Then the extreme closeup of the black pupil cuts to an explosion and the iconic mushroom cloud of an atomic bomb. An excerpt from one of Lyndon B. Johnson's speeches is heard over the rolling fiery clouds: "These are the stakes: to make a world in which all of God's children can live, to go into the dark, we much either love each other or we must die."[36] These words are then followed by: "Vote for President Johnson on November 3rd. The stakes are too high for you to stay home."

The juxtaposition of a symbol of innocence with the very real threat of nuclear war resonated with an American public in the midst of the Cold War, just two years after the Cuban missile crisis. Even though it aired only once and did not name the opponent, the message was clear: there is too much at stake to vote for Goldwater. This juxtaposition is also important for notions of twentieth-century flower-bearing terrorists[37] or films like James Whale's *Frankenstein* (1931), which famously features a daisy in the scene in which the monster meets the young girl, Maria, and throws her into the river where she drowns.[38] Although these examples do not directly quote *Faust*, it is likely that they draw their impact from the enduring juxtaposition of Gretchen and the daisy oracle alongside the demon Mephistopheles. Combining a countdown and the little girl with a daisy under the threat of nuclear annihilation alongside the excerpt from Johnson's speech, that "we must love each other or we must die," is a decidedly Faustian gesture.

It is hardly surprising that a scene from Goethe's Faust—one of the most scrutinized dramas in the world—has had such a pronounced impact on popular and consumer culture, but it is remarkable that the significance of the daisy oracle has gone unnoticed for so long. In addition to being one of the first literary references to flower divination in this manner, Goethe's use of the daisy oracle is notable for: (1) his deviation from its folk form (from "von Herzen / mit Schmerzen" to "Er liebt mich / liebt mich nicht"); (2) the tension created by the juxtaposition of the daisy oracle in the presence of the demon Mephistopheles; (3) the significance of the oracle in the action of the plot as the inciting incident of the first part of the drama, the so-called Gretchen tragedy that demonstrates Gretchen's agency and desire and; (4) the legacy of the daisy oracle in post-Goethean popular culture. Reading the causality of action in Goethe's *Faust* in terms of the daisy oracle reveals the nuances of Gretchen's highly ambivalent character and renders her autonomy and desire in terms of her transgression, transience, and destruction. The daisy oracle is the inciting incident that sets the plot in motion and provides mutual access for both Gretchen and Faust to love, desire, the divine, and eternity while simultaneously serving as an allegory for the self-destructing potential of humankind's striving to manifest its own ideals, and still achieve redemption.

*Portland State University*

## NOTES

1. Translation of the scene's name is by Walter Kaufman, *Goethe's Faust* (New York: Anchor, 1990). Further references to this source will appear parenthetically in the text.

2. Gustav Freytag, *Die Technik des Dramas* (Leipzig: S. Hirzel, 1863) 199.

3. Freytag, *Die Technik des Dramas*, 105. For translation see Gustav Freytag, *Technique of the Drama: An Exposition of Dramatic Composition and Art*, trans. Elias J. MacEwan (Chicago: Scott, Foresman & Company, 1900) 121.

4. Freytag acknowledges that the love scene is "von wunderbarer Schönheit" (extraordinarily beautiful) but also that the scenes "nicht viel Anderes sind als Selbstgespräche Gretchens" (not much more than Gretchen's soliloquies). Freytag, *Die Technik des Dramas*, 106.

5. Wolfgang Mieder, "Modern Variants of the Daisy Oracle 'He loves me, he loves me not,'" *Midwestern Journal of Language and Folklore*, 11 (1985) 65-115. See also Wolfgang Mieder, *Liebt mich, liebt mich nicht: Studien und Belege zum Blumenorakel* (Vienna: Edition Praesens, 2001); Wolfgang Mieder, "Moderne Varianten des Blumenorakels: 'Er (sie) liebt mich, er (sie) liebt mich nicht,'" in *Festschrift für Lutz Röhrich zum 60. Geburtstag*, ed. Rolf Wilhelm Brednich und Jürgen Dittmar (Berlin: Erich Schmidt, 1982) 335-45. See also Ignaz Zingerle, *Das deutsche Kinderspiel im Mittelalter* (Innsbruck: Wagner, 1873) 32; and Iona and Peter Opie, *The Oxford Dictionary of Nursery Rhymes* (Oxford: Clarendon, 1951) 331-32 and 404-5.

6. Walter von der Vogelweide, "Mich hat ein Halm froh gemacht," in *Deutsche Dichtung des Mittelalters: Von den Anfängen bis zum Mittelalter*, vol. 1, ed. Michael Curschmann and Ingeborg Glier (Munich: Carl Hanser, 1980) 606-7.

7. Goethe also collaborated with Herder on *Von deutscher Art und Kunst (1773)*— an essay whose focus on primitive poetry features Ossian and many children's songs. Although Vogelweide's poem was not published in Herder's text, the children's songs in *Von deutscher Art und Kunst* demonstrate the likeliness of a relationship between their collaboration and Goethe's own work. For example, see Herder's recorded *Fabelliedchen* that begins "Es sah ein Knab' ein Röslein stehn / Ein Röslein auf der Haiden" is almost exactly Goethe's poem "Röslein auf der Heide."

8. "Mich hât ein halm gemachet frô / er giht, ich sül genâde vinden. / Ich maz daz selbe kleine strô, / als ich hie vor gesach von kinden. / Nû hoeret unde market, ob siz denne tuo: / "sie tuot, sie entuot, sie tuot, sie entuot, sie tuot!— / swie dicke ich also maz, so was daz ende ie guot. / daz troestet mich: dâ hoeret ouch geloube zuo." Vogelweide, "Mich hat ein Halm froh gemacht," 606-7.

9. Albrecht Schöne, *Johann Wolfgang Goethe Faust Kommentare*, in Johann Wolfgang von Goethe, *Sämtliche Werke* (Frankfurt/Main: Deutscher Klassiker Verlag, 1999) volume vol. 7.2, here 309. Goethe's deviation from the Alexandrine and Marigold forms in "Garten" might be explained if we read Gretchen's lines in dactylic hexameter, which is the meter Greeks would use to interpret Pythia's oracles. If so, this would further emphasize the significance of the oracle.

10. *Wer rupffs plümen tregt, maint, er sey in zweifel, ob In sein lieb gerecht main! Wer sy aber tregt gerupfft vsz, on die zwey pletter, vnd die geleich stand, Bedeüttet, das er gantzer gerechtikaitt gewert ist von seinem liebsten! Wellichern aber ain plettlin allain ist beliben stan, Das maint, Im sey vngeleich geschehen!* Mieder, *Liebt mich*, 4. See also Carl Haltaus, ed., *Liederbuch der Clara Hätzlerin* (Quedlinburg: Gottfried Basse, 1840) 173.

11. Hätzlerin's version differs from other references to daisy oracles at that time. A tapestry from Strasbourg circa 1430 depicts a man and a woman sitting under a tree and removing the petals from a flower together. They appear to be playing the same game depicted in *Faust*. Malcolm Jones, "Lovers grafting clasped hands of fidelity, and 'daisy oracle': tapestry (detail) Strasbourg, c. 1430" in *The Secret Middle Ages* (Connecticut: Praeger, 2003) 165-67. See Jean-Baptiste Greuze, "La Simplicité" (1759) for another example of the daisy oracle in painting. Cited in Mieder, *Liebt mich*, 86.

12. Johann Wolfgang von Goethe, *Urfaust, Faust Fragment, Faust I: Ein Paralleldruck*, ed. Werner Keller (Frankfurt a/M: Insel, 1985) 408-11.

13. Mieder, "Götzenhain, Anfang August 1858 (DVA E12388)," in *Studien und Belege*, 7.

14. Mieder, *Liebt mich*, 5, 45. Wolfgang Amadeus Mozart, *Briefe und Aufzeichnungen*, vol. 2, ed. Wilhelm A. Bauer und Otto Erich Deutsch (Kassel: Bärenreiter, 1962) 139.

15. In "Straße," when Mephistopheles asks Faust whether he will swear his love to Gretchen, Faust responds: "Und zwar von Herzen" (3054; and indeed with all my heart). Later, after their kiss, Gretchen declares her love to Faust: "Bester Mann! Von Herzen lieb ich dich!" (3206; Dear Man, I love you with all my heart!). The other two instances are also related: (1) When Faust tells Wagner about the passion needed to study, he says: "Doch werdet ihr nie Herz zu Herzen schaffen, / Wenn es euch nicht von Herzen geht." (544-45; But from heart to heart you will never create. / If from your heart it does not come.); and (2) When Faust demands that Mephistopheles find more jewels, Mephistopheles responds sarcastically: "Ja, gnäd'ger Herr, von Herzen gerne." (2861; Yes, gracious lord, it is a pleasure.). In *Urfaust*, Goethe uses "Bester Mann schon lange lieb ich dich" but returns to the "Bester Mann! Von Herzen lieb' ich dich!" in *Fragment* and *Faust I*.

16. See Ann White, *Names and Nomenclature in Goethe's "Faust"* (Doctoral dissertation, University of London, 1980).

17. See Rowena and Rupert Shepherd, "Daisy," in *1000 Symbols: What Shapes Mean in Art & Myth* (London: Thames & Hudson, 2002) 264.

18. See also "I'm afraid!" and "Read the look on my face." (completely omitting Faust's response) in Martin Greenberg's translation of *Faust: A Tragedy* (New Haven, CT: Yale UP, 2014) 114; and "I'm shuddering!" and "Oh do not shudder!" in Walter Arndt's translation of *Faust* (New York: Norton, 2000) 87.

19. Paul Fischer, "Schauder," in *Goethe-Wortschatz: Ein sprachgeschichtliches Wörterbuch zu Goethes Sämtlichen Werken* (Leipzig: Emil Rohmkopf Verlag, 1929) 524-25. All translations, unless otherwise noted, are my own.

20. Mieder, "Kempten, 21. November 1902 (DVA H4709)," in *Liebt mich*, 24.

21. See Ann White's insightful analysis of the connection between daisies and pearls with regard to Gretchen's character in *Names and Nomenclature*, 64-95.

22. Christoph E. Schweitzer, "Gretchen and the Feminine in Goethe's Faust," in *Interpreting Goethe's Faust Today*, ed. Jane K. Brown, Meredith Lee, and Thomas P. Saine (Columbia, SC: Camden House, 1994) 134.

23. Barbara Becker-Cantarino, "Witch and Infanticide: Imaging the Female in Faust I," *Goethe Yearbook* (Columbia, SC: Camden House, 1994) 1-22.

24. Becker-Cantarino, "Witch and Infanticide," 18. See Hermann Weigand, "Goethe's Faust: An Introduction for Students and Teachers of General Literature," *The German Quarterly* 37 (1964): 467.

25. Benjamin Bennett, *Goethe as Woman: The Undoing of Literature* (Detroit: Wayne State UP, 2001).

26. Adrian Del Caro, "Margarete-Ariadne: Faust's Labyrinth," *Goethe Yearbook* 18, 2011, 223-43.

27. Gail Hart, "Das Ewig-Weibliche nasführet dich: Feminine Leadership in Goethe's Faust and Sacher-Masoch's Venus," in Brown, Lee, and Saine, *Interpreting Goethe's Faust Today* (Columbia, SC: Camden House, 1994) 112-22.

28. Lilian R. Furst, "The Problem of Gretchen," in Approaches to Teaching Goethe's Faust, ed. Douglas J. McMillan (New York: Modern Language Association, 1987) 49.

29. For a reading of Gretchen's agency and relationship to allegory, see Patricia Anne Simpson, "Gretchen's Ghosts: Goethe, Adorno, and the Literature of Refuge," in *Goethe's Ghosts: Reading and the Persistence of Literature*, ed. Simon Richter and Richard Block (NY: Boydell & Brewer, 2013) 168-85.

30. Benedikt Jeßing, Bernd Lutz, and Inge Wild, eds. "Religionsgespräch," in *Metzler Goethe Lexikon* (Stuttgart: Verlag J. B. Metzler, 1999) 411.

31. I am indebted to Wolfgang Mieder for his insight and feedback in our correspondences about this paper. Special thanks to the students in my Fall 2018 Age of Goethe class, especially to Christine Claringbold, whose poetry and initial question about Gretchen and the daisy oracle inspired this paper as my response.

32. Mieder, *Liebt mich*, 87–95.

33. Mieder, *Liebt mich*, 102–60.

34. The ad ran once on September 7, 1964. It was made by the advertising firm Doyle Dane Bernbach (DDB) and was part of a larger campaign whose shock value was earned in the manipulation of other sacred images of purity (daisy oracle, licking ice cream, sawing up a US map, and hands ripping up social security cards). Robert Mann, "How the 'Daisy' Ad Changed Everything about Political Advertising," *Smithsonian Magazine*, April 13, 2016.

35. See Edwin Diamond and Stephen Bates, *The Spot: The Rise of Political Advertising on Television* (Cambridge, MA: MIT Press, 1992) 128.

36. The words are from a speech Johnson gave on April 17, 1964. The excerpt was adapted from W. H. Auden's poem "September 1, 1939," which Auden adapted from scripture (John 3:14).

37. See Patricia Melzer, *Death in the Shape of a Young Girl* (New York: New York UP, 2015).

38. This differs from Mary Wollstonecraft Shelly's *Frankenstein* where there is no daisy. Instead, Frankenstein saves a young girl from drowning only to be shot by a "rustic" who mistook his resuscitation for murder, which in turn leads to Frankenstein's resolve to "vow eternal hatred and vengeance to all mankind." Mary Shelley, *Frankenstein* (New York: Bantam Dell, 2003) 130.

HANS LIND

# Goethes *Der Zauberflöte zweyter Theil* als Bruch: Zur Semantik des Zauberbegriffs im ausgehenden 18. Jahrhundert

**Abstract:** Der Beitrag wendet sich gegen einen Teil der Forschung zu Goethes *Der Zauberflöte zweyter Theil* (entstanden 1795–1802), der eine ungebrochene Kontinuität zwischen der *Zauberflöte* von Mozart und Schikaneder und Goethes Fortsetzung annimmt. Es ist These dieses Beitrags, dass sich Goethes Fortsetzung von der Vorlage in einem äußerst maßgeblichen Detail unterscheidet: Während Schikaneders Libretto in einem Kontinuum verankert ist, welches den Zauberbegriff seit dem Barock rationalisiert und empfindsam umgeprägt hat, hat Goethe sich mit seiner Fortsetzung nicht nur graduell von der Tradition eines rationalisierten Verständnisses des Zaubers gelöst, sondern vielmehr kategorisch. Goethes *Der Zauberflöte zweyter Theil* erweist sich als Absage an eine semantische Tradition, die sich noch in der zweiten Hälfte des 18. Jahrhunderts in einem inflationären Schrifttum in verschiedensten Dimensionen entfaltet hatte. Um diesen Bruch nachzuweisen, wird der Beitrag eine Einführung in die etablierte semantische Praxis eines ausschließlich wirkungsästhetisch verstandenen Begriffs des "Zaubers" bieten (von Musik/Dichtkunst über Psychologie bis hin zur Anthropologie), die sich teils geographisch, teils gattungsspezifisch ausdifferenziert hat, und von der sich Goethes Verwendung des Begriffs in seiner *Zauberflöte* dezidiert absetzt.

**Keywords:** *Zauberflöte*, Schikaneder, Mozart, Zauber, Semantik, Wirkungsästhetik, Psychologie, Musik, Liebe, *Magic Flute*, magic, semantics, aesthetics, psychology, music, love

G OETHES *DER ZAUBERFLÖTE ZWEYTER THEIL*[1] (entstanden 1795–1802)[2] markiert das Ende einer Zeit, die als Rückkehr der Zauberspiele in die Annalen der Theatergeschichte eingegangen ist, wobei sich der Musikzauber als fast wichtigster Gemeinplatz etabliert hat. Dabei scheint sich dieser Diskurs der zweiten Hälfte des 18. Jahrhunderts in einer Hinsicht nicht maßgeblich vom Spätbarock zu unterscheiden: Mit einer fast naiv anmutenden Ernsthaftigkeit werden noch bei den Enzyklopädisten die Mythen der Zauberkraft der Musik abgearbeitet und bestätigt,[3] und dies bis hin zur "Huldigung der Macht der Musik (als anthropologische Konstante)"[4] in Goethes *Novelle*. Zwar existieren im 18. Jahrhundert durchaus kritische Gegenstimmen. Indes sind diese eher verhalten. Und, wie ich an anderer Stelle zeige,[5] ist ein Dissens gerade in den letzten zwei Jahrzehnten des 18. Jahrhunderts tatsächlich auch eine Gattungsfrage: Während im Sprechtheater der Orpheus-Mythos und damit die Macht der Musik ironisch-kritisch relativiert wird, findet letztere sich hingegen im Musiktheater emphatisch bestätigt (von Christoph Willibald Gluck[6] bis Ferdinand Paer[7]).

Dies sollte indes nicht darüber hinwegtäuschen, dass, auch wenn in der zeitgenössischen Diskussion die Spanne der Macht und Wirkungen der Musik auffallend identisch geblieben ist,[8] nichtsdestoweniger der Rationalismus der Aufklärung in diesem Diskurs ebenso deutliche Spuren hinterlassen hat, wie die Empfindsamkeit. Ebenso wenig sollte übersehen werden, dass in den 1790er Jahren mit der Romantik eine wesentliche semantische Umwertung stattfinden wird, die diesen stetigen Rationalisierungsprozess, der in den 1780er Jahren auch im Hinblick auf die Thematisierung des Topos in den Künsten inflationäre Züge annimmt, abrupt beendet—wobei für diesen Bruch mit der semantischen Praxis Goethes *Der Zauberflöte Zweyter Theil* durchaus als paradigmatisch verstanden werden kann.

Diese Gemengelage ist Ausgangpunkt meines Beitrages. Seine These ist, dass Goethes *Zauberflöte* von der Vorlage Schikanders und Mozarts im Hinblick auf die Semantik des "Zaubers" tatsächlich eine Kluft trennt: Während Schikaneders Text in einem Kontinuum verankert ist, welches den Zauberbegriff seit dem Barock rationalisiert und empfindsam umgeprägt hat, hat Goethe sich mit seiner Fortsetzung nicht nur graduell von der Tradition eines rationalisierten Verständnisses des (Musik-)Zaubers gelöst, sondern vielmehr kategorisch. Goethes *Der Zauberflöte zweyter Theil* erweist sich hier als Absage an die Tradition einer Rationalisierung des Musikzaubers, die sich in einem inflationär erscheinenden Schrifttum in verschiedensten Dimensionen entfaltet hatte. Und es ist dieser Bruch, der leicht übersehen wird, wenn Goethes Fortsetzung der *Zauberflöte* in einer Kontinuität mit der *Zauberflöte* von Schikaneder und Mozart gelesen wird. Um ihn herauszuarbeiten, werde ich zunächst meine These im Kontext bisheriger Forschung darstellen. Danach soll die Ubiquität einer Rationalisierung des Zauberbegriffs nachgewiesen werden, was neben einem kurzen Abriss der Behandlung des Musikzaubers in wissenschaftlichem Schrifttum und Dichtung gerade auch eine diachrone Analyse erfordert, die die zeitgenössische Verwendung des Begriffs in seiner Breite abarbeitet und die zugrundeliegenden rationalistischen Erklärungsmodelle freilegt—und hier auch darlegt, inwieweit die Zaubermetapher in den verschiedenen Sparten (von Rhetorik und Poetik bis hin zu Psychologie und Anthropologie) eine vergleichbare Verwendung gefunden hat. Es ist meine Überzeugung, dass die Tragweite des Bruchs von Goethes *Der Zauberflöte zweyter Theil* mit dieser semantischen Tradition, in der sich Schikaneders *Zauberflöte* bewegt, erst angemessen erfasst werden kann, wenn die Allgegenwärtigkeit einer bestimmten semantischen Praxis etabliert ist, die sich teils geographisch, teils gattungsspezifisch ausdifferenziert hat, und von der sich Goethes Verwendung des Begriffs in seiner *Zauberflöte* dezidiert absetzt. Der Beitrag wird dann in einem kurzen Abriss den Wandel der Semantik von Schikaneder und Mozarts *Zauberflöte* über Christian

August Vulpius' Weimarer Fassung bis hin zu Goethes Fortsetzung darstellen, um hier die Diskontinuitäten offenzulegen, die in dieser Hinsicht zwischen den verschiedenen Behandlungen des Zauberflötenthemas bestehen.

## Stimmen

Die in der Forschung immer wieder beobachtbare Annahme einer Kontinuität von Vorlage und Fortsetzung ist bei oberflächlicher Betrachtung zunächst durchaus zutreffend. Bereits mit dem Titel schließt Goethe an Schikaneders Erfolgsoper an, und sowohl stoff- als auch motivgeschichtlich bestehen viele Gemeinsamkeiten.[9] Ein solches war aus wirkungsästhetischer Perspektive durchaus intendiert, sollte doch laut Goethe die "Erinnerung an die erste *Zauberflöte* . . . immer angefesselt bleiben."[10] Und auch aus einer formgeschichtlichen Perspektive besteht eine nicht zu leugnende Verwandtschaft.[11] Gemeinsamkeiten ergeben sich zudem im Hinblick auf einen auch zeitgeschichtlich deutbaren "Schatten" beider Opern.[12]

Der Fehler eines Teils der Anhänger einer Kontinuitätsthese besteht indes darin, aus stoff-, form- und motivgeschichtlicher Verwandtschaft auch auf eine ideengeschichtliche, wenn nicht gar ideologische Kontinuität zu schließen, welche zumindest im Hinblick auf die Semantik des Musikzaubers, der bei Schikaneder und Mozart als wesentliches Thema der Oper verstanden werden muss, nicht besteht.[13] Goethe hat für diesen Anschein einer Kontinuität tatsächlich selbst den Grundstein gelegt: mit seiner Aussage, dass er mit seiner Fortsetzung Schikaneders "Verhältnisse" einer Steigerung unterziehen wolle.[14] Goethes Diktum entsprechend wird Goethes *Zauberflöte* dann auch als "gesteigerte Wiederholung"[15] der Vorlage gelesen,[16] bis hin zu deren "Vervollkommnung,"[17] wobei sich hier eine Steigerung nicht nur aus wirkungsästhetischer Perspektive,[18] sondern durchaus auch ideologisch gedacht findet: als "Steigerung der Humanitätsidee."[19] Verleitet hat einen Teil der Forschung zudem eine weitere vermeintliche Kontinuität, die mit der Semantik des Zauberbegriffs in enger Verbindung steht, und zwar hinsichtlich der Mysterienkonzeption der beiden Opern.[20]

Jane Brown hat das Verhältnis dagegen zutreffender als "Ausbeutung seines Vorgängers" beschrieben,[21] und auch andere haben bei Goethe eher eine funktionale Approbation des Materials festgestellt.[22] Teils hat es dabei sogar den Anschein, als ob Goethe, indem er in der Schikaneder'schen *Zauberflöte* eine Präfiguration seiner eigenen Überzeugungen erblickte,[23] die Vorlage selbst einer Fehllektüre unterwirft, was gerade auch den "höheren Sinn" der "Erscheinungen"[24] betrifft, die Goethe in Schikaneders Text erkannt haben will. Teile der Forschung sind dann mit mystizistischen oder pantheistischen Lektüren von Schikaneders Vorlage auch "Goethes eigenem Wink"[25] gefolgt[26] und haben einen gemeinsamen geistigen "Wurzelgrund"[27] von Vorlage und Fortsetzung angenommen[28] bzw. Goethes Fortsetzung als "konzentriertes Abbild der *Zauberflöte* Mozart-Schikaneders" verstanden.[29]

Dass sich Goethes "Wiederholung" mit "verändertem Text, doch in unveränderter Stimmung"[30] durchaus maßgeblicher von ihrer Vorlage unterscheidet, ist indes meine These. Dieser Beitrag bietet nicht ausreichend Raum, um die Kluft zwischen Schikaneders Vorlage und Goethes Fortsetzung auszuführen—ein solches beabsichtige ich an anderer Stelle zu leisten.[31] Ich will diesen Beitrag aber dazu nutzen, mit dem Wandel der Semantik des "Musikzaubers" von Schikaneder zu Goethe zumindest einen Aspekt dieses Bruchs nachzuweisen.

## Von der Leidenschaft zur Seelenkraft: Musikzauber im rationalen Diskurs

Wie ich an anderer Stelle ausführe,[32] bietet das 18. Jahrhundert im Hinblick auf den Musikzauber äußerst vereinfacht gesagt zwei Modelle zur Erklärung an: Auf der einen Seite ein mechanistisches Modell, welches, teils an die galenische Humoralpathologie angelehnt, die Musikwirkung als Affektwirkung grundsätzlich passiv versteht, und welches über das Saitengleichnis noch in der Empfindsamkeit fortwirkt. Und auf der anderen Seite ein dieses Modell teils ablösendes, teils mit diesem Modell verbindendes Verständnis der Musikwirkungen als Folge einer aktiven Produktivität der Seele. Beide Modelle fügen sich dabei in eine stetige Entwicklung und Ausdifferenzierung der Semantik des Zauberbegriffes ein, die im Spätbarock längst an Form gewonnen hatte, und sich bis zum nächsten Jahrhundertende fortsetzt. Der erste Schritt einer mechanistischen Erforschung des Wirkungsgrundes war dabei bereits vom barocken Rationalismus vorgegeben und hatte mit den barocken Affekte(n)lehren[33] auch eine Ausdifferenzierung respektive der übrigen Künste gefunden. War bei Athanasius Kircher nicht nur Orpheus' Person, sondern auch sein Instrument vom Vorwurf echter Zauberei freigesprochen worden, musste unter Zugrundelegung obiger Rationalisierungsleistung für die die Macht der Musik verhandelnden Diskurse in der Aufklärung notwendigerweise dasselbe gelten: Die Wirkungsmacht der Musik sollte nicht nur gepriesen, und dabei vielleicht gar mythisch verklärt, sondern vielmehr erforscht und begründet werden.

Dies bedeutete indes nicht, dass die Bezeichnung der Musik als Zaubermittel, bzw. das Verständnis ihrer Macht als Zaubermacht, in der Aufklärung ausgedient hätte. Das Gegenteil ist vielmehr der Fall: In der Literatur erlangte die Verwendung des Begriffs des "Zaubers" und seiner Kognaten als Begriff für die Wirkungsmacht der Musik im engeren Sinne, bzw. der Künste im weiteren Sinne, vielmehr gerade in der zweiten Jahrhunderthälfte erst ihren Höhepunkt. Und es ist meine These, dass die entscheidende Voraussetzung hierfür gerade war, dass durch die rationalen Bemühungen der Aufklärung jeglicher echter Zauber ausgeschlossen wurde; der Begriff den respektiven Diskursen nunmehr unzweideutig als Metapher gänzlich zur Bezeichnung der Wirkungsmacht eines Mediums zur Verfügung gestellt werden konnte, anstatt wie bisher zur Bezeichnung eines unerklärlichen, wenn nicht gar überirdischen Kausalverhältnisses.

Schon bei Kircher, der in seinem Traktat noch Raum für (Musik-)"Zauber" bzw. "Wunder" im ursprünglichen Wortsinn ("übernatürlich") gelassen hatte, konnte der Begriff lediglich das Wirkungsverhältnis bezeichnen. Und entsprechend wirkungsästhetisch stellt Kircher bei der Darlegung seines Programms, die "wunder-würkende Musica Krafft und Macht" bzw. die "wunderliche Kraft in Würkung" der Musik, mit der der Mensch zu "allerley Gemüthsbewegungen" gebracht werden könne, zu ergründen, fest, dass sie "desto grösseres wundern verursacht je weiter und verborgener sich etwa solche Stimm Thon und Music dem Gehör präsentiert."[34] Dass der Nexus dabei mechanisch ist, führt Kircher unter Zugrundelegung galenischer Humoralpathologie aus, und endet schließlich mit dem noch in der Empfindsamkeit beliebten Resonanzmodell als Bild für die Erklärung der Wunderwirkungen der Musik auf die menschliche Seele: "Wann 2 Instrument gantz rein und gleich gestimmet seyn und nur das eine wird geschlagen mit harmonischem modulis, so bringts eben auch dieselbe harmoniam heraus in dem andern Instrument. ... Vide magiam musicam."[35]

Entsprechend folgerichtig können dann auch "Kunst-Bezauberung" und "starcke Bewegung," die sich "nach denen verschiedenen und mannigfaltigen Thon- [u]nd Stimm-Arten richtet und ändert," bei Kircher nicht nur im Satzgefüge, sondern auch im Hinblick auf den Kausalzusammenhang eng beieinanderstehen.[36] Wird mit Zauber nunmehr lediglich eine Wirkung, und nicht deren (übernatürlicher) Ursprung referiert, kann dann in der Folge der Begriff rationalisiert verwendet werden.[37] Weiterhin war es bei Kircher nicht widersprüchlich gewesen, anlässlich der Musik von einer "wunderwürckenden Krafft" zu sprechen, gleichzeitig aber in kartesischer Manier[38] als Programm zu setzen, "gründlich darthun und eröffenen [zu] wollen; daß was wir von dieser an sich ziehenden Music-Krafft / und Gemüths-Zwang halten / wie und auf was Weis dieselbe so mancerley starcke Würkung / so wohl bey den Menschen / als auch bey den unvernünfftigen Thieren habe."[39]

Dieses grundlegende mechanistische Verständnis wirkt durchaus umfassend in die zweite Hälfte des achtzehnten Jahrhunderts fort. Noch bei Johann Gottfried Herder kann dann die Zauber- bzw. Wundermetapher (Herder spricht in der *Abhandlung vom Ursprung der Sprache* in der kurzen Spanne von gerade einmal zwei Seiten[40] von "Wunder," "Zaubermomenten," "Zauberkraft" und "Zauberliedern") ebenso selbstverständlich für Wirkungen gebraucht werden, "deren Ursprung eher natürlich" ist, d.h. "nicht bloß nicht übermenschlich" "sondern offenbar thierisch," womit diese lediglich dem "Naturgesetz einer empfindsamen Maschine" entsprängen.[41] Ebensowenig ist es in der von Johann Adam Hiller besorgten Ausgabe von Jacob Adlungs *Musicalischer Gelahrtheit* (1783) ein Widerspruch, wenn der "Zauber" auf seine genaueren physiologischen oder psychologischen Ursachen zurückgeführt werden wird.[42] Bei Herders Zeitgenosse Johann Joseph Kausch, der in seiner *Psychologischen Abhandlung* (1782)[43] ebenfalls die Ursache einer evidenten Macht der Musik untersucht hat, und hier den Begriff des "Zaubers" für die Wirkungen der Musik fast inflationär verwendet,[44] ist der Wandel der Semantik des Zauberbegriffs besonders deutlich. Spricht Kausch von der "Zauberkraft der Musik in unserem Busen" (94), oder der "Zauberkraft der himmlischen Harmonien" (59), die wie ein "Zauberstab" auf unser Gemüt wirken (95), steht dahinter nichts Unerklärliches. Vielmehr ist es ein klar analysierbarer psychologischer Wirkungsmechanismus, den Kausch minutiös sezieren wird. Für Kausch handelt es sich dann auch bei der "Kraft der orpheischen Zaubertalente" (173) um nichts anderes, als eine durchaus im Sinne Johann Georg Sulzers verstandene "ästhetische Kraft, welche uns bewegt"

(47). Kausch hat indes bereits den Schritt von einer passiven Affektion zu einer produktiven Tätigkeit der Seele vorgenommen, indem er nicht von einer einfachen Seelenmechanik ausgeht, sondern vielmehr die besondere Wirkungsmacht der Musik der aktiven assoziativen Tätigkeit des Rezipienten zuschreibt, und dies durchaus analog zu Sulzers aktivistischer Erklärung der Schönheit im Allgemeinen.[45] Findet die Zauberwirkung ihre eigentliche Ursache in der tätigen Seele des Empfängers, kann sich die "Bezauberung" auch gänzlich von einer gezielt produzierenden (Künstler-)Autorität gelöst finden, oder der Künstler lediglich "zufällig die empfindsame Seite des Herzens rühren." Auf der anderen Seite gibt es bei Kausch eine universellere Wirkungsgarantie, wenn das Wohlgefallen als die "andere" Zauberquelle des redenden Künstlers wie der Tonkunst identifiziert wird:[46] Assoziative Tätigkeit einerseits und auf einfacher Seelenmechanik beruhender (lediglich passiver) Effekt andererseits stehen bei Kausch als Wirkungsquellen nebeneinander. Aber auch die assoziative Wirkung als erste der beiden möglichen Ursachen einer "Bezauberung" ist bei Kausch nicht gänzlich unberechenbar, könne doch davon ausgegangen werden, dass die "Nachahmung der Thierakzente" ein sicheres Mittel zu jenen Gemütsbewegungen sei, "die die Zauberkraft der Musik in unserem Busen oft wache macht."[47] Dies entspricht einer nicht unbedeutenden Tendenz im Schrifttum, Herder gemäß das mittels der Musik bewirkte "Wunder"[48] auf die Ähnlichkeit bestimmter Tonfolgen der Musik mit den natürlichen Affektausdrücken gegründet zu sehen.

Die aktive Tätigkeit der Seele im Falle der Assoziation soll auch dafür verantwortlich sein, dass nicht nur der Laie, sondern auch der Kenner durch die Kunst der Musik "bezaubert" zu werden vermag,[49] dann hier aber die Regeln für beide Rezipiententypen notwendigerweise voneinander abweichen müssen.[50] Diese Unterscheidung zwischen einfacher und höherer Ursache der Zauberwirkung bei Kenner und Laie hindert indes Kausch nicht, "Zuckerbrote" und "Zaubereien" bisweilen als Begriffe fast tautologisch aneinanderzufügen.[51] Dass solch "Zauberton," sei es aufgrund seiner Schönheit, sei es aufgrund seiner Ähnlichkeit zu den natürlichen Affektausdrücken, in der Rhetorik ein machtvolles Mittel sein muss, ist evident. Und auch Sulzer versäumt es nicht auszuführen, dass in der Rede der Ton oft mehr Wirkung entfalte, als sein Inhalt.[52] Für Herder findet sich der Ton der Rede bei Platon gar zur "Sylben-Musik" gesteigert.[53]

Diesen psychologischen bzw. psychomechanistischen Untersuchungen ist es zu verdanken, dass auch in der Musikgeschichtsschreibung die Zaubermetapher äußerst präsent ist. So wird etwa in Forkels umfassender und grundsätzlich nüchtern gefasster Historiographie der Musik der "mächtige Zauber" der Musik beschrieben[54] und Burney formuliert in seiner *Abhandlung über die Musik der Alten*: "Ich will diese Anmerkungen noch mit einem Beyspiele schließen … um daran allen Zauber seiner Kunst, und alle Wunder des Rhythmus zu zeigen."[55]

Es muss insoweit nicht überraschen, dass die Zauberkraft, nunmehr als Metapher verstanden, zu einem ausgeprägten Gemeinplatz werden musste, wenn über die Musik gesprochen wird. Sprach Johann Nicolaus Forkel vom "musicalischen Wunder" in einem sozialen Kontext, wenn die Musik "mit mächtigem Zauber unter allen Gliedern einer ganzen Versammlung eine solche Übereinstimmung der Gefühle [bewirke], dass gleichsam die Herzen aller in ein einziges zusammenzuschmelzen zu scheinen,"[56] avancierte die Zaubermetapher schnell zum Mittel der Lobpreisung jeglicher besonders machtvoller Komposition. Und fand die Metapher bereits Verwendung, wenn Christoph Martin Wieland Glucks wirkungsmächtige Setzkunst lobte, füllt sie schnell auch die die Musikaufführungen begleitenden Rezensionen.[57]

Bereits Michel de Chabanon wusste, die Leistung, die erforderlich ist, um einen solchen Zauber zu bewirken, unter Gebrauch der etablierten begrifflichen Terminologie zu preisen: "Eine Arie rührt euch auf dem Theater in einem sehr hohen Grade der heftigsten Leidenschaft: der Sänger, der ein solches Wunder thut, ist ein Zauberer, dessen Kunst euch lieb und werth seyn muss; es besitzen nicht alle diese so schwere Kunst."[58] In der Empfindsamkeit findet sich das Wirkungsverhältnis dabei in ein Gleichgewicht gebracht: Erfordert die angemessene Produktion eine empfindsame Seele, muss Gleiches auch für den Rezipienten gelten; der Reiz der Musik bleibt wenig Empfindsamen notwendigerweise verschlossen. In diesem Sinne kann es in *Adelheit von Veltheim* (1781) heißen: "Die Liebe herrschst sonst überall, / Herrscht über alle Erdensöhne; / Doch ihre süßen Zaubertöne / Bethören einen Achmet nicht."[59]

Dass mit "Zauber" oder "Bezauberung" oft nicht mehr gemeint ist, als ein (wenn auch bisweilen qualifizierter) Reiz, zeigt nicht nur Sulzers synonyme Verwendung der beider Termini hinsichtlich der Musik.[60] Auch bei den übrigen Autoren können sich "Reiz" und "Zauber" nicht nur gegenseitig vertreten, sondern finden sich auch immer wieder gepaart, etwa als "bezaubernder Reiz." Bei Johann Mattheson kann ferner "erstaunenswert" die sonst üblichen Prädikate "bezaubernd" und "zauberhaft" im Satzgefüge problemlos ersetzen.[61] Und auch bei Wieland schließlich wird deutlich, dass mit dem "Zauber" nichts anderes gemeint ist, als eine der Optik vergleichbare sinnliche Wirkung, die lediglich ein anderes Organ betrifft: "Wer wird mit einem Blinden über die Wirkung von Licht und Farben, oder mit einem Stocktauben über den Zauber der Musik hadern?"[62]

In der Dichtkunst findet sich der Musikzauber nicht weniger häufig vertreten. Neben den häufigen Referenzen auf Orpheus, sowie den Lobpreisungen von Dichtung und Musik in den Preisgedichten Christlob Mylius' und Gotthold Ephraim Lessings,[63] ist es der Zauber von Damons Flöte, auf den Wieland im *Agathon* (1766) verweist.[64] Und in mythischer Verklärung erscheint die Musik schließlich im *Oberon* (1780). Aber selbst hier ist die Musik nicht davor gefeit, zum Mittel degradiert zu werden.[65] Julius von Soden schließlich sieht in seiner *Anna Boley* mit dem Menschsein ein nicht uneingeschränkt positiv verstandenes Unterworfensein unter die Macht des Musikers verbunden.[66]

## Zur Ubiquität des Zauberbegriffes in Kunst und Wissenschaft

Der physiologische und psychomechanische Grund des Musikzaubers und damit die semantische Verschiebung des Zauberbegriffs weg von seiner Bedeutung der Unerklärlichkeit bzw. Übernatürlichkeit der Ursache führt dabei schnell zu einem Verständnis einer strukturalen Verwandtschaft der Wirkungen von Musik und Rhetorik, die sich von den barocken Affektenlehren[67] bis zu den Assoziationstheorien des späten 18. Jahrhunderts fortsetzt und eine analoge Behandlung auch in anderen Sparten bewirkt: Vom Zauber der Dichtkunst über den Zauber der Liebe bis hin zum Zauber der Wissenschaften wird ein und dieselbe Wirkung mit derselben Metapher belegt.

Schon Kausch findet das von ihm festgestellte Wirkungsverhältnis nicht auf den Bereich der Musik beschränkt. Vielmehr soll auch die mächtige "Zauberkraft der redenden Künste" in denselben psychologisch begriffenen Mechanismen ihren Grund haben.[68] Kann in Friedrich Klingers *Faust* die Zaubermetapher gar die Wirkungsmacht der Wissenschaften bezeichnen,[69] vertritt sie in der Dichtung indes wohl am häufigsten die Wirkungsmacht der Liebe (und dies durchaus auch in ihrer hohen Variante). Die Verweise sind hier äußerst zahlreich, was auch darin begründet liegt, dass die Tradition dieser Metapher in der deutschsprachigen Literatur bis in die mittelalterliche Dichtung zurückreicht, und noch Immanuel Kant wird in seiner *Anthropologie in pragmatischer Hinsicht* (1798) im Hinblick auf die Leidenschaften von "Zauber" sprechen.[70] Für die Dichtung des 18. Jahrhunderts hat Klopstock mit den "Verwandlungen ihres mächtigen Zauberstabs"[71] ein prominentes Beispiel geliefert, und diskurskonform heißt es in Goethes *Stella* (1775): "Oh wenn ich manchmal von Gedanken in Gedanken sinke, . . . den Zauber der Liebe vergebens mit einem Drang, einer Fülle ausspreche, dass ich meine ich müsste den Mond herunter ziehen."[72] Selbst im Lustspiel findet der Zauber als Metapher der Liebeswirkungen eine nicht unbeachtliche Verbreitung, etwa wenn klagend auf die unentrinnbare Verstrickung verwiesen wird.[73] Am häufigsten findet sich die Zaubermetapher dabei auf den Moment der oft sinnlichen Auslösung der Liebe und ihrer Wirkungen bezogen.[74]

In Wielands *Oberon* schließlich erweist sich der Musikzauber lediglich als Steigerung eines Versuchs allgemeiner sinnlicher Manipulation: Nachdem Almansaris damit gescheitert war, das Auge und die Einbildungskraft Oberons mittels einer perfide organisierten Inszenierung ihrer schönen Person zu verzaubern, greift sie als letztes Mittel zur Musik.[75] Und obwohl Wieland im *Oberon* die Zaubermetapher für die rechte Liebe eher vermeidet,[76] kann bei anderen durchaus auch die keusche Liebe mit denselben Attributen belegt werden. In dem von Wieland herausgegebenem Briefroman Sophie von La Roches (*Geschichte des Fräulein von Sternheim*, 1771) wird selbst die "jungfräuliche Schamhaftigkeit" nicht ungefährliche sinnliche Reize entfalten, welche es verdienen, mittels der Zaubermetapher bezeichnet zu werden. In Johann Andrés *Die Bezauberten* (1777, nach Marie Justine Favart) bewirkt gar das "artige Wesen" des Gegenübers einen betörenden "Zauber."[77]

## Gattung, Geographie, Reiz

Die Unterschiede innerhalb einer solchen allgemeinen Semantik sind hier teils gattungsbezogen, teils geographisch bedingt. Während im französisch geprägten Lustspiel, und hier insbesondere im Volkstheater, die sinnliche Zauberwirkung der Liebe durchaus kritisch bewertet wird (etwa in

Charles-Simon Favarts *La fée Urgèle*, 1765),[78] hat sich vor allem das Singspiel für eine eher empfindsame Ausdeutung des Liebeszaubers entschieden. Gerade dort kommt es zu einer fast inflationären Abarbeitung des Topos, wobei es oft zu einer interessanten Verschränkung von Zauber und Liebe kommt, bei der Zauber von Musik und optischem Reiz entweder gleichgeordnet als Mittel gegenüberstehen, oder aber gar sich gegenseitig bedingen, bzw. aufeinander zurückgeführt werden können. Im Volkstheater findet sich ebenso oft eine interessanten Amalgamierung, nunmehr empfindsamer und kritisch-distanzierter Positionen, was gerade auch durch die vielfältigen intertextuellen Einflüsse bedingt ist: als Nachwirken der *Commedia dell'arte* sowie aufgrund des zeitgenössischen Einflusses von *Opera buffa* und *Opera comique* als Werkformen. Heißt es in einer Marinelli'schen Kasperliade (die Wirkungen der Musik und der sinnlichen Liebe gänzlich deckungsgleich präsentierend) "Süße Worte, sanfte Blicke . . . Das sind deine Zauberstricke,"[79] wird hier eine Gleichsetzung begründet, die sich in anderen Lustspielen ebenso manifestiert. So kann dann auch Julius von Sodens Don Quichotte, nachdem er der Aufführung einer Symphonie beigewohnt hat, ausrufen: "Dank dir weise Urganda! Ohne Zweifel ist dies dein Werk!—Aber umsonst!—Umsonst bietest du alle Reize der Natur, umsonst den Zauber der Musik auf."[80]

Dass es hier immer wieder zu Gleichstellungen der Wirkungsmächte von körperlicher Schönheit und Musik kommt, liegt indes nicht nur darin begründet, dass es sich bei den verschiedenen Referenten der Zaubermetapher um vergleichbare Wirkungsphänomene handelt, denen es zudem gemein ist, dass sie oft in der Sinnlichkeit ihre Grundlage finden—wie dies bei Adolf von Knigge[81] erkennbar wird, wenn dieser die "sinnlichen Mittel" eines "Zaubers" von "Musik," "Baukunst" und "Malerey" gleichordnet, oder aber in St. Pauls Lustspiel *Wahnsinn aus Liebe*[82] (1787), in dem sich ebenfalls Ton- und Augenzauber gleichgesetzt finden, die beide zwangsläufig in Liebe münden:

> (Blanka singt eine Arie und accompagniert sich auf der Zitter.)
> Wolser. (nachdem Blanka aufgehört hat zu singen) Der Ton ihrer Stimme ist wie Zaubertrank, der das Gift der glühendsten Liebe in alle meine Adern gießt.
> Blanka. Ihre Blicke haben den nemlichen Zauber in mein Herz gegossen.[83]

Vielmehr können der Zauber der Liebe und der Zauber der Musik durchaus gegenseitig aufeinander als Wirkungsgrund zurückgeführt werden: Gilt, wie Sulzer ausführt, dass allein der Ton der Stimme schon unabhängig vom Inhalt mächtige Wirkungskraft entfalten kann, was Sulzer dazu führt, für die Rhetorik die Aufgabe zu formulieren, "was . . . nützlich ist, angenehm zu machen und allen seinen Pflichten [damit] einen bezaubernden Reiz zu geben,"[84] führt umgekehrt die Liebe selbst zu ihrer wirkungsmächtigen Entäußerung in Zaubertönen. In Konsequenz kann Musik auch als Medizin gegen den Liebeskummer dienen, wobei in nachfolgender Passage der Topos der sich in Musik entäußerten Liebe zudem beiläufig noch mit aufgerufen wird:

> Da fand ich—dich Friede
> des Herzens—wie süß!
> Begeisterung zum Liede Kam wieder—Sie riß

> Mich hoch zu den Sternen,
> In Seligkeit schwang
> ich mich in die Fernen
> zum Sphärengesang.
> Nun rührt mich dein Zauber
> O Liebe nicht mehr!
> Wohl girret der Tauber
> sein Treuelied her.[85]

Aufgrund dieser Verschränkungen ist es dann auch nicht verwunderlich, wenn in Karl Friedrich Henslers *Sonnenfest der Braminen* (1790) die Wirkung einer bar jeder Sinnlichkeit stattfindenden Menschenliebe ebenfalls als "Zauber" bezeichnet wird, nachdem schon Mendelssohn vergleichbar der "Zauberkraft der Sympathie"[86] gehuldigt hatte—und hier auch noch denselben Begriff benutzt, den er an anderer Stelle für die Musik gebraucht: "Zauberkraft der Harmonie."[87] Die Macht der Musik, die Macht der Liebe und die Macht der Sympathie werden hier nicht nur mit denselben Metaphern beschrieben, sondern können aufgrund ihrer Verwandtschaft nicht nur in Anbetracht ihrer Wirkungen, sondern im Hinblick auf ihre Ursache und ihr Wesen durchaus gemeinsam verhandelt werden. Regelmäßig wird dabei ein ästhetisches Wirkungsverhältnis bezeichnet, das als natürlich, oft sogar als mechanisch verstanden wird.

Was hier bereits anklingt, lässt sich mit weiteren Belegen bestätigen: In Schikaneders und Mozarts *Die Zauberflöte* findet die Zaubermetapher, nunmehr als "Zauberton," eine Verwendung, und von Friederike Sophie Seylers *Hüon und Amande* (1789)[88] bis zu Schikaneders *Stein der Weisen* (1790)[89] ist nicht echte Zauberei durch den Begriff bezeichnet, sondern ein besonders qualifizierter Reiz. Selbst in den "echten" Zauberstücken[90] des ausgehenden 18. Jahrhunderts kann es zu einer interessanten Koexistenz von buchstäblicher und übertragener Verwendung des Zauberbegriffes kommen, wenn die durch Zauber geschaffene Schönheit ihrerseits den der Schönheit natürlich eigenen Reiz entfaltet, etwa in Schikaneders Fortsetzung der *Zauberflöte* (*Das Labyrinth oder Der Kampf mit den Elementen*, 1798) oder aber in Joachim Perinets *Die Zauberzither* (1791).[91]

Nach dem gerade Gesagten muss auch bereits erahnbar werden, welches Potential einer Zauberwirkung gerade dem multimedialen Musiktheater zukommen muss. Und es entfaltete sich zeitgleich tatsächlich ein kleiner Wettstreit zwischen Sprech- und Musiktheater,[92] wobei Wieland dem Singspiel gerade aufgrund seiner Fähigkeit zum "großen Zweck der Täuschung und innigsten Theilnehmen auf Seiten der Zuschauer" sogleich das Recht auf einen "Platz unter den verschiedenen dramatischen Gattungen" zuwies.[93]

Wichtiger ist aber in unserem Kontext, dass ein psychologisches Verständnis der Ursachen des "Zaubers" es gerade auch erlaubt, die einzelnen Konstituenten des Musiktheaters jeweils gesondert mit der Zaubermetapher zu belegen.[94] Dass die gepriesene Wirkung durchaus auch Kaltblütigkeit erfordert, wird dabei nicht verhehlt: "Kurz, die Illusion geht verloren, wenn der Künstler nicht das lebhafte, anhaltende Feuer eines Brandes, oder Ekhofs und Schräders Zauberkraft besitzt, mit kaltem Blute zu täuschen."[95]

Poetischer, aber nicht weniger rationalisierend, findet sich die Illusionsmacht der Musik unter Verwendung der Zaubermetapher indes von Johann Heinrich Voss in Sprache gesetzt, wenn er Blackwell übersetzt.[96] Aber auch hier ist deutlich: Der "Zauber" des Theaters ist das Resultat einer gezielten Steuerung von Wahrnehmungsapparat und Affekthaushalt des Rezipienten, und erfordert, um nun die Worte einer der Quellen von Schikaneders *Zauberflöte* zu benutzen, ein detailliertes "Wissen … über die Neigungen des menschlichen Körpers und der Seele," wobei die praktische Erprobung der Wirkungen von "Dekoration und Musik" es sichert, Schauspiele zu schaffen, bei denen "die Sinne den Betrug mit Wahrheit sahen," als "unüberwindliche Illusion,"[97] die jedoch als medial vermittelt nicht von Dauer sein kann:

> Orpheus Geliebte war die Musik. Wer kennt nicht ihre bezaubernde Gewalt? Sie singt die Vernunft in den Schlaf, und erhöht die Phantasie auf eine so angenehme Art, dass wir uns selbst in ihrem Zauberkreise vergessen … Aber kaum schweigt die Musik, so hört der Zauber auf, und die Bilder verfliessen. Wir sehn uns wieder im Getümmel des Lebens, uns jammern nach der glänzenden Täuschung zurück.[98]

## Trügerische Kontinuitäten: Von "Zauberzithern" und "Zauberflöten" zwischen Schikaneder und Goethe

Die Omnipräsenz der Musikmacht in den zeitgenössischen Diskursen, verbunden mit der fast inflationären Verwendung der Zaubermetapher als nunmehr rationalisierte Beschreibung dieser Wirkungsmacht hat sich insbesondere in Schikaneder und Mozarts *Zauberflöte* niedergeschlagen.

Nicht nur, dass die *Zauberflöte* selbst die Macht der Musik behandelt, und zwar durchaus unter Zuhilfenahme obiger Metaphorik (als "Zauberton"),[99] und dabei noch diskurstypisch die Wirkung der Musik der des "bezaubernden" Bildnisses Paminas gleichsetzt. Vielmehr finden sich, auch wenn dem Flöteninstrument noch ein irrationalen Ursprungsmythos mitgegeben wurde, die Zauberwirkungen in der *Zauberflöte* gänzlich im rationalen Register verortet.[100] Assmann urteilt insoweit durchaus zutreffend, wenn er ausführt, dass den Musikinstrumenten in der *Zauberflöte* keine Macht zugeschrieben wird, die nicht der zeitgenössische rationale Diskurs der Musik bereits zugewiesen hat.[101] Und selbst wenn teils darauf insistiert wird, dass die *Zauberflöte* keine Zauberflöte sei,[102] d.h. sich eine Gleichsetzung von Diegese-Instrument und Oper[103] verbieten soll: die *Zauberflöte* ist nichtsdestotrotz eine rationalisierte Reflektion über die Macht der Musik,[104] wenn nicht gar ein Metakommentar der Oper als Gattung, und zwar gänzlich wie dieses sich in obigen Diskursen des 18. Jahrhunderts etabliert hat—was sicher auch Borchmeyer dazu veranlasst hat, das Flöteninstrument der Vorlage als "Symbol der Musik als tönende Humanität" zu bezeichnen.[105]

Dies ändert sich auch nicht dadurch, dass motivgeschichtlich die Zauberspiele der 1780er/frühen 1790er Jahre, wie Otto Rommel festgestellt hat, als Fortführung einer irrationalen Barocktradition erscheinen: Hinsichtlich der Motive besteht zwar eindeutig eine ungebrochene Kontinuität mit der Tradition des barocken Zauberspiels, hinsichtlich ihrer Semantik jedoch

keinesfalls.[106] Entsprechend ordnet auch Rommel Schikaneders Vorlage
implizit in jene rationalistische Tradition von Zauber- und Feenliteratur der
zweiten Hälfte des 18. Jahrhunderts ein, in der sich Übernatürliches "rationalisiert und humanisiert" findet, oder aber "skeptisch-ironisch" entwertet
wird—und verweist dezidiert darauf, wie wenig diese Zauberliteratur mit der
Romantik gemein hat.[107]

Die Zugehörigkeit der *Zauberflöte* zu einer rationalisierten, ver-
mittelnd empfindsam-aufgeklärten Semantik eines Verständnisses des
Musikzaubers wird dadurch bestätigt, dass sowohl im Unterschied zu
den "echten" Zauberspielen des Barock als auch zu Goethes Fortsetzung
auf jeglichen anderen Zauber verzichtet wurde: Einzig die Wirkung der
Musikinstrumente sowie Paminas sinnlicher Reiz werden diskurskonform
mit der Zaubermetapher belegt. Womit Schikaneder seine *Zauberflöte* gerade auch wesentlich von der Vorlage August Jacob Liebeskinds (*Lulu oder die
Zauberflöte*, 1786) entfernt hat, die neben dem Musikzauber auch echten
Zauber kennt.[108] Selbst Goethes erste Auseinandersetzung mit Schikaneders
Libretto (die Beauftragung seines Schwagers Christian August Vulpius mit
einer Umarbeitung desselben) wird diese Topoi lediglich fortschreiben,
und teils sogar dezidiert verstärken, wenn im Hinblick auf die genutzte
Metaphorik "der Flöte Zauberklang"[109] der "Liebe Zaubermacht"[110] ebenso
gleichgestellt wird wie dem "holde[n] Zauberbild" Paminas, das das "Herz mit
süßer Sehnsucht füllt." Und in Vulpius' Weimarer Fassung der *Zauberflöte* finden sich, der Tradition entsprechend, dann auch die übrigen Gemeinplätze
der Musikwirkungen aufgerufen: Neben der Macht über die menschlichen
Leidenschaften[111] und dem Einsatz der Flöte als Mittel des Gotteslobs[112]
wird auf die Besänftigung von Löwen[113] ebenso wenig verzichtet, wie auf
die Anlockung von Tieren, die ebenfalls in orpheischer Manier als Zuhörer
verzeichnet werden.[114] Noch in Goethes Fortsetzung der *Zauberflöte* darf
die Musik nicht nur ihre bewegenden, sondern gerade auch heilenden Kräfte
beweisen—ein Nutzen, dem sich eine Fülle zeitgenössischer medizinischer
Veröffentlichungen zugewandt haben.[115]

## Anstelle eines Fazits: Brüche

Aus obiger Darstellung des Feldes einer rationalisierten Semantik des
Zauberbegriffes im 18. Jahrhundert muss gleichzeitig evident werden, wie
weit sich Goethe mit seiner Fortsetzung der *Zauberflöte* von dieser Tradition
entfernt hat. Während sich alle bei Schikaneder zu findenden Zaubereien
widerspruchslos in die rationalisierte Semantik des Zauberbegriffes ein-
gliedern lassen, und Schikaneder in seiner Fortsetzung (*Das Labyrinth*) die
Rationalisierung des Topos zumindest in Teilen forttreibt, indem er auch den
Zauber der Liebe in Anlehnung an die französische Tradition deutlich stärker als im ersten Teil kritisch seziert, reichert Goethe seine Fortsetzung mit
einer Fülle von Zauberphänomenen an, die keineswegs in obiger Tradition
einer rationalen Erklärung zugeführt werden können: Nicht nur, dass die beiden Musikinstrumente und Paminas sinnliche Reize ihre Alleinstellung im
Hinblick auf eine Attribution der Metapher verloren haben. Wie Goethes
andere Zaubergegenstände ist vielmehr auch der Musikzauber als "echter,"

d.h. übernatürlicher Zauber zu verstehen. Vulpius stärkte bereits deutlich die Bedeutung echter "Zauberdinge" (293) im Geschehen: Neben Zauberflöte und Zauberglöckchen ist der Sonnenkreis wieder zum "mächtigen Talismann" geworden (276). Hinzugefügt ist zudem der Hinweis auf den weisen Seher Arasmeno (150). Bei Goethe kommen ein goldener Sarg hinzu, dem Finsternis entströmt und der in ständiger Bewegung gehalten werden muss (302); ein "Zaubersigel," das den Sarg verschließt, und welches niemand lösen kann (303), sowie ein "Zauberkristall," der die moralische Wertigkeit einer Person anzeigt (311). Hinzu kommen Zaubersprüche, wie Sarastros "Zaubersegen," der einen Anschlag vereitelt (303) und "Sarastro's lösend Götterwort," auf das alle zur Rettung hoffen (306), sowie die Versetzung des Liebespaares in einen "Zauberschlaf" (313). Die Trennung der Liebenden ist dann auch keine Probe, sondern "Fluch" (304). Und wo sich doch diskursentsprechend die rationalisierten Kräfte der Musik bei Goethe aufgerufen finden, werden diese ironisiert bis hin zur "Groteske."[116] Allem Zauber Goethes ist dabei gemein, dass sich die Wirkung gerade nicht diskursentsprechend humoralpathologisch oder psychologisch fassen lässt. Jaeckle hat sehr scharfsinnig darauf verwiesen, dass die Zauberdinge in Goethes Zauberflötenfortsetzung (wie ihre geheimnisvollen Pendants in den *Wahlverwandtschaften*, dem *Wilhelm Meister* sowie der *Natürlichen Tochter*) vielmehr eine topische Verwandtschaft mit der Büchse der Pandora aufweisen[117]—und Goethes Fortsetzung der *Zauberflöte* in den Kontext von Goethes Wissenschaftslehre und Naturwissenschaft gestellt (Metamorphosestudien, Farbenlehre, Dualität der Erscheinungen).[118]

Aber nicht nur im Hinblick auf den Musik- und Instrumentenzauber löst sich Goethe von der gemäßigt-empfindsamen Tradition des Singspiels, in der sich Schikaneders *Zauberflöte* in der Forschung immer wieder verortet findet (cf. Borchmeyer, Krämer, Matt). Auch die Wirkungsmacht der Liebe will Goethe, wie die Paralipomena zeigen, nicht, wie im ausgehenden 18. Jahrhundert üblich, mit der Zaubermetapher belegt finden. Goethe scheidet hier vielmehr Liebe und Zauber ausdrücklich voneinander.[119]

Der Zauberbegriff von Goethes Fortsetzung erweist sich insoweit als gänzlich einer anderen Semantik verhaftet, die keinerlei Kontinuität zu der Entwicklungslinie aufweist, in der Schikaneder und Mozarts Vorlage verortet ist. Mit dem Musikinstrument von Schikaneder und Mozarts *Zauberflöte* teilt Goethes Fortsetzung lediglich den Namen, nicht jedoch die zugrundeliegende Semantik. Unter dieser Maßgabe ist der leider in der Forschung bisher nicht in diesem Kontext thematisierte, abweichende ursprünglich intendierte Titel von Goethes Fortsetzung ("Die Zauberharfe")[120] durchaus bezeichnend: Goethes Fortsetzung steht im Hinblick auf die Behandlung der "Zauberdinge" Perinets Version des Lulu-Stoffes deutlich näher, die anstelle der Flöte ebenfalls ein Saiteninstrument im Titel trägt.

Goethe hat mit seiner *Zauberflöte* den rationalisierenden Charakter der Vorlage Schikaneders (und sogar von Schikaneders Fortsetzung) getilgt—eine Tilgung, die anderweitig als "geistige Entleerung des Zaubers" bei "Schikaneders Nachtretern" kritisiert wurde[121]—um hinsichtlich des Zauberbegriffes wieder in einer Ambivalenz zu münden, die durchaus auch das Potential eines erneuten Mystizismus in sich birgt. Parallel zu einer Wiederkehr der "dunkle[n] imaginative[n] Verhältnisse,"[122] die sich gerade auch infolge eines semantischen

Wandels des Geheimnisbegriffs ergeben, welchen ich in meinem jüngsten
Aufsatz im Lessing-Jahrbuch beschrieben habe,[123] und die im Widerspruch
noch zu Goethes zehn Jahre älterem Text *Die Geheimnisse* steht,[124] durf-
te auch die Zaubermetapher in Form ihrer rationalisierten Semantik bei
Goethe nicht überdauern. Es ist gerade die Diskontinuität hinsichtlich des
Mysterienverständnisses beider Opern,[125] die mit Goethes Bruch mit einer
rationalisierten Semantik des Musikzaubers gleichläuft, und die in dem "dai-
monischen Wesen" des Genius der Fortsetzung als Repräsentation eines ele-
mentaren Lebensprinzips[126] und "Zentralgestalt der 'neuen Mystik' Goethes"
kulminiert.[127] Und die in der Ambivalenz der Semantik des "Wunders" in
Goethes *Märchen* eine weitere Parallele findet—womit sich die in der
Forschung immer wieder betonte Zusammengehörigkeit von Goethe selbst
als "Märchen" bezeichneten *Der Zauberflöte zweyter Theil* mit dem *Märchen*
und dem *Faust* bestätigt.[128] Der Bruch hinsichtlich der Semantik des
Musikzaubers, ebenso wie hinsichtlich des Mysterienverständnisses, spiegelt
sich dabei auch in einem äußerst bedeutsamen Topos der Oper. Schikaneders
Vorlage steht nämlich unter dem Primat von Kontrolle, Goethes dagegen von
Unkontrollierbarkeit: Das Paar bei Goethes *Zauberflöte* ist dem Wirken höherer Mächte und elementarer Prinzipien gänzlich unterworfen, Determinierung
und Fatalismus sind maßgebliche Topoi, die sich lediglich in der Figur des
geflügelten Genius gebrochen finden.[129]

Die semantische Neubestimmung des Musikzaubers in den 1790er Jahren
mag zwar nicht notwendig, aber durchaus hilfreich für die Fortführung des
Topos im frühen 19. Jahrhundert gewesen sein, wurde die Zaubermetapher
schließlich erst dadurch für die Bestrebungen der Romantik anschluss-
fähig. Hierzu musste aber erst einmal jener vorhergehende, mehr als ein
Jahrhundert dauernde graduelle semantische Wandel notwendigerweise
wieder rückgängig gemacht werden, und der Zauberbegriff wieder in das
Spannungsverhältnis einer Ambivalenz zwischen natürlicher und übernatürlicher Erklärung der Wirkungsmacht zurückgebracht werden.[130] Die eigen-
tümlich Stellung der *Zauberflöte* "zwischen Barock und Romantik"[131] ist
dabei durchaus wörtlich zu nehmen, und zwar nicht nur aus einer rein chro-
nologischen Perspektive, sondern im Hinblick auf eine topische: Goethes
*Der Zauberflöte zweyter Theil* steht nicht nur wieder jenen Zauberspielen
des Barocks nahe, die in der Forschung als Motivschatz der Zauberspiele
des 18. Jahrhunderts entschlüsselt wurden, sondern fügt sich zu einer Fülle
von zeitgenössischen Zauberspielen auf den Vorstadtbühnen, die, anstelle
an den aufklärerisch-empfindsamen Wandel anzuknüpfen, in den sich das
Singspiel im 18. Jahrhundert noch bereitwillig eingefügt hatte,[132] sich statt-
dessen direkter auf die Barocktradition beziehen,[133] oder aber bereits einem
genuin romantischen Mysterienverständnis verhaftet sind.[134] Hier konnte
es im Hinblick auf die Semantik des Zauberbegriffes durchaus bereits im
ausgehenden 18. Jahrhundert zu Überschneidungen von alter und neuer
Verwendung kommen. Wenn im *Ulldolini* (1790) der Anblick der Geliebten,
ihre "Engelgestalt" eine "Allmacht" entfaltet, die das Erlebnis zu einer quasi-sa-
kralen Erfahrung macht, welche auch tatsächlich in "Anbetung" mündet,[135]
ist die Grenze des etablierten semantischen Spektrums bereits überschritten.
Und auch Perinets Version der *Zauberflöte* nimmt bereits Topoi auf, die von

der Diskussion des 18. Jahrhunderts bewusst ausgeschlossen worden waren. Indes musste hierfür nicht erst auf die Romantik gewartet werden. Bereits im Zeichen des Sturm und Drang finden sich deutlich früher auch Ausdeutungen des Zauberbegriffs, die dessen Begriffsgrenzen zurück zu der ursprünglichen Ambivalenz von mechanischer und übernatürlicher Wirkungsursache verschieben. Eine Rezension im *Teutschen Merkur* des Jahres 1773[136] beschreibt etwa die Musikwirkungen als Folge einer schöpferisch-treibenden Kraft gänzlich im Geiste der Genieästhetik des Sturm und Drang, was mit dem eingeschränkten semantischen Spektrum des Zauberbegriffes nicht mehr fassbar ist, vielmehr Goethes Verständnis von Mozart als dämonischem Charakter[137] vorwegnimmt.

Es mag primär ein Problem der Librettoforschung sein, bzw. von musikwissenschaftlichen Beiträgen im Speziellen, dass Goethes *Der Zauberflöte zweyter Theil* teils in eine falsche Kontinuität gestellt wird. Germanistische Beiträge sind sich einer abweichenden Verortung von Goethes Fortsetzung—und deren Verwandtschaft eher zum *Faust*,[138] denn zu Schikaneder und Mozart—stärker bewusst. Ein Problem ist indes auch hier oft bereits ein falsches Verständnis von Schikaneders Vorlage als "romantische Oper,"[139] welches sich in einer unzutreffenden Einordnung von Schikaneders Mysterienkonzeption spiegelt[140]—und teils auch aus problematischen gattungsgeschichtlichen Einstufungen resultiert, die sich in der Parallelbildung von Weimarer und Wiener Klassik äußern. Gerade die Frage, ob Schikaneders *Zauberflöte* (ebenso wie die Weimarer Klassik) epochengeschichtlich in der Romantik zu verorten ist, oder aber eine genuine Oper der Aufklärung bzw. einer aufklärerisch-rationalisierten Empfindsamkeit ist,[141] ist hier für die Kontinuitätsfrage von besonderer Relevanz. Gänzlich unschuldig am Übersehen des Bruchs ist hier aber sicher auch Goethes deutlich spätere *Novelle* nicht, die in der Forschung als "letzte und schönste Huldigung an die *Zauberflöte*"[142] verstanden wurde, und in der sich die Macht der Flötenmusik und die "Macht der Liebe" wieder enggeführt finden. Indes bleibt der mehr als ein Vierteljahrhundert nach Goethes *Zauberflöte* fertiggestellte Text[143] selbst nicht ohne Ambivalenz, wenn laut Goethes Aussage[144] eigentlich die "Macht von Liebe" gepriesen werden sollte. Vielmehr wird dort in einer interessanten Parataxe, die überdies eine Parallele zu Kleists späterer Cäcilienerzählung[145] aufweist, unentscheidbar, ob die "Macht der Liebe" oder die der "Frömmigkeit" das Thema der *Novelle* ist, womit sich mit der Flötenmusik natürliche (d.h. psychomechanische) Verursachung und übernatürliche (theologische) Erklärung wieder gegenüberstehen.

*Universität Wien / Yale University*

## ANMERKUNGEN

1. Werner Wunderlich, Doris Ueberschlag und Ulrich Müller, *Die Zauberflöte und ihre Dichter: Schikaneder, Vulpius, Goethe, Zuccalmaglio: Faksimiles und Editionen von Textbuch, Bearbeitung und Fortsetzungen der Mozart-Oper* (Salzburg et al.: Anif, 2007) 300–323.

2. Markus Waldura, "Die Singspiele," in *Goethe-Handbuch*, hrsg. von Bernd Witte et al. (Stuttgart und Weimar: Metzler, 1997) 2:188.

3. Ich bereite hierzu gerade einen zweiten Aufsatz vor, der unter dem Titel "*Musurgia universalis*: Zum Orpheusmotiv als Indikator einer *contentio palliata* in der Dramatik des ausgehenden 18. Jahrhunderts" erscheinen soll.

4. Gernot Gruber, "Zu Goethes Mozartverständnis," in *Eine Art Symbolik fürs Ohr. Johann Wolfgang von Goethe. Lyrik und Musik*, hrsg. von Hermann Jung (Frankfurt a/M: Peter Lang, 2002) 84.

5. S. supra Fn. 3.

6. *Orfeo ed Euridice* (1762) / *Orphée et Euridice* (1774).

7. *Orphée et Euridice* (1791).

8. Zur Macht der Musik im 18. Jahrhundert vgl.: Rainer Bayreuther, "Theorie der musikalischen Affektivität in der frühen Neuzeit," in *Musiktheoretisches Denken und kultureller Kontext*, hrsg. von Dörte Schmidt (Schlingen: Edition Argus, 2004) 69-92; Fritz Beinroth, *Musikästhetik. Von der Sphärenharmonie bis zur musikalischen Hermeneutik* (Aachen: Shaker, 1995) insbes. Kapitel 4; A. Schering, "Die Musikästhetik der Aufklärung," *Zeitschrift der Internationalen Musikgesellschaft* 8 (1906-7) 263-322; Nicola Gess, *Gewalt der Musik. Literatur und Musikkritik um 1800* (Freiburg und Berlin: Rombach, 2011). Zu Goethes Musikverständnis vgl. hingegen Dieter Borchmeyer, "'Eine Art Symbolik fürs Ohr.' Goethes Musikästhetik," in *Goethe und das Zeitalter der Romantik*, hrsg. von Walter Hinderer (Würzburg 2002) 413-58; sowie speziell zur Oper: Bodo Plachta, "Goethes Bezeichnungsvielfalt musiktheatralischer Genres" in: Gabriele Busch-Salmen, *Goethe-Handbuch. Supplemente. Band 1: Musik und Tanz in den Bühnenwerken* (Stuttgart und Weimar: Metzler, 2008) 1:75-76. Zum dämonischen Charakter der Musik vgl. Gespräch mit Eckermann v. 8. März 1831.

9. Walter Weiss, "Das Weiterleben der Zauberflöte bei Goethe," in *Studien zur Literatur des 19. und 20. Jahrhunderts in Österreich. Festschrift für Alfred Doppler zum 60. Geburtstag*, hrsg. von Johann Holzer, Michael Klein und Wolfgang Wiesmüller (Innsbruck: Institut für Germanistik, 1981) 18; Victor Junk, *Goethes Fortsetzung der Mozartschen Zauberflöte* (Berlin: Duncker, 1899) 51.

10. Goethe, zitiert bei: Paul Nettl, *Goethe und Mozart. Eine Betrachtung* (Esslingen: Bechtle: 1949) 18, Hervorhebung hinzugefügt.

11. Vgl. hierzu: Markus Waldura, "Der Zauberflöte zweyter Theil," *Archiv für Musikwissenschaft* 1993, 271-72, 290 (wo auch die relevanten Abweichungen von der Vorlage behandelt werden).

12. Jean Starobinski. "A Reading of the Magic Flute," *The Hudson Review* 31, Nr. 3, 422 (als "return of the shadow;") Brown nimmt hingegen eine "Verdunkelung" erst bei Goethe an: Jane Brown, "'The Monstrous Rights of the Present:' Goethe and the Humanity of 'Die Zauberflöte'," *The Opera Quarterly*, 28 (2012), 18.

13. Joseph Müller-Blattau, "Der Zauberflöte Zweiter Teil. Ein Beitrag zum Thema Goethe und Mozart," *Goethe. Jahrbuch der Goethe-Gesellschaft* 18 (1956), 162. Dagegen: Dieter Borchmeyer, *Mozart oder die Entdeckung der Liebe* (Frankfurt a/M: Insel, 2005) 277.

14. Brief an Paul Wranitzki v. 24.01.1796.

15. Nicholas Boyle, *Goethe. Der Dichter in seiner Zeit* (Frankfurt a/M: Insel, 2004) 2:379.

16. Junk 55; Richard Samuel, "Goethe and 'Die Zauberflöte,'" *German Life and Letters* 10, Nr. 1, 32; Gruber 80; Hans-Albrecht Koch, "Goethes Fortsetzung der Schikanederschen

Zauberflöte. Ein Beitrag zur Deutung des Fragments und zur Rekonstruktion des Schlusses," *Jahrbuch des Freien Deutschen Hochstifts* 8 (1969), 165; Emil Staiger, *Musik und Dichtung* (Zürich: Atlantis, 1966) 54; Otto Conrady, *Goethe—Leben und Werk* (Düsseldorf: Artemis & Winkler, 1994) 735–36 ("reflektiertes Nachspiel").

17. Junk 76.

18. Hermann Abert, *Goethe und die Musik* (Hamburg: Severius, 2013) 101–2 ("Bühnenwirksamkeit," "Kontrastwirkung"); Otto Rommel, *Die Alt-Wiener Volkskomödie. Ihre Geschichte vom barocken Welt-Theater bis zum Tode Nestroys* (Wien: Anton Schroll, 1952) 49 ("Steigerung" "ganz im Geiste barocker Theatralik"); Gruber 80 (Steigerung der "Kontrasthaftigkeit der Handlung"); Matthew Birkhold, "Goethe and the Uncontrollable Business of Appropriative Stage Sequels," *Goethe Yearbook* 25 (2018), 111, 122.

19. Hans-Georg Gadamer, "Die Bildung zum Menschen. Der Zauberflöte anderer Teil," in *Vom geistigen Lauf des Menschen. Studien zu unvollendeten Dichtungen Goethes* (Tübingen: Mohr, 1967) 126, 133; Gruber 84; Arthur Henkel, *Goethe-Erfahrungen. Studien und Beiträge* (Stuttgart: Metzler, 1982) 1:149, 157, 159; Müller-Blattau 162–136. Borchmeyer sieht eine Kontinuität im "Triumph der Mutterliebe über die Elemente" (Borchmeyer, *Mozart* 269), nicht aber hinsichtlich der Macht der Musik (277).

20. Alfons Rosenberg, "Alchemie und Zauberflöte," *Mozart-Jahrbuch* (1971/72): 402–14; George Cebadal, *Goethes Die Zauberflöte II. Die Entdeckung von Goethes ägyptischen Mysterien im Bindeglied zwischen Mozarts "Zauberflöte" und der "Faust"-Dichtung* (Norderstedt: Bod, 2016). Cf. infra Fn. 100, 125 und zugehörigen Text.

21. Jane Brown, "An den Grenzen des Möglichen. Goethe und 'Die Zauberflöte,'" in *Modell "Zauberflöte": der Kredit des Möglichen*, hrsg. von Matthias Mayer (Hildesheim: Echo, 2007).

22. Werner Michler, "'Die Zauberflöte' und das Problem der literarischen Gattungen. Zu Mozart und Goethe," in *Mozarts literarische Spuren*, hrsg. von Lucjan Pachalski (Wien: Praesens, 2008) 25, 28; Rosenberg, "Alchemie und Zauberflöte," 268; Andreas Blödorn, "Fortgehn ins Unendliche. Goethes 'Der Zauberflöte Zweyter Theil' als kosmologische Allegorie auf Mozarts Oper," *Jahrbuch für Internationale Germanistik* 89 (2007), 127 ("Kontrafaktur"), 146 ("mystischer Eklektizismus"). Seidlin hat ebenfalls schon früh die "Entmenschlichung" von Goethes Fortsetzung gesehen: Oskar Seidlin, "Goethes Zauberflöte," *Monatshefte für Deutschen Unterricht* 35, Nr. 2 (1943), 56.

23. Weiss geht hier sogar so weit anzunehmen, dass Goethe sich in Mozart (und dessen *Zauberflöte*) selbst erkannte: Weiss 23. Auf die enge "geistige Verwandtschaft Goethes und Mozarts" verweist neben Staiger auch Nettl, *Goethe und Mozart*, 39, und dies durchaus auch im Hinblick auf den "Todesgedanken," den auch andere in Goethes *Zauberflöte* als Motiv herausgearbeitet haben (u.a. Seidlin 58).

24. Gespräch mit Eckermann v. 29.01.1827.

25. Koch 130.

26. Paul Nettl, *Mozart and Masonry* (New York: Dorset, 1957), 40; Rosenberg, "Alchemie und Zauberflöte"; Nicholas Till, *Mozart and the Enlightenment: Truth, Virtue, and Beauty in Mozart's operas* (London: Norton, 1992) 292–308. Siehe auch: Paul Nettl, "Deutungen und Fortsetzungen der 'Zauberflöte,'" in *Die Zauberflöte*, hrsg. von Attila Csampai (Reinbeck: Rowohlt, 1982) 183–200.

27. Rosenberg, "Alchemie und Zauberflöte," 270.

28. Allegorie: Joseph Szöverffy, "Zauberflöte und Welttheater. Begegnung von Barock und Aufklärung," *Archiv für Kulturgeschichte* 48 (1966), 275; Jane Brown, "The

Queen of the Night and the Crisis of Allegory," *Goethe Yearbook* 8 (1996), 142–56; Symbol: Rommel, *Volkskomödie*, 526; Seidlin 54; Nettl, "Deutungen," 194; Conrady 735–36. Freimaurertum: Seidlin 53–54.

29. Weiss 16, der aber durchaus zutreffend erkennt, dass sich bei Goethe "Natur" durch "Elementarmächte" ersetzt findet (Weiss 18). Ähnlich Borchmeyer mit Verweis auf Gadamer: Borchmeyer, *Mozart*, 269.

30. Staiger 49.

31. Meine Monografie zu Schikaneder und Mozarts *Zauberflöte* befindet sich gerade in Überarbeitung für eine Verlagsveröffentlichung.

32. S. supra Fn. 3.

33. Vgl. Hubert Meister, *Musikalische Rhethorik und ihre Bedeutung für das Verständnis barocker Musik* (Regensburg: Feuchtigner & Gleichlauf, 1995); Dénes Zoltai, *Ethos und Affekt: Geschichte der philosophischen Musikästhetik von den Anfängen bis zu Hegel* (Berlin: Akademie-Verlag, 1970; Hans-Heinrich Unger, *Die Beziehungen zwischen Musik und Rhetorik im 16.-18. Jahrhundert* (Hildesheim: Olms, 1941; Zur Nachwirkung im 18. Jahrhundert: Ernest Harries, "Johann Mattheson and the Affekten-, Figuren-, and Rhetoriklehren," in *La musique et le rite sacré et profane*, hrsg. von Marc Honegger and Paul Prevost (Straßburg 1986) 2:517–31; Gottfried Scholz, "Affekte und rhetorische Figuren in Mozarts frühen Konzertarien," in *Neue Musik und Tradition. Festschrift Rudolf Stephan zum 65. Geburtstag* (Laaber: Laaber-Verlag, 1990) 135–48.

34. Athanasius Kircher, *Neue Hall- und Thon-Kunst* (Nördlingen: Heylen, 1684) 124.

35. Athanasius Kircher, *Musurgia Universalis* (Schwäbisch Hall: Laidigen, 1662) 139.

36. Kircher, *Musurgia Universalis*, 139.

37. Unter anderem in Johann Adolph Scheibe, *Critischer Musikus* (Leipzig: Bernhard Christoph Breitkopf, 1745) 683–84.

38. René Descartes, *Musicae Compendium* (1618).

39. Kircher, *Tonkunst*, 125.

40. Johann Gottfried von Herder, *Abhandlung über den Ursprung der Sprache* (Berlin: Christian Friedrich Voß, 1772) 21–22.

41. Herder 23. Zu Herder vgl. auch Harmut Krones, "Johann Gottfried Herder, die Affektenlehre und die Musik," in *Ideen und Ideale. Johann Gottfried Herder in Ost und West*, hrsg. von Peter Andraschke und Helmut Loos (Freiburg im Breisgau: Rombach, 2002) 71–88.

42. Jacob Adlung, *Anleitung zur musikalischen Gelahrtheit* (Dresden und Leipzig: Breitkopf, 1783) hier insbesondere S. 37, 80–84.

43. Johann Joseph Kausch, *Psychologische Abhandlung über den Einfluß der Töne und insbesondere der Musik auf die Seele* (Breslau: Johann Friedrich Korn 1782). Angaben im Folgenden nach dieser Ausgabe, mit Verszählung in Klammern im Text.

44. Kausch 4, 8, 14–15, 23, 28, 47, 72, 89, 105, 113, 131, 160, 196, 196.

45. Vgl. hierzu u.a. Johann Georg Sulzers "Untersuchung über den Ursprung der angenehmen und unangenehmen Empfindungen" in *Vermischte Philosophische Schriften* (Leipzig: Weidmanns Erben und Reich, 1773) 1–98).

46. Kausch 169.

47. Kausch 89.

48. Kausch 21.

49. Kausch 160.

50. Sulzer, "Untersuchung," 40.

51. Kausch 47.

52. Lemma "Ton (redende Künste)," in Johann Georg Sulzer, *Allgemeine Theorie der Schönen Künste* (Leipzig: Weidemann, 1774) 4:451–52.

53. Johann Gottfried Herder, *Ideen zur Philosophie der Geschichte der Menschheit von. Dritter Theil* (Riga: Johann Friedrich Hartknoch, 1787) 155.

54. Johann Nicolaus Forkel, *Allgemeine Geschichte der Musik* (Leipzig: im Schwickertschen Verlage, 1788) 1:125.

55. Karl Burney, *Abhandlung über die Musik der Alten*, übers. Johann Joachim Eschenburg (Leipzig: im Schwickertschen Verlage, 1781) 87.

56. Forkel 1:125 (§ 38).

57. Vgl. etwa *Musicalische Real-Zeitung* 20 (20.05. 1789), 32.

58. Michel Paul Guy de Chabanon. *Ueber die Musik und deren Wirkungen* (Leipzig: Friedrich Gotthold Jacobäer & Sohn, 1781) 172.

59. *Adelheit von Veltheim. Ein Schauspiel mit Gesang in vier Akten* (Leipzig: im Verlage der Dykischen Buchhandlung, 1781) 33.

60. Das Lemma "Musik" der *Allgemeinen Theorie der Schönen Künste* spricht vertretend etwa von der "wahren Natur dieser reizenden Kunst," Sulzer, *Allgemeine Theorie*, 3:347.

61. Johann Mattheson, *Der Vollkommene Capellmeister* (Hamburg: Christan Herold, 1739).

62. *Sammlung der besten deutschen Schriftsteller und Dichter 59. Band 6: Wielands Neue Götter-Gespräche* (Karlsruhe: Christan Gottlieb Schmieder, 1791) 49.

63. Mylius' "An die deutschen Dichter"; Lessings "An den Herrn Marpurg über die Regeln der Wissenschaften zum Vergnügen; besonders der Poesie und Tonkunst."

64. Christoph Martin Wieland, *Geschichte des Agathon* (Frankfurt a/M: Orell & Geßner, 1766) 1:71.

65. "Indem erfüllt, wie aus der höchsten Sfäre, / die lieblichste Musik der Lüfte stillen Raum; / Es tönt als ob ringsum auf jedem Baum / Ein jedes Blatt zur kehlen worden wäre, / Und Mara's Engelston / der Zauber aller Seelen, / Erschallte tausendfach aus allen diesen kehlen," Christoph Martin Wieland, *Oberon*, hrsg. von Wolfgang Jahn (München: Goldmann, 1964) Nr. 56; dagegen abwertend: Wieland, Oberon, 226–27.

66. Julius von Soden, *Anna Boley Königin von England* (Nürnberg: Felßeckersche Buchhandlung, 1791) 51.

67. Vgl. supra Fn. 33.

68. Kausch 169; Sulzer äußert sich ebenfalls zum Thema im Lemma "Ton (redende Künste)" der *Allgemeine Theorie der Schönen Künste*.

69. "In seiner Lage schien ihm der kürzeste und bequemste Weg zum Glück und Ruhm die Wissenschaften zu sein; doch kaum hatte er ihren Zauber gekostet, als der heftigste Durst nach Wahrheit in seiner Seele entbrannte": Friedrich Klinger, *Faust's Leben, Thaten und Höllenfahrt in fünf Büchern* (St. Petersburg: Kriele, 1791) 6.

70. Immanuel Kant, *Anthropologie in pragmatischer Hinsicht* (Königsberg: Friedrich Nicolovius, 1798), 237.

71. Friedrich Gottlieb Klopstock, *Elegien der Deutschen* (Lemgo: Meyersche Buchhandlung, 1776) 220.

72. Johann Wolfgang von Goethe, *Goethes Werke*, ed. im Auftrag der Großherzogin Sophie von Sachsen Weimar (Weimar: Böhlau, 1887–1919) I/11:150. Nach dieser Ausgabe wird im Folgenden mit der Sigle "WA" zitiert.

73. "Unglücklicher Zauber der Liebe, welchen Drang hast Du in mein Herz gegossen," Johann Thiard Gräz, *Das Bild ächter Liebe oder die Stiefmutter. Ein Originallustspiel in 5 Aufzügen* (Leipzig: Ferstli, 1790) 28.

74. "Dieser Zauber in den Blicken / Dieser schöne Rosenmund, / Auf der Wang das blüh'nde Bund / In dem Lächeln dies Entzücken, / Dieses Busenschleyers Geiz, / Dieses schlanken Wuchses Reiz, / Dieses Zauberfüßchens Schweben, / Diese runde volle Hand, / … Steckt mein Hirn und Herz in Brand": Johann Gross, *Die Illuminaten. Ein komisches Original-Singspiel in zwey Aufzügen* (Wien, o.A.: 1787) 42.

75. Wieland, *Oberon*, 226–27.

76. Im *Oberon* erscheint die durch sinnlichen "Zauber" induzierte Liebe keineswegs als erstrebenswert und wird von der keuschen, rechten Liebe geschieden.

77. Johann André *Die Bezauberten. Eine komische Oper in einem Aufzuge. Nach dem Französischen der Madame Favart* (Berlin: Himburg, 1777) 24.

78. *La fée Urgèle, ou Ce qui plaît aux dames* (UA Frankreich 1765, Deutschland 1773).

79. Leopold Huber, *Kasperl der Lustige Schaahfhirt, oder das Mayfest auf den Alpen. Ein komisches Singspiel in zwey Aufzügen* (Wien: mit Goldhannschen Schriften 1791) 51.

80. Julius von Soden, *Schauspiele* (Berlin: Friedrich Maurer 1788) 1:104.

81. Benjamin Noldmann [Adolf von Knigge], *Geschichte der Aufklärung in Abyssinien* (Frankfurt a/M: o.A., 1791) 2:83.

82. *Le Fou par amour ou la fatale épreuve.*

83. François-Marie Mayeur de St. Paul, *Wahnsinn aus Liebe, oder die fatale Probe. Ein Lustspiel in zwei Aufzügen* (Strasburg: in der akademischen Buchhandlung, 1789) 5.

84. Johann Georg Sulzer, *Vermischte Schriften. Zweyter Theil* (Leipzig, Weidmanns Erben und Reich: 1781) 120. Vgl. hierzu auch Sulzers Lemma "Ton" in der *Allgemeine Theorie der Schönen Künste*.

85. Johann Michael Armbruster *Gedichte* (Kempten: Typographische Gesellschaft, 1785) 1:44–45.

86. Moses Mendelssohn, *Jerusalem oder überreligiöse Macht und Judenthum* (Frankfurt a/M: o.A., 1791) 77.

87. "Wundert man sich noch über die Zauberkraft der Harmonie?" (Moses Mendelssohn, *Philosophische Schriften* (Berlin: Voß 1761) 1:150); an anderer Stelle heißt es allgemeiner für die schönen Künste: "Wenn der Künstler uns durch seine Zauberkraft in seine solche Gemüthsverfassung setzen kann, so hat er den Gipfel seiner Kunst erreicht, und den würdigsten Bestimmungen der schönen Künste Genüge getahn," Mendelssohn 130.

88. Friedrike Sophie Seyler *Hüon und Amande. Ein Romantisches Singspiel in Fünf Aufzügen nach Wielands Oberon* (Flensburg, Schleswig und Leipzig: in der Kortenschen Buchhandlung, 1789)—und zwar als "Zauberblicke," vor denen schon Gellert im *Das Orakel* warnt.

89. *Der Stein der Weisen oder Die Zauberinsel* (UA: Wien, 1790)

90. Vgl. hierzu etwa die Klassifikation Rommels: Otto Rommel, *Die romantisch-komischen Original-Zauberspiele* (Darmstadt: Wissenschaftliche Buchgesellschaft, 1974).

91. *Kaspar, der Fagottist, oder: Die Zauberzither.*

92. S. supra Fn. 3.

93. Christoph Martin Wieland, "Versuch über das deutsche Singspiel und einige dahin einschlagende Gegenstände," *Der Teutsche Merkur* 1775, Drittes Vierteljahr, 83.

94. Vgl. etwa die Rezension in *Der Teutsche Merkur*, 1787, 2.Vj, 260.

95. Johann Christian Brandes, *Sämtliche dramatische Schriften* (Hamburg: Dykschen, 1790) 1:xxxiv.

96. Thomas Blackwell, *Untersuchung über Homers Leben und Schriften*, transl. Johann Heinrich Voß (Leipzig: Weygandsche Buchhandlung, 1776).

97. Jean Terrasson, *Geschichte des egyptischen Königs Sethos*, transl. Matthias Claudius (Breslau: Gottlieb Löwe, 1777) 267-73.

98. Blackwell 260.

99. Christian August Vulpius, *Die Zauberflöte. Eine Oper in drei Aufzügen* (Leipzig: Johann Samuel Heinsius, 1794) 41.

100. Gemeint ist das Rudiment einer magischen Herstellung der Flöte durch Paminas Vater als Vorgeschichte der Oper. Rationalisiert versteht die Oper dagegen: Otto Jahn, *Mozart* (Leipzig: Breitkopf und Härtel, 1867) 2:530-31. Auch Rommel ordnet die *Zauberflöte* in jene Zauber- und Feenspiele ein, die sich dem Thema aus einer gänzlich rationalen Perspektive nähern: Rommel, *Volkskomödie* 487-89. Gleiches gilt für Assmann (Jan Assmann, "'Die Zauberflöte.' Märchen oder Mysterium?" in *Mozart. Experiment Aufklärung im Wien des ausgehenden 18. Jahrhunderts*, hrsg. von Herbert Lachmayer, 761-69 (Wien: Hatje Cantz, 2006), sowie Jan Assmann, *Die Zauberflöte. Oper und Mysterium* (München: Hanser, 2005) 68. Henkel übersieht dies, wenn er gerade die Marginalisierung des Zauberflöteninstruments bei Goethe als Beleg für einen "antimagisch, sittlich-human[en] Zug" sieht (157)—und ignoriert überdies die Steigerung des Magischen bei Goethe durch die Hinzufügung eines ganzen Arsenals "echter" Zaubermittel. Rosenberg versieht die Flötenmusik ebenfalls mit einer mythischen Deutung; Alfons Rosenberg, *Die Zauberflöte. Geschichte und Deutung von Mozarts Oper* (München: Prestel, 1964) Kapitel 5. Ähnlich urteilt Siegfried Morenz: *Die Zauberflöte. Eine Studie zum Lebenszusammenhang Ägypten—Antike Abendland* (Münster: Böhlau, 1952) 59.

101. Assmann, *Die Zauberflöte*, 68.

102. Marianne Tettlebaum, "Whose Magic Flute?" *Representations* 102, Nr. 1 (2008): 90.

103. Auf die *Zauberflöte* als Ritual und dessen verändernde Wirkung auf den Zuschauer, nebst der Rolle der Musik in diesem Prozess, verweisen u.a.: Assmann, *Die Zauberflöte*, 22, 65, 70-71; Assmann, "'Die Zauberflöte.' Märchen oder Mysterium?"; sowie: Jan Assmann, "Kunst und Rituale: Mozarts Zauberflöte," in *Die neue Kraft der Rituale*, hrsg. von Axel Michaels (Heidelberg: Winter, 2007) 111.

104. Cf. Assmann, *Die Zauberflöte*, 68-71, 294. Eine kritische Betrachtung der Macht des Flöteninstruments und der Frage der "agency" bieten: Tettlebaum, "Whose Magic Flute?"; Rose Rosengard Subotnik, "Whose 'Magic Flute?' Intimations of Reality at the Gates of the Enlightenment," *19th-Century Music* 15, Nr. 2 (1991) 132-50; Carolyn Abbate, *In Search of Opera* (Princeton, NJ: Princeton UP, 2003) Kapitel 2.

105. Borchmeyer, *Mozart*, 275.

106. Dies ist eine der Thesen meiner noch zu veröffentlichenden Monografie zur *Zauberflöte*, s. supra Fn. 31.

107. Rommel, *Volkskomödie* 488, 491, 493.

108. Unter anderem einen "Zauberring."

109. Vulpius 255.

110. Vulpius 275.

111. "Du kannst mir ihr allmächtig handeln, / der Menschen Leidenschaft verwandeln. / Bei deiner Flöte Zauberklang, / verwandelt Drohn sich in Gesang," Vulpius 255.

112. "Mein Dank soll mit der Flöt' erklingen / so will ich eine Hymne singen," Vulpius 263.

113. Vulpius 238.

114. Vulpius 263.

115. Vgl. hierzu etwa Sulzers Lemma "Ton (heilende Wirkung)" der *Allgemeine Theorie der Schönen Künste*.

116. Gruber 81; Borchmeyer, *Mozart*, 275.

117. Erwin Jaeckle, *Goethes Zauberflöten-Fragment*, in *Die Elfenspur*, 19–43 (Zürich: Atlantis, 1958) 33–34.

118. Jaeckle 34–38; ähnlich: Borchmeyer, *Mozart* 272. Auf die Bedeutung der "Elementarmächte" in Goethes Fragment verweisen auch Weiss 18 und Borchmeyer, *Mozart* 269, 275.

119. Paralipomena Nr. 5, zitiert bei Koch 141 ("Und Menschenlieb und Menschenkräfte, sind mehr als alle Zauberey … Nein durch keine Zaubereyen darf die Liebe sich entweihen").

120. Boyle 2:378.

121. Rommel, *Volkskomödie*, 530.

122. WA III/1:92–93.

123. Hans J. Lind, "Geheimnisse bei Terrasson und Lessing," *Lessing Yearbook/ Jahrbuch* 40, Nr. 6 (2019): 153–174.

124. Ich lege für die *Geheimnisse* ein anti-alchemistisches, rationalisiertes Verständnis des "echten" Rosenkreuzertums zugrunde, wie es Hans-Dietrich Dahnke (*Goethe-Handbuch*, 550) und Julius Goebel ("Goethe's 'Geheimnisse,'" *The Journal of English and Germanic Philology* 15 [1916]: 339) herausgearbeitet haben.

125. Assmann hat im 4. Kapitel seiner Monografie zur *Zauberflöte* (147–66) sowie in mehreren Essays beschrieben, wie rationalisiert gerade in Freimaurerkreisen lang tradierte Mysterien neu gelesen wurden, von Ignaz von Born bis Warburton (s. Assmann, supra Fn. 100). Eine kurze Liste relevanter Autoren bietet zudem Jan Assmann, "Schiller, Mozart und die Suche nach neuen Mysterien," in *Athenäum. Jahrbuch für Romantik* 16 (2006), 20.

126. Vgl. Michler 20; Weiss 16; Borchmeyer, *Mozart* 269, 275.

127. Rosenberg, "Alchemie und Zauberflöte," 276.

128. Rosenberg, "Alchemie und Zauberflöte," 269–70; Seidelin 60; Szvöfferly 275; Brown, *Monstrous Right* 11; Brown, "An den Grenzen" 194; Koch 156; Borchmeyer, *Mozart* 259.

129. So auch: Jaeckle 24, Koch 149, Michler 20, Borchmeyer, *Mozart* 265, 275. Vgl. auch Boyle 2:401; Matthew H. Birkhold, "Goethe and the Uncontrollable Business of Appropriative Stage Sequels," *Goethe Yearbook* 25 (2018): 109–31.

130. Vgl. etwa Wilhelm Heinrich Wackenroders Essay "Die Wunder der Tonkunst. Das eigentümliche innere Wesen der Tonkunst und die Seelenlehre der heutigen

Instrumentalmusik," in: *Sämtliche Werke und Briefe. Historisch-kritische Ausgabe*, Bd. 1, *Werke*, hrsg. von Silvio Vietta. Heidelberg: 1991.

131. Rosenberg, "Alchemie und Zauberflöte," 268.

132. Vgl. Jörg Krämer, *Deutschsprachiges Musiktheater im späten 18. Jahrhundert: Typologie, Dramaturgie und Anthropologie einer populären Gattung* (Tübingen: De Gruyter, 1998).

133. Rommel, *Volkskomödie* 486.

134. Vgl. die Einführung von Otto Rommel in *Die romantisch-komischen Original-Zauberspiele.* (Reprint; Darmstadt: Wissenschaftliche Buchgesellschaft, 1974), sowie: Rommel, *Volkskomödie* 488-93 und 559-79.

135. Freyherrn von Lehndorff, "*Ulldolini.* Ein Schauspiel in 5 Aufzügen," *Deutsche Schaubühne* 18, Nr. 3 (1791): 6.

136. *Der Teutsche Merkur* 1: 191.

137. Gespräch mit Eckermann v. 6. Dezember 1829. Hierzu fügt sich Goethes Verständnis der Musik als dämonisch: Gespräch v. 8. März 1831.

138. Supra Fn. 128.

139. E. T. A. Hoffmann, *Die Serapions-Brüder* (Berlin: G. Reimer: 1819) 212); Franz Hermann, *Ideen über das antike, romantische und deutsche Schauspiel* (Breslau: o.A., 1820) 26 ("wahrhaft romantisch"). In den 1830er Jahren erhält Mozarts Zauberflöte selbst in Theateranzeigen den Untertitel "romantische Oper in zwei Akten" (vgl. etwa *Didascalica* 45 (1835) 3; *Frankfurter Konversationsblatt* v. 1. Dezember 1833 (Nr. 98): "ächt romantische Oper."

140. S. supra Fn. 20, 100, 125 und zugehöriger Text.

141. Zur Aufklärung gehörend liest die *Zauberflöte* dagegen die Mehrheit des Schrifttums, von Branscombe bis Assmann. Krämer sieht die *Zauberflöte* als Teil einer aufgeklärten Empfindsamkeit (Krämer, *Deutschsprachiges Musiktheater im späten 18. Jahrhundert*), ebenso Borchmeyer (Borchmeyer, *Mozart* 29); von Matt hat ebenfalls empfindsame Tendenzen in Mozarts Opern herausgearbeitet: Peter v. Matt, "Papagenos Sehnsucht," in *Mozarts Opernfiguren. Grosse Herren, rasende Weiber—gefährliche Liebschaften*, hrsg. von Dieter Borchmeyer, 153-66 (Bern: P. Haupt, 1992). Auch für Rommel ist die "Zauberflöte" nur aus einer wirkungsästhetischen Dimension ("barocke Theatralik"; "Bildbarock") eine "deutsche Barockoper," hinsichtlich der Humanisierung indes eindeutig Teil der Aufklärung (Rommel, *Volkskomödie* 493-95; 512-14).

142. Borchmeyer, *Mozart* 279, Hervorhebung hinzugefügt. Allgemeiner zum Verhältnis von Goethe und Mozart siehe: Robert Spaethling, *Music and Mozart in the Life of Goethe* (Columbia: Camden House, 1987); sowie Abert, *Goethe und die Musik*.

143. Der Beginn des Projekts (unter dem Arbeitstitel "Die Jagd") fällt indes ebenfalls in die Zeit von Goethes *Zauberflöte*.

144. "Zu zeigen wie das Unbändige, Unüberwindliche oft besser durch Liebe und durch Frömmigkeit als durch Gewalt bezwungen werde, war die Aufgabe dieser Novelle," Eckermann, 18. Januar 1827.

145. Heinrich von Kleist, *Die heilige Cäcilie oder die Gewalt der Musik* (1810).

LESLEY FULTON

# "Ächt antike Denkmale"?: Goethe and the Hemsterhuis Gem Collection

**Abstract:** The small collection of engraved gems selected by Dutch philosopher and connoisseur Frans Hemsterhuis was, for more than thirty years, a source of fascination for Johann Wolfgang von Goethe. This article examines the aesthetic principles on which Hemsterhuis based the formation of his collection and traces the collection's reception and influence on Goethe. Motifs illustrating the classical ideal, be they of Greek or modern origin, were the primary justification for inclusion, with authenticity playing a subsidiary role in the collection. Hemsterhuis's appreciation of the Greek ideal was based purely on stylistic characteristics, formal components dependent entirely on observation. Analysis of the dating attributions for this collection since its formation demonstrate claims of authenticity based on connoisseurship to be permanently in a state of flux. The collection also informs aspects of Goethe's own principles of classification.

**Keywords:** engraved gems, aesthete, classical ideal, eighteenth-century replica, connoisseurship.

GOETHE, THE COLLECTOR, and Goethe, the "universal man" of his time—these two facets of Goethe's identity are intrinsically linked; his collections played a decisive role in his scientific achievements and in molding his aesthetic sensibility. The range of Goethe's collections reflect his interests in both the natural and physical worlds—with a black-figured Greek vase being just as much an object of curiosity as a block of feldspar. The development of Goethe's collections was dependent upon his keen observational skills, trained through learning to draw. In a conversation with Chancellor von Müller towards the end of his life, Goethe recalls: "Meine eignen Versuche im Zeichnen haben mir doch den grosen Vortheil gebracht, die Naturgegenstände schärfer aufzufassen; ich kann mir ihre verschiednen Formen jeden Augenblick mit Bestimmtheit zurückrufen" (My own attempts at drawing have given me the particular advantage that I am able to observe natural objects in a more penetrating way; I can recall, at any moment, their varying forms with absolute certainty).[1] Goethe interpreted and recorded any object of interest to him, capturing the image on paper either as a simple sketch or as an outline drawing. These accurate observations were the records he made to grasp the form of an object, its external structure or morphology, slight variations in appearance indicating a close relationship between two objects. Goethe went on to develop a system of classification for each of his collections. Since every additional item was placed in the hierarchy based on its similarity or difference in form, the larger the collection, the more accurate its classification system.[2] By imposing order on the natural environment through his classification schemes based on form, Goethe aspired to make sense of nature in all its diversity.

Goethe likely applied the same methodology to his collections of gem impressions—casts made using a variety of materials such as sealing wax, sulfur, plaster, and glass paste that played an important role in his art historical research. He amassed a vast number of these replicas, often complete collections, organized in dactyliothecae. He personally owned as many as 5,000 of these casts[3] and also had access to the ducal collection.[4] In addition to his cast collection, Goethe also possessed a small collection of engraved gems, many of which he had purchased on his first Italian journey. He realized while a student in Adam Friedrich Oeser's atelier at Leipzig that it was only through the study of the original engraved gem that the art of the gem cutter could be fully understood. When the opportunity to study the renowned gem collection of the Dutch philosopher and aesthete Frans Hemsterhuis arose, Goethe found himself in possession of a set of intaglios that would become an important tool for his appreciation and interpretation of the classical world of the Greeks.

My argument hinges on the perplexing question of connoisseurship and authenticity and is based on Goethe's claim that the aesthetic qualities of a finely carved stone would always be apparent to the connoisseur through intuition supported by a practiced eye. The subjective essence of this assertion is emphasized in his qualifying statement that a man might be able to convince himself but be unable to justify his claims to another.[5] I seek to link the formation of Hemsterhuis's collection of engraved gems with Goethe's aesthetic concept of the beautiful and demonstrate its dependence on the practices discussed by Pierre-Jean Mariette in his *Traité des Pierres Gravées* (Treatise on Engraved Gems).[6] That Goethe should prize the collection as he did is understandable, given his and Hemsterhuis's shared aesthetic appreciation of beauty and its relation to the Greek ideal—ideas upon which Hemsterhuis expounded in his essay "Lettre sur la sculpture" (Letter Concerning Sculpture). For this reason, I begin by examining connoisseurship and its methodology from the mid-eighteenth century to the early 1800s: first, regarding its characterization of the Greek ideal and, second, in terms of its stylistic assessment of early modern gems. The raison d'être of Hemsterhuis's collection was that the gems illustrate the Greek ideal, and the aesthete, believing himself to be a true Greek and therefore perfectly attuned to the mores of the classical Greek world, had little difficulty identifying what, for him, were authentic artifacts. Goethe, however, appears to have exercised more caution in his assessment of Hemsterhuis's gems and, in the next section, I discuss conflicting opinions concerning the dating of gems in terms of notions of authenticity and connoisseurship that have been generated over a period of more than 250 years. Such attributions, based on connoisseurship, move from ancient Greek artifacts in the eighteenth century to renaissance material in the twentieth century and, finally, to eighteenth-century copies of Greek and renaissance gems in the present century. These differences of opinion highlight the fluidity of such methods of scholarship. I conclude with a comment on the value of an "open" collection for scholarship today.

## Formation and Composition of the Hemsterhuis Collection

As son of the Greek philologist Tiberius Hemsterhuis, Frans Hemsterhuis inherited a lifelong passion for classical scholarship. However, it was Greek culture, particularly its aesthetic and ethical values, that dominated his reception of antiquity. The younger Hemsterhuis did not read classical authors primarily as a philologist, but to appreciate their remarks on the beauty of form. His admiration for antiquity culminated in his enthusiasm for Homer and Plato, referring to the language of Homer as "the language of the gods." Hemsterhuis's aesthetic sensibility, particularly attuned to an appreciation of form in ancient art, became especially apparent in the small collection of precious gems that he gradually acquired, which alone satisfied his desire for the beautiful.[7] The importance of such fine feelings had been identified by Mariette, along with taste, as essential for the appreciation of the art of glyptics: "I acknowledge it is engraved gems alone that are of sufficient merit to affect someone who prides himself in possessing both taste and fine feelings. Happy is he who contemplates those precious remnants of antiquity: they will be for him the source of infinite knowledge, they will perfect his taste, and without his noticing, his imagination will be filled with the most noble and magnificent thoughts" (Mariette 1:34).[8] Indeed, Hemsterhuis seems to have assembled his collection based on the same aesthetic ideals as those of Mariette.

Mariette's *Traité*, intended for collectors such as Hemsterhuis who wished to gain greater insight and appreciation of their miniature works of art, represents a milestone in the study of antique and modern engraved gems.[9] Hemsterhuis made many references to *Traité* in his own catalogue, *Pierres Gravées Antiques* (Antique Engraved Gems)[10] and also included material from *Traité* in his dissertation on sculpture.[11] Indeed, a reading of Mariette's advice to the would-be connoisseur of glyptics,[12] suggests that he exercised considerable influence on Hemsterhuis, particularly with regard to an appreciation of style in relation to historicity. Thus, it would seem perfectly reasonable that Hemsterhuis should choose to include in his own collection a number[13] of the gems illustrated in the second volume of *Traité*, the majority of which were examples from the French royal cabinet. With these fine examples available to him, he could make stylistic comparisons and experience the work of individual artists.

Further examples of gems from other distinguished collections that appeared in Hemsterhuis's own collection include examples from the Stosch, Farnese, and Marlborough collections.[14] Hemsterhuis appears to have had a particular penchant for signed intaglios and maintained a lively dialogue about them in his correspondence[15] with the gem engraver Lorenz

Natter.[16] On his travels through Europe, Natter had frequently visited the Dutch Republic, and his talents as medalist and engraver secured employment at the court of William IV of Orange as well as the friendship of Frans Hemsterhuis. Natter was on good terms with Hemsterhuis; he taught him the art of modeling in wax and, in return, Hemsterhuis promoted Natter's art in the Dutch Republic.[17] In addition to engraving gems, Natter also acted as an agent for their sale and Hemsterhuis was more than ready to take advantage of any information he might pass on should a favorable opportunity arise to enrich his collection.[18]

The collection of about seventy engraved gems might be described as eclectic, since there was no apparent system involved in Hemsterhuis's selection of individual pieces: for example, gods and heroes from Greek mythology lie alongside an almost equal number of portrait gems of Greek philosophers, sovereigns, and soldiers, as well as Roman heads of state. Thus, one must question what unites this seemingly unrelated group of carved stones and what criteria Hemsterhuis used when purchasing a gem to add to his collection. His choice appears to be governed simply by the aesthetic quality of the gems—they had to be beautiful,[19] the finest examples of the engraver's art. By applying his aesthetic principles to these carved images, Hemsterhuis evoked his personal vision of the Greek ideal, concepts he developed in his essay, "Lettre sur la sculpture."

"Lettre sur la sculpture" was written in response to a request from the banker Theodorus de Smeth that he present his ideas on sculpture. Three years earlier, in 1762, Hemsterhuis had described de Smeth's collection in his first published work "Lettre sur une pierre antique" (A Letter Concerning an Antique Gem).[20] The subject of "Lettre sur la sculpture" is discussed in a very broad sense—Hemsterhuis includes references to both bas relief sculpture and carved stones as well as free-standing works. Indeed, his drawing introducing the essay (Fig. 1) is based on such an interplay of the art of sculpture; the relief represented on the pedestal is derived from the motif of a gem he possessed[21]—the notion of *disegno* (design) relates them and also unites them with the art forms of painting and architecture.[22]

In the essay, Hemsterhuis develops his notion of beauty, defined as that which allows us to grasp the greatest number of ideas in the shortest amount of time (*Sculpture* 5-6). Beauty is unity in variety, and it is the contour, through its finesse and fluency, that enables the observer to grasp within a moment, the idea of beauty (*Sculpture* 9-10). Clarity of the outline is essential if a work of art is to reach its optimum; if contours are confused, then attainment of the ideal will be jeopardized (*Sculpture* 10). To illustrate his point, Hemsterhuis uses an engraving made after an intaglio in the cabinet of Louis XV of France (Fig. 2). He declares the composition to be marred by lack of clarity in the contours of the individual components, thereby making it difficult to interpret, even for a connoisseur (*Sculpture* 10-11).

Using both a solitary figure and a group as examples, Hemsterhuis then proceeds to refine his thesis further, describing how the fundamental principles of sculpture—the unity or simplicity of the subject, combined with the delicacy and finesse of the contour—might be achieved in order to produce a work of total perfection. An example from Hemsterhuis's collection,

Figure 1. Frontispiece to François Hemsterhuis' *Lettre sur la sculpture* engraved after a drawing by Hemsterhuis. Source: http://digi.ub.uni-heidelberg.de/diglit/hemsterhuis 1769/0001.

his "Adonis"[23] (Fig. 3), demonstrates how the carving of this gem fulfills the above criteria for a solitary figure. The intaglio represents in full-length, a young male nude in three-quarter view holding an unstrung bow in his right hand; he is turned to the left, leaning on a column, a mantle extends from his left arm, behind his back and onto the top of this support, where it is held in place by his right arm. Hemsterhuis himself described the engraving as "très belle" (very fine), qualifying the remark with the comment that the nature of the stone itself, a garnet, made its working extremely difficult. The carving of the gem has a sketch-like quality: the outlining contours are bold, emphasizing the form of the figure as does the drapery, its folds adding variety. The soft curves describing the young hero are complemented by the perpendicular column he leans on, the total effect being one of grace and tranquility.

Following from his discussion of the representation of a solitary figure, Hemsterhuis describes the qualities required for the success of a group: of prime importance was the choice of subject—it had to be imposing, the action of the scene simple, with all members of the group adopting natural poses and depicted as if reinforcing the action. The figures had to be as varied as possible, of different sexes, ages, and proportions (*Sculpture* 23–24). These constraints were applied by Hemsterhuis in his selection of

Figure 2. *Venus et Vulcain*: Pl.XXI in Pierre-Jean Mariette's *Traité des pierres gravées*, Tome II, 1750. Source: http://catalogue.bnf.fr/ark:/12148/cb30884683j.

gems—he owned very few multifigured intaglios and seems to have preferred those scenes composed of only two well-contrasted figures. Analysis of his "Sacrifice de Silene & Bacchus" (Sacrifice of Silenus & Bacchus, *Catalogue* 4-6, no. 5) demonstrates the particular properties he is seeking when selecting a gem of this type (Fig.4). What is most striking about

Figure 3. *Adonis*. Wine-red garnet set in a gold-plated ring. Vertical oval. 17.5 × 13.5 × 4.5 mm., National Museum of Antiquities, Leiden, Inv. Nr. GS-10784.

the composition of the motif is the manner in which the entire surface of the gem is dominated by the two figures. The boundary of the design is enclosed by the perimeter of the stone and the carving of the motif complements its curvature. The scene is set simply by the attitudes of the protagonists, Bacchus and Silenus, together with the sacrificial altar, its bacchanal-like character underlined by the presence of the thyrsos. Hemsterhuis described it himself as:

A young man making a sacrifice before an altar, with a Silenus behind him. In one hand, he is holding a cup or patera, as he lifts the other to the heavens. The Silenus has put his thyrsos aside, to be prepared to carry out whatever the priest asks of him. A ring is carved on one side of the altar. The two figures are totally nude and of the greatest beauty. The Silenus is crowned with laurel. (*Catalogue* 4–5)

Figure 4. *Bacchus and Silenus*. Yellow-brown carnelian. Vertical oval. 19 × 16 × 4.5 mm., National Museum of Antiquities, Leiden, Inv. Nr. GS-10662.

The figures must have fulfilled Hemsterhuis's requirements, as he states that they are of the greatest beauty: they are both absorbed in the sacrifice at the altar, their gaze focused on the flames. The outlining contours of the youthful Bacchus represent those of the Greek ideal, his perfect form is thrown into contrast by the heavy, fleshed-out proportions of the old satyr who stands close behind him. The sinuous curve of the contour running from his shoulder to his left foot is accentuated by the corresponding profile of the Silene, and the pose of the figures in three-quarter view increases the number of ideas available to the observer, as does the contrast of their soft, wave-like outlines with those of the regular architectural elements included in the scene. The overall effect is one of pure harmony.

Hemsterhuis concludes the catalogue entry, stating, "my gem is a Greek work of the highest quality" (*Catalogue* 6). His collection was composed mainly of gems carved in the style of the finest period of Greek art, they, above all, demonstrated the aesthetic qualities he sought. He did include a few examples from the Roman period, but those of Etruscan provenance scarcely corresponded to his taste. He rejected Etruscan workmanship, stating that because it originates not from nature but from Egyptian art, it is simply the work of copyists and therefore has no soul (*Sculpture* 17–18).

## Goethe and the Hemsterhuis-Gallitzin Gem Collection

Hemsterhuis formed his collection based on his desire to possess what was beautiful—he sought aesthetic pleasure through these miniature works of art. Having analyzed and assimilated their qualities, he was prepared to part with them;[24] for example, he happily presented his friends, Fagel and Benthink, with valuable pieces. Only a few years after meeting the Princess Adelheid Amalia von Gallitzin[25] in 1775, he handed over his entire collection of about seventy gems to her,[26] abandoning his collection for good. A close platonic relationship developed between Hemsterhuis and the princess, demonstrated by their frequent correspondence.[27] In 1785, he and the princess met Goethe in Weimar while on a tour of central Germany. That she invoked a positive impression on the poet is made clear in a letter dated October 21, 1785, from Goethe to a mutual acquaintance, Friedrich Heinrich Jacobi (1743–1819):

> Diese herrliche Seele hat uns durch ihre Gegenwart zu mancherley Gutem geweckt und gestärckt, und die Ihrigen haben uns schöne Stunden und Freude gegeben. Du kennst mich und sie und wenn ich dir sage daß wir diesmal ganz natürlich gegen einander und offen gewesen sind; so kannst du dir das übrige wohl dencken. (WA IV/7:109)

> This delightful, faithful soul has, by her presence, awoken and strengthened our resolve for goodness, and her family and companions have given us great pleasure. You are acquainted with both she and myself and when I tell you that on this occasion we were quite natural and open with one another, I am certain that you will be able to fill in the rest for yourself.

Despite intermittent inquiries from Goethe, several years passed before the princess renewed her contact with him. Their reunion is detailed by Goethe in his *Campagne in Frankreich* (*Campaign in France*) of 1792 (WA 1/33:229–44), when he visited Münster for a few days as a guest of Princess Gallitzin. There he became acquainted with the Hemsterhuis gem collection; he had earlier attempted to obtain a set of sealing wax impressions of it through Jacobi, but without success: "Verschaffe mir doch Abdrücke in Siegellack von der Fürstinn geschnittenen Steinen. Mich interessiren jetzt diese Kunstwerke mehr weil ich sie beßer verstehe" (WA IV/9:23; Procure for me impressions in sealing wax from the princess's intaglios. My interest in these works of art has grown as I now have a better understanding of

Figure 5. Johann Heinrich Meyer: *Theseus and the Marathonian Bull*, (1796?). Pen and wash in gray ink with white highlights over graphite underdrawing. Klassik Stiftung Weimar, Inv. Nr. KK 2592.

them). The princess observed Goethe's fascination for the gems and, on the day of his departure, insisted that they accompany him to Weimar. The collection remained in his possession until 1797, and during that time, "den geistig ästhetischen Mittelpunct verlieh, um welchen sich Freunde . . . mehrere Tage gern vereinten" (WA I/49.2:101; became an intellectual and aesthetic focus, uniting and occupying friends over a period of several days).

Goethe, being very much aware that at any moment he might have to return his treasure to its rightful owner, planned to make impressions of the collection with the help of his advisor on artistic matters, Heinrich Meyer.[28] A recipe for glass pastes[29] was sent to him from Rome.[30] Goethe had previously commented on the fine quality of gem impressions manufactured there: "Man kann von Rom nichts Kostbares mitnehmen, besonders da die Abdrücke so außerordentlich schön und scharf sind" (WA I/32:82; From Rome one cannot acquire anything more precious, as there in particular, the quality of the casts is so fine and sharp). In addition to sets of impressions, Karl August Böttiger noted that Heinrich Meyer had also made drawings of several of the intaglios (Fig. 5).[31] Princess Gallitzin had hoped that Goethe might help her find a suitable buyer for the collection to raise money needed for charitable work,[32] but events in Europe at the time made such an opportunity unlikely. The princess finally requested that the gems be returned to her when it appeared likely that they could be sold at the Russian court following Paul I's succession to the throne in November 1796. The following February, Goethe wrote to the princess:"Heute früh ist die Sammlung mit der fahrenden Post abgegangen" (Early this morning I sent off your collection with the postchaise). After five years of having the gems in his possession, he gratefully acknowledges:

> daß Ihre Wohltat sehr groß war, sowohl des Vertrauens, das Sie mir zeigten, als des Kunstgenusses den Sie mir gewährten. Die Kenntnisse, die ich mir dadurch erwarb, werden mich mein ganzes Leben begleiten, so wie Ihnen das Bewußtseyn bleiben muß einen Freund ganz auf seine eigenste Weise glücklich gemacht zu haben. (WA IV/12:32–33)

> that your kindness was truly great, as was your trust in me when you allowed me the experience of such great art. The knowledge that I acquired will accompany me throughout my life, just as for you, the awareness will always remain of your having made a friend happy quite after his own fashion.

The princess's attempt to sell the collection in Russia failed, as did Goethe's over year-long attempt to arouse the interest of the Duke of Gotha in 1801.[33] While informing the princess of his failure in this regard, he proposes the following plan to make the gems more widely known:"Wir [Goethe and Heinrich Meyer] dachten auch schon Umrisse von den Gemmen mit einer kurzen Rezension herauszugeben, um dadurch die Sammlung bekannter zu machen, so wie überhaupt die Menschen etwas mehr Respect vor den Dingen haben, wenn sie in Kupfer gestochen, oder im Druck irgendwo angeführt sind" (WA IV/16:104;We also thought of publishing outline engravings of the gems accompanied by a short review, in order to make the collection better known, as people on the whole will pay more attention to things if they are engraved in copper or printed by any means available). An article advertising the gems was eventually published in 1807, a year after the princess's death, and was included as part of the "Programm" of the *Jenaische Allgemeine Literatur-Zeitung*[34] under the title:"Nachrichten von einer Sammlung meistens antiker geschnittener Steine" (Report of a Collection, Composed in the Main, of Antique Engraved Gems). Sixty intaglios were described, some in considerable detail, and the article also included a page of five engravings illustrating the "preiswürdigsten Stücke" (most impressive pieces).[35]

The collection was eventually sold by the princess's daughter, Marianne, to William I, king of the Netherlands, in 1819.[36] News of the royal owner finally reached Goethe in 1823 through the Landgrave of Hessen-Darmstadt,[37] who, on command of the king, forwarded to the poet a copy of the catalog of the medals and gems held in the royal cabinet.[38] Overjoyed, he learned that the collection had remained intact and was in safe keeping, to be displayed with objects of similar worth for the education of the public (WA IV/37:246–47). Soon thereafter, an announcement of the catalog was published in the journal *Über Kunst und Altertum* with a German translation of part of the original preface and a commentary on the history of the Hemsterhuis collection.[39] In the announcement's conclusion, Goethe punctuates the value of public collections and art institutions, quoting the epigraph that had been selected to introduce the publication: "Die Werke der Kunst gehören nicht einzelnen, sie gehören der gebildeten Menschheit an" (Works of art do not belong to individuals, they are the property of all educated people).[40] Today, the Rijksmuseum van Oudheden (National Museum of Antiquities) in Leiden houses the Hemsterhuis gem collection. It remains more or less complete and as Goethe knew it over two-hundred years ago.[41]

## Hemsterhuis, Goethe, and "das Schöne"

That Goethe should occupy himself with this small collection of gems over a period of more than thirty years would confirm its importance to him.[42] Prior to borrowing this collection from Princess Gallitzin in 1792, his experience with glyptics had been mainly confined to working with impressions. Hemsterhuis's reputation as a collector was a guarantee of the quality of the gems and Goethe commented that "hier für uns das Studium der geschnittenen Steine zu gründen sei" (WA I/33:253; here for us is the basis for the study of engraved gems). Upon returning it to the princess, five years later, Goethe stated: "Die Kenntnisse, die ich mir dadurch [Ihre Sammlung] erwarb, werden mich mein ganzes Leben begleiten" (WA IV/12:32–33; The knowledge which I gained from it, will remain with me throughout my life).

As well as perhaps providing evidence of lost works of art from the past, these creations of art in miniature represented for Goethe a series of images from ancient Greece that he could analyze and place in a historical sequence[43]—the classical ideal representing for him the peak of artistic achievement. He recognized the ideal in many of the gems in Hemsterhuis's collection as those that fulfilled his aesthetic vision of beauty. That the two scholars shared similar notions on the interpretation of these images is hardly surprising, as they also entertained comparable ideas on the discernment of the beautiful. Commenting on Hemsterhuis's aesthetic in his autobiographical work of 1821, *Campagne in Frankreich 1792*, Goethe wrote:

> Hemsterhuis Philosophie, die Fundamente derselben, seinen Ideegang konnt'ich mir nicht anders zu eigen machen, als wenn ich sie in meine Sprache übersetze. Das Schöne und das an demselben Erfreuliche sei, so sprach er sich aus, wenn wir die größte Menge von Vorstellungen in Einem Moment bequem erblicken und fassen; ich aber mußte sagen: das Schöne sei, wenn wir das gesetzmäßig Lebendige in seiner größten Thätigkeit und Vollkommenheit schauen, wodurch wir, zur Reproduktion gereizt, uns gleichfalls lebendig und in höchste Tätigkeit versetzt fühlen. Genau betrachtet ist eins und ebendasselbe gesagt, nur von verschiedenen Menschen ausgesprochen, und ich enthalte mich mehr zu sagen; denn das Schöne ist nicht so wohl leistend als versprechend, dagegen das Häßliche, aus einer Stockung entstehend, selbst stocken macht und nichts hoffen, begehren und erwarten läßt. (WA I/33:234)

> Hemsterhuis's philosophy, the basis of it, and his thought processes I could only adopt by translating them into my own language. The beautiful and how we might best enjoy it, so he said, depends upon our exposure to as many

ideas as possible that we can comfortably perceive and apprehend within a single moment. I however must say: beauty is revealed when we observe a likeness made after the laws of nature displaying a precise balance of functionality and perfection of form, and through this exposure, we experience a drive to reproduce it as well as a sense of liberation, or release, leading to a heightening of our emotions. Considered closely, one and the same thing is expressed but stated by different men, and I refrain from saying more; for the beautiful does not so much deliver as promise, whereas the ugly, arising from an impasse, is itself constrained and does not permit hope, desire, nor expectation.

As Goethe here acknowledges, Hemsterhuis shares his aesthetic of the beautiful, but their ideas evolved from different principles. Hemsterhuis's theory is based on two interrelated premises: the artwork as a "Ganzheit" (totality) and the "Reproduktionsfähigkeit dem Geist des Betrachters" (capacity to emulate by the spirit (soul) of the observer). Looking more closely at the former, as expressed by Hemsterhuis in his "Lettre sur la sculpture": the artwork is represented by the union of its corresponding parts—it is the diversity of the components that, when united in a rational and harmonious manner, create an object of beauty—that is, beauty is unity in diversity.

These same sentiments are echoed by Goethe, but their origins are found in his morphological studies of the life processes, according to which he viewed the beautiful human being as "das letzte Produkt der sich immer steigernden Natur" (WA I/46:28; the ultimate goal of evolving nature). Thus, Goethe's statement that beauty is revealed only in the most complex forms of nature is perfectly in accord with Hemsterhuis's aesthetic of unity in diversity. Hemsterhuis expounds his second premise on how the vision of the beautiful is internalized, stating: "the soul is able to reproduce the idea of the object; this reproduction or transformation by the soul results in an image quite different from that generated by the object itself" (*Sculpture* 6). Goethe takes up Hemsterhuis's proposition, in his statement on the psychic effects of the beautiful, declaring that we are stimulated through the transformation of the object by the soul to an elevated perception of it, as quoted above.

Through his reading of Hemsterhuis's works, Goethe developed his ideas on beauty defining the concept through his perception of nature and her associated laws. Although Goethe had previously avoided defining the beautiful, in considering the philosopher's words, he formulates a personal view of beauty. Over a period of forty years, this "fein gesinnt" Dutchman (WA I/33:233), both through his philosophical essays and his cultivated taste in the arts, influenced Goethe's aesthetics and broadened his understanding of glyptics.

## Connoisseurship and Authenticity: Dating the Hemsterhuis Gem Collection

In this section, I investigate the nature of connoisseurship and attempt to relate its methods to the extraordinary differences it has generated over a quarter of a century on the dating of the gems in Hemsterhuis's collection. I begin by analyzing connoisseurship from the mid-eighteenth century to the first quarter of the nineteenth century regarding (1) its characterization of the Greek ideal and (2) its stylistic assessment of early modern gems.

Hemsterhuis's judgment as a connoisseur was founded on his perception of beauty, and the gems he regarded as fulfilling his criteria of the beautiful were mostly those he believed to illustrate the classical Greek ideal. It was these remnants of antiquity, carved at the time of the flowering of ancient Greek civilization, that Hemsterhuis desired, above all, to include in his collection. In the descriptions he gives of his gems, we frequently encounter such phrases as "L'air d'antiquité y est parfait" (its expression of antiquity is perfect) and "très belle gravure, et grecque" (very fine engraving and Greek). However, such remarks can scarcely be used as guidelines for comprehending his preference for any one of the gems he selected for inclusion in his collection. Many of those he chose were to be found in some of the great glyptic collections of the day. One such intaglio, a black agate stone carved with an image of a faun seated on a panther skin, was included in the Stosch publication of 1724. Hemsterhuis comments: "Mr. Stosch calls it a masterpiece with good reason, for it does not cede to any other engraving we know" (*Catalogue* 25–26, no. 25) and he then proceeds to list the factors that contribute to the outstanding nature of the engraving:"be it for the composition, the design, the lightness of the work, its polishing and finish, the flowing contours, the precise workmanship."

Here, finally, we have some notion of the qualities he was seeking in the gems he sought to possess above all others.[44] It is obvious that Hemsterhuis was not concerned that both he and Stosch possessed a gem with an identical motif;[45] in fact, there were quite a number of replicas of this particular design in circulation.[46] The Comte de Caylus, commenting on the number of copies in existence worldwide, attributed them to the ancients:"the repetition and imitation of motifs is one of the reproaches that one can make concerning the Ancients: whereby one often sees several originals carved with the same figure, made by different artists, dealt with identically, or at least with scarcely any essential differences."[47] In his own *Catalogue raisonné*, Hemsterhuis frequently compares a gem in his collection with that from another, both being carved with the same motif;[48] in his account of an amethyst engraved with a scene he describes as "Fête de Cybele" (Festival of Cybele), he makes comparisons with a cameo signed with the name "Alexandre" that belonged to the Earl of Carlisle, stating:

> This intaglio, which is without any doubt antique, quite surpasses the fine cameo that I am about to discuss. Here again is proof that the great artists of antiquity never tired of repeating appealing compositions. . . . I have no doubt that the maker of the Alexander cameo is also the same engraver of my own gem. It is broken on its lower margin but the engraving itself is intact. (*Catalogue* 17–18)

These remarks on the copies made by antique engravers are very much in line with those of both Mariette and Caylus; Hemsterhuis was convinced of the authenticity of his Greek gems.

There can be no doubt that the author of the article published in the *Jenaische Allgemeine Literatur-Zeitung* (1807) who described these sixty engraved gems was of the same opinion as Hemsterhuis regarding the age of the specimens in this collection.[49] Again, exactly why a gem was considered antique remains obscure, as very little information is presented to the reader concerning style, a formal description of the motif being, in general, complemented with only a few words relating to its style, e.g., "vortrefflich" (of outstanding quality), "fleißig" (diligent), "vorzüglich" (exquisite).[50] Toward the end of the article, Goethe declares once more that: "Aus inneren Gründen der Kunst sehen wir uns berechtigt, wo nicht alle, doch bey weitem die größte Zahl Steine . . . für ächt antike Denkmale zu halten" (From the central concepts of art we feel ourselves justified in maintaining that if not all, then the majority of the gems be regarded as genuine antiques).[51] However, an additional comment demonstrated that he was well aware of the possibility that some of those gems might be replicas but that he himself chose to reject such an idea. Rather, he preferred, like Hemsterhuis, to acknowledge these replicas as being of ancient Greek workmanship but was nevertheless aware of the mass production of popular motifs in his own century. He goes on to assure the reader that several of the gems, at least, may be regarded as ancient imitations rather than modern copies. For example, Goethe describes the "Bacchus no. 5" gem as: "Arbeit, wie auf den Stein gehaucht, und in Hinsicht auf die idealen Formen eines der edelsten antiken Werke"[52] (Work so fine, it appeared that the motif had been breathed onto the stone, and in terms of ideal form, one of the most noble works of antiquity). Similarly, he describes gem no. 13, featuring Dionysos and a silen, as follows: "Beiden Figuren sind mit Geist und Kunst in sehr gutem Stil gearbeitet" (Both figures are worked with spirit and artistry in a very good style). Based on these descriptions emphasizing the finesse of the engraving and their stylistic representation of the classical ideal, we might infer that these are factors are definitive for their recognition as examples of art of the finest period.

I explore this proposition further by analyzing a gem that was also regarded as demonstrating "la grande manière" (the grand manner), a carnelian carved by Dioscoride illustrating "Diomedes with the Palladium" (Fig. 6). There is a replica in the Hemsterhuis collection, and in the *Jenaische Allgemeine Literatur-Zeitung* article Goethe remarks: "dass dieses nicht der schon bekannte Diomedes des erwähnten Künstlers ist . . . aber er hat beynahe dieselbe Grösse, und nicht viel geringeres Ku[n]stverdienst" (that this is not the Diomedes by Dioscoride already known to us . . . but it is similar in size, and of not much less artistic merit). Mariette discusses the same gem in his *Traité* but his comments are rather more informative; he pinpoints the stylistic differences between the original gem belonging to the Duke of Devonshire and a replica of it, which he considers to be antique, held in the French royal cabinet.[53] The refinements of these qualities presented by Mariette offered the connoisseur guidance when faced with a gem of questionable origin. His comparison sheds a great deal of light on the characteristics he uses to differentiate the prototype from a copy in terms of style (see Table 1).

Figure 6. Johann Heinrich Meyer: *Diomedes with the Palladium*, (1796?). Pen in gray and black with washes in gray ink and highlights in white over graphite underdrawing. Klassik Stiftung Weimar, Inv. Nr. KK 9400/68.

Table 1. Pierre-Jean Mariette's stylistic analysis of Dioscoride's *Diomedes with the Palladium*

| Stylistic characteristic | Original: Duke of Devonshire | Replica: Louis XV of France |
| --- | --- | --- |
| l'attitude (mien, pose) | animée (animated) | languissante (languid) |
| les proportions générales (overall proportions) | grand & majesteuses [mais] svelte (tall and majestic, slender) | pesant (heavy) |
| membres de la figure (limbs of the figure) | allongées (elongated) | ramassés (thickset) |
| contours | coulans (flowing) | arides (dry) |
| carrure (stature) | un guerrier illustre: le corps s'est formé (an illustrious warrior: the body is trained) | un homme du commun: les muscles trop ressentis (common man: the muscles over-emphasised) |

# Stylistic Characteristics of Early Modern Gems: Renaissance and Eighteenth Century

In his *Jenaische Allgemeine Literatur-Zeitung* article, one of the few gems Goethe excludes from those characterized as antique is gem no. 19, the representation of a mask. He describes the "etwas fratzenhaften Züge" (somewhat grotesque features) as Florentine work of the sixteenth century.[54] Further affirmation that the gem is from this period is provided by:"die feste Zeichnung, das Belebte im Ausdruck, die meisterhafte Behandlung mit vielem Fleiß verbunden" (the sound drawing, the animated expression, the masterly handling associated with considerable diligence)—qualities that offer "das Recht einen der vorzüglichsten Künstler jener Zeit als Urheber dieses Werkes zu vermuthen." (the license to presume one of the finest artists of that time to be the creator of this work). Clearly, Goethe must have had a considerable understanding of renaissance style; his collections of medals and bronzes from that period as well as his study of the master craftsman Cellini all bear witness to this.[55] Furthermore, the Florentine gem collections had been a subject of study and discussion following Heinrich Meyer's sojourn in Florence in 1796.[56] Of the sixty intaglios in the Hemsterhuis collection, Goethe identified only two examples as renaissance work, the mask described above and a centaur (RMO Leiden Inv.Nr. GS-10480), whereas Hemsterhuis disregarded this period completely. Today, almost half of the gems are regarded as being of renaissance craftsmanship; discriminating between that period and the antique was obviously problematic and, as Goethe clearly realized that there would always remain cases in which judgment criteria could only be subjective (WA I/49.2:103).

As for gems of the eighteenth century, again Hemsterhuis does not acknowledge a single intaglio in his collection as being of contemporary origin, even though he had ordered copies of antique stones from the celebrated engraver Natter for himself and for friends.[57] Hemsterhuis was well-acquainted with Natter's quality of workmanship and was seduced into possessing some of these modern replicas himself. However, he was convinced that he could distinguish a modern work from a genuine antique, as evidenced by his correspondence with Princess Gallitzin. He appears to have introduced her to the study of glyptics early on in their acquaintance by sending her what he regarded as thirteen of the best-engraved gems in the Cabinet du Prince.[58] Indeed, after Hemsterhuis gave his collection to her, Princess Gallitzin became something of a connoisseur and was perfectly capable of discussing the qualities that distinguished an antique engraving from a modern copy. Their correspondence in 1785 provides some insight into their opinions, which can perhaps clarify some of the glaring differences in the current dating of these gems. Hemsterhuis writes:

> a gemstone that, as a stone, is very fine, and good enough as an example of modern engraving provided that you do not intend to compare it rigorously with your Diomedes, your fauns, your sacrifices. . . . It is a copy of Stosch' celebrated Meleager . . . you have without doubt 12 to 16 gems that are more classic and renowned, or more beautiful and unmatched for their workmanship.[59]

Having received the intaglio, the princess replies that although "modern in every respect," she wishes to retain it, and adds the following:

> We have become so attuned to using the lens to examine our gems that even when our eyes are unaided, we still imagine that we can distinguish the shadows of muscles, veins, arteries in modern examples; less so with antique stones. If the outline is sufficiently well copied, our imagination will provide whatever else may be required to endow a modern gem with an all-embracing beauty. This is the case with the Meleager, he appears charming to the unaided eye, but through the lens, one experiences a certain disagreeable sensation that might be compared to one's emotions on hearing a fine, noble countenance speaking coarsely.[60]

Hemsterhuis replies: "I am delighted that the Meleager gives you pleasure. . . . What pleases you is not the work of the artist, rather the poesie given to the prototype through the original creator. Our modern artists are not wanting in skill but they lack a Greek soul." He considers modern artists to simply be copyists, suggesting that their work, be it good or bad, will always be recognizable as such. He then comments on the work of several modern engravers: Sirletti, Natter, Pichler, and Marchant, declaring only Pichler as a possible "poëte à la grecque" (artist of the Greek manner), since the slavish style of the copyist was absent from his gems.[61]

How was Hemsterhuis able to identify "une âme grecque" (a Greek soul)? He obviously felt himself sufficiently capable; in a later letter to the princess he confides in her: "I have only ever known three people, be it personally or by their works, who were born truly Greek, and they are you, Goethe and myself."[62] At another point he declares "I was born Greek, Platonic, and Tyrannoctonic."[63] Later, he clarifies these statements as follows:

> When I spoke to you of a certain trio . . ., I wished to say that those three people were born with something in their intellect, in their soul or in their faculties, that I have not seen in others, and by which they see, experience and consider the arts with the same hindsight and with the same point of view as the Greeks.[64]

According to Hemsterhuis, he, Goethe, and Princess Gallitzin were capable of appreciating the fine arts in the same way as the ancient Greeks had themselves.

It is remarkable that Hemsterhuis who was clearly well-acquainted with the work of a number of highly esteemed modern engravers, never mentions eighteenth-century gems in his own collection. On the other hand, Goethe, in his *Jenaische Allgemeine Literatur-Zeitung* article, proposed that at least two were of recent origin: a Medusa by Sirletti, of the type engraved by Sosocles and "eine der vortrefflichsten neueren Nachahmungen nach antiken Werken"[65] (one of the most exquisite new replicas after antique work), and Neptune riding three dolphins for which "die Erfindung und Anordnung des Ganzen unverkennbar moderne Züge [hat]"[66] (the concept and composition of the design had unmistakeable modern characteristics). Obviously, the two men viewed the collection very differently: Goethe believed it to be composed of mainly antique Greek gems, based primarily on Hemsterhuis's reputation as a connoisseur and aesthete, when it was in fact a collection of gems from a variety of periods. Hemsterhuis' desideratum was simply that they were created by an artisan who had a "Greek soul" and was therefore able to emulate the style of a classical Greek engraver.

## "Ächt antike Denkmale"?: The Connoisseur and Authenticity

In 1823, Goethe reflecting on the problem of authenticity comments: "Nun aber findet die Zweifelsucht kein reicheres Feld sich zu ergehen als gerade bei geschnittenen Steinen; bald heißt es eine alte, bald eine moderne Kopie, eine Wiederholung, eine Nachahmung; bald erregt der Stein Verdacht, bald eine Inschrift, die von besonderem Werth sein sollte" (WA I/49.2:103; Now, however, as far as skepticism is concerned, there is no richer field for indulgence than that of engraved gems; one minute it's an antique, the next a modern copy, a replica, an imitation; one moment the gem arouses suspicion, the next has an inscription which should be of particular value). Such skepticism had plagued Goethe's glyptic studies for over two decades; for his second stay in Italy, he had planned, together with Heinrich Meyer, to compare impressions of the better-known gems in his collection with the examples on display in Florence, "damit man . . . vielleicht zu mehrer Klarheit über diese Sachen gelangt"[67] (so that one . . . perhaps gains more insight into these things). Meyer continues:

> Ich meines Orts bin nie weniger als jetzt geneigt gewesen zu glauben, daß Betrug dieser Art geübte Augen hintergehen kann. Es sind mir einige von den neusten nachgearbeiteten Pasten gezeigt worden und wurden für Wunder ausgegeben, allein es erfordert einen Strohkopf, wenn man ihn nur eine Minute lang betrügen will. Das Schöne und Gute bleibt immer der wahre Prüfstein, und wenn diese ersten Bedingungen erfüllt sind, so fragen wir auch nicht weiter nach Alterthum oder Neuheit.

> For myself, I have never been more confident than I am today that fraud of this type can escape the experienced eye. I have been shown a few of the latest examples of reworked pastes that were passed off as a marvel, but you would have to be very undiscerning to be taken in by them even for a minute. The beautiful and good always remain the true touchstone, and if these first requirements are fulfilled, we do not need to inquire further with regard to age or novelty.

The aesthetic qualities of a finely carved stone will always be apparent to the connoisseur through "ein[em] inner[en] Gefühl, begünstigt durch ein geübtes Auge" (WA I/49.2:103; intuition endorsed by a practiced eye). And Goethe appears, in fact, to have had considerable success in this field; one hundred years later, Adolf Furtwängler described 32 of the 58 intaglios and cameos in his collection as "bemerkenswerten echt antiken"[68] (noteworthy genuine antiques).

## **Conclusion**

Classical Greek antiquities, such as the Elgin Marbles, were to be a regular subject of discussion for the Weimarer Freunde (Weimar Circle) for the rest of Goethe's life, their style no doubt aiding him in his subsequent appreciation of engraved gems, the study of which remained a life-long interest for him. The Hemsterhuis collection of gems that fascinated Goethe has remained more or less intact for over 250 years and has existed as part of a public collection for more than two centuries. The conflicting opinions it has generated over this time recall the words of Goethe in his "Skizzen zu einer Schilderung Winckelmanns" (Notes for a Portrayal of Winckelmann) of 1805, where, in his reflections on collectors and collections he comments:

> Traurig ist es, wenn man das Vorhandne als fertig und abgeschlossen ansehen muß. Rüstkammern, Galerien und Museen, zu denen nichts hinzugefügt wird, haben etwas Grab- und Gespensterartiges; man beschränkt seinen Sinn in einem so beschränkten Kunstkreis, man gewöhnt sich solche Sammlungen als ein Ganzes anzusehen, anstatt daß man durch immer neuen Zuwachs erinnert werden sollte, daß in der Kunst, wie im Leben, kein Abgeschlossenes beharre, sondern ein Unendliches in Bewegung sei.[69]

> How sad it is if our collections are regarded as complete and self-contained. Armories, galleries, and museums to which nothing more will be added, are rather grave- and ghost-like; in such an enclosed environment, their meaning is restricted, and one becomes accustomed to regarding such collections as complete in themselves when instead, one ought to be reminded with every new addition that in art as in life nothing should be regarded as final, but rather as ever-changing.

*Brandenburg, Germany*


## **NOTES**

1. Ernst Grumach, ed., *Kanzler von Müller Unterhaltung mit Goethe* (Weimar: Böhlau, 1956) 185. Unless otherwise indicated, all translations are my own.

2. It was for this reason that Goethe never regarded his collections as complete; additional information derived from new items meant constant revision of his classification schemes.

3. See Christian Schuchardt, *Goethe's Kunstsammlungen, Zweiter Theil* (Jena: Frommann, 1848) 344–46.

4. With such a sizable collection, he had a stock of closely related motifs available, which he hoped to classify into a historical sequence according to variation in style.

5. Johann Wolfgang von Goethe, *Goethes Werke*, ed. im Auftrag der Großherzogin Sophie von Sachsen Weimar (Weimar: Böhlau, 1887–1919) I/49.2:103. Hereafter abbreviated as WA and cited parenthetically.

6. Pierre-Jean Mariette, *Traité des pierres gravées* 2 vols. (Paris: Mariette, 1750).

7. See here Leendert Brummel, *Frans Hemsterhuis, een philosofenleven* (Haarlem: Tjeenk Willink, 1925) 68–69.

8. Mariette 1:34.

9. See Salomon Reinach, *Pierres gravées des collections Marlborough, et d'Orléans, des recueils d'Eckhel, Gori, Levesque de Gravelle, Mariette, Millin, Stosch réunies et rééditées avec un texte nouveau* (Paris: Firmin-Didot, 1895) 85–87 for an analysis of its contents.

10. Hemsterhuis had begun to compose a catalogue raisonné of his gem collection shortly before his death. This document, together with a copy of it in another hand, are today part of the National Numismatic Collection located at De Nederlandsche Bank, Amsterdam.

11. François Hemsterhuis, *Lettre sur la sculpture, à Monsieur Théod. De Smeth, Ancien Président des Echevins de la Ville d'Amsterdam* (Amsterdam: Rey, 1769).

12. Mariette 1:93–104; at the end of this section, he neatly summarizes the qualities required "to develop ones' taste and become a good judge" as "knowledge of drawing in association with style and working method."

13. Hemsterhuis's collection included the following intaglios illustrated by Mariette in the second volume of his *Traité*: Pl. 14 Apollon & Cupidon; Pl. 19 Mars & Venus; Pl. 27 L'amour sur un cheval marin; Pl. 33 Sacrifice; Pl. 41 Sorcière; Pl. 42 Taureau d'Epyre; Pl. 64 Initiation d'un Luperque; Pl. 80 Cerbere enchaine par Hercule; Pl. 94 Diomede enlevant le Palladium; Pl. 125 Adonis.

14. Gems from Stosch's publication *Gemmae antiquae caelatae* (Amsterdam: Picart, 1724): Pl. 6 L'amour domptant un lion; Pl. 11 Taureau couche par terre; Pl. 37 Harpocrates; Pl. 40 Le Taureau Dionysiaque; Pl. 44 Faune; Pl. 46 Hercule couronne d'olive; Pl. 53 L'amour domptant un lion; Pl. 60 Silenus; Pl. 64 Cupidon; Pl. 65 Meduse de Sosocle. Examples from the Marlborough collection in Reinach 115–116: 1, Pl. 36 Mercure; 1, Pl. 42 Soldat qui secourt son camarade; those of the Farnese: Inv. 26278 Afrodite, Eros, donna e leone (Stosch Pl. 6); Inv. 25889 Centauro; Inv. 26071 "Platone" (Hemsterhuis, *Catalogue* 28, no. 29, as "Aristophane").

15. For example, in the letter, Klassik Stiftung Weimar GSA 33/509: L. Natter to F. Hemsterhuis, London, November 24, 1752, where Natter mentions a list of names of ancient Greek engravers sent to him by Hemsterhuis, four of which he cannot identify; another, ΩΣΤΡΑΤΟΥ, he recognizes as the signature, Sotrati [Sostratos] engraved on the "Meleager and Atalanta" cameo (Inv.Nr.:BM1913,0307.326); a further comment he makes referring to the signature engraved on the collar of the dog Sirius (Marlborough 293) which Hemsterhuis had transcribed incorrectly, his ΓΝΑΙΟC should be read as ΓΑΙΟΣ ΕΠΟΙΕΙ.

16. See Elisabeth Nau, *Lorenz Natter. 1705–1763. Gemmenschneider und Medailleur* (Biberbach an der Riß: Biberbacher Verlag, 1966) for the first comprehensive account of Natter's life and work. Also, and more recently, John Boardman, Julia Kagan, Claudia Wagner, *Natter's Museum Brittanicum* (Oxford: Archaeopress, 2017), for a more detailed approach, concentrating on Natter's catalogues of private English gem collections, which he aimed to collate and publish as his "Museum Britannicum."

17. See François Hemsterhuis, "[Brief] Aan Petrus Wesseling, 7 februari 1757," University of Gröningen Library Hemsterhuis's Letters Project, ed. Jacob van Sluis (2017) 12.8:17–19, https://www.rug.nl/library/heritage/hemsterhuis/12_overige_correspondentie.pdf, a letter from Hemsterhuis to the Utrecht professor, Petrus Wesseling, recommending Natter for a position in the royal mint. Subsequent letters from the project are referred to as Sluis, *Hemsterhuis's Letters Project*.

18. Brummel 71.

19. See here Mariette 1, 104 and Annie Zadoks-Josephus Jitta, *La Collection Hemsterhuis au Cabinet Royal des Médailles à la Haye* (La Haye: Imprimerie de l'Etat, 1952) 18–19.

20. The gem, an amethyst, is today held in the gem cabinet of the National Museum of Antiquities, Leiden, Inv.Nr. GS-01167.

21. The gem is listed in the auction catalogue of 1791, compiled following Hemsterhuis's death the previous year; it is described as "Een [ring] Antique Gravure in Sarde, verbeelende een Beeldhouwer, die een Vaas, voor zig hebbende, schynt te bewerken, in 't goud gemonteerd" (150, no. 15; an antique intaglio in sardonyx mounted in gold, depicting a sculptor working on a vase).

22. The concept of *disegno* had been formulated by Giorgio Vasari in his *Vite de'più eccellenti Pittori Scultori e Architetti* of 1568, as the idea conceived by the artist that is expressed through his hands. It applied to all three branches of the arts—architecture, sculpture and painting—and was the prerequisite of all creative processes. For a more detailed appraisal of Mariette's concept of artistic style, see Valérie Kobi, *Dans l'œil du connaisseur. Pierre-Jean Mariette (1694–1774) et la construction des savoirs en histoire de l'art* (Rennes: UP Rennes, 2017) 98–99.

23. National Museum of Antiquities (RMO) Leiden, Inv.Nr. GS-10784. The figure was identified as "Adonis" by Hemsterhuis, although he states in his catalogue (9, no. 11), that the pose resembles that often given to Meleager by other gem cutters. Today the gem held in the Cabinet des Médailles, Paris, inv.58.1460, is labelled "Apollon."

24. Goethe appears to have shared Hemsterhuis's opinions on collecting and collections; in a conversation with Chancellor von Müller he states that possession was for him: "Nötig, um den richtigen Begriff der Objekte zu bekommen . . .: Und so liebe ich den Besitz, nicht der beseßnen Sache, sondern meiner Bildung wegen" (Grumach, 9).

25. See Heinz Moenkemeyer, *François Hemsterhuis* (Boston: Twayne, 1975) 14–25, for a detailed account of the Princess Adelheid Amalia von Gallitzin's life and her relationship with Hemsterhuis.

26. Brummel 73, and a letter dated "15 avril 1777" in Sluis, *Hemsterhuis's Letters Project* (2017) 17, 4.37:56–57 (https://www.rug.nl/library/heritage/hemsterhuis/lettres4_diotime_1775-1788.pdf) in which the princess [Diotime] assures Hemsterhuis she had only been willing to accept his gem collection "en depot" over the past year and that she wishes to continue to regard her possession of it in the future as such. It would appear that she was only willing to acknowledge the collection as being on loan to her.

27. Hemsterhuis and the princess exchanged letters regularly between 1775 and 1790, the year of Hemsterhuis's death.

28. Johann Heinrich Meyer (1760–1832) was a Swiss artist and art historian, adviser to Goethe on all artistic matters; for a complete account of his life, see Jochen Klauß, *Der "Kunschtmeyer": Johann Heinrich Meyer. Freund und Orakel Goethes* (Weimar: Böhlau, 2001).

29. On the manufacture of impressions in glass paste and its advantages over softer materials such as sealing wax and sulphur, see Peter und Hilde Zazoff, *Gemmensammler und Gemmenforscher. Von einer noblen Passion zur Wissenschaft* (Munich: Beck, 1983) 151–52.

30. J. H. Meyer to Goethe, May 4, 1796, in *Schriften der Goethe-Gesellschaft* 32 (1917): 237–38.

31. In *Karl August Böttiger. Literarische Zustände und Zeitgenossen. Begegnungen und Gespräche im Klassischen Weimar*, ed. Klaus Gerlach und René Sternke (Berlin: Aufbau, 1998) 77. The drawings to which Böttiger refers are today held in the department of prints and drawings, Klassik Stiftung Weimar, seven of which I have so far identified: KK 9400/61 Kopf Herkules; KK9400/62 Kopf eines alten Mannes; KK9400/63 Portrait-Kopf mit überzogener Löwenhaut; KK9400/64 Profil eines Unbekannten; KK9400/67 Brustbild des Bacchus; KK9400/68 Diomedes mit Palladium; KK2592 Theseus und marathonische Stier. Several of these were engraved and later published in the *Jenaische Allgemeine Literatur-Zeitung*, a journal founded in 1804 on Goethe's own initiative.

32. Letter from Fürstin Gallitzin to Goethe, January 20, 1794, *Goethe-Jahrbuch* 3 (1882): 284–85.

33. For the history of these transactions see: WA IV/15:265; WA IV/16:2–3; letter from Herzog Ernst II von Gotha to Goethe, January 14, 1802, quoted in Erich Trunz, ed., *Goethe und der Kreis von* Münster (Münster: Aschendorff, 1974) 112–13.

34. *Jenaische Allgemeine Literatur-Zeitung* 4, no. 1 (1807): i–v, http://zs.thulb.uni-jena.de/rsc/viewer/jportal_derivate_00237128/JALZ_1807_Bd.1_003.tif.

35. Goethe repeated the descriptions of twenty of those gems he regarded as the most exquisite in his "Campagne in Frankreich 1792" (WA I/33:255–59).

36. Its purchase on May 13, 1819, is recorded in a diary of the royal treasury: Johannes C. de Jonge, *Uitgaande Brieven 1788–1823*.

37. Letter from Christian Ludwig von Hessen-Darmstadt to Goethe, September 20, 1823: Klassik Stiftung Weimar, GSA 28/104 Bl.322; in Gerhard Femmel and Gerald Heres, *Die Gemmen aus Goethes Sammlung* (Leipzig: Seemann, 1977) 266–67 (Z488).

38. Johannes C. de Jonge, *Notice sur le cabinet des médailles et des pierres gravées de sa Majesté le Roi des Paijs-Bas* (La Haije: La Veuve Allart et Comp., 1823).

39. *Über Kunst und Altertum* 4, 3.Quartal (1823).

40. The quotation is extracted from A. H. L. Heeren, *Ideen über Politik, den Verkehr und den Handel der vornehmsten Völker der alten Welt* 3,1 (Göttingen: Vandenhoeck & Ruprecht, 1812).

41. Fifty-six intaglios were catalogued by Dr. A. N. Zadoks-Josephus Jitta in 1952 (*Collection Hemsterhuis*), the keeper of the royal cabinet at that time, four additional former pieces she could trace solely as plaster impressions, and a further two engraved stones as well as four cameos were untraceable. Hemsterhuis listed sixty-two intaglios and four cameos in his own catalogue raisonné. With the aid of the online database of the RMO, Leiden, I have traced one of her plaster impressions, a cornelian depicting a "Bacchus sacrifiant," Inv.Nr. GS-10662, which I have discussed in this paper. Of the two gems that were untraceable, one I have located, again in the online database, Inv.Nr. GS-10770: "Männliches Porträt/Priester"; the second, a mask representing the head of an old man, his hair dressed "la même que celle de Venus deMedicis" (Hemsterhuis, *Catalogue* 13–15, no. 18), can perhaps be located in de Jonge's set of impressions of the royal cabinet, published in 1837.

42. Femmel and Heres 40–41.

43. Kristel Smentek, *Mariette and the Science of the Connoisseur in Eighteenth-Century Europe* (Farnham: Ashgate, 2014) 193, for earlier ideas on this point—those of the connoisseurs Pierre Crozat and Mariette, as well as the importance of these engraved gems for Winckelmann's analyses of ancient art.

44. Those attributes listed by Hemsterhuis that marked a gem of the finest quality are identical to those which Mariette describes, in considerable detail, as characteristics of "la gravûre Grecque" in his *Traité* 1:56–57.

45. Mariette explains the existence of such replicas in his *Traité* 1:39, declaring that the Ancients had always demonstrated a great willingness to copy those works which had merited universal approbation.

46. For a history of this gem and a list of replicas made after it, see Reinach 173, no. 44.

47. Anne-Claude-Philippe de Tubières, Comte de Caylus, "Mémoire sur les Pierres gravées," *Mémoires de Litterature, tirés des Registres de l'Académie Royale des Inscriptions et Belles-Lettres* 19 (1753): 249.

48. Hemsterhuis makes comparisons in his *Catalogue* with the following, the source/owner is indicated in parentheses following the subject of the engraving, no. 3, Apollon & Cupidon (Mariette); no. 5, Sacrifice de Silene & Bacchus (Mariette); no. 7, Mars & Venus (Mariette); no. 12, Tête de Ptolomée Philopator; no. 14, Buste de Papirius (Stosch); no. 16, Vache d'Apollonides (Stosch); no. 20 Fête de Cybele (Stosch); no. 25, Faune assis (Stosch); no. 26, Tête de Silène (Stosch); no. 27, Taureau d'Epyre (Mariette); no. 30, Tête de jeune Hercule (Stosch); no. 44, Diomede enlevant le Palladium (Stosch, Mariette).

49. Authorship of the articles published in the "Programm": *Unterhaltung über Gegenstände der bildenden Kunst* is acknowledged by the initials "WKF" (Weimarer Kunstfreunde), and usually identified as Goethe, Heinrich Meyer, and their associates.

50. Analysis of this very loose terminology as used by Hemsterhuis and Goethe to describe the characteristics of Greek engraving demonstrates their similarity.

51. *Jenaische Allgemeine Literatur-Zeitung* 4, no. 1 (1807): v.

52. The same metaphor was used by Winckelmann in his description of the execution of the Niobe group, its effortless perfection, as it were: "von einem Hauche geblasen": see Johann Joachim Winckelmann, *Geschichte der Kunst des Alterthums* (Dresden: Walther, 1764) 226–27, quoted after Humphry Trevelyan, *Goethe and the Greeks* (Cambridgs: Cambridge UP, 1942) 141.

53. Mariette 1: 62–63.

54. His dating of this gem, RMO, Leiden Inv. Nr. GS-10696, still stands today.

55. See here "'*Goethe und die Renaissance' ein Vortrag im Wiener Goethe-Verein von Ludwig Geiger*" (Berlin: Haack, 1887) 15–16.

56. Meyer's detailed notes of reference to these collections are held by the Klassik Stiftung Weimar, GSA Bestand 64.

57. In the letter to Hemsterhuis dated November 24, 1752 (Klassik Stiftung Weimar, GSA 33/509, Note 14), Natter discusses the following intaglios: a copy of the Othyrade gem; the prices he is asking for copies of a Socrates and a Sosocles's Medusa; the possibility of cutting a gem with the motif of Cassandra after a design by Hemsterhuis.

58. Cabinet du Prince; i.e., William V, Prince of Orange collection of antiques. See the undated letter in Sluis, *Hemsterhuis' Letters Project* (2011) 1.1:13–14 (https:// www.rug.nl/library/heritage/hemsterhuis/01_diotime_1775_1778c_neo.pdf) in which he describes the most salient characteristics of each intaglio, whereby he is perhaps hoping to develop the princess' taste for and appreciation of these miniature works of art.

59. Hemsterhuis is here referring to his own collection, which, by this time, he had gifted to the princess. Sluis, *Hemsterhuis's Letters Project* (2010) 6.11: 41–44 (https:// www.rug.nl/library/heritage/ hemsterhuis/06_diotime_1785f.pdf).

60. Sluis, *Hemsterhuis's Letters Project* (2015) 16.11: 25–26 (https://www.rug.nl/library/heritage/hemsterhuis/lettres3_diotime_1785-1790c.pdf).

61. Sluis, *Hemsterhuis's Letters Project* (2010) 6.13: 47–49 (https://www.rug.nl/library/heritage/ hemsterhuis/06_diotime_1785f.pdf).

62. Sluis, *Hemsterhuis's Letters Project* (2011) 7.17: 52–54 (https://www.rug.nl/library/heritage/hemsterhuis/07_diotime_1786b.pdf).

63. Sluis, *Hemsterhuis's Letters Project* (2011) 3.61: 147–49 (https://www.rug.nl/library/heritage/hemsterhuis/03_diotime_1780a_neo.pdf).

64. Sluis, *Hemsterhuis's Letters Project* (2011) 7.19: 56–58 (https://www.rug.nl/library/heritage/hemsterhuis/07_diotime_1786b.pdf).

65. RMO, Leiden Inv.Nr. GS-10547; Goethe in his *Jenaische Allgemeine Literatur-Zeitung* article misread the letter engraved at the base of the carnelian, his "Σ" was in fact Natter's initial, "N." He corrected this error in his *Campagne in Frankreich 1792*, of 1820–22.

66. Johannes C. de Jonge, *Catalogue d'Empreintes du Cabinet des Pierres Gravées de sa Majesté le Roi des Pays-Bas, Grand-Duc de Luxembourg* (La Haye: Imprimerie d'état, 1837) 20, no. 417; today the gem is out of sight and can be identified solely by the plaster impression.

67. J. H. Meyer to Goethe, November 7, 1796 in *Schriften der Goethe-Gesellschaft* 32 (1917): 384–85.

68. Adolf Furtwängler, *Die Antiken Gemmen. Geschichte der Steinschneiderkunst im Klassischen Altertum* Bd.2 (Leipzig: Giesecke & Devrient, 1900) 280.

69. Johann Wolfgang Goethe, *Faust*, in *Sämtliche Werke. Briefe, Tagebücher und Gespräche*, hrsg. Friedmar Apel et al., 40 Bde. (Frankfurt a/M: Deutscher Klassiker-Verlag, 1985–2013) 19: 198. Qtd. in Markus Bertsch und Johannes Grave, "Einleitung: 'Ein Unendliches in Bewegung,'" in *Räume der Kunst. Blicke auf Goethes Sammlungen*, ed. M. Bertsch and J. Grave (Göttingen: Vandenhoeck & Ruprecht, 2005) 7.

MONIKA NENON

# Bestseller und Erlebniskultur: Neue medienästhetische Ansätze bei Gisbert Ter-Nedden und Robert Vellusig verdeutlicht an Romanadaptionen von Franz von Heufeld

**Abstract:** In diesem Artikel werden neue medienwissenschaftliche Ansätze von Gisbert Ter-Nedden und Robert Vellusig vorgestellt, die den medientechnologischen Wandel im 18. Jahrhundert ergründen und dessen Wirkung bis in die Gegenwart verfolgen. Ausgehend von der Briefkultur und dem Briefroman des 18. Jahrhunderts zeigt dieser Ansatz, wie in der Literatur eine neue Erlebniskultur geschaffen wird, die den Menschen zum "Augen- und Ohrenzeugen" des Geschehens macht und Emotionen weckt, wobei diese Rezeptionsweise vergleichbar mit derjenigen von Filmen und den neuen sozialen Medien sei. Durch Elemente der Mündlichkeit wird eine Unmittelbarkeit des Daseins geschaffen, die Einblick in das Bewusstsein anderer Menschen ermöglicht und eine neue Dimension des Erlebens erreicht. In einem zweiten Schritt wird dieser theoretische Ansatz auf Bestseller wie Rouseaus *Julie, ou La Nouvelle Héloïse* oder Henry Fieldings *The History of Tom Jones, a Foundling* angewandt und gezeigt, dass deren Anziehungskraft gerade in den Merkmalen der Mündlichkeit liegt, die diese Unmittelbarkeit des Erlebens erzielen. Durch Elemente wie kurze Briefe, monologähnliche Reflektionen oder Dialoge wird eine Dramatisierung des Romans erreicht, die, wie anschließend ausgeführt wird, den umgekehrten Schritt, nämlich die Adaption dieser Romane für das Drama erlaubt, den Franz von Heufeld in einigen seiner Komödien für die Wiener Bühne erfolgreich vollzogen hat.

**Keywords:** Mediengeschichte, Erlebniskultur, Mündlichkeit, Briefroman, Romanadaption, Drama, history of media, culture of experience, orality, epistolary novel, adaption of the novel

FILME, DIE SCHWIERIGKEITEN und Auseinandersetzungen von Menschen, ihre Leiden und Freuden zeigen, laden das Publikum zur Teilnahme an dem Schicksal der Protagonisten ein und rühren dabei nicht selten zu Tränen. Gebannt folgen wir dem Geschick der Menschen, versetzen uns in ihre Lage, haben Mit-Leid und werden emotional bewegt. Filme dieser Art—man denke an Klassiker wie *Casablanca, Love Story* oder *Titanic*—machen den

Zuschauer zum "Augen-und Ohrenzeugen" eines fiktiven Geschehens, wie
Gisbert Ter-Nedden und in seiner Nachfolge Robert Vellusig sagen würden. Diese Medienwissenschaftler fragen nach der Wirkung von Medien
und ihrer Geschichte. Ter-Nedden bezeichnet das Kino als "eine neuar-
tige Bewusstseinsdroge,"[1] die auf die Zuschauer durch technische Mittel
audio-visueller Art wirke. Dass Kunst, vor allem Dichtung und Drama die
Leidenschaften der Menschen aufrührt, ist bekanntlich ein wichtiges
Konzept in der Antike und schon da werden Geschichten erzählt, die den
Zweck haben, bei den Zuschauern Lachen oder Furcht und Mitleid zu
erregen. "Mit den Lachenden lacht, mit den Weinenden weint, das Anlitz
des Menschen,"[2] sagt Horaz und die Poetiken beschäftigen sich mit der
Frage, wie die jeweils angestrebte Wirkung zu erzielen sei. Während die
Wirkung—die Erregung der Leidenschaften—nicht neu ist, so Ter-Nedden,
ändern sich aber die technischen Mittel im Lauf der Geschichte. Die Kultur,
die sich "die Gestaltung des Erlebens" des einzelnen Menschen zur Aufgabe
macht, bezeichnet der Soziologe Gerhard Schulze als "Erlebniskultur."[3]
Im Folgenden soll nun dieser neue medienästhetische Ansatz von
Ter-Nedden und Vellusig vorgestellt werden, der ausgehend von dem
Luhmannschen Verständnis, dass Gesellschaft Kommunikation sei, nach
dem medientechnischen Wandel im 18. Jahrhundert fragt. Dabei soll der
Blick auf bestimmte Gattungen wie Brief, Briefroman und Drama gelenkt
werden. Am Beispiel von Jean-Jacques Rousseaus *Julie, ou La Nouvelle
Héloïse* und Henry Fieldings *The History of Tom Jones, a Foundling*
und deren Dramatisierungen von Franz von Heufeld möchte ich nach
dem Zusammenhang von den Gattungen fragen und dabei besonders die
Themen Mündlichkeit und Schriftlichkeit ansprechen.

## Die Verschriftlichung der Kultur

Ter-Nedden betont, dass die klassische Rhetorik in den deutschen Ländern
bis zum 18. Jahrhundert dominiert. Die Sprache der Gelehrten war bekanntlich Latein und beherrschte das Bildungssystem bis zum 18. Jahrhundert. Ter-
Nedden sieht (und damit ist er natürlich nicht allein) die große medientech-
nische Erneuerung im Buchdruck, der die Kommunikation von "direkter
Interaction"befreie und gleichzeitig die Herrschaft des Latein effektiv beende.
"Die Medienrevolution im 16. Jahrhundert entgrenzt die Leistungsfähigkeit
der Schrift als Speichermedium."[4] Die Alphabetisierung lässt das
Nationalbewusstsein der europäischen Länder und die Nationalsprachen
emporkommen. Die Kultur verschriftlicht sich, wobei Ter-Nedden drei
"epochale Innovationen" hervorhebt: den Aufstieg der Zeitung, den Aufstieg
der Zeitschrift und den Aufstieg des Romans als Leitgattung der Literatur.
In allen drei Medien werden bis zum 17. Jahrhundert Wissensbestände und
neue Informationen gespeichert und massenhaft verbreitet. "Sowohl die
Zeitung wie der Roman tauchen im Alltag dort auf, wo vorher nicht Schrift,
sondern Rede war";[5] sie gelten als wesentliche Träger der Verschriftlichung
der Kultur.

## Brief und Briefroman

Eine der zentralen Thesen von Robert Vellusig lautet nun: "In dem Maße, in dem das 18. Jahrhundert Formen des Wissens entwickelt, die strukturell apersonal sind, beginnt sich die Literatur als das Andere des Wissens zu begreifen: Sie findet ihren mimetischen Bezugspunkt im personalen Erleben."[6] Was ist damit gemeint? Während die Zeitungen, Zeitschriften und Enzyclopädien das gesamte Wissen der Zeit speichern, konzentrieren sich die Romane in der zweiten Hälfte des 18. Jahrhunderts vor allem auf das Leben des einzelnen Menschen. Welche Ereignisse und Erfahrungen das Leben der Menschen bewegen, wie sie sich dazu verhalten und welche Gedanken und Gefühle das "Innere" der Menschen ausmachen, kann der Mensch nur in der Literatur, vor allem im Drama und nun auch in der emporkommenden Gattung des Romans erfahren. Friedrich von Blanckenburg schreibt in seinem die Gattung legitimierenden *Versuch über den Roman*, dass "das Seyn des Menschen, sein innrer Zustand" sein Hauptwerk sei.[7] "Gefühle und Handlungen der Menschheit" seien der eigentliche Inhalt der Romane.[8] Um diese These zu stützen, nimmt Blanckenburg seine Beispiele aber nicht vornehmlich aus Romanen, sondern aus den Dramen von Shakespeare und Lessing. Im Theater, wo Handlungen und Gefühle auf der Bühne aufgeführt werden, findet er die intendierte Wirkung—die innere Bewegung der Zuschauer—am besten verwirklicht: "Das Innre der Personen ist es, das wir in Handlung, in Bewegung sehen wollen, wenn wir bewegt werden sollen."[9] Als performative Kunst verfügt das Theater darüber hinaus über Mittel, die dem Romandichter nicht zustehen; die Körpersprache von Gestik und Mimik und den Ton der Stimme. "Und wenn wir, zu diesem Vorzuge des Drama, die wirkliche Vorstellung, Miene, Ton der Stimme, Stellung der Person hinzudenken, wie sie jedem Ausdruck mehr Kraft, mehr Leben geben, und auf diese Art natürlich mächtiger ins Herz dringen: so ists kein Wunder, daß der Romanendichter so weit zurück bleibt."[10] Der Zuschauer wird im Theater "zum Augen-und Ohrenzeugen" des Geschehens auf der Bühne. Dieser visuelle und akustische Eindruck hinterläßt stärkere Wirkung als beim Lesen durch bloße Beschreibungen im Roman erzielt werden kann. Aus diesem Grund schlägt Blanckenburg sozusagen eine Dramatisierung des Romans vor, indem er für den Roman "in heftigen Situationen" den Einsatz von Dialogen und Monologen empfiehlt.[11] Wie deutlich wird, bringt Blanckenburg nun Elemente von Mündlichkeit und direkter Kommunikation in die Schriftlichkeit des Romans zurück. Der Romanerzähler soll seelische Vorgänge in dramatischer Unmittelbarkeit darstellen.

Ter-Nedden und Vellusig gehen nun gleicherweise in ihren Thesen zum Briefroman dem Inhalt und der Form nach. Wie Blanckenburg bestätigen Stiening/Vellusig die Bedeutung der "empirischen Individualität des einzelnen Subjekts" für den Briefroman.[12] Schon Goethe hat die Bedeutung des Subjekts hervorgehoben und betont, dass das Dasein des Menschen in seiner Unmittelbarkeit in Briefen aufbewahrt werden kann:

Wie bedeutend das Leben eines Menschen sei, kann ein jeder nur an ihm selbst empfinden, und zwar in dem Augenblick, wenn er auf sich selbst zurückgewiesen das Vergangene zu betrachten und das Künftige zu ahnen genötigt ist. Alle spätere Versuche, solche Zustände darzustellen, bringen jedoch jenes Gefühl nicht wieder zurück. Deshalb sind Briefe so viel wert, weil sie das Unmittelbare des Daseyns aufbewahren, und der Roman in Briefen war eine glückliche Erfindung.[13]

Das Unmittelbare des Daseins, d.h. die Gedanken und Gefühle eines Menschen können in Briefen festgehalten werden und deshalb werden Briefe zu Augenblicksdokumenten des gelebten Lebens.

Wie wird nun formal diese Unmittelbarkeit des Daseins in Briefen erzielt? Die Antwort lautet: durch die (Wieder-)Einführung von Mündlichkeit in die Schriftlichkeit. Im 18. Jahrhundert definiert Gellert Briefe als "freye Nachahmung des guten Gesprächs" und als "Gespräche mit Abwesenden."[14] Schon in der Antike wird ein Brief als "halbierter Dialog"[15] bezeichnet. Goethe sieht den Brief "als eine Art von Selbstgespräch,"[16] bei dem sich der Briefeschreiber "einen abwesenden Freund als gegenwärtig" vorstelle. Briefkunst im 18. Jahrhundert wird als natürliche Fortsetzung des Gesprächs, des mündlichen Austauschs unter Kommunikationspartnern betrachtet. Gideon Stiening und Robert Vellusig definieren den Briefroman demnach folgendermaßen: "Briefromane sind Romane, die eine Geschichte *in einer* und *als eine Folge von Briefen* präsentieren und so ein schriftliches Äquivalent für die kommunikative Rahmung des mündlichen Erzählens bilden."[17] Von diesen schriftlichen Gesprächen ging große Faszination aus. Die Wirkung auf das Publikum der Briefromane von Richardson und mehr noch von Jean-Jacques Rousseaus Briefroman *Julie, ou La Nouvelle Héloïse* war überwältigend. So berichtet Rousseau in seinen *Bekenntnissen* von der Prinzessin von Talmont, die den Roman zu lesen begann, während sie für den Opernball angekleidet wurde; doch obwohl die Kutsche schon bereit stand, konnte sie mit dem Lesen nicht aufhören. Morgens um 4 Uhr las sie immer noch, legte die Ballkleider ab und las die Geschichte von Julie und ihrem Geliebten St. Preux ungestört weiter.[18] Die Gebanntheit einer solchen Leserin hat Ter-Nedden als "den Kino-Effekt" des Briefromans beschrieben. Bei der Lektüre von Briefen, die das Unmittelbare des Daseins vorführen wie Goethe sagt, werden die Leser und Leserinnen in die Geschichten von Menschen aktiv miteinbezogen. Sie erhalten Einblick, wie andere Menschen ihr Leben leben, welche Leidenschaften sie entwickeln, was sie begehren, welche Konflikte damit verbunden sind, welche Schmerzen sie erleiden und wie sie damit umgehen. Viele Menschen waren fasziniert von der Liebesgeschichte von Julie und St. Preux. Jean-Jacques Rousseaus Briefroman *Julie, ou La Nouvelle Héloïse*, der 1761 im Amsterdamer Verlagshaus von Marc Michel Rey erschienen war, erwies sich als einer der ersten Bestseller im 18. Jahrhundert. Bis 1800 kamen mehr als 70 Auflagen heraus, die noch durch zahlreiche Raubdrucke ergänzt wurden, die in einem unregulierten Buchmarkt vertreten waren. Die Nachfrage der Leserschaft war so groß, dass die Buchhändler das Werk sogar tage-bzw. stundenweise—man spricht von 12 Sous pro 60 Minuten—ausliehen. Die Leser und vor allem auch die Leserinnen rissen sich das Buch förmlich aus den Händen und konnten nicht aufhören, die Liebesgeschichte von Julie und St. Preux zu verfolgen.[19] "Lebendig erzählen heißt, eine Geschichte so zu schreiben, dass sie den Leser nicht zum Adressaten von Informationen über eine Vergangenheit, sondern zum Augen-und Ohrenzeugen einer imaginierten Gegenwart macht" schreibt Robert Vellusig.[20] Wie wird dieses lebendige Erzählen erreicht? Eine Antwort darauf hat Rousseau selbst in der Vorrede zur *Julie* gegeben, in der er über den empfindsamen Brief schreibt:

> Ein Brief hingegen, den die Liebe wirklich in die Feder diktiert hat, ein Brief eines wahrhaftig leidenschaftlich Liebenden wird nachlässig, weitschweifig, voller Unordnung und Wiederholungen sein. Sein von Gefühlen überströmendes Herz sagt immer wieder das gleiche und kann nie ein Ende finden; wie eine lebendige Quelle, die ohne Aufhören fließt und sich niemals erschöpft. Da ist nichts Hervorstechendes, nichts Bemerkenswertes; man behält weder Worte noch Wendungen, noch Sätze; man bewundert nichts, man wird durch nichts erstaunt. Indessen fühlt man doch seine Seele gerührt; man fühlt sich bewegt, ohne zu wissen warum. Wenn die Stärke der Empfindungen uns auch nicht trifft, so rührt uns doch ihre Wahrheit; und auf solche Art kann das Herz zum Herzen reden.[21]

Rousseau beschreibt anschaulich die neue (sprechende) Sprache des Herzens, die die Gedanken und vor allem die Gefühle des Schreibenden/ Sprechenden ausdrückt. Informationen oder Argumente sind bei dieser Art des Sprechens nicht wichtig, sondern die ständige Wiederholung der Empfindungen gegenüber dem Anderen werden immer wieder aufs Neue ausgedrückt. Bei der Lektüre bekommt der Lesende Einblick in die Zustände des Bewusstseins anderer Menschen. Die Leser werden durch diese sprachlichen Eindrücke emotional bewegt, obwohl sie nicht die gleiche Stärke der Empfindungen fühlen, also eine emotionale Distanz besteht, wie Rousseau feststellt; sie sind aber gerührt durch die Wahrheit der Empfindung und nehmen Anteil an den Freuden und Leiden der Anderen. Ter-Nedden bezeichnet diese Art von Literatur als "neuartiger, süchtig machender Typ von poetischer Literatur" und zieht davon ausgehend die Verbindung zum Kino, das auf ähnliche Weise wirkt und wie schon erwähnt zur "Bewusstseinsdroge" werden kann. Die Briefromane werden die ersten internationalen Bestseller und stehen "am Anfang der modernen Erlebnisgesellschaft," zu der später der Film, das Radio, das Fernsehen, das Internet etc. gehören werden. Nicht die Macht zu rühren, sondern die Entwicklung neuartiger technischer Mittel fördern diese Entwicklung.[22]

## Vom Roman zur Komödie: Franz von Heufelds Adaptionen

Rousseaus Briefroman zeitigte gerade in den deutschen Ländern große Wirkung und regte auch zu deutschen Briefromanen an—man denke nur an Sophie von La Roches *Geschichte des Fräuleins von Sternheim*, Friedrich Heinrich Jacobis Romane und vor allem Goethes *Werther.* Rousseaus international bekannter Briefroman ist auch erfolgreich für die Bühne adaptiert worden. Im Folgenden sollen nun Franz von Heufelds dramatische Bearbeitungen von Rousseaus Briefroman *Julie, ou La Nouvelle Héloïse* und von Henry Fieldings *The History of Tom Jones, a Foundling* im Mittelpunkt meiner

Überlegungen stehen. Diesem in der fachwissenschaftlichen Diskussion noch sehr wenig beachteten Adaptionsprozess von Roman zum Drama möchte ich mich im Folgenden zuwenden, wobei zwei Fragen im Mittelpunkt stehen werden.

Erstens soll die Verschiebung inhaltlicher Schwerpunkte vom Roman zum Drama herausgearbeitet und gezeigt werden, dass Heufeld sich in den Lustspielen auf die Liebes- und Familienthematik konzentriert, während historisch-politische sowie philosophische Inhalte der Romane keine Berücksichtigung finden. Zweitens soll nach den formalen Prozessen gefragt werden, die bei dem Wechsel der Gattungen im Gange sind. Dabei soll die These verfolgt werden, dass gerade die Romane, die sich durch diskursive Elemente auszeichnen, wie z.B. der zeitgenössische Briefroman, besonders für eine dramatische Bearbeitung geeignet sind und gezeigt werden, nach welchen Methoden Franz von Heufeld bei der Umsetzung verfährt. In dem Zusammenhang stellt sich auch die Frage nach der dramatischen Konzeption und der Wirkungsästhetik Heufelds angesichts eines Publikums, das zunehmend an zwischenmenschlichen Themen interessiert ist.

Franz Ulrich von Heufeld[23] (1731–1795) wurde am 13. September 1731 auf der Insel Mainau geboren. Siebzehnjährig kam er nach Wien und studierte dort Philosophie und Rechtswissenschaften. Danach war er in verschiedenen Staatsämtern im Bereich der Finanzverwaltung tätig und wurde auch Mitarbeiter bei den von Christian Gottlob Klemm herausgegebenen Wochenschriften *Die Welt* (1762) und *Der österreichische Patriot* (1764/65). Wie Josef von Sonnenfels setzte sich Franz von Heufeld insbesondere für die Reformierung der Schaubühne in Wien ein. Er war 1769 und 1774–1776 als künstlerischer Leiter am Kärntnertortheater tätig. Das Repertoire des deutschen Theaters, das noch sehr stark vom Stegreiftheater, d.h. von den Hanswurststücken, geprägt war, sollte dabei durch neue regelmäßige Stücke ersetzt werden, die sich an den Reformvorschlägen von Gottsched orientierten, doch genau daran mangelte es. Um das Schauspielangebot zu erweitern, schrieb Heufeld Komödien und adaptierte auch fremdsprachige Theaterstücke und Romane. Einen wichtigen Kulturtransfer leistete er durch die erste deutsche *Hamlet*-Adaption,[24] die sich an der Shakespeare-Übersetzung von Christoph Martin Wieland orientierte und Friedrich Ludwig Schröder zu weiteren *Hamlet*-Bearbeitungen anregte, die sehr erfolgreich in Hamburg aufgeführt wurden. Außer *Hamlet* bearbeitete Heufeld auch Rousseaus Briefroman *Julie, ou La Nouvelle Héloïse* und Henry Fieldings Roman *The History of Tom Jones, a Foundling*, denen ich mich im Folgenden zuwenden möchte.

Heufelds Stück *Julie, oder Wettstreit der Pflicht und Liebe* wird am 6. Dezember 1766[25] zum ersten Mal in Wien gegeben und wird 1769 dreimal gespielt. Im April 1767 kommt das Stück in Hamburg zur Aufführung, worüber Lessing in der *Hamburgischen Dramaturgie* eine ausführliche Rezension schreibt.[26] Franz von Heufeld nimmt als Vorlage für die Konzeption seines Stückes die deutsche Übersetzung von Rousseaus Roman *Julie, ou La Nouvelle Héloïse*, wobei die Bearbeitung eines 800 seitigen Romans in ein kurzes Lustspiel natürlich nur einige wichtige Themen des Stoffs behandeln kann. Inhaltlich konzentriert sich Heufeld auf die ersten drei Teile des

Romans, in denen die Liebesbeziehung zwischen der adligen jungen Dame Julie zu ihrem bürgerlichen Hauslehrer St. Preux thematisiert werden. Julie und St. Preux, der in Heufelds Stück Siegmund heißt, lieben sich, aber Julie soll nach dem Willen ihres Vaters eine standesgemäße Heirat mit dem sehr viel älteren Wolmar eingehen, dem Julie aus Dankbarkeit versprochen wurde. So steht natürliche Liebe, die Ständeschranken überwindet, gegen Konventionsehe, die an den gesellschaftlichen Unterschieden festhält, was für die Zeit eines der wichtigsten gesellschaftlichen Themen darstellt. In ihrer Liebe zu Siegmund befindet sich die junge Julie im Konflikt zwischen Pflicht und Neigung, der verschärft wird, als sie das Angebot eines Freundes Mylord Eduard erhält, durch seine Unterstützung mit ihrem Geliebten nach England zu fliehen. Da diese Flucht das Verlassen ihrer alten Eltern zur Folge haben würde, lehnt Julie dieses Angebot aus kindlicher Liebe und Verpflichtung gegenüber den Eltern ab. Siegmund dagegen kämpft um seine Liebe, indem er Wolmar zum Duell herausfordert und droht sogar mit Selbstmord, wenn er Julie nicht erhalten kann. Die Themen Duell und Selbstmord werden ausführlich in Rousseaus Roman diskutiert, während andere Romanthemen wie Gesellschaftskritik, Religion, Natur, Erziehung, Politik, sowie die Gesellschaftsutopie von Clarens im Drama keine Berücksichtigung finden. Auffallend ist, dass Rousseaus radikale Gesellschaftskritik in das Stück keinen Eingang findet, was keine Überraschung ist, da es sonst der scharfen Zensur in Wien zum Opfer fallen würde. Doch der Ausgang von Heufelds Stück ist mit der letztlichen Zustimmung des Vaters zur ständeüberwindenden Liebesheirat seiner Tochter modern und fortschrittlich. Der Wert des Individuums unabhängig von Stand und Vermögen und sein Anspruch auf individuelles Glück werden im Drama in den Mittelpunkt gestellt. Mit der Intention des Abbaus von Vorurteilen Adliger gegenüber Bürgerlichen und der Betonung individueller Autonomie hat das Stück eine klare gesellschaftskritische, aufklärerische Dimension.

## Heufelds Adaption von Rousseaus *Julie, ou La Nouvelle Héloïse*

Mein Interesse ist nun zu zeigen, wie sprachliche und dramatische Elemente des Briefromans erfolgreich in ein Theaterstück umgewandelt werden können oder anders gewendet, wie Elemente von Mündlichkeit im Roman eine dramatische Bearbeitung ermöglichen. Was die Form angeht, so würde die Fokussierung auf den Familienkonflikt eher ein bürgerliches Trauerspiel nahelegen. Doch Heufeld macht aus dem Stoff ein rührendes Lustspiel, wobei er in der Vorrede das Publikum auf einen "ernsthaften Stoff" vorbereitet, der "nichts Lustiges"[27] bringen wird, sondern die Menschenliebe und den Abbau von Vorurteilen befördern soll. Im Folgenden möchte ich zeigen, wie Heufeld bei der Ausgestaltung der Aufzüge und Auftritte im Drama die Textstellen von Rousseau übernimmt, die im Briefroman Rousseaus schon mündlichen Charakter haben. Dass Briefe eine Ähnlichkeit mit Gesprächen aufweisen, hat im 18. Jahrhundert bereits schon Gellert festgestellt, wenn er formuliert: "Das erste, was uns bey einem Briefe einfällt, ist dieses, daß er die Stelle eines

Gesprächs vertritt. . . . und deswegen muß er sich der Art zu denken und
zu reden, die in Gesprächen herrscht, mehr nähern, als einer sorgfältigen
und geputzten Schreibart."[28] Nun finden sich bei Rousseau z. B. kurze Briefe,
genannt Billete, die bereits Dialogcharakter haben. Als St. Preux sich von Julie
entfernen möchte und mit Selbstmord droht, schreibt Julie:

## Rousseau: 1. Teil, 3. Brief

Erstes Billett:
Nehmen Sie nicht die Meinung mit sich, Sie hätten Ihr Weggehen notwendig
gemacht! Ein tugendhaftes Herz könnte sich überwinden oder aber schweigen
und wäre dann vielleicht zu fürchten. Sie aber—Sie können bleiben.
Antwort St. Preux:
Ich habe lange geschwiegen; am Ende hat mich Ihre Kälte zum Reden
gebracht. Wenn man sich auch um der Tugend willen überwinden kann, erträgt
man doch nicht die Verachtung derer, die man liebt. Ich muß fort.
Zweites Billett von Julien:
Nein, mein Herr; nach dem, was Sie zu empfinden schienen, nach dem, was Sie
mir zu sagen sich erkühnt haben, reist ein Mensch, wie Sie zu sein vorgeben,
nicht fort; er tut mehr.
Antwort:
Ich habe nichts vorgegeben als eine gedämpfte Leidenschaft in einem verzwei-
felden Herzen. Morgen werden Sie befriedigt sein; und Sie mögen sagen, was
Sie wollen, ich werde weniger getan haben, als fortgereist zu sein.
Drittes Billett von Julien:
Unsinniger! Ist Dir mein Leben lieb, so scheue Dich, Hand an das Deinige zu
legen!—Ich bin von Gesellschaft umringt und kann bis morgen weder mit
Ihnen sprechen noch an Sie schreiben. Haben Sie Geduld! (37–38)

## Heufeld: 1. Aufzug, 1. Auftritt

Julie. Nehmen Sie nicht die Meynung mit sich hinweg, als ob sie Ihre Entfernung
nothwendig gemacht hätte. Ein tugendhaftes Herz kann sich überwinden, oder
schweigen: und dann wird es vielleicht furchtbar werden: Aber Sie! Sie können
bleiben.
Siegmund. Ich habe lange geschwiegen: aber nun gebeut Ihr Kaltsinn zu
reden. Wenn man sich auch um der Tugend Willen überwinden kann: so erdul-
det man doch die Verachtungen seines Geliebten nicht. Ich muß fort.
Julie. Nein mein Herr! Nach dem, was Sie zu empfinden schienen; nach dem,
was Sie mir zu sagen sich erkühnt haben, reist ein Mensch, wie Sie erdichtet,
daß Sie wären, nicht fort: er thut mehr.
Siegmund. Ich habe nichts erdichtet als eine gemäßigte Leidenschaft in einem
Herzen voller Verzweiflung. Bald werden Sie befriedigt seyn: und was Sie nun
auch sagen mögen; ich werde dann stets weniger gethan haben, als von Ihnen
mich entfernt. Leben Sie wohl! (will abgehen)
Julie. Bleib Unsinniger! ist dir mein Leben theuer, ach! so scheue dich, das deinige zu verkürzen . . . (218–19)

Es wird deutlich, dass die Billette, die zwischen Julie und St. Preux ausge-
tauscht werden, im Grunde einen Dialog darstellen, den Heufeld fast wörtlich
in sein Stück einfügt. Gellius' Übersetzung von Rousseaus Roman wird sprachlich mit wenigen die Kommunikativität fördernden Umformulierungen über-
nommen. So machen dramatische Elemente im Roman eine Überführung
ins Drama sehr leicht möglich, wie auch folgendes Beispiel demonstriert. In
einem Brief von Clare an Julie zitiert Clare ein Gespräch zwischen Mylord
Eduard mit Julies Vater, indem es um eine Charakterisierung von St. Preux
geht:

## Rousseau: 1. Teil, 62. Brief

Alle die Gaben, die nicht in menschlicher Macht stehen, hat er von der Natur
erhalten und sie durch alle andern Talente, die von ihm abhingen, vermehrt. Er
ist jung, hochgewachsen, wohlgestaltet, stark, gewandt, hat Erziehung, Verstand,
Lebensart, Mut, einen gebildeten Witz, ein reines Herz; was fehlt ihm also, um
Ihr Jawort zu verdienen? Vermögen? Das soll er haben. (169)

## Heufeld: 2. Aufzug, 1. Auftritt

Alle Gaben, die nicht von uns abhängen, hat er von der Natur erhalten, und er hat
sie durch diejenigen, die nur von ihm abhängen, vermehret. Er ist jung, ansehn-
lich, wohlgebildet, ein Mann von Geschicklichkeit; er hat Erziehung, Verstand,
Sitten, Umgang; er hat wahren Muth … Was fehlt ihm, um Ihr Jawort zu erhalten—Vermögen? das soll er haben. (234–35)

Wiederum übernimmt Heufeld mit einigen sprachlichen Vereinfachungen
und Verkürzungen die Beschreibung von Rousseau/Gellius fast wörtlich. Ein
anderes Beispiel zeigt einen Gedankengang Julies in einem Brief an Mylord
Eduard, in dem sie über ein mögliches Verlassen der Eltern nachdenkt:

## Rousseau: 2. Teil, 6. Brief

Unbarmherzig sollte ich diejenigen verlassen, denen ich das Leben verdanke,
die es mir erhalten und lebenswert machen, deren ganze Hoffnung und Freude
in mir allein ruht? Einen fast sechzigjährigen Vater! Eine stets kränkliche Mutter!
Ich, ihr einziges Kind, sollte sie hilflos der Einsamkeit und den Beschwernissen
des Alters preisgeben, da eben die Zeit kommt, ihnen die zärtlichen Sorgen, die
sie mir verschwenderisch zuteil werden ließen, zu erwidern! (213)

## Heufeld: 2. Aufzug, 2. Auftritt

ach ich Undankbare sollte diejenigen verlassen, von denen ich das Leben erhalten? Diejenigen, welche keine andere Hofnung, kein anders Vergnügen, als in
mir allein haben? einen sechzigjährigen Vater? eine stets kränkliche Mutter!
Ich—ihr einziges Kind, sollte sie hülflos der Einsamkeit, und dem Überdrusse
des Alters überlassen, eben itzt, da die Zeit kömmt, ihnen die zärtliche Sorge, die
sie an mich verschwendet haben, zu erwidern? (239)

Dieser Gedankengang ähnelt einem Monolog im Drama und kann deshalb sehr leicht in das Stück aufgenommen werden. Heufeld fügt diejenigen Briefstellen aus Rousseaus Roman ein, die bereits Dialogen oder Monologen ähneln und geht damit den umgekehrten Gang wie Friedrich von Blanckenburg, der eine Dramatisierung des Romans durch diese Methode vorschlug. Um die Kommunikationsfähigkeit zu fördern, kürzt Heufeld gelegentlich den Satzbau oder nimmt Umstellungen vor. Umständliche sprachliche Wendungen werden vereinfacht; Nominalstil wird in Verbalstil umgewandelt. Heufelds Intention ist dabei, den Rousseauschen "Ton" beizubehalten (215). Die Auswahl bühnentauglicher Stellen ist nach Heufeld keine leichte Aufgabe, wenn er in der Vorrede betont, dass es ihm schwerer fiele "wegzulassen, als herauszunehmen" (215). Ein Stück dieser Art soll auf ein Publikum zielen, dass "bereits bey dergleichen Stücken, und bey Trauerspielen gezeiget, daß es mit einem edlen Gefühle begabet, daß es sanfter Empfindungen fähig ist, die einen angenehmern Eindruck, als selbst der Ausbruch der Freude machen? Eine stille Thräne, über die verfolgte Unschuld, über die gedrückte Tugend, ist eine Wollust eines guten Herzens, die nur kleinen Seelen unbekannt bleibet" (214). Wie deutlich wird, ist die intendierte Wirkung der Komödie nicht Lachen, sondern Mitleid. Diese auf Identifikation mit den Hauptpersonen beruhende Wirkung soll vor allem Affekte der Zuschauer ansprechen und in Bewegung bringen. Die emotionale Wirkung auf den Zuschauer ist damit vergleichbar mit derjenigen eines Lesers eines zeitgenössischen Briefromans, die auf die Rührung der Sinne zielt, wie Rousseau in der Einleitung zu seinem Roman formuliert. Auch den Gegenstand der Darstellung, nämlich "die Wirklichkeit des Lebens" teilen Briefroman und Drama.[29] Rolf Tarot weist darauf hin, dass z.B. schon Diderot Richardsons Briefromane als "grands drames" bezeichnet habe. Auch Friedrich von Blanckenburg zeige in seinem Werk *Versuch über den Roman*, wie im Roman Unmittelbarkeit mit Hilfe von Dialogisierung erreicht werden kann und der Leser damit "in den Zuschauer verwandelt" werde. Richardson selbst bezeichnete seine *Clarissa* in einem Nachwort als "dramatic narrative" und nicht als eine Geschichte.[30] Diesen Vorgang, der das Publikum am Erlebten teilhaben lässt und emotional miteinbezieht, beschreibt Gisbert Ter-Nedden als den "Kino-Effekt des Briefromans"[31] und genau darin liegt, wie deutlich gemacht werden sollte, die Möglichkeit einer Dramatisierung.

## Heufelds Adaption von Henry Fieldings
### *The History of Tom Jones, a Foundling*

Auch bei Heufelds Dramatisierung von Henry Fieldings Erfolgsroman *The History of Tom Jones, a Foundling*, der 1749 erschienen ist und sofort überall in Europa bekannt wurde, lassen sich ähnliche Verfahrenstechniken feststellen. Heufelds Stück *Tom Jones*[32] wurde am 10. September 1767 zum ersten Mal im Burgtheater aufgeführt. Wie schon bei der Adaption von Rousseaus *Julie* konzentriert sich Heufeld auf den Familienkonflikt, der durch Standesunterschiede verursacht wird. Sophie Western soll aus familienpolitischen, ökonomischen Gründen den ihr widerwärtigen Neffen von

Allworthy namens Blifil heiraten, doch ist sie in den jungen, gutaussehenden Tom Jones verliebt, der vermeintlich ein Findelkind ist und der von dem Adligen Allworthy zusammen mit Blifil erzogen wurde. Die Handlung setzt mit dem 14. Kapitel des Vierten Buches von *Tom Jones* ein und spielt ausschließlich auf dem Landgut von Sophies Vater, das neben dem von Allworthy liegt. Neben der Einheit des Ortes ist auch die Einheit der Zeit gewahrt, denn die Handlung konzentriert sich auf einen einzigen Tag. Damit werden weite Teile des Romans—Tom Jones Jugendgeschichte, seine Reise durch England und sein Aufenthalt in London, die die große, gesellschaftliche Welt in satirischem Licht zeigen—nicht im Drama berücksichtigt. Heufeld führt inhaltlich dagegen den ersten Teil mit dem Romanschluss (2. Kapitel des 12. Buches) zusammen, wo sich herausstellt, dass Tom Jones ein Kind aus einer heimlichen Verbindung von Allworthys Schwester ist und damit ein Neffe von Allworthy und Blifils Bruder. Dadurch erweist sich der Standeskonflikt als nichtig und einer Heirat steht nichts mehr im Wege. Es ist aber hervorzuheben, dass in diesem Stück brisante Themen wie die patriachalische Familienstruktur, die Stellung der Frauen und die freie Partnerwahl sehr deutlich angesprochen werden, wobei im Gegensatz zu Heufelds *Julie* schärfere Töne angeschlagen werden. Sophies Vater Western spielt die Rolle des sturen, komischen Alten, der auf seine väterliche Autorität pocht und von seiner Tochter unbedingten Gehorsam erwartet. Die Tochter Sophie folgt ihrem Gefühl und betont ihr Recht auf freie Partnerwahl und auf eine Liebesheirat. Die vermittelnde Schwester von Sophies Vater zeigt sich dagegen in einer zweideutigen Rolle. Sie präsentiert sich einerseits als kluge, welterfahrene Frau, die explizit die Geschlechtergleichheit hervorhebt. Als ihr Bruder Sophie mit Freiheitsberaubung und Enterbung bedroht, hält sie ihm entgegen:"Wir sind so frey, wie die Männer; und wollte Gott! ich dürfte nicht sagen, wir verdienen diese Freyheit besser. Noch einmal Bruder! wir sind keine Sklavinnen, die man einsperrt, wie die türkischen Weiber."[33] Andrerseits versucht sie, Sophie von den Vorteilen einer Konventionsehe mit Blifil zu überzeugen.

In formaler Hinsicht verfährt Heufeld in ähnlicher Weise wie bei der Rousseauadaption, indem er einige von Fieldings Romandialogen ziemlich wörtlich übernimmt. Ob Heufeld dabei die erste 1750 erschienene deutsche Übersetzung benutzt oder die englischen Exzerpte selbst überträgt oder übersetzen läßt, läßt sich nach Foltinek[34] nicht mehr feststellen. Im Folgenden möchte ich nun drei Textbeispiele heranziehen, um die Verfahrensweise Heufelds zu verdeutlichen.

Das Lustspiel beginnt mit einem Gespräch von Sophie und ihrem "Mädchen" Honora, in dem Honora ihrem "Fräulein" von Szenen berichtet, die als Liebesbeweise von Toms Neigung zu Sophie interpretiert werden können.

## Heufeld: Tom Jones, 1. Aufzug, 1. Auftritt

Soph. Ich will es wissen, Honora! sag es den Augenblick!
Hon. Je nu! aber werden Sie nicht böse! Er kam jüngsthin zu mir ins Zimmer. Da lag ihr Fächer auf dem Tische, den nahm er in die Hände, und spielte damit—das war dieser nämliche Fächer, den sie mir vorgestern geschenkt

haben. Wie nu, Herr Jones, sagte ich! Sie werden meines Fräuleins Fächer verderben. Darauf machte er ihn sanft zu, und küßte ihn—ich versichre sie gnädi-
ges Fräulein! in meinem Leben sah ich keinen so feurigen Kuß, als er diesem
Fächer gab—[35]

## Fielding: 4. Buch, 14. Kapitel

"Prithee tell me," says Sophia,—"I will know it this Instant," "Why, Ma'am," ans-
wered Mrs. Honour, "he came into the Room, one Day last Week when I was at
Work, and there lay your Ladyship's Muff on a Chair, and to be sure he put his
Hands into it, that very Muff that your Ladyship gave me but yesterday"; La, says
I, "Mr. Jones, you will stretch my Lady's Muff and spoil it"; but he still kept his
Hands in it, and then he kissed it—to be sure, I hardly ever saw such a Kiss in
my Life as he gave it." (206-7)[36]

Mit einigen Änderungen ist die Szene genauso gestaltet wie Fielding sie
beschrieben hat. Heufeld macht aus dem Muff einen Fächer, doch sprachlich
folgt Heufeld weitgehend der Vorlage. Der Handlungsablauf und der umgang-
sprachliche Ton des Mädchens sind ebenfalls gewahrt. Heufeld zeichnet
in dieser Szene und auch im ganzen Stück Tom Jones als gefühlvollen und
leidenschaftlichen Mann, der seine wahren Gefühle zeigen kann, während
Jones' Promiskuität und Draufgängertum im Drama keine Berücksichtigung
finden.

In dem nächsten Beispiel unterrichtet die Schwester ihren Bruder über
die Verliebtheit ihrer Nichte, wobei sie sich in der vermeintlichen Person
täuscht, denn es ist nicht Blifil, in den Sophie verliebt ist, sondern Jones:

## Fielding: 6. Buch, 2. Kapitel

but I believe, Brother, you are convinced I know the World, and I promise
you I was never more deceived in my Life, if my Niece be not most desperately
in Love." "How! in Love," cries Western, in a Passion, without acquainting me!
I'll desinherit her, I'll turn her out of Doors, stark naked, without a Farthing. Is
all my Kindness vor'ur, and vondness o'ur come to this, to fall in Love without
asking me Leave!" (274-75)

## Heufeld: 1. Aufzug, 4. Auftritt

Fr. West. Ich glaube, Bruder, sie sind überzeugt, daß ich die Welt kenne: Ich
versichere sie, in meinem Leben ward ich nicht mehr betrogen, wenn meine
Nichte nicht verzweifelt verliebt ist.

West. (aufgebracht) Verliebt? ohne mein Wissen? Ich will sie enterben, ich
will sie aus dem Haus stossen, ohne einen Pfennig Geld will ich sie fort jagen.
Erhaltet alle meine Liebe für sie so viel, daß sie sich verliebet ohne mich um
Erlaubniß zu fragen?

Es wird erkennbar, dass Heufeld sich genau an die englische Vorlage hält,
indem er die Komik der Szene, die in der drastischen Reaktion Westerns

liegt, bewahrt. Die kräftige Wortwahl, die im Orginal die Derbheit Westerns zum Ausdruck bringt, wird in der deutschen Übertragung abgemildert, was auch in anderen Adaptionen von Heufeld üblich ist, da er einem gereinigten Stilideal zu folgen sucht.

In diesem letzten Beispiel versucht die Tante von Sophie, ihre Nichte von den Vorteilen einer Konventionsehe zu überzeugen, indem sie ihr erklärt, dass Abneigung gegenüber dem künftigen Ehemann kein Grund gegen Eheschließung sei.

## Fielding: 7. Buch, 3. Kapitel

Sophia:
"Indeed, Madam,"cries Sophia, "this is the only Instance in which I must disobey both yourself and my Father. For this is a Match which requires very little Consideration in me to refuse."

"If I was not as great a Philosopher as Socrates himself," returned Mrs. Western,"you would overcome my Patience. What Objection can you have to the young Gentleman?"

"A very solid Objection, in my Opinion,"says Sophia,—"I hate him."

"Will you never learn a proper Use of Words?" answered the Aunt. "Indeed Child, you should consult Bailey's Dictionary. It is impossible you should hate a Man from you have received no Injury. By Hatred, therefore, you mean no more than Dislike, which is no sufficient Objection against you marrying of him. I have known many Couples, who have entirely disliked each other, lead very comfortable, genteel Lives. Believe me, Child, I know these Things better than you. You will allow me, I think, to have seen the World, in which I have not an Acquaintance who would not rather be thought to dislike her Husband, than to like him. The contrary is such out-of-Fashion romantic Nonsense, that the very Imagination of it is shocking." (333–34)

## Heufeld: 2. Aufzug, 5. Auftritt

Soph. Es thut mir leid, gnädige Tante! dieß ist der einzige Fall, in welchem ich beyden, ihnen und meinem Vater ungehorsam seyn muß. Denn diese Heurath braucht meiner Seits sehr wenig Ueberlegung sie auszuschlagen.

Fr.West. Wäre ich nicht eine so große Philosophinn als Sokrates selbst, so würdest du meine Geduld ermüden. Was für Einwürfe kannst du wider den jungen Edelmann machen?

Soph. Sehr gründliche—ich hasse ihn!

Fr. West. Wirst du nimmermehr den eigentlichen Gebrauch der Wörter lernen? Wahrhaftig, gutes Kind! du solltest Bayls Wörterbuch zu Rathe ziehen. Es ist schlechterdings unmöglich, daß du einen Mann hassen solltest, von dem du nie beleidiget worden. Durch Hassen also verstehest du nichts anders, als nicht lieben? dieses ist kein hinlänglicher Grund, ihn auszuschlagen. Ich habe manches Paar gekannt, die sich ganz und gar nicht liebten, und dem ungeachtet sehr glücklich lebten. Glaube mir, gutes Kind! ich verstehe diese Dinge besser als du. Du wirst mir, hoffe ich, zugestehen, daß ich die Welt gesehen? Ich habe in dieser, ich versichere dich, nicht eine einzige bekannte Dame, die ihrem

Ehemanne nicht lieber mißfallen, als gefallen wollte. Das Gegentheil ist ein solches aus der Mode gekommenes romanenhaftes Zeug, daß sogar die Einbildung davon anstößig wird.

Heufeld orientiert sich wiederum inhaltlich und sprachlich an der Vorlage Fieldings. Sophies kurze, bündige Aussage "Ich hasse ihn" wird mit einer weitläufigen Erklärung der Tante kontrastiert, warum Heirat ohne Liebe möglich und sogar "in der großen Welt" üblich sei, womit sie angesichts der zeitgenössischen adligen Heiratspraktiken nicht ganz Unrecht hat. Die Komik liegt in der Ironie, die zwischen dem überzogenen Selbstbild der Tante entsteht, die sich mit Sokrates vergleicht und auf ihre Welterfahrenheit pocht und der lächerlichen Aussage, dass ihre Bekannte das Missfallen der Ehemänner vorziehen. Vergleicht man die Übersetzung, so fällt hier eine interessante Umkehrung auf, denn im englischen Text lieben die Ehefrauen die Männer nicht und man kann fragen, ob es sich bei Heufeld um einen Übersetzungsfehler handelt oder um eine patriachalische Umdrehung. Die Tante behandelt ihre Nichte nicht als autonome Person, wenn sie sie herablassend als "Kind" bezeichnet, ihre Wortwahl maßregelt und ihre Position vollkommen ablehnt. Inhaltlich folgt Heufeld demnach der Vorlage Fieldings weitgehend. Sprachlich fällt die Höflichkeit des Tons und die gereinigte Wortwahl gegenüber dem Orginal auf.

Wie schon bei der Adaption von Rousseaus Bestseller *Julie* verwendet Heufeld ähnliche Verfahrenstechniken. Inhaltlich konzentriert sich Heufeld auf die Liebesgeschichte der Romanvorlagen, die durch Standeskonflikte kompliziert wird, aber bei ihm gemäß der Lustspieltradition nach Überwindung der Schwierigkeiten in der Eheschließung endet. Aus den Romanvorlagen werden die Teile entnommen, die dramatischen Charakter haben wie z.B. Dialoge, Monologe, wörtliche Berichte, Briefe, die das Publikum direkt am Geschehen teilhaben lassen und emotional miteinbeziehen. Diese Textausschnitte, in denen der "Kinoeffekt" der Romane liegt, wie Ter-Nedden sagen würde, machen den Kern der neuen Lustspiele von Franz von Heufeld aus. In sprachlicher Hinsicht nimmt Heufeld oft Textkürzungen, grammatische und stilistische Änderungen vor, die einem neuen Stilideal im Gottschedschen Sinne entsprechen, das in Wien propagiert wird.

Heufeld schafft durch die Adaption erfolgreicher, zeitgenössischer Romane neue, regelmäßige Komödien für die deutschsprachige Bühne in Wien. Mit diesen Adaptionen leistet er nicht nur einen Beitrag zur Erweiterung des Repertoires, sondern auch zur Reform des Wiener Theaters.[37]

Werke wie Heufelds rührendes Lustspiel *Julie, oder Wettstreit der Pflicht und Liebe* werden allgemein zur Literatur der Empfindsamkeit gerechnet und hier nun teilen Robert Vellusig und Gisbert Ter-Nedden eine sich von der traditionellen Literaturwissenschaft absetzende Meinung. Für Robert Vellusig ist Empfindsamkeit "keine literarische Strömung,"[38] sondern eine Bezeichnung für die "moderne, massenmedial gestützte Erlebniskultur." Seiner Meinung nach hat sich in der Mitte des 18. Jahrhunderts nicht die Bedürfnislage der Menschen geändert, sondern die "Möglichkeiten ihrer Befriedigung."[39] Das heißt gesellschaftlicher Wandel kann durch "neue Kommunikationsmedien- und technologien" herbeigeführt werden. Diese These ist bestechend, doch meiner Meinung nach greift sie etwas zu kurz, denn sicherlich tragen auch andere Faktoren zu dem großen Kulturwandel im 18. Jahrhundert bei: man denke dabei nur an die Entwicklung der Naturwissenschaften, das Entstehen einer Konsumgesellschaft, die Ausweitung der Wirtschaft, die Erweiterung des Handels, der Ausbau der Städte, der Verwaltungsinstitutionen, des Bildungswesens, politische Umwälzungen, Kriege etc. Das alles, so meine ich, führt in der "Sattelzeit"[40] zu großen Gesellschaftsveränderungen. Eine ähnliche Position wie Vellusig vertritt Gisbert Ter-Nedden. Er grenzt sich dabei insbesondere von Gerhard Sauder ab, indem er bestreitet, dass die Empfindsamkeit ein im wesentlichen bürgerliches Phänomen sei.[41] Seiner Meinung nach ist die Strömung der Empfindsamkeit ständeübergreifend und damit vertritt er die Position Pikuliks.[42] Dazu kann man sagen, dass sicherlich Leser und Leserinnen unterschiedlicher Stände und Schichten von den Briefromanen angezogen werden, doch inhaltlich propagieren die oben genannten Romane und die Dramen oft als bürgerlich zu bezeichnende Werte und weisen meiner Meinung nach häufig eine deutlich antihöfische Stoßrichtung auf. So ist bei Rousseau eine klare Kritik am Lebenswandel des Pariser Adels erkennbar, wenn er Verschwendung, Luxus und "Sittenverfall" der Pariser Welt kritisiert, während Werte wie Leistung, Bildung, Maßhalten, Arbeit, Freundschaft und die Liebesehe in der idealen Gemeinschaft von Clarens propagiert werden. Wie die Analyse von Heufelds Stücken zeigt, geht es darin ebenfalls um die Überwindung von Standesschranken, um die Hervorhebung von bürgerlichen Werten und um die Betonung von individuellen Glücksansprüchen.

Diese Einwände sollen nun nicht den Beitrag, den Gisbert Ter-Nedden und Robert Vellusig leisten, schmälern, denn dieser medienästhetische Ansatz stellt mit seinem Interesse an der Wirkungsästhetik einfach andere Fragen als ein historisch-sozialer. Mit der Untersuchung des technischen Wandels eröffnet dieser neue medienästhetische Ansatz einen frischen Blick auf die Genres des 18. Jahrhunderts, insbesondere auf die Briefkultur und auf den Briefroman. Der faszinierende Gedanke dabei ist das Konzept einer international massenhaft geteilten "Erlebniskultur," die mit dem Briefroman beginnt und sich heute über den Film bis hin zu den neuen sozialen Medien technisch in immer neuer Weise weiterentwickelt. Es sollte gezeigt werden, dass die Wirkungsweise des Briefromans, des Romans, des Dramas und des Films sich darin ähnelt, dass die Unmittelbarkeit des menschlichen Daseins so präsentiert wird, dass das Publikum direkt bei der Lektüre oder beim Zuschauen emotional in das Geschehen mithineingezogen wird. Formen der Mündlichkeit werden dabei in den Adaptionsprozessen vom Bestseller zum Drama kreativ eingesetzt, so dass neue Erlebnismöglichkeiten eröffnet werden.

*University of Memphis*

## ANMERKUNGEN

1. Gisbert Ter-Nedden, "Der Kino-Effekt des Briefromans. Zur Mediengeschichte der Empfindsamkeit am Beispiel von Richardsons *Clarissa* und Lessings *Miss Sara*

*Sampson,*" in *Poetik des Briefromans. Wissens-und Mediengeschichtliche Studien,* hrsg. von Gideon Stiening und Robert Vellusig (Berlin: de Gruyter, 2012) 85–129, hier 86.

2. Horaz, Poetic, zit. nach Robert Vellusig, "Si vis me flere … revisited," in *Das Erlebnis und die Dichtung. Studien zur Anthropologie und Mediengeschichte des Erzählens* (Göttingen: Wallstein, 2013) 166.

3. Gerhard Schulze, *Die beste aller Welten. Wohin bewegt sich die Gesellschaft im 21. Jahrhundert?* (München, Wien, 2003) zit. nach Robert Vellusig, "Anthropologie und Mediengeschichte des Erzählens," in *Das Erlebnis und die Dichtung,* 20.

4. Vgl. Gisbert Ter-Nedden, "Das Ende der Rhetorik und der Aufstieg der Publizistik," in Hans-Georg Soeffner, *Kultur und Alltag* (Göttingen: Schwarz, 1988) 171–91, 172.

5. Gisbert Ter-Nedden, "Der Kino-Effekt des Briefromans," 96.

6. Robert Vellusig, "Anthropologie und Mediengeschichte des Erzählens," 22.

7. Friedrich von Blanckenburg, *Versuch über den Roman.* Faksimiledruck der Orginalausgabe von 1774. Mit einem Nachwort von Eberhard Lämmert (Stuttgart: Metzler, 1965) 18.

8. Blanckenburg 19.

9. Blanckenburg 58.

10. Blanckenburg 99.

11. Blanckenburg 99.

12. Stiening und Vellusig, "Einleitung," in *Poetik des Briefromans,* 10.

13. Johann Wolfgang von Goethe, Autobiographische Einzelheiten. Aristeia der Mutter (1831). Zit. nach Goethe, *Briefe* 4, 488, zit. nach Robert Vellusig, "Werther muss—muss seyn!," in *Das Erlebnis und die Dichtung,* 238.

14. Gellert, zit. nach Robert Vellusig, *Schriftliche Gespräche. Briefkultur im 18. Jahrhundert* (Wien: Böhlau, 2000) 8.

15. Vgl. Vellusig, *Schriftliche Gespräche,* 26.

16. Johann Wolfgang von Goethe, zit. nach Vellusig, "Werther muss—muss seyn," 237.

17. Stiening und Vellusig, *Poetik des Briefromans,* 7.

18. Vgl. Jean-Jacques Rousseau, *Les Confessions,* in *Oeuvres Complètes,* Bd. 1, hrsg. von Bernard Gagnebin und Marcel Raymond (Paris: Éditions Gallimard, 1959) 547. Zur Wirkung Rousseaus auf die Leserschaft vgl. auch Robert Darnton, "Rousseau und sein Leser" in *Literatur und Linguistik* 15, Nr. 57–58 (1985): 111–46.

19. Siehe Darnton, "Rousseau und sein Leser," 135.

20. Vellusig, "Werther muss—muss seyn," 150.

21. Zitiert wird nach der ersten deutschen Übersetzung von Johann Gottfried Gellius, die 1761 erschienen ist. Jean-Jacques Rousseau, *Julie oder Die neue Héloïse. Briefe zweier Liebenden aus einer kleinen Stadt am Fuße der Alpen.* (München: Winkler, 1988) 12, die die Vorlage von Franz von Heufeld dramatischer Adaption war.

22. Vgl. Ter-Nedden, "Der Kino-Effekt des Briefromans," 86.

23. Siehe zur Bedeutung des österreichischen Autors Franz von Heufeld für die Wiener Bühnen: Walter Rogan, *Franz von Heufeld. Ein Beitrag zur Geschichte der Wiener Sittenkomödie und des Wiener Burgtheaters,* Phil. Diss., Wien, 1932. Jüngst auch Johann Sonnleitner, "Nachwort. Franz von Heufeld. Ein Wiener Theaterdichter zwischen Posse und Lustspiel," in *Franz von Heufeld. Lustspiele,* hrsg. von Johann Sonnleitner (Wien: Hollitzer Wissenschaftsverlag Verlag Lehner, 2014) 498–532.

24. Vgl. dazu: Monika Nenon, "Hamlets Anfänge. Zu Wielands Übersetzung und Franz von Heufelds Hamletadaption," in *Wieland-Studien Bd. 8* (Heidelberg: Winter, 2013) 73–89 und Monika Nenon, "Christoph Martin Wielands Hamletübersetzung und ihre Bühnenwirkung: Zu Franz von Heufelds und Friedrich Ludwig Schröders Hamlet-Adaptionen," in *Shakespeare as German Author. Reception, Translation Theory and Cultural Transfer*, hrsg. von John McCarthy (Amsterdam: Brill/Rudopi, 2018) 92–115.

25. *Julie, oder Wettstreit der Pflicht und Liebe. Ein rührendes Lustspiel von drey Aufzügen*. Aufgeführt von der K. K. privil. Schaubühne in Wien, im Jahre 1766. Gedruckt mit den Ghelischen Schriften. Der Text wurde vor kurzem von Johann Sonnleitner in *Franz von Heufeld. Lustspiele* neu herausgegeben, 211–60.

26. Vgl. zur Rezeption des Stückes ausführlicher: Monika Nenon, "Rousseau-Adaption und Lessings Rousseaukritik in der *Hamburgischen Dramaturgie*," in *Lessing Yearbook/Jahrbuch 41*, hrsg. von Monika Fick (Göttingen: Wallstein, 2014) 139–61.

27. *Julie, oder Wettstreit der Pflicht und Liebe*, 214.

28. C. F. Gellert, *Briefe, nebst einer praktischen Abhandlung von dem guten Geschmacke in Briefen* (Leipzig: Johann Wendler 1751) in *Die epistolographischen Schriften*. Faksimiledruck nach den Ausgaben von 1742 und 1751, hrsg. von Reinhard M. G. Nickisch (Stuttgart: Metzler, 1971) 2–3.

29. Zur Verbindung zwischen Drama und Roman im 18. Jahrhundert vergleiche: Rolf Tarot, "Drama—Roman—Dramatischer Roman: Bemerkungen zur Darstellung von Unmittelbarkeit und Innerlichkeit in Theorie und Dichtung des 18. Jahrhunderts" in *Momentum dramaticum. Festschrift für Eckehard Catholy*, hrsg. von Linda Dietrick und David G. John (Waterloo: University of Waterloo Press, 1990) 241–71, hier 245–47.

30. Siehe dazu Ian Watt, *The Rise of the Novel* (Berkeley: University of California Press, 1967) 209.

31. Ter-Nedden, "Der Kino-Effekt des Briefromans," 85–129.

32. Franz von Heufeld, *Tom Jones. Ein Lustspiel von fünf Aufzügen nach dem englischen Roman* (Wien: n.p., 1767).

33. Heufeld, 4. Aufzug, 5. Auftritt.

34. Siehe dazu Herbert Foltinek, "Dramatische Ansätze in der englischen Romanliteratur des achtzehnten Jahrhunderts: Ein Beitrag zur Geschichte der literarischen Gattungen," in *Österreichische Akademie der Wissenschaften. Philosophisch-Historische Klasse*. Sitzungsberichte 417 (1983): 3–28, hier 24. Herbert Foltinek, "Franz von Heufeld und seine Beziehung zur englischen Literatur," in *Die Österreichische Literatur. Ihr Profil an der Wende zum 18. zum 19. Jahrhundert (1750–1830)*, hrsg. von Herbert Zeman (Graz: Akademische Druck-und Verlagsanstalt, 1979) 445–63.

35. Heufeld, *Tom Jones*, 1. Aufzug, 1. Auftritt.

36. Henry Fielding, *The History of Tom Jones, a Foundling*, hrsg. von Fredson Bowers (Middleton: Wesleyan University Press, 1983) 207.

37. Siehe zur Theaterentwicklung in Wien: Hilde Haider-Pregler, *Des sittlichen Bürgers Abendschule. Bildungsanspruch und Bildungsauftrag des Berufstheaters im 18. Jahrhundert* (München: Jugend & Verlagsgesellschaft, 1980). Franz Hadamowsky, *Wien. Theatergeschichte. Von den Anfängen bis zum Ende des Ersten Weltkriegs* (Wien: Jugend & Volk, 1988).

38. Vellusig, "Si vis me flere . . . revisited," 182.

39. Vellusig, "Si vis me flere … revisited," 183.

40. Reinhart Koselleck, *Kritik und Krise* (Frankfurt: Suhrkamp, 1959). Vergleiche auch den kulturellen Überblick über das Zeitalter von Steffen Martus, *Aufklärung. Das deutsche 18. Jahrhundert—Ein Epochenbild* (Berlin: Rowohlt, 2015), der viele historisch-politische und wissenschaftsgeschichtliche Aspekte miteinbezieht.

41. Gerhard Sauder, *Empfindsamkeit*, Bd. 1. Voraussetzungen und Elemente (Stuttgart: Metzler, 1974).

42. Lothar Pikulik, *Frühromantik* (München: Beck, 1992) 25–33.

ILINCA IURASCU

# *Papierdenken*: Blasche, Fröbel, and the Lessons of Nineteenth-Century Paper Modeling

**Abstract:** This article focuses on paper modeling as a theoretical subject and material practice at the center of nineteenth-century pedagogical reform debates in Germany and beyond. Tracing a brief history of paper-based craft instruction after 1800—from Heinrich Blasche to Friedrich Fröbel—it shows how the plastic and haptic capabilities of paper and pasteboard modeling are understood as the basis for new, often radical educational models. Such models implicitly short-circuit the principle of alphabetical learning to propose instead the possibility of fundamental relations between "making" and "thinking."

**Keywords:** history of paper, paper modeling, Heinrich Blasche, Friedrich Fröbel, history of education, nineteenth-century crafts

A BOOK-REVIEW PRINTED IN 1820 in the *Jenaische Allgemeine Literatur-Zeitung* under the heading "Pedagogy" announces the publication of a new manual on paper modeling: Bernhard Heinrich Blasche's *Der Papierformer, oder Anleitung allerley Gegenstände der Kunstwelt aus Papier nachzubilden* (The Paper Modeler, or How to Reproduce All Manners of Artistic Objects from Paper, 1819).[1] Both the volume and its presence in the journal are part of a larger trend. As one of the many crafts involving techniques of paper manipulation[2] (such as scrapbooking and silhouette art), paper modeling, defined here as the construction of three-dimensional models from paper and pasteboard, gains increasing attention among early nineteenth-century educators, practitioners, and readers. But the 1820 review seems vehemently critical toward Blasche's manual: "Es ist durchaus nicht zu billigen, wenn man das Mechanische zum Wissenschaftlichen hinaufziehen will" (237; The attempt to raise the mechanical to the level of science can under no circumstance be sanctioned). The book's treatment of paper modeling as "more" than just a "mechanische Fertigkeit" (235; mechanical skill) and its elevation from an activity dedicated to "der Erholung und dem Zeitvertreibe" (relaxation and passing the time) to a "wahrhaft bildend und mathematisch" (236; truly educational and mathematical) practice are plainly dismissed. In the same negative vein, the article also comments on Blasche's suggestion that, qua manual craft, paper modeling can ultimately be exercised as a "freye Thätigkeit" (236; free activity)—a formulation that signals the potential for intellectual and creative autonomy. From the reviewer's perspective, any affinity between manual craft and intellectual pursuit is rejected from the start.

The critical tone of the review invites a closer look at some of the specific cultural developments associated with the paper-craft boom of the early nineteenth century. With historical ties to educational practice, paper modeling, in particular, becomes a platform for intense debate during this period, a critical ground where the limits of craft pedagogy, as taught by Blasche and his followers, are theorized, tested, and challenged. Indeed, if the "paper consciousness" of the age may be understood, at least in part, around "notion[s] of manipulability—around finger mind-relationships and the technologies that mediate between them,"[3] Blasche's manuals are central to this reorientation. For Blasche, as I will show, paper modeling, the crafting of three-dimensional paper objects involving technical instruments and measurements, can amount to what may be called *Papierdenken*, a process of thinking directly anchored in the materiality of paper, in the concrete gestures and operations that allow for its transformation. A closer look at the institutional contexts that inform Blasche's ideas may also lead to a better understanding of later developments in nineteenth-century educational theory. More specifically, I will suggest, Blasche's insistence on the affinity between mechanical skill and intellectual labor finds new expression in Friedrich Fröbel's craft pedagogy and its focus on the interrelation between processes of "making" and "thinking."

## Rethinking Crafts

In line with the didactic emphasis on manual work and craft-based activities promoted by pedagogic reformer and Rousseau follower Johann Bernhard Basedow, several authors of instructional literature around 1800 bring pasteboard and paper modeling to the attention of a broader audience. Notable among them is Bernhard Heinrich Blasche (1766–1832), instructor of arts and crafts at the renowned pedagogical institution led by Christian Gotthilf Salzmann (1744–1811) in Schnepfenthal. Prefiguring ideas that would be amply theorized by Fröbel and his followers, Blasche's notion of education challenges neat distinctions between manual occupation and labor of the mind, offering, instead, concrete applications for "die intellektuelle Bildung durch mechanische Beschäftigungen zu befördern" (how intellectual education can be conveyed via mechanical activities).[4] But as the review from the *Jenaische Allgemeine Literatur-Zeitung* suggests, the notion that the former could somehow derive from the latter is still a matter of debate. At the Philanthropinum, the boarding school experiment launched by Basedow in 1774, manual work is framed as an essential component of educational practice but crafts are still clearly distinguished from "Studienarbeit" (study work) and the higher activities of the mind.[5]

Blasche's understanding of the pedagogical role of manual crafts goes further than Basedow's. Drawing on the classic Rousseauist notion that in-depth knowledge presupposes the direct interaction with matter, Blasche brings the importance of object lessons to bear upon "minor" craft activities and manual work. Unmediated observation is the first step in that process, as he points out in the introduction to *Der technologische Jugendfreund* in 1804: Illustrated books "können den Mangel des Anschauns der Gegenstände . . . durchaus nicht völlig ersetzen" (cannot fully replace the experience of . . . seeing things firsthand).[6] Direct observation, however, turns out to be only the start of a complex pedagogical agenda with far-reaching implications.

Newly employed to teach arts and crafts at the Schnepfenthal school, the former student of theology and philosophy Blasche responds to the institutional aims expressed by director Salzmann himself: to devise a program which "die Kinder an eigenes Beobachten und Denken gewöhnt und auf die Ausbildung und Übung der Sinne . . . hingearbeitet" (habituates children to observe and think for themselves, aimed to develop and train their senses).[7] At Schnepfenthal, children are encouraged "selbst etwas zu verfertigen" (to make something on their own) thereby enabling the fusion of eye, hand and mind with the express purpose of producing independent, self-sufficient learners.

> Der Geist . . . lebt dabei auf, faßt eigene Ideen und erfindet Mittel sie auszuführen. Das Auge übt sich, die Größen zu messen, um jedem Teile des auszuführenden Werkes das nötige Verhältnis zum Ganzen zu geben, und die Muskeln der Hände werden auf so mannigfaltige Art geübt, daß sie . . . sich selbst zu helfen im Stande sind.[8]

> The spirit . . . is thereby enlivened, attains its own ideas and finds ways to fulfill them. The eye becomes skilled in measuring sizes, in order to lend each part of the work that is to be done its necessary relation to the whole, and the hand muscles are trained in so many different ways that they are able to help themselves.

Salzmann ascribes to manual work a vital pedagogical function, a role that requires the participation of both students and teachers. Not merely children, but their instructors too, he argues, must once more become learners of "making." "Es gibt da keinen Ausweg" (There is no other way), he concludes. It is therefore not without managerial pride that he lists the different types of manual occupations students can learn at Schnepfenthal: "allerlei Spielereien aus Papier und Netzstricken"; "allerlei Dinge aus Holz zu schnitzen, Korbflechten, Papparbeiten" (all sorts of playthings made from paper and netting—wood carving, basket-weaving, pasteboard modeling).[9] In other words, precisely the kind of activities Blasche is hired to teach.

For his part, Blasche is fully aware of the mission entrusted to him, both as an instructor educating children, and an educator instructing other educators. In *Werkstätte der Kinder* (Children's Workshops, 1800), published only a few years after his arrival at Schnepfenthal, he calls on the teaching community to recognize manual crafts not "als blos zufälliges Erziehungsmittel, sondern selbst . . . einen wesentlichen Zweig der Pädagogik" (as a merely accidental means of instruction, but rather . . . an essential branch of pedagogy).[10] Central to Blasche's argument is a subtle but important shift, signaled for the first time in 1797, in a volume that marks the start of his theoretical engagement with paper crafts: *Der Papparbeiter* (The Pasteboard Worker). While here he continues to speak of crafts in terms of "mechanische Arbeit" (mechanical work), thus returning to the distinction between "körperliche Übung" vs. "Kopfarbeit" (physical exercise vs. intellectual labor), he also introduces the formula "mechanische Kunst" (mechanical art) which places the discussion in a different frame of reference: aesthetic theory.[11] Indeed, "mechanical art" is a term with unmistakable Kantian resonances. According to the Kantian classification, "wenn die Kunst, dem Erkenntnisse eines möglichen Gegenstandes angemessen, bloß ihn wirklich zu machen die dazu erforderlichen Handlungen verrichtet, so ist sie mechanische; hat sie aber das Gefühl der Lust zur unmittelbaren Absicht, so heißt sie ästhetische Kunst" (if art merely performs the acts that are required to make a possible object actual, adequately to our cognition of that object, then it is mechanical art; but if what it intends directly is [to arouse] the feeling of pleasure, then it is called aesthetic art).[12] Blasche's point, then, is not to claim a place for manual crafts among the "fine arts" but, rather, to align them more closely with the Kantian "mechanical arts," and thereby confirm their educational relevance and capacity to skillfully produce objects that are "fully adequate to their concept."[13]

## Pasteboard before Paper

Nowhere are these ideas more clearly illustrated than in *Der Papparbeiter*, Blasche's only book dedicated entirely to the subject of pasteboard modeling. It is here that he proposes, for the first time, that crafts can be successfully used to convey abstract knowledge: "In der Folge aber kann man die Anleitung zu dieser Kunst auch dazu benutzen, den Kindern die ersten Anfangsgründe der Geometrie auf eine leichte und angenehme Art beyzubringen" (One can further use the instructions to this art to teach children the first principles of geometry in an easy and agreeable manner).[14] Armed with pasteboard, pen, ruler, scissors, and glue, students are instructed to build various spherical, cylindrical, and cuboid shapes, to cut, bend, mold, measure angles and circumferences, attach, and fit individual parts together. In this manner, suggests Blasche, the principles of geometry become "anschaulich" (accessible to the imagination).[15]

But around 1800 (and even later in the century), pasteboard modeling is still often seen as a means of passing the time, with "wenig oder gar keinen Werth" (little or even no worth) attached to it. Instead, as Blasche argues, "Erfahrung und Nachdenken . . . lehrten mich das Gegentheil" (experience and reflection . . . taught me the opposite).[16] If Blasche's reformulation of the role and meaning of pasteboard modeling provokes critical reactions (as seen in the case of the *Jenaische Allgemeine Literatur-Zeitung* review), his manuals also seem to have become increasingly popular, judging by the number of editions, reprints, and translations published until the end of the century. This wave of textual dissemination goes hand in hand with a process of literary validation. From Goethe to Fontane, pasteboard modeling enters the German autobiographical canon as an early sign of future artistic endeavors.

"Pappenarbeiten konnten mich höchlich beschäftigen" (I occupied myself greatly with pasteboard work) declares the former Schnepfenthal school visitor Goethe in 1811 in *Dichtung und Wahrheit*. Almost taking a page out of Blasche's book, Goethe evokes not just a simple scene of childhood play, but an exemplary scenario of progression from technical execution to imaginative creation:

> Ich hatte früh gelernt, mit Zirkel und Lineal umzugehen, indem ich den ganzen Unterricht, den man uns in der Geometrie ertheilte, sogleich in das Thätige verwandte. . . . Doch blieb ich nicht bey geometrischen Körpern, bey Kästchen und solchen Dingen stehen, sondern ersann mir artige Lusthäuser, welche mit Pilastern, Freytreppen und flachen Dächern ausgeschmückt wurden.[17]

> I had early learned to use compasses and ruler, because all the instructions they gave me in geometry were forthwith put into practice. . . . I did not stop at geometrical figures, little boxes, and such things, but invented pretty pleasure houses, adorned with pilasters, steps, and flat roofs.[18]

Placed in dialogue with manuals like *Werkstätte der Kinder* and *Der Papparbeiter*, however, Goethe's personal narrative of creative exceptionalism reads differently: namely, as the direct application of a method already launched and taught at Schnepfenthal.

Significantly, Blasche inaugurates his career as arts-and-crafts educator precisely with a manual on pasteboard modeling. The form, texture, and substance of the material itself play an intrinsic part in developing his method. Due to its physical properties—lightness, pliancy, compactness—pasteboard presents a series of important advantages for teachers and learners alike. Blasche extolls its virtues in the preface, exclaiming that "die ganze Werkstatt läßt sich . . . in ein Kästchen oder in eine große Mappe bringen, ist folglich tragbar und kann überall aufgeschlagen werden" (the entire workshop . . . fits in a small box or a large folder and can therefore be easily transported and opened everywhere).[19] To borrow Anke te Heesen's formulation: here, boxes and folders become "easily graspable equivalent[s] of the complex world,"[20] not merely in the sense of acting as capacious objects, but also as material representations of the extreme versatility and applicability of pasteboard.

At least starting with Jérôme de Lalande's *Art du cartonnier* (The Art of the Pasteboard Maker, 1762) and its subsequent German translation, pasteboard garners the attention of writers and technologists as a discrete category of the paper industry. In Lalande's presentation, pasteboard is the ultimate product of recycling, a material processed from low-quality rags, along with the scraps discarded by hatmakers and bookbinders.[21] In its finished state, the material then returns to the bookbinder's shop, where it is reintegrated into the process of book production. In Blasche's own interpretation, however, pasteboard seems to acquire a different meaning. Its traditional ties with bookbinding, and implicitly with the print industry, are now reoriented towards a new purpose. For Blasche, pasteboard is first and foremost a teaching material, not for the dissemination of the "higher" cultural techniques of reading and writing, but the "basic" skills of folding, cutting, and pasting. Even within the family of experimental educators around 1800, that gesture is bold. If Pestalozzi still speaks of pasteboard, quite literally, as a support for letters and the process of alphabetization,[22] Blasche's *Papparbeiter* elevates it to the status of a pedagogical material in its own right. Just as the "Kinderpappe, . . . der dickliche Mehlbrey, womit man Kinder zu nähren pflegt, ehe sie Zähne bekommen" (the mush, . . . the thick porridge fed to children before their teeth grow in)[23] provides nourishment for infants, the *Pappe* used for modeling nourishes the young students' imagination.

In a double sense then, Blasche's *Papparbeiter* lays the groundwork for a new model of learning. Starting with pasteboard, Blasche redirects the attention of students and educators from paper as surface of inscription to its three-dimensional capabilities. And in this manner, he prefaces a significant development in nineteenth-century pedagogy: Friedrich Fröbel's systematic treatment of manual crafts as elementary cultural techniques that predate and, in a sense, short-circuit alphabetic education.[24]

## Thinking (with) Paper

After his departure from Schnepfenthal in 1806, Blasche returns once more to the topic of paper modeling with the publication of *Der Papierformer* (1819; The Paper Modeler), described in the preface as "[die] Ergänzung meines Papparbeiters von mathematischer Seite" (a companion to the *Papparbeiter* from a mathematical perspective). Both manuals, argues Blasche, serve the same goal, for both represent in essence "nur eine Kunst" (the same art).[25] That goal is formulated as the act of bringing forth a "freie Thätigkeit" (independent action), not merely the "blinde Nachahmung" (blind imitation) of steps and operations.[26] As with *Der Papparbeiter*, the new manual firmly asserts the strong ties between paper crafts and abstract knowledge, and warns that, should those ties be severed, modeling would result in "werthlosen Zeitvertreib" (worthless diversion).[27]

In *Der Papierformer*, Blasche imagines a method based on elementary geometric forms as representations of mathematical "archetypes." Echoing notions of classic geometry going as far back as Pythagoras and Plato, Blasche sees the world as mathematically grounded, and everything in it—from trees to machines—as variations of a limited set of shapes and the combinations thereof:

> Alle Formen, welche die technischen Künstler . . . aufstellen, lassen sich . . . auf wenige Grundformen zurückführen; diese Grundformen sind als die mathematischen Urbilder zu betrachten, nach welchen die Natur sowohl als die ihr folgenden Künstler bilden. . . . Man betrachte die verschiedenen Kunsterzeugnisse . . . so wird man allemal die geometrischen Körper und deren Combinationen darinn finden. . . .[28]

> All forms . . . constructed by technical artists can be . . . traced back to a small number of basic shapes; these basic shapes must be regarded as mathematical archetypes which both nature and the artists that follow her use as their model. . . . Looking at the diverse artifacts produced . . . one can identify therein those geometrical forms and combinations.

The manual traces a gradual progression from observation (of basic solids—tetrahedra, cones, cubes, cylinders, etc.) to drafting (of polyhedral nets), assembly, and construction, and in this manner proposes a systematic and "allseitigen Kenntnis des Gegenstandes . . . womit man es zu thun hat" (comprehensive understanding of its object of study).[29] The act of looking at, drawing, and then modeling shapes out of paper thus amounts to a complex pedagogic experience where materiality and abstraction are coextensive, and the acquisition of manual dexterity goes hand in hand with processes of conceptual articulation. Paper modeling—in the sense of a guided method of creating and transforming paper objects—is, at the same time, a source book for thinking (with) paper, a manual for *Papierdenken*.

This reformulation can also be understood in light of Blasche's engagement with transcendental idealism, and especially with the philosophy of Friedrich Schelling after 1800. Amply manifest in Blasche's later work on educational theory, Schelling's ideas also inform the notion of "Konstruktion" (construction) at the heart of the paper modeling manual. According to Schelling's *System des transzendentalen Idealismus* (1800; *System of Transcendental Idealism*), "die Transzedental-Philosophie geht . . . von keinem Dasein, sondern von einem freien Handeln aus, und ein solches kann nur postuliert werden" (transcendental philosophy . . . proceeds from no existent, but from a free act, and such an act can only be postulated).[30] In a similar manner, argues Schelling, geometry also proceeds from postulates and pupils themselves must bring forth (*hervorbringen*) "die ursprünglichste Konstruktion" (the most primary construction). Schelling's analogy between transcendental inquiry and geometry takes on concrete form in Blasche's paper modeling. Here, too, its object is brought forth, rather than "als schon vorhanden voraussetzen" (presupposed as already present). To put it differently, in Blasche's vision, craft-making does not primarily produce technical artists, but philosophers.

## Papyro-Plastics

Over the course of the following decade, several translations and compilations render Blasche's work more accessible to a broader international audience. Aiming for wider appeal, the English editor and translator of *Der Papierformer*, Daniel Boileau, adds a new introduction and changes the title of Blasche's manual to *Papyro-Plastics or the Art of Modelling in Paper* (1824). "We have first to account for its name," Boileau explains:

> We are aware that the term Plastics is generally confined to the modelling of sculptors and statuaries in gypsum, clay, wax & c. But as the art of making cork models of architectural monuments on a small scale has obtained on the continent the appellation of Phelloplastics from the Greek word φέλλος, cork; we think ourselves warranted by this analogy in denominating the art of modelling in paper Papyro-plastics.[31]

Boileau's pseudo-Greek neologism invokes a genealogy that goes back to an elementary cultural technique, namely "molding" or "forming" (πλάσσειν). According to the preface, papyro-plastics offers a "natural" access point into the study of arts and a "love of reality" "characteristic of the infancy of nations," illustrated by "the Greeks [who] had clever statuaries long before they had able painters."[32] But not the idea of Winckelmannian imitation of classical antiquity is at stake here. Rather, Boileau proposes something akin to recapitulation theory in childhood education avant-la-lettre: by being instructed in the art of paper modeling, pupils are supposedly rehearsing no less than an "original" aesthetic impulse, the drive to shape and mold matter into things. Thus, Boileau concludes, paper modeling caters in particular to "the youthful mind," protecting it from "that listless indolence, that pernicious love of cards or that rage from indiscriminately reading any book at random ... unfortunately tolerated in many respectable families."[33] Here, both card playing and arbitrary reading amount to modern addictions that result in ignorance, miseducation, and the misuse of paper.

With its focus on handiwork and construction, papyro-plastics now offers to correct such mistakes. Boileau obviously departs from the more elaborate methodological principles upheld by Blasche. Nevertheless, he also follows in the tradition of the nineteenth-century pedagogical reformer in at least one regard: highlighting the educational importance of working with and on paper, not as a surface of inscription, but rather as an endlessly moldable and modular substance. Over the course of the nineteenth century, paper modeling continues to be adopted by various new pedagogical initiatives. To be sure, the basic techniques that constitute it (folding, cutting, pasting) can be found across a range of different paper-based crafts and arts—from collage to silhouette cutting. Yet the systematic focus on the plasticity of the material itself, the intersections between geometric theory, philosophy, and handiwork, and, more broadly, the idea of a pedagogy built around the manipulation of matter, set it apart, both in terms of method and content.

Royal Society Fellow John Ayrton Paris (1785–1856) subscribes precisely to these principles in his fictionalized guide for the young learners of science. The book's title echoes some of Blasche's and Boileau's own theoretical premises: *Philosophy in Sport Made Science in Earnest. Being an Attempt to Illustrate the First Principles of Natural Philosophy by the Aid of the Popular Toys and Sports* (1827). In Paris's account, building a paper kite becomes an opportunity for the fictional instructor to discuss papyro-plastics and its relevance for understanding basic mathematical principles.[34] At the same time, the act of construction also enables a dialogue about the "uses" of philosophy and the role of playful paper manipulation in providing direct access to them. The book's protagonists are shown at work, cutting, folding, and assembling the kite's tail out of waste paper. While examining the sheets, they find them filled with "every description of scientific and literary works," leading one character to conclude that: "if you compose the tail of your kite with these papers ... it will certainly vie with that of Scriblerus himself; you will have a knot of divinity, a knot of physic, a knot of logic, a knot of philosophy, a knot of poetry and a knot of history."[35] But Paris takes a different route than Carlyle or Jean Paul, whose "paper" satires trace endless cycles leading from print to waste and back to print matter. The textual paper trail is irrelevant here. Instead, it is the very construction of the paper object—the kite—that moves to the center of attention along with the technical lessons learned from measuring and modeling its different parts. Such lessons enable the understanding of concepts of gravity, velocity, action, and reaction. From there, Paris's fictional teacher and students proceed with questions about the history of science and culture. As the teacher presents his pupils with various gadgets and tools (like the paper they use for building the kite), the key aspect of his method remains the progression from "making" to "understanding" via a process of guided and playful self-learning.

## Gift Pedagogy

Paris's instructor refers to the tools and gadgets he offers his students as "gifts," a term which yet another nineteenth-century German reformer eventually turns into a key feature of modern pedagogical practice. In 1838, decades after Blasche publishes his first manual on craft education, a land surveyor and former student of crystallography named Friedrich Fröbel releases a series of articles on what he calls "Gaben und Beschäftigungen" (Gifts and Occupations).[36] Along with the institution created to accommodate them—the kindergarten—these objects and activities can be productively understood in terms of the cultural techniques of early childhood education.

The publication of Fröbel's first articles on play gifts coincides with the opening of a *Pflege-, Spiel- und Beschäftigungsanstalt* (Care, Play, and Activity Center) in Bad Blankenburg. Under the new name it adopts in 1840—*Allgemeiner deutscher Kindergarten* (The General German Kindergarten)—the Blankenburg institution will become known as Fröbel's most significant pedagogical invention. The idea of a "garden for children" as Fröbel conceives it is unprecedented: not in the least since it transposes the principles of guided self-learning to the pre-elementary stage and imagines an almost exclusively craft-based model of instruction, supported by an ample philosophical framework. At the same time, Fröbel's project can be seen as a conceptual hybrid, a distillation of the various theoretical sources available to him: a blend of enlightened humanism (Rousseau), Weimar classicism (Schiller), liberal nationalism (Jahn), ethical idealism (Fichte) and Romantic pedagogical practice (Pestalozzi and Blasche). The kindergarten is not invented in a vacuum.

Some of these sources and the theoretical directions deriving from them have received more critical attention than others. Thus, while the link with Blasche is not immediately visible, the connection between Fröbel and his mentor Johann Heinrich Pestalozzi has been repeatedly invoked. There are obvious parallels, for instance, between Pestalozzi's foundational work on modern pedagogy *Wie Getrud ihre Kinder lehrt* (*How Gertrud Teaches Her Children*, 1801) and Fröbel's *Mutter- und Kose-Lieder* (*Mother-Play and Nursery Songs*, 1843), a guide to mothers teaching their children by means of play and song.[37] Both volumes can be read against the background of Kittler's "discourse network 1800," which aligns education with the pedagogical and bureaucratic invention of the "Muttermund" ("Mother's Mouth") and the maternal "gifts" as the origin of all discourse.[38] But if Pestalozzi stresses the preeminence of maternal orality in the training of early learners,

for Fröbel this aspect no longer fully answers the question about early
childhood pedagogy. Already in the description of the first gift and occupation—the child handling a ball of yarn—Fröbel shifts the focus to the
material interaction with the object itself as an extension of the child's own
corporeality:

> Sehen wir doch, wie das kleine Kind alles umfasst und umspannt, und hat
> es nichts anderes, seinen kleinen Daumen, seine eigene zweite Hand und
> Faust. Auch sehen wir . . . wie sowohl jede Hand für sich allein, als beide
> gemeinsam, recht eigentlich dazu gebildet sind, eine Kugel, einen Ball in sich
> einzuschließen.[39]

> We see how the little child likes so much to seize and grasp everything, even
> its own thumb or its other hand or fist if it has nothing else. We also see . . .
> how each hand by itself is well adapted to enclose a ball, as are also both hands
> together.[40]

In their most basic form, Fröbel's gifts can be described as "playthings, such
as balls, blocks in different shapes, paper, sticks and tiles—all abstract, geometrical objects designed to stimulate the child's imagination." In their turn,
the occupations comprise "carefully structured activities" involving those
very objects: "building with blocks, weaving strips of paper, folding paper,
creating geometric patterns with blocks, papers and tiles, rolling balls."[41] As
Norman Brosterman notes, none of the materials used in the Fröbelian curriculum are essentially new.[42] Rather, the novelty resides in the way they are
applied and integrated into systematic units, which are themselves part of a
carefully designed and conceptually coherent whole. Ideas of oneness, unity,
and synthesis (of life and nature) dominate Fröbel's vision, in line with his
training as a student of idealist philosophy in Jena. Nature, Fröbel writes in
*Die Menschenerziehung* (1826; *The Education of Man*), is "Ein Lebganzes"
(a living whole), characterized by "der innere lebendige Zusammenhang" (living inner connection) of its objects and manifestations, as well as a sense of
organization that pervades all its parts: "die Kräfte, die Stoffe, die Töne und
Farben [haben] wie die Formen und Gestalten ihre innere Einheit, ihren leb-
endigen innern Zusammenhang in und unter sich und mit dem Ganzen" (the
various forces, materials, sounds, colors, have—like the forms—their inner
unity, their living inner connection in and among themselves and with the
whole).[43]

By the time the accounts of the first gifts and occupations appear in the
*Sonntagsblatt* journal in 1838, the theoretical basis of the project, with its
focus on conceptual integration on the one hand, and systematic praxis on
the other is fully developed.[44] And it is especially this second aspect that contemporary reviewers identify as distinctive of Fröbel's approach. An article
released in Arnold Ruge and Theodor Echtermeyer's *Hallische Jahrbücher
für deutsche Wissenschaft und Kunst* (Halle Yearbooks of German Science
and Art) in 1839 defines the project in terms of scientific practice: "Die
Erziehungskunst [ist] nicht die schöne, die der Titel dieser Zeitschrift meint,
aber diese Praxis mit der wir es hier zu thun haben, stützt sich auf die
Wissenschaft" (The art of education is not an aesthetic one, as the title of

this journal suggests; the practice which is examined here is grounded in science).[45]

Implicit in this assertion is a reference to Fröbel's own professional trajectory, at the intersection between educational and scientific training. Following his teaching assignment in Frankfurt and apprenticeship at Johann Pestalozzi's institute at Yverdon, Fröbel is employed as an assistant at the University of Berlin's *Mineralogisches Museum* (Mineralogical Museum), formerly the *Königliches Mineralienkabinett* (Royal Mineral Cabinet) under Friedrich II. In that capacity, he works on the classification of the museum's vast collection and attends Christian Samuel Weiss's mineralogy and crystallography lectures at the University of Berlin. According to Michael Friedmann, it is via Weiss's work on the geometrical laws of crystal formation that Fröbel's ideas on pedagogy gain their systematic coherence and the project of the gifts and occupations finds its methodological basis: "The crystals, with their regular, ordered axes systems" become for Fröbel the "express[ion] of the basic order of nature."[46] Their symmetry and regularity is an expression of mathematical harmony, which, for Fröbel, also represents the original principle of creation in continuous transformation. In the autobiographical "Brief an den Herzog von Meiningen" ("Letter to the Duke of Meiningen"), Fröbel speaks of his encounter with the "Mineralien, diesen stummen Zeugen einer stillen, tausendfach schaffenden Thätigkeit der Natur" (minerals, these silent witnesses of the quiet, endlessly creative activity of nature) in terms of the revelation of "ein auf das verschiedenste modificirtes Gesetz der Entwicklung und Entfaltung" (under all kinds of various modifications one law of development).[47] Implicitly, for Fröbel, mathematics is not "ein Todtes, in sich Abgeschlossenes" (dead, self-limited) or a "Summe äußerlich, ein anander gereiheter, einzelner wie einzeln und zufällig gefundener Formen und Wahrheiten" (certain sum of . . . forms and truths found separately and accidentally and put on file). Rather, it represents "ein lebendiges, ununterbrochen sich neu wieder aus sich selbst gestaltendes . . . Ganzes" (a living whole . . . continually regenerating itself anew).[48]

Fröbel's mathematical vision of organic unity and transformation could hardly be understood in its full complexity without its grounding in the geometric principles of crystallography. In the pedagogical system of the gifts launched in 1838, those principles become manifest in full force. Significantly, Fröbel's gift system progresses from solids (ball, sphere, cube, and cylinder) to plane geometry (activities involving parquetry, slat-work, pricking, and sewing) to then come full circle with the construction of complex three-dimensional structures using peas-work and clay.[49] Weiss's geometric analyses of crystalline forms starting from three-dimensional grids, and his classification of specimens according to axes, facets, and angles translate into his student's own system of crafts: from the first gift of the ball as the *Bild vom All* (image of the whole) through various unfoldings that reveal multiple planes and points of intervention and, ultimately, to their regrouping into endlessly new spatial configurations.

## Lessons on Paper

On the surface then, there is no immediately visible link between Blasche's manuals on pasteboard and paper modeling, and Fröbel's system of gifts and occupations, involving a broad range of materials and activities. The paper-based crafts included in Fröbel's method are only featured in the thirteenth, fourteenth, and eighteenth gifts, in the form of folding, cutting, and weaving techniques, as well as stymography, or paper punch work on perforated sheets. According to Brosterman, their "introduction near the end of the [twenty] gift sequence" suggests that Fröbel understands these activities, given the attention to detail, precision, and elaborate technique they entail, as only "recommended for older children."[50] More importantly, in contrast to what Blasche, Boileau, and the other authors of papyro-plastics manuals propose, "what link[s] [Fröbel's] paper occupations, besides the material of their manufacture, [is] flatness."[51] The spherical, cylindrical, and cuboid objects that Blasche invites his students to observe, fold, and unfold into geometric grids in his *Papparbeiter* and *Papierformer* seem drastically different from the flat pinwheels and woven and punched patterns that Fröbel's children create with strips, needles, and colored squares of paper. In other words, Fröbel's paper-play occupations appear to have borrowed little, if anything, from the already established tradition of paper modeling and its bold theoretical scope, at the intersection between aesthetic theory, philosophy, and geometry.

This apparent discrepancy deserves a closer look, however. Written a decade before the first account on gifts and occupations, an autobiographical fragment from 1827 suggests a much closer link between Blasche's theories and Fröbel's quest for a new curricular design. According to Fröbel's own account, that quest is motivated by a growing dissatisfaction with Pestalozzi's methods, and its "Mangel eines organischen Zusammenhangs der Unterrichtsgegenstände" (utter absence of any organized connection between the subjects of education).[52] Instead, invoking a classic autobiographical trope, Fröbel draws on his own childhood experience in his search for answers: "Die Forderung meiner Zöglinge ward mir zu folgender Frage: Was thatest du als Knabe? Was geschah für dich um deinen Thätigkeits- und Darstellungstrieb zu beleben? Wodurch wurde dieser Trieb in diesem deinem Alter am entsprechendsten befriedigt?" (The demand of my pupils set me upon the following question: "What did you do as a boy? What happened to you to satisfy that need of yours for something to do and to express?").[53] The questions lead Fröbel back to the topic of paper crafts, and the importance of the plasticity and manipulability of matter:

> Da trat mir etwas aus meiner frühesten Knabenzeit entgegen, was für mich in diesem Augenblick Alles abgab dessen ich bedurfte. Es war die leichte Kunst, in glattes Papier durch geordnete Striche Zeichen und Gestalten einzuprägen. . . . Von diesem Formen aus Papier stiegen wir zum Formen des Papiers selbst empor, dann zum Formen aus Pappe und endlich aus Holz. Meine spätere Erfahrung hat mich noch viel Gestaltungs—und Formungsmaterialien kennen lernen.[54]

> Then there came to me a memory from out my earliest boyhood, which yielded
> me all I wanted in my emergency. It was the easy art of impressing figures and
> forms by properly arranged simple strokes on smooth paper. . . . From these forms
> impressed upon paper we rose to making forms out of paper itself, and then
> to producing forms in pasteboard, and finally in wood. My later experience has
> taught me much more as to the best shapes and materials for the study of forms.[55]

As Fröbel imagines it in 1827, the idea of a systematic progression of learning is closely linked to the malleability of paper and some of the elementary
techniques of paper and pasteboard modeling. And, as archival documents
suggest, it is precisely via Blasche's manuals that Fröbel begins to consider
the full implications of a rigorous approach to crafts. During that very same
year (1827), Fröbel contacts the former Schnepfenthal educator with the
proposal of initiating a "freier Verein deutscher Erzieher" (an independent
union of German educators) that would reflect a new, collective vision of
pedagogical reform.[56] The brief correspondence does not result in any concrete plans, yet the familiarity with Blasche's work and theories is evident.
In the same autobiographical fragment, Fröbel insists on the significance
of paper crafts for early childhood education in a language that echoes the
discourse of papyro-plastics, filtered through his own crystallographic training. The "höchst einfache Beschäftigung des Formens auf Papier" (simple
occupation of impressing forms on paper) has the ability to fully engage the
child's imagination. That is precisely because it gives

> ein bestimmtes und klares und zugleich ungesehen ein mehrfaches Erzeugniß
> der Thätigkeit hervor. Das gleichsam Auf- und aneinander [*sic*]- Bauende der
> Thätigkeit und das durch Hinzufügen entstehende Erzeugnis scheint dem jun-
> gen Menschen besonders zuzusagen . . . Der Mensch ist bestimmt, nicht allein
> die Natur in der Mannigfaltigkeit ihrer Formen und Gestalten zu erkennen,
> sondern sie auch in der Einheit . . . zu verstehen. . . . Die ersten Naturgebilde,
> die Festgestalten (Krystalle) der Natur erscheinen als ein durch innere Kraft
> bedingtes, äußeres Aneinander. . . . Baut der junge Mensch nicht gern, und sind
> nicht die ersten Festgestalten der Natur Bauwerke?[57]

> precise, clear and many-sided results due to its own creative power. The con-
> structive and connective nature of the activity and the object thereby created
> seem particularly appealing to a young person. . . . Man is compelled not only
> to recognize nature in her manifold forms and appearances, but also to under-
> stand her in the unity of her inner working. . . . The earliest natural formations,
> the fixed forms of crystals, seem as if driven together by some secret power
> external to themselves. . . . Does not the child take pleasure in building, and
> what else are these earliest fixed forms of nature but built-up forms?[58]

Once again, the autobiographical letter indicates the major role Fröbel
ascribes to paper as a prime mover of the idea of systematic play pedagogy.
If, in the final rendition of Fröbel's system, paper-based gifts seem to occupy
a more advanced stage in the process of object manipulation, here paper
crafts reveal their function as elementary cultural techniques: the "constructive and connective" impulse of "impressing forms on paper" "brings forth"
creative transformations that endlessly rehearse the unity of all things. Not

unlike crystallography, paper modeling unveils basic geometric principles and, at the same time, explores new patterns, angles, and facets of matter. But it is Heinrich Blasche who first introduces these notions into the realm of German Romantic pedagogy. His ideas of folding and unfolding geometric grids and exploring the plastic qualities of paper with the aim of producing independent thinkers are recaptured and continued in Fröbel's vision. The material itself, paper, and its creative capacity remain centrally important throughout this conceptual development.

*University of British Columbia*

## NOTES

1. Unsigned review of *Der Papierformer, oder Anleitung allerley Gegenstände der Kunstwelt aus Papier nachzubilden* by Bernhard Heinrich Blasche, *Jenaische Allgemeine Literatur-Zeitung* 148 (1820): 235–37. Subsequent references to this review are given parenthetically in the text. All translations are my own unless otherwise indicated.

2. For aspects of this discussion see, for example, the section on "Paper" in The Multigraph Collective, *Interacting with Print: Elements of Reading in the Era of Print Saturation* (Chicago: U of Chicago P, 2018) 223–42. Also see Lothar Müller, *Weisse Magie. Die Epoche des Papiers* (Munich: Carl Hanser, 2012) as well as Anke te Heesen, *The World in a Box: The Story of an Eighteenth-Century Picture Encyclopedia*, trans. Ann M. Hetschel (Chicago: U of Chicago P, 2002).

3. The Multigraph Collective 225.

4. Johann Christian Gottlob Schumann, *Lehrbuch der Pädogogik* (Hanover: Carl Meyer, 1874) 340.

5. See Johann Bernhard Basedow, *Das in Dessau errichtete Philanthropinum* (Leipzig: Crusius, 1774) 17.

6. Bernhard Heinrich Blasche, *Der technologische Jugendfreund oder unterhaltende Wanderungen in die Werkstätte der Künstler und Handwerker, zur nöthigen Kenntniß derselben* (Frankfurt a/M: Wilmans, 1804–10) iv–v.

7. Blasche, *Der technologische Jugendfreund*, 27.

8. Quoted in Karl Richter, ed., *Pädagogische Bibliothek* (Berlin: Klönne & Meyer, 1869) 60.

9. Quoted in Richter 60–62.

10. Bernhard Heinrich Blasche, *Werkstätte der Kinder. Ein Handbuch für Eltern und Erzieher, zu zweckmäßiger Beschäftigung ihrer Kinder und Zöglinge* (Gotha: Justus Perthes, 1800) iii.

11. Bernhard Heinrich Blasche, *Der Papparbeiter, oder Anleitung in Pappe zu arbeiten* (Schnepfenthal: im Verlage der Buchhandlung der Erziehungsanstalt, 1797), iii–iv.

12. Immanuel Kant, *Kritik der Urteilskraft* in *Werke*, Akademie-Textausgabe, vol. 5 (Berlin: De Gruyter, 1968) 305; Immanuel Kant, *Critique of Judgement*, trans. Werner Pluhar (Indianapolis: Hackett, 1987) 172.

13. Rodolphe Gasché, *The Idea of Form: Rethinking Kant's Aesthetics* (Stanford, CA: Stanford UP, 2003) 182.

14. Blasche, *Papparbeiter*, xi.

15. Blasche, *Papparbeiter*, xii.

16. Blasche, *Werkstätte*, iii.

17. Johann Wolfgang von Goethe, *Dichtung und Wahrheit* (Weimar: Hermann Böhlau, 1889) 75.

18. Johann Wolfgang von Goethe, *The Autobiography of Goethe: Truth and Poetry*, trans. John Oxenford (London: Bell and Sons, 1897) 35.

19. Blasche, *Papparbeiter*, viii.

20. As Anke te Heesen has shown, "the concept of a box as a material and easily graspable equivalent of the complex world" (194) is closely linked to the didactic reforms of the late eighteenth century. Blasche's pasteboard models give concrete meaning to that very notion.

21. Jérôme de Lalande, *Art du cartonnier* (Paris: Desaint & Saillant, 1772).

22. See Heinrich Scherer, *Die Pädagogik vor Pestalozzi* (Leipzig: Brandstetter, 1897) 454.

23. Johann Christoph Adelung, *Versuch eines vollständigen grammatisch-kritischen Wörterbuches der Hochdeutschen Mundart*, vol. 3 (Leipzig: Breitkopf, 1777) 959.

24. See also te Heesen on the development of "educational materials" around 1800: "besides the appropriation of the world by reading, there was an autonomous appropriation supporting, among other things, the motor skills of the child" (58–59).

25. Bernhard Heinrich Blasche, *Der Papierformer oder Anleitung, allerlei Gegenstände der Kunstwelt aus Papier nachzubilden* (Schnepfenthal: Buchhandlung der Erziehungsanstalt, 1819) 2.

26. Blasche, *Papierformer*, 5.

27. Blasche, *Papierformer*, iii–iv.

28. Blasche, *Papierformer*, 5-6.

29. Blasche, *Papierformer*, 41.

30. F. W. J. Schelling, *System des transzendentalen Idealismus* (Hamburg: Felix Meiner, 1962) 38; F. W. J. Schelling, *System of Transcendental Idealism*, trans. Peter Heath (Charlottesville: U of Virginia P, 1978) 28.

31. Daniel Boileau's *Papyro-plastics or the Art of Modelling in Paper* (London: Boosey & Sons, 1824) 5.

32. Boileau vi.

33. Boileau vii–viii.

34. John Ayrton Paris, *Philosophy in Sport Made Science in Earnest. Being an Attempt to Illustrate the First Principles of Natural Philosophy by the Aid of the Popular Toys and Sports* (London: Longman, 1827) 134-35.

35. Paris 86.

36. There is a vast literature on Friedrich Fröbel and his pedagogical legacy. For a list of relevant titles, see, for instance, Helmut Heiland, M. Gebel, and Karl Neumann, eds., *Perspektiven der Fröbelforschung* (Würzburg: Königshausen & Neumann, 2006); Ann Taylor Allen, *The Transatlantic Kindergarten: Education and Women's Movements in Germany and the United States* (New York: Oxford UP, 2017); Norman Brosterman, *Inventing Kindergarten* (New York: Harry Abrams, 1977).

37. See Friedrich Fröbel, *Mutter- und Koselieder. Dichtung und Bilder zur edlen Pflege des Kindheitlebens. Ein Familienbuch* (Blankenburg: Anstalt zur Pflege des

Beschäftigungstriebes der Kindheit, 1843); Heinrich Pestalozzi, *Wie Gertrud ihre Kinder lehrt. Ein Versuch den Müttern Anleitung zu geben, ihre Kinder selbst zu unterrichten. In Briefen* (Bern: Heinrich Geßner, 1801).

38. Friedrich Kittler, *Discourse Networks 1800/1900*, trans. Michael Metteer (Stanford, CA: Stanford UP) 54.

39. Fröbel, *Mutter- und Koselieder* 10.

40. Friedrich Fröbel, *Friedrich Froebel's Pedagogics of the Kindergarten: Or, His Ideas Concerning the Play and Playthings of the Child*, trans. Josephine Jarvis (New York: Appleton, 1895) 35.

41. Allen 27.

42. See Brosterman 35.

43. Friedrich Fröbel, *Ideen Friedrich Fröbels über Die Menschenerziehung und Aufsätze verschiedenen Inhalts. Friedrich Fröbel's gesammelte pädagogische Schriften,* vol. 1.2, ed. Wichard Lange (Berlin: Enslin, 1863) 149; Friedrich Fröbel, *The Education of Man. International education series*, vol. 5, ed. W.T. Harris, trans. William Nicholas Hailmann (New York: Appleton, 1887) 198–99.

44. Friedrich Fröbel, *"Kommt, laßt uns unsern Kindern leben!" Keime, Knospen, Blüthen und Früchte aus dem Leben für Bethätigung dieses Wechselzurufes geeinter Familien in Deutschland, in der Schweiz und in Nordamerika. Ein Sonntagsblatt für Gleichgesinnte* (Leipzig: Dörffling, 1838).

45. See *Hallische Jahrbücher für deutsche Wissenschaft und Kunst* 56 (1839): 4.

46. Michael Friedman, *A History of Folding in Mathematics. Mathematizing the Margins* (Basel: Birkhäuser, 2018) 214. Friedman discusses Weiss's contribution as one of the founders of modern crystallography and main source of Fröbel's engagement with the earlier work of French mineralogist René Just Haüy, who lays the bases of the geometrical laws of crystallization.

47. Friedrich Fröbel, *Aus Fröbels Leben und erstem Streben. Autobiographie und kleinere Schriften*, ed. Wichard Lange (Berlin: Enslin, 1862) 111–12; Friedrich Fröbel, *Autobiography of Friedrich Froebel*, trans. Emilie Michaelis and H. Keatley Moore (London: Swan Sonnenschein, 1892) 97.

48. Fröbel, *Menschenerziehung*, 154–55; Fröbel, *Education*, 205–6.

49. See also Brosterman 84 and Friedman 215.

50. Brosterman 78.

51. Brosterman 83.

52. Fröbel, *Aus Fröebels Leben*, 90; Fröbel, *Autobiography*, 70.

53. Fröbel, *Aus Fröebels Leben*, 94; Fröbel, *Autobiography*, 75.

54. Fröbel, *Aus Fröebels Leben*, 94–95.

55. Fröbel, *Autobiography*, 75.

56. See Enrique Menéndez Ureña, *Philosophie und gesellschaftliche Praxis. Wirkungen der Philosophie K. C. F. Krauses in Deutschland* (Stuttgart-Bad Cannstatt: Frommann-Holzboog, 2001) 224–25.

57. Fröbel, *Aus Fröebels Leben*, 95.

58. Fröbel, *Autobiography*, 76.

ETHAN BLASS

# The Men Who Knew Too Much: Reading Goethe's "Erlkönig" in Light of Hitchcock

**Abstract:** There are a number of resonances between Goethe's ballad "Erlkönig" and Hitchcock's 1934 film *The Man Who Knew Too Much*. Most strikingly, the father figures in these works can both be understood as having "too much" knowledge. Drawing on the work of René Girard, this article accounts for such resonances by showing that both the film and the poem trace a set of relations between knowledge, ritual, and violence. While, in both works, the knowledge of these fathers prevents a ritual from taking shape, without the outlet of ritual, violent tensions only build. In the poem, this leads to the death of a child, whereas the film obviates a similar catastrophe by subtly allowing ritual to resurface.

**Keywords:** Goethe, Hitchcock, "Erlkönig," ritual, sacrifice, knowledge, violence

## Introduction

THOUGH IT IS WELL-KNOWN that the cinema of Alfred Hitchcock owes a great debt to German art and culture, it is by no means intuitive to see a relationship between this filmmaker and the poetry of Goethe. Understandably, studies of the "German Hitchcock" focus typically on Hitchcock's early work in Weimar Germany,[1] or on the powerful influence that directors such as F.W. Murnau and Fritz Lang had on his conception of cinema.[2] That Hitchcock is an heir not only of the cinematic but also of the German literary tradition is sometimes noted, but attention is given primarily to the more uncanny or horrific manifestations of German Romanticism. Authors like E.T.A Hoffmann or The Brothers Grimm come across as more relevant than Goethe.[3] I suggest that Goethe deserves a more salient place in the broader discussion of Hitchcock vis-à-vis the German-speaking world. And the particular case in point that I examine is a subtle network of correspondences between Hitchcock's 1934 (and 1956) *The Man Who Knew Too Much* and Goethe's 1782 ballad "Erlkönig."

By bringing "Erlkönig" into dialogue with the film, I neither claim direct influence nor imply that Hitchcock definitely read this poem. Admittedly, given the widespread renown of "Erlkönig," it indeed seems quite likely that he would have indeed been familiar with it.[4] Nevertheless, there are no direct references to "Erlkönig" in any of Hitchcock's writings or interviews. And while the two works in question resonate with each other in a variety of ways, it would be wrong to say that the film somehow alludes to the poem.[5] Nevertheless, regardless of whether Hitchcock ever actually read "Erlkönig," attending to the *resonances* between them can elevate the understanding of both works.[6] The comparison that this article pursues might thus be understood as an interpretive lens. By recognizing aspects of "Erlkönig" within the images and story line of the Hitchcock film, the film can be seen in a fresh light and from a new vantage point. Consider, for instance, the father's attempts in the poem to explain away the boy's fears. Numerous readings of "Erlkönig" take for granted that the father's quasi-scientific explanations are indicative of an Enlightenment worldview.[7] As I will argue, however, the film implies a way of thinking about the father that draws on an alternative vocabulary; it suggests that the father explains things as he does because he is a "man who knows too much." In short, in comparing the film and the poem, it becomes evident that the film's title is an apt description for the father in either work.

On the surface, of course, the knowledge of the two fathers pertains to very different things: the father in Goethe knows about a forest landscape; the father in Hitchcock knows about an assassination plot. However, a more careful comparison reveals that such differences are only secondary. At a fundamental level, there is a common object or theme upon which the knowledge of these fathers converges. I argue here that to know too much in both Goethe's poem and Hitchcock's film is ultimately tantamount to inhibiting or standing in the way of a ritual. Indeed, the world of both of these works is charged by forces driving toward the completion of some sort of ritual—celebrants are taking their places, so to speak; the ceremony is about to begin. In their own ways, however, the father figures become obstacles to the unfolding of the ritual. They know too much to indulge in the ritual, or they perceive a hidden link between ritual and violence. In the following, I bolster my argument by drawing on the anthropological writings of René Girard. For Girard, the categories of knowledge, violence, and ritual are inextricably entwined and bear heavily on each other. Girard theorizes that knowledge or awareness of the violent core of ritual traditions brings the practice of ritual to a halt or renders it ineffectual. As I show, both the poem and film essentially put this type of knowledge on display.

The argument proceeds through the following stages. To begin, I outline some of the most striking resonances between these works. As will become clear, the film parallels the poem in ways that a mere plot synopsis could never convey. Second, I give an overview of the place of knowledge in Girard's thoughts on ritual and violence. This will entail, more specifically, a discussion of Girard's theory of the origin and function of sacrifice. The argument's focus then shifts back to the two works. With Girard in the background, I develop readings of the film and the poem, highlighting, in particular, the extent to which the violence pervading these works can be understood as sacrificial in nature. Finally, I consider not only the resonances between these works but also the most crucial differences. Although the poem and the film give expression to the same problematic, I argue that, by virtue of embodying different literary forms or genres, these works address this problematic and come to terms with it in slightly different ways. While the escalation of tensions in the poem leads to catastrophe, the film avoids a similar fate by subtly allowing aspects of ritual to resurface.

## Echoes of "Erlkönig" in *The Man Who Knew Too Much*

The scene in the 1934 rendition of *The Man Who Knew Too Much* that most immediately brings "Erlkönig" to mind revolves around the kidnapping of a child. To contextualize this scene, Bob and Jill Lawrence are vacationing in Switzerland with their young daughter Betty. One evening, a man whom the family has befriended there, Louis Bernard, is mysteriously shot and killed. With his dying words, he asks Bob to look for a note in his hotel room and then deliver it to the British consul—as it turns out, the note contains information about a plan to assassinate a "statesman." Bob indeed finds a cryptic note in Louis's room. However, before he can speak with the British consul, a bellhop arrives with a message that has just been left for him: "Say nothing of what you found or you will never see your child again." Realizing that Bob has acquired information about their plan, it seems that the film's villainous conspirators have kidnapped Betty and are holding her hostage. It is at this point that Hitchcock presents a visually stunning sequence that portrays the child's plight: Betty is seen with a male figure—evidently her captor—riding in moonlight through a forest (Fig. 1).

Beyond the general setting and dramatic scenario here, there are a number of details in this sequence that resonate with the poem. The father in the

Figure 1. *The Man Who Knew Too Much* (1934). Wer reitet so spät durch Nacht und Wind? Here, it is the child together with a member of the film's villainous circle. DVD screenshots.

poem, for instance, "faßt" (grasps) the child, has the child "wohl in dem Arm" (safe in his arms).[8] The male figure in the film similarly envelops Betty with his arm and gloved hand. In the poem, the father tells the child: "Sei ruhig, bleibe ruhig" (Be calm, stay calm). It is interesting, therefore, that Betty's mouth is initially covered, as if she too is being told or forced to keep quiet. Warmth figures in the poem as well—the child is held "warm." In a similar vein, Betty is resting against some sort of enormous fur. And Betty's eyes, casting their worried glance beyond the edge of the frame, are also noteworthy considering that "seeing" is also crucial for the poem—"Siehst, Vater, du . . . siehst du nicht dort . . ." (Do you see, father . . . do you see there . . .). Naturally, the sequence here does not evoke the poem in every respect. For example, Betty is not a "Knabe" (boy). Remarkably, however, from a certain angle, this difference vanishes. Indeed, Betty appears somewhat androgynous in these shots. It is telling that, in Hitchcock's 1956 version of this film, the child is a son rather than a daughter.

Another moment that is subtly evocative of "Erlkönig" occurs later in the film's story line. In a central scene, Betty's mother goes to a concert at London's Albert Hall because she has learned that the assassination is to occur there. The villainous plan involves a sharpshooter firing his gun in synchrony with the crash of cymbals in order to effectively silence the fatal shot. For the present context, however, the performed music is significant not only for its cymbals but also for the lyrics presented by chorus and soloist accompanying the orchestra:

> There came a whispered terror on the breeze
> And the dark forest shook
> And on the trembling trees
> Came nameless fear, and panic overtook
> Each flying creature of the wild
> And when they all had fled
> God save the child
> Around whose head screaming
> The night birds wheel and shoot away
> God save the child
> Finding release from that which drove them onward like their prey
> [God save the child, God save the child . . .]
> Finding release the storm clouds broke
> And drowned the dying moon
> The storm clouds broke, the storm clouds broke
> Finding release[9]

While these lines are far from a direct quotation of "Erlkönig," there are a number of ways in which they invoke the same atmosphere present in Goethe's poem. Like "Erlkönig" the setting of the song is a windy night in a forest. The air is thick with "fear" and "panic," and, most importantly, the song features a child in danger. Further, the relationship between the song lyrics and "Erlkönig" is strengthened by the dramatic scenario in which this text is presented: these lyrics are presented in a work of classical music. "Erlkönig" is similarly associated with the tradition of the *Lied* in a way that few other poems are.[10] The resonance between these two texts is strengthened through their inherent relationship to music: on some level, both texts are song lyrics.

The examples noted thus far are moments in the film where the themes and imagery of "Erlkönig" bubble to the surface. But other moments in the film also recall the poem, showing that the link in question can be drawn through the entirety of these works. One aspect to consider in this regard is the film's title. The film is evidently about a "man who knew too much." Stated most simply, what this means in terms of the plot is that the father's knowledge about international intrigue puts his child in danger. Similarly, in "Erlkönig," the poem's father figure is commonly associated with knowledge and understanding. Critics call him "der verstandeskühle, dem Tag angehörende Mensch des Lebens" (the coolly rational man, belonging to the light of day),[11] and the embodiment of "ein[e] . . . wissenschaftlich[e] Naturbetrachtung" (a scientific approach to observing nature).[12] Furthermore, the poem also suggests that he "knows too much"—like in the film, the excessive knowledge of the poem's father contributes to the child's plight. His ready explanations for the nocturnal sights and sounds only serve to increase the danger the child is in. Despite the obvious differences between the film and the poem, both works are attuned to a fundamental issue, namely the problem of knowledge. One way to paraphrase this issue is to refer again to the film's title: apparently, there is a point at which knowledge becomes excessive or problematic. Yet what exactly does this mean? What kind of knowledge? In what sense does it become a problem?

These two works express and articulate this problem in a variety of ways. For instance, the possibility of knowing too much lends itself to a reading that invokes the topic of the subconscious, and both "Erlkönig" and *The Man Who Knew Too Much* have, of course, been interpreted in this vein quite brilliantly.[13] For the purpose of the present comparison, however, I turn not to Freud but rather to one of Freud's most original readers: René Girard.[14] Invoking Girard here helps to draw out thematic strands in these works that are not commonly highlighted—namely, that the threat of violence pervading these works is related to the trappings of ritual festivity. Girard's anthropological framework furthermore facilitates characterizing this festivity as essentially sacrificial—as rites revolving around the selection of a sacrificial victim. Beyond casting a new light on just these two particular works, however, incorporating Girard into my analysis offers a foundation for the suggestion that, to some extent, Goethe and Hitchcock might be interpreted as developing an anthropological perspective. In this respect, the present article corroborates and extends recent work in both Goethe and Hitchcock scholarship.[15] I argue that these artists trace not only the structure and dynamics of the human psyche but also of human culture and social formations.

## René Girard on Ritual and Knowledge

Most relevant to the notion of knowing too much are Girard's anthropological writings on the origin and purpose of sacrificial ritual. According to Girard, sacrifice is ubiquitous in human cultural history because it serves a social function of the utmost importance. Namely, it protects a given community from its own violence. When conflict erupts between the members of a community, it has the potential to spiral out of control. It can lead to a cycle of violent reprisals that leave no one standing at the end. Ritual sacrifice, however, is an "instrument of prevention" in the struggle against this dangerous tendency.[16] By killing a sacrificial victim, Girard claims, a community is essentially redirecting the violence that would otherwise manifest itself as civil strife. Instead of killing each other, the members of the community appease their violent impulses by participating in a sacrificial rite. Girard thus claims that sacrifice actually works, in a certain sense, in that it truly does "restore harmony to the community" (8). However, Girard emphasizes that the ritual celebrants are necessarily deluded as to *why* sacrifice works. In their eyes, the resulting harmony is a sign that their deity is pleased and appeased: "It is the god who supposedly demands the victims; he alone . . . savors the smoke from the altars" (7). Lost from view is the fact that the deity appeased here is really nothing more than the community's own violence. In other words, the community itself does not perceive the ritual as a violent act—the community does not realize that it is essentially committing a kind of collective murder and fails to understand that this murder secures the foundation of its social harmony. In truth, the sacrificial rite is just as violent as any act of vengeance that would normally lead to a cycle of reprisals. As Girard writes, however, "the covert appropriation by sacrifice of certain properties of violence . . . is hidden from sight by the awesome machinery of ritual" (19).

This concealment of violence is necessary in order for ritual to function. If sacrifice itself is perceived as violent, it can no longer serve the function of expelling violence from the community. Thus, for societies that practice sacrifice, peace and harmony are ultimately dependent upon a "misunderstanding," or upon a certain lack of knowledge. As Girard observes, this runs counter to the usual assumptions about the value and importance of knowledge:

> Because modern man clings to the belief that knowledge is in itself a "good thing," he grants little or no importance to a procedure . . . that only serves to conceal the existence of man's violent impulses. The optimistic falsification could well constitute the worst sort of ignorance. Indeed, the formidable effectiveness of the process derives from its depriving men of knowledge: knowledge of the violence inherent in themselves with which they have never come to terms (82).

If the sacrificial mechanism only works by means of "depriving men of knowledge," an obvious implication suggests itself. Within a sacrificial framework, namely, it becomes eminently possible, as the film would put it, to "know too much." Knowledge, in other words, can disrupt the workings of ritual, rendering it ineffective. This is to say that, in an indirect manner, too much knowledge can actually give rise to violence.

It is worth dwelling on this apparent paradox. To the extent that knowledge disrupts ritual, it might seem that knowledge would thus prevent violence, because to disrupt ritual here is to throw a wrench into the process whereby sacrificial victims are offered. What must be remembered, however, is that the social cohesion of the community rests upon the completion of this process. Ritual sacrifice operates as a means of channeling violence beyond the bounds of the community; therefore, when this process is compromised, violence has nowhere to go. It is in this sense, Girard argues, that knowledge about the violent nature of ritual sacrifice can threaten a community and leave it helpless: "Demystification leads to constantly increasing violence, a violence perhaps less 'hypocritical' than the violence it seeks to expose, but more energetic, more virulent, and the harbinger of something far worse—a violence that knows no bounds" (24–25). What ultimately becomes clear is that "men cannot confront the naked truth of their own violence without the risk of abandoning themselves to it entirely" (82). Put somewhat differently, so long as sacrifice is viable, violence still occurs but it is directed into "proper" channels: it falls only upon ritually determined victims who stand at the community's edge (10). When the ritual mechanism is demystified, however, it is as if these "proper" channels get blocked. At this point, violence overflows such channels, and the community's violent impulses are forced to seek out new kinds of victims. In this case, there is now nothing preventing these victims from coming from within the community itself.

## Knowing Too Much in Hitchcock

To what extent does this account of sacrificial ritual help make sense of the two works under consideration? Beginning with the film, the basic plot of the film already maps onto the model developed by Girard. By acquiring knowledge about the conspiracy, the father is endowed with the ability to prevent a murder; yet it seems that by preventing a murder, he risks actually triggering a type of violence that is even worse: the death of his own child. Beyond the confines of the basic plotline, however, if Girard's analysis can truly be applied to the film, then the villainous conspiracy that the father uncovers should somehow be related to ritual. In this case then, what the father comes to understand would essentially be that the "awesome machinery of ritual" is a cover for violence. Some remarkable details from the film suggest that this description is indeed valid.

For example, the father's pursuit of the villains, at one point, leads him to a building called "The Tabernacle of the Sun," the meeting place of a sun-worshipping cult. Just as the father goes inside, it seems that a ritual ceremony of some sort is about to begin. The congregation sings a hymn of praise to its deity. When silence falls, the presiding priestess figure announces from the pulpit:

> Perhaps those who may be among us tonight for the first time, and who have not yet become initiated into the mysteries of the first circle of the sevenfold ray, may be wondering what is going to happen now. I will tell them. Before proceeding to the mysteries, which are only for the initiate, it is of course necessary for the minds and souls of us all to become purged and to be made clean. I'm therefore going to ask anyone here who is not in tune with us to submit to a very simple process of control. Merely place him or herself under the guidance of the fourth circle.

Figure 2. *The Man Who Knew Too Much* (1934). A ceremony inside "The Tabernacle of the Sun." DVD screenshot.

Though this is said to be an initiation ritual, there is clearly a sacrificial cast about it. In asking "anyone . . . who is not in tune with us" to "submit . . . to a process of control," the priestess is essentially scanning the crowd for potential victims. Most significant in terms of Girard here is that the "Tabernacle of the Sun" is indeed where the assassination conspirators are hiding. There is thus a literalization in this scene of the relationship between violence and ritual that Girard describes. A ritual ceremony *literally* functions as the cover for a murderous operation. And this is of course exactly what the father suspects. To be "the man who knew too much," in short, is to know that these "sun-worshippers" are actually assassins.

The sense that this ritual ceremony is linked to violence is strengthened by what might seem to be a rather unassuming detail. As the above quotation already suggests, this scene refers to the shape of the circle numerous times. The priestess speaks of "the mysteries of the first circle" and of "the guidance of the fourth circle." Notable as well is that these scattered references are echoed visually by a remarkable piece of circular metalwork (Fig. 2) The invocation of circles here can be interpreted as an invitation to look through them. According to Girard, circles are a common feature of the myths that sacrificial societies tell. They are a trace, in his view, of the circular mob formation that originally engulfed the first victims. In reference to one myth in particular, Girard notes: "two parallel lines of gods . . . form a circle and push the victim into the fire by closing in on him. I would like the reader to remember this circular or almost circular configuration which will reappear . . . in a great many of the myths I shall be discussing."[17] Against this backdrop, the recurring circular shapes in the film operate as one more symbol suggesting that the film's villains are main players in a system of community sacrifice.

Many of these same themes that characterize the scene in the "Tabernacle" appear as well when the film's setting shifts to Albert Hall. For one thing, Albert Hall, both inside and out, is an emphatically circular structure. Even more important, however, is the role of ceremony and ritual in the Albert Hall scene. Consider what the villains plan to do here. The sharpshooter is about to fire his gun when the music calls for a cymbal crash. "At such a moment," the leader of the gang explains, "your shot will not be heard. No one will know." This somewhat ridiculous tactic accords perfectly with the logic traced here. For, as one critic puts it, the concert here "is a staid ritual of refined society."[18] Once again, this "ritual" literally serves as a cover for violence. In a certain sense, the concert and all of its trappings become unwitting accomplices to the crime. The montage in this sequence renders this especially clear, as Hitchcock cuts from the musicians getting ready to play their instruments directly to the gun emerging into view. The same hands that are about to crash the cymbals or play the drums become nearly identical with the hands pulling the trigger.

## Knowing Too Much in Goethe

Could one argue that a similar dynamic animates Goethe's poem? Does the link between ritual and violence that the film suggests cast the poem in a new light? Indeed, traces of ritual do subtly pervade the poem. For instance, consider the following image? "Meine Töchter führen den nächtlichen Reihn, / Und wiegen und tanzen und singen dich ein" (My daughters lead the nocturnal round dance / They will rock you and dance you and sing you to sleep).[19] To be sure, an alluring spectacle is presented, evidently intended to tempt the child. However, this spectacle could also be described as a festivity or rite. What the child is sensing in the night, in other words, are the preparations for a ritual of some sort, or the stirrings of ritualistic tendencies.[20] Other aspects of the poem's imagery point in a similar direction. Though it is perhaps only natural for an *Erlkönig* to wear a crown, it is notable that the "Kron' und Schweif" (crown and train)—as well as the mother's "gülden Gewand" (golden robe)—are essentially ceremonial trappings. The realm of the Erlkönig is thus one in which the forces of ceremony and ritual are still active or potent. And while the poem of course never mentions the notion of ritual or rite explicitly, what it does explicitly mention are "Spiele" (games), already gesturing to what contemporary anthropology sees as the deep-seated relationship between ritual and play.[21] Thus, at a fundamental level, the playing of games in the third stanza belongs to the same ritualistic register as ceremonial finery and nightly festivities.

That these ritualistic elements in the poem are implicated in violence is fairly transparent. For example, even the ominous undertones of "wiegen und tanzen und singen dich ein" (rock you and dance you and sing you to sleep) could be interpreted as a kind of death by ritual, a death by song and dance. This evokes the Hitchcock scene in which the distinction between the musicians on stage and the assassin in the balcony begins to blur. Similarly notable in this context is the specific type of dance associated with the Erlkönig's daughters. Translated into English, a "Reihn" or "Reigen" is a round dance. In short, it is a dance that produces, by definition, a circular formation. This, too, recalls the numerous circles presented in the film. Like the film, "Erlkönig" presents the same sort of circular formation that, according to Girard's, operates as the trace of an original act of collective violence. In the particular image of the "Reihn," ritual's basis in violence becomes more apparent because the violent act, at its core, begins to shine through the veneer of celebration. In this sense, the "Reihn" subtly prefigures the violence that is fully exposed only in the poem's subsequent course.

Yet is this relationship between ritual and violence something that the father in the poem knows about? To reiterate, this indeed seems to be the case in the film. To "know too much" in Hitchcock is to perceive the violent underbelly of a ritualistic practice. To some extent, the father in "Erlkönig" also "knows too much." He perceives the nightly landscape in the light of "der kühle Verstand" (cool rationality);[22] his rational explanations of things prevent him from seeing or entertaining what the child sees. This kind of knowledge evidently pertains, however, to something like a natural science. It is not obvious that myth or ritual is anything this father knows about directly. On the contrary, these things don't even seem to appear on his radar. In order to account for how the father's quasi-scientific responses pertain to ritual at a deeper level, it will be necessary to take a step back and consider the poem's narrative structure. Of particular interest in this regard is an aspect of the poem encountered already in the "Volkslied" upon which Goethe's "Erlkönig" is loosely based.

In Herder's translation of the Danish folk ballad, "Erlkönigs Tochter" ("Erlking's Daughter"), a figure named "Herr Oluf" ventures out on horseback in order to summon guests for his impending wedding.[23] When he encounters Erlkönig's daughter, however, it turns out she has other plans for him. She asks him to dance with her, to join her in the "Reihen." And, after he declines three such offers, she delivers a violent blow to his heart: "Sie tät einen Schlag ihm auf sein Herz" (She struck him in the heart" Herder 335). At this point, Herr Oluf returns home for the wedding. The following morning, however, as the bride and wedding guests prepare for the festivities, they find that the groom is dead: "Die Braut hob auf den Scharlach rot / Da lag Herr Oluf, und er war tot" (The bride lifted the scarlet cloth / There lay Sir Oluf, and he was dead" 336).

Clearly, Goethe departs from this plot in significant ways, as his own variation on the Erlkönig theme tells a different story. But there are basic structural moments in the original poem that Goethe retains even while reworking them. For example, Herr Oluf refusing to dance with Erlkönig's daughter three times is intriguing because Goethe's poem can also be interpreted as having a three-part structure: the father in "Erlkönig" makes three attempts to explain what the boy is seeing or hearing. In this sense, Herr Oluf's three refusals to join the dance become in Goethe, the father's three explanations. Furthermore, wariness of the round dance, on the one hand, and knowledge of the landscape, on the other, occupy the same structural position in the two poems.

This particular poetic transformation is telling. What makes it possible? In moving from Herder's poem to Goethe's, what steers the course of the transformation? One answer is that the latter poem is animated by an insight into the role that knowledge plays in the breakdown or failure of ritual. In Goethe's poem, rather than objecting directly to any nightly festivities, the father simply issues laconic statements of a knowing or quasi-factual nature. Implied here is that disrupting a ritual practice and having too much knowledge are, on some level, the same thing. Indeed, Goethe's poem makes it especially clear that when the machinery of ritual becomes clogged, knowledge or awareness is to blame. It could therefore be argued that Goethe anticipates the insight that Girard arrives at in an anthropological register: namely, the functioning of ritual ultimately depends on "ignorance" or "misunderstanding." By inserting his rationalistic perspective into the nocturnal economy, the father hinders a ritual from taking shape. The problem with this, however, is that, far from being mere child's play, ritual actually accomplishes something; it actually serves a purpose. Speaking with Girard, it channels a community's violent impulses so that the community can survive.

At this stage in the argument, it is clear that there is a direct relationship between the father's repeated explanations and the growing threat of violence, and it is *because* of his explanations that violence has nowhere to go. Without a ritualistic outlet, internal tensions build. The father is thus responsible for the very violence he is trying to thwart. The poem's striking repetition of "fassen" (grasp)—the verbs appears in lines 4 and 27—serves as one last indication of this. If the father and the Erlkönig share a grasp on the child, it is because violence is emanating equally from them both. The course of the poem, in short, exposes these two figures as doubles.

## Generic Considerations: The Ballad and the Thriller

All resonances and similarities aside, Goethe's poem and Hitchcock's film are, of course, not the same work. Simply in terms of the basic shape of the stories they tell, there is at least one glaring difference between them that must be addressed. Considering the course of the film more carefully, one way to describe the film's arc is to say that, while the father begins to know too much, he gradually learns how to know less. The father gradually comes to acknowledge—with the mother also playing a crucial role[24]—the necessity of coping with violence, or of giving violence some sort of outlet. The father comes to cede a certain legitimacy to ritual. This is made especially clear in the finale of the 1956 version of *The Man Who Knew Too Much*. In this version of the film, the father pushes the villain down a grand staircase in the embassy, evidently causing him to fall on his gun and shoot himself. As his body comes to a stop near the floor, a crowd of people from a nearby concert gather around it, quickly forming a mob (Fig. 3). This scene creates the subtle impression that the villain has become a sacrificial victim. There is something distinctly ceremonial about how he rolls down the grand staircase between marble pillars and candelabras. His death similarly serves the function of strengthening a community, specifically, of reuniting the members of the film's central family. In short, it serves the function that a ritual

Figure 3. *The Man Who Knew Too Much* (1956). Pushed down the stairs by the father, the child's kidnapper takes a fatal fall. DVD screenshot.

sacrifice *should* serve. Obviously, none of this happens in the poem. There is no moment in the poem where the father's perspective shifts, where he learns to "know less" or to entertain the legitimacy of ritual play. The father's inability to learn to "know less" results in the tragic ending of the poem: in contrast to the film, the child in the poem does not survive. If these two works indeed address a similar problematic throughout, what is one to make of this striking contrast?

My answer is that, though the two works here may share a problematic, they do not share a genre: "Erlkönig" is a lyrical ballad, whereas the film is perhaps best referred to as the Hitchcock thriller. These distinct narrative forms aim at different effects; moreover, they quite simply function differently. To begin with, a number of Goethe's ballads emphasize or are structured around some type of violent collision of opposing poles. The specific nature of these poles or the labels one might give them vary from case to case. For example, Goethe's poem "Heidenröslein" ("Wild Rose") stages a violent back-and-forth—"Ich breche dich . . . Ich steche dich" (I will break you . . . I will prick you)[25]—between Röslein and Knabe. In "Die Braut von Corinth" ("The Bride of Corinth"), the poles that collide are characterized as Christianity and paganism. "Erlkönig," of course, is based on an opposition between the father's perspective and the son's. Regardless of what, exactly, the two poles or extremes are, the poem generally thrives on the strong tension between them; it brings these poles together in order to watch them clash. The point, it seems, is to generate something of a violent oscillation. At any moment, all the energy could suddenly shift from one extreme to the other.

Such a description also applies in some measure to the Hitchcock thriller. Or, to be more precise, it applies to a certain part or aspect of the

Hitchcock thriller. In many of Hitchcock's films, there is a scene—usually at the end of the plot's exposition—in which the film's central conflict first flares up, or where the threat posed by the dark forces in the film openly present themselves. In *The 39 Steps*, for example, Annabella Smith, spending the night in Richard Hannay's apartment, mysteriously emerges into his room with a knife in her back. The corresponding scene in *The Lady Vanishes* occurs when Gilbert comes into Iris's hotel room at night while she tries to find a way to get rid of him. (As these examples suggest, the moment in question often occurs in or near a bedroom at night.) An abiding characteristic of these initial scenes of conflict is that they generally have a particular lyrical density. The images are often some of the most powerful in the film, defying subservience to the horizontal narrative flow and taking on a life of their own. Beyond the examples just cited, one might think of the doors opening one after another in *Spellbound*, or of the enormous and astonishing close-up of Grace Kelly that first introduces Lisa Fremont in *Rear Window*'s version of this scene. In the 1934 *Man Who Knew Too Much*, the nocturnal ride through the forest that is so peculiarly reminiscent of "Erlkönig" occurs at this moment. What these observations are driving at is that this point in the Hitchcock thriller's structure, in some sense, encapsulates a Romantic-style lyric in that the film harnesses the same sort of tension—and, in some cases, the very same imagery—on which the lyric thrives.

Following this point in its structure, the film typically has about an hour and ten minutes left to go. In the remainder of the film, the violent clash of extremes eventually occurs, concluding the film's main plotline, and a subsequent narrative ensues in which the focus is not so much on highlighting the opposition between the two poles as it is on investigating how mediation between them might be possible.[26] A kind of dance takes place as the opposing poles in the film begin to approach and interact. For instance, two figures that embody extremes become chained together—sometimes literally—in a common pursuit, or become partners in a shared adventure (as in *The 39 Steps, The Lady Vanishes, Saboteur, Rear Window*).[27] This process generally brings about a transformation or allows a new type of relationship to form. It is also in the course of such a transformation that the father in *The Man Who Knew Too Much* arrives at a perspective that evidently eludes the father in "Erlkönig." In the film, there is time for the father to become acquainted with the forces of the villainous underworld. To some degree, he learns to see what the child sees and thus learns to incorporate the child's perspective into his own. An extended shot of father and daughter both looking at the villainous ringleader is quite literally illustrative of this point (Fig. 4). Obviously, this is not to say that the film succeeds where the poem fails, or that the film is better than the poem because it enables the child to live. The difference in plot, rather, indicates a generic fault line because these two narrative forms have different tendencies or strengths. A poem failing to bring about mediation only renders it more capable of giving expression to an explosive volatility.

Figure 4. *The Man Who Knew Too Much* (1934). The father sees what the child sees. DVD screenshot.

## Hitchcock's "Pixyish" Cinema

At the beginning of this article, I suggested that influence alone cannot account for the relationship between the poem and the film. The specific nature of the resonances and similarities I have traced only adds further weight to this suggestion. These works are linked not only by intertextual references or a set of isolated motifs; rather, their commonalities reach down to the most basic level of narrative structure. In light of such fundamental parallels, the category of influence becomes insufficient. That said, however, it is of course still plausible that Hitchcock had read "Erlkönig," making it possible that the poem had a significant and direct impact on him. Sure enough, among the archive of Hitchcock's statements and recollections—specifically, in the audio recordings of the 1962 conversation between Hitchcock and François Truffaut—there is at least one statement that is curious and noteworthy in this regard.[28]

When discussing with Truffaut the latter part of his British period—the period in which the 1934 *Man Who Knew Too Much* was made—Hitchcock defines this period in terms of a peculiar strain of "ideas." As he puts it: "The latter period was the beginning of the formation of ideas. The ideas began to come. Offbeat, pixyish idea[s]." Offbeat and pixyish—these adjectives are interesting. What exactly could Hitchcock be referring to? He unfortunately does not elaborate. However, his use of the word "pixyish" is particularly striking. Citing from a variety of dictionaries, a "pixie" is defined as follows: "In folklore and children's stories: a supernatural being with magical powers";[29] "A fairy-like or elfin creature, especially one that is mischievous";[30] "A cheerful sprite like an elf typically conceived of as playing mischievous tricks on householders or as dancing in the moonlight."[31] Indeed, the Erlkönig figure is technically an *Elfen*könig (king of the elves).[32] Both Goethe's "Erlkönig" and Herder's "Erlkönigs Tochter," in short, draw on something of a mythology surrounding elves.[33] In this sense, one could almost say that they are poems about pixies. Some English-German dictionaries even translate pixie as "Elf" or "Elfe."[34]

While this does not directly equate to Hitchcock speaking about Goethe's poem in particular, it still suggests something about the kind of literature from which Hitchcock's cinema takes its cue. When thinking of the "ideas" of his latter British period, Hitchcock evidently was thinking of the same sorts of themes, or of the same sort of imagistic reservoir, upon which Goethe's "Erlkönig" also draws. In other words, these "ideas" and Goethe's poem come from the same storytelling universe.[35] This is especially interesting given that, on the surface of things, there is no reason that this should be the case. Hitchcock's films are not straightforward adaptations of fairy tales or ballads—something akin to "Erlkönig" would be a natural title for none of his films. Instead, the films from this period—which are the first to establish the typical "Hitchcock thriller" plotline—deal mainly with international intrigue. The mysterious forces that wreak havoc in the world are not elves and fairies but rather enemy governments or scheming anarchists. Based on how Hitchcock describes the essential "ideas" behind the films from this period, however, there are hints that this apparent distinction is not all too relevant. Regarding its most fundamental problematic and imagistic network, *The Man Who Knew Too Much* crosses paths in the night with "Erlkönig." In closing, it is notable that Goethe's poem has, of course, given rise, not only to countless *Vertonungen*, but also to a large body of illustrations.[36] By virtue of the ideas and images at its core, *The Man Who Knew Too Much* makes a—perhaps unintentional—cinematic contribution to this tradition.

*University of Oklahoma*

# NOTES

1. See Joseph Garncarz, "German Hitchcock," in *Framing Hitchcock*, ed. Sidney Gottlieb and Christopher Brookhouse (Detroit: Wayne State UP, 2002), 59–81.

2. See Sidney Gottlieb, "Early Hitchcock: The German Influence," in *Framing Hitchcock*, ed. Sidney Gottlieb and Christopher Brookhouse (Detroit: Wayne State UP, 2002), 35–58.

3. See Donald Spoto, *The Dark Side of Genius: The Life of Alfred Hitchcock* (New York: Ballantine, 1983), 77–78.

4. And to be clear, it is possible that he could have been familiar with it in the original language. Hitchcock was fairly fluent in German, as is evidenced by his 1966 appearance on the German television program "Frankfurter Stammtisch." As of April 2021, the entirety of this interview is accessible on the "Deutsche Fernsehgeschichte" channel on YouTube.

5. For a comprehensive account of the sources and historical events that more certainly impacted Hitchcock's work on this film, see Mark Glancy, "*The Man Who Knew*

*Too Much* (1934): Alfred Hitchcock, John Buchan, and the Thrill of the Chase," in *Hitchcock at the Source: The Auteur as Adaptor*, ed. R. Barton Palmer and David Boyd (Albany, NY: SUNY Press, 2011).

6. My understanding of the kind of comparison I pursue is indebted to Stanley Cavell's essay "A Matter of Meaning It," in *Must We Mean What We Say?* (Cambridge: Cambridge UP, 2002). Comparing the myth of Philomel to Federico Fellini's *La Strada*, Cavell suggests that the film's apparent references to the myth can be thought of as intentional even if Fellini wasn't exactly thinking of them. My sense is that Cavell's remarks could apply as well to the relationship between "Erlkönig" and *The Man Who Knew Too Much*.

7. Representative of this approach is Erich Trunz's suggestion that "der Vater" is "historisch gesprochen . . . der Aufklärer." (The father is, historically speaking, the Enlightenment force) Johann Wolfgang von Goethe, *Werke*, Hamburger Ausgabe (Munich: Beck, 1981) 1:564. Hereafter abbreviated as HA and cited parenthetically.

8. All quotations of "Erlkönig" are from Johann Wolfgang Goethe, *Sämtliche Werke. Briefe, Tagebücher und Gespräche*, hrsg. Friedmar Apel et al., 40 Bde. (Frankfurt a/M: Deutscher Klassiker-Verlag, 1985–2013) 1:303–4. Hereafter abbreviated as FA. Unless otherwise indicated, all translations are my own.

9. My transcription of the lyrics—which are not always easy to understand—follows the subtitles provided by The Criterion Collection edition of the film. *The Man Who Knew Too Much*, directed by Alfred Hitchcock (1934; New York: Criterion Collection, 2013), DVD.

10. For a fascinating reading of the poem's most well-known *Vertonung*, see Christopher H. Gibbs, "'Komm geh' mit mir': Schubert's Uncanny 'Erlkönig,'" *19th-Century Music* 19, no. 2 (1995): 115–35.

11. Erich Trunz, "Balladen," in HA 1:564.

12. Max Kommerell, *Gedanken über Gedichte* (Frankfurt a/Main: Vittorio Klostermann, 1956) 355.

13. Regarding the poem, see Kenneth S. Calhoon, *Fatherland: Novalis, Freud, and The Discipline of Romance* (Detroit: Wayne State UP, 1992) 25–48. In a footnote to chapter one, "The Politics of Infanticide: Goethe's 'Erlkönig,'" Calhoon provides an overview of psychoanalytic readings of the poem (4n). Regarding the film, see Robin Wood, *Hitchcock's Films Revisited* (New York: Columbia UP, 1989) 358–70.

14. See, for example, Girard's chapter on "Freud and The Oedipus Complex" in *Violence and the Sacred*, trans. Patrick Gregory (Baltimore: Johns Hopkins UP, 1977).

15. See Michael Saman, "Towards Goethean Anthropology: On Morphology, Structuralism, and Social Observation," *Goethe Yearbook* 27 (2020): 137–63. For Hitchcock scholarship, see David Humbert, *Violence in the Films of Alfred Hitchcock: A Study in Mimesis* (East Lansing: Michigan State UP, 2017).

16. René Girard, *Violence and the Sacred*, trans. Patrick Gregory (Baltimore: Johns Hopkins UP, 1977) 17.

17. René Girard, *The Scapegoat*, trans. Yvonne Freccero (Baltimore: The Johns Hopkins UP, 1986) 62.

18. Elisabeth Weis, "Consolidation of a Classical Style: The Man Who Knew Too Much," in *A Hitchcock Reader*, ed. Marshall Deutelbaum and Leland Poague (Ames: Iowa State UP, 1986) 104.

19. FA 1:304.

20. Geoffrey Hartman's reading of "Erlkönig" points at times in a similar direction. Hartman describes the poem in such a way that its proximity to sacrifice and ritual becomes apparent. As he writes: "The shudder comes when we realize that we knew from the start a sacrifice would be required: that the boy must die, and voice fail. Something in the form itself compels this awareness. 'Wer reitet so spät durch Nacht und Wind?' is, in retrospect, more than a functional device allowing the narrative to unfold. It is as much a challenge as a question, a *qui vive* indicating a satisfaction to be exacted, if only in the form of an appropriate answer. And the answer we then hear is indeed strangely impersonal, cold, ritualistic" (192). *The Fate of Reading* (Chicago: U of Chicago Press, 1975).

21. *Ritual, Play and Belief, in Evolution and Early Human Societies*, ed. Colin Renfrew, Iain Morley, and Michael Boyd (Cambridge: Cambridge UP, 2018).

22. Emil Staiger, *Goethe*, vol. 1 (Zürich: Artemis, 1981) 345.

23. Citations of "Erlkönigs Tochter" refer to Johann Gottfried Herder, *Werke in zehn Bänden*, vol. 3, *Volkslieder, Übertragungen, Dichtungen*, ed. Ulrich Gaier (Frankfurt a/M: Deutscher Klassiker Verlag, 1990) 335–36.

24. Robin Wood emphasizes the mother's role in counteracting the father's blind rationality. As he notes in reference to the 1956 version: "It is a structuring motif of the film . . . that Jo knows better than Ben. Her insights and decisions . . . can all be justified rationally, but they are reached 'intuitively.' Ben, limited to the purely rational, understands very little, though he can ring bells and burst open doors when required." *Hitchcock's Films Revisited* (New York: Columbia UP, 1989) 369–70.

25. FA 1:278.

26. To be sure, one might also find a tendency toward mediation in Goethe's ballads. See R. Ellis Dye, "Goethe's 'Die Braut von Korinth': Anti-Christian Love Poem or Hymn of Love and Death," *Goethe Yearbook* 4 (1988): 83–98. As Dye argues, "despite an overlay of anti-Christian polemics, the primary emphasis in the poem is on the bridging of distance and difference, on conjunction and integration" (83). I would simply suggest that this sort of conjunction and integration is easier to observe in the Hitchcock thriller. The fact that "Die Braut von Corinth" has so often been interpreted as straightforwardly anti-Christian is already telling in this respect.

27. As John A. Bertolini describes this process, "one member of a couple usually has to persuade the other member to believe him or her, and then they together have to prove to the world that they are right. In doing so, by working together, they develop their romantic relationship until the end of the film when they can join together in love. For love to be created, Hitchcock suggests that the man or the woman has to enter into the private mental world of the other; their fantasy lives must be shared" (234–35). "Rear window, or The Reciprocated Glance," in *Framing Hitchcock*, ed. Sidney Gottlieb and Christopher Brookhouse (Detroit: Wayne State UP, 2002).

28. The passage in question can be found in its entirety only on the audio recordings. It seems to have been partially edited out of the printed version of the conversation in Truffaut's *Hitchcock: Revised Edition* (New York: Simon & Schuster, 1984) 123. The audio recording of the discussion of the latter British period is part of the special features included in the Criterion Collection edition of *The Lady Vanishes*, directed by Alfred Hitchcock (1938; New York: Criterion Collection, 2007), DVD.

29. *The Oxford English Dictionary* (Oxford: Oxford UP, 1989) s.v. "pixie."

30. *The American Heritage Dictionary* (Boston: Houghton Mifflin Company, 2006) s.v. "pixie."

31. *Webster's Third New International Dictionary* (Springfield, MA: Merriam-Webster Inc., 1986) s.v. "pixie."

32. See the commentary on "Erlkönig" (FA 1:1022): "Herder hatte eine dänische Ballade *Erlkönigs Tochter* übersetzt und dabei "Ellerkonge" (von 'Elverkonge', 'Elfenkönig') mit der Erle in Verbindung gebracht, die früher auch 'Eller' hieß."

33. This is easier to see in Herder's poem, where we read: "Da tanzen die Elfen auf grünem Land.'" (There elves are dancing in the green meadows.) Though elves make no explicit appearance in "Erlkönig," Goethe does refer to them in texts that are linked to the poem. Writing about "Um Mitternacht wenn die Menschen erst schlafen" (Around midnight when humans are barely asleep)—a poem that is in certain respects something of a proto-"Erlkönig"—Goethe explains: "Der Mond ist unendlich schön, Ich bin durch die neuen Wege gelaufen da sieht die Nacht himmlisch drein. Die Elfen sangen." FA 1:970. (The moon is unbelievably beautiful. I ventured through new terrain, with the night appearing like heavenly sky. The elves sang.)

34. *Collins German Dictionary* (New York: HarperCollins, 2007) s.v. "pixie."

35. Noteworthy with respect to the theme of elves and pixies is the peculiar brooch that the mother gives to Betty. The small figure on the brooch is arguably just a girl dressed to go skiing—the brooch has at least been described like this before. See Ina Rae Hark, "Revalidating the Patriarchy: Why Hitchcock Remade *The Man Who Knew Too Much*," in *Hitchcock's Rereleased Films: From Rope to Vertigo*, ed. Walter Raubicheck and Walter Srebnick (Detroit: Wayne State UP, 1991) 215. Yet there is simultaneously something rather elfin and mischievous about the brooch. The figure's winter hat is reminiscent of the sorts of pointed hats that are associated with pixies. It is furthermore with a close-up of the brooch that the sequence presenting the nocturnal ride through the forest begins. A certain thematic link is thus suggested between this peculiar figure and the kidnapping of the child.

36. See Brigitte Buberl, *Erlkönig und Alpenbraut: Dichtung, Märchen und Sage in Bildern der Schack-Galerie* (Munich: Lipp, 1990).

ELISABETH KRIMMER

# Genius and Bloodsucker: Napoleon, Goethe, and Caroline de la Motte Fouqué

**Abstract:** This article provides an overview of the starkly divided responses of German intellectuals to Napoleon and contrasts Goethe's and Caroline de la Motte Fouqué's representations of the French emperor, arguing that Goethe's perception of the foreign ruler is linked to his notion of genius. Goethe saw in Napoleon the embodiment of strong leadership and considered him capable of containing violence and anarchy. While Goethe's response is marked by his cosmopolitan attitude, de la Motte Fouqué's attitude toward Napoleon is characterized by pronounced nationalism and violent hatred of the French. Her novel *Edmund's Wege und Irrwege* champions warfare as a means of personal catharsis and national rejuvenation.

**Keywords:** Napoleon, Caroline de la Motte Fouqué, warfare, nationalism

WE HAVE COME TO THINK OF our current moment as one of singular polarization. And yet, if we survey the political climate of early nineteenth-century Europe in general and the responses of German writers and thinkers to the momentous changes embodied by Napoleon in particular, we encounter an ideological landscape that is marked by stark contrasts and fierce opinions. These conflicting attitudes were rooted not only in Napoleon's personality (in what Byron called Napoleon's "antithetically mixed" spirit) and in the ideological and temperamental dispositions of his contemporaries, but also in the nature and impact of Napoleon's rule and policies in Germany.

In order to illuminate the division engendered by Napoleon, this article contrasts Goethe's response to the French emperor with that of Caroline de la Motte Fouqué. Much previous research on Goethe and Napoleon has focused on their personal encounter and on the import of Napoleon's comments on *Werther*. In contrast, I am interested in the larger significance of the figure of Napoleon for Goethe's thinking. I link Goethe's perception of Napoleon to his notion of genius, arguing that Goethe admired the Corsican's Faustian energy and saw in him an exemplary incarnation of a "Tatmensch." But his response to the French emperor was also informed by his conviction that only strong centralized leadership grounded in military success can contain violence and guarantee order and stability. Whereas Goethe found much to admire in the French emperor, Caroline de la Motte-Fouqué professed her hatred for him and used all poetic resources at her disposal to call for the eradication of the foreign tyrant. Before I begin my discussion of Goethe and de la Motte Fouqué, I offer a brief overview of the social, political, and economic impact of Napoleonic rule on Germany that helps to contextualize the differing responses to him in a divided intellectual climate.

## Napoleon in Germany

Even a cursory survey of the intellectual landscape in early nineteenth-century Germany shows that Napoleon inspired both ardent admiration, typically expressed in hyperbolic terms, and violent hatred, but never indifference. Not infrequently, adulation and rejection were combined in one and the same person. The group of admirers includes not only the young Ludwig van Beethoven who dedicated his *Eroica* to him but also Johann Wolfgang von Goethe who, in his conversations with Johann Peter Eckermann on March 11, 1828, referred to Napoleon as a demigod who strides from battle to battle: "Sein Leben war das Schreiten eines Halbgottes von Schlacht zu Schlacht und von Sieg zu Sieg. Von ihm könnte man sehr wohl sagen, daß er sich im Zustande einer fortwährenden Erleuchtung befunden, weshalb auch sein Geschick ein so glänzendes war" (His life was the striding of a demi-God from battle to battle and from victory to victory. One might very well say about him that he was in a perpetual state of enlightenment, which is why his destiny was so splendid).[1] Napoleon enthusiasm also inspired Christoph Martin Wieland who, on February 11, 1798, wrote, "Ich interessiere mich höchlich für Buonaparte, der, seit dem es Menschen gibt, vielleicht nicht drey seinesgleichen gehabt hat, und der Frankreichs u des ganzen Europa Heiland werden würde, wenn die Franzosen den Verstand hätten, ihn auf Lebenslang zu ihrem Dictator zu machen" (I am most interested in Buonaparte; since there have been humans, there have perhaps not been three like him. He could become a messiah for France and all of Europe if the French were clever enough to make him dictator for life).[2] Similarly, the poet Friedrich Hölderlin wrote an ode entitled "Buonaparte" in which he characterized poets as vessels that contain the spirit of heroes and Napoleon as a spirit so great that it would shatter every vessel.[3]

In some cases, such admiration persisted even in the face of Germany's defeat and occupation. The philosopher Georg Friedrich Wilhelm Hegel wrote a fervent letter to Friedrich Immanuel Niethammer, dated October 13, 1806, in which he called Napoleon "diese Weltseele" (this world soul) and professed that "es ist in der That eine wunderbare Empfindung, ein solches Individuum zu sehen, das hier auf einen Punkt concentrirt, auf einem Pferde sitzend, über die Welt übergreifft und sie beherrscht . . . sind solche Fortschritte nur diesem ausserordentlichen Manne möglich, den es nicht möglich ist, nicht zu bewundern" (it is indeed a wondrous sensation to see such an individual, concentrated here in one point, sitting on a horse, surveilling the world and dominating it . . . such progress is possible only in such an extraordinary man; it is impossible not to admire him).[4] Even Napoleon's enemies succumbed to his charms when they met him in person. Johannes von Müller, for example, the most important historian of his time and a European celebrity, initially referred to Napoleon as "Attila Bonaparte" and "Barbar,"[5] but changed his mind when he met him in the flesh during the occupation of Berlin. In a letter to his brother, dated November 25, 1806, Müller reports on a meeting in the Berliner Schloss that left him deeply impressed with Napoleon's intellect: "Durch sein Genie und seine unbefangene Güte hat er auch mich erobert" (With his genius and his simple kindness he conquered me too).[6] Smitten, Müller expressed his desire to seek employment in the French empire. Later in the century, Heinrich Heine completed Napoleon's apotheosis when he exclaimed that "Napoleon war nicht von dem Holz, woraus man die Könige macht;—er war von jenem Marmor, woraus man Götter macht" (Napoleon was not made of the wood that makes kings—he was formed from that marble with which Gods are made).[7]

Clearly, the list of German admirers of the French emperor is long, but so is the list of his enemies. To the volunteers in the Wars of Liberation, Napoleon was Attila the Hun, the devil, a son of hell, a demon, the anti-Christ, the lord of darkness, a seven-headed dragon, Cain's descendent, and the beast of the apocalypse.[8] A little ditty by Johann Friedrich Schink entitled "Dem Korsen. Schand- und Schimpfode" (To the Corsican. Ode of Shame and Insult) reads thus: "Abschaum der Menschheit . . . Wütrich, Ungeheuer, . . . Blutsauger, Völkergeißel, Weltzertreter, Pest, Räuberhauptmann, Henker und Bandit, Du Mensch gewordner Satan, Missethäter . . . Die Tamerlane, Attila, Tibere, Caligula und Nero—Engel sind! Die Höll' ist selbst nicht schwarz genug an Farben, zu schildern dich" (scum of mankind . . . berserk, monster . . . bloodsucker, scourge of nations, world crusher, plague, robber captain, executioner and bandit, you Satan become man, evildoer . . . The Tamerlanes, Attilas, Tiberii, Caligulas and Neros—they are angels! Hell itself does not have colors black enough to describe you).[9] It would seem that, when dealing with Napoleon, only superlatives will do. He is God or monster, but never ordinary.

Among German writers, Heinrich von Kleist was most violent in his hatred for Napoleon. He considered Napoleon a tyrant who sought to dominate and exploit German lands. On October 24, 1806, Kleist wrote to his sister:

> Es heißt ja, daß der Kaiser den Franzosen alle Hauptstädte zur Plünderung versprochen habe. Man kann kaum an eine solche Raserei der Bosheit glauben . . . Es wäre schrecklich, wenn dieser Wüterich sein Reich gründete. Nur ein sehr kleiner Teil der Menschen begreift, was für ein Verderben es ist, unter seine Herrschaft zu kommen. Wir sind die unterjochten Völker der Römer. Es ist auf eine Ausplünderung von Europa abgesehen, um Frankreich reich zu machen"[10]

> It is said that the emperor has promised the French all capital cities for plunder. It is hard to believe such raging evil exists . . . It would be horrible if this brute were to found his empire. Only a very small segment of the people understands what ruin it is to be governed by him. We are the subjugated peoples of the Romans. It is his design to plunder Europe in order to make France rich).

In a letter to Rühle von Lilienstern, written in late November 1805, Kleist suggests taking drastic action against the foreign oppressor: "Warum sich nur nicht einer findet, der diesem bösen Geiste der Welt die Kugel durch den Kopf jagt. Ich möchte wissen, was so ein Emigrant zu tun hat?" (Why can we not find someone who shoots a bullet through the head of this evil world spirit. I would like to know what such an emigrant does all day?).[11]

If German responses to Napoleon were contradictory, so was the nature of Napoleonic rule in Germany, which bestowed great benefits but also wrought serious harm. Napoleon was not only a brilliant military leader, but also an unusually talented administrator who implemented reforms inspired by revolutionary ideals. The little corporal instituted equality before the law, improved and rationalized legal codes and state and local administrations, secured property rights, including intellectual property, abolished feudalism, championed a meritocracy that contributed to the leveling of class differences, encouraged science and the arts, and instituted secular education and religious toleration along with civil liberties for Jews.[12] In order to understand Napoleon's accomplishments and his outsized energy, it is helpful to consider the situation on the island of Malta as a case study. On his way to Egypt, Napoleon spent six days on Malta. During these six days, he "replaced the island's medieval administration with a governing council; dissolved the monasteries; introduced street lighting and paving; freed all political prisoners; installed fountains and reformed the hospitals, postal service and university, which was now to teach science as well as the humanities . . . he abolished slavery, liveries, feudalism, titles of nobility . . . allowed the Jews to build a hitherto banned synagogue."[13] In light of such enlightened activism, it is hardly surprising that some countries were quite happy with Napoleonic rule. In Italy, for example, there never was a rebellion against the French for the simple reason that the French were better administrators than the Austrians.

Such reforms, and Napoleon's talents, are impressive in and of themselves, but they shone all the more brightly when compared to the rather mediocre talents of the Prussian King and the Austrian emperor. While Napoleon was known for his decisiveness, Friedrich Wilhelm III of Prussia had earned the nickname the "Kunktator," which translates roughly to "he who hesitates." The dashing Prince Louis Ferdinand, a nephew of Frederick the Great, believed that the Prussian king's "feige und schwächliche Politik Europa ins Verderben gestürzt hat" (cowardly and weak politics has caused Europe's ruin).[14] While Napoleon modernized Europe in a whirlwind of action, Friedrich Wilhelm never followed through on promises of reform made in 1813, and the reactionary policies associated with the Austrian diplomat Klemens von Metternich offer some evidence that there was less freedom after than during Napoleon's reign. If we look East, we find the autocratic Tsar Alexander I who relied on serfdom, which was to persist in Russia until 1861, while Napoleon abolished it.

To be sure, Napoleon was a reformer as well as a despot and imperialist, but so were the rulers of Britain and Russia. Napoleon's wars cost millions of lives but they were not always of his making. As Roberts points out, "war was declared on him far more often than he declared it on others."[15] And while Napoleon was known for censorship and propaganda, there was no freedom of the press in Prussia, Austria, and Russia either.[16] Unlike other European sovereigns, Napoleon, who was utterly self-made, was acutely aware of the need to please his subjects. In a letter to his brother Jerome, whom he appointed

King of Westphalia, he admonished his wayward proxy: "What the people of Germany ardently desire is that those who are not noble and who have talent should have an equal right to your respect and to employment."[17]

Clearly, there were great advantages to Napoleonic rule, while its negative aspects were not unique to French governance but rather common across Europe. Even so, the positive features of Napoleonic rule were, as Jeffrey Sammons points out, "submerged in the miseries of conscription, taxation, censorship, arrests and forced labor, the violent destruction of economic life at every level."[18] Zamoyski makes a similar point: "the benefits of emancipation, equality before the law, and a functioning administration based on a solid constitution, not to mention the spread of education for all, were generally appreciated, those who had bestowed them were increasingly resented for their arrogance and their financial demands."[19] Tellingly, the conflict between Napoleon and his brother Louis, whom he had appointed King of Holland, was rooted in the fact that Louis felt beholden to his Dutch subjects whereas Napoleon ordered him to exploit them ruthlessly. Similarly, in Prussia, Napoleon demanded war contributions of such a magnitude that they sucked the country dry and reduced "much of the population to poverty and even starvation."[20] Since Germany was both the site of many battles and a waystation to Russia, there was a constant coming and going of French and allied soldiers who requisitioned food and were billeted in the houses of average civilians. Weimar, for example, had to house 6,108 French officers and 203,617 soldiers in 1813. Charlotte Schiller alone had to provide for 100 soldiers.[21] Moreover, the violence and hardships of billeting were often exacerbated by anger about French arrogance and a sense that French geopolitical ambition was paired with cultural imperialism. And yet, in spite of experiencing the French occupation firsthand, some residents of Weimar remained smitten with the French emperor.

## Napoleon and Goethe

In Weimar, the disadvantages of a war that had started with the allied response to the French Revolution and ultimately lasted until Napoleon's defeat at Waterloo in 1815 were all too palpable. In the wake of the battles of Jena and Auerstedt on October 14, 1806, some 15 and 17 miles from Weimar, an army of 40,000 soldiers, possibly as many as 50,000, descended upon the 7,000 inhabitants of Weimar. Goethe's entry in his diary reads as follows: "Abends um 5 Uhr flogen die Kanonenkugeln durch die Dächer. Um ½ 6 Einzug der Chasseurs. 7 Uhr Brand, Plünderung, schreckliche Nacht. Erhaltung unseres Hauses durch Standhaftigkeit und Glück" (In the evening at 5 cannonballs were flying through the roofs, at half past five the chasseurs entered town. Seven o'clock fire, plunder, horrible night. Our house saved through steadfastness and luck).[22] The French army was known to live off the land, and its impact was felt deeply. Houses were broken into, furniture destroyed, valuables and food damaged or taken. Johanna Schopenhauer, mother of the philosopher Arthur Schopenhauer and a resident of Weimar, notes that nothing could be done "gegen 50,000 wütende Menschen, die diese Nacht hier frei schalten und walten durften" (against 50,000 angry men who were free to do what they liked this night), and used this freedom to "mangeons, buvons, pillons, brulonts tout les maisons" (eat, drink, plunder, burn all the houses). Schopenhauer also conveys a drastic image of billeted soldiers: "Denk Dir dabei die gräßlichen Gesichter, die blutigen Säbel blank, die weißlichen, mit Blut bespritzten Kittel, die sie bei solchen Gelegenheiten tragen, ihr wildes Gelächter und Gespräch, ihre Hände mit Blut gefärbt" (think of the horrid faces, the bloody sabers drawn, the white tunic, such as they wear for such occasions, spattered with blood, their wild laughter and conversation, their hands drenched in blood).[23]

The loss in property was significant: the French requisitioned 3,000 animals, including over one hundred horses, large quantities of grain, hay, and straw, along with over 40,000 liters of wine and 25,000 liters of beer. They also set fire to some houses, which thankfully did not spread because there was no wind. While significant and even crushing, these material damages were dwarfed by injuries to life and limb. The French officer caste was known for its chivalry; the common soldiers, however, availed themselves of all the spoils of war. Some inhabitants of Weimar took refuge in the castle, but those who did not were exposed to violent mistreatment. The painter Georg Melchior Kraus died as a result of injuries inflicted by French soldiers, and many women, including the wife of the writer Christian August Vulpius, were victims of rape.[24] Discipline in Weimar was restored on October 15, 1806, when Napoleon arrived in town. It bears mention that this devastation of the town of Weimar followed on the heels of a severe loss of lives in the course of the Napoleonic wars: 998 soldiers from Carl August's duchy died in the fight against Andreas Hofer's rebellion in Tyrol and, of the 2,000 soldiers from Thuringia who joined the Russian campaign, only 550 returned.[25]

Goethe's response to the occupying force was characterized by a willingness to cooperate and appease. He warned against resistance which he considered futile and ultimately self-destructive—though a certain distance to the occupying force is indicated by the fact that he refused to meet Napoleon during these days even though he was presented with an opportunity to do so. When the first soldiers arrived, Goethe and his son's tutor Friedrich Wilhelm Riemer greeted them at the Frauentor, offering wine and beer.[26] In accordance with his reputation and social standing, Goethe did not have to put up ordinary soldiers in his house. Rather, he was assigned Marshall Ney. During the night of October 14, however, before Ney arrived and imposed order, several infantrymen demanded entry to Goethe's home and threatened Goethe in his own bedroom, where, according to Weimar gossip, they placed bayonets on his chest.[27] Goethe reports that he was particularly worried about his unpublished manuscripts, and with some right. Johanna Schopenhauer informs us that Herder lost most of his papers during these turbulent days. As is well known, this encounter with French soldiers, which was quite possibly a brush with death, made a profound impact on Goethe and motivated him to get his affairs in order: he married his long-time mistress Christiane Vulpius and shored up his finances.

One might expect Goethe to dislike a foreign ruler who was the root cause of so much hardship. And yet, during his first personal encounter with Napoleon at the Congress of Erfurt, an illustrious gathering of two emperors, four kings, and numerous other sovereigns in 1808, Goethe found much to admire in the French emperor. The Congress of Erfurt was initiated by Napoleon, who sought to reaffirm his alliance with Russia (although his efforts were undermined by his own foreign minister Talleyrand). Goethe was present because his sovereign, Duke Carl August of Weimar, had requested that he accompany him to help navigate the precarious position of his duchy: Weimar was a member of the Rheinbund and thus allied with Napoleon, but it was also linked to Russia through Maria Paulowna, the sister of the Tsar and wife of Carl August's son. Goethe's infamous meeting with Napoleon took place on October 2. It was followed by a second meeting on October 6, 1808 in Weimar, which Napoleon visited after the Congress of Erfurt. Entire books have been written about the first encounter, but there is precious little information about it. Goethe himself did not publish a full account of his conversation with Napoleon and seemed to take an impish delight in being vague and enigmatic about it. Still, there are two drafts, which Goethe wrote in 1819 and 1822/23 in the context of the *Tag- und Jahreshefte* (Day- and Yearbooks). They were edited posthumously by Goethe's secretary Eckermann and published in 1836 as "Skizze" (Sketch) in the *Nachgelassene Werke* (Posthumous Works). In addition, there is an account, written in French, by Friedrich von Müller, who had been asked by Talleyrand to produce a description of Napoleon's conversations with Wieland and Goethe, but this narrative does not offer much additional information. Finally, there are sundry references in various letters of Goethe's friends and acquaintances.

Based on these sources, we know that Napoleon greeted Goethe with the words "Vous etes un homme" (You are a man), inquired about his age, and, when informed that he was 60 years old, remarked that he looked well (MA 14:576-81). When Napoleon's intendant-general Daru mentioned Voltaire's Mahomed, which Goethe had translated, Napoleon gave voice to his displeasure, remarking that it is highly objectionable that a conqueror such as Mahomed should offer such a negative account of himself. The poet and the emperor then discussed *Werther*. Napoleon—who was, according to Roberts, a voracious reader who traveled with a carefully curated library and read *The Sorrows of Young Werther* six times during his Egyptian Campaign,[28]— singled out a particular passage in the text that he claimed was unnatural. Tantalizingly, Goethe never revealed which passage they were talking about—"ob aber Napoleon dieselbe Stelle gemeint hat oder eine andere halte ich für gut nicht zu verraten" (I consider it opportune not to reveal whether Napoleon meant this passage or another one)—but notes that he conceded Napoleon's point: the passage in question was indeed untrue ("etwas Unwahres") but was necessary to achieve a certain effect.[29]

Napoleon then expressed his disapproval of tragedies that highlight the role of destiny. "Was, sagte er, will man jetzt mit dem Schicksal, die Politik ist das Schicksal" (MA 19:579; What do you want with destiny now, he said, politics is destiny). After a brief interlude during which Napoleon discussed political affairs with his aides, the meeting concluded with questions about Goethe's family, children, and hobbies along with polite wishes for various members of the Weimar court. During the entire conversation, Napoleon took great interest in what Goethe had to say, repeatedly asking "Qu'en dit

Mr. Göt?" (What does Mr. Goethe say?). So far Goethe's account. According to Friedrich von Müller's *Erinnerungen aus den Kriegszeiten 1806-1813*, Napoleon invited Goethe to move to Paris, which the latter considered seriously, and asked him to write a drama about Julius Caesar that portrayed Caesar as a benefactor whose assassination harmed the empire.[30] In a letter to his wife Caroline, dated November 19, 1808, Wilhelm von Humboldt adds that Goethe was particularly impressed with Napoleon's intimate knowledge of French drama and with the fact that he never criticized without offering constructive advice on how to improve matters.[31]

To Goethe, the conversation with Napoleon remained a highlight of his life. In a letter to Cotta, written on December 2, 1808, he described Napoleon's impact on him:

> Ich will gerne gestehen, daß mir in meinem Leben nichts Höheres und Erfreulicheres begegnen konnte als vor dem französischen Kaiser, und zwar auf eine solche Weise zu stehen ... mich noch niemals ein Höherer dergestalt aufgenommen, indem er mit besonderem Zutrauen mich, wenn ich mich des Ausdrucks bediene darf, gleichsam gelten ließ ... wo ich ihm auch irgend wieder begegne, ich ihn als meinen freundlichen und gnädigen Herren finden werde.[32]

> I will happily confess that nothing higher or more delightful could have occurred to me in my life than standing before the French emperor in such a manner ... never has anybody in such an elevated position received me in this way, insofar as he, if I may put it like this, received me so to speak with a special intimacy and let me be myself ... wherever I may meet him again, I will find him to be my kind and merciful lord.

Four years after this encounter, in 1812, Goethe again gave voice to his admiration for Napoleon in stanzas dedicated to Marie Louise of Austria, the French emperor's second wife:

> Was Tausende verwirrten, löst der *Eine*.
> Worüber trüb Jahrhunderte gesonnen,
> *Er* übersiehts in hellstem Geisteslicht
> Das Kleinliche is alles weggeronnen,
> . . . . . . . . . . . . . . . . . . . . . . . . . . . . .
> Und wenn dem Helden alles zwar gelungen,
> Den das Geschick zum Günstling auserwählt,
> Und Ihm vor allen alles aufgedrungen,
> Was die Geschichte jemals aufgezählt;
> Ja reichlicher als Dichter je gesungen!—
> *Ihm* hat bisher das Höchste noch gefehlt;
> Nun steht das Reich gesichert wie geründet
> Nun fühlt *Er* froh im Sohne sich gegründet. (MA 9:66)

> What thousands have confounded, one disentangles
> What centuries have pondered gloomily
> He surveils all with brightest light of mind.
> All that is petty is melted away,
> . . . . . . . . . . . . . . . . . . . . . . . . .

> And when the hero has succeeded in everything
> He whom destiny chose as favorite
> And before others bestowed upon him everything
> That history ever had enumerated!—
> Yes, more plentiful than poets have ever sung
> Until now he lacked the highest good
> Now the empire is secure and rounded
> Now he happily feels grounded in his son.

Upon reading this ode, which contributed to Goethe's reputation as a "Fürstenknecht" (prince's servant), Dorothea Schlegel, in a letter to Varnhagen von Ense, dated September 2, 1812, remarked dryly: "Ist er durch keine Marter zu diesen Stanzen gezwungen worden, so will ich Gott bitten, daß sie ihm verziehen werden" (If he was not forced by torture to write these stanzas, I will ask God to forgive him for this).[33] Goethe, however, was not bothered by his detractors. To him, Napoleon remained an exemplary human being who had developed his inborn talent to the fullest possible degree. In a conversation with Eckermann on March 11, 1828, Goethe expresses his admiration for Napoleon's seemingly infinite energy, calling him "einer der produktivsten Menschen … die je gelebt haben" (MA 19:605–6; one of the most productive people … who have ever lived). Goethe is similarly enthusiastic in a conversation with Sulpiz Boisserée, recorded by the latter: "Napoleon hat ihm imponirt, er habe den größten Verstand, den je die Welt gesehen" (Napoleon impressed him; he has the greatest mind the world has ever seen).[34] As far as Goethe was concerned, all opposition to Napoleon was rooted in petty impulses: "Es sind zwey Formeln, in denen sich die sämmtliche Opposition gegen Napoleon befassen und aussprechen läßt, nämlich: Afterredung (aus Besserwissenwollen) und Hypochondrie" (There are two formulas that characterize and label all opposition to Napoleon, namely slander [due to a know-it-all attitude] and hypochondria).[35] Goethe, who was awarded the Cross of the Legion of Honor, continued to wear it conspicuously and frequently, even after Napoleon's downfall. He also kept a flask with a stopper in the form of a Napoleon bust on his desk until he died.[36]

Goethe's remarks suggest that he saw in Napoleon a fellow genius. Indeed, unlike Arthur Schopenhauer who believed that true genius is incompatible with politics and warfare,[37] Goethe perceived an affinity between genius in art and genius in political affairs. In a conversation with Eckermann, he identified the same greatness in a wide variety of intellectual and practical pursuits: "Ob Einer sich in der Wissenschaft genial erweiset, wie Oken und Humboldt, oder im Krieg und der Staatsverwaltung, wie Friedrich, Peter der Große und Napoleon, oder ob Einer ein Lied macht wie Béranger, es ist Alles gleich und kommt bloß darauf an, ob der Gedanke, das Apercu, die Tat lebendig sei und fortzuleben vermöge" (Whether one proves a genius in science, such as Oken and Humboldt, or in war and governance, such as Frederick, Peter the Great, and Napoleon, or whether one makes a song such as Béranger, it is all the same and the only thing that matters is whether the thought, the apercu, the deed is alive and capable of persistence).[38] Goethe was not blind to Napoleon's faults, but he came to see in him a force of nature that transcends common categories of morality. "Außerordentliche Menschen, wie Napoleon, treten aus der Moralität heraus. Sie wirken zuletzt wie physische Ursachen, wie Feuer und Wasser" (Extraordinary people like Napoleon leave morality behind. They ultimately act like physical forces, like fire and water).[39] Goethe recognized the ruthlessness in Napoleon's behavior, noting that "was ihn in den Weg tritt wird niedergemacht, aus dem Weg geräumt—und wenn es sein leiblicher Sohn wäre" (whatever stands in his way will be destroyed, cast aside—and even if it were his own son), but he believed that such ruthlessness was inextricably linked to Napoleon's energy and the force of his intellect and willpower. Thus, he compared Napoleon to the director of an orchestra who uses every instrument for his own grander purpose, the creation of a masterpiece. According to Falk, Goethe even approved of the execution of opponents, such as that of the bookseller Johann Philipp Palm or of Louis Antoine Duke d'Enghien, because they stood in the way of a genius's desire to create.[40] In Goethe's pantheon, Napoleon occupied the same elevated rank as Mozart, Byron, and, of course, Goethe himself. According to Sulpiz Boisserée, Goethe also perceived an intimate relation between Napoleon and Faust.[41] Both are defined by a striving that knows no bounds and both violate common norms of decency and morality on their path to greatness. To the end, Goethe maintained Napoleon's superiority, mocking the detractors: "Getraust du dich, ihn anzugreifen, / So magst du ihn nach der Hölle schleifen" (MA 18.1:77; If you dare attack him, you can drag him to hell).

Goethe's admiration for a foreign conqueror has incurred the wrath of many contemporaries and nineteenth-century scholars, whereas those who were pleased that Napoleon had singled Goethe out were far and few between. Karl Ludwig Knebel, tutor to Carl August's younger brother, was impressed that a sovereign ruler participated so actively in the life of the mind: "Mit unserem Goethe hat er sich schon ein paarmal ziemlich lange unterhalten und vielleicht dadurch auch deutschen Monarchen das Exempel gegeben, daß sie sich nicht scheuen dürften, ihre vorzüglichsten Männer zu erkennen und zu ehren" (Several times he talked with our Goethe for quite a long time and perhaps, in doing so, has set an example for German monarchs that they should not hesitate to recognize and honor their most accomplished men).[42] Knebel, however, remained a rather lonely voice in this debate. More common were those who found Goethe's openly expressed admiration for the French emperor objectionable. In a letter to his wife written on January 9, 1809, Wilhelm von Humboldt takes umbrage at Goethe's habit of parading his Cross of the Legion of Honor and referring to Napoleon as "mein Kaiser" (my emperor).[43] Goethe was known to regard nationalist impulses with a great deal of skepticism and kept his distance from the freedom fighters of the Wars of Liberation, even stopping his own son from joining the volunteers. He felt sympathy for those who had suffered personal harm during the wars but professed his impatience with those who lamented the loss of a German fatherland, which he considered largely imaginary:

> Wenn Jemand sich über das beklagt, was er und seine Umgebung gelitten, was er verloren hat und zu verlieren fürchtet, das hör' ich mit Teilnahme und

> spreche gern darüber und tröste gern. Wenn aber die Menschen über ein
> Ganzes jammern, das verloren sein soll, das denn doch in Deutschland kein
> Mensch sein Lebtag gesehen, noch viel weniger sich darum bekümmert hat; so
> muß ich meine Ungeduld verbergen, um nicht unhöflich zu werden.[44]

> If anybody complains about what he and his environment have suffered, what
> he has lost and fears to lose, I listen with sympathy and willingly talk about it
> and willingly offer comfort. But when people lament a wholeness that we have
> supposedly lost and that no man in Germany has seen in his lifetime, much less
> cared about; then I must hide my impatience so as not to be impolite.

Goethe, whose outlook was essentially cosmopolitan, could not embrace a
critique of Napoleon that objected first and foremost to his foreignness.

While Goethe's appreciation of Napoleon's talents was rooted in his cosmopolitanism, it was also connected to his rather pessimistic outlook on
politics. Goethe considered war and violence to be ineradicable features of
society. To him, the best chance for peace lay not in the avoidance of war but
in its containment, and the best chance for such containment consisted in
strong, centralized leadership. For this reason, Goethe believed in the superiority of monarchies over parliamentary rule, as evidenced in his remarks on
the French military triumph in Spain in 1824:

> Ich muß die Bourbons wegen dieses Schrittes durchaus loben, sagte er, denn
> erst hierdurch gewinnen sie ihren Thron, indem sie die Armee gewinnen. Und
> das ist erreicht. Der Soldat kehret mit Treue für seinen König zurück, denn er
> hat aus seinen vielen Siegen, so wie aus den Niederlagen der vielköpfig befeh-
> ligten Spanier die Überzeugung gewonnen, was für ein Unterschied es sei,
> einem Einzelnen gehorchen oder Vielen. (MA 19:82).

> I truly must praise the Bourbons for this step, he said, because they win their
> throne only by winning over the army. And that is done. The soldier returns
> with loyalty for his king because his many victories, along with the defeats of
> the Spaniards, who followed multiple commanders, have convinced him that it
> makes a difference whether one obeys one or many.

Goethe's appreciation for the soldier-king Napoleon is inspired by similar
convictions: only strong leadership is capable of preventing the Hobbesian
*bellum omnium contra omnes*: "Mit dem Säbel in der Faust an der Spitze
einer Armee, mag man befehlen und Gesetze geben, und man kann sicher
sein, daß man gehorcht werde; aber ohne dieses ist es ein mißliches Ding.
Napoleon, ohne Soldat zu sein, hätte nie zur höchsten Gewalt emporsteigen
können ... es liegt in der Natur der Dinge und ist nicht anders möglich" (With
the saber in one's fist at the head of an army, one may command and pass
laws, and one can be sure that one will be obeyed; but without this it is a piti-
ful thing. Napoleon, if he had not been a soldier, could never have risen to the
highest power ... it is in the nature of things and is not possible in any other
way).[45] Without such a leader, the mob rules: "Frankreichs traurig Geschick,
es mögen's Große bedenken; / Aber bedenken fürwahr sollen es Kleine noch
mehr. / Große gingen zu Grunde: wer aber schützte die Menge / Gegen die
Menge? Da war Menge der Menge Tyrann" (France's sad destiny, great people

may consider it;/ but in truth the little people should think on it even more. / Great ones perished: but who protected the crowd against the crowd? Thus the crowd was the tyrant of the crowd).[46] In other words, Goethe saw in Napoleon a force against chaos and mob rule, and he was willing to tolerate a degree of violence if it served the greater purpose of stability.[47]

Even so, in the last decades of his life, Goethe's admiration of the little corporal was frequently interwoven with a subtle criticism. Tellingly, Goethe added stanzas to his infamous ode to Marie Luise that speak to the incompatibility of boundless striving and a desire for peace. "*Den Frieden* kann das Wollen nicht bereiten: / Wer Alles will will sich vor allen mächtig, / Indem er siegt, lehrt er die andern streiten" (MA 9:195; Desire cannot clear the path for peace: He who wants everything wants to be powerful above all. In winning, he teaches others to fight). Goethe's contradictory impulses are best expressed in a conversation with Eckermann on February 10, 1830. Goethe remarked that the exiled Napoleon was unable to procure a new uniform in his preferred color when his old one had become threadbare and commented: "Ist es nicht rührend, den Herrn der Könige zuletzt soweit reducirt zu sehen, daß er eine gewendete Uniform tragen muß? Und doch, wenn man bedenkt, daß ein solches Ende einen Mann traf, der das Leben und Glück von Millionen mit Füßen getreten hatte, so ist das Schicksal das ihm widerfuhr, immer noch sehr milde" (MA 19:355; Is it not touching to see the master of kings so reduced at last that he must wear a uniform that has been turned inside out? And yet, if we consider that such an end befell a man who trampled on the lives and happiness of millions, then the destiny that he incurred, is still rather mild). In the later years of his life, a recognition of the suffering and loss of lives caused by the French emperor appears to have tempered Goethe's admiration. The discomfort with Napoleon's particular kind of genius finds its most sardonic expression in Goethe's poem "Etymologie spricht Mephistopheles": "Ars Ares wird der Kriegsgott genannt, Ars heißt die Kunst und Arsch ist auch bekannt" (MA 18.1:57; We call the god of war Ars Ares, ars is art and ass is also well known).

## Caroline de la Motte Fouqué

While Goethe's admiration for and Kleist's fierce opposition to Napoleon are widely discussed, it is little known that some of Napoleon's most outspoken critics were women. This is hardly surprising if we recall Napoleon's disregard for the intellectual and political abilities of the fairer sex. When the Napoleon biographer Andrew Roberts notes that "Napoleon generally saw women as lesser beings," he is not offering a supposition but merely citing Napoleon himself who proclaimed that "women should not be looked upon as equals of men . . . they are, in fact, only machines for making babies."[48] Napoleon was convinced that "women are at the heart of all intrigues" and therefore believed that they "should be kept in their family circles."[49]

Clearly, such opinions were not likely to garner much support among Napoleon's female contemporaries although there was the occasional admirer. Dorothea Veit-Schlegel, for example, wondered in a letter to Carl Friedrich Zelter, dated April 4, 1800, "Können Sie sich wohl ein herrlicheres Loos denken, als Buonapartes Mutter zu sein?" (Can you think of a more glorious destiny than to be Buonaparte's mother?).[50] For the most part, however, German women did not take kindly to the French emperor. The hatred of Maria Carolina, Queen of Naples, for the foreign tyrant is legendary. A daughter of Empress Maria Theresia of Austria, Maria Carolina referred to Napoleon as "that ferocious beast . . . that Corsican bastard, that parvenu, that dog."[51] She also called him a devil, which, as Waltraud Maierhofer points out, made her the devil's grandmother since her favorite grandchild, Marie Louise of Austria, became Napoleon's second wife.[52] Interestingly, however, even Maria Carolina grudgingly admitted that she felt admiration for the little corporal: "I admire him, and my sole regret is that he serves so detestable a cause."[53] In Weimar, Duchess Anna Amalia remained unimpressed with the foreign conqueror. In a letter to Karl von Knebel, dated October 29, 1805, she writes: "Im Grunde wissen sie alle nicht, was sie wollen, auch selbst Buonaparte, der nur seinem tollen und blinden Stolz und Übermut den Zügel laufen läßt und sucht, wie weit er kommen kann" (Fundamentally they all do not know what they want, not even Buonaparte who gives his mad and blind pride and folly free rein and probes how far he can go).[54]

Among German royalty, the fiercely anti-French Queen Louise of Prussia was Napoleon's most formidable enemy. Unlike her peace-loving husband, Louise called for war and, at Tilsit, personally pleaded with the emperor to return the city of Magdeburg to Prussian governance. Napoleon blew her off; he objected to the Prussian "petticoat government" and, when asked whether he was swayed by the queen's charm, said that she was "as handsome as could be expected at thirty-five."[55] To this list of female opponents, one might add Madame de Staël and Maria Paulowna, a sister of Tsar Alexander I and the daughter-in-law of Carl August of Weimar and Eisenach, or Schiller's sister-in-law, Caroline von Wolzogen who writes, "dieser Charakter ist mir durchaus zuwider" (I find this character utterly detestable).[56]

Among Napoleon's female detractors, Caroline de la Motte Fouqué (1775–1831), wife of Friedrich de la Motte Fouqué and author of more than twenty novels, occupies a prominent position. De la Motte Fouqué, an aristocrat who moved in "the highest court circles,"[57] is known for her active interest in politics and her pronounced nationalism.[58] Like Johanna Schopenhauer, she experienced Germany's occupation firsthand. French soldiers were billeted in her house in 1806, and her husband and sons fought in the Prussian army in 1813.[59] Unlike Goethe, however, de la Motte Fouqué responded to the foreign conquest with fierce resistance.

Her opposition to the French emperor is evident in her *Edmund's Wege und Irrwege: Ein Roman aus der nächsten Vergangenheit* (Edmund's Paths and Misadventures: A Novel from the Recent Past), published in 1815. *Edmund's Wege und Irrwege*, a meandering novel with minimal plot, combines a narrative of the hero's amorous entanglements with his political *Bildung*. At the beginning of the text, Edmund, a young count, is quite literally lost. Throughout the text, he wanders aimlessly until his life gains purpose when he joins the fight against Napoleon. As he matures and finds his true calling as a soldier and patriot, Edmund abandons unsuitable romantic companions and settles on a German maiden who exudes the "Maienduft der Jugend und Unschuld" (May scent of youth and innocence).[60] Edmund's *Bildung* gives occasion to descriptions of travels, chance acquaintances, masked balls, duels, and love affairs, as well as prolonged conversations about sculpture, art, religion, nature, and poetry. This social portrait unfolds in a gothic atmosphere. There are ghost stories, lonely castles in the forest, ruins, a witch, gypsies and soothsayers, ominous prophecies, a comet that portends the coming war and revenge against the French, and scholars of magic.

In its aimlessness and lack of action, de la Motte Fouqué's narrative mimics the disorientation of Germany's male youth and the political stagnation of German life under French occupation. De la Motte Fouqué aims to show how the passion and thirst for action of a whole generation of young men are stifled by foreign oppression. Thus, Edmund, who is described as "dies jugendliche Flammenmeer" (this youthful sea of flames), vacillates between bursts of enthusiasm and melancholy despondence. Deeply depressed about the "Schmach des Vaterlandes und die eigenen gebundenen Hände" (1:104; the shame of the fatherland and their own tied hands), Edmund and his friends indulge in fantasies of violent retribution against the French tyrant: "ich möchte den fremden Blutsauger durch und durch stechen" (1:35; I want to run the foreign bloodsucker through and through). This pent-up energy finally erupts in the cataclysmic battle of Leipzig that concludes the novel.

De la Motte Fouqué champions a conservative agenda that derides the abolition of class boundaries. This is evident in a conversation with an admirer of Napoleon who praises his regime because it is such that "die verächtliche Scheidewand indischer Kastenverfassung zusammenstürzen müsse" (1:113; the despicable dividing wall of the Indian caste system must collapse). While this comment champions the advent of social equality, Edmund honors societal stratification as a valuable national heritage while characterizing its abolishment as a form of imprisonment: "daß man einerseits ehrwürdige Schranken niederreißt und sich unter ihren Trümmern ein schmähliches Gefängnis bauen will" (1:114; that one wants to tear down venerable barriers on the one hand and build a shameful prison on their ruins). To de la Motte Fouqué, serfdom is acceptable as long as one is subordinated to native, not foreign, rulers. Moreover, her feudalism is accompanied by antisemitism. She refers to the "schmutzigen Schacherjuden" (1:148; dirty haggling Jews) and considers a willingness to associate with Jews a sign of untrustworthiness: "Solchem Kerle traue ich nicht über den Weg, das hält's mit Juden und Christen!" (3:182; I don't trust such a guy; he deals with Jews and Christians).

Throughout, *Edmund's Wege und Irrwege* is steeped in nationalist rhetoric and violently anti-French and antirevolutionary sentiments. De la Motte Fouqué acknowledges Napoleon's epochal importance. He is a man, "der so einer ganzen Zeit eine Physiognomie aufdrücke, und wie das unerbittliche Geschick mit ehrnem Tritt von West nach Ost über Königshäupter hinschreite, mit blutgetränktem Griffel seine Gesetze in die zitternden Menschenherzen grabe" (1:112; who thus impresses his physiognomy on an entire era, and, like inexorable destiny, strides with iron step from West to East across the heads of kings, inscribing his laws with blood-drenched stylus in trembling human hearts). In spite of such acknowledgments of Napoleon's great impact on his time, she remains firm in her hatred of the French emperor, likening him to various animals. He is an "angeschossener Eber" (3:142; wounded boar) who needs to be put down and a snake whose head must be crushed (3:207).

While Napoleon is a wild beast, his army is satanic: they are French Satans (3:11), devils (3:208), blood hounds (3:209), "wilde Bursche" (2:62; wild fellows), "Streiter der Hölle" (3:155; warriors from hell) and "Höllengeister" (3:141; ghosts from hell) who exude the "Gifthauch satanischen Lebens … Ein Pestnebel" (3:154; the poisonous stench of satanic life … a plague mist), and, in doing so, poison healthy German blood ("verpestete Luft das gesunde Blut angesteckt hat," 2:85). De la Motte Fouqué emphasizes that French skin is of a brown and yellow sheen (2:64), and French faces are grimaces ("Ueberall Fratzen," 2:64). In contrast to the "einfach stillen deutschen Mann" (simple, quiet German man), the French enjoy "rastloses Geschnatter" and indulge in "jede Ungezogenheit trotzenden Uebermuthes" (2:103; restless chatter … every naughty behavior of defiant excess). In short, they are amoral miscreants whose wanton behavior is marked by "Verderbtheit und ausmergelnde Ueberfeinerung" (3:163; corruption and corrosive excessive refinement) and, as such, degrades every village they occupy: "Der tonlosen Sprache dumpfes Gemurmel, verpestete Luft, fratzenhafte Neckereien und liederliche Späße zogen durch alle Gassen" (2:52; the dull murmur of a toneless language, plague-infested air, grimacing pranks and dissolute jokes roamed through all the streets).[61] In short, they are "Ungeziefer" (3:198; vermin) that need to be exterminated. Prussia, in contrast, is a divine entity even in its defeat: "Preußen stand da wie ein gefallener Engel, in dessen letzten Zuckungen man noch die Spuren eines göttlichen Daseyns ahnete" (3:155; Prussia stood there like a fallen angel in whose last stirrings one could intimate the traces of a divine existence).

In order to remedy Germany's misfortune, de la Motte Fouqué champions warfare as a means of both personal catharsis and national rejuvenation. Although *Edmund's Wege und Irrwege* borrows heavily from Goethe's *Wilhelm Meisters Lehrjahre* (*Wilhelm Meister's Apprenticeship*), the text is less interested in its hero's *Bildung* than in his gradual transformation into a soldier. In his early years, characterized as "eine verhunzte Kindheit" (1:33; ruined childhood), Edmund was prevented from pursuing a military career by a mother who lost her husband in the Napoleonic wars and who did not want to lose her son as well. The rectification of this maternal failure of judgment forms the arc of a novel that ends with Edmund's decision to fight, followed by France's ultimate defeat. Throughout, de la Motte Fouqué glorifies a culture of violence. Toward the beginning of the book, Edmund challenges a stranger to a duel, an act that is celebrated not only as the "erste[ ] freie[ ] That seines Lebens" (1:52; the first free deed of his life), but as a great way to make friends. The duel ends when Edmund wounds his opponent and they promptly fall into each other's arms and cry: "Die kleine Begebenheit hatte indeß Edmund mehrere Freunde gewonnen" (1:64; meanwhile the little event had won Edmund several friends).

Throughout, the text's main concern is honor, not victory, and this honor can be restored only through an "ungeheures Blutbad" that would "unsre Schmach ertränken" (2:54; monstrous bloodbath … drowns out our shame). Such a bloodbath is meaningful even if victory is out of reach because its ultimate purpose is to redeem future generations. *Edmund's Wege und Irrwege* endows death in battle with a transcendental dimension, noting that the corpses of dying soldiers build a bridge to heaven ("Mit ihren geweiheten Leibern die Brücke zum Himmel bauend," 3:191). Given a choice between servitude and death, a nation must choose the latter to preserve its national honor:"Ein Volk muß sterben können für seine Ehre, oder dienen, ein Drittes giebt es nicht" (2:55;A nation must be able to die for its honor, or serve, there is no third option).[62] The life of an individual matters little in this scheme: "Das Individuum soll alles und ist nichts" (3:153; the individual must do everything and is nothing). Repeatedly, warfare is imagined as a creative, healing, and life-giving endeavor—German blood is said to fertilize the soil from which German freedom grows (2:28; see also 3:178)—and battle effects a reawakening in which the new man is born (3:199–200).

Interestingly, de la Motte Fouqué suggests that it falls to women to instill such bloodthirsty nationalism.[63] Thus, the text charges women with a national mission even as it ostensibly promotes female subordination and denies women the right to develop their individuality:"Frauen dürfen aber nicht solche abgeschlossene Art und Weise, solche prononcirte Individualität haben wollen, das giebt eigensinningen Trotz" (3:147; women are not allowed to have such a closed-off manner, such pronounced individuality, that leads to obstinate defiance). And yet, subverting the gender ideology that the text explicitly sets out, de la Motte Fouqué introduces a matronly mentor figure who guides Edmund on his path towards patriotic resistance. The epitome of maternal benevolence and unassuming intelligence, Frau General Nordheim takes Edmund under her wing and, offering the use of her extensive library, introduces him to the German classics, including Stolberg, Ramler, and Klopstock. Under her tutelage, Edmund decides to fight for the fatherland and becomes engaged to Frau Nordheim's granddaughter Agnes. Clearly, *Edmund's Wege und Irrwege* stresses the importance and legitimacy of women's participation in the political life of the nation, but it weds its protofeminism to a highly problematic agenda of militaristic nationalism.

## Conclusion

As the preceding analysis shows, Goethe's and de la Motte Fouqué's responses to Napoleon differ in fundamental ways. De la Motte Fouqué's exuberant celebration of warfare constitutes the polar opposite of Goethe's desire to keep violence in check. Goethe tolerates some forms of bloodshed in the service of stability; de la Motte Fouqué promotes quasi-apocalyptic warfare for the greater good of Germany's honor. Both Goethe and de la Motte Fouqué speak in favor of social hierarchies and monarchic rule, but Goethe's cosmopolitanism contrasts sharply with de la Motte Fouqué's chauvinism. *Edmund's Wege und Irrwege* is filled with xenophobic comments, sentiments, and characterizations. To de la Motte Fouqué, the quality and nature of governance are less important than the bloodline that links the sovereign to his subjects. While Goethe makes allowance for any man of genius, de la Motte Fouqué is willing to tolerate structures of abuse and servitude as long as the ruler is native born. Much like Goethe, de la Motte

Fouqué recognized Napoleon's extraordinary gifts but, to her, nationality trumped talent. And yet, it is her chauvinistic mission that invites female participation, whereas women do not feature at all in Goethe's notion of genius.

*University of California, Davis*

## NOTES

1. Johann Wolfgang von Goethe, *Johann Peter Eckermann, Gespräche mit Goethe in den letzten Jahren seines Lebens*, ed. Heinz Schlaffer, vol. 19 of *Sämtliche Werke nach Epochen seines Schaffens*, Münchner Ausgabe (Munich: btb, 2006) 605. Further references to this edition appear as MA with volume and page number. All translations, unless otherwise noted, are my own.

2. Christoph Martin Wieland, *Wielands Briefwechsel*, vol. 14.1, ed. Hans Werner Seiffert and Siegfried Scheibe (Berlin: Akademie, 1963) 189.

3. Friedrich Hölderlin, *Sämtliche Werke*, Grosse Stuttgarter Ausgabe, vol. 1.1, *Gedichte bis 1800*, ed. Friedrich Beissner (Stuttgart: W. Kohlhammer, 1946) 293.

4. Georg Wilhelm Friedrich Hegel, *Briefe von und an Hegel*, vol. 1, ed. Karl Hegel (Leipzig: Verlag von Duncker & Humblot, 1887) 68.

5. Johannes von Müller, "Letter to Gentz, December 19, 1805," in *Schriften von Friedrich von Gentz. Ein Denkmal*, ed. Gustav Schlesier, vol. 4, *Briefwechsel zwischen Gentz und Johannes v. Müller* (Mannheim: Heinrich Hoff, 1840) 171.

6. J. D. F. Rumpf, ed., *Dreihundert und achtzehn Briefe berühmter und geistreicher Männer und Frauen* (Berlin: A. W. Hayn, 1829) 136.

7. Heinrich Heine, *Vermischte Schriften*, vol. 8 of *Sämmtliche Werke. Ausgabe in zwölf Bänden* (Hamburg: Hoffmann & Campe, 1876) 205.

8. See Andreas Fischer, *Goethe und Napoleon. Eine Studie von Andreas Fischer* (Frauenfeld: J. Huber, 1900) 6; see also Eckart Kleßmann, ed., *Deutschland unter Napoleon in Augenzeugenberichten* (Düsseldorf: Karl Rauch, 1965) 28.

9. Cited in Fischer 133.

10. Letter to Ulrike von Kleist, October 24, 1806, Heinrich von Kleist, *Sämtliche Werke und Briefe*, vol. 2, ed. Helmut Sembdner (Munich: Carl Hanser, 1993) 770-71.

11. Kleist 761.

12. See Andrew Roberts, *Napoleon: A Life* (New York: Penguin, 2014) xxxvi.

13. Roberts 167; See also Zamoyski's description of Napoleon's time on Elba: "He set about making roads . . . went on to building aqueducts, organizing drainage, sanitation, wheat cultivation, dictating letters on the subject of poultry farming, tuna fisheries, and horticulture," Adam Zamoyski, *Napoleon: A Life* (New York: Basic, 2018) 624.

14. Kleßmann 61.

15. Roberts xxxviii.

16. Roberts 243.

17. Cited in Zamoyski 474.

18. Jeffrey L. Sammons, "Fighting Napoleon—Loving the French: Friedrich Spielhagen, Noblesse Oblige (1888)," in *Women against Napoleon: Historical and Fictional*

*Responses to his Rise and Legacy*, eds. Waltraud Maierhofer, Gertrud M. Roesch, Caroline Bland (Frankfurt a/M: Campus, 2007) 247–63, here 256.

19. Zamoyski 476.

20. Zamoyski 477.

21. See Gustav Seibt, *Goethe und Napoleon. Eine historische Begegnung* (Munich: Beck, 2008) 199.

22. Johann Wolfgang Goethe, *Sämtliche Werke, Briefe, Tagebücher und Gespräche*, Frankfurter Ausgabe, ed. Friedmar Apel, vol. 33 (Frankfurt am Main: Suhrkamp, 1994) 128.

23. Johanna Schopenhauer, *Ihr glücklichen Augen. Jugenderinnerungen, Tagebücher, Briefe* (Berlin: Verlag der Nation, 1978) 329, 330, and 328.

24. See Seibt 10 and 11.

25. See Seibt 161 and 191.

26. Seibt 21.

27. See L. Bobe, ed., "Tagebuchaufzeichnungen des Dänischen Archäologen Johann Heinrich Carl Koes, 8–23. October, 1806, Weimar," *Goethe-Jahrbuch* 27 (1906): 118–24, here 122.

28. See Roberts 62.

29. MA 19:578; Napoleon's comment on Werther has inspired a number of scholarly contributions, including Bernd W. Seiler, "Goethe, Napoleon und der 'junge Werther,'" *Deutsche Vierteljahrsschrift für Literaturwissenschaft und Geistesgeschichte* 83, no. 3 (2009): 396–407; Pierre Grappin, "Goethe und Napoleon," *Goethe-Jahrbuch* 107 (1990): 71–80; Gonthier-Louis Fink, "Goethe und Napoleon," *Goethe-Jahrbuch* 107 (1990): 81–100; Lieselotte Blumenthal, "Zur Textgestaltung von Goethes 'Unterredung mit Napoleon,'" *Goethe-Jahrbuch* 20 (1958): 264–76.

30. Friedrich von Müller, *Erinnerungen aus den Kriegszeiten 1806–1813* (Hamburg: Alfred Janssen, 1907) 139. Fischer notes that, in his youth, Goethe had plans to write a Caesar drama that cast his assassination as the fruit of envy (21).

31. *Wilhelm und Caroline von Humboldt in ihren Briefen 1788–1835*, ed. Anna von Sydow (Berlin: Mittler & Sohn, 1920) 108.

32. Kleßmann 337.

33. Dorothea v. Schlegel geb. Mendelssohn und deren Söhne Johannes und Philipp Veit, *Briefwechsel*, ed. J. M. Raich, vol. 2 (Main: Franz Kirchheim, 1881) 99.

34. Sulpiz Boisserée, *Sulpiz Boisserée* (Stuttgart: Cotta'scher Verlag, 1862) 265.

35. Letter to Riemer, August 8, 1807, *Goethe, Begegnungen und Gespräche*, ed. Renate Grumach, vol. 6 (Berlin: De Gruyter, 1999) 324.

36. See Seibt 248. Seibt notes that when the Austrian quartermaster Reichsgraf Hieronymus II. Colloredo was quartered in his house, Goethe greeted him wearing the Cross of the Legion of Honor (204).

37. Fischer v.

38. MA 19:617. See also his comments on Byron: "Byrons Kühnheit, Keckheit und Grandiosität, ist das nicht alles bildend?—Wir müssen uns hüten, es stets im entschieden Reinen und Sittlichen suchen zu wollen.—Alles Große bildet, sobald wir es gewahr werden" (MA 19:277; Byron's audacity, cockiness, and grandiosity, is not all that educational?—We must take care not always to look for it in strict purity and morality—All greatness educates as soon as we become aware of it).

39. Friedrich Wilhelm Riemer, *Mitteilungen über Goethe, auf Grund der Ausgabe von 1841 und des handschriftlichen Nachlasses*, ed. Arthur Pollmer (Leipzig: Insel, 1921) 268.

40. *Goethe, Begegnungen und Gespräche*, ed. Renate Grumach, vol. 6 (Berlin: De Gruyter, 1999) 566.

41. See "Faust bringt mich dazu, wie ich von Napoleon denke und gedacht habe" (Faust reminds me of how I think and have thought about Napoleon), conversation dated August 3, 1815, in *Goethes Gespräche*, ed. Woldemar Freiherr von Biedermann (Leipzig, 1889-96) 191, http://v1.faustedition.net/testimony/graef_1162.

42. Kleßmann 331.

43. Anna von Sydow, ed., *Wilhelm und Caroline in ihren Briefen*, vol. 3 (Berlin: Mittler und Sohn, 1909) 66.

44. Letter to Zelter, July 27, 1807 (MA 20.1:155).

45. MA 19:300; see also "Die Tüchtigen sie standen auf mit Kraft / Und sagten: Herr ist der uns Ruhe schafft" (MA 18.1:291, lines 10278-79; Men of ability rebelled, and said: / Let him be ruler who'll establish order).

46. *Venezianische Epigramme* 53 (MA 3.2:137).

47. See, for example, Goethe's thoughts on Napoleon's execution of 800 Turkish prisoners in Egypt (MA 19:314).

48. Roberts 56 and 278.

49. Zamoyski 184.

50. Cited in Eva Walter, *Schrieb oft, von Mägde Arbeit müde. Lebenszusammenhänge deutscher Schriftstellerinnen um 1800—Schritte zur bürgerlichen Weiblichkeit* (Düsseldorf: Schwann, 1985) 146.

51. Cited in Roberts 394.

52. Cited in Waltraud Maierhofer, "Maria Carolina, Queen of Naples: The 'Devil's Grandmother' Fights Napoleon," in *Women against Napoleon: Historical and Fictional Responses to his Rise and Legacy*, eds. Waltraud Maierhofer, Gertrud M. Roesch, Caroline Bland (Frankfurt a/M: Campus, 2007) 57-78, here 58. Napoleon called her "that whore," see Roberts 394.

53. Maierhofer, "Maria Carolina, Queen of Naples," 67.

54. Amalie, Herzogin von Weimar, "Briefe der Herzogin Amalie aus den Jahren 1788-1807," in Wilhelm Bode, *Amalie, Herzogin von Weimar. Ein Lebensabend im Künstlerkreise* (Berlin: Mittler & Sohn, 1908) 179-210, here 203.

55. Roberts 460.

56. Seibt 43.

57. Carol Diethe, *Towards Emancipation: German Women Writers of the Nineteenth Century* (New York: Berghahn, 1998) 32.

58. On de la Motte Fouqué's advocacy of monarchy and aristocracy, see Helmut Peitsch, "Caroline de la Motte Fouqués *Magie der Natur. Eine Revolutionsgeschichte*," in *Geschichte(n)—Erzählen. Konstruktionen von Vergangenheit in literarischen Werken deutschsprachiger Autorinnen seit dem 18. Jahrhundert*, eds. Marianne Henn, Irmela von der Lühe, and Anita Runge (Göttingen: Wallstein, 2005) 265-85 and Elisabeth Krimmer, "Officer and Lady: Pants and Politics in Caroline de la Motte-Fouqué's *Das Heldenmädchen aus der Vendée*," *Studies in Eighteenth-Century Culture* 30, no. 1 (2001): 165-81.

59. See Julie Koser, *Armed Ambiguity: Women Warriors in German Literature and Culture in the Age of Goethe* (Evanston, IL: Northwestern UP, 2016) 140–41.

60. Caroline de la Motte Fouqué, *Edmund's Wege und Irrwege. Ein Roman aus der nächsten Vergangenheit*, 3 vols. (Leipzig: Gerhard Fleischer dem Jüng., 1815) 3:62. Further references appear in the text with volume and page number.

61. See also de la Motte Fouqué's comments that Frenchmen lack "das lebendige Element der Poesie" (2:88; the living element of poetry), and that even their "Verstand" is limited (2:89).

62. See also Kontje who notes the text's "stress on subordination, coupled with an unbridled hatred of the French and a boyish enthusiasm for war," Todd Kontje, *Women, the Novel, and the German Nation 1771–1871: Domestic Fiction in the Fatherland* (Cambridge: Cambridge UP, 1998) 100.

63. See Baumgartner who argues that in de la Motte Fouque's texts "wives were to keep watch over their husbands' patriotic spirit," Karin Baumgartner, "Valorous Masculinities and Patriotism in the Texts of Early Nineteenth-Century German Women Writers," *German Studies Review* 31, no. 2 (2008): 325–44, here 333.

ROBERT KELZ

# Instrument or Inspiration? Commemorating the 1949 Goethe Year in Argentina

**Abstract:** This essay examines commemorations of the 1949 Goethe Year in postwar Peronist Argentina. Its purview includes numerous musical performances, theatrical presentations, academic lectures, and written scholarship. Most activities occurred in the capital city of Buenos Aires; however, this investigation also makes excursions beyond the epicenter to Mendoza, La Plata, and Rosario, as well as neighboring Uruguay, Chile, and Brazil. There was no German author so broadly recognized and esteemed as Goethe, so the plethora of tributes to him represent an opportunity to analyze the resonance of a German figure among the full diversity of Argentina's educated population, including Argentines of all political persuasions, European nationals and immigrants, and large, conflictive German-speaking blocs of antifascist, Jews, nationalists, and recently arrived Nazis. The sweeping range of homages permits an analysis of Goethe's reception among all these groups while providing insights into their perspectives on Peronism, Nazism, postwar European politics, and, especially, Argentine literary history. Argentina and Goethe are twin lenses for exploring the role of art as an instrument and an inspiration in the cultural contact zones that existed among immigrant groups, their hosts, and nations of origin.

**Keywords:** intercultural, humanism, nationalist, Peronism, postwar, reconciliation

Against the backdrop of the 1949 Goethe Year in Argentina, this essay investigates several core themes across host and immigrant populations. The commemoration of the 1949 bicentenary of Goethe's birth depicts a bidirectional relationship that informs both how Argentines interpreted and deployed Goethe locally and, reciprocally, sheds light on how he influenced national literary history.[1] No figure in German literature had such wide, intercultural appeal as Goethe, so the tributes to him also document German-speakers' integration into Argentine cultural life and the positions that Argentines took toward the immigrants among them. Furthermore, the commemorations in 1949 track the trajectory of ongoing disputes and shifting alliances within German Buenos Aires as well as transatlantic projects between immigrants and their European Fatherland. Notably, Argentines and immigrants alike often compared Goethe with other singular national icons, such as Dante, Shakespeare, and Cervantes. Goethe was the exception, not the rule, so this article, the first in a two-part series, also investigates whether the Goethe Year represents an outlier amid broader social, political, and cultural developments. Finally, for reasons of language, geography, and otherwise, Latin American Germanists have a scant presence in German studies in the USA. Nevertheless, the history of German studies in Latin America is rich and the accomplishments of its scholars are worthwhile, so this essay is a small gesture to facilitate more flow of ideas from south to north.

Tensions in German Buenos Aires arose during the interwar period and continued after the Second World War. Having risen to power as a military officer and Secretary of Labor, Juan Perón became President of Argentina in 1946 and held power until 1955. Catalyzed by Eva Perón, the government granted women's suffrage and funded an array of social welfare programs, subsidizing access to housing, health care, education, and leisure activities. Simultaneously, the regime vigorously purged dissidents from government, media, and education sectors. Elected democratically, Perón had populist tendencies and some scholars have identified parallels between his Third Way and fascism.[2] He also allowed many nationalist German media and cultural organizations to reemerge in the postwar period and actively encouraged German immigration to Argentina. During the 1949 Goethe Year, Perón was at the apex of his power. Cultural, educational, and media organizations existed at his whim and they knew it.

## The 1949 Goethe Year: Hispanic Perspectives from Peronist Argentina

Commemorations of the 1949 Goethe Year were accompanied by a great deal of scholarship appearing in Argentine media, including various books and special editions of journals[3] and a plethora of newspaper articles,[4] as well as many events celebrating his accomplishments, such as scholarly lectures and representations in the performing arts. Considered Latin America's preeminent musical institution at the time, the Teatro Colón held a tribute to Goethe on November 2, 1949, featuring artists such as Carlos Feller, a Jewish immigrant from Lviv and bass singer in the Colón ensemble who achieved later achieved great success at the Cologne Opera from 1969 to 1996,[5] and female vocalist Olga Chevaline, a Russian immigrant to Argentina and member of the Colón choir before becoming a professor of voice at Rosario National University,[6] who performed the songs "Dem Musensohn" (The Son of the Muses) and "Heidenröslein" (Rose on the Heath) by Schubert, "Talisman" by Schumann, and Hugo Wolf's "Gretchen am Spinnrad" (Gretchen at the Spinning Wheel) and "Die Bekehrte" (The Encounter). The event also featured a speech by Guillermo Thiele, a philosophy professor at the University of Buenos Aires, entitled "Goethe ayer, hoy y mañana" (Goethe Yesterday, Today, and Tomorrow). Focusing on the world's struggle to surmount the postwar malaise, Thiele emphasized the solace that these musical interpretations of Goethe's verse offered in such dispiriting times. Goethe's ability to overcome despair caused his art to be eternally inspirational.[7] On August

28, the independent ensemble at the theater Florencio Sanchez performed dramatized passages from *Wilhelm Meister, Gespräche mit Eckermann* (*Conversations with Eckermann*), as well as "Vorspiel auf dem Theater" ("Prelude in the Theater") under the direction of Ruben Pesce, a prolific actor and director who worked with the influential Teatro de los Independientes (Theater of the Independents) and the Teatro Cervantes, Argentina's national theater.[8] Even conservative German media concluded that the performance demonstrated the enduring universalism that Goethe still signified, 200 years after his birth.[9]

The importance of Goethe's intertextual presence in Argentine dramas in 1949 was punctuated when Arturo Berenguer Carisomo, a lawyer and professor of Hispanic literature at the University of Buenos Aires, won the year's Premio Nacional de Teatro (National Theater Prize) for his play, *La piel de la manzana* (The Skin of the Apple, 1943). A modernized adaptation of Goethe's *Faust*, Berenguer's drama features innovative depictions of Goethean personages, including the businessman Fausto Segundo and his secretary, Wagner, as well as Mr. James Devil and Margarita. The updates to Mr. Devil and Fausto Segundo illustrate the drama's intertextuality by alluding to their literary origins while also conveying localized, contemporary implications. Mr. Devil, in particular, obviously alludes to Goethe's drama, but his style of dress, "a la moda de principios del siglo XVI" (in the fashion of the early sixteenth century),[10] deliberately recalls the age of Spanish colonization in the Americas.[11] An insidious financier, Mr. Devil's anglicized name also connotes the expansionist, predatory capitalism associated with Great Britain and the United States vehemently denounced by Peronism. Perón even framed his election campaign as a choice between Argentine and US-American values, with the slogan "Braden o Perón" (Braden or Perón) referring to Spruille Braden, the interventionist ambassador from Washington, DC. Moreover, in *La piel de la manzana* Fausto Segundo reflects the materialism of the Argentine bourgeoisie that Eva and Juan Perón attacked by inciting crowds to "quemar el Barrio Norte" (burn down Barrio Norte), a wealthy district in Buenos Aires that the drama's setting evokes.[12] As the Mendozan Germanist Claudia Garnica de Bertona has noted, Berenguer demystifies Goethe's *Faust* insofar as the pact is solely motivated by Fausto Segundo's rapacity. Fausto is an absolutely flat character. Although he is married to Margarita, he expresses no emotional warmth nor the slightest spiritual and psychological depth.[13] His figure parodies its Goethean inspiration through an acerbic satire of the *porteño* bourgeoisie, who is guided solely by wealth and is willing to sacrifice love, spirituality, and even his soul for the happiness that only money can buy.

The figure of Margarita undergoes perhaps the most radical transformation. Unlike Goethe's Gretchen, she is an educated, resilient woman with an upper middle-class background who scorns Fausto and repels the romantic advances of Mr. Devil. In Berenguer's drama, too, Margarita saves Faust's soul, but not by interceding mercifully. Instead, she tears up his pact with the devil to secure dominance over her husband, vowing "no voy a cometer la torpeza de crearme un rival serio, devolviéndole a usted la juventud" (I'm not going to be so inept as to create a serious rival for myself by restoring your youth).[14] Disdainful of her husband and Mr. Devil's promises of riches, Margarita prefers the modest, prudent, sensitive Wagner. Her wink when she invites him to a cup of tea at the drama's close betrays a person who has made her choice.

*La piel de la manzana* is a milestone along the trajectory of the Faustian myth within Argentine literature.[15] Berenguer enriched the canonical German drama with sharp social criticism and political messaging that welded his interpretation to the volatile environment of mid-twentieth-century Buenos Aires. His reinvention of the Gretchen figure dovetailed with the rise of Eva Perón and Argentina's legalization of women's suffrage in 1947. First staged in 1942, the drama's success in Peronist Argentina—it not only won the National Theater Prize in 1949 but was also named best drama for the 1948-1950 triennium by the Comisión Nacional de Cultura (National Commission of Culture)—is testimony to its provocative interplay with the *porteño* zeitgeist of the 1949 Goethe Year.

Meanwhile, the Andean city of Mendoza celebrated a full week of lectures by academics from Argentina, Uruguay, Spain, Portugal, and Germany, as well as musical performances by the municipal orchestra of Beethoven's *Egmont* and Wagner's "Faust Overture." On August 19, across the River Plate in neighboring Uruguay, the University of Montevideo featured a speech in Spanish by the exiled German poet and intellectual, Werner Bock, followed by a performance of Schumann and Schubert's musical arrangements of Goethe's verse by the soprano Olga Linné, later known for her interpretations of Mozart with the ensemble of the Teatro Solis, Uruguay's premier theater and the oldest in South America.[16]

Bock was a prolific voice during the 1949 celebrations, and one week following the homage in Montevideo, he lectured at the Argentine Writers Society. After its president, the philosopher Carlos Alberto Erro, gave a brief overview, Bock spoke about Goethe's concept of the fatherland: "das nach ihm dort liege, wo man wirke und nützlich sei" (that according to him was located where one was influential and useful). Imagining Goethe in a nation of immigrants such as Argentina, Bock's vision resonated with the illustrious audience, which included many of the most renowned names in Argentine intellectual life. In attendance were the essayist and cultural critic for *La Nación*, Eduardo Mallea; the vehement anti-Peronist biographer, poet, and professor of literature at the National University of La Plata, Ezequiel Martínez Estrada; the journalist and literary critic known especially for his work with the antifascist newspaper *Argentina Libre*, Luis Emilio Soto; the anti-Peronist Spanish philosopher, Francisco Romero; and finally, the famous author, Jorge Luis Borges, who was also a passionate anti-Peronist and would succeed Erro as president of the Argentine Writers Society the next year.[17] Beyond their intellectual prestige, these individuals were united by their mistrust of nationalism, abhorrence of authoritarianism, and steadfast affirmation of humanist convictions in their professional activities. Notably, Bock (from Germany to Argentina), Mallea (to France), Martínez Estrada (to Cuba and Mexico), Romero (from Spain to Argentina), Borges (to Switzerland and Spain) all had past or future trajectories of migration. Their collective admission into the newly founded South American Goethe Academy, whose president was Werner Bock, represented an intellectual and political commitment to Goethe's intercultural legacy.

The Goethe Academy ran a varied series of radio programs in Buenos Aires and collaborated with the immigrant Hermann Gebhardt's antifascist, *La voz del día*, broadcast from Uruguay since 1938. Albert Theile, cofounder (with Udo Rukser) and editor of the exilic magazine *Deutsche Blätter* in Chile from 1943 to 1946, curated a book exhibit on Goethe at the Casa del Escritor (House of the Writer) in Buenos Aires. The newly admitted members to the academy, Romero, Martínez Estrada, and Borges held a symposium at the Argentine PEN-Club in the Colegio de Estudios Superiores (College of Advanced Studies). Finally, Juan Pablo Keins, a Berlin-born translator and antiquarian bookseller who had emigrated from Madrid in 1937, organized an exhibit of Goethe-themed manuscripts and artifacts in the Witcomb Gallery.[18] The Goethe Academy also held events to celebrate its inaugural year in Montevideo, Santiago de Chile, and its seat in Sao Paulo.

Having hoped futilely for a Goethean solution to the world's maladies in the 1932 Goethe Year, Argentine scholarship in 1949 testified to the tumultuous intervening seventeen years.[19] The biographer Antonio Herrero instrumentalized Goethe's internationalism to buttress Peronism in a two-part contribution for the state-sponsored literary magazine, *Cultura*, with his essay, "Goethe como símbolo posible de la argentinidad" (Goethe as a possible symbol of Argentineness). According to Herrero, Goethe's unlimited idealism, infinite curiosity, and creative potency rendered him an archetype of humanity that, sadly, Europe was now neglecting.[20] Steeped in Catholic dogma, Herrero cited the current irrefutable fact of European moral bankruptcy, as well as the fact that this attitude of supreme resignation had transferred the torch of culture so imperiled on Goethe's continent to "nuestra" (our) Argentina: "nada, pues, más apropiado y requerido que utilizar la oportunidad de este centenario . . . para proyectar un breve resumen de los valores goethianos con la índole Argentina" (Nothing, therefore, more appropriate and required than to use the opportunity of this centenary . . . to project a brief summary of Goethean values with the Argentine character).[21] Argentina, thanks to its vivacious diversity, could recover and confirm Goethe's vision for mankind. Herrero found the literary representation of Argentina in *Faust*, because just as Goethe's protagonist had opened fertile ground for human habitation, Argentina, too, offered new territory for millions of men to live freely, work, and thrive. While there was no figure in Argentine history equivalent to Goethe, a composite could be formed from the independence fighter, José de San Martín, and the political theorist and diplomat, Juan Bautista Alberdi. Herrero also proposed as further Goethean halves the literary characters Martín Fierro and Don Segundo Sombra.[22] The former is the brave, uncouth, violent, musically gifted gaucho protagonist of José Hernández's epic poem, *Martín Fierro* (1872), Argentina's national poem; the latter is the eponymous personage in Ricardo Güiraldes's novel, who is also a gaucho, but functions as a reflection on the ethical implications and impact of Gaucho lore on Argentine history. Taken as complementary—one embodying vitality and passion, and the other ethics and knowledge—these pairs of famous Argentines expressed the full range of Goethean virtues. According to Herrero, there was an infinite list of possible duos in Argentina, a country with an expectant curiosity, insatiably open spirituality, and tireless vitality could be defined as a "pueblo goethiano" (Goethean people).[23]

The parallels between Herrero's essay and the internationalism of other tributes, such as Werner Bock and Guillermo Thiele's speeches at the Argentine Writers Society and the Teatro Colón, respectively, is deceptive. Bock and Thiele perceived in Goethe an exemplary, inspirational model for Latin American art and society. Herrero twisted this analysis to suit a fundamentally nationalist agenda; for him, Goethe did not inspire Argentine virtues but rather manifested them. He represented a set of ideals that Europe had abandoned and Argentina had already achieved. Goethe was a foil to gloss Argentina's luster, not a dream awaiting fulfillment. Herrero's output suggests opportunism; he hailed President Hipólito Yrigoyen as a master of democracy in 1927, and then advocated for Argentine spiritual imperialism during the military dictatorship of the 1930s.[24] His essay on Goethe in *Cultura*, a publication funded by Argentina's Ministry of Education and thus beholden to the national government, brandishes tropes of Argentine chauvinism, including Alberdi's maxim "gobernar es poblar" (to govern is to populate), gaucho folklore, Catholic dogma, revolutionary icons, even—at least under Peronism—the exaltation of the working class.[25] Herrero conscripted Goethe to propagandize for Peronist Argentina.

Numerous academics contradicted Herrero's thesis and approach, including the Spanish linguist and historian, Antonio Tovar. Tovar, at the time affiliated with the University of Buenos Aires and the University of Salamanca, had served as undersecretary of Media and Propaganda from 1938 to 1941 in Francoist Spain and participated in diplomatic missions to Nazi Germany. Later, he became disillusioned with Francoism and supported student protests as a faculty member at the University of Madrid in 1965. In 1981, Tovar won the Goethe Prize for his support of freedom in academic research and instruction. In a volume published by the University of Cuyo, Tovar argued that Goethe's relevance and lesson to the postwar world was to have understood that the path to erudition was synonymous with humility. Only by grasping his limitations and learning from other examples, such as English and classical models, could Goethe achieve his greatest accomplishments. Therefore, it was backward to arrogate Goethe to contemporary modes of thought and political agendas.[26]

In his conclusions, Tovar evoked the German author, Hans Carossa. An updated version of his speech to the Goethe Society in Weimar in 1938, Carossa'a essay, "La Significación de Goethe para la Actualidad" (Goethe's Significance for the Present), appeared in the *Estudios Germanicos* publication of the University of Buenos Aires. Carossa, who chose inner emigration after 1933 and walked a moral tightrope throughout the Nazi period, had brazenly criticized the Nazi regime's exploitation of Goethe for political motives. He advanced this view in 1949, arguing that any endeavor to politicize Goethe exposed a fundamental misunderstanding and disrespectful instrumentalization of his work.[27] Likewise in his "Goethe frente a Shakespeare" (Goethe versus Shakespeare), Juan C. Probst affirmed Carossa in his view that the Bard and Goethe were united by a timelessness that political movements consistently attempted to exploit for their own aims, thus debasing the work and revealing their own philosophical poverty and incoherence.[28]

The Mendozan professor of German, Alfredo Dornheim, bolstered this view by inveighing against the compartmentalization and mobilization of the German poet for individualist and materialist objectives, which he described as "deliberadamente antigoetheana" (deliberately anti-Goethean).[29] Still, the homages in 1949 had to transcend the past and influence the "forma y el contenido spiritual de nuestra cultura" (spiritual form and content of our culture).[30] For Dornheim, Goethe represented affirmation of the world and of life, reconciliation of contrasts, and liberation of the spirit based on love and beauty. In a deranged and tormented world, Dornheim continued, the objective of the Mendozan commemorations was to affirm solidarity with Goethe's ideals and activate them to achieve a better future.

Kantian scholar and professor at the University of Buenos Aires Federico Korell advanced this thinking with his theories on contemporizing Goethe. A consequence of current civilization, Korell asserted, is that pseudoscholars seize upon artistic creations as delimited objects to suit a preconceived agenda, placing them at the service of lies, hate, and infamy. This perverts Goethean virtues, inverting the relationship between inspiration and instrumentalization, value and utility, liberty and bondage. Explicitly contravening Herrero, and also to an extent Berenguer, Korell specified: "estamos en presencia de este abuso toda vez que se supedita lo poético a lo político . . ., sean los fines perseguidos positivos o negativos, bien o mal intencionados" (we are in the presence of this abuse whenever a poet is subordinated to the political purposes . . ., be the ends pursued positive or negative, well or ill-intentioned).[31] The pernicious effect is that the personality or the work is attributed a valuation alien to its nature—art becomes a secondary instance that is "para" (for) something, it becomes an instrument.[32] Korell warned that homages to Goethe risked instrumentalization in place of inspiration. The more an artwork is detached from utilitarian considerations, the better it will serve humanity. His urgent advice was to read the poet with one's soul in a state of "tabula rasa," almost as infants, so that each person could "vivir" (live) the poet in their own, true way.[33] Korell's thesis was in good faith but, in the wake of global catastrophe, his conclusion represents a contrivance. Korell fantasized a willful amnesia by admonishing readers to purge their minds of what could never be forgotten.

A final, distinct contribution for the 1949 Goethe Year was the Spanish Civil War refugee Guillermo de Torre's essay, "*Clavijo* o los límites olvidados" (*Clavigo*, or the Forgotten imits), in *Atenea*, an academic journal published by the Chilean University of Concepción. The cultural critic, poet, and future chair of the Department of Literature at the University of Buenos Aires, Guillermo de Torre adhered to the model of *Werkinterpretation*, a text-centered approach later exemplified by Emil Staiger's three-volume study, *Goethe* (1952–59). Focusing on his tragedy, *Clavigo* (1774), de Torre analyzed Goethe with rigor and, to a degree, censure. A youthful diversion, Goethe wrote *Clavigo* in eight days, taking creative liberty to retell the encounter between the Spanish journalist and man of the theater, José Clavijo y Fajardo,

and Pierre-Augustin Caron de Beaumarchais, who coincided at the court of
Carlos III in 1764. According to his memoirs, the Parisian courtier, playwright,
and spy Beaumarchais had traveled to Spain to convince his friend, Clavijo
to keep his promise to marry his sister, Louise Claron. He was unsuccessful,
returned to Paris shortly thereafter, and lived for many more eventful years
before dying there in 1799. In Goethe's narration, however, Beaumarchais
manipulates Clavigo into promising to marry his sister, blackmails him when
he demurs, and ultimately murders Clavigo in a duel. Beaumarchais's sister
dies from grief when Clavigo reneges on his word, uttering his name with
her last words as her brother absconds.

Aghast at Goethe's treatment, de Torre charged that the drama brings
together all the most nonsensical elements of degenerate post-Romanticism
although it was written in the pre-Romantic era. All the tropes are there: the
struggle between love and ambition, magnification of a minuscule point of
honor, alleged morality, simultaneous death of lovers, and hyperbolic, con-
trived language and modes of literary expression. In fact, De Torre charged,
*Clavigo* does not even serve for a chapter on Goethe and Spain because
there is not the slightest effort to characterize Spanish culture—Goethe's
misspelling of Clavijo divulges his negligence. In the 1949 Goethe Year, de
Torre's examination of *Clavigo* exposed the forgotten or sometimes deliberately overlooked limitations and flaws of a poetic idol.

The drama's lone value, de Torre declared, was that it demonstrated how,
in 1774, Goethe was cultivating the skills he would refine in Weimar classicism. A genuine Romantic aspired to absolute originality, but Goethe showed
little regard for this attribute in *Clavigo*. His approach was closer to classicism
which, according to de Torre, draws from any model where it finds inspiration. This was typical of Goethe's works, which borrowed from Richardson's
*Pamela*, the Faust legends, and Shakespeare's *Hamlet* and *Macbeth*. To his
credit, Goethe freely admitted such practices and did not criticize others for
borrowing from him, even congratulating Walter Scott for effectively reworking a scene from *Egmont*. In de Torre's eyes, Goethe's greatest accomplishment was that through his openness and humility, he showed the way toward
a vibrant and mutually beneficial interchange among cultures. De Torre welcomed this enthusiastically: "Que la corriente de transferencias e influjos de
espíritu a espíritu sea más intensa cuanto mayor riqueza posean éstos, es una
realidad tan cierta como poco reconocida" (That the flow of transfers and
influences from spirit to spirit intensifies according to the wealth they possess is a reality as certain as little recognized). Goethe comprehended both
his role as a hub for ideas and his propensity for gathering impulses and fash-
ioning them into his own creations. In the poet's own words, his oeuvre was
"la de un ser colectivo que lleva el nombre de Goethe" (that of a collective
being carrying the name of Goethe).[34] In de Torre's estimation Goethe was
a pathbreaker not only for the concept of world literature but also, perhaps
even more importantly, for its application.

The varied contributors to Argentine commemorations of the 1949
Goethe Year display a tension between instrumentalization and inspira-
tion. Whereas especially Herrero and, to a lesser extent, Berenguer, recast
Goethe to suit the environment and exigencies of Peronist Argentina, most

participants in the Goethe Year activities rejected this tendency. Repulsed by egoism, exclusion, jingoism, and expediency, their diversity coalesced around the mantras of humility, inclusion, interculturalism, and sincerity. Notably, they avoided condemning Nazism specifically, pointing instead toward broad deficiencies in politicized interpretations of Goethe. Disillusioned by the recent past, Argentine and immigrant artists and scholars remained resilient. They still found inspiration in Goethe to chart a hopeful, proactive course toward a promising future in what they perceived to be the poet's own image.

## Vying for an Icon: Goethe in German Buenos Aires, 1933–1945

More than any other country in Latin America at the time, Argentina had thriving, diverse, and conflictive populations of German-speaking nationalists, antifascists, and Jews. Argentina had remained neutral in World War II until late 1944 and, in consequence, factional German-speaking nationalist, Zionist, and antifascist schools, media, and cultural institutions had existed for nearly the entirety of Hitler's reign. Nationalist German propagandists conscripted Goethe into their glorification of National Socialism. The Goethe bookstore sold posters of the European war theater and tapestries with Hitler's maxims.[35] One teacher in the Goethe School taught from Hans Grimm's *Volk ohne Raum* (People without Space, 1926),[36] other instructors were fired for inadequate loyalty to Hitler,[37] and multiple schools received funding from Nazi Germany and celebrated Hitler's birthday as a holiday.[38] The Goethe bookstore and the Goethe School publicly conscripted Goethe into the National Socialist propaganda campaign.

Funded by Joseph Goebbels's Ministry of Propaganda, director Ludwig Ney's Deutsches Theater played for the nationalist colony, including Goethe's *Faust* and *Götz von Berlichingen*. The nationalist press ratified Goethe's dramatic works as cultural birthrights shared by all Germans, maintaining that mutual bloodlines bequeathed ownership of the work to them.[39] The *Deutsche in Argentinien*, the media arm of the German Labor Front in Argentina, argued that the eternal German spirit inspired Goethe to articulate inchoate ethnic impulses toward National Socialism in *Götz*. During the siege of the Jagsthausen castle, for example, the Knight of Iron Hand expressed a growing intuition of Germanic strength.[40] Goethe foreshadowed a National Socialist community, which was racially exclusive but admitted all adherents of Hitlerism into its ranks. In German Buenos Aires, this exclusion found expression in racial antisemitism and xenophobia. Celebrating *Götz* as an exemplary German, the *Deutsche La Plata Zeitung* lauded the knight's hatred of foreign influence, vilifying Metzler and Link as democratic-Jewish agitators driven by sadism, lust for power, and greed.[41] Ludwig Ney himself asserted that Götz's reverence for the Kaiser reflected the poet's intuitive, Teutonic longing for an authoritarian state.[42] The premiere of *Götz*, attended by 1,450 spectators, substantiated Goethe's resonance among the nationalist colony.[43] German nationalists in Argentina excluded all other interpretations of Goethe's works to secure their links to a National Socialist worldview; any perspective not attuned to Nazism only masked Goethe from true understanding. Goethe was the exclusive domain of the nationalist colony, favored by race, nationhood, and allegiance to Hitler.

Meanwhile, just blocks away, the antifascist Freie Deutsche Bühne also performed German drama. Composed of thespian refugees, during its first two seasons the theater staged playwrights of twelve nationalities, almost of whom were banned in Nazi Germany. Within four months, its performances had been reviewed by local media in seven languages.[44] In contrast to the exclusionary mission of the Deutsches Theater, the antifascist ensemble committed to inclusion and interculturalism. Although its humanist program aligned with multiple Goethean dramas, the Freie Deutsche Bühne did not perform him until 1949. After Schiller's *Maria Stuart* flopped in 1940, the ensemble eschewed the German classics.[45] The largely Jewish antifascist colony rejected dramatists staged in Nazi Germany, and the troupe's precarious finances precluded presentations of Goethe until the 1949 bicentenary.

Nonetheless, antifascists deployed Goethe to fight Nazism. Marketing materials for the Freie Deutsche Bühne featured his programmatic statement, "Das Theater bleibt immer eine der wesentlichsten Angelegenheiten" (theater always remains one of the most essential matters).[46] At commencement ceremonies for the Pestalozzi School, created in 1934 to resist the Nazification of German schools in Buenos Aires, founder Ernesto Alemann read verses from "Allen," excerpted from Goethe's musical comedy, *Lila* (1777).[47] The antitotalitarian *Argentinisches Tageblatt*, too, leveraged Goethe against German nationalists, arguing, for example, that coordinated schools were responsible for legislation prohibiting untranslated foreign language materials translation. The new laws impacted instruction in all schools; however, the *Tageblatt* ran the headline, "Shakespeare, Dante, Goethe, Voltaire verboten," to add emotional indignation to the pronouncement.[48]

## Above the Fray? The 1949 Goethe Year in German Buenos Aires

Many of the same individuals who sowed the bitter conflicts during National Socialism took on leading roles in the commemorations of the 1949 Goethe Year. Several nationalist institutions persevered in the postwar period while new rightwing actors emerged, including the magazine, *Der Weg*. Founded in 1947 by the Hitler Youth leader and Nazi pedagogue Eberhard Fritsch, *Der Weg* was banned in Germany and Austria in 1949, but the Dürer Press published the magazine in Argentina until it folded in 1957. No newspaper or magazine execrated the occupational powers, distorted and reversed the charges of war crimes, denounced the restoration of democracy and citizens' rights, and exalted National Socialist leaders so blatantly and forcefully.[49] Among its staff and contributors were such notorious individuals as Reinhard Kopps, Johann Leers, Mathilde Ludendorff, Hans Grimm, and Hans-Ulrich Rudel. Worldwide, *Der Weg* was among the most unapologetically fascist publications in the postwar period.

Known for its political content, *Der Weg* was initially mainly an arch-conservative monthly cultural magazine. Its coverage of the 1949 Goethe Year was the most robust among all media sources based in Argentina. The August issue was devoted to Goethe, and he figured in most other months, too. Considering the magazine's deserved reputation for unabashed Nazism, the balance of its August issue is astonishing. No exiles ever appeared in its pages, but the homage to Goethe featured the aforementioned Hans Carossa, an ambivalent but frequently critical voice during Hitler's regime; the classical archeologist Ludwig Curtius, who the Nazis stripped of his professorship at the University of Heidelberg in 1938; Wilhelm Flitner, a Germanist whose seminars became meeting points for the Hamburg White Rose resistance group; and the respected philologist, Richard Benz, who had lectured under the auspices of the Propaganda Ministry, but also received the West German Order of Merit in 1952 and honorary citizenship of the city of Heidelberg two years later. Utterly anomalous for *Der Weg*, these figures suited the anti-fascist *Argentinisches Tageblatt* more than Fritsch's magazine. There were also incorrigibles, including the novelist and cultural critic, Will Vesper, and the Austrian-German author Guido Kolbenheyer, whose steadfast propagandistic output earned him a place with Carossa on Hitler's Important Artist Exempt List. Nonetheless, *Der Weg*'s eulogy was characterized by balance. Distinguishing his magazine from earlier nationalist media, Fritsch emphasized that *Der Weg* would neither worship Goethe as a deity nor make him out to be "einen rechthaberischen Propheten" (dogmatic prophet). He added that although Goethe was quintessentially German, his genius was equally founded on "weltweiter Kultur" (worldwide culture). Fritsch's introduction was laced with Nazi ideological binaries, such as "die egozentrische Überwertung des Materialismus" (egocentric overvaluation of materialism) versus "werteschaffenden Idealismus" (value-creating idealism) or "gegen die geistesstumpfende Vermassung die Achtung vor der eigengearteten Persönlichkeit" (respect for the singular personality against the stupefying dimensioning) and, aesthetically, "die Schönheit der edlen Gestaltungsform" (beauty of noble form of creation) over the "den Wahn von Halt- und Formlosigkeit" (the delusion of instability and formlessness). Despite this outburst, in general, the ensuing articles showed restraint. Thus, Fritsch concluded, readers should avoid skimming the issue hurriedly. Instead, they should take time to contemplate its meaning in moments of calm and harmony.[50]

Many readers likely were quite surprised by what awaited them. Hans Carossa narrated the execution of jurist and secret KPD member Arvid Harnack, who requested that the jail priest read from the "Prolog im Himmel" ("Prologue in Heaven") in *Faust* to give him courage before the Nazis murdered him. Ludwig Curtius lamented conditions in Germany, citing Goethe's rueful diary entry from 1817 that, "Friede selbst keinen friedlichen Charakter annimmt" (peace itself lacks the character of peace).[51] Then, recurring to the poet's correspondence with Schiller, he discovered edification: "Ein Jahrhundert kann man nicht verändern, aber man kann sich dagegen stellen und glückliche Wirkungen vorbereiten" (it is impossible to alter a century, but one can oppose it and prepare felicitous effects).[52] Notably, Curtius's conclusion dovetailed with the Argentine scholar Alfredo Dornheim, who also saw in Goethe a path out of the current global malaise. Wilhelm Flitner drew inspiration from Goethe's enhancement of autochthonous "Volkstümlichkeit" (folklore) with internationalism, a universal epiphany initiated when foreign literature is translated into a nation's mother tongue. The resulting insights catalyzed a new national literature distinguished by a "freien, weit umherblickenden Humanität" (free, far-sighted humanity).[53] Here again, the contents of *Der Weg* overlapped with its Latinx counterparts. Guillermo de Torre had identified Goethe as a germinal model for an internationalist approach to literary studies. In Victoria Ocampo's esteemed journal, *Sur*, the Frenchman and recent Nobel Prize winner, Andre Gide, concurred. Gide explained that foreign writers, such as Goethe, were inestimably enriching because they compelled authors to expand their cross-cultural awareness.[54] Even the Nazi novelist Guido Kolbenheyer, poised Goethe's "volksbewusste" (nationally conscious) output with internationale Geistigkeit" (international spirituality) as foundational for the future German nation.[55] For all their differences, Gide, de Torre, Flitner, and Kolbenheyer each deemed Goethe a seminal impulse for an intercultural turn in twentieth-century humanism. Finally, Will Vesper's short story about an aging Goethe, too, posited Goethe's timeless capacity for love as the guiding impulse for mankind. Startlingly, the August 1949 issue of *Der Weg* broadly coincided with Hispanic authors about Goethe's internationalism, humanism and—they hoped—formative significance for the future. Furthermore, its homage was characterized by restraint. There were neither diatribes against the occupation nor panegyrics to Nazi henchmen nor even xenophobic and antisemitic race baiting. In this special edition of Eberhard Fritsch's fascist megaphone, Goethe was above the fray.

*Der Weg* was a stridently pro-Nazi publication and articles commemorating Goethe in other months corresponded to this ideology. Contributors included Hans Grimm, author of the foundational German expansionist text *Volk ohne Raum* and the Silesian Germanist, Herbert Cysarz, a Nazi collaborator and fervent participant in the Sudeten German Volkskampf. Cysarz and Grimm exploited Goethe to rage against the Allied occupation. In one representative passage, Grimm seethed that Germans possessed neither freedom of speech nor the ability to travel and could not even choose what newspapers and magazines they wanted to read. Worse still: "es darf von fremder Meinungsmache und Propaganda . . . uns als Volk nicht nur als Sündenbock der Geschichte erscheinen zu lassen, sondern als schmutzig vor aller Welt und vor uns selbst" (Foreign opinion-making and propaganda . . . are permitted to make us as a people appear not only as the scapegoat of history, but as foul to the whole world and to ourselves).[56] Cysarz's tellingly entitled article, "Goethe und der Selbstmord des abendländischen Geistes" (Goethe and the Suicide of the European Spirit), adopted a similar tone and perspective.[57] Another contributor was Hans Naumann, a speaker at the 1933 book burnings and enthusiastic participant in the humanities war effort. His essay in *Der Weg* was an ethnocentric examination of the Germanic origins of Goethean poetry, but without overt references to National Socialism.[58]

*Der Weg*'s August tribute to Goethe demonstrated a nuanced position in which internationalism and humanism were predominant; however, its release just after the magazine had been prohibited in Germany urges suspicion. Fritsch was working to overturn the ban at the time, which may explain the diplomacy of the August issue.[59] Contributions in other months by Grimm, Cysarz, and to a lesser extent, Naumann, confirmed the magazine's hardline position. Moreover, the essays in *Der Weg* were written exclusively by Europeans. Although it was not hostile to the host country, *Der Weg* never saw itself as an Argentine or even a German-Argentine publication, and the authors in its pages verified this identity. Rather than an immigrant magazine, *Der Weg* aimed to be a Nazi organ for Germans everywhere. After Perón's downfall in 1955, various antifascist, Jewish, and governmental groups campaigned against *Der Weg*. Increasingly isolated, it lost many advertisers and folded in 1957. *Der Weg* may have survived had it heeded the appeals for internationalism and humanism that characterized its own commemorations of Goethe in August 1949. Instead, its demise underscores the imperative of cross-cultural alliances to overcome the multifold challenges of exile and emigration.

Another new player in the media landscape of German Buenos Aires was the *Freie Presse*. Established in December 1945, it employed mostly the same staff as the Nazified *Deutsche La Plata Zeitung*, and its founder, Frederico Müller, likely was a proxy for Hermann Tjarks, who had owned the *La Plata Zeitung*.[60] The *Freie Presse* not only inherited its predecessor's public but, like the antifascist *Argentinisches Tageblatt* in the 1930s, also garnered new readers and writers by targeting recent German immigrants to Argentina. Its circulation rose steadily, reaching 30,000 in the 1950s, the highest of any German-language newspaper printed outside of Europe.[61] The *Freie Presse* saw itself as a conservative, patriotic outlet targeting an immigrant readership in Argentina. Politically, it flattered the Peronist regime and became vehemently anticommunist to curry favor with Bonn after the West German embassy opened in 1952. While the paper eventually distanced itself from fascist publications like *Der Weg*, it feuded bitterly with the *Argentinisches Tageblatt*, whose antifascism and anti-Peronism were often irreconcilable with its own platform.[62] During the 1949 Goethe Year, the *Freie Presse* was a young, rapidly growing paper negotiating a complex and shifting external environment.

The *Freie Presse* launched its coverage of the Goethe Year with a preview for an upcoming celebratory performance of *Iphigenie* by Ludwig Ney's Neue Bühne, successor to the Deutsches Theater. Indicating Ney's ongoing alliances with fascist organizations, tickets for the performance were available at the Dürer publishing offices and the Goethe bookstore. Both *Der Weg* and the *Freie Presse* previewed the event,[63] but the *Argentinisches Tageblatt* did not and in fact refused to report on Ney's stage until 1956.[64] *Der Weg*'s coverage attacked the antifascist, Jewish, "wurzellos" (rootless), and "zufällig" (coincidental) audience and ensemble of the Freie Deutsche Bühne, comparing them unfavorably with the true theater community drawn to the Neue Bühne.[65] The *Freie Presse*, by contrast, focused on *Iphigenie*, emphasizing that the drama would be an enlightening experience "für jeden aufgeschlossenen Menschen" (for every open-minded person) and was "gerade in unserer heutigen Zeit besonders geeignet" (especially appropriate for our current time).[66] The *Freie Presse* differentiated itself from *Der Weg* (and the *La Plata Zeitung*) by foregrounding inclusion and even intimating reconciliation.

Its review of the performance buttressed this position by praising Goethe's "entsühnende, Liebe und Frieden verschenkende Werk" (expiatory, love and peace-giving work). Without confronting the antifascist and Jewish German-speaking populations, the *Freie Presse* subtly defined its allegiance. Its critic excluded Jews by defining *Iphigenie* as "bewusst abendländisch und christlich geweiht" (consciously consecrated as occidental and Christian). Likewise, the timeless protagonist, who symbolizes love, reconciliation, and peace, was "christlich in ihren Gedankengängen" (Christian in her line of thought). Echoing conservative drama theory from Nazi Germany, the *Freie Presse* emphasized the spoken dramatic word in the sold-out presentation with remarks such as "atemversetzende Versprache" (breathtaking verse), "sprachlich vollendet modulierten Grundton" (linguistically perfectly modulated tone), "Rhythmik des Sprachlichen" (linguistic rhythm), "sprachlich höchst kultivierte Leistung" (highly cultivated linguistic accomplishment), "hohe sprachliche Kultur" (high linguistic culture)—all in a single review.[67] Citing Nazi poet laureate Hanns Johst and the Germanist Julius Petersen, theater scholar Gaetano Biccari has described the primacy of the spoken word as a hallmark of theater under Nazism.[68] Reviewers and theatergoers alike ratified Ney's approach—the presentation in the 900-seat Teatro Smart was sold out, and his troupe played *Iphigenie* on tour in Chile that spring.[69] For the *Freie Presse*, the sanctity of the word continued unabated into the postwar period. Moreover, its insistent affirmations of a Christian-European worldview undercut the paper's overtures of inclusion and reconciliation.

Despite instances of ambivalence, the *Freie Presse* did promote integration and interculturalism. It reported on various events held by Argentine organizations in Goethe's honor, including praise for the performance at the Teatro Colón featuring several Jewish musicians.[70] It also confirmed that Ruben Pesce's sketches at the Florencio Sanchez Theater illustrated the transnational pollination that Goethe, "der Weltbürger (nicht Kosmopolit) Zeit seines Lebens vertrat" (the global citizen [not cosmopolitan] represented throughout his life).[71] Semantic grumblings notwithstanding, the *Freie Presse* surpassed the rigid insularity of *Der Weg* and its predecessors from the Nazi period.

The paper also ran a piece, "Goethe in Buenos Aires," by Juan Probst, a professor of German at the University of Buenos Aires and pioneer for the field in Latin America. Born to Argentine diplomats in Hamburg, Probst investigated Goethe's impact on Argentine authors. One example is Estanislao del Campo, author of *Fausto. Impresiones del gaucho Anastasio el Pollo en la representación de esta ópera* (Faust: Impressions of the Gaucho Anastasio the Chicken in the Representation of the Opera, 1866). A touchstone in Argentine literature, del Campo's narrative in verse sometimes is referred to as the Creole Faust after Luis Saslavsky's cinematic adaptation *El Fausto criollo* (The Creole Faust, 1979). *Fausto* chronicles two gauchos' accidental visit to Charles Gounod's opera *Faust* (1859) at the Teatro Colón. Initially, its relevance to Goethe's work seems only superficial; however, the Faustian material is a foil for the salient theme of the 1,278-verse poem—to mock the gauchos' ignorance. It also discloses the long history of Goethe's *Faust* as a layered reference point for refinement and cosmopolitanism among Argentina's upper classes. Del Campo's adaptation is a commentary on *porteño* worldliness, rural unsophistication, and the cultural gulf between them that continues shape Argentine society even today.

Probst himself explored the Romantic poet, novelist, and political activist Estebán Echeverría's engagement with Goethe.[72] A prominent proponent of Latin American Romanticism, when Echeverría first read Goethe as a student in Paris he exclaimed:"Wenn ich doch die deutsche Sprache beherrschte, um so viel Schönheit besser genießen zu können!" (If only I knew the German language to be able to better enjoy so much beauty!). Echeverría later drafted a political, satirical drama entitled *Mefistófeles* (1833). In this fragment, a demon visits the poet while he is translating not the New Testament, but the Prolog to *Faust*. Although Mephisto belittles the poet's undertakings, Echeverría's labor to disseminate *Faust* to the Spanish-speaking world put into action the theory of literary sociologist Wiebke Sievers that even famous authors are unlikely to receive full recognition for their artistic merits unless they are published in a nation's mother tongue.[73] In his own output, too, Echeverría's work bears traces of Goethe. His *Cartas a un amigo* (Letters to a Friend, 1835) clearly draws from *Die Leiden des jungen Werthers* (*The Sorrows of Young Werther*). Beyond their formal similarity as epistolary novellas, Echeverría's nameless protagonist reads James Macpherson's cycle of epic poems, *Ossian* (1760), as deeply emotional reactions to nature and nearly commits suicide during a trip through the Pampas. Unlike Werther, his mother persuades him against it by convincing him that the woman he loves, Luisa, will bring him happiness. He had met Luisa at a ball, recalling Werther's first encounter with the alliterative Lotte. The plot, personages, and Romantic themes present in Werther also pervade the *Cartas*.

Echeverría's interest in Goethe, Jean Paul, Schiller, and Friedrich and August Wilhelm Schlegel also led him to establish a literary salon at a bookstore in Buenos Aires, which was frequented by German employees of the nearby Bunge firm.[74] According to Probst, some of them procured translations of German authors for the group, thus sustaining a circum-Atlantic literary exchange beyond Echeverría's own travels. Akin to its European contemporaries, the salon evolved into a political group dedicated to restoring humanist ideals in the national government. This was a dangerous agenda during Juan Manuel de Rosas's totalitarian regime, which soon banned the salon. Foreshadowing many German speakers' routes to Buenos Aires a century later, Echeverría's opposition to a dictatorship forced him into Uruguayan exile in 1840. Although the *Freie Presse* did not break with its nationalist past, the 1949 Goethe Year reveals that the newspaper had evolved from its predecessor's fascist dogma and was not in the same category as *Der Weg*. The *Freie Presse* foregrounded Argentine commemorations of Goethe and highlighted his presence in Argentine literature. By tending bridges to Argentine cultural history, the *Freie Presse* opened pathways for its readership to engage and perhaps to integrate with the host society.

When Wilfred von Oven, formerly press adjutant to Joseph Goebbels, became the editor in chief of the *Freie Presse* in 1952, he defined the paper as a National Socialist publication.[75] In the preceding paragraphs, I have debunked this claim as an exaggeration, but the paper's refusal to address Nazi crimes including the Shoah and its placement of former Nazis like von Oven in leadership positions betray lingering nationalist inclinations.[76] Unsurprisingly, conflicts frequently arose between the *Freie Presse* and the antifascist *Argentinisches Tageblatt*; however, during the 1949 Goethe Year the two newspapers found a measure of common ground. While the *Tageblatt* still refused to cover the nationalist Neue Bühne even for performances such as *Iphigenie*, the *Freie Presse* developed an unlikely collaboration with the antifascist, predominantly Jewish Freie Deutsche Bühne. From the *Freie Presse*'s inception in 1945, it reported on the exilic theater.[77] Founder and director Paul Walter Jacob also advertised regularly in the *Freie Presse*, which he perceived as a conduit to new spectators and healthier finances. Admired internationally for its accomplishments as the world's only regularly performing exilic theater during World War II, after the conflict Jacob hoped the Freie Deutsche Bühne could become the theater of all German speakers in Buenos Aires.[78]

To this end, the stage featured guest performances by some of the most famous names in German theater, including Ernst Deutsch (1946), Ellen Schwanneke (1946), Hans Moser (1948), and Viktor de Kowa (1949), lead actor and director of the Berlin Tribune Theater. De Kowa's visit coincided with Freie Deutsche Bühne's performance on August 28, "Der unbekannte Goethe" (The Unknown Goethe), featuring the one-act play, *Die Geschwister* (*Brother and Sister*, 1776), *Was wir bringen* (*What We Bring*, 1802), and the fragment, *Pandora* (1810). The *Freie Presse* and the *Tageblatt* both had lukewarm reviews for the performances, agreeing that the actors were challenged by Goethean prose. The *Tageblatt*'s comment on the "oft schwierige Diktion der Goetheschen Sprache" (often difficult diction of Goethean language) was corroborated by the *Freie Presse*: "Goetheprosa ist nicht leicht zu sprechen" (Goethean prose is not easy to speak). In resemblant wording, each newspaper commended de Kowa's introductory speech, which the *Freie Presse* described as a "Friedensbotschaft an die Menschen" (message of peace to the people) and the *Tageblatt* an "Appell an die Menschlichkeit" (appeal to humanity).[79] Unfortunately, noting the "kaum zur Hälfte besetzte Saal" (hardly half-filled auditorium), the *Freie Presse* lamented that more people had not heard de Kowa's words. Such poor attendance indicated the unhealed rifts in German Buenos Aires. This explains the unconventional repertoire for the presentation, an unsuccessful tactic to avoid works stigmatized by Nazi propaganda. While the nationalist population still abstained from visiting the Freie Deutsch Bühne, the mostly Jewish antifascist colony repudiated canonical German dramatists, including Goethe. Furthermore, de Kowa was a problematic figure. Unlike guests such as Deutsch and Schwanneke, de Kowa had not emigrated from Nazi Germany. Instead, he had featured in thirty-five films from 1933 to 1945 and was named to the Important Artist Exempt List to shield him from military service. Despite de Kowa's public repentance, many theatergoers were not ready for reconciliation even with Goethe, let alone an actor irredeemably tarnished for making a career under Hitler.

Likely anticipating controversy—a visit by the Viennese comic Hans Moser had provoked similar strife in 1948—Paul Walter Jacob had attempted to preempt the polemics in the Freie Deutsch Bühne's theater almanac previewing the Goethe Year.[80] In one chapter, "Goethe als Theaterleiter" (Goethe as Theater Manager), the director and theater scholar Carl Hagemann explained that the labor and costs of producing and attending dramatic performances rendered the theater at once an artistic proving ground, a cultural institute, and a business enterprise. Thus, a successful theater must reflect the artistic and cultural life of the individual city or country where it performs. Despite these layered challenges, there has existed an ideal theater director, who balanced artistic, business, and representative responsibilities—Goethe.[81] Paul Walter Jacob strove to meet these obligations in the polarized environment of postwar German Buenos Aires, and his selection of Hagemann's essay implies that he looked to Goethe for guidance in the endeavor. This was a mistake, because in Jacob's situation Goethe's tactics were doomed. By mirroring the cultural life of Buenos Aires, the Freie Deutsche Bühne also—inevitably—delineated its divisions. The lackluster attendance at "Der unbekannte Goethe" added to mounting evidence that 1949 was too soon for the rapprochement that Jacob and Viktor de Kowa wished to attain.

The *Tageblatt* itself showed nuance on the issue of guilt for artists under the swastika. Although it refused to report on Ludwig Ney until 1956, already in 1949, it found sympathy for Gustaf Gründgens. In an interview with the paper after a presentation of Goethe's *Tasso* in Düsseldorf, Gründgens pleaded with its journalists to understand his plight. Despite his work as artistic director of the Prussian State Theatre and member of the Prussian state council under Hermann Göring, the *Tageblatt* accepted Gründgens's contrition, recognized his moral quandary, and lauded his interventions to protect thespians from Nazi persecution.[82] While it was willing to consider forgiveness for repentant individuals, the newspaper relentlessly prosecuted fascist transgressors. An article entitled, "Weimar und Buchenwald," laid bare its tenacity. The *Tageblatt*'s final piece on commemorations for the 1949 Goethe Year chronicled a speech by the immigrant journalist, Ernst Feder, at the Teatro Serrador in Rio de Janeiro for Goethe's 200th birthday. A daily columnist for the widely read newspaper, *Diario De Noticias*, Feder already had spoken about the luminous German in Portuguese; however, this event, organized by the local antifascist Freies Europäisches Künstlertheater (Free European Artists Theater), was his first lecture in German. Like Feder and the *Tageblatt*'s readership, most members of the audience had arrived in Brazil as refugees from Nazi persecution, and his speech dovetailed with their mutual experiences of terror, oppression, and flight. Feder began with a wistful account of the previous Goethe Year, held in 1932 on the 100th anniversary of the poet's death and still present in the minds of many attendees at the Serrador that evening. A century after his death, Feder asserted, much of Goethe's mission had appeared fulfilled. German Goethe scholars had participated in celebrations throughout Europe and beyond, including Gerhart Hauptmann in Boston and New York, Thomas Mann in Prague, Emil Ludwig in Rome and Florence, Ernst Cassirer in Pairs, Max Dessoir in Belgrade, and Kurt Wolff in Budapest. Albert Bassermann, too, had starred in a performance of *Faust* in Antwerp. Museums across the globe featured exhibits in Goethe's honor and the director of the French National Library, Julian Cain, curated one of the most lustrous collections in the Parisian Mazarine Gallery.

Then, within months, the barbarians seized power. Other than Hauptmann, all the German artists and intellectuals on Feder's list emigrated, and the Nazis banned and burned many of the books in the Mazarine. Before long Cain was jailed and deported to Buchenwald, an injustice from which the *Tageblatt*'s article drew its title. From this point on, Feder transitioned to a seething diatribe, lambasting Hitler and his comrades for a litany of abuses against Germany's most famous author. He was distressed by Mathilde Ludendorff's conspiracy theory of Goethe's complicity in Schiller's murder by the Free Masons, outraged at the credence her accusations gained in Germany after 1933, and, livid about the Nazi ban on Max Hecker's book in Goethe's defense.[83] It seems, the immigrant journalist concluded, "als sei mit der geistigen Elite Deutschlands auch der Geist Goethes außer Landes gegangen" (as if along with Germany's intellectual elite Goethe's spirit, too, had left the country).[84] Feder honored Goethe, but his focus was on Nazi crimes. Furthermore, there was no mention of Goethe's role in postwar Germany nor reconciliation with the victims of National Socialism. More than a homage, his speech was a reckoning.

Perhaps the most famous German-speaking exile in Brazil after Stefan Zweig, Ernst Feder marked a decidedly partisan tone at the close of the 1949 Goethe Year. The article, "Weimar und Buchenwald" brought an end to the *Tageblatt*'s coverage of the 1949 Goethe Year commemorations. The paper's reporting had been varied, pluralistic, and in certain instances even conciliatory yet, attesting to the enduring rancor in German Buenos Aires, its last word was indignation.

*The University of Memphis*

## NOTES

1. I am indebted to my Argentine colleagues Silvia Glocer of the University of Buenos Aires, and Claudia Garnica de Bertona and Lila Bujaldón de Esteves of the University of Cuyo for helping me procure sources for this project during the 2020 pandemic. Regula Rohland de Langbehn, founder of the Documentation Center of German-Speaking Immigration at the University of General San Martín, has been extremely helpful.

2. Marcos Novaro, ed., *Peronismo y democracia: historia y perspectivas* (Barcelona: Edhasa, 2014).

3. In Argentine media and foreign media by Argentine authors: José María Gallegos Rocafull et al., eds., *Homenaje a Goethe: En el II centenario de su nacimiento* (La Plata: Escuela Superior de Lenguas Vivas de la Universidad Nacional de La Plata, 1949); León Pagano and Ilse Brugger, eds., *Estudios Germanísticos* 9. Número especial dedicado a Johann Wolfgang Goethe (1950); Alfredo Dornheim, ed., *Goethe 1749—28 de agosto—1949* (Mendoza, Argentina: Facultad de Filosofía y Letras de la Universidad de Cuyo, 1949); Guillermo de Torre, "*Clavijo* o los límites olvidados," *Atenea* 26, no.

154 (1949): 30–42; Guillermo de Torre, "Goethe y la 'literatura universal,'" *Realidad: Revistas de Ideas* 17–18, no. 6 (1949): 260–268; Werner Bock, "La juventud de Goethe en su segundo Centenario," *Revista Faluctad de Humanidades y Ciencias* 3 (1949), n.p.; Lorenzo Luzuriaga, "Goethe, educador de nuestro tiempo," *Realidad: Revistas de Ideas* 17–18, no. 6 (1949): 198–204; Alfonso Reyes, "Goethe y la filosofía del dibujo," *Realidad: Revistas de Ideas* 15, no. 5 (1949): 258–263; Antonio Herrero, "Goethe como símbolo posible de la argentinidad," *Cultura* 1 (1949): 61–77; Andre Gide, "Goethe," *Sur* (August 1949): 15–22; Juan P. Ramos, "La Sabiduria de la Vida en Goethe," *Boletín de la Academia Argentina de Letras* 28, no. 70 (1949): 459–484; Francisco Romero, "Jerusalem-Werther Aprendiz de Filósofo," *Ideas y Figuras* (Buenos Aires: Editorial Losada, 1949) 71–83; José Vasconcelos, "Goethe y el Derecho," *Revista de la Universidad de Buenos Aires* 5, no. 1 (1949): 65–82; Roberto Paine, "Goethe y la Aventura Italiana," *Revista de la Universidad de Buenos Aires* 5, no. 1 (1949): 83–98; Emilio Estíu, "La Concepción del Hombre en Goethe," *Humanidades. Universidad Mar del Plata* 33 (1949): 83–100; Alejandro Ruiz-Guiñazu, "Nota preliminar," in *German y Dorotea* by Johann Wolfgang von Goethe (Buenos Aires: Editorial Emecé, 1949) 5–32.

4. For the leading newspaper, *La Nación*, in August see Werner Bock, "Sobre las huellas de Goethe en Wetzlar," *La Nación*, August 14, 1949; Werner Bock, "Goethe el genio e los ojos," *La Nación*, August 28, 1949; Fausto Nicolini, "Goethe y Gaetano Filangieri, *La Nación*, August 28, 1949; Guillermo de Torre, "Clasicismo y romanticism en Goethe," *La Nación*, August 28, 1949.

5. Ana E. Weinstein, Robrto Nasatsky, and Miryam Gover de Nasatsky, *Trayectorias musicales judeo-argentinos* (Buenos Aires: Editorial Milá, 1998) 58.

6. Emilio Casares Rodicio, *Diccionario de la música espñola e hispanoamericana.* 10 vols. (Madrid: SAGE, 2000) 3:613.

7. "Goethe-Ehrung im Teatro Colón," *Freie Presse*, November 4, 1949.

8. Osvaldo Pellettieri, *Historia del teatro argentino en Buenos Aires: La segunda modernidad, 1949–1976* (Buenos Aires: Editorial Galerna, 2001) 50, 64, 108, 242.

9. "Argentinier feiern Goethe," *Freie Presse*, August 30, 1949.

10. Unless otherwise indicated, all translations are my own.

11. Arturo Berenguer Carisomo, "Advertencia del autor," in *Teatro de Camara* (Buenos Aires: edición del autor, 1943) n.p.

12. Norberto Galasso, Perón: Formación, ascenso y caída, 1893–1955 (Buenos Aires: Ediciones Colihue, 2005) 302.

13. Claudia Garnica de Bertona, "Otro Fausto argentino: *La piel de la manzana* de Arturo Berenguer Carisomo," in *Literatura: Espacio de contactos culturales. Actas Cuartas Jornadas Nacionales de Literatura Comparada*, ed. Olga Steimberg de Kaplán (Córdoba: Editorial Comunicarte, 1999) 1041–1054, here 1047.

14. Berenguer Carisomo 103.

15. Ana María Llurba, "*La piel de la manzana* o el triunfo de la mujer," *Gramma* 40 (2005): 35–39, here 38.

16. Susana Salgado, *The Teatro Solís: 150 Years of Opera, Concert and Ballet in Montevideo* (Middletown, CT: Wesleyan UP, 2003) 447.

17. "Goethe-Feier in der argentinischen Schriftstellergesellschaft," *Argentinisches Tageblatt*, August 26, 1949.

18. "Die südamerikanische Goethe-Akademie und Goethe-Gesellschaft im ersten Jahr ihres Bestehens," *Argentinisches Tageblatt*, December 31, 1949.

19. Augusto Bunge, "Goethe: de su vida y su obra," *Nosotros* 26, no. 75 (1932): 5–14; Marcos Victoria, "El Centenario de Goethe," *La Literatura Argentina* 43 (1932): 197–198; Ardoino Martini, *La personalidad de Goethe* (Rosario: Colegio Libre de Estudios Populares, 1933).

20. Herrero, "Goethe como símbolo posible," 64.

21. Herrero, "Goethe como símbolo posible," 65.

22. Herrero, "Goethe como símbolo posible," 70–71.

23. Herrero, "Goethe como símbolo posible," 64.

24. Antonio Herrero, Hipólito Yrigoyen, maestro de democracia (La Plata: Olivieri y Dominguez, 1927); Antonio Herrero, *Imperialismo espiritual: misión de la Argentina* (Buenos Aires: Editorial Almafuerte, 1936).

25. Juan Bautista Alberdi, *Bases y puntos de partida para la organización política de la República Argentina* (Buenos Aires: Ediciones Jackson, 1938) 66.

26. Antonio Tovar, "Goethe, mejor que Goethe," in Dornheim, *Goethe 1749—28 de agosto—1949*, 96.

27. Hans Carossa, "La significación de Goethe para la actualidad," *Estudios Germanísticos* 9 (1950): 208–222, here 210.

28. Juan C. Probst, "Goethe frente a Shakespeare," *Estudios Germanísticos* 9 (1950): 91–102.

29. Alfredo Dornheim, "Goethe, voilà un homme," in *Goethe 1749—28 de agosto—1949*, 19.

30. Dornheim, "Goethe, voilà un homme," 27–28.

31. Korell, "¿Cómo actualizar a Goethe?," in Dornheim, *Goethe 1749—28 de agosto—1949*, 146.

32. Korell 142.

33. Korell 147.

34. de Torre, "*Clavijo* o los limites olvidados," 41.

35. Advertisements in: *Deutsche La Plata Zeitung*, December 11, 1938; September 9, 1939.

36. Mariana González Lutier, "La Comisión de Investigación de las Actividades Anti-argentinas: El caso de la Goethe Schule," *Cuadernos DIHA* 5–6 (2019): 98–110.

37. Claudia Garnica De Bertona, "Max Tepp, un intermediario entre dos mundos," *Anuario Argentino de Germanística* 5 (2009): 313–22, here 314.

38. Annual report, Humbodlt-Schule (1939), Goethe School Archive, Vicente López, Argentina.

39. "Warum spielt das Deutsche Theater Buenos Aires *Faust*?," *Deutsche La Plata Zeitung*, March 12, 1942.

40. "*Götz von Berlichingen* und der Bauernkrieg," *Der Deutsche in Argentinien*, June 1940.

41. "Goethes *Götz von Berlichingen*," *Deutsche La Plata Zeitung*, May 26, 1940.

42. "*Götz von Berlichingen* und der Bauernkrieg."

43. "Deutsches Theater," *Deutsche La Plata Zeitung*, June 19, 1940.

44. "Jean," *Jüdische Wochenschau*, April 26, 1940; "Dos Funciones de Teatro Alemán Ofrecerán Hoy," *Noticias Gráficas*, April 27, 1940; "Niezaleny Teatr Niemiecki," *Kurjer Polski*, August 16, 1940; "Free German Stage," *Buenos Aires Herald*, April 30, 1940;

"Freie Deutsche Bühne," *Di Presse*, August 13, 1940; "Szinház," *Délamerikai Magyarság*, August 15, 1940; "Lide Na Kre," *Checoslovaquia Libre*, July 22, 1940.

45. "Maria Stuart," *Jüdische Wochenschau*, July 19, 1940.

46. Programmhefte 1940-1945, Paul Walter Jacob-Archiv, VI b) 281.

47. Hermann Schnorbach, *Por la otra Alemania: El Colegio Pestalozzi en Buenos Aires, 1934-2004* (Buenos Aires: Asociación Pestalozzi, 2004) 116.

48. "Shakespeare, Dante, Goethe, Voltaire verboten," *Argentinisches Tageblatt*, September 3, 1942.

49. Holger Meding, *"Der Weg." Eine deutsche Emigrantenzeitschrift in Buenos Aires 1947-1957* (Berlin: Wissenschaftlicher Verlag Berlin, 1997) 116.

50. Eberhard Fritsch, *Der Weg* (August 1949): 584.

51. Ludwig Curtius, "Goethe in unserer Zeit," *Der Weg* (August 1949): 588-604, here 596.

52. Curtius 600.

53. Curtius 614, 616.

54. Curtius 15-16.

55. Guido Koblenheyer, "Goethes Weltbürgertum und die internationale Geistigkeit," *Der Weg* (August 1949): 626-628, here 626.

56. Hans Grimm, "Eine dörfliche Goethe-Rede," *Der Weg* (October 1949): 792-797, here 796.

57. Herbert Cysarz, "Goethe und der Selbstmord des abendländischen Geistes," *Der Weg* (September 1949): 688-694.

58. Hans Naumann, "Goethe und seine Verwendung einiger Frühformen unserer Poesie," *Der Weg* (July 1949): 483-488.

59. Meding, 117.

60. Georg Ismar, *Der Pressekrieg. Argentinisches Tageblatt und Deutsche La Plata Zeitung, 1933-1945* (Berlin: Wissenschaftlicher Verlag Berlin, 2006) 197.

61. Ismar 198-199.

62. West German Embassy to Federal Foreign Office, November 16, 1962, Bestand B33, Band 248, Politisches Archiv des Auwärtigen Amtes.

63. "Neue Deutsche Bühne von Ludwig Ney: Festvorstellung von Goethes *Iphigenie auf Tauris*," *Freie Presse*, May 31, 1949.

64. "Axel an der Himmelstür," *Aregntinisches Tageblatt*, July 8, 1956.

65. "Zufällige Zuschauermenge oder Theatergemeinschaft?" *Der Weg*, April 1949; "Aus dem deutschen Theaterleben in Buenos Aires," *Der Weg*, June 1949.

66. "Goethe: *Iphigenie*," *Freie Presse*, May 27, 1949.

67. "Festvorstellung von Goethes *Iphigenie auf Taurus*," *Freie Presse*, May 21, 1949.

68. Gaetano Biccari, *"Zuflucht des Geistes." Konservativ-revolutionäre, faschistische und nationalsozialistische Theaterdiskurse in Deutschland und Italien 1900-1944* (Tübingen: G. Narr 2001) 85, 136.

69. "Großer Erfolg der Ney-Bühne in Chile," *Freie Presse*, November 15, 1949.

70. "Argentinier feiern Goethe," *Freie Presse*, August 30, 1949; "Goethe-Ehrung im Teatro Colón," *Freie Presse*, November 4, 1949.

71. "Argentinier feiern Goethe," *Freie Presse*, August 30, 1949.

72. "Goethe in Buenos Aires," *Freie Presse*, August 28, 1949.

73. Wiebke Sievers, *Grenzüberschreitungen. Ein literatursoziologischer Blick auf die lange Geschichte von Literatur und Migration* (Vienna: Böhlau, 2016) 13–16.

74. The German immigrant Carl Bunge would later move the firm to Buenos Aires, where it became the enormously influential firm, Bunge and Born.

75. Holger Meding, *Flucht vor Nürnberg? Deutsch und österreichische Einwanderung in Argentinien 1945–1955* (Cologne: Böhlau, 1992) 268.

76. In Argentina, Kopps obscured his identity under the pseudonym Juan Maler.

77. "FDB: *Marilou*," *Freie Presse*, December 3, 1945.

78. Jacob to Alexander Berger, November 22, 1943, Paul-Walter-Jacob-Archiv, Korrespondenz.

79. "Der unbekannte Goethe in der FDB," *Argentinisches Tageblatt*, August 30, 1949; "Der unbekannte Goethe: Feier in der F. D. B.," *Freie Presse*, August 30, 1949.

80. "Carta a la redacción," *Revista Familiar Israelita del Uruguay*, August 27, 1948.

81. Carl Hagemann, "Goethe als Theaterleiter," in *Theater Almanach auf das Goethe-Jahr 1949*, ed. Paul Walter Jacob (Buenos Aires: Editorial Jupiter, 1948) 20–22.

82. "Wiedersehen mit Gustav Gründgens," *Aregntinisches Tageblatt*, March 7, 1949.

83. Mathilde Ludendorff, *Der ungesühnte Frevel an Luther, Lessing, Mozart und Schiller im Dienste des allmächtigen Baumeisters aller Welten* (Munich: Ludendorff, 1929); Max Hecker, *Schillers Tod und Bestattung. Nach den Zeugnissen der Zeit im Auftrag der Goethe-Gesellschaft dargestellt* (Leipzig: Insel, 1935).

84. "Weimar und Buchenwald," *Argentinisches Tageblatt*, September 18, 1949.

SEAN FRANZEL, ILINCA IURASCU, AND PETRA MCGILLEN

# Media Inventories of the Nineteenth Century: A Report from Two Workshops

THE FIRST SELF-PROCLAIMED *General Bibliography of Printed Inventories* (*Bibliographie générale des inventaires imprimés*) (1892–1895), arduously compiled by Fernand de Mély and Edmund Bishop, starts with an immediate disclaimer: "If the fear of incompleteness had deterred its two authors, th[is] publication . . . would have never seen the light of day."[1] "We have only included inventories properly speaking," the preface states, leaving aside "manuscript and library" catalogues, "mere lists of relics," and "testaments and literary descriptions," which "would have carried us too far." De Mély and Bishop's pointed reference to "proper" inventories (as distinct from other types of itemized written records) calls for further examination. While the volume does not offer any definitions for the terms it invokes, the commentary here can be considered against the background of nineteenth-century dictionary entries. In Larousse's *Great Universal Dictionary*, for example, the term "inventory" is primarily understood as a "catalogue, a record that inscribes and describes, article by article, all the objects, immovable and movable property, goods, titles, papers, belonging to a person, or found in a house or residence."[2] But during the nineteenth century, a growing interest in inventories of artifacts associated with historical sites or collections (such as those announced in the *Bibliographie générale*) gives rise to the need for more diverse and, at the same time, more systematic approaches.[3] In the process, categorical limits are continuously tested and reexamined. By their own admission, de Mély and Bishop are "compelled to admit some exceptions," challenging their own self-imposed criteria and thus returning to the impossible task of not going "too far." Inventories, as de Mély and Bishop's efforts suggest, promise an overview and a systematic organization of accumulations of discrete objects, yet are based in a sense of incompleteness vis-à-vis the excess of practices of storing, listing, ordering, and recording with which they are confronted.

De Mély and Bishop's multivolume undertaking thus serves as an apt starting point for a discussion around the slippery margins of inventorying categories, their nineteenth-century histories, media practices, and techniques. What cultural premises mark the increased awareness of the importance of inventorying that gives rise to metaprojects such as the *Bibliographie générale des inventaires imprimés*? How do inventories work against and in dialogue with other media of storage and retrieval such as catalogues, indexes, bibliographies, and archives? What new media configurations do techniques of inventorying enable and how, in turn, are such techniques shaped by the media channels and formats they employ? What is at stake in the critical effort of "taking stock"—whether as commercial, bureaucratic, literary, historiographical, or scientific undertakings—and what does this tell us specifically about the nineteenth century?

These questions were at the forefront of two research workshops organized at Dartmouth College (March 2018) and the University of Missouri (February 2020) under the title "Media Inventories of the Nineteenth Century," with participation from scholars in German studies and related fields. One of our expressed goals has been to go beyond certain canonical accounts in German media studies that have tended to favor construing the beginning and end of the nineteenth century ("around 1800" or "around 1900") as foundational breaks or turning points. Instead, our working principle has been to explore multiple historical trajectories, to engage with local and temporal configurations of objects and actions, and to expand the range of critical interventions. As a cultural mode, model, and medium, inventorying is a felicitous category for thinking about nineteenth-century studies, not least because there is a marked interest in its (re)definition throughout the century. Furthermore, inventorying operates in conjunction (and tension) with related cultural techniques and media of collection, classification, preservation, and distribution (from lists to catalogues and beyond) that likewise invite modular approaches and new critical tactics.

Focusing on the particular semantics and connotations of the inventory, it is worthwhile to consider briefly the conceptual history of the term in the German cultural context. The term inventory (*inventarium*) arises in the early modern period, based on the Latin *invenire*: to come upon or across, to find. Inventorying goes hand in hand with different cultural techniques of finding, collecting, and bringing different things together that are more or less unrelated. The term's primary *legal meaning* pertains to the list of the property of a deceased or convicted person, a list of "what is found" in the estate or belongings of said person, and extends to churches, museums, and other state and private institutions.[4] Along with related techniques of ordering such as the catalogue, inventories are of particular importance in practices of *collecting and displaying art*.[5] In the *scientific realm*, the inventory was aligned in the seventeenth and eighteenth centuries with the "table" as a mode of formalizing and representing "what is found" in the physical world.[6] These connotations make their way into nineteenth-century scientific projects of global measurement and mapping, as in geological and geographical tectonic and glacial inventories or the plant inventories of Alexander von Humboldt. The term is also essential in the *commercial realm*, referring to a list of goods in a merchant's storehouse. In his early nineteenth-century dictionary, J. H. Campe suggests German equivalents for *Inventur* (inventory) and *Inventur machen* (taking inventory) such as *Bestandbuch* (ledger) and *Lagerbestand aufnehmen* (recording stock), which he strongly associates with the business of print: "Inventur ... nennen die Buchhändler und andere Kaufleute das Verzeichniß der auf ihrem Lager noch vorräthigen Bücher oder Waaren" (inventory is what booksellers and other merchants call the list of books or other goods that they have in stock).[7] In the world of the nineteenth-century serial print, commercial inventories, and catalogues take on particular importance as tools that consumers encounter in newspapers, journals, bookstores, and other sites where the surplus of print products calls out for organization. Notions of finding and ordering specific items are also closely related to the *rhetorical* concept of invention: as Campe notes, *Inventieren* can mean both *Überlieferungsstücke verfertigen* (to compile an inheritance), and *Erfinden* (invent, create). This is the epoch in which the model of rhetorical invention is supplanted by aesthetics of genius/originality, yet inventorying and invention persist as techniques into the nineteenth century, with various formats such as anthologies, florilegia, pocket books, and more, presenting readers with aides in finding specific kinds and topics of writing.[8] Practices of taking inventory are also implicated in nineteenth-century *philological* projects of establishing national *literary traditions*.

Eighteenth- and nineteenth-century reference works and later historiographical interventions alike tell us certain things about *what* an inventory is, but they also give us crucial information about *when* an inventory is. Taking stock commonly comes after (or in anticipation of) some kind of event; it is the result of a process of some sort that surveys "what is found." In the commercial realm, inventories are commonly made "bei dem Schluß des Jahres" (at the end of the year)[9] as well as ahead or after trade fairs. In the legal realm this relates to a notion of transition and handing or taking over (*Übergang / Übergabe / Übernahme*) commonly related to death, with the act of inventorying commonly serving as a proactive step to prepare the estate. In the literary realm, this is an epoch in which the modern awareness of literary estate and legacy (*Nachlassbewußtsein*) emerges.[10] Being aware of how inventories are timed, how stock is taken at specific moments, tells us something about the eventfulness of techniques of inventorying and their partial, often necessarily incomplete status. This brings us back to the historiographical stakes of inventorying and its role in negotiating historical transitions.

If we understand inventories as inherently modular, and the practices and objects involved as operating across diverse registers, the critical work that they invite must inevitably bear certain traces of this modularity and adaptability. The research presentations at the two workshops therefore considered the implications of "taking stock of taking stock," so to speak. Along with focusing on specific techniques and objects, projects have made various inroads into the "what, when, where, why and how" of inventorying, with initial results crystallizing around questions of: (1) categorical demarcations and confluences (*What* are inventories, how do they intersect with related categories, and what types of cultural techniques mobilize them?); (2) localities and spatial constructions (*Where* are inventories, how do they negotiate and reconfigure notions of space, what sites have been traditionally affiliated with inventorying practices, and what sites newly emerge in the nineteenth century?); (3) temporal dimensions (*When* are inventories, how do they articulate notions of memory and recollection as well as "legacy" and the future, and what temporal figures do they coalesce?); and (4) modalities (*How and why* do inventories exist; how are practices of inventorying deployed and to what ends?). Each presentation engaged each of these questions to some degree. Nevertheless, to highlight common threads running through the discussions, we grouped the presentations around the four clusters delineated above.

To explore the *"what" of inventories*, we begin with Jocelyn Holland's research on the technological lexica of the late eighteenth and early nineteenth centuries and the ways in which these reference works collect and organize distinct technical objects and craft concepts of technology (*Technologie*) more generally. In her presentation, Holland addressed questions of technological terminology and practices of ordering, which coalesce in part around the problem of genre: whereas the technological "dictionary" prevails in the eighteenth century, after 1800 it faces competition by other genres such as the *Hausbuch* (house book), the *Kunstbuch* (art book), the *Handbuch* (handbook), the *Taschenwörterbuch* (pocket dictionary), and the *Lexikon* (lexicon). Notable in this context is the work of Johann Beckmann, which includes the massive 23-volume *Physikalisch-ökonomische Bibliothek* (Physical-Economic Library) (1770–1807). Holland addressed how strategies of collecting and ordering technological language and practices evolve, and what role genre constraints play in this process.

Grant Wythoff was similarly interested in nineteenth-century practices of inventorying technical objects, focusing his presentation on the work of the nineteenth-century archaeologist Augustus Pitt-Rivers, who collected and catalogued over 50,000 technical artifacts from around the world over the course of his life. Wythoff also sought to position Pitt-Rivers's inventorying practices vis-à-vis his own research, which involves using text mining to write a cultural history of "the gadget." The term originally emerged in the context of nautical slang as early as the 1850s and would gain widespread acceptance in the twentieth century, being used to describe objects as diverse as dashboard gauges and atomic bombs, can openers and smartphones. While "gadget" can be a placeholder for any kind of object, even imaginary ones, Wythoff argued that the gadget's evolving application to particular tools and techniques reveals important lessons about our relationship to technology.

The *"where" of inventories* is also highly pertinent to the literary realm, something that Petra McGillen addressed in her discussion of the literary list. Engaging with Robert E. Belknap's 2004 *The List: The Uses and Pleasures of Cataloguing*, McGillen sought to explore what distinguishes a list from an inventory, situating this question in the context of the vast literary tradition of the list as well as the generative potential of different kinds of accumulations. As McGillen put it, it is not the content as such of lists, catalogues, and inventories that makes them unique, but the interactions between the different items within that content. Thus, the relationship of the literary list to the inventory pertains to what one might call a poetics of enumerative forms.

In terms of the literary realm, several presentations explored the potential of using the concept of inventory to examine literary forms and genres not typically conceived of as inventories. This includes Jessica C. Resvick's presentation on the theatrical adaptation of Hoffmann's *Das Fräulein von Scuderi* (*Mademoiselle de Scuderi*) by the dramatist, novelist, and critic Otto Ludwig, one of the first nineteenth-century German realists. Poetic realist works take recognizable reality (*finden*) and transform it (*erfinden*), thus engaging with inventorying in the sense of *inventio*, and Ludwig's oeuvre is uniquely poised to offer insight into the medially specific practices that make such endeavors possible. It is striking that his theory of poetic realism finds unexpected expression in the theory and practice of dramatic adaptation. As Resvick argued, the interplay of prose fiction and drama in Ludwig's work reveals the necessity of expanding traditional generic and media historical conceptions of the period. Generic cross-pollination is central to his adaptation of *Das Fräulein von Scuderi* (whose Serapiontic frame narrative, in fact, addresses the medial constraints of drama). If largely prose-specific practices like serialization allow individual installments to join into a coherent whole, then the performative realizations of a drama, an infinite number of which are possible, can never achieve this same totality. By tracing out Ludwig's reworking of the serial structure and contextualizing it within his theoretical writings on drama and poetic realism, Resvick explored the possibility of a generic inventory of the period.

In his presentation on Heine's poetics of combination and allegory, Roger Cook proposed ways in which inventorying functions both as a feature of nineteenth-century poetics and as a tool of contemporary criticism. For Cook, creating an inventory of the multifaceted elements of Heine's writing—in particular, his widespread use of allegory—can circumvent certain narratives in Heine scholarship that obscure the progressive thrust of his Romantic aesthetics. This entails looking at specific literary texts as inventories, as well as a body of work as inventory. A critical overview of the different forms of allegory he creates helps distinguish his poetics from mainstream (non-Jewish) German Romantics, and shifts the focus more to Heine's interest in the unconscious impulses that are the binding other to consciousness—including dream images and the sensory stimuli that accompany and shape comprehension, in short, all manner of affect. A method that focuses on Heine's poetic inventories could bring scholarly work in alignment with Heine's attempts to use allegorical *Bildlichkeit* (figurativity) to create new meaning and gain knowledge in ways that conceptual language cannot.

Turning to aspects of temporality and historiography, the *"when" of inventories* is also quite pertinent to the business of print, literary and otherwise, a topic explored by Sean Franzel in his presentation on reports on the Leipzig book fairs by the publicist and antiquarian Carl August Böttiger. Böttiger organizes his reports around the catalogue (*Meß-Katalog*) of products for sale, a print object produced twice a year in tandem with the spring and fall fairs. Böttiger cultivates a distinctive style of commentary, taking the seasonally recurring fairs and the constant need for new catalogues as an occasion for producing new reports. These reports straddle journalistic digests of commercially relevant information and satirical *Unterhaltung* (entertainment). In a sense, Böttiger's reports are quite typical of nineteenth-century serial print, which constantly called upon readers to digest a range of actual and hypothetical lists, catalogues, and inventories and to imagine broader literary, commercial, scholarly networks that they were more or less directly a part of. Given that these catalogues were published twice a year and that Böttiger's digests of them appeared in installments spaced out over time, they model a kind of literary production—and a concomitant need for inventorying it—based in serialized continuation over time.

Birgit Tautz also addressed the temporalities of readers' material encounters with books in her discussion of marginalia as practices that should be situated in the orbit of inventorying. Tautz's interest in marginalia stems from their role as small genres that nonetheless fulfill central communicative functions and also from their indexical operations. Marginalia are indices pointing to a network of read books and resonances and to ideals of individuality (of the author, annotator, and/or owner of the book). They thus manifest various temporalities of reader encounters and of layered encounters of previous readers. They serve crucial functions in the reader's engagement with texts regarding, for example, impulse control and mediation, expressions of ambivalence when reading, asserting readers' expertise, and identity and individuality. Marginalia thrive on the private/public threshold and yet disrupt the conventional understandings of this duality in important ways. In sum, marginalia become important ancillary tools or concepts in further understanding practices of inventorying tied to books as material objects.

Working with notions of intermediality and "minor" temporalities, Ilinca Iurascu took a closer look at the popular entertainment form of the toy theater (*Papiertheater*), focusing particularly on its remediated character: from dramatic publicity to domestic performativity, and from stage to page (i.e., cut-out sheet) and back to the (miniature) stage. Such transfers and transitions, however, can hardly be understood outside the commercial context of toy-theater catalogues, as well as the circulation of printed lists, props, and advertising model sheets that often featured interchangeable paper figures. In the world of *Papiertheater*, this modular character is central to the idea of theatrical inventories and to the way they restructure temporal relations on and beyond the stage. Drawing on toy-theater adaptations of Schiller's *Die Räuber* (*The Robbers*), Iurascu ultimately asked what happens to the melodramatic mode and its engagement with historical change when transposed into the realm of the *Papiertheater*, built around notions of miniature time and mobile, modular inventories.

In his presentation, Matt Erlin took up historiographical questions underlining many of the presentations, namely the distinction between nineteenth and twenty-first-century practices of inventorying. Taking a second-order perspective on the topic of media inventories, he first considered how the widespread current efforts to digitize nineteenth-century (and not just nineteenth-century) resources are themselves an inventorying practice, and one that can be placed into a productive dialogue with nineteenth-century concerns about information management. He then turned to several concrete instances of digital inventories (e.g., *Nineteenth-Century Collections Online*, *Zeitschriften der Aufklärung, The Corvey Collection*), considering how the metadata from these collections can be used to illuminate and analyze key features of the nineteenth-century media archive. Erlin worked with a concrete example from the cusp of the nineteenth century, exploring how information on reviewed titles for the entire run of Friedrich Nicolai's *Allgemeine Deutsche Bibliothek* (General German Library, 1765–1806) can be mined for author demographics as well as frequent keywords.

The *"where" of inventories* led us to consider questions regarding spatial and "natural" reconfigurations in conjunction with gestures of collecting and archiving, while highlighting the disciplinary and epistemic dimensions of systems of storage and classification. Samuel Frederick explored the inventorying capabilities of media of plant collecting, both in the concrete form of the vascula (*Botanisiertrommel*) and similar containers created to store and transport botanical specimens and as part of broader discursive networks, as in the case of nineteenth-century botanical collecting guides. Frederick considered the ways in which the accumulation, dissemination, and preservation of data on plants (typically the indexing of new species) intersected with concerns for the gathering and preservation of actual specimens, which inevitably perish and wither as collected things. In the case of moss, however, this outcome is overcome by way of its unique collectability, which allows for complete desiccation and (apparent) death followed by the potential of resuscitation through contact with water.

Matthew H. Birkhold's presentation inquired about the different media inventories that have shaped our perception and knowledge of glaciers. The question of how to realistically represent these icy masses first arose in the nineteenth century, when a convergence of interests met in the Alps: the need to navigate troops safely over glaciers, a desire to sell travel guides to Germans seeking entertainment in the mountains or quick passage to Italy, the pursuit of scientific knowledge, the hubristic attempt to scale the world's tallest peaks, and the creation of works of art. The result was a proliferation of glacier depictions and catalogues. By examining these historical records, Birkhold ultimately directed our attention to the current moment and the question of how to best portray the dwindling stocks of glacier inventories today.

Continuing with the theme of nature inventories, Vance Byrd discussed the archival techniques of Romeyn Beck Hough's *The American Woods* (1888–1913), framing them as part of a media genealogy including cabinets of curiosity, scientific collections, and xylotheques. Hough's work does not illustrate its subject using contemporary illustration processes (engravings or photomechanical reproduction). Instead, it showcases the materiality of trees as natural objects by publishing natural-wood preparations of tree species and varieties in each of its fifteen fascicules. As Byrd pointed out, the manufacture of wood veneers for Hough's *American Woods* produced material carriers that determine how knowledge about the forest was stored and represented. The archival techniques driving the material and media transformations of the publication capture a nostalgic mode in which taking stock of North American forests was in tune with the work of late nineteenth-century conservation movements. The consumption of authentic wood veneers for Hough's serial publication was a synecdochic measure to store and disseminate fragments of a natural world increasingly dominated by monoculture rather than the biodiversity presented by the publication's pages.

Shifting attention to questions of institutional location, Paul Babinski presented on the manuscript collection of Vienna's *Orientalische Akademie* (Oriental Academy). Founded in 1754 on the model of the French *École des jeunes de langues*, the *Orientalische Akademie* became a center of

Orientalist knowledge production in nineteenth-century Europe. Working from the materials preserved in the school's manuscript collection, and considering them alongside the documents found in its archives, Babinski situated the material inventory of Vienna Orientalism at a critical time in the history of Europe's relationship with the Ottoman Empire: a moment when European states, hoping to train young men to replace the Levantine dragomans that mediated diplomatic communication in multilingual Istanbul, were confronted with the challenge of teaching the languages of the Near East in the heart of Europe. This process entailed experimenting with new forms of writing and engagement with both a real and imaginary "Orient." As students took over work once performed by Ottoman contacts, and generations of diplomat-scholars from the school built careers as Orientalists on the basis of their engagement with Ottoman philological and literary traditions, the transcultural character of Orientalist collaboration—once built into the scholarly division of labor itself—became progressively more textual and imaginary.

Returning to the subject of inventorying practices associated with specific cultures and sites of performance, Mary Helen Dupree's presentation focused on the German recitation anthology, which functioned both as a textual archive and a source of "scripts" and cues for the oral performance of literature in the long nineteenth century. German recitation anthologies remediated and promoted a culture of literary declamation that emphasized the musicality of literature as well as its sensual and affective dimensions. From 1800 to 1914, recitation anthologies compiled by editors such as Friedrich Eberhard Rambach, Betty Gleim, Karl Friedrich Solbrig, and Maximilian Bern (to name but a few) made the practice of literary declamation readily accessible to a broad audience of professionals and laypeople. These anthologies supported a practice of reading literary texts as scripts or scores for performance, thus mirroring processes of textualization at work in musical cultures of the nineteenth century. Recitation anthologies also had a commercial function, indexing the larger inventories of texts for performance available from publishers and sellers, such as the Bloch Theaterbuchhandlung (Theater Bookstore) in Berlin. As objects of popular consumption, recitation anthologies were themselves subject to extensive inventorying in the nineteenth century, a process that continues today with the cataloging of recitation anthologies in bibliographies and full-text databases.

In her presentation, Catriona MacLeod reframed the question of "locating inventories" by approaching it from the margins, via the subject of nineteenth-century papercraft. Unlike literary products during the same period, craft practices around paper situated themselves precariously around inventorying, as indeed might be expected given their ephemeral and marginal status as art objects. Working with papercuts (*Scherenschnitte*) by figures such as Luise Duttenhofer, Adele Schopenhauer, and Hans Christian Andersen, MacLeod showed how their diverse relationships with the inventory reveal much about the gendering of craft and creativity, the role of salons, and questions of literary canonicity. Schopenhauer's works, for the most part, vanished into the albums of female friends and were not published until the 1910s, whereas Duttenhofer retained copies of her papercuts for her personal inventory, suggesting a different conception of her oeuvre as a comprehensive archive. In the case of Andresen's prolific production of papercuts, a complex relation to media inventories is captured in the ways that he critically disrupted the print culture of his day. Such gestures of disruption ultimately also interrogate contemporary archival efforts centered around his canonical status. The three figures at the center of MacLeod's investigation created private inventories that refuse and undermine the usable inventory of the periodical, library, or reading room.

Further pressing the question of *how* practices of inventorying are deployed and to *what* ends, several presenters focused on tactics of cultural display and the role of print media accompanying exhibition spaces and collections. Peter M. McIsaac looked into the functions of sales catalogues and guides to popular anatomical exhibitions in terms of their different material composition and representational strategies. Both, however, served as crucial contributors to the respective scenes of exhibition and the multimedialized discourse they established. Beyond their immediate marketing and documenting functions, their changing material composition and use of text and image were devised with respect to both changing exhibition practices and shifting legal and social expectations regarding the exhibits and the contents they represented. Partly as a result of the charged nature that came with open sexually related content, deliberate choices had to be made in terms of the cost and quality of the materials and, indeed, the basic question of text vs. image. Beyond the exhibition venues themselves, their accompanying print media were also subject to constraints with regard to who might have access to the displayed content and in what form, as even textual descriptions of risqué material could generate legal penalties if they fell into the hands of minors. At the same time, new ideas of public health communication and changing exhibition strategies led to changes in related paper-based media. By considering catalogues and guidebooks as complex media, McIsaac developed an approach that links medial materiality to the functions, audience, and status of the objects and moments of reception both inside and outside of display settings.

Wallis Miller's presentation likewise focused on the prominent role of print inventories and catalogues in architecture exhibitions that accompanied and provided the conceptual and medial underpinnings for the emergence of modernism in architecture. Beginning "around 1800" and ending in 1932, Miller argued that exhibitions of architecture revealed transformations that other ways of communicating architectural ideas did not, not least in cases where unbuilt architectural models were exhibited. A key part of such exhibitions included catalogues and the inventories that served as their backbone. Tracking the development of catalogues across the nineteenth century, Miller likewise sketched the strongly intermedial stakes involved with practices of inventorying and displaying revealed in the cultural and political debates surrounding modern architecture.

In her case-study analysis of Prussia's efforts to reclaim cultural property after the Napoleonic Wars, Alice Goff focused on the politics of cultural restitution and the tactical mobilization, rewriting, and unwriting of inventories. In 1814, Prussian delegates in Paris began the process of identifying and reclaiming cultural property seized from German states by the French, a process involving complex undertakings, diplomatic finesse, deep historical knowledge, and vast logistical resources. Among the most challenging classes of objects to be reclaimed were those taken out of churches, many of which had been secularized during the Napoleonic period: such works were frequently un-inventoried, known only to local clerical officials and parishioners, and difficult to describe with definitive authority. Goff focused on the array of media drawn up by local administrators in the new Prussian Rhineland in order to support the reclamation of their missing church property in France. These included lists, sketches, affidavits, seals, citations, and painstaking text descriptions intended to communicate the identity of altars, reliquaries, architectural elements, and miscellaneous *Kirchengeräthe* (church objects) to the Prussian delegation in Paris. At the beginning of the post-Napoleonic era, during which Prussia would come to consider the cultural property of churches as part of a national patrimony, these media drew attention to the larger challenge of pinning words to objects and enlisting works of art into the bureaucratic regime of the Prussian state.

Finally, the *"how" of inventories* can also be understood at the level of multiple intersections between textual, visual, and aural platforms and operations, which, in turn, may ultimately help reconceptualize the inventory not only along media-historical lines but also along media-theoretical lines. In his presentation on the digital edition of the eighteenth-century print series Vetusta Monumenta, Noah Heringman argued that the engraver George Vertue made embedded media history a hallmark of the style he developed during his four decades of producing antiquarian engravings for the journal. Using several specific plates as case studies, particularly Vertue's 1741 engraving of a sixteenth-century decree, Heringman pointed to the interaction of different media from different periods (including coinage, seal engraving, secretary hand, and copper engraving itself) in the composition of these plates, suggesting that both the print series as a whole and the individual prints within it might be read as inventories of current and ancestral media.

In his presentation, Nikolaus Wegmann explored the ongoing fascination with medial techniques of self-documentation since the eighteenth century. Departing from Diderot's 1762 question: "How is it, I asked myself, that . . . nobody has the courage to keep for us an exact register of all the thoughts running through his mind, all the movements of his heart, all his sorrows, all his pleasures," Wegmann discussed different strategies of writing oneself down entirely on paper with a notebook, as well as documenting oneself with a camera and tape recorder, exploring the emergence of this idea in notions of self-improvement and *Bildung* as well as in terms of more contemporary applications involving digital media. Practices of inventorying become important in the fascinating yet likely impossible project of self-documentation, especially in cases necessitating the collection of unmanageable amounts of data required for fuller self-understanding.

Bryan Klausmeyer's presentation examined the discursive and medial strategies of inventorying employed by Alexander von Humboldt in his *Ideen zu einer Geographie der Pflanzen* (Essay on the Geography of Plants) (1807) and *Kosmos: Entwurf einer physischen Weltbeschreibung* (Cosmos:

a Sketch of a Physical Description of the Universe) (1845–58, 1862). In Klausmeyer's reading, Humboldt sought to integrate an abundance of facts and observational data into his natural-scientific writings by developing an unusual editorial strategy of constant revision and republication. At the same time, in a critique of the Enlightenment encyclopedia, he also attempted to dynamize the classificatory enterprise by introducing motion into his representation of nature. From there, Klausmeyer examined the differences in medial strategy between Humboldt's early and late work, showing how each "takes stock" of the medial situation in different ways, drawing first on the techniques of landscape painting and later on the new technical media of the mid-nineteenth century (cyclorama, panorama, and daguerreotype) to generate "moving" or "magic" images. The presentation thus argued for the particular importance of Humboldt as a transitional figure within the media history of the nineteenth century since, in addition to registering major changes in the media landscape, his work also offers unique insights into the unexplored potential of new technical media before their solidification into stable and historically recognizable forms.

Finally, Tyler Whitney approached the topic of inventories through the media and literary histories of phonography as an amalgamation of print, image, and sound in the late nineteenth century. More specifically, he examined two gramophone recordings originally published as visual images in the periodicals *Über Land und Meer* (Over Land and Sea, 1890) and *Prometheus* (1890), which were "educed," that is, transformed from high-resolution digital image files into playable sound recordings over one hundred years later by the research group First Sounds Initiative. Taking this technical achievement as his starting point, he further situated such initially inaudible visual representations of mechanical sound within the broader medial economy of print and serial publication in nineteenth-century Germany, showing how early encounters with and thoughts about phonography occurred outside of the domain of the strictly audible and relied instead on an "auditory imagination" activated by a combination of text and image. On the one hand, he showed how the two recordings can be used as a way to push back against contemporary critiques of a textually grounded approach to sound studies, articulated most forcefully with reference to deconstruction and affect theory. On the other hand, Whitney concluded, it is imperative that we borrow from the conceptual resources of media theory in order to complicate traditional notions of textual analysis and replace a naive hermeneutics or mere historicization with a more media-theoretical approach to texts and textual practices in terms of paperwork, transduction, intermediality, sonification, and the archive.

The working group's goals for the future include an edited volume that will take more extensive stock of the projects outlined here, attempting to profile the nineteenth century as an epoch captivated by the *Wille zum Inventar* (will to inventory) across a wide range of cultural, commercial, scientific, political, and aesthetic contexts.

*University of Missouri*
*University of British Columbia*
*Dartmouth College*

# NOTES

1. Fernand de Mély and Edmund Bishop, *Bibliographie générale des inventaires imprimés*, vol. 1. (Paris: Ernest Leroux, 1892) v. Unless otherwise indicated, all translations are our own.

2. Pierre Larousse, *Grand dictionnaire universel du XIXe siècle: français, historique, géographique, mythologique, bibliographique, littéraire, artistique, scientifique*, vol. 9, *H-K* (Paris: Administration du grand dictionnaire universel, 1866–1877) 769.

3. See Corina Heß, *Danziger Wohnkultur in der Frühen Neuzeit Untersuchungen zu Nachlassinventaren des 17. und 18. Jahrhunderts* (Berlin: LIT, 2007) 15.

4. Johann Heinrich Zedler, "Ein schrifftliches Verzeichniß, in welchem die Dinge, so in der Erbschafft sich befinden, sie seyen an beweg- oder unbeweglichen Gütern, aussenstehenden und Gegen-Schulden, beschrieben und verzeichnet werden," in *Grosses vollständiges Universal-Lexikon Aller Wissenschafften und Künste* (Leipzig: Zedler, 1732–54) 796.

5. Anke te Heesen, for example, tracks the rise of the art-historical exhibition catalogue over against the inventories of private collections. Anke te Heesen, "Der Ausstellungskatalog als Monographie. Über Kataloge und ein neues Format des geisteswissenschaftlichen Publizierens," *Kodex. Jahrbuch der Internationalen Buchwissenschaftlichen Gesellschaft*, vol. 5, *Bleiwüste und Bilderflut. Geschichten über das geisteswissenschaftliche Buch*, ed. Carlos Spoerhase and Caspar Hirschi (2015): 231–248. See also Peter McIsaac, who writes of the "inventoried consciousness" at work in the intersection of literature and modern museums. Peter McIsaac, *Museums of the Mind. German Modernity and the Dynamics of Collecting* (University Park, PA: Penn State UP, 2007).

6. Cornelia Vismann, *Akten. Medientechnik und Recht* (Frankfurt a/M: Fischer, 2000) 208.

7. J. H. Campe, *Wörterbuch zur Erklärung und Verdeutschung der unserer Sprache aufgedrungenen fremden Wörter.* 2 vols (Braunschweig: Schulbuchhandlung, 1801) 1:432.

8. See, for example, the essays on catalogues and anthologies in The Multigraph Collective, *Interacting with Print: Elements of Reading in the Era of Print Saturation* (Chicago: U of Chicago P, 2018).

9. Johann Heinrich Zedler, "Inuentarium," in Zedler, *Grosses vollständiges Universal-Lexikon*, 796.

10. Kai Sina and Carlos Spoerhase, eds., *Nachlassbewusstsein: Literatur, Archiv, Philologie, 1750–2000* (Göttingen: Wallstein, 2017).

BIRGIT TAUTZ AND PATRICIA ANNE SIMPSON

# Forum: (New) Directions in Eighteenth-Century German Studies

**Abstract:** This volume's Forum seeks to promote the discussion of (new) directions in eighteenth-century (German) studies. Envisioned as a dialogue with similar fora in other venues, as well as with prolific publication and conference activities, this topic engages a wide range of contributors working through recent research in part to chronicle the state of the field and, more importantly, to redefine and reimagine its objects of study. These eight short essays illustrate inter- and cross-disciplinary work, but also foreground the capacity for academic activism. The contributors reflect on eighteenth-century German (Goethe) studies in dialogue with disability studies and medical humanities, music and sound studies vis-à-vis the spoken word/orality, (post)colonialism/decoloniality and the environment, abolitionist discourse as an important literary impetus, and, finally, legacies and reverberations of the eighteenth century in late twentieth- and early twenty-first-century cultures. Individually and collectively, these contributions open up new lines of inquiry and dialogue with other periods of German literary and cultural history. At the same time, they expose erstwhile blind spots and thus task universities and colleges with turning to new areas of inquiry in order to promote diverse areas of scholarship.

**Keywords:** eighteenth-century German studies, Goethe studies, medical humanities, disability studies, orality/sound studies, postnational approaches, interdisciplinary, state of the field

Tʜɪs ᴠᴏʟᴜᴍᴇ's Fᴏʀᴜᴍ, "(New) Directions in Eighteenth-Century (German) Studies," has evolved over time; it is at once urgent and obsolete—because whatever we present here is a mere snapshot in time. The topic resonates with a panel and a roundtable we organized at the German Studies Association (GSA) conference in 2019. And while only a few of the original contributors are included in this volume of the *Goethe Yearbook*—Monika Nenon presented the initial ideas for her article and Bridget Swanson and Peter Höyng participated in the roundtable—the GSA discussions led to further directions and invitations that contributed to the Forum.

This Forum is a snapshot in yet another sense of the word: it exists in the company of other fora, such as the *German Quarterly*'s 2020 special issue (vol. 93.2) on the eighteenth century, which includes articles and investigations about the role, importance, and relevance of the eighteenth century to German studies, as well as recent pathbreaking articles published in *The Eighteenth Century* (previously *Eighteenth Century Theory and Interpretation*), which, for some time, has provided impulse, provocations, and insights into specialized eighteenth-century topics, often from a comparative perspective. The eight contributions in this volume provide a glimpse into an expanse: they point to many books, journal issues and special sections, research projects, and groups. In short, they refer to an abundance of work that has been done and is about to begin that intersects, challenges, and deepens what our colleagues sketch here. The contributions resonate broadly with an array of interdisciplinary and intersectional approaches, and they probe the temporal contours of periodization by challenging preoccupations with the twentieth- and twenty-first centuries in German studies while exploring strategies for "modernizing" and translating (adapting) the eighteenth century for twenty-first-century sensibilities. In this way, the Forum authors initiate a stimulating, entirely unmediated and unorchestrated dialogue not only with one another but also with the examples of scholarship merely referenced in the notes or even seemingly neglected that often go beyond the examples and framework the contributors sketch here. Openness, nonexclusiveness, and the necessary incomplete would serve as an apt motto for this dialogue.

This characterization applies to varying directions of research in Anglo-American scholarship vis-à-vis *Germanistik*, in German studies and German literature versus other Western and increasingly non-Western national literary traditions, as well as to the various ways of reading interdisciplinary scholarship from their different yet constitutive disciplinary angles. The latter include, aside from the aforementioned special issue of *German Quarterly*, books on alternative medicine, heredity, and public health, translation and transcontinental or transatlantic perspectives, as well as anthropology and geography, popularization and historiography. Readers of our Forum will notice the absence of New Materialism and object studies, New Formalism, and work intersecting visual studies, architecture, and exhibition or museum studies. Nevertheless, we certainly did not neglect these important new directions, some of which are represented elsewhere in this volume. In particular, New Materialism and object studies were foremost in our minds when this Forum was in the planning stages: we intended it as a kick-off to and ongoing dialogue with the Atkins Goethe Conference 2020 on *Goethe's Things*, before pandemic redirections affected conference as well as printing and production schedules. We are looking forward to devoting (part of) the next two volumes to these important (and novel) directions.

The finished contributions, to our surprise, formed pairs. Their arrangement in the Forum section reflects an unintended serendipity. However, we do hope that pairing them truly invites further work, for example, on expanding the field of health studies/medical humanities (Stephanie Hilger) while challenging the erstwhile absorption of disability studies within it (Eleoma Bodammer), leading to transformative effects on pedagogy and institutions of higher learning and thus creating new questions and fields of inquiry not represented here. Similarly, Mary Helen Dupree's and Peter Höyng's dialoguing on orality/sound studies/musicology suggests that "detours" through new directions not only fortify tasks for book history and musicology, respectively, but may also serve to reinvoke older questions and tear away the veil of history, exposing what has been eclipsed in disciplinary canon formations. Obenewaa Oduro-Opuni and Matthew Birkhold remind us not only how adjacent (and not so adjacent) disciplines open up novel pathways to materials but also show how national divisions—themselves an outgrowth of the eighteenth century—may have imposed a constricting order onto texts, thoughts, and concepts around 1800. This order, in turn, may have implied causalities where there were at best networks, and coexistences that produced chaos from which innovation, systems, and ideas suggesting progress emanated but not without creating blind spots and biases along the way. And finally, Brent Peterson's and Bridget Swanson's essays illustrate, respectively, the remediation of entrenched eighteenth-century concepts of migration (*Auswanderung*) and education (*Bildung*) today, along with popularization, *Geschichtsvergessenheit* (historical amnesia), and new forms of instrumentalization in the public sphere. As we circle back to the practices of pedagogy and the structure of institutions, perhaps we sense not only a historical continuity with fault lines and fractures but also an enormous potential for debate and insight into innovative learning and creative scholarship—in short, the modernity of the eighteenth century.

*Bowdoin College*
*University of Nebraska-Lincoln*

STEPHANIE M. HILGER

# Medical Humanities and the Eighteenth Century

THE ACADEMIC SEPARATION of the sciences and the humanities makes it difficult to explore the connection between the various aspects of the human condition, not least in the discipline of medicine. Even though medicine is not a hard science per se but an interpretive approach that combines scientific and humanities-based modes of knowledge and therefore also experiences what Catherine Belling has called the "hermeneutic anxiety" that informs humanities research,[1] it is firmly located among other science buildings whose literal and figurative gates are jealously guarded. The current academic focus on evidence-based medicine further increases the distance between medicine and humanities-based approaches to the human body by implying that the humanities do not produce real evidence. At the same time, calls for narrowing this distance are intensifying. Reestablishing the connection between the humanities and the sciences has become more important than ever because of global processes of corporatization that affect both health care institutions and universities. Cost efficiency in medical education has made it increasingly difficult to offer courses that focus on the human aspect of medicine within the medical curriculum itself. At the same time, the perceived crisis in the humanities has encouraged literary scholars to emphasize that their work is not a self-referential field of inquiry but that it engages broad social and political processes. As a result of the convergence of these two trends, the need for interdisciplinary spaces in teaching and research has grown over the past years.

The most forceful calls for bridging disciplinary divides already occurred in the 1970s, when the practice of "literature and medicine" gained ground as a reaction to the transformation of medical schools into high-powered research centers in the previous decade. As Anne Hudson Jones outlines, Edmund Pellegrino called upon medical educators to refocus their attention on the moral dimension of medicine.[2] At the same time, Joanne Trautmann Banks highlighted the necessity of "read[ing], in the fullest sense" in order to increase medical practitioners' "tolerance for ambiguity" with the goal of improving patient care.[3] With the establishment of the journal *Literature and Medicine* in 1982, these interdisciplinary endeavors found a home. The name of the journal reflected the reality that the majority of these interdisciplinary ventures originated in literature departments. In addition, literature, in the sense of *belles lettres*, is perhaps the most "humanistic" of all humanities disciplines because it is often considered a production of art for art's sake. However, the contributors to the first issues of the journal demonstrated the exact opposite of this common notion. In fact, Rita Charon vehemently opposed an instrumentalization of literature that provided medical doctors merely with "a civilizing veneer" by arguing that writing a poem or quoting a philosopher does not necessarily make a better doctor.[4] Many of the early scholars working in the field focused on the textual features not only of literature but also of other types of discourse, including medical texts. One incarnation of this practice is Rita Charon's concept of "narrative medicine," which puts medical practitioners face to face with the textuality of their patients' experiences. These close reading practices were geared at simultaneously uncovering the textual dimension of medical discourse and demonstrating that literature does not constitute a self-referential aesthetic discourse but a powerful vehicle for social commentary. Gradually, the designation "literature and medicine" became limiting in view of other humanities-based approaches to medicine such as history, philosophy, and theology, which do not necessarily focus on medicine's narrative dimension. As a result, the designation "medical humanities" began to be used with increasing frequency. The founding of journals such as *Medical Humanities*, published by the Institute of Medical Ethics in the UK (2000), and the *Journal of Medical Humanities*, based in the Center for Bioethics and Humanities at the University of Colorado (1981),[5] signaled the expansion of the field and its increasing academic institutionalization. More recently, as Paul Crawford has observed, "medical humanities" has been replaced by "health humanities" to encompass not only the full range of disciplines involved in the delivery of healthcare but also the patients themselves.[6]

This brief overview shows that even though there is some slippage between the designations "literature and medicine," "narrative medicine," "medical humanities," and "health humanities," they are not synonymous; each highlights a specific approach in the effort to overcome strict disciplinary separations.[7] Scholars and teachers in these fields have been exploring a wide range of interrelated topics: the history of medicine, the social impacts of health policy, the therapeutic uses of reading and writing literature (biblio- and scriptotherapy), writing about disease (pathography), graphic medicine, the pedagogical uses of literature courses in the medical curriculum, the role of doctor-writers, the representation of the medical encounter in literary texts, the medical case history as a literary genre, changing literary depictions of disease, and social determinants of health, just to name a few of the most prevalent areas of inquiry. Through their exploration of these topics, scholars have sought to connect the sciences with the humanities.

But how should we imagine the relationship between medical humanities/health humanities and eighteenth-century studies, and German studies of that century in particular? Much of the work in health humanities performed by literary scholars centers on the twentieth and twenty-first centuries. From this perspective, the divide between the sciences and the humanities appears as an immutable reality. Approaching the effort to connect the sciences and the humanities from an eighteenth-century vantage point, however, demonstrates that the separation of these realms of knowledge, and its institutionalization, is a relatively recent phenomenon, mainly of the nineteenth century. The eighteenth century constitutes a transitional period between the *de facto* interdisciplinarity that had reigned until the Early Modern period and the separation of the sciences and the humanities that was institutionalized in the European system of higher education in the nineteenth century and its eventual global dissemination by way of Anglo-American research universities in the twentieth century. Eighteenth-century thinkers reacted to the beginnings of this disciplinary specialization, when the Cartesian mind-body dichotomy was mapped onto the separation of the humanities and sciences, which were eventually characterized as "soft" and "hard," respectively.[8]

One of the most famous eighteenth-century writings on this topic is Friedrich Schiller's inaugural lecture as a professor of history at the University of Jena in 1789, "Was heißt und zu welchem Ende studiert man Universalgeschichte?" ("What is and to what End do we Study Universal History?"). Addressed to his fellow historians and students, Schiller contrasts the "Brotgelehrte" (the scholar who works for his bread) with the "philosophische Kopf" (5; philosophical head).[9] Schiller argues that the scholar who works primarily to earn an income is interested in separating his discipline from all others so as to protect his academic territory and carefully circumscribe his tasks. By contrast, the philosophical head incarnates the Enlightenment ideal of the universal scholar whose goal is to connect his studies to different disciplines in an effort to insert them into the "große Ganze der Welt" (7; the wholeness of the world). While Schiller specifically addresses his fellow historians, his lecture highlights the inadequacy of any type of epistemological endeavor that does not strive to understand the "Zusammenhang der Dinge" (7; connection between things) by failing to embed discipline-specific knowledge within a broader context. Schiller's positing of the ideal of the philosophical head acknowledges the reality that, in the late eighteenth century, disciplinary boundaries had become jealously guarded by those working within their comforting confines. Schiller's reflections on scholarship and research were shaped profoundly by the disciplinary rift that he experienced in his own life. In addition to being a historian and playwright, Schiller was also a physician; he therefore had to straddle the gap between medicine and literature/history. In his lecture, Schiller explicitly mentioned medical doctors, alongside lawyers and theologians, as those suffering acutely from the separation of their discipline from other fields of knowledge that explore the human condition.

Schiller wrote three medical dissertations. The first one, "Philosophie der Physiologie" (Philosophy of Physiology), of which only eleven paragraphs survive, was rejected for its holistic approach and his writing style. His second attempt, "Tractatio de Discrimine Febrium Inflammatoriarum et Putridarum" ("Über den Unterschied zwischen entzündlichen und fauligen Fiebern" / On the Difference between Inflammatory and Putrid Fevers), written in Latin, suffered the same fate. In it, Schiller critiqued medical textbooks and did so by embedding literary citations. His third attempt, *Versuch über den grossen Zusammenhang der thierischen Natur des Menschen mit seiner geistigen* (Essay on the Connection between Man's Animal and Mental Nature), was more successful and was accepted by his professors in Stuttgart; it was printed by Cotta in 1780, but only after Schiller was forced to remove formulations that were deemed too literary.[10] The juxtaposition of Schiller's play *Die Räuber* (The Robbers) which was written during the author's medical studies and sometimes at his patients' bedside, with his third dissertation demonstrates the interpenetration of medical and literary discourse in Schiller's oeuvre.[11] As a subject of the Duke of Württemberg, however, Schiller could not live up to his own ideal of the "philosophische Kopf." The Duke prohibited Schiller, whom he had hired as an army surgeon, to produce nonmedical writings. Their conflict eventually escalated, leading to Schiller's escape from Stuttgart and his position at the University of Jena. Schiller's inaugural lecture and his suspicion of the "Brotgelehrte" function as a criticism of the separation of those disciplines that we now call the sciences and the humanities. Schiller's dissertation already strove to reconnect the two poles in the Cartesian dichotomy—body ("thierisch") and mind ("geistig")—by promoting a psychosomatic approach to human life, not unlike Karl Philipp Moritz's "Erfahrungsseelenkunde." Schiller warns of the separation of mind and matter, body and soul, sciences and humanities. That he was not the only one worried about this development can be seen in the writings of the prominent Paris surgeon Sauveur François Morand. Morand's *Discours dans lequel on prouve qu'il est nécessaire au chirurgien d'être lettré* (Treatise in which it is Proven that a Surgeon Needs to be Lettered, 1743) registers the anxieties about a shift towards pure materialism that excludes any *lettres*.

The fact that Schiller has been described as a "Philosoph und Mediziner" (philosopher and physician) in twentieth-century scholarship testifies to the institutionalized division of the sciences and the humanities.[12] Inquiries into Schiller's writings therefore provide a particularly fruitful ground for research. Physician-writers such as Schiller and Albrecht von Haller, however, only constitute one field of inquiry in eighteenth-century health humanities. Any of the topics mentioned in the introduction to this essay—ranging from literary representations of medical encounters to medical case studies as a hybrid form—will broaden the field of health humanities by positioning the eighteenth century as a time that registered the anxieties about the beginning disciplinary fragmentation that current health humanities seeks to overcome.

While the eighteenth century provides a fruitful vantage point from which to approach the health humanities, the health humanities allow for a fresh perspective on the eighteenth century. Eighteenth-century thinkers wrestled with the separation of the humanities/mind from the sciences/body, yet they rarely questioned the supremacy of the mind:

> Historically, the division of labor between faculties of arts and faculties of science emerged in the 18th century, alongside the idea that humans are more than mere nature—that there are human-exclusive capacities that set us apart from "mere" animals and plants. More specifically, the argument was that reason, language, and art had liberated the human from the contingencies of nature and had gradually given rise to a uniquely human world of "culture" that is irreducible to the laws of nature and that therefore requires its own set of sciences (the term "culture" was first used to mark a distinctive human world in the late 1770s).[13]

The supremacy of the human mind was, of course, a cornerstone of the Enlightenment and its philosophical heads. The humanities catered to the intellectual needs of humans, who were perceived not only as superior to animals but also as nonanimal. The implicit assumption was that humans were more humane and that the humanities promoted the humanistic ideals of liberty, equality, and fraternity promoted during the Enlightenment. The Enlightenment's self-perception has significantly shaped the scholarship of this period. Daniel Gordon argues that there are two stances towards the Enlightenment.[14] The first is critical of the Enlightenment's claims, informed by a postmodernist approach. The second one, by contrast, idealizes the era's assertations and builds a teleological bridge to the French Revolution. Analysis beyond this polarized thinking has become crucial in uncovering the discontinuities and tensions in eighteenth-century thought so as to "illuminat[e] the obscure aspects of an era whose primary metaphor was one of light."[15] The medical humanities, seeking to rebuild the bridge between the sciences and the humanities, is one of the paths to a more holistic understanding of the eighteenth century beyond those two opposing poles.

*University of Illinois at Urbana-Champaign*

## NOTES

1. Catherine Belling, "Hypochondriac Hermeneutics: Medicine and the Anxiety of Interpretation," *Literature and Medicine* 25, no. 2 (2006): 376–401, here 376.

2. Anne Hudson Jones, "Why Teach Literature and Medicine? Answers from Three Decades," in *New Directions in Literature and Medicine Studies*, ed. Stephanie Hilger (London: Palgrave Macmillan, 2017) 31–48.

3. Joanne Trautmann Banks, "The Wonders of Literature in Medical Education," in *The Role of the Humanities in Medical Education*, ed. Donnie J. Self (Norfolk: Bio-Medical Ethics Program, Eastern Virginia Medical School, 1978) 32–44, here 36.

4. Rita Charon, *Narrative Medicine: Honoring the Stories of Illness* (Oxford: Oxford UP, 2006) 226.

5. The *Journal of Medical Humanities* was first published under the title *Bioethics Quarterly* (1981). In 1982, the name was changed to the *Journal of Bioethics.* Then, in 1985, it became the *Journal of Medical Humanities and Bioethics* before assuming its current title, *Journal of Medical Humanities* in 1989.

6. See Paul Crawford et al., "Health Humanities: The Future of Medical Humanities?" *Mental Health Review Journal* 15 (2010): 4–10.

7. For a more detailed history of the field, see Anne Jones; also see Ronald Carson, Chester Burns, and Thomas R. Cole, eds., *Practicing the Medical Humanities. Engaging Physicians and Patients* (Hagerstown, MD: University Publishing Group, 2003); Thomas Cole, Nathan Carlin, and Ronald Carson, *Medical Humanities: An Introduction* (New York: Cambridge UP, 2015); Martyn Evans and Ilora G. Finlay, eds., *Medical Humanities* (London: BMJ, 2001); Therese Jones, Delese Wear, and Lester D. Friedman, eds., *Health Humanities Reader* (New Brunswick, NJ: Rutgers UP, 2014).

8. Recent examples in Anglo-American scholarship defining the juncture of health sciences and eighteenth-century studies from my own work include Stephanie Hilger "Epistemological Anxiety: The Case of Michel-Anne Drouart," in *Intelligible States:*

*Bodies and/as Transitions in the Health Humanities*, ed. Stephanie Hilger and Lisa DeTora (London: Routledge, 2019); Stephanie Hilger, "Enlightenment Angst: James Parsons' *A Mechanical and Critical Enquiry into the Nature of Hermaphrodites* (1741)," in *Taking Stock: Twenty-Five Years of Comparative Literary Research*, ed. Norbert Bachleitner, Achim Hölter, and John McCarthy (Leiden: Brill, 2020) 247-69. Also see Alice Kuzniar, *The Birth of Homeopathy out of the Spirit of Romanticism* (Toronto: U of Toronto P, 2017)

9. All translations are my own.

10. Friedrich Schiller, *Versuch über den grossen Zusammenhang der thierischen Natur des Menschen mit seiner geistigen.* (Tübingen: Cotta, 1780); Friedrich Schiller *Was heißt und zu welchem Ende studiert man Universalgeschichte? Eine akademische Antrittsrede* (Jena: In der akademischen Buchhandlung, 1789).

11. Hans Sutermeister discusses Schiller's career as a physician and its intertwinement with his work in the humanities. See his *Schiller als Arzt: Ein Beitrag zur Geschichte der psychosomatischen Forschung* (Bern: Haupt, 1955).

12. Wilfried Noetzel, "Friedrich Schiller. Philosoph und Mediziner," *Internationale Zeitschrift für Philosophie und Psychosomatik* 1 (2009): 1-15, here 1.

13. Tobias Rees, et al. "How the Microbiome Challenges Our Concept of Self," *PLoS Biology* 16, no. 2 (2018). https://doi.org/10.1371/journal.pbio.2005358.

14. Daniel Gordon, "Introduction: Postmodernism and the French Enlightenment," in *Postmodernism and the Enlightenment* (New York: Routledge, 2001) 1-6.

15. Andrew Curran, *The Anatomy of Blackness: Science and Slavery in an Age of Enlightenment.* (Baltimore: Johns Hopkins UP, 2011) xi.

ELEOMA BODAMMER

# Disability Studies and New Directions in Eighteenth-Century German Studies

THE FORUM TOPIC "(New) Directions" is an opportunity to draw attention to the need to integrate disability studies more into Goethe scholarship and research on eighteenth-century German literature. However, going in a new direction within the discipline should not only mean an impulse for discussion; it should have a transformative impact that causes positive changes in the place where the discipline is housed, namely, at the university itself. My thoughts on this new direction therefore play out against the need for and move toward broader, more inclusive perspectives in the field of German studies and its institutional frameworks. Admittedly, I reflect on this topic from the distinct perspective of German in the United Kingdom.

As German studies expands to explore wider and newer fields, academics are using the many opportunities available to openly and publicly reflect on this transformation, for example, via blogs, social media, and in new spaces in academic journals, such as the Forum section of the *Goethe Yearbook*. In such spaces, amplifying the voices of those with protected characteristics (in the UK, the Equality Act 2010 lists these as age, disability, gender reassignment, marriage and civil partnership, pregnancy and maternity, race, religion or belief, sex, and sexual orientation) and reflecting on positionality is also part of this new approach to diversifying both research and the curriculum. Furthermore, as with other "expanding" German studies pathways (e.g., gender and race) that address underrepresentation, a more emphatic focus on disability should be intersectional and can also have a transformative and inclusive impact on university curricula, pedagogy, assessment, and course design.

Disability studies and literary disability studies scholars are often agents of change and academic activists. As such, they are sensitive to the real-world relevance of their research focus. Whether identifying as disabled, not disclosing, or nondisabled allies and advocates, they often bring a commitment to challenging prejudice, stigma, injustice, and bias in relation to disability, to supporting disability pride and visibility, and to amplifying the voices of disabled people. These individuals can actively bring about institutional change by creating opportunities for disabled people (or people with disabilities) to teach and conduct research, and by educating the next generation of students to use disability theory for literary study and to be knowledgeable about inclusive terms and ableist structures.[1] Disability studies scholars can transform work environments both within and outside the academy, for example, by fighting for civil rights, accommodations and adjustments, physical access, safe spaces, content warnings, universal and equitable design, fair assessment, etc., and by attending to language that may intend to assure fairness and "objectivity," but nevertheless often fails to secure inclusiveness.[2] The academic discipline of disability studies generally seeks to go beyond research, aiming instead to serve as a holistic approach that informs many aspects of academic life.

Much can be gained from examining the eighteenth-century concept of *Behinderung* before it evolved into a collective idea in the twentieth century through examining period-specific uses of alternative words and concepts. According to Felix Welti in *Behinderung und Rehabilitation im sozialen Rechtsstaat* (Disability and Rehabilitation in the Social Constitutional State, 2005), the terms *Behinderung* and *Behinderte* have only been in use in the modern-day sense of disability and disabled people in Germany since around 1919, just after World War I, after being popularized by the Otto-Perl-Bund, a self-help group for physically disabled people in Berlin. Welti maintains that the word *Gebrechen* (affliction) was the term most commonly used as an overarching term for disability prior to the modern era.[3] Grimms' *Wörterbuch* defines "Behinderung" and "behindern" as preventing someone from doing something (in the sense of "verhindern"), deriving from the Latin "impedimentum" and "impedire."[4] Similarly, the online Adelung dictionary classifies "behindern" as to impede, in the context of legal impediments.[5] The online Goethe *Wörterbuch* defines "Behinderung" in relation to its use in a theater context for an incapacity caused, for example, by illness, and clarifies the meaning of "behindern" through the example of preventing others from developing or educating themselves.[6] Alternative words, such as the word "Invalide" are documented in the online Goethe *Wörterbuch* and Adelung to describe those unable to work or serve as a result of an illness, disability, or an injury in the context of war.

When tracing the origins of the meanings of *Behinderung* and related terms we find a focus on prevention, barriers, and obstacles to progression. There is some correspondence between the range of meanings that *Behinderung* and *behindern* have in the German language in the eighteenth century and their historical equivalents in English: namely, the noun *disability* and the verb *to disable*. These include the sense of preventing a person from performing an action, an inability to act, a temporary impairment, and a soldier discharged due to injury.[7] Eighteenth-century engagements with aesthetic and political debates surrounding physical, mental, cognitive, and social impairments, and ableism made use of a wide range of terms specific to the period and context. Tracing how literary representations of disability in German-language writing evolved and intersected with other characteristics, such as class, race, gender, etc., can reveal lost period- and country-specific concepts.

How then can Goethe studies and eighteenth-century German studies engage more directly with the well-established theoretical framework of disability studies and catch up, in this sense, with the field of English literature? Taking eighteenth-century German studies in a new direction could mean using disability theory to interpret both canonical and noncanonical literary texts from this period with the aim of retrieving protodisability concepts. Such interpretations might focus on disability metaphors, negative images, and cultural attitudes toward disability and disabled people, using the approach described by Mitchell and Snyder as the "negative image school" with its "dehumanizing representations."[8] Alternatively, they might seek to uncover what Lennard J. Davis refers to as "the hegemony of normalcy" and its fragility in relation to disability.[9] Approaches might emphasize that disabled and nondisabled bodies and minds are constructed socially and by the other. They might examine the use of disability as a trope or "narrative prosthesis," which Mitchell and Snyder argue is the "crutch" on which disability narratives "lean for their representational power, disruptive potentiality, and analytical insight."[10] Mitchell and Snyder's concept of narrative prosthesis involves a disabled character being "artificially" used to tell a story of curative intervention and restored functionality.[11] Without a disability studies framework, narratives about curing impairments or disabilities may be received as positive; however, through the lens of such a framework, they are challenged and critiqued as having ableist objectives, thus reinforcing the supremacy of normalcy and erasing the lived experiences and identities of disabled people. Raising concerns about the dominance of the idea of the restoration of normalcy as a master narrative is one of the many focuses of disability studies.

Traversing the entire theoretical history of the discipline can obviously not be accomplished here; the scope of this paper limits discussion to flagging a few milestones in this history, such as the use of models in the social, cultural, and literary debates on disability. The medical model of disability defines disability as a medical issue and focuses on prevention, cures, and rehabilitation; however, it is criticized for foregrounding the impairment, disadvantages, and weaknesses of disabled individuals. The social model of disability, pioneered by Michael Oliver, offers a response to the medical model and assesses disability as a problem within society rather than within the individual. Furthermore, the social model examines the disabling effects of social environments and focuses on social inequality, exclusion, and discrimination.[12] Through changes in social attitudes, as well as improvements in access, inclusion, and participation, the social model aspires to achieve reforms and secure human rights.[13]

The cultural model emerged in the 1990s and identified the need to include cultural and intersectional perspectives; it is now also known as critical disability studies.[14] As part of this development, as Meekosha and Shuttleworth argue, scholars challenged the social model for the way it differentiated between impairment and disability as nonreciprocal concepts, where the former is viewed as "a functional limitation" and the latter "a socially generated system of discrimination."[15] In this critical disability studies context, we also find the idea of disability as a complex embodied identity[16] that is fluid and context related. Here, there is a rejection of binaries as oppositional elements, such as impairment/disability and disability/ability; instead, these poles are seen as in dialogue with each other.[17] The cultural model of disability introduced the idea that culture influences our understanding of disability and called for cultural and literary analysis.[18] This approach examines disability as a cultural and political experience and locates sites of discrimination, violence, restriction, resistance, liberation, and agency.[19] It recognizes that the analysis of disability reveals responses to ethics, values, ideals, morals, identity, social relations, and lived and embodied experiences.[20] In this context, the slash in dis/ability is used to signify the breaking down of the binary of ability and disability and to punctuate the understanding of an interplay between disabled and nondisabled experiences.[21]

More discussion of the ways in which disability was mediated in eighteenth-century literature refines not only the theoretical foundation of these social and cultural models but also diversifies approaches to rethinking models for literary history. Such discussion could take a variety of directions that might help to explain responses to disability in aesthetic theories, debates on humanity, and the history of emotions. To help disability studies make a more pronounced transdisciplinary leap from the social sciences to literary studies, more work is needed on research topics such as hidden or nonvisible disabilities, passing as disabled or nondisabled, the idea of "assimilation" into environments designed for nondisabled people, performing disability, disability drag (where a nondisabled actor plays a disabled character),[22] narratives of reverse prejudice against nondisabled characters, and the broader field of the historical construction and evolution of disability as a collective term in the context of medical, cultural, religious, and supernatural epistemes.

Period-specific books on disability in German literature continue to be lacking. However, Carol Poore's *Disability in Twentieth-Century German Culture* (2007) is an important milestone in relation to cultural history, and Peter Lang has introduced a new book series called "Disability, Media, Culture," which is open to German studies proposals.[23] Conversely, theoretically driven approaches broaden the purview of particular periods. For example, editing a volume of the *Edinburgh German Yearbook on Disability in German Literature, Film, and Theater* with German sociologist Michael Schillmeier was one way in which I was personally able to contribute to offering a platform to scholars of modern German literature working on disability.[24] Overall, North American and British disability theory has heavily influenced the critical engagement with disability in German Studies; the latter relies on Anglo-American scholarship for its foundational terms and discourse. Yet eighteenth-century German studies, and German studies in general, would benefit from a better integration of German-language scholarship on disability that could mitigate the disconnect between the cultural context of the theory and its application in literary studies.[25]

Theoretical approaches in literary studies that relate to diversity, inclusion, and accessibility have made a successful transition from the periphery to the center by changing the environment and context in which this research is received. This context shifting involved work focused on creating more inclusive environments in which to work and study as well as commitments to promoting equality, diversity, and inclusion in the curriculum, which is often an institutional objective for learning and teaching strategies.

With the advent of decolonizing and diversifying movements at universities, diversity and inclusivity goals are now informing our thinking about course design, ensuring that women writers, working-class writers, and writers of color are represented. Students from a variety of backgrounds are beginning to see themselves reflected in study material and relevant theoretical frameworks are being taught and put to good use. However, when it comes to the subject of disability, the goal of inclusion must not just be about addressing physical barriers to participation, it must also be about changing the curriculum to make it more disability-inclusive through, for example, teaching texts about and by disabled people, promoting the work of disabled academics, and using the critical theoretical framework of disability studies. From a disability studies perspective, not including disability is a form of exclusionary behavior that reinforces an ableist curriculum; it means we are not training future scholars in the field of disability studies, helping them become agents of change, or educating and raising awareness among students about how to respond to students with disabilities in the classroom and beyond. To grow disability studies within German literary studies we need research-led teaching on the subject. A shift in academic culture that diversifies disability in a way that includes literature about and by disabled people could have a transformative impact on the academy and take it in a new direction.

*University of Edinburgh*

## NOTES

1. The term "disabled people" places the identity marker first, whereas a person-first approach uses the term "people with disabilities."

2. For example, where noninclusive language is encountered within the institution, it is important to challenge it by raising smaller questions about whether terms such as "blind or double-blind peer reviewing" is still acceptable language, and making cases for neutral and inclusive adjectives, such as "anonymous" and "independent," which do not reinforce the idea that not seeing is equal to not knowing, and do not claim a problematic metaphorical link to the lived experience of being visually impaired or blind.

3. Felix Welti, *Behinderung und Rehabilitation im sozialen Rechtsstaat: Freiheit, Gleichheit und Teilhabe behinderter Menschen* (Tübingen: Mohr Siebeck, 2005) 55.

4. http://www.woerterbuchnetz.de/DWB?lemma=behinderung; http://www.woert erbuchnetz.de/DWB?lemma=behindern.

5. http://woerterbuchnetz.de/cgi-bin/WBNetz/wbgui_py?sigle=Adelung&lemma=be hindern.

6. http://woerterbuchnetz.de/cgi-bin/WBNetz/wbgui_py?sigle=GWB&lemma= behindern.

7. For a discussion of the concept of disability in the context of literary studies, before it acquired its modern meaning, see Essaka Joshua, *Physical Disability in British Romantic Literature* (Cambridge: Cambridge University Press, 2020) 1–2.

8. David T. Mitchell and Sharon L. Snyder, *Narrative Prosthesis: Disability and the Dependencies of Discourse* (Ann Arbor: University of Michigan Press, 2000) 15.

9. Lennard J. Davis, *Enforcing Normalcy: Disability, Deafness and the Body* (London: Verso, 1995) 49.

10. Mitchell and Snyder 49.

11. Mitchell and Snyder 53.

12. Anne Waldschmidt, "Disability Goes Cultural: The Cultural Model of Disability as an Analytical Tool" in *Culture—Theory—Disability: Encounters between Disability Studies and Cultural Studies*, ed. Anne Waldschmidt, Hanjo Berressem, Moritz Ingwersen (Bielefeld: transcript, 2017) 19–28, here 20–21.

13. Waldschmidt 21.

14. For an overview of the history of the formation of the field of critical disability studies and the way it has re-evaluated the social model of disability and incorporated discussions of diversity, gender, race, and class into the concepts of disability, see Helen Meekosha and Russell Shuttleworth, "What's So 'Critical' about Critical Disability Studies?," in *The Disability Studies Reader*, ed. Lennard J. Davis, 5th ed. (New York: Routledge, 2017) 175–94.

15. Meekosha and Shuttleworth 177.

16. See Liat Ben-Moshe, "'The Institution Yet to Come': Analyzing Incarceration Through a Disability Lens" in *The Disability Studies Reader*, 119–30, here 120. This is in reference to Rosemarie Garland-Thomson, *Extraordinary Bodies: Figuring Physical Disability in American Culture and Literature* (New York: Columbia UP, 1997).

17. Meekosha and Shuttleworth 182.

18. On the call to revise the social model and include cultural analysis, see, for example, Tom Shakespeare, "Cultural Representation of Disabled People: Dustbins for Disavowal?" *Disability & Society* 9, no. 3 (1994): 283–99. For the inclusion of disability in feminist studies and the cultural and literary analysis of disability, see Garland-Thomson, *Extraordinary Bodies* and Rosemarie Garland-Thomson, "Integrating Disability, Transforming Feminist Theory," *NWSA Journal* 14, no. 3 (2002): 1–32. For the development of the cultural model of disability, see Sharon L. Snyder and David T. Mitchell, "Re-engaging the Body: Disability Studies and the Resistance to Embodiment," *Public* Culture 13, no. 3 (2001): 367–89. For research on nonnormative embodiment, sexuality, and subjectivity, see Margrit Shildrick, in particular, *Dangerous Discourses of Disability, Subjectivity and Sexuality* (Basingstoke: Palgrave Macmillan, 2009) and Tobin Siebers, *Disability Aesthetics* (Ann Arbor: U of Michigan P, 2010). For work in the field of feminist philosophy and disability, see Shelley Lynn Tremain, *Foucault and Feminist Philosophy of Disability* (Ann Arbor: U of Michigan P, 2017); Davis *Enforcing Normalcy*; and Lennard J. Davis, *The End of Normal: Identity in a Biocultural Era* (Ann Arbor: U of Michigan P, 2014). This is not a comprehensive list, but a suggestion for further reading.

19. Waldschmidt 22–24.

20. Waldschmidt 23.

21. Waldschmidt 25–26.

22. Tobin Siebers, *Disability Theory* (Ann Arbor: U of Michigan P, 2008) 114.

23. Carol Poore, *Disability in Twentieth-Century German Culture* (Ann Arbor: U of Michigan P, 2007).

24. *Edinburgh German Yearbook: Disability in German Literature, Film, and Theater*, 4 (2010).

25. See, for example, work on the complex disabling relations between the social, nonsocial, and the individual, and the impairment/disability binary, by Michael Schillmeier, *Rethinking Disability: Bodies, Senses and Things* (London: Routledge,

2010). For the sociology of disability and the social construction of disability, see Anne Waldschmidt and Werner Schneider, eds., *Disability Studies, Kultursoziologie und Soziologie der Behinderung: Erkundungen in einem neuen Forschungsfeld* (Bielefeld: transcript, 2007). For disability history, see Elsbeth Bösl, Anne Klein, and Anne Waldschmidt, eds., *Disability History: Konstruktionen von Behinderung in der Geschichte: Eine Einführung* (Bielefeld: transcript, 2010) and Jutta Jacob, Swantje Köbsell, and Eske Wollrad, eds., *Gendering Disability: Intersektionale Aspekte von Behinderung und Geschlecht* (Bielefeld: transcript, 2010). For disability master narratives, see Petra Lutz, Thomas Macho, Gisela Staupe, and Heike Zirden, eds., *Der [im-] perfekte Mensch: Metamorphosen von Normalität und Abweichung* (Cologne: Böhlau, 2003) and Markus Dederich, *Körper, Kultur und Behinderung: Eine Einführung in die Disability Studies* (Bielefeld: transcript, 2007). For a recent theoretical overview of German-language Disability Studies, see David Brehme, Petra Fuchs, Swantje Köbsell, and Carla Wesselmann, eds., *Disability Studies im deutschsprachigen Raum: Zwischen Emanzipation und Vereinnahmung* (Weinheim: Beltz Juventa, 2020). This is not a comprehensive list, but a suggestion for further reading.

MARY HELEN DUPREE

# Goethe's Talking Books: Print Culture and the Problem of Literary Orality

OVER THE PAST TWO DECADES, there has been an upswing in scholarship on literary orality in the long eighteenth century, focusing in particular on the recitation and declamation of poetry. Much of this research takes as its starting point the reassessment of the "ear" and a related concern with the "tones" of language in Herder and Klopstock's poetics. In an analysis of Klopstock's 1774 *Gelehrtenrepublik* (The Republic of Letters), Karl-Heinz Göttert summarizes this shift:

> Nicht das—aufklärerische—Auge, sondern das Ohr wird das entscheidende Organ der sinnlichen Wahrnehmung, und nicht auf die "körperliche" *Unterstützung* der Sprache z.B. durch hohe oder tiefe Stimmlage kommt es an, sondern der Ton hat ein *eigenes* Leben, deren Zeichenhaftigkeit gerade keinen Regeln folgt.[1]

> Not the—Enlightened—eye, but rather the ear becomes the decisive organ of sensual perception; at stake here is not the "physical" *supporting* of language, for example, by pitching the voice high or low, but rather tone has its *own* life, whose semiotic character does not follow any rules.

As Göttert and others have shown, the revaluation of the ear in the eighteenth century was by no means limited to poetological theory, but also provided the impetus for a wide spectrum of acoustic performance and composition practices, which, in turn, inspired thousands of pages of commentary in instructional handbooks, journals, and correspondences. In his 2004 monograph *Ins Ohr geschrieben. Lyrik als akustische Kunst von 1750 bis 1800* (Written Into the Ear. Lyric Poetry as Acoustic Art from 1750 to 1800), Joh. Nikolaus Schneider draws on this enormous wealth of primary source material to show how the acoustic dimensions of language informed the composition and reception of German-language lyric poetry from 1750 to 1800.[2] Meanwhile, the impact of popular literary reading practices around 1800 has been central to my own research as well as that of scholars such as Reinhart Meyer-Kalkus, Hans-Joachim Jakob, and Martin Danneck. For example, Meyer-Kalkus's *Geschichte der literarischen Vortragskunst* (History of Literary Elocution, 2020) integrates popular practices of literary declamation and recitation into a broader history of oral reading that encompasses the reading practices of Goethe, Tieck, and Kleist.[3] Other scholars working at the intersection of media studies and the history of science have noted that the ascendancy of the acoustic in the domain of eighteenth-century aesthetics, poetics, and performance coincided with the rise of acoustic science as a discipline.[4] In her introduction to the 2015 edited volume *Dichtung für die Ohren. Literatur als tonale Kunst* (Poetry for the Ears: Literature as Tonal Art), Britta Herrmann reflects on the physiological and cultural implications of *das innere Hören* (interior or virtual hearing) around 1750 and the sense of loss that it generated, which itself had important consequences for literary culture.[5] In a somewhat similar vein, Tyler Whitney has revisited Herder's *Viertes Kritisches Wäldchen* (*Critical Forests: Fourth Grove*) in order to show that Herder's depictions of the ear were not simply abstractions, but were grounded in contemporary physiological discourse.[6]

The current wave of scholarship on literary orality in the long eighteenth century has been bolstered by the "acoustic turn" in literary studies and an expansion of interdisciplinary research under the aegis of Sound Studies since the early 2000s.[7] All of the abovementioned scholars have grappled in some way with the narrative of the ascendancy of silent reading, or *Verschriftlichung*, that has become entrenched in eighteenth-century German studies scholarship since the publication of Friedrich Kittler's *Aufschreibesysteme 1800/1900* (*Discourse Networks 1800/1900*) in the 1980s.[8] This discourse continues to exert a strong pull over discussions of literary orality in the German-speaking world, even as some media-studies scholars have shifted towards less exclusionary and more holistic approaches to orality and literacy. While scholars working on literary orality in Germany have tended by and large to reinforce the dominant narrative of *Verschriftlichung*, they have also rightly argued for the significance of orality as a factor in processes of literary communication, thereby opening up space for a wealth of groundbreaking research that traces the impact of literary orality on literary composition, intermedial encounters, knowledge production, and cultural change.

However, the task of unpacking literary orality in the long eighteenth century presents some uniquely tricky methodological and theoretical problems for scholars. The massive amount of primary source material available is itself an obstacle: How can one begin to sort through and evaluate the many lengthy—and often very repetitive—theoretical treatises, declamation handbooks, recitation anthologies, reviews, and related texts that appeared from 1750 onward, many of which are now available as full-text online resources? Can the source material be mined for information about performance practices without resorting to neopositivism, and without reproducing the aesthetic biases and blind spots of eighteenth- and nineteenth-century editors and journalists? As Schneider has argued, historical accounts of oral performances such as declamatory concerts or Klopstock recitations can only provide interpretations of those performances; they do not provide direct access to the performances themselves.[9] And of course, there are no audio recordings of eighteenth- and early nineteenth-century oral performances, although modern technology has made it possible to at least imaginatively recreate some historical soundscapes and sound artifacts.[10]

An even thornier problem has to do with the complex performance situations involved in recitation and declamation, in which speakers read literary texts aloud without inhabiting a role. These types of performances were staged in a variety of institutional and architectonic settings, from theaters and schools to private homes and outdoor venues. An approach grounded in performance studies would seem to be most useful for analyzing such situations. Yet, as Meyer-Kalkus has pointed out, the theoretical categories of German performance studies, such as co-presence and performativity (as the term was developed in the early 2000s by Erika Fischer-Lichte), emerged in response to twentieth-century avant-garde theater and performance art; they do not always map well onto more traditional, "rhetorical" or interpretive speaking practices.[11] The interdisciplinary field of sound studies offers some useful terminologies, such as Jonathan Sterne's concept of "ensoniment," which postulates the emergence of "sound" as a separate domain of inquiry in the mid-eighteenth century.[12] However, the topic of literary orality in the eighteenth century remains somewhat marginalized in sound studies, compared with the much larger number of studies on acousmatic sound, soundscapes, and acoustic technologies.

The binaries of traditional literary history and eighteenth-century studies can also prove unhelpful where literary orality is concerned. For example, separating "theory" from "practice" is not always useful in historical contexts where theoretical questions were often worked out in performance spaces. A more dynamic model of "praxis" is outlined by Hans-Joachim Jakob in his study of literary declamation in nineteenth-century Prussian school programs:

> Die Vermittlung von Deklamationswissen wird . . . keineswegs im Sinne einer folgenlosen, abstrakten und zweckfreien Kunstfertigkeit gedacht, sondern als Bestandteil einer lebendigen und "in allen Lebenslagen" nutzbaren kulturellen Praxis, die als Bestandteil nicht nur des bildungsbürgerlichen Alltagslebens im 19. Jahrhundert fungierte.[13]

> The communication of knowledge about declamation is . . . understood here not in the sense of an abstract and pure artistic skill without consequences, but rather as a component of a lively cultural practice that was useful in all life situations and whose function was not limited to the everyday life of the educated middle classes in the nineteenth century.

Like the theory-practice divide, the public-private distinction that has informed so much scholarship on the long eighteenth century may also prove of limited usefulness when dealing with the nontheatrical oral performance of literature, which often occupied a middle ground between publicity and intimacy.

Recent scholarship on eighteenth- and nineteenth-century literary communication networks and the history of the book offers some conceptual models that may be more useful for thinking about the "elective affinities" between orality and print culture. As Andrew Piper argues in his groundbreaking 2009 monograph, *Dreaming in Books: The Making of the Bibliographic Imagination in the Romantic Age*, the period around 1800 was one of both "bibliographic surplus" and "diversity"; a sense that there were "too many books" fueled anxieties about their circulation and proliferation.[14] Although literary orality remains marginal to Piper's study, it maps onto the concept of "sharing" that he develops to characterize practices such as the compiling of texts and text fragments in literary "miscellanies" or anthologies. "Sharing" complicates traditional notions of authorship: "the more writing was shared and shareable, the more difficult it became to claim something as one's own."[15] More recently, studies such as the Multigraph Collective's *Interacting with Print* (2018) and Abigail Williams's *The Social Life of Books* (2017) have applied the concept of "sharing" directly to the oral performance of literature. The Multigraph Collective, itself a collaborative endeavor, situates oral reading practices within a larger ecology of interactions between people and print: "To speak of shifting from an oral to a textual culture overlooks the extent to which conversations, lectures, sermons, and public readings persisted in the age of print and gained currency from their relationships with print."[16] Meanwhile, Williams calls attention to the impact of oral reading practices on the materiality of books:

> By considering the life of books read out loud, we can also start to see and hear the orality in the history of the book. The sharing of reading is evident both in the material form of books and in their reception history. Print sizes, book formats, and genres of writing were shaped by their suitability for performance. Large text, small books, short extracts, episodic structure, epigrammatic snippets: all made text more portable or more adaptable for use in company. Focusing on the performed and spoken nature of printed text gives us new insights into the way eighteenth-century literature was valued by its readers, forcing us to think about texts with audiences rather than readers, texts that were, as the great cultural historian Robert Darnton puts it, "better heard than seen."[17]

The "life of books read out loud" was a critical factor in the book trade in eighteenth-century Germany and even played a part in Goethe's own self-marketing practices. For example, when Goethe announced the new, twenty-volume Cotta edition of his collected works in the issue of the *Morgenblatt für gebildete Stände* (Morning Paper for the Educated Classes) dated April 26, 1816, he cited the oral and sociable performance of his poems as a justification for separating them into a single volume: "Der Componist, Sänger, Declamator will die Lieder, die kürzern Gedichte beisammen, um sich deren auf Reisen, in Gesellschaften bedienen zu können" (The composer, the singer, the declamator wants the songs and shorter poems kept together, so as to make use of them while traveling and in sociable circles).[18] Here, Goethe invalidates the notion that his works were only meant for silent, cloistered reading. He appears here as one of several actors in a creative circuit that brings together readers, composers, singers, and declamators, all of whom influenced the way(s) in which Goethe's poems were "shared." Thinking about orality as part of a larger ecology of "sharing" practices can help us to reassess the function and purpose of books and the contributions of multiple actors in eighteenth- and nineteenth-century literary communication networks.

Recent scholarship on orality in the *Goethezeit* has made valuable connections between orality and text circulation, highlighting important points of connection such as the popular practice of reading Klopstock's Christian epic poem *Der Messias* (*The Messiah*) aloud[19] and the instruction of literary declamation in nineteenth-century German schools.[20] Much of this scholarship centers on questions about authors and authorship, canon building, the rise of nationalism, and institution formation. While these are vitally important questions, there is also more work to be done in uncovering less hegemonic and even subversive aspects of the interface between orality and print, such as local and regional cultures of reading or the uses of the recitation anthology by female readers and members of ethnic and religious minorities. As Vance Byrd and Ervin Malakaj have argued, an approach that favors "a holistic model and a diffuse notion of authorship" can help us to capture the complexity and diversity of literary communication networks pre-1900.[21] Researching these hidden corners of literary history requires a rigorous and critical examination of existing sources, bibliographies, and archives, which are often shaped by hegemonic notions of canonicity. As Julie Koser points out in her contribution to last year's *Goethe Yearbook* forum on "Canon versus 'The Great Unread,'" such questions are made more urgent by the recent flourishing of computational criticism and distant reading practices.[22]

Looking at Goethe and his works alone, one can quickly find many examples of the interface between orality and print culture. Such examples include Goethe's somewhat skeptical depiction of a declamatory concert in *Die Wahlverwandtschaften* (*Elective Affinities*), his practice of reading his own works prior to publication, and his staging of a melodramatic reading of "Das Lied von der Glocke" ("The Song of the Bell") in Bad Lauchstädt following Schiller's death.[23] Moreover, orality is an important part of the story of Goethe's long literary afterlife: literary declamation practices and their remediation in recitation anthologies played a significant part in the shaping of the cult of Goethe in the nineteenth century. At the same time, one must be careful about eliding some of the lesser-known contributors to these networks. An examination of Goethe's relationship to orality can help to uncover previously unheard voices, like that of Emilie Herold, who performed Goethe's "Legende vom Hufeisen" ("The Legend of the Horseshoe") along with ballads by Schiller and Collin in a declamatory concert in Munich on December 12, 1809, while she was visibly pregnant.[24] Literary orality also connected networks of texts and actors in Germany with other regional and national networks, such as the communities of readers throughout the world that staged "Schiller-Feier" (Schiller memorials) upon the 100th anniversary of the poet's birth in 1859.

As Piper argued in 2009, revisiting the process of "becoming bookish" around 1800 is a necessary step towards understanding "the future of the book" (which some more pessimistic voices have presumed to be "the end of the book").[25] Similarly, taking stock of literary orality in the eighteenth and nineteenth centuries can help us to sound out present and future media ecologies, which are in the process of being transformed by the proliferation of "bookish" acoustic media such as podcasts and e-books. For all of these reasons, a reconsideration of literary orality in the larger context of literary communication networks of the so-called "Age of Goethe" is a key desideratum of Goethe studies in the twenty-first century.

*Georgetown University*

## NOTES

1. Karl-Heinz Göttert, *Geschichte der Stimme* (Munich: Fink, 1998) 381; see also Göttert, "Wider den toten Buchstaben. Zur Problemgeschichte eines Topos," in *Zwischen Rauschen und Offenbarung. Zur Kultur- und Mediengeschichte der Stimme*, ed. Friedrich Kittler, Thomas Macho, and Sigrid Weigel (Berlin: Akademie-Verlag, 2008) 93–113. On Klopstock's impact on practices of oral reading, see Johannes Birgfeld, "Klopstock, the Art of Declamation and the Reading Revolution: An Inquiry into One Author's Remarkable Impact on the Changes and Counter-Changes in Reading Habits between 1750 and 1800," *British Journal for Eighteenth-Century Studies* 31, no. 1 (2008): 101–17. Unless otherwise indicated, all translations are my own.

2. Joh. Nikolaus Schneider, *Ins Ohr Geschrieben. Lyrik als akustische Kunst zwischen 1750 und 1800* (Göttingen: Wallstein, 2004).

3. Reinhart Meyer-Kalkus, *Geschichte der literarischen Vortragskunst* (Berlin: Metzler, 2020). The book expands on the history of "Sprechkünste" (the art of speaking) that Meyer-Kalkus developed in *Stimme und Sprechkünste im 20. Jahrhundert* (Berlin: Akademie-Verlag, 2001). See also Mary Helen Dupree, "From 'Dark Singing' to a Science of the Voice: Gustav Anton von Seckendorff and the Declamatory Concert Around 1800," *Deutsche Vierteljahrsschrift für Literaturwissenschaft und Geistesgeschichte* 86, no. 3 (2012): 365–96; Hans-Joachim Jakob, *Der Diskurs über Deklamation und über die Praktiken auditiver Literaturvermittlung. Der Deutschunterricht des höheren Schulwesens in Preußen (1820–1900)* (Frankfurt a/M: Peter Lang, 2017); and Martin Danneck, "Lebendige Rede, tote Buchstaben und die Normierung des Sprechens im Schrifttum zur Deklamation um 1800," in *Belebungskünste. Praktiken lebendiger Darstellung in Literatur, Kunst, und Wissenschaft um 1800*, ed. Nicola Gess, Agnes Hoffmann, and Annette Kappeler (Munich: Fink, 2019) 43–60.

4. On acoustics and the performance of knowledge around 1800, see Viktoria Tkaczyk, "The Making of Acoustics around 1800, or How to Do Science with Words," in *Performing Knowledge 1750–1850*, ed. Mary Helen Dupree and Sean Franzel (Berlin: De Gruyter, 2015) 27–55. The intersection of acoustic science and aesthetic and practical knowledge from the eighteenth century onward is also a key concern of the interdisciplinary DFG network "Hör-Wissen im Wandel," which met from 2013 to 2016 and produced the collective volume *Wissensgeschichte des Hörens in der Moderne* (Berlin: De Gruyter, 2017).

5. Britta Herrmann, "Auralität und Tonalität in der Moderne. Aspekte einer Ohrenphilologie," *Dichtung für die Ohren. Literatur als tonale Kunst*, ed. Britta Herrmann (Berlin: Vorwerk 8, 2015) 9–32, here: 16–17. The term "das innere Hören" is also deployed by Albrecht Koschorke to account for the interiorization of listening in the eighteenth century. See Koschorke, *Körperströme und Schriftverkehr. Mediologie des 18. Jahrhunderts* (Munich: Fink, 1999) 337.

6. See Tyler Whitney, "Herder's Tympanum: Sound and Physiological Aesthetics 1800/1900," *Goethe Yearbook* 25 (2018): 11–29. On Herder and orality, see e.g., Martin

Danneck, "Johann Gottfried Herders Forderung einer Berücksichtigung der musikalischen Aspekte von Sprache in Wissenschaftstexten," *German Life and Letters* 70, no. 4 (2017): 456–65; and Tanvi Solanki, "Cultural Hierarchies and Vital Tones: Herder's Making of a German *Muttersprache*," *German Studies Review* 41, no. 3 (2018): 551–65.

7. The "acoustic turn" in German literary and cultural studies has also precipitated a wave of edited volumes and special issues devoted to unpacking the cultural and media-historical meanings of "sound." See e.g., *Sound Matters: Essays on the Acoustics of Modern German Culture*, ed. Nora M. Alter and Lutz Koepnick (New York: Berghahn, 2006); *Acoustic Turn*, ed. Petra Maria Meyer (Munich: Fink, 2008); also the special issue on *Sound Studies in German Contexts*, ed. Joy Calico and David Imhoof, *Colloquia Germanica* 46, no. 4 (2013).

8. Friedrich A. Kittler, *Aufschreibesysteme 1800/1900* (Munich: Fink, 1985); *Discourse Networks 1800/1900*, trans. Michael Metteer (Stanford, CA: Stanford UP, 1992).

9. Schneider 157.

10. See e.g., Patrick Feaster, *Pictures of Sound: One Thousand Years of Educed Audio: 980–1980* (New York: New York Distributed Art Publishers, 2013).

11. Meyer-Kalkus, *Vortragskunst*, 27.

12. Jonathan Sterne, *The Audible Past. Cultural Origins of Sound Reproduction* (Durham, NC: Duke UP, 2003) 2.

13. Jakob 55.

14. Andrew Piper, *Dreaming in Books: The Making of the Bibliographic Imagination in the Romantic Age* (Chicago: U of Chicago P, 2009) 5.

15. Piper 125.

16. The Multigraph Collective, *Interacting with Print: Elements of Reading in the Era of Print Saturation* (Chicago: U of Chicago P, 2019) 10.

17. Abigail Williams, *The Social Life of Books: Reading Together in the Eighteenth-Century Home* (New Haven and London: Yale UP, 2017) 3–4.

18. Johann Wolfgang von Goethe, *Goethes Werke*, ed. im Auftrag der Großherzogin Sophie von Sachsen Weimar (Weimar: Böhlau, 1887–1919) I/41:98.

19. See e.g., Birgfeld; also Meyer-Kalkus, *Vortragskunst*, 96–107.

20. See e.g., Jakob; also Meyer-Kalkus, *Vortragskunst*, 288–300.

21. See Vance Byrd and Ervin Malakaj, "Introduction," in *Market Strategies and German Literature in the Long Nineteenth Century*, ed. Vance Byrd and Ervin Malakaj (Berlin: De Gruyter, 2020) 3.

22. Julie Koser, "Recovery and Obsolescence: Feminist Scholarship, Computational Criticism, and the Canon," *Goethe Yearbook* 27 (2020): 197–203.

23. Mary Helen Dupree, "Radical Intermediality: Goethe's Schiller Memorials as Experimental Theater," in *The Radical Enlightenment in Germany. A Cultural Perspective*, ed. Carl Niekerk (Leiden and Boston: Brill/Rodopi, 2018) 353–81.

24 "Deklamatorium der Madame Emilie Herold. München, den 12. Dezember," *Journal des Luxus und der Moden* 25 (January 1810): 33–34; see also *Baierische National-Zeitung* 281, December 5, 1809, 1177–178.

25. Piper 4–8.

PETER HÖYNG

# Three Observations and Three Possible Directions: Musical and Eighteenth-Century Studies

IN PREPARING MY OBSERVATIONS on and considering the possible directions for musical studies in relation to eighteenth-century (German) studies, my choice of departure was browsing issues of the international journal *Eighteenth-Century Music.*[1] My premise was that a simple perusal would provide a sense of how musicologists and musical historians have shaped the field over the past decade or so. *Eighteenth-Century Music* is a relatively new journal; its first biannual volume came out only in 2004. This fact alone is surprising for a number of reasons. In the words of Richard Taruskin, "the eighteenth century provides the unshakeable bedrock of our scholarly and performing canons—canons that started forming precisely during the eighteenth century . . ., and continue, for better and worse, to sustain our musical occupations and institutions."[2] Following Taruskin's line of thought, one wonders why it took so long to establish an international journal of and for eighteenth-century music? One might argue that precisely because the music of the eighteenth century carries such a foundational weight for the field of musicology as a whole, it does not need special or specialized attention. Assuming that this is the case, the journal's existence then indicates, as a flipside and first observation, a shift within the larger field of classical musicology: no longer is eighteenth-century music the omnipotent authority; rather, it has become merely a foundational platform within the field of musicology.

Taruskin's extensive review of *The Cambridge History of Eighteenth-Century Music* (2009) also helps to develop a second observation. He begins his major argument with the bold statement that "since the late 1960s the status of the eighteenth century as a music-historical period has been very much in question."[3] The reason for facing this uncertainty derives from the fact "that all attempts at writing the history of eighteenth-century music . . . have been misguided because all had been looking for ways of connecting the style of Bach and Handel to the style of Haydn and Mozart."[4] In the recent past, one way of overcoming or at least sidestepping this trap has been to organize musical history by genre, as the *Cambridge History of Eighteenth-Century Music* and the *New Oxford History of Music* have both done. Pursuing this method is, at least in the eyes of Taruskin, "a deplorable decision, because it prevents (or absolves) this purported history of eighteenth-century music from ever engaging with the historiographical problems."[5] Ultimately, he criticizes the *Cambridge History of Eighteenth-Century Music* for a lack of providing a comprehensive or overarching narrative for a unifying development for the century in question.[6]

Taruskin's issues with the musical history of the eighteenth century allow me to introduce my second observation: namely, quarreling about the proper form of historiography seems to be from a bygone era. After all, we have entered an age of post-theory in which "post" can signal both abandoning a heightened claim to the necessity of practicing literary studies with a valued theoretical underpinning in mind, or entering a new era in which previous theoretical paradigms (e.g., Frankfurt School, Foucault's discourse analysis, postcolonialism, etc.) are available without claiming to be the dominant or absolute framework. In short, within the broader discourse of eighteenth-century studies, we have more or less reached scholarly consensus on what has been obvious to everyone who has experienced the past two decades: we live in postmodern times, never more so than long *after* the theoretical fad of postmodernism ended.[7]

While acknowledging the variety of theoretical frameworks at our disposal does not absolve anyone for a lack of sophistication, the recognition of a post-theoretical age is nevertheless liberating. A single overbearing theoretical framework no longer dictates how cultural, literary, or musical history should be done or, for that matter, how and what various approaches' co-, inter-, or transdisciplinary interactions might look like. With Taruskin's thundering verdict in mind, I therefore dare to say: we should not be overly concerned with how to find the historiographical nexus from Bach to Mozart on grounds of style alone, but we should continue to see the practices of music making within larger social, philosophical, and anthropological contexts. We should use methods borrowed from cultural studies, sociology, and literary theory—which, as the following, somewhat prototypical recent books and journal contributions show, can be done with exemplary success: Stephen Rose, *The Musician in Literature in the Age of Bach* (2011); Matthew Pritchard, "'The Moral Background of the Work of Art': 'Character' in German Musical Aesthetics, 1780–1850" (2012); David Wyn Jones, *Music in Vienna: 1700, 1800, 1900* (2016); Andrew Talle, *Music and Everyday Life in the Eighteenth Century* (2017); Emily H. Green and Catherine Mayes, *Consuming Music: Individuals, Institutions, Communities, 1730–1830* (2017); Daniel Chua, *Beethoven and Freedom* (2017); and the 2018 special issue of *Music and German Culture*.

These seven examples underscore not only the diversity of scholarly work over the past decade but also demonstrate that literary historians share enough interest and scholarly acumen with musical historians to allow for trans- if not interdisciplinary and collaborative work. The selection furthermore shows that today's musical historiography borrows from cultural studies as much as it continues to rely on some of the staples of the eighteenth century: Bach and Beethoven. Furthermore, the lives of these two prolific composers gesture toward another issue altogether within the field of eighteenth-century studies, namely that literary scholars view the eighteenth century as a rather stretchable period, well beyond its obvious dates (1700–1799) and easily embrace the vague, and often ill-defined attribute of "long."

A third and final point is worth making about some peculiarities of scholarship devoted to the eighteenth century. In the past decade, cultural as well as musical historians have begun to expand their field into sound studies. Befitting the self-understanding of this new mode of investigation, sound studies draws on science and technology studies, along with communication studies and other complementary fields. German studies, as a whole, has embraced sound studies, as use of this name as part of a German Studies Association Network evinces. However, recent scholarship such as Kata Gellen's *Kafka and Noise: The Discovery of Cinematic Sound in Literary Modernism* (2019) and Tyler Whitney's *Eardrums: Literary Modernism as Sonic Warfare* (2019) also indicate that sound studies has been an affair largely associated with modernism.[8] Thus far, musical historians of the eighteenth century seem to have avoided this new approach. However, within German studies there is one notable exception in terms of sound studies within eighteenth-century studies: as demonstrated by her introductory overview, "Music and Sound in Eighteenth-Century German Studies" (2020), Mary Helen Dupree has established herself within the US as the foremost and most innovative researcher on this topic.

The expansion of German studies into sound studies and Dupree's scholarship with its focus on orality and *Hör-Wissen*—on which she elaborates in the present Forum—also steer us toward the first of three possible new approaches to musical studies within eighteenth-century studies. In analogy to the new works on sound studies within modernist writings vis-à-vis acoustic phenomena, a recent call for papers by the International Society for Eighteenth-Century Studies (ISECS) demonstrates how eighteenth-century studies, with their logo- and ocular-centric focus, can expand toward the exploration of acoustic dimensions, namely when encounters with the other take into account "acts of hearing and listening, whether performed or narrated, real or imaginary. These occur, for example, in conversations, philosophical dialogues, sermons, speeches, musical performances (both religious and secular), theatrical performances, and literary declamation."[9] Evidently, sound studies has been firmly established as an interdisciplinary approach to the phenomenon of sound, and it seems therefore rather natural that eighteenth-century studies would find many pathways into various phenomena and practices of sound. Dupree's contribution to this Forum highlights one, long-eclipsed dimension of sound and the production of sound in literary performance: the persistence of orality. The latter aspect is supported by an "almost endless supply of textual sources," as Dupree rightly observes, including, for example, "literary representation of hearing and listening, treatises on music and declamation," yet they are waiting to be interpreted by scholars of the eighteenth century.[10]

Placed in the context of musical studies, sound studies in the eighteenth century defers to the field of music technology and media, as exemplified by the transition of the keyboard instrument from the cembalo to the ever-larger-sounding pianoforte. The genealogy of the piano as an instrument shows how technology and aesthetic production evolved inter-dependently. However, sound studies also provides new avenues into the understanding of performing arts. More closely emerging from within tra-ditional musical studies is research on the intermediality of the performing arts. After all, from the late 1760s on, the so-called *Nationaltheater* within German-speaking cultures often performed the typical range of theatrical and operatic genres and had to strike a balance between actors who also performed as singers and vice versa. The practice (and the legacy) of these newly established theaters—often in conjunction with or in competition with established opera houses—offered a fertile breeding ground for a host of questions that eighteenth-century studies has all too often ignored, remaining fixated on the meanings of canonical, printed texts rather than turning to the manifold aspects present in performance arts. Here again, Dupree, along with her coeditor Sean Franzel, offers insight into this prob-lem, opening the door for such an expanding view in their edited volume *Performing Knowledge 1750–1850* (2015). This shift in focus from the fixed text to the dynamic aspects of performing literary texts musically invites collaboration from such fields as sociology, philosophy, translation studies, network studies, intermedial aesthetics, art history, and, last but not least, music history. In this regard, the field of performance praxis paves the way. For example, the renewed interest in performing operas by Georg Friedrich Handel highlights the fascinating performative aspects of eighteenth-century music. The burgeoning interest in eighteenth-century musical performance is also demonstrated by the revival of music writ-ten and performed by countertenors in recent years as well as the forma-tion of ensembles specializing exclusively in historical performance tech-niques. Whereas the latter stresses how musical performance continued to rely on textual production throughout the eighteenth century, Boris Previšić's research derives from the opposite pole in his exploration of "the transfer of musical concepts into literary discourses, beginning around 1750."[11] According to Dupree, Previšić's scholarly work resulted in "the most focused, large-scale project on sound and music in the eighteenth century to date."[12]

This rich spectrum of possible intersections between sound/musical studies and cultural/literary studies brings me to my final suggestion of pos-sible, new directions for musical studies in relation to eighteenth-century (German) studies. In a 2020 special issue of the *German Quarterly*, editors Caroline Kita, Francien Markx, and Carl Niekerk correctly observe in their introduction that film and visual studies "have become more or less perma-nent presences in many German studies programs ..., the same cannot, or at least not yet, be said of music, musical history, or the intersections of music and German culture more broadly."[13] Nevertheless, I find the editors' claim that "since the early 2000s, German music studies has rapidly developed into a vibrant interdisciplinary field," a bit premature, and perhaps overly opti-mistic.[14] Indeed, I would be most pleased if, in analogy to German film stud-ies, one might imagine German music studies as a subdiscipline in its own right, with eighteenth-century studies being an integral part. German stud-ies as well as German music studies would therefore benefit from such an intra- and interdisciplinary move. After all, German eighteenth-century music will undoubtedly remain an integral part of music history, even if it is no longer serves as the center or springboard of all approaches.

*Emory University*

## NOTES

1. The editorial board is comprised of 28 members from 13 different countries.

2. Richard Taruskin, review of *The Cambridge History of Eighteenth-Century Music*, ed. by Simon P. Keefe (Cambridge: Cambridge UP, 2009) xvii + 798, in *Eighteenth-Century Music* 8, no. 1 (2011): 117–29, here 117.

3. Taruskin 118.

4. Taruskin 118.

5. Taruskin 121.

6. In comparison, I would argue that a scholarly community of German studies should be able to answer the following question: What makes the period from Lessing to Novalis, from Gottsched to the Schlegels, etc., a defining moment in German literary history. Furthermore, I would hope that we could agree that what binds an unusually rich and creative period goes beyond the dominant author who is used as a placeholder for that age.

7. See for example the discussion by eight scholars in *PMLA* "On Rita Felski's *The Limits of Critique*," *PMLA* 132, no. 2 (2017): 331–91.

8. Other scholarship that documents this burgeoning field include Lutz Kopenick and Nora Alter's edited volume *Sound Matters* (2005), or the 2013 special issue "Sound Studies in German Studies" in *Colloquia Germanica*, edited by Joy Calico and David Imhoff, the two co-organizers of the GSA Network "Music and Sound Studies."

9. Call for Papers for an ISECS panel in Edinburg (January 15, 2019), entitled: "Enlightenment for the Ears: Negotiating Identities Through Acts of Listening in the Long Eighteenth-Century."

10. Helen Mary Dupree, "Music and Sound in Eighteenth-Century German Studies," *The German Quarterly* 93, no. 2 (2020): 270.

11. Dupree 271.

12. Dupree 271.

13. Caroline Kita, Francien Markx, and Carl Niekerk, "Introduction," *The German Quarterly* 91, no. 4 (2018): 364–76, here 364.

14. Kita, Markx, and Niekerk 365.

OBENEWAA ODURO-OPUNI

# Lessing and Kotzebue: A Black Studies Approach to Reading the Eighteenth Century

## Introduction

*D*IE *NEGERSKLAVEN. Ein historisch-dramatisches Gemählde in drey Akten* (1796; The Negro Slaves. A Dramatic-Historical Painting in Three Acts) by German author August von Kotzebue (1761–1819) belongs to the German eighteenth- and nineteenth-century dramatic genre of *Sklavenstücke* (slave plays).[1] *Sklavenstücke* articulate a nuanced critique of slavery and the transatlantic slave trade and thus bear witness to an early German-language discourse indicative of abolitionist currents. As a German-language transcultural contribution within the larger discursive abolitionist context, Barbara Riesche categorizes *Die Negersklaven* within the subgenre of plantation plays. Texts belonging to this subgenre are mostly set in the West Indies; the majority of characters are enslaved Black Africans, with a few white Europeans in positions of power, such as slaveholders and/or plantation owners. In these texts, visiting Europeans are confronted with the horrors of slavery through their interactions with enslaved Black Africans. The perspectives shared by the enslaved people compel the visiting Europeans to work on their behalf to facilitate domestic and romantic reunions while also working to end the brutal treatment they endure on the plantations, thus promoting the humane treatment of enslaved Black Africans.[2]

This article addresses the marginalization and scarcity of scholarship on German-language abolitionist efforts and sentiments within German studies. I argue for an overall inclusion of slave plays in literary conversations concerning the Age of Goethe. Bringing slave plays and canonical literary works into dialogue with each other offers another layer of enlightened understanding through abolitionist advocacy. Slave plays confirm German-language critical engagements with slavery and abolition and allow for enriching interdisciplinary and intersectional approaches and methods in the field of German studies by way of broader, comparative examinations of race, gender, and social class. This engagement would yield insights relevant to transatlantic American studies, Black studies, and diaspora studies, all of which do not typically consider German-language contributions. Therefore, such engagement would not only expand the scope of German studies by including additional voices on slavery and abolition that are generally associated with American literature and history, but would also speak to the transcultural dynamics of American studies.

Kotzebue's play serves as an important case study in the *Sklavenstücke* genre. In *Die Negersklaven*, Kotzebue's articulation of a sociopolitical critique of slavery and the transatlantic slave trade according to transcultural and abolitionist literary conventions resonates strongly with Gotthold Ephraim Lessing's (1729–81) *Mitleidskonzept*,[3] presented, for example, in his play *Emilia Galotti* (1772). The *Mitleidskonzept* provides an understanding of humanity and human nature through a capability and capacity to feel and extend empathy. Both *Die Negersklaven* and *Emilia Galotti* are contextualized by the German eighteenth-century discourse on theatrical ethical education and the emergence of essential humanistic ideals. In line with an awakening bourgeois consciousness, Lessing centers his works on bourgeois, middle-class protagonists and foregrounds the sentimental and sociocritical educational function of theater. Thus, Lessing's bourgeois tragedy is reflective of distinct literary strategies and thematic discourses, which also resonate with those exhibited in Kotzebue's *Die Negersklaven*. I analyze *Die Negersklaven* as also surfacing within the framework of the bourgeois tragedy. Drawing on Ashraf H.A. Rushdy's conceptual framework of intertextuality, which posits that cultural productions emerge from and simultaneously contribute to social conditions, I discuss a "continuation" of bourgeois tragic understandings within *Die Negersklaven* as a transcultural abolitionist literary production.[4]

## Humanistic Ideals: Lessing's Bourgeois Tragedy

Lessing's understanding of the tragedy foregrounds the purpose of *Mitleid*. *Mitleid*, in turn, is understood as having inherent moral implications for the theater audience. In this context, Lessing assigns to the theater the educational function of presenting the moral, and therefore proper, world order: "In der moralischen [Welt] muß alles seinen ordentlichen Lauf behalten, weil das Theater die Schule der moralischen Welt seyn soll" (In the moral [world], everything must remain in its proper order, because theater shall be the school of the moral world).[5] Lessing claims the educational purpose of theater operates through tragedy.[6] Accordingly, the rationale of the tragedy is to establish an identification between the on-stage characters and the audience. This identification is facilitated by the development of Lessing's bourgeois tragedy, which centers the experiences of ordinary citizens alongside bourgeois ideals, and elicits in the theater audience intense feelings of fear and pity caused by an empathetic and sentimental identification with the characters on stage. This ultimately allows for an educational application to the real-life world of the audience through the contemplation of "was ein jeder Mensch von einem gewissen Charakter unter gewissen Umständen tun [würde]" (what any individual of a certain character would do under certain circumstances).[7] Lessing considers this mode of identification to be an essential means of sustaining attention and achieving a moral impact on the audience. Because the scenarios presented on stage could easily befall the everyday people of the audience, engaging emotionally allows the audience to learn life lessons on how to best resolve the real-world issues that they might potentially face.[8]

According to Horst Steinmetz, compassion toward stage characters "garantiert . . . menschliches Sozialverhalten . . . ls Anwendung höchster humaner Qualität . . . [und] verspricht eine allgemeine Humanisierung der Gesellschaft und ihrer Umgangsformen" (guarantees in its application the highest human quality, human social behavior, and has the promise of a general humanization of society and its modes of behavior).[9] Thus, the basic "Fähigkeit des Menschen zum Leiden . . . [ist die eigentliche] Basis aller tragischen Vorgänge. . . . Als ein Wesen, das des Leidens fähig sei, qualifiziere sich der Mensch als Mensch" (capability to endure suffering is the actual foundation of all tragic processes. . . . Being a creature capable of suffering marks the human as human).[10] Hence, the very nature of humanity can only be attained by empathizing with others and their circumstances, which is facilitated and driven by a sentimental and emotional identification: "Der Appell an die sich im Leiden manifestierende Menschlichkeit sowie die Darstellung des leidenden Menschen sei darum als die tragende Basis des Tragischen zu betrachten, gelte darum für alle Formen der Tragödie, insbesondere auch für das bürgerliche Trauerspiel" (The appeal to humanity, which is manifested through suffering, as well as the representation of humans who endure suffering should therefore be seen as the foundation of the tragedy and applies to all types of tragedies, particularly the bourgeois tragedy).[11]

Steinmetz describes how Christian Schmid argues that the bourgeois tragedy gives insight into the human heart. Similarly, Karl Guthke emphasizes the importance of the humanity of the ordinary citizen in relation to his fellow humans in his discussion of the bourgeois tragedy. The sentimental human strives to lead a virtuous life that is influenced by sentimentalism, which Guthke identifies as [eine] "Gesinnung, die als grundsätzlich allen Ständen zugänglich dargestellt wird, ist das Ethos der 'Empfindsamkeit'" (The ethos of sentimentalism is a disposition that is essentially presented as accessible to all social classes).[12] Steinmetz also mentions the importance of societal obligations and responsibilities, which echo an understanding of implications for human social behavior and thus a larger advancement of society through an empathetic identification. As such, the nature of the human and its humanity is not necessarily limited to the bourgeois class but also extends to the nobility, as long as a sentimental identification based on compassion occurs. This directly relates to the notion of a sentimental humanistic identification of slaveholders and plantation owners with the suffering of enslaved Black Africans, which will be addressed in the following section.

## An Appeal to Humanity: Intertextuality in Eighteenth-Century Literary Conventions

In the chapter "Master Texts and Slave Narratives: Race, Form, and Intertextuality in the Field of Cultural Production," Rushdy[13] asserts that intertextuality should also include an understanding of "the ways texts mediate the social conditions of their formal production." Cultural productions would then be explored as emerging from and contributing to a particular social condition. Rushdy states that "to read intertextually is to discern how a given text creatively alludes to and possibly rewrites a predecessor text, evokes the political dynamic in the field of cultural production, and inscribes into that dialogue its concerns with the social relations in the field of power." Cultural productions should therefore be considered social and material, because they clearly reveal "the way a culture thinks about itself, articulating and proposing solutions for the problems that shape a particular historical moment." This approach is of interest for this article because it emphasizes the "social forces that condition the relationships between (and within) texts."[14]

In this context, Kotzebue draws on bourgeois dramatic and literary conventions through emphasizing humanity and morality. Like Lessing, Kotzebue views theater as the most effective way to voice his opinions about German wrongdoings. As Chunjie Zhang states, "Kotzebue claimed that theater was the place where human sympathy, empathy and fine feelings can be educated and influenced."[15] Similarly, Brycchan Carey describes various forms of communication that abolitionists employed to spread their message, relying heavily on graphic accounts of the horrors of slavery to evoke and engage their audience's pity:

> Eighteenth-century British abolitionism was acted out on many stages. From the mid-1760s, when the new and, at the time, rather eccentric antislavery ideals of American Quakers began to reach the British public, to 1807, when parliament voted to outlaw the trade in human beings in British ships, the reading public were bombarded with thousands of poems, pamphlets, novels, tracts, sermons, articles, treatises, and essays offering reasons why, or why not, the slave trade should be abolished. Some of these were performed: essays read out at public meetings, speeches delivered to parliament, poems and novels shared among family members, sermons intoned before pious congregations, tracts read aloud to illiterate village swains.[16]

Stephen Ahern also considers the workings of affect in this vein—"the fleeting, volatile registers of embodied subjectivity"—with regard to abolitionism and points to abolitionist accounts in which "invoking the language of feeling might wield a political force beyond appeals to mere reason."[17] Works promoting the abolition of the slave trade and the emancipation of enslaved Black Africans were often intended to speak to the audience's emotions through displays of the unstable, ephemeral nature of the lives of enslaved individuals.

However, as Charles T. Davis and Henry Louis Gates, Jr. note, one of the most effective means of appealing to the morality of readers and slaveholders through narrative content was the slave narrative. These "truthful" firsthand accounts of slavery and the slave trade were either written directly by enslaved people or dictated to abolitionists who then put pen to paper: "This fugitive slave literature is destined to be a powerful lever. We have the most profound conviction of its potency. We see in it the easy and infallible means of abolitionizing the free States. Argument provokes argument, reason is met by sophistry. But narratives of slaves go right to the hearts of men."[18] Ahern emphasizes the importance of an "affective identification" between enslaved Black Africans and European audiences that is capable of "lead[ing] to action that could alleviate a situation," which, I argue, requires an understanding of compassion, pity, and empathy.[19] My analysis applies Ahern's theorization of affect to Kotzebue's play. In this sense, then, Kotzebue employs abolitionist strategies by accentuating the emotional and physical suffering of enslaved Black Africans in the play.

Kotzebue also condemns the institution of slavery as a terrible cruelty to appeal to what Ahern characterizes as "a shared human capacity for affective response, especially for a fellow-feeling that wells up in encounters with the suffering of others."[20] Accordingly, Kotzebue punctuates this sentiment by emphatically drawing attention to the condition of the marginalized Other by explicitly referring to enslaved people as "unsre [*sic*] schwarzen Brüder" (our Black brothers),[21] which establishes a connection between the European reader and the suffering and enslaved Black African in the New World. In this sense, Kotzebue seeks to generate sufficient empathy to encourage the reader "to try to relieve the conditions that produced the pain," as Ahern describes, and employs a visual rhetoric that is used to "engage in imaginative identification with the plight of the victim," which is further intensified by the disclosure of Kotzebue's personal sentiments.[22] Kotzebue states at the beginning of the play: "Der Verfasser schämt sich nicht zu gestehen, daß er, während er dieses Schauspiel schrieb, tausend Thränen [*sic*] vergossen hat. Wenn des Zuschauers Thränen [*sic*] sich mit den seinigen mischen, so ist seine Mühe belohnt" (The author is not ashamed to confess that he shed a thousand tears while he wrote this play. If the spectator's tears mix with his own, then his efforts will be rewarded).[23] Kotzebue's emotional outburst could be interpreted as an attempt to elicit political action with reference to the unjust enslavement of Black Africans. This disclosure by the author, then, may be a strategic move that further embeds *Die Negersklaven* within the traditions of abolitionist sentimental literature and shows how the author steers his audience toward a proper, moral human response to slavery and the transatlantic slave trade.

Kotzebue guiding his audience in this manner also aligns with Steinmetz's argument that there are societal obligations and responsibilities that are expected of humans and can only be fulfilled by affectively identifying and suffering someone else's pain. This will ultimately lead to wanting to engage in ending this pain as well as altering the oppressive societal structures that allow for abuses of power by nobility and the enslavement of Black Africans by bourgeois protagonists. Any call for action to end these injustices is understood to be a direct result of empathizing with one's fellow human being.

In the preface to the play, Kotzebue assumes an educational and lecturing role that reveals similarities to Lessing's views of the moral and educating function of theater. Kotzebue's appeal to humanity can be read as intended to further a betterment of society and humanity in accordance with humanistic Enlightenment ideals. These appeals on behalf of and by enslaved Black Africans (via slave narratives) addressed free Blacks; white, bourgeois, middle-class individuals; and especially slaveholders and plantation owners, who were part of the bourgeois class. Steinmetz's understanding of human suffering as something that characterizes members of all social classes, not just the higher classes, is essential here[24] because abolitionist literature is not limited to a particular social group; it aims at a sentimental and compassionate emotional "human" identification in response to the horrors of slavery, regardless of gender, nationality, race, or social class.[25]

## Conclusion

Drawing on Rushdy's notion of intertextuality, I have shown that Kotzebue employed eighteenth-century literary conventions that are strikingly similar to those used by Lessing. Considering that Lessing's theory of the bourgeois tragedy lends itself in its sentimental function to abolitionist purposes, it could be argued that Kotzebue drew on the literary conventions employed by Lessing's tragedies when writing his play *Die Negersklaven*. However, a larger understanding of human nature and its moral function within the world that is expressed by compassion and sentimentalism is what ties Lessing and Kotzebue together: Both authors emphasize a human capacity for affective identification and compassion that must be activated through emotional appeals. This common perspective of humanity regarding the advocacy of enslaved Black Africans in *Die Negersklaven* and an abuse of power by the nobility in Lessing's *Emilia Galotti* warrants a larger examination of Enlightenment ideals of humanity in a Black studies context that might include abolitionist discussions of Black identity and humanity.

Regardless of whether these texts have long been part of the canon or have only recently entered it, further examination of these late eighteenth-century and early nineteenth-century German-language works would benefit from an interdisciplinary approach rooted in Black thought and theories. This article already extends beyond the confines of bourgeois identity formation—and the field of German national identity formation, which instrumentalizes this category—into transatlantic studies and American studies. By considering *Sklavenstücke* alongside other canonical German-language literary contributions, future research can further broaden the understanding of German Enlightenment texts in an interdisciplinary manner, thus raising the impact of eighteenth-century studies on other, closely aligned disciplines.

*University of Arizona*


## NOTES

1. August von Kotzebue, *Die Negersklaven. Ein historisch-dramatisches Gemählde in drey Akten.* (Leipzig: Kummer, 1796).

2. Barbara Riesche, *Schöne Mohrinnen, Edle Sklaven, Schwarze Rächer: Schwarzendarstellung Und Sklavereithematik Im Deutschen Unterhaltungstheater (1770–1814)* (Hanover: Wehrhahn, 2010) 122.

3. A conceptualization of pity, empathy, or compassion. The German word for sympathy, *Mitleid,* more explicitly suggests suffering with (someone), i.e., suffering explicitly what another is suffering. Unless otherwise indicated, all translations are my own.

4. Ashraf H.A. Rushdy, *Neo-Slave Narratives: Studies in the Social Logic of a Literary Form*. (Oxford: Oxford UP, 1999).

5. Lessing qtd. in Karl Siegfried Guthke, *Das deutsche bürgerliche Trauerspiel* (Stuttgart: Metzler, 2006) 19.

6. Thomas Martinec, "Lessing's Dramatic Theory," in *Lessing and the German Enlightenment*, ed. Ritchie Robertson (Oxford: Voltaire Foundation, 2013) 119-37. Thomas Martinec describes several of these texts, including *Correspondence on Tragedy* (1756-1757), which is a set of letters between Lessing, Moses Mendelsohn, and Friedrich Nicolai, and *Hamburg Dramaturgy* (1767-1768), which is a collection of theater reviews that Lessing compiled while being a dramatic theater adviser in Hamburg. Martinec describes the *Hamburg Dramaturgy* as "a compilation of diverse ideas" (22).

7. Lessing qtd. in Inge Stephan, "Die aufklärerischen Literaturtheorien von Gottsched über Lessing bis zum Sturm und Drang," in *Deutsche Literaturgeschichte: Von den Anfängen bis zur Gegenwart*, edited by Inge Stephan (Stuttgart: Metzler, 2001) 156-171, here 157.

8. Stephan 157. Lessing's conceptual notion of the tragedy was inspired by Aristotle's *Poetics*, in which catharsis (purification) is a marking feature of the tragedy. Through the audience having experienced pity and fear, a purification of these very emotions is understood to occur (https://www.britannica.com/art/catharsis-criticism).

9. Horst Steinmetz, *Das Deutsche Drama von Gottsched Bis Lessing: Ein Historischer Überblick* (Stuttgart: Metzler, 1987) 86.

10. Steinmetz 85.

11. Steinmetz 85.

12. Guthke 42.

13. Rushdy elaborates on "intertextuality" in the context of debates on slavery in African American fiction in the 1960s that illustrate the "contemporary narrativity of slavery." He titled these "neoslave narratives." Having emerged from ongoing political and academic debates in the 1960s, these initial original debates on slavery are mirrored by Rushdy by way of an intertextuality that focalizes the political function of these debates. In my discussion, I primarily draw on Rushdy regarding discursive interactions between texts of political significance. In this sense, Kotzebue becomes part of an overall political and discursive dialogue through fictional and nonfictional textual elements of his play, which highlight an intertextual approach. See Rushdy 3.

14. Rushdy 14-16.

15. Chunjie Zhang, *Transculturality and German Discourse in the Age of European Colonialism* (Evanston, IL: Northwestern UP, 2017) 91.

16. Brycchan Carey, "To Force a Tear: British Abolitionism and the Eighteenth-Century London Stage," in *Affect and Abolition in the Anglo-Atlantic, 1770-1830*, ed. Stephen Ahern (Aldershot, UK: Ashgate, 2013) 109-28, here 109.

17. Stephen Ahern, "Introduction: The Bonds of Sentiment," in *Affect and Abolition in the Anglo-Atlantic, 1770-1830* (Aldershot, UK: Ashgate, 2013) 1-19, here 1.

18. Charles T. Davis and Henry Louis Gates, Jr., eds., *The Slave's Narrative* (Oxford: Oxford UP, 1985) xiv-xvii, here xvii.

19. Ahern 6.

20. Ahern 5.

21. Kotzebue 3.

22. Ahern 2, 5.

23. Kotzebue 4.

24. Steinmetz 85.

25. This point is discussed by Michael Craton, James Walvin, and David Wright in *Slavery, Abolition and Emancipation: Black Slaves and the British Empire: A Thematic Documentary* (London: Longman, 1976) 195.

MATTHEW H. BIRKHOLD

# Law and Literature: Codes as Colonizing Texts and Legal Ideas in Anthropocene Works

THE STUDY OF LAW AND LITERATURE has a rich history in *Germanistik* and promises a bright future. As Elizabeth S. Anker and Bernadette Meyler note in their introduction to *New Directions in Law and Literature* (2017), myriad new interdisciplinary methodologies and inquiries have proliferated over the past decade.[1] For my contribution to this Forum, I do not wish to recite the long list of *Dichterjuristen* (lawyer-poets) who inspired the first generation of scholars to investigate this intersection.[2] Nor is my goal to review the recent work of our colleagues who have examined the interrelationships of law and humanistic inquiry more broadly. Rather, I seek to encourage continued innovation by highlighting a largely overlooked genre that may be especially fruitful for scholars of the *Goethezeit* (Age of Goethe) to explore and by adumbrating an emerging legal question into which we, as literary scholars, may have special insight.

"Law and Literature" has often been conceived of as having two branches: law in literature and law as literature. This distinction has, thankfully, been challenged to reveal the complex entanglement of laws and literatures in their various forms. After all, law also shapes literature, literature influences the law, and both share a number of imaginative and narrative capacities. To name just two terrific, recent studies, Chenxi Tang thoroughly examines how literature has shaped international law in *Imagining World Order* (2018) and Javier Samper Vendrell's fourth chapter in *The Seduction of Youth* (2020) considers the ways in which the Weimar Republic's Gesetz zur Bewahrung der Jugend vor Schund- und Schmutzschriften (Law for the Protection of Youth Against Trash and Smut) shaped queer periodicals. Yet the root division—"law in" and "law as"—helpfully draws attention to the tendency of most scholars to focus primarily on one object—the law or literature. Indeed, the ideas discussed below might each be thought to fall into just one of these traditional categories. But this distinction should compel us to interrogate the consequences of that focus and what else might be missing. As we continue to study the interrelationships of law and literature in the Age of Goethe, I hope we will increasingly attend to bigger questions about colonialism and the environment, in particular.

## Law Code as Literature

The juridical debates that occurred throughout the German territories in the final decades of the eighteenth century resulted in the creation of several new legal codes, the most famous of which is the Allgemeines Landrecht für die Preußischen Staaten (Prussian General Law Code). For this reason, Theodore Ziolkowski describes the period as "the age of the great codes" in his classic work of law and literature, *The Mirror of Justice: Literary Reflections of Legal Cases* (1997). In his estimation, earlier codes like the Sachsenspiegel and Lex Burgundionum lacked the hallmarks of modern codes: "substantive completeness, logical systematization, and terminological clarity."[3] Positioned in this *Sattelzeit*, Goethe and his contemporaries witnessed "the unstable transition from the old order to a new, unknown one," as Sean Franzel nicely put it in a recent issue of this journal.[4] For that reason, the literary products of the time have been productively read as commentaries and meditations on the period's shifting juridical notions. Less scholarly attention, however, has been devoted to the new codes themselves as a form of literature.

In his 2019 article, "Legal Codes as Cultural Products," Heikki Pihlajamäki urges literary scholars and cultural historians to read codes likes the Prussian General Law Code.[5] Supposedly "mature" codifications, "based on a scientific system, and meant as comprehensive and exclusive," Pihlajamäki reminds us, nevertheless contain lacunae.[6] How should we read these silences and the narrative and rhetorical choices that create them? Approaching codes as literature further opens up possibilities for comparative research: how do German codes, not just in content but in form, differ from those written elsewhere? Finally, Pihlajamäki notes that "scholars have not given enough attention to European codifications as export products."[7] The German and French civil codes spread to nearly every continent, shaping and controlling other laws and other peoples. Codes could therefore be read as a type of colonizing literature.

To offer one example, the drafters of the Prussian General Law Code were plainly concerned with the language and style of the code as they sought to make the new law understandable to the public.[8] The publication patent from March 20, 1791 even claimed the new code "in der Sprache der Nation und dergestalt allgemeinverständlich vorgetragen werde, daß ein jeder Einwohner des Staats . . . die Gesetze, nach welchen er seine Handlungen einrichten und beurteilen lassen soll, selbst lesen [und] verstehen . . . könne"[9] (was presented in the language of the nation and in a generally understandable way so that every inhabitant of the state . . . can read [and] understand the laws, according to which he should conform his behavior and be judged). What were the implications of the language and form of the Prussian General Law Code?

The laws regulating discipline of servants in Prussia are instructive. Reformist bureaucrats and conservative estate owners compromised in the creation of the Prussian General Law Code II, Title 7, §227, which granted the master the right to hold "faules, unordentliches, und widerspenstiges Gesinde . . . durch mäßige Züchtigungen zu seiner Pflicht" ("lazy, disorderly, and unruly servants . . . to their duty through moderate punishment"). Already upon its creation, however, this article was thought likely to be repealed.[10]

Consequently, Title 5, §77 was included, codifying an indirect right of punishment. "Reizt das Gesinde die Herrschaft durch ungebührliches Betragen zum Zorn, und wird in selbigem von ihr mit Scheltworten, oder geringen Thätlichkeiten behandelt: so kann es dafür keine gerichtliche Genugthuung fördern" (If, through improper behavior, the servant provokes the master to anger and is resultingly treated with abusive words or minor violence, [the servant] cannot demand legal redress for this [treatment]). This article assured that, even if Article 277 were removed, masters would maintain the negative freedom from prosecution for this particular kind of physical harm, which arguably amounted to a sort of positive right to discipline.[11] At least with regard to this article, there is not clarity in the code, as Ziolkowski claims, but intentional ambiguity. The Prussian jurist and General Law Code drafter Carl Gottlieb Svarez noted this gap at the time of the law's creation: "Der Paragraph ist so vorsichtig gefaßt, daß er zwischen beiden Extremis die richtige Mittelstraße hält, und dem *arbitrio iudicus*, das sich ohnehin immer mehr auf die Seite der Herrschaft neigen wird, Raum genug läßt, das nöthige Ansehen derselben zu mainteniren" (The paragraph is so carefully formulated, that it assumes the correct middle way between both extremes and leaves enough room to *arbitrio iudicus*, which will anyway always tend to favor the side of the masters, to maintain the necessary regard [owed the masters]).[12] Legal and literary ambiguity, of course, open the text to interpretation.

In 1899, Article 95 of the Introductory Act to the German Empire's new *Bürgerliches Gesetzbuch* (Citizens' Book of Laws) banned corporal punishment (except in schools and prisons), explicitly eradicating the direct right to punish servants: "Ein Züchtigungsrecht steht dem Dienstberechtigten dem Gesinde gegenüber nicht zu" (An employer does not possess the right to discipline vis-à-vis servants).[13] The *Bürgerliches Gesetzbuch* and *Strafgesetzbuch* (Book of Legal Punishments) from 1871, however, did not address the indirect right to punish servants arguably created by the Prussian General Law Code II, Title 5, §77. This right consequently remained in force for the duration of the German Empire's existence. Thus, when the German Empire sent its laws overseas, in addition to its soldiers and settlers, it also exported the juridical ambiguity about corporal punishment.[14]

German settlers in present-day Namibia regularly physically abused African workers on farms and in mines.[15] In *Violence as Usual* (2020), Marie Muschalek documents the pervasive slapping, kicking, beating, shoving, dragging, and cuffing.[16] As employers in German South-West Africa, these private German citizens used corporal punishment with impunity thanks to the peculiar drafting of the eighteenth-century laws that provided the foundation for colonial administration.[17] As Harry Schwirck illuminates, "the right to discipline stands as the most obvious instance of a white civil right weakening the protection of Africans under criminal law; it redefined a range of criminal activity as a civil right of white adults vis-à-vis natives. In so doing, the right to discipline cleared a space in which much mistreatment of Africans could take place without social or legal sanction."[18]

The laws written around 1800 would go on to enable colonial violence but were also immediately part of a larger global discourse. The literature of the *Goethezeit* was occupied with colonial fantasies, as Susanne Zantop long ago demonstrated, and German thinkers of the period were influenced by non-European cultures, as Chunjie Zhang shows in *Transculturality and German Discourse in the Age of European Colonialism* (2017). How do the legal codes produced in the Age of Goethe—as export products and literary forms—fit into these global connections? What logics do law and literature share as they create negative spaces for *arbitrio iudicus* or literary interpretation?

## Environmental Law in Literature

In addition to living through the "age of the great codes," Goethe and his contemporaries wrote at the beginning of the Anthropocene.[19] This proposed geological epoch, named for the global impact of humanity on the planet, is thought to have begun with the Industrial Revolution and emerged alongside Europe's Enlightenment, secularization, the rise of modern capitalism, and the emancipation of the bourgeoisie.[20] This epoch also purportedly witnessed the advent of a new "environmental reflexivity," that is, a critical awareness of the ways in which human activities affect the environment.[21] Borrowing insights from New Materialisms, our colleagues have written compelling accounts of such proto-ecological thinking around 1800 and parsed the way that authors like Goethe documented "the material interactions of all living and nonliving things," in the words of Heather Sullivan, and revealed the "distributed agency among humans and non-humans."[22]

These same New Materialist insights have led to something of a crisis in law's existing ontology, as scholars question "what matter *is* and, relatedly . . . what the implications of matter are."[23] If rocks and trees are agentic, how should law reconfigure legal subjectivities to make room for the trans- and posthuman? This work seems to have changed the way we think about rights and responsibilities in exciting new ways, particularly in the realm of environmental law. In the past three years, for instance, the High Court of Uttarakhand, India, granted legal personhood to the glaciers feeding the Ganges and Yamuna rivers and the Whanganui River was granted legal personhood in Aotearoa, New Zealand.[24]

However, after taking a wrecking ball to the edifice of the legal subject, as Edward Mussawir and Connal Parsley assert, critical legal scholars have rightly questioned whether considering a river a legal human is the victory it is often touted to be.[25] Slavoj Žižek argues in *Absolute Recoil: Towards a New Foundation of Dialectical Materialism* (2014) that New Materialisms "reinscribe[ ] subjective agency into natural reality as its immanent agential principle."[26] In other words, by extending agency and vitality to nonhuman material, such environmental law "wins" actually maintain humanist values that may continue to prove destructive. Moreover, as Gwen Gordon reminds, "theories of these rights of nature may be deployed in ways that shift with [social, political and material] circumstances," so the better question is not the ontological one, but the practical concern of "how easily will we be able to imagine nature as a rights holder in each regime, and how will that imaginatory space energize the will to protect nature by means of these varied rights arguments?"[27] Consequently, scholars have called for law to "start experimenting with different assemblages that include the non-human."[28] At this juncture, law and literature scholarship in the *Goethezeit* may be poised to make an exciting contribution. Namely, Germanists studying authors and artists who consciously or unconsciously embodied this ostensibly new environmental reflexivity might question whether their cultural products criticize, extol, or otherwise comment on the legal consequences of the distributed agencies and material interactions they document. Literature offers the experimental space to explore the quandaries that environmental law faces today and we—not lawyers—have the training to mind the aesthetic, historical, cultural, and rhetorical details essential to a convincing analysis of these conceptual questions.

To what extent can literary engagements with posthumanist subjectivities and ecocritical ideas trouble or advance the law's concerns with New Materialisms? Do authors writing at the start of the Anthropocene offer special insights, poetologial or otherwise? Caroline Schaumann indicates how Tieck's *Der Runenberg* (*Rune Mountain*) delineates "the creative force of plants, rocks, earth, and gems" while distorting and questioning various categories and classifications.[29] Classifications, I will add, upon which the law relies to this day. To supply yet another example, Jason Groves convincingly argues for Goethe's "openness to the planet's inherent instability" and the development of an environmental aesthetics that embraces "the fragmented, displaced, and unconsolidated."[30] He demonstrates how *Wilhelm Meisters Wanderjahre* (*Wilhelm Meister's Journeyman Years*) "relinquishes a subject function, which is redistributed among the various characters and interpolated novellas."[31] Are there lessons for legal thinking here?

Of course, one might contend that this question instrumentalizes literature for the sake of law, which it might. But conducting such law and literature analyses would also test the conceptual reach and rigor of *Goethezeit* scholarship on the Anthropocene while reaffirming its relevance to the legal arena, which has long been skeptical of outside voices. In addition, posing such questions will further reveal the shared logics of literary and legal thinking while perhaps exposing the limitations of each.[32] Scholars in our field, I believe, may offer precisely the sorts of new ideas needed to conduct legal experiments that may guide environmental law in the future.

*The Ohio State University*

## NOTES

1. Elizabeth S. Anker and Bernadette Meyler. *New Directions in Law and Literature* (Oxford: Oxford UP, 2017).

2. Thomas O. Beebee provides a nice overview in the introduction to *Citation and Precedent: Conjunctions and Disjunctions of German Law and Literature* (New York: Bloomsbury, 2014).

3. Theodore Ziolkowski, *The Mirror of Justice: Literary Reflections of Legal Cases* (Princeton, NJ: Princeton UP, 1997) 188.

4. Sean Franzel, "Koselleck's Timely Goethe?" *Goethe Yearbook* 26 (2019): 283–99, here 287.

5. Heikki Pihlajamäki, "Legal Codes as Cultural Products," in *The Oxford Handbook of Law and Humanities*, ed. Simon Stern, Maksymilian Del Mar, and Bernadette Meyler (Oxford: Oxford UP, 2019) 703–817.

6. Pihlajamäki 705.

7. Pihlajamäki 705.

8. For an in-depth discussion, see: Hans Hattenhauer, "Berlin und die deutsche Rechtssprache," in *Rechtsentwicklungen in Berlin*, ed. Friedrich Ebel and Albrecht Randelzhofer (Berlin: De Gruyter, 1988) 99–120.

9. Hattenhauer 106. Unless otherwise indicated, all translations are my own.

10. For more see, Reinhart Koselleck. *Preussen Zwischen Reform Und Revolution: Allgemeines Landrecht, Verwaltung und Soziale Bewegung von 1791 bis 1848* (Stuttgart: Klett, 1967) esp. 641–569.

11. This article was later incorporated into the Prussian *Gesinderecht*. For how later courts preserved Article 77, see Thomas Vormbaum, *Politik und Gesinderecht im 19. Jahrhundert* (Berlin: Duncker & Humblot, 1980) 356–57.

12. Qtd. in Vormbaum 90.

13. Qtd. in *Bürgerliches Gesetzbuch nebst Einführungsgesetz* (Berlin: Guttentag, 1901) 181.

14. As Nils Ole Oermann reminds us in "The Law and the Colonial State: Legal Codification versus Practice in a German Colony," in *Wilhelminism and Its Legacies: German Modernities, Imperialism, and the Meaning of Reform, 1890–1930*, ed. Geoff Eley and James Retallack (New York: Berghahn, 2008) 171–84.

15. For an early academic account of German colonialism, see Fritz F. Müller, *Kolonien unter der Peitsche: Eine Dokumentation* (Berlin: Rütten & Loening, 1962).

16. Marie Muschalek. *Violence as Usual: Policing and the Colonial State in German Southwest Africa* (Ithaca, NY: Cornell UP, 2020).

17. For an explanation of the complicated legal framework, see Harry Schwirck, "Law's Violence and the Boundary Between Corporal Discipline and Physical Abuse in German South West Africa," *Akron Law Review* 36, no. 1 (2002): 81–132.

18. Schwirk 132.

19. Here, I follow the dating proposed by Crutzen and Stoermer. See their "The 'Anthropocene.'" *Global Change Newsletter* 41 (2000): 17–18.

20. Eva Horn and Hannes Bergthaller, *The Anthropocene: Key Issues for the Humanities* (New York: Routledge, 2020) 26.

21. See Christophe Bonneuil and Jean-Baptiste Fressoz, *The Shock of the Anthropocene: The Earth, History and Us*, trans. David Fernbach (London: Verso, 2016).

22. Heather I. Sullivan, "Goethe's Concept of Nature: Proto-Ecological Model," in *Ecological Thought in German Literature and Culture*, ed. Gabriele Dürbeck, et. al. (Lanham, MD: Lexington Books, 2017) 17–31, here 18, and Heather I. Sullivan, "Agency in the Anthropocene: Goethe, Radical Reality, and the New Materialisms," in *The Early History of Embodied Cognition 1740–1920: The Lebenskraft-Debate and Radical Reality in German Science, Music, and Literature*, ed. John A. McCarthy, et. al. (Leiden: Brill Rodopi, 2016) 285–304, here 297.

23. Anna Grear, "'Anthropocene, Capitalocene, Chthulucene': Re-encountering Environmental Law and its 'Subject' with Haraway and New Materialism," in

*Environmental Law and Governance for the Anthropocene*, ed. Louis J. Kotzé (Oxford: Hart, 2017) 77–95, here 92.

24. For more, see: Cristy Clark, et. al. "Can You Hear the Rivers Sing? Legal Personhood, Ontology, and the Nitty-Gritty of Governance," *Ecological Law Quarterly* 45 (2019): 787–844.

25. Edward Mussawir and Connal Parsley. "The law of persons today: at the margins of jurisprudence," *Law and Humanities* 11, no. 1 (2017): 44–63, here 61.

26. Slavoj Žižek, *Absolute Recoil: Towards a New Foundation of Dialectical Materialism* (New York: Verso, 2014) 12.

27. Gwen Gordon, "Environmental Personhood," *Columbia Journal of Environmental Law* 43, no. 1 (2019): 49–91, here 91.

28. Andreas Philippopoulos-Mihalopoulos, "Critical Environmental Law in the Anthropocene," in *Environmental Law and Governance for the Anthropocene*, ed. Louis J. Kotzé (Oxford: Hart Publishing, 2017) 117–35, here 126.

29. Caroline Schaumann, "Tracing Romanticism in the Anthropocene: An Ecocritical Reading of Ludwig Tieck's Rune Mountain," in *Romantic Legacies: Transnational and Transdisciplinary Contexts*, ed. Shun-liang Chao and John Michael Corrigan (New York: Routledge, 2019) 195–212, here 208.

30. Jason Groves, "Goethe's Petrofiction: Reading the *Wanderjahre* in the Anthropocene," *Goethe Yearbook* 22 (2015): 95–113, here 98, 109.

31. Groves 107.

32. See, for example, Simon Stern, "Legal and Literary Fictions," in *New Directions in Law and Literature*, ed. Elizabeth S. Anker and Bernadette Meyler (Oxford: Oxford UP, 2017) 313–26.

BRENT PETERSON

# Johann Wolfgang Goethe, Migrant? or Debunking the Myth of 1955

IN 1749, WHEN GOETHE WAS BORN in Frankfurt am Main, his hometown was one of the hundreds of more or less independent states that made up the Holy Roman Empire. By our standards, Frankfurt was a modestly sized town of about 36,000 inhabitants but, at the time, it was surprisingly cosmopolitan. Not only was it the site of the emperor's coronation, but, according to Nicolas Boyle, trade with England was handled by the descendants of Dutch immigrants and Huguenots, who were French Protestants who fled their homeland in 1685 rather than convert to Catholicism. According to Philipp Ther, Huguenots gave French and English the word refugee.[1] Frankfurt was also home to a community of Italian importers of Mediterranean fruit and Jewish families that had been expelled from elsewhere in Germany. A little more than a decade after Goethe's birth, the local Rothschild family founded a bank that became one of the world's leading financial institutions, with branches in London, Vienna, Paris, and Milan.

The contrast between Frankfurt and the bulk of the empire could scarcely have been greater. The empire's population was overwhelmingly rural and most people lived and died inside a ten-mile radius around their home villages. They also spoke a bewildering array of mutually incomprehensible dialects, and the idea of a common German identity had not yet been invented. E. J. Hobsbawm estimates that in 1789 only 300,000 to 500,000 people read *Hochdeutsch*, and far fewer of the people who were "German" spoke the language that supposedly united them.[2] In other words, the cultural prerequisites for the nation as a cultural community were not yet present. What we now think of as Germany was an agglomeration of places that were foreign to one another. Although this history is often overlooked, it should be common knowledge; even more pertinent are the questions it raises: first, why do situations in Goethe's birthplace and the rest of the empire matter to the legacy of the eighteenth century in scholarly research? And, second, what does the particular context into which Goethe was born have to do with thinking about him as a migrant?

The answer to the first question challenges well-worn assumptions about the history of migration to Germany; indeed examining eighteenth-century Frankfurt helps to reframe the entire narrative, because for too many Germans, as well as for quite a few of us who study German culture and history, the country's experience of migration appears to have begun in 1955,

when the Federal Republic began recruiting *Gastarbeiter* to satisfy a boom-
ing economy's need for labor. Soon, laborers from Italy, Spain, Greece, Turkey,
Morocco, Portugal, Tunisia, and Yugoslavia joined a workforce supposedly
made up, until then, entirely of ethnic Germans. When these officially temporary migrants started bringing their families to Germany, that is, when they
shifted from being guests to long-term and then permanent residents and
citizens, German society changed in ways that were both familiar and different. While it is certainly true that today's Germany differs markedly from
what it had been before 1955, this widely accepted story of how migration
affected German society is, at best, only partially true. It is also dangerously
misleading and in need of correction. Reading Goethe, his hometown and
peripatetic early life within the cultural and political context of migration
strikes me as a perfect opportunity to start that narrative in the eighteenth
rather than the middle of the twentieth century and to connect migration
with the idea of Germany, which arose at roughly the same time.

Part of the problem that I want to explore here lies in the interpretation
of German homogeneity in the decade after the Second World War. What I
call the myth of 1955 posits a Germany filled exclusively with Germans as
the normal state of affairs rather than the result of a dozen years of Nazi ethnic cleansing and genocide. Until 2000, when the laws governing German citizenship changed, Germany did not regard itself as a nation of immigrants—
and an alarmingly large portion of the political spectrum still denies that
Germany is in fact that. But the makeup of Goethe's hometown during his
life already testifies to a much longer history of migration. One of the services that ought to be part of historical and literary scholarship—and a fundamental direction of eighteenth-century studies—would be to make sure
that people know about the nonhomogeneity not just of Germany today but
also of its historical culture. I will address one of many possible examples
below but, before doing so, I ask: What about Goethe? Was Goethe himself a
migrant?

When speaking of an era that preceded nations and passports, it might
seem strange to claim that movement within the Holy Roman Empire constituted migration, but if the aim is to shift our thinking away from the paradigm
of German homogeneity, then it makes sense to at least raise the possibility
that when Goethe left for Weimar in 1775, he was traveling to a foreign country. In fact, when moving to Weimar, the capital of the Duchy Saxe-Weimar-
Eisenach and, according to the constitution of the empire, a sovereign state,
Goethe was already a repeat migrant. He was thus in the enviable position
of having attempted migration before, albeit only temporarily. Leipzig, where
he began his university studies, was located in Electoral Saxony; Straßburg,
where he finished his studies, had been part of France since 1681. After his
study abroad experiences in larger, more cosmopolitan cities, Weimar might
have seemed disappointing. Goethe also may have experienced difficulties
that would be familiar to most of today's migrants. He certainly wasn't poor,
nor did he have to search long for a job, but the wild life that he led with the
young duke, "flirting incognito with the peasant girls, swimming naked in
the duchy's chilly rivers," and playing practical jokes that made their objects
blush for years afterwards, in Boyle's cleansed version of events,[3] might well

have led the locals to wish he had never shown up. On the one hand, then, thinking about Goethe as a migrant both normalizes migration as a fact in German history and also suggests that the unfortunate questioning or even rejection of migrants is nothing new. On the other hand, for Goethe, at least in Boyle's estimation, Weimar was the right place to be. It was little more than a village, top-heavy with aristocrats, but "political power—and so the political, and ultimately the cultural future of the nation—lay not with the empire and not with the burghers of Germany's city republic, but with the Enlightened autocracies ruled by Germany's princes."[4] Goethe's goals were, to be sure, lofty, but they echo the dreams and aspirations of millions of migrants before and since who left their homelands in search of opportunities that were otherwise missing.

Although he was himself a migrant, Goethe did not make the topic a central element of his writing. His only foray into the topic came in the unfinished collection *Unterhaltungen deutscher Ausgewanderten* (*Conversations of German Refugees*, 1794). Although lost interest in the project, the word *Ausgewanderten* found a new home not quite two centuries later as the title of a volume of four longish stories by W. G. Sebald. The English translation bears the unfortunate translation *The Emigrants*, which suggests free will on the part of the people who find themselves outside of their home country. However, both Goethe and Sebald use the term to show how, in the first instance, French troops forced Germans from their homeland along the Rhine, and, in the second instance, how Jews were either expelled or escaped from Nazism, never to find a real home again. The semantic-conceptual link shows a consciousness of forced migration that expands beyond the usual, twentieth-century time frame that we consider in the history of migration.

My own interest in that history is mainly concerned with literary and filmic migration narratives, and while they are scarcer in the eighteenth and early nineteenth century, they are far from nonexistent. Such texts are worthy objects of inquiry in their own right, but they are doubly important in my project of pushing the history of migration well beyond the usual starting point of 1955. A contemporary of Goethe's who would be worth considering as a migrant is Solomon Maimon. Unlike Moses Mendelssohn, whom I have also argued was a migrant,[5] Maimon migrated from Poland and thereby marks the early, difficult relationship between Polish and German Jews. In the literary realm, I have argued elsewhere that Chamisso's *Peter Schlemihl* is one of the founding documents of migration and German culture, while the Chamisso Prize, which was awarded between 1985 and 2017 for works "from the outside" but written with a "German pen," was a noble, but intellectually incoherent attempt to incorporate texts by migrant authors into the corpus of German literature. At the moment, I am working on a book, tentatively titled, *Beyond the Myth of 1955: Rethinking Migration and German Culture.*[6] It therefore makes sense to me to close this short essay with a look at a more obscure migration narrative from the Age of Goethe: Friedrich de la Motte Foqué's 1824 novel, *Der Refugié oder Heimath und Fremde: Ein Roman aus der neuern Zeit* (The Refugee, or Home and Strangers: A Novel from Recent Times).[7] Here, as with Chamisso, who fled the French Revolution as a boy, the claim is not that the author was a migrant, in part because one of the

shortcomings of the early scholarship of migrant literature is that it searched
in authors' lives for the meaning of their work, as if Goethe could only write
the *Unterhaltungen* if he had himself been expelled from the Rhineland by
French forces. My aim is, on the one hand, to extend the historical sweep of
migration and German culture, and, on the other hand, to insist that "migration narratives" rather than "migrant literature" can help us explore the discursive universe of migration and show how migrants were co-constitutive
of German culture, rather than contributors to it, long before *Gastarbeiter*
first arrived in Germany and began writing.

Fouqué was himself the descendent of prominent Huguenots. His grand-
father served with distinction as a general in Friedrich the Great's army, but,
rather than depicting its author's personal history, *Der Réfugié* revolves
around Robert Gautier, the son of a Huguenot pastor in a village in the
Prussian provinces. The narrative begins around 1800, when Huguenots had
been in Prussia for roughly 115 years, and ends during the Wars of Liberation
1813–1815, at the moment when Prussian forces first cross the border into
France. On the novel's first page, readers encounter Pastor Gautier, sitting
outside his parsonage on a summer Sunday evening. Members of his rural
congregation walk by and greet him affectionately as "Herr Jottjé," using
the Plattdeutsch pronunciation of his French name. Readers learn that he
comes from a long line of pastors, but his ancestors had all served churches
in the "sogenannten Refugié-Kolonie" (1:2 so called refugee-settlement). This
particular Pastor Gautier is the first "der einen Ruf als deutscher Prediger
angenommen hatte" (1:2 who followed the call as a German preacher). He
also married his predecessor's daughter, which means that he not only wed a
German, but he also must have converted to Lutheranism. Owing to the lack
of suitable partners, particularly in the countryside, intermarriage was more
common than we might otherwise imagine. Such marriages are an important
sign of acceptance, and Pastor Gautier appears to have been well integrated
into German society. However, in the book's second chapter he shares his
anxiety with a German friend. The problem, which migrants and refugees
frequently experience, is that Gautier worries about losing the worldview
he inherited in the *Kolonie* (1:52–53). More than a century after the initial
migration, Gautier still feels like a guest. Germans are his comrades, but he
and they nevertheless remain separate. He feels welcomed and well treated, but never quite accepted as a native. Germans allow him and his fellow
Huguenots to flourish so long as they remain apart, living as they did in what
we would now call a parallel society, but, after having taken a step into their
midst, a step that is probably not reversible, Pastor Gautier is afraid of losing
his connection to French culture. Readers never learn about relationships
that he might have had with his fellow Huguenots, but his marriage and service to a rural German congregation suggest that he is relatively isolated.

What we might not expect is the pastor's continuing desire to be French
at a time when he lives in an almost completely German context. Being both
French and German—that is, creating an identity that embraces intersection-
ality—appears to be impossible for Pastor Gautier and undesirable in most
hegemonic cultures, which view integration as a one-way street. Only the
migrant has to adapt, which might seems logical until we think about the

cultural and economic advantages of migration for both sides. Moreover, it is worth asking whether any culture can or should demand assimilation. Even if it were possible for Pastor Gautier to abandon his previous cultural affiliations would anyone profit from that bargain? Again, one of the reasons to read *Der Refugié* is to learn that these issues did not simply spring into existence after the massive flows of migrants after 1955 and 2015. In addition, at least in the case of the Huguenots, resolving these questions, to the extent that they ever were resolved, took generations.

This snippet comes at the beginning of a novel that stretches through three volumes to a total of over 1200 pages. I do not recommend that everyone rush order a copy of *Der Refugié* on interlibrary loan. You could wait to see if *Beyond the Myth of 1955* ever appears, or, for a very different reading of the novel, my book on how Germans learned to be German has been available for some time (*History, Fiction, and Germany: Writing the Nineteenth-Century Nation*). In many respects, the book is an early critique of excessive nationalism, which also makes Foqué's novel worth discovering. And, even if it is something of a stretch to accept Goethe as a migrant, using him and the cultural and political context in which he lived to imagine centuries rather than decades of migration not only provides a new way of exploring old texts, but it also offers a way to rethink current debates in a far more productive manner than accepting the mythical narrative of 1955.

*Lawrence University*

## NOTES

1. Philipp Ther, *Die Außenseiter: Flucht, Flüchtlinge und Integration im modernen Europa* (Berlin: Suhrkam, 2017) 42; in English translation as *The Outsiders: Refugees in Europe since 1492* (Princeton NJ: Princeton UP, 2019) 28.

2. E. J. Hobsbawm. *Nations and Nationalism since 1780* (Cambridge: Cambridge UP, 1990) 61.

3. Nicholas Boyle, Goethe, The Poet and the Age, vol. 1, The Poetry of Desire (Oxford: Oxford UP, 1991) 243.

4. Boyle, 248.

5. Brent O. Peterson, "Moses Mendelssohn, Germany's First Migrant," *German Quarterly* 90.2, Spring 2017, 141–56.

6. See Brent O. Peterson, *History, Fiction and Germany: Writing the Nineteenth-Century Nation* (Detroit: Wayne State UP, 2005). Brent O. Peterson, "Peter Schlemihl, the Chamisso Prize, and the Much Longer History of German Migration Narratives," *German Studies Review* 41, no. 1, February 2018, 81–98.

7. Friedrich de la Motte Foqué, *Der Refugié oder Heimath und Fremde: Ein Roman aus der neueren Zeit* (Gotha und Erfurt: in der henning'schen Buchhandlung, 1824; facsimile reprint, *Friedrich de la Motte Foqué Sämtliche Romane und Novellenbücher* (Hildesheim: George Olms, 1990) 10.1–2). All subsequent references are given parenthetically in the main text; translations are my own.

BRIDGET SWANSON

# "Goethe Boom" Films: *Bildung* Reloaded

THE PROJECT OF GERMAN REUNIFICATION in the 1990s coincided with a marked decline in film adaptations based on German canonical texts. The move signified a turn away from classical literary adaptations and broke with a longstanding trend in the German film industry. Whereas previous eras of cultural crisis and change, such as during the 1930s and 1970s, had often prompted renewed interest in classical adaptations, changes in funding structures in the early 1990s shifted the German adaptation industry's attention away from eighteenth-century *Dichter und Denker* (poets and thinkers) to the works of contemporary bestselling authors. With these sorts of book-to-film endeavors proving economically successful on the global market, in part due to financially advantageous changes in the book publishing industry,[1] such adaptations promised Germany's film industry a strengthened foothold in commercially successful entertainment cinema. From Joseph Vilsmaier's *Schlafes Bruder* (*Brother of Sleep*, 1995) to Tom Tykwer's *Parfüm. Die Geschichte eines Mörders* (*Perfume: The Story of a Murderer*, 1995), the adaptations created during this era indeed garnered national and international acclaim, with Caroline Link's *Nirgendwo in Afrika* (*Nowhere in Africa*, 2001) even winning the Academy Award for Best Foreign Language Film in 2002. At this point, it seemed that the relevance of Weimar classicism had waned.

Starting in the early 2000s, however, German film studios began to return to canonical texts and have released numerous adaptations based on the works of Goethe, Lessing, Schiller, and Kleist, among others. Loosely grouped under the umbrella term "contemporary classical adaptations," these films range from more conservative theater-based productions like Leander Haußmann's *Kabale und Liebe* (*Intrigue and Love*, 2005), to modernizations such as Christoph Stark's *Julietta* (2001), Sebastian Schipper's *Mitte Ende August* (*Sometime in August*, 2005) and Uwe Janson's *Werther* (2008), to biopic-oriented heritage films like Philipp Stölzl's *Goethe!* (*Young Goethe in Love*, 2010) and Dominik Graf's *Die geliebten Schwestern* (*Beloved Sisters*, 2014). As suggested by Paul Cooke, Randall Halle, and Brad Prager and Jaimey Fisher, the cultural shift toward eighteenth-century German literature in the early twenty-first century complicates scholarly treatments of the current transnational German film market.[2] Whereas these scholars outline contemporary German film output as increasingly outward-looking, with Germany's traumatic twentieth-century past and contemporary multiculturalism often stylized for consumption by global markets, the contemporary classical adaptations discussed here point toward a pervasive national preoccupation with two intertwined endeavors that can be traced back to production and reception processes of the eighteenth century. First, German cinema has sought to rival Hollywood's successful "Shakespeare boom" period via acts of emulation and appropriation reminiscent of Enlightenment-era German literary practices. Second, the contemporary German film industry has been engaged with concerns about the perceived need and mandate for the media literacy of young Germans—doing so in a manner that co-opts aspects of the discourses of *Bildung* inherent to the very texts upon which the contemporary classical adaptations were based. The resulting adaptations are thus culturally unique compared with earlier eras of German *Literaturverfilmungen*, as they emphasize, across both aesthetic and industrial lines, figurations of transnational pop culture, national *Bildung*, and pedagogy.

In terms of the appropriative practices at play in the initial emergence of this genre, eighteenth-century Shakespeare emulation resurfaces as twenty-first-century Shakespeare boom emulation. That the German film industry has channeled Hollywood Shakespeare film adaptations to create contemporary cinematic fare based on Germany's literary trove is, from a film historical perspective, distinctive, contrasting with most other national cinema contexts. Here, filmmakers imitate the translocation and modernization of Baz Luhrmann's *Romeo + Juliet* (2006) and Michael Almereyda's *Hamlet* (2000) and fit Shakespeare's works to their geographical and linguistic contexts, examples of which are described at length by Mark Thornton Burnett, Maurizio Calbi, and Sonia Massai.[3]

However, in Germany, where the Hollywood Shakespeare boom films garnered the greatest profits of any foreign market, several German critics and filmmakers immediately responded with laments that "die Amerikaner und die Engländer 'ihren' Shakespeare rauf und runter verfilmen, mal klassisch, mal modern, mal experimentell, während sich bei uns kaum einer mit Goethe, Schiller oder Lessing beschäftigt" (the English and Americans endlessly adapt 'their' Shakespeare in film, be it classical or modern or avantgarde, whereas hardly any of us is dealing with Goethe, Schiller or Lessing).[4] With the strong conviction that Goethe and his contemporaries were just as much writers of important world literature as Shakespeare, German directors charted a different path in the 2000s, co-opting the aesthetics, stylistics, and marketing campaigns of the Hollywood genre to feature German canonical works, promoting their films with taglines on the DVD jackets such as "So nah an Shakespeare—und an Hollywood—war Schiller nie!" (Never before was Schiller so close to Shakespeare or—for that matter—to Hollywood). Indeed, the films that were produced in Germany recycle in their advertising materials and DVD covers the precise layout, sizing, and position of main and supporting characters that were popularized by the Shakespeare boom films. In terms of speech acts (dialogue, narration, and voice-overs), the films intermix noticeably archaic spoken German and direct quotes from the original texts with modern slang; they integrate textual overlays with antiquated orthography; and musically, they juxtapose pop music with traditional folk songs and ballads. These films also include pronounced collisions between historical fact and contemporary values, with some films transposing historical settings to the contemporary Berlin metropolis and its outskirts.

By revivifying longstanding German canonical works through contemporary popular culture frameworks so that they speak to contemporary national viewers and of national concerns, these films' model of aesthetic emulation calls to mind the *Sturm und Drang* treatises that outlined best practices for the appropriation of Shakespeare in the eighteenth century. The overarching message across Lessing's "Siebzehnter Brief" (Seventeenth Letter, 1759), Goethe's "Zum Schäkespears Tag" (For Shakespeare's Day, 1771), Herder's "Shakespeare" (1773) and Lenz's "Anmerkungen über das Theater" (Notes on Theater, 1774), is that the genius of Shakespeare resides not simply in the works he produced but in his approach to creating a literary output that spoke to his context and time. These treatises therefore discouraged simple transpositions of plot and characters from Shakespearean to German-speaking locales as well as slavish word-for-word translations from the original English to German. They instead put forth the argument that German authors should approach their own national literary production akin to Shakespeare by mining German cultural history for themes and characters whose stories resonate with present, that is, eighteenth-century, concerns and to write them in a way and with stylistic attention devoted to the sociohistorical context of contemporary readers. At times, proper content was even identified as ideal material for such future narratives. Lessing, for example, directly called for the revival of the longstanding *Faust* legend by dint of the adaptive process he outlined.[5]

In addition to demonstrating what Shakespeare-related emulation looks like today, transposed from the eighteenth-century German page to the twenty-first-century German screen and subtly reflective of Hollywood simultaneously as model and contrast, the "Goethe boom" films also foreground a motif central to many of the Enlightenment works upon which they are based: the importance of reading critically to thwart the impact of unfettered words. As David Wellbery explains, given fears about the suggestive power of literature and its increased availability to the middle class, "during the period extending from the first publication of Werther roughly to the century's end, the pedagogical establishment waged a campaign against excessive, uncontrolled reading."[6] As he demonstrates, *Die Leiden des jungen Werther* (*The Sorrows of Young Werther*) showcases the dangers of excessively and uncontrollably consuming literature: Werther is a victim of *Lesesucht* (reading addiction), and his overidentification with the titular Emilia Galotti at the end of Goethe's epistolary novel leads him to his untimely and gruesome end. Moving back a few years to the 1772 publication of *Emilia Galotti*, the death of Lessing's protagonist—Werther's role model—can be understood as an appropriation of the martyrdom of the narrative figure Virginia. Although Emilia's chosen literary role model proves a more valiant and appropriate choice than Werther's, the effect of literary identification in both cases is similarly substantial, and fatal.

In the Goethe boom films that reimagine Werther, Emilia, and others through the dual lens of historical and contemporary issues, eighteenth-century wariness about the power of the printed word and literary overidentification is repackaged as twenty-first-century concerns about the suggestive power of the visual medium and appropriate ways to engage with the canon. Drawing, in part, from their source texts, Goethe boom films often include sequences in which the main characters position themselves as visual consumers of eighteenth-century German literary works. Yet, to underscore the problems of overidentification, the films also incorporate a variety of self-reflective devices premised upon revealing the visual as a medium warranting critical engagement by viewers via distancing techniques that momentarily suspend the films' verisimilitude. Such sequences include the breaking of the fourth wall, the inclusion of notably high-angle shots that position the viewer as a sort of knowing audience member, intertextual citations, or references to other works, identifiably altered *tableaux vivants*, and protagonists who represent the films' own viewers.

For example, Henrik Pfeifer's *Emilia* (2005) foregrounds the affect and education of an audience member who engages with a canonical theatrical work. Viewers of the film first encounter Pfeifer's protagonist, Emilia, via an extended close-up that positions her as an audience member in a dimly lit theater. Offscreen sound signals that she is attentively watching a stage production of *Emilia Galotti*; the film's viewers, however, are alone privy to Emilia's position as spectator of this canonical play; the camera seldom cuts to the stage, allowing viewers only a brief peek at what Emilia is observing. Instead, viewers primarily see and hear Emilia seeing, hearing, and weeping as the play reaches its tragic conclusion. After this establishing sequence, viewers watch as Emilia increasingly perceives and positions herself as Lessing's classic protagonist in modern-day Berlin. Her dilemmas, behaviors, and desires align with those of the titular Emilia Galotti, and at the film's climax, she cites from Lessing's play in order to save herself. Unsatisfied with her fiancé (whom her parents are pressuring her to marry) and in love with another man, Emilia stages a simulated suicide during a phone call with her father in which she quotes directly from the final act of *Emilia Galotti*. Her words conjure up powerful images in her father's mind of Emilia Galotti's death, which then frees our modern Emilia from having to live out life with the wrong partner. For the film character of Emilia, viewing an adaptation of Lessing's bourgeois tragedy entails her internalization of the moral of the play. But she also applies that moral in her own life—a life whose circulation through the "everyday," in this case, characterizes "popular culture" as a space where viewers, like Pfeifer's Emilia, also often engage and interact with circulating canonical works, however co-opted or transformed.

A second poignant example of how Goethe boom films signal the contemporary power of transmediated canonical works in popular culture is Rolf Teigler's *Penthesilea-Moabit* (2008). Like *Emilia*, this film foregrounds the experience of audience members viewing an adaptation, but portrays such engagement with adaptations as acts of civic duty. Drawing on Kleist's use of teichoscopy, by which the events of the main figures are reported on by secondary characters peering at the action from behind a barricade, Teigler's film begins and ends with a frame story that accentuates the manner in which the circulation of canonical stories and their contemporary relevance occurs and is sustained through popular culture. At the film's center is a journalist intent on publishing a critical review of a staging of Kleist's work in an abandoned park in the Moabit district of Berlin. During the play, he and his companion stand in the bleacher section, behind a barricade and well above the action, but nevertheless are deeply moved by the work. Numerous cuts break away from the onstage occurrences to register the journalist's and—in particular—his companion's disgust at the grotesque acts unfolding on stage. Though this canonical text had been unknown to the companion, both parties leave determined to relate their experience of the work; the journalist writes up his review of the adaptation, while the companion, we learn, creates the very film product we have just watched, a product that questions and, in fact, condemns cross-cultural violence in contemporary Berlin. The emotional and pedagogical effect of literature and film on audiences both *in* the film and *of* the film highlights the imperative for a modernized *Penthesilea* to challenge viewers to engage critically. These actual and implied audience members exemplify the role that real-world viewers might be expected to play as part of a contemporary education in which they are required to engage with and make meaning of contemporary adaptations of canonical German literary works.

By foregrounding the *Bildung* of the spectator, and repeatedly drawing attention to practices of critical engagement with narratives that are already central to the source texts, contemporary classical adaptations point toward an important sociocultural component that has helped prompt the film industry to revisit, adapt, and update eighteenth-century texts: the Bundeszentrale für politische Bildung (Federal Agency for Civic Education), which we might see as the contemporary instantiation of the eighteenth-century "pedagogical establishment" of which Wellbery speaks. While German critics and filmmakers were encountering Hollywood Shakespeare boom films, a nationwide movement to address concerns about media literacy and its role in the state was simultaneously underway. In 1998, Chancellor Gerhard Schröder established Die Beauftragte der Bundesregierung für Kultur und Medien (Federal Commissioner for Culture and the Media) in the Bundeszentrale "in order to bring together the responsibility for the cultural and media policy of the Federal Government."[7] As explored by Susanne Unger, only five years later under the leadership of the newly appointed commissioner Christina Weiss, a specialist in childhood visual processing, the Bundeszentrale published a mandate for film competence, requiring that primary and secondary school students throughout Germany receive instruction in film appreciation and media analysis in all subjects capable of integrating the medium.[8] This, in turn, resulted in the founding of the Filmkompetenzagentur (Agency for Film Competence) in 2005, a separate entity that worked closely with both the Bundeszentrale and members of the German film industry to standardize film education nationwide, including the publication of numerous didacticized materials known as *Filmhefte* (companion materials for the teaching of film) and the organization of class trips to the cinemas tied to public lectures. As this occurred, private distribution companies, including Concorde Verleih and Warner Brothers Germany, likewise began to produce pedagogical materials corresponding with several of their films as part of a marketing strategy. The multifaceted, multi-institutional approach taken nationwide was considered necessary, given that many teachers had never received explicit training in film and media pedagogy but nevertheless needed to engage in the project of increasing students' media literacy.

Film adaptations of canonical works were seen as an ideal vehicle for the new undertaking; after all, the literary texts were already part of the general curriculum and often required for the *Abitur.* Thus, the media literacy project across Germany provided film studios with an additional financial incentive to produce films about or on canonical German texts and writers, beyond the proven success of the Shakespeare boom. Yet what remains most intriguing for understanding the continued relevance and role of the eighteenth century in Germany's contemporary film industry is how recent government-mandated curricular policies have come to shape contemporary German film aesthetics in ways that indeed bring back the "Enlightenment ideal of moral-ethical pedagogy through art," which, according to Randall Halle, had been "nullified" in favor of melodramatic works shaped for mere entertainment purposes.[9] Instead, the post-1989 German film market is one which—at least via contemporary classical adaptations—still draws from the Enlightenment in order to support an ethical, pedagogical agenda focused on educating German citizens not only through their own literary trove, but also in ways of looking, seeing, and engaging with the canonical, the pedagogical, and the transnational in contemporary times.

*University of Vermont*

## NOTES

1. Simone Murray, *The Adaptation Industry: The Cultural Economy of Contemporary Literary Adaptation* (London: Routledge, 2012).

2. Paul Cooke, *Contemporary German Cinema* (Manchester, UK: Manchester UP, 2012); Randall Halle, *German Film after Germany: Toward a Transnational Aesthetic* (Chicago: University of Illinois Press, 2008); Brad Prager and Jaimey Fisher, *The Collapse of the Conventional: German Film and Its Politics at the Turn of the Twenty-First Century* (Detroit: Wayne State UP, 2010).

3. Mark Thornton Burnett, *Filming Shakespeare in the Global Marketplace* (Houndmills, UK: Palgrave Macmillan, 2007); Maurizio Calbi, *Spectral Shakespeares: Media Adaptations in the Twenty-First Century* (New York: Palgrave Macmillan, 2013); Sonia Massai, "Defining Local Shakespeares," in *World-Wide Shakespeares: Local Appropriations in Film and Performance* (London: Routledge, 2005) 3–14.

4. Ulli Pascal, "Vorwort" in *Emilia—Der Film*. http://www.emilia-der-film.ch/pages/02_03.htm. Unless otherwise indicated, all translations are my own.

5. Gotthold Ephraim Lessing, "Siebzehnter Brief," *Werke*, vol. 5, ed. Herbert G. Göpfert (Munich: Hanser, 1973) 73.

6. David Wellbery, "Pathologies of Literature," in *New History of German Literature*, ed. David Wellbery and Judith Ryan (Cambridge, MA: Harvard UP, 2005) 386–92.

7. "Cultural and Media Policy of the German Federal Government," *Presse- und Informationsamt der Bundesregierung, 2020*. https://archiv.bundesregierung.de/archiv-de/meta/startseite/cultural-and-media-policy-of-the-german-federal-government-470768.

8. Susanne B. Unger, "Cultivating Audiences: *Filmbildung*, Moral Education, and the Public Sphere in Germany" (Doctoral dissertation, University of Michigan, 2011).

9. Halle 114.

Johann Wolfgang von Goethe. **West-Eastern Divan. Complete, Annotated New Translation, including the "Notes and Essays" & the Unpublished Poems.** Translated by Eric Ormsby. Berkeley, CA: Gingko, 2019. xlii + 595 pp.

Barbara Schwepcke and Bill Swainson, eds. **A New Divan: A Lyrical Dialogue Between East & West.** Berkeley, CA: Gingko, 2019. xvii + 187 pp.

These two complementary volumes were published in 2019 in connection with the 200th anniversary of Goethe's *West-östlicher Divan*. Schwepcke and Swainson's *A New Divan: A Lyrical Dialogue Between East & West* is composed of two parts. The first part consists of twenty-four poems by twenty-four poets from both "East" and "West" who were invited to enter into a dialogue with Goethe on themes of his *Divan*: namely, the poet, love, the tyrant, faith, and paradise. The poems appear in their original language with facing-page English translations. The second part of *A New Divan* contains six exciting essays that examine issues of translation involving both East and West, including those raised by Goethe in the *Divan's* "Noten und Abhandlungen" ("Notes and Essays"). These essays help to situate Eric Ormsby's prose translation of Goethe's entire *Divan* (including the "posthumous" poems and the "Notes and Essays").

Ormsby's bilingual *Divan* reproduces Goethe's original poems and, on facing pages, an English translation in paragraph form without lineation. For the poems, Ormsby relied on the two-volume Hendrik Birus edition of the *Divan* (1994/2010), and for the "Noten und Abhandlungen" (English text only) on Max Rychner's edition (1963). Although Ormsby studied in Germany, his scholarly background is in Islamic studies. Thus, he knows the languages in question, differentiating, for instance, the poetic forms in Goethe's *Divan* from the inexhaustible prosody of Hafiz's Persian. His familiarity with the commentaries on Hafiz's work and on the "Eastern" context of the traditions on which Hafiz himself drew (and Hammer and Goethe in turn) is evident in accompanying footnotes that, among other things, annotate Arabic, Persian, or Turkish references to unfamiliar persons and places, while also referring to "Goethe's own sources in the German translations he used."

The introduction informs in short order of the background of Goethe's interest in Persian poetry, including pre-Hafiz (William Jones's translation of Arabic poetry; pre-Islamic odes; knowledge of Orientalist scholarship). Alongside themes Goethe himself identified in his *Divan*, Ormsby adds three others: song itself, longing, and the "Sufi vision of personal transformation." He also discusses the incidence of "doubling" in the *Divan* (e.g., East-West, Marianne-Suleika, Goethe-Hafiz, Goethe-Hatem), and its "voices," mentioning that many of its poems are "little recitations or arias, momentary solos and duets" that acknowledge the singing of poetry in the Muslim world.

It is an odd publishing fate that, while the world went without a translation of the "Noten und Abhandlungen" for almost two hundred years, one appeared in 2010, by Martin Bidney, along with his *rhymed* translation of Goethe's *Divan* (but without the original). Bidney's translation has been differently received (*Goethe Yearbook*, vol. 19; *Translation and Literature*, vol. 22). To distinguish the two versions, one might say that Bidney is entering into dialogue with Goethe (in the manner of Goethe with Hafiz), while Ormsby's version, despite some inevitable translation errors, offers an excellent introduction to a large body of Goethe's poetry that makes it accessible in a way that a rhymed translation does not.

To evaluate Ormsby's translation and the essays in *A New Divan*, it will be helpful to consider the three *epochs* of translation that Goethe wrote about in the "Noten und Abhandlungen." On its face, Ormsby's translation fits the definition of the first epoch, which according to Goethe, makes "a foreign country known to us," and on its own terms, for which a prose translation is most suitable. As Ormsby writes, it effaces "the idiosyncrasies of any sort of poetic art," while at the same time "surpris[ing] us with foreign excellence . . . and conferring a more exalted state of mind as it edifies." Goethe's own example was Luther's Bible translation. Ormsby is himself a poet but, as he writes, his translation gives "a closer appreciation of the original than a verse translation."

In the second translation epoch, a translator transposes himself to a foreign country but, at the same time, adapts the works to his own particular perspective and time. Goethe's examples include French translators of works of all epochs, which become "Frenchified" (my term), and Wieland, who for Goethe presented Shakespeare and antiquity in light of his own time. Although Goethe doesn't classify it as such, Hammer's translation would seem to fit in here. Thus, Sylvia Wentker's essay on Hammer ("Bringing Persia to Germany") counters the received view of his translation as one-dimensional, especially among Germanists (she includes Hendrik Birus) who are ignorant of Oriental languages. She locates Hammer's verse translation and his interpretation of Hafiz within the context of the Ottoman connoisseurship Hammer encountered in Constantinople, with its preference for the elaborately nuanced and artificial style of Persian poetry. Hafiz's attacks on authority, especially religious figures, found a welcome response in the era of the Enlightenment, and, similarly, because of his reliance on the sixteenth-century nontheological, "philologically based" commentary of Hafiz by Ahmad Sudi (d. 1591), Hammer glossed over the Sufi content of the ghazals. Thus, a worldly Hafiz, a "Persian Anacreon."

The challenges noted in the title of Narguess Farzad's essay ("Hafiz and the Challenges of Translating Persian Poetry into English") concern "the excessively emotive aspects of classical Persian poetry" and the issues of Persian prosody and scansion. Ormsby's translation, by avoiding the challenges, linguistic and cultural, of Goethe's German, again underlines its categorization within Goethe's first epoch, at the same time introducing a major writer of the Western canon to a great number of readers who would otherwise find a poetic translation tiring (an effort that could, however, be furthered by the publication of a more public-friendly edition.)

The third epoch, Goethe's "highest," seeks to make the translation identical to the original, abandoning the perspective of one's own nation, in the process introducing a style that may be unpalatable to a poet's contemporaries but that, according to Ormsby, will offer future poets new "rhetorical, rhythmic, [and] metrical advantages." Goethe's example is Johann Heinrich Voss, translator of Homer. Stefan Weidner (in "The New Tasks of the Translator") takes apart this last category through the prism of Walter Benjamin's "idea of a 'pure language' . . . a vision of overcoming Babelesque linguistic diversity." As Weidner points out, Goethe himself must have been "perfectly aware that neither Oriental literature in German translation nor the *Nach-Dichtung* it inspires, such as the *Divan*, has any chance of finding readers and being appreciated other than by specialists if it is offered up completely unmediated simply for what it is." Had Goethe (or Hammer) sought to be faithful to the third paradigm, as did Hölderlin in his translations of Greek or Rückert in *his* German translation of Hafiz, the results might have been "originals," but they would be basically unreadable, appreciated only by specialists. All of this again underlines the pitfalls that Ormsby has avoided.

Robyn Creswell ("Playing a Part: Imru' al-Qays in English") deals with the translation efforts of poets, beginning in the eighteenth century, to create new styles and poetic forms from Eastern models. Although he begins with the "spiritual sympathy" Goethe found in Hafiz, comparing it to the flinty, self-reliant Hafiz of Emerson (yes, that Emerson), he moves on to a discussion of the sympathetic bond that English-language poets and translators have forged with the pre-Islamic prince and poet, from the philologist William Jones to Alfred Lord Tennyson and the contemporary American poet Frederick Seidel. Working in the other direction, Khadim J. Hassan ("On the Translation of European Poetry into Arabic Culture") explores the revolutionary effect on modern Arabic poets of acquaintance with Western poetic models. It began in the late nineteenth century with translations of the *Iliad*, Lamartine, and even Khayyam's quatrains, all rendered respecting "the laws of Arabic meter" and highlighting the translator's precocity. The "Apollo school," which emerged in the 1930s, initiated a new approach, which led to non-metric translations that "were the first of their kind." Moreover, in the majority of cases, as Creswell notes, "the translator demonstrates richness of vocabulary, powerful syntax, supplements of rhythm and a profound grasp of the work's meanings, evident in their critical commentaries and explanatory notes which involve both interpretation and critical appreciation."

The poets discussed in *A New Divan*, both Eastern and Western, testify to the elective affinities felt between poets. Such an affinity is at the center of Rajmohan Gandhi's essay ("Goethe and 'the East' of Today") on the fractured nature of discourse, past and present, between East and West and among the Muslim world itself. He describes the discovery of Goethe's *Divan* in 1923 by Muhammed Iqbal, "one of South Asia's greatest poets and the man who would give Pakistan its ideological foundation." Influenced by Goethe's appreciation of "Islam's message of submission to God," Iqbal's response, the Persian-language *Payam-i-Mashriq* ("Message of the East"), highlights the "realities common to all," absent labels, that are inherent to the *Divan*.

Such an elective affinity among poets and translators was the case in the development in the early modern era of the different European vernaculars, which constantly interacted with one another via translations, a process that continued with the "discovery" of the non-Western idioms in Goethe's day. Now that the Arab literary world is catching up, one cannot help but feel that the process may be coming to an end. Where once William Jones encouraged translation of "the poetry of Eastern nations" in order to discover new forms and "new images and similitudes that future poets might emulate," by the late twentieth century, Arab poets, according to Hassan, have increasingly thrown off the yoke of meter, favoring, for instance, prose poems, and thereby eroding the vibrancy of literary models that once characterized Eastern cultures.

Bidney's mammoth translation project includes a 200-page section of his own *rhymed* commentary on each of the twelve books of Goethe's *Divan*, which indicates that English-language poets continue to experiment with foreign poetic forms in an aspirational manner. To the extent that such poetry enriches the resources of English as a poetic medium, the result may be reserved for cognoscenti. This is where Goethe's use of the term *epochs* in connection with literary translation is apt. As Weidner writes, Goethe assumed that "languages and literatures follow a 'natural' course of development which is reflected . . . ultimately in a continuous assimilation of the various national literatures into each other, a process for which Goethe later coined the term 'world literature.'" Did Goethe think that national literatures would die out, that they would be replaced by a world language, for example, by English, which is becoming the kind of "pure" language of which Benjamin wrote, one that could overcome "Babelesque linguistic diversity"? To the extent that English is on its way to becoming everyone's "original," Ormsby's translation might be placed in Goethe's third epoch.

*New York, New York*                                    *Elizabeth Powers*

Stefan Hajduk, **Poetologie der Stimmung. Ein ästhetisches Phänomen der frühen Goethezeit.** Bielefeld: transcript, 2016. 513 pp.

The notion of *Stimmung* is in the air, it is all around us. After having been pushed aside in the late twentieth century, *Stimmung* has returned as a priority for architecture, city planning, environmentalism, and literary criticism. The term has become the progressive angle from which diverse movements have sought to reverse the functionality of modernism without falling into retrograde traditionalism. The eighteenth-century affinity for nurturing *Stimmung*, first articulated in landscape gardening and sentimental prose, has been mobilized into a more active climate awareness, both local and global.

Stefan Hajduk's massive *Poetologie der Stimmung* covers much more than the literature of the early Goethezeit, as it addresses the 250-year history of scholars who have sought to characterize the illusive quality. He engages earnestly with Leo Spitzer's articles on *Stimmung*'s relation to ancient ideas of cosmological harmony while proposing Heidegger's *Befindlichkeit* as conceptually superior to nineteenth-century aesthetic articulations. He is also fully conversant with Gernot Böhme's more recent appeal to foster *Atmosphäre* in architecture. Most importantly for Goethe scholars, Hajduk builds his argument on David Wellbery's definitive essay on the subject in *Aesthetische Grundbegriffe*, providing interpretations and examples that augment Wellbery's reconstruction of the term's semantic field. For all his thoroughness, Wellbery's succinct review of Goethe's remarks on *Stimmung* leaves room for many more investigations into the term's poetic use around Strasbourg and Weimar. Hajduk's book takes up the challenge by finding diverse forms of *Stimmung* in the early *Goethezeit*, not just those that proffer a lyrical perception of nature. The core of Hajduk's book is organized around lengthy close interpretations of three texts: Goethe's *Die Leiden des jungen Werthers*, Karl Philipp Moritz's *Andreas Hartknopf* novels, and Ludwig Tieck's short drama, "Der Abschied."

Hajduk agrees with Wellbery's opening claim that the difficulty in translating *Stimmung* into other European languages reflects the manner in which the German term integrates both subjective and objective references. *Stimmung* appears both within the perceiving individual as well as in the surrounding environment. "Mood" and "atmosphere" capture different portions but by no means the full range of aesthetic connotations in *Stimmung*. Because the term is often invoked in such a manner as to take advantage of its rich metaphorical allusions, no single other word comes close to its fullness. Agreeing with Wellbery's *Begriffsgeschichte*, Hajduk reviews the many connotations of *Stimmung*, landing at the conclusion that "mood," "milieu," "ambience," "atmosphere," or "attunement" do not adequately correspond to the word's musical-cosmological resonance nor its indeterminate sense of an emotional landscape.

Demonstrating the inadequacy of many translation choices makes clear how many diverse and complex connotations are carried by the word. Indirectly, both Wellbery and Hajduk underscore the distinctiveness of the German word. For both scholars, contextual usage remains vital to understanding the particular meanings invoked at any given instance. Wellbery refrains from offering a conceptual definition but turns instead to a history of its metaphorical application. In this regard, both critics agree with Spitzer that *Stimmung*'s lexical career takes off in the eighteenth century. In building off his predecessors, Hajduk points out that Wellbery's focus on aesthetic theory serves an entirely different purpose than Spitzer's reconstruction of cosmology. Hajduk goes further than Spitzer and Wellbery in highlighting the inadequacy of all translations and conceptualizations of *Stimmung* to argue that philosophical definitions around 1800 were ultimately incomplete and poetic articulations increasingly subjective, thereby losing the term's spatial and natural dimensions. For Wellbery, the indeterminacy is a source of fruitful variation, whereas Hajduk sees a problem that ultimately requires Heidegger to provide an adequate answer.

Contrary to Wellbery's conceptual history, Hajduk argues that from Kant to Humboldt, *Stimmung* loses its position within the aesthetic space of nature as something external to the subject, such as a musical tone or atmosphere—decisive connotations for Goethe, Moritz, and Tieck. The poetic texts Hajduk cites differ substantially from the established philosophical definitions of *Stimmung*. For much of his book, Hajduk traces the shifting meanings of the term by focusing on discrepancies between poetic practice and philosophical conceptualizations of *Stimmung*. After much effort, he concludes that there is little to be gained from a synchronic contextualization of the term around 1800. Frustrated with the classical era, Hajduk moves on to Heidegger's *Sein und Zeit* (1927) after critically reviewing Vischer, Kierkegaard, Nietzsche, Simmel, and Dilthey. Heidegger's adaptation breaks with earlier forms grounded in subjectivity, thereby removing its link to feeling or affect through a phenomenology of existential space. For the sake of performing literary interpretations, Hajduk further adapts Heidegger's existentialism into hermeneutics. Like many other commentators, Hajduk reveals his aversion to holding a position that could, in any manner, be subject to Hegel's critique of Romantic *Stimmung* as a mere projection of interiority onto nature. It has to be more than a poetic expression of emotions.

Hajduk works valiantly to bridge the yawning gap between Heidegger's ontological interest and Romantic subjectivity. The account of *Stimmung* provided in *Sein und Zeit* avoids the old problem of differentiating between subject and object as the source of *Stimmung*, yet the differences between Romanticism and phenomenology remain so vast that one struggles to believe that Heidegger and Goethe are contemplating the same question when they use the term. One must ask why such an amorphous term should require an exact delineation: What does Hajduk attain by identifying a certain definition? Why not allow its indeterminacy?

As with *Weltliteratur*, Germanists share a critical interest in the concept's origins. Hajduk traces the first metaphorical use of *Stimmung* to Herder's *Reisejournal* (1769), while Wellbery ascribes it to Goethe's Falconet essay published in 1776 in the collection *Aus Goethes Brieftasche*. Hajduk resolves the difference by offering the general claim that Herder announces *Stimmung* in aesthetic theoretical terms, while Goethe offers its first poetic articulation. *Stimmung*, for Herder, describes the condition of suspension (*Schwebezustand*), a position that Anne McCarthy (*Awful Parenthesis: Suspension and the Sublime in Romantic and Victorian Poetry*, 2018) has recently isolated in British Romanticism. English also lacks a comparable word. The possibilities for cross-cultural readings are probably only enhanced by the difficulty in finding fulfilling translations between German and English. One could argue that its untranslatability befits its home in *Sturm und Drang* literature. As a difficult term to define, *Stimmung* emerged in literary history in much the same manner as it operated—diffusely. The fact that Herder and Goethe are seen as having first invoked *Stimmung* as an aesthetic idea and practice shows how much the mediation between these two authors cannot be explained through textual evidence alone, but rather through some diffuse sense of *Stimmung*, the nineteenth century would have called it *Geist*.

Hajduk's reconstruction shows that a literary usage for the term established itself well before *Stimmung* appeared in ordinary or philosophical speech. The first poetic articulation as a self-conscious aesthetic position can be found in Werther's discourse of feeling as it arises from the phenomenological experience of space and media, nature and letters. In Karl Philipp Moritz's two novels, *Andreas Hartknopf. Eine Allegorie* (1785) and the accompanying *Predigerjahren* (1790), Hajduk detects a "Stimmung der Seele" that looks very much like the ancient macro-micro-cosmological model of harmonious spheres, which would later prove so important to Romantics such as Tieck, Novalis, and Eichendorff. In all these texts, music remains the expression of feelings that have a universal resonance. Hartknopf's discussion of musical tones and compositions is derived from terms associated with the historical semantics of *Stimmung*, ideals such as harmony, symphony, sympathy, and concord. By articulating ideas ranging from an emotional aesthetics of sympathetic souls to formal principles of autonomous art, Moritz's novels provide a historical transition from sentimentalism and Weimar classicism.

By focusing on *Stimmung* single-mindedly, Hajduk offers a new interpretation of Werther and allows for insights previously overlooked. Werther's letters describe the environmental context within which he has experiences; thus, they situate feeling within natural space. Hajduk argues against equating *Stimmung* solely with sentimental emotions, "Rührung" "Herz" "Empfinden" or "Tränen." He argues instead that Werther produces *Stimmung* on multiple levels. Hajduk is particularly keen on demonstrating the media operation in its historical usages. He wants to show that *Stimmung* can describe an event or a mood within a media network, without being reduced to a particular historical context, such as the publication of a best-selling book that captures the mindset of an audience. The reader is left balancing between *Stimmung*, as providing ontological insight in the manner of *Befindlichkeit*, and its place within a historically changing semantic field (*Begriffsgeschichte*). Does *Stimmung* reveal an existential condition or does it belong to a cosmological tradition that stretches back to antiquity but no longer resonates within our media-driven society? Hajduk answers this query by showing the media character of both sides of the question. For eighteenth-century *Germanistik*, this means reorienting *Werther* scholarship in line with Albrecht Koschorkes's "Mediologie des 18. Jahrhunderts." *Werther*'s appearance at the right historical moment (Lukács) elevated the experience to a privileged form of social-historical perception. After *Werther*, readers became sensitive to its binding operation, linking subjectivity, nature, history, media. Hajduk interprets *Werther* as a text in which the position of sender and receiver collapse together. Werther's outpourings exist as information (*Mitteilungen*) that are extended within a logic of readerly participation. His letters create an accord within the communication channel—in other words, they set up a consensus (*Zusammen-Stimmung*) that in turn avows a new mediation between natural space and perception. In a double move, *Werther* manages to both formalize the aesthetics of *Stimmung*, while also embodying it as an entity within the history of reading.

Moritz's great psychological novel, *Anton Reiser*, presents *Stimmungen* in the form of fluctuating moods, or *Launen*, which, as Christiane Frey has argued (*Laune: Poetik der Selbstsorge von Montaigne bis Tieck*, 2015), the protagonist seeks at first to understand and then later to regulate. Moritz shifts away from *Stimmung* as emotional states and back to more archaic teachings in his *Andreas Hartknopf: Eine Allegorie* and *Andreas Hartknopfs Predigerjahre*. Leo Spitzer's essays on the relation between *Stimmung* and Greek metaphysics become important again for Hajduk's interpretations. At the conclusion of the first *Hartknopf* novel, the narrator describes his mystical encounter with the protagonist as a synthesis of music and cosmology. Unlike in *Werther*, *Stimmung* in *Hartknopf* does not manifest itself as a configuration of love in nature, but more as the personal experience of universal harmony.

Hajduk's somewhat esoteric choice of Tieck's minor drama "Der Abschied" draws a parallel between an out-of-tune piano and a tragic lovers' triangle. The two-act play shows its *Sturm und Drang* lineage quite clearly—imagine if Albert had eavesdropped on Werther and Charlotte embracing for one last goodbye and then murdered them in sequence. On the other side, Tieck's marital psychology anticipates the unhappy unions of Henrik Ibsen. By tracing how different literary epochs reconfigured an established form, Hajduk exposes the continuities between them. Even within literary history, the term continues its mediating function, bridging the generations. Hajduk's analysis quite compellingly isolates the bourgeois repression and denial that turns a supposedly idyllic retreat into a "*Stimmungstragodie*."

The important innovation in Hajduk's book lies in his introduction of media theory within the conceptual history of *Stimmung*. His interpretations layer meanings together, so that media operations and poetic expression are enmeshed as different aspects of the same phenomenon. For all his insistence on defining *Stimmung* conceptually, his writing plays whimsically with its many connotations. The dispersion of Hajduk's many insights across his tome only confirms how difficult it is to pin down a certain definition of *Stimmung*, whether cosmological, ontological, or aesthetic.

*Pennsylvania State University*                                    *Daniel Purdy*

Sebastian Kaufmann. **Heidegger liest Goethe. Ein vielstimmiges "Zwiegespräch" (ca. 1910–1976).** Heidelberg: Universitätsverlag Winter, 2019. 100 pp.

It is difficult to speak of what this book does without also speaking of what it doesn't do. We know well that Heidegger's work is deeply informed by a philosophical dialogue with poets, but there remain details to be filled in as to what that rapport looks like in the case of Goethe. In *Heidegger liest Goethe*, Sebastian Kaufmann presents the results of locating all passages that mention Goethe in the almost one hundred volumes of the Heidegger *Gesamtausgabe*. The substantive backbone of the contribution is a *Stellenkonkordanz* that lists such passages volume by volume, while the main body of the book consists of Kaufmann's selective overview of the material. Heidegger's mentions of Goethe are generally brief, but they are spread throughout his writings, so that, taken together, there is a significant body of material to be dealt with. What do we learn from Kaufmann's research?

As other scholars have already shown, Heidegger did not always engage with Goethe's writings with a keen interest in the specificity of Goethe's own thought. Rather, the general pattern that emerges is of Goethe being cited approvingly when his ideas can be made to harmonize with Heidegger's own, and disapprovingly when he runs athwart of Heidegger's intellectual allegiances. Heidegger's discussions of the poem "Ein Gleiches," for example, serve to exemplify his "Tendenz zur 'Gleichschaltung' unterschiedlichster lyrischer Texte, die nach demselben simplen Schema (durch Hervorhebung des Verbs 'sein') auf die Seinsfrage umgebogen werden," as Kaufmann notes. Heidegger focuses, namely, on the verb in the opening line: "Über allen Gipfeln ist Ruh," thereby presenting Goethe's poem as an instantiation of a Heideggerian paradigm. Similarly, Kaufmann documents Heidegger's several citations of "Wär das Auge nicht sonnenhaft," a poem adapted from the Hellenic tradition, with Heidegger being interested in its function as a modern German expression of a Greek idea. Here again, what Kaufmann calls the "projektive[r] Selbstbespiegelungs-Charakter seiner Interpretationen" is on display.

But most mentions of Goethe prior to the 1950s are considerably less favorable than the above examples. Many of Heidegger's judgments were formed under the influence of voices in early twentieth-century German intellectual culture that not only commentated and critiqued but indeed variously mythologized and demonized Goethe. In the work of Simmel and Gundolf, for example, Heidegger appreciated the "künstlerische[s] Moment," whereby often overwrought and overdetermined constructions of the cultural figurehead "Goethe" take the upper hand over sober interpretation of his actual writings. (In that era, the name "Goethe" signified a sometimes wildly contradictory manifold; as Heidegger succinctly observes: "Goethe und Goethe ist nicht das Selbe"). More strongly at work, though, is a decided "Abwertung gegenüber Hölderlin," influenced by Norbert von Hellingrath and operating on the logic that if one is to be truly pro-Hölderlin, then one must necessarily be anti-Goethe. This peculiar literary tribalism, which Heidegger held to for decades, has been a central point in previous scholarship on Heidegger and Goethe.

Unlike Hölderlin's putatively authentic relationship to ancient Greece, Goethe's classicism offered, in Heidegger's view, an inauthentic counterfeit of classical culture. And unlike Hölderlin's voicing of distinctive qualities of the modern German nation, Goethe is seen as representing a universal cosmopolitanism that threatens national authenticity. There follow from these viewpoints Heidegger's sometimes almost abusive treatments of Goethe, which reach their crescendo in the 1940s, most nakedly in the *Schwarzen Heften*. To Goethe—seen as *Weltbürger* and proponent of *Weltliteratur*—Heidegger ascribes "geradezu metaphysische Verantwortung für das völlige In-Vergessenheit-Geraten jenes 'anfänglichen Seins' in der Neuzeit." After 1945, when Goethe is fashioned into a cultural icon for the democratization of Germany, Heidegger holds him to be complicit in an annihilation of true Germanness that makes the crimes of the Nazis look, in comparison, like "die reine Harmlosigkeit."

Kaufmann does passingly acknowledge the presence of "faschistoiden Züge" in Heidegger's work, but his characterization of the above remark as being merely "absonderlich" is the closest he comes to a political judgment in this book. Yet trying to speak of shifts in Heidegger's thought while shying away from politics is, in some cases, rather like trying to speak of sailing without mentioning wind. Hobbled by this omission, Kaufmann is unable to truly get a handle on the highly disparate mass of material he has gathered and is able ultimately to offer no more satisfying judgments than that Heidegger's readings of Goethe are "ausgesprochen ambivalent, ja geradezu gespalten," or, aestheticizing things, that they occur "in mehrfach wechselnden Tonlagen." Yet it is altogether possible to identify and discuss certain influences and motivations from which those contradictions arise. This would mean, among other things, addressing Heidegger's politics candidly.

From the 1950s onward, there finally appear "Spuren einer vertieften und erweiterten Goethe-Lektüre": whereas in 1949, Heidegger concedes to Karl Jaspers that he had "noch kein zureichendes Verhältnis zu Goethe," in 1950, he writes to Hannah Arendt, "Mit den Jahren lerne ich Goethe verstehen." Until then, he simply hadn't read Goethe attentively. Among the intriguing evidence Kaufmann presents of more serious engagement with Goethe's thought after 1950 is, for example, a late philosophical poem prominently referencing ideas from the introduction to the *Propyläen*. In general, one can say that in matters of science, epistemology, and observation, Heidegger cites Goethe as a genuine intellectual ally: aspects of the *Farbenlehre*, or notions such as the *Urphänomen* or "gegenständliches Denken," for example, seem to be evoked sincerely and without antagonism. This direction, however, is not thoroughly explored in *Heidegger liest Goethe*, and readers wishing to know more about the intellectually fruitful aspects of Heidegger's readings will wish to have been offered more in this regard.

As Heidegger admonishes at one point, "Auch die Beziehung zu einem Dichter hat ihre Geschichte," and the work of reconstructing how Heidegger read Goethe necessarily involves embedding the available textual evidence within the salient specifics of its history. Other scholars, such as Clemens Pornschlegel and Günther Martin, have already covered much of what Kaufmann expounds and have also explored dimensions that he sidesteps. But, with this book, the way is opened for scholars to continue the interpretive work, equipped with Kaufmann's very helpful appendix.

*NYU Berlin*                          *Michael Saman*

Mattias Pirholt. **Grenzerfahrungen. Studien zu Goethes Ästhetik**. Heidelberg: Universitätsverlag Winter, 2018. 267 pp.

One might expect that a study of Goethe's aesthetics would arrive at a set of logically connected general statements establishing the concept of art, discriminating its kinds, explicating its relation to the world, and comparing it to such other important human domains as morality and knowledge. The grounds for judgment of individual works and the role of such judgments outside the arts—for example, vis-à-vis nature or technical artifacts—might also be considered. Such expectations are called forth by the concept of aesthetics itself, which, at least in its initial and primary meaning, designates a philosophical discipline, contributions that have roughly the shape I have sketched in the foregoing sentences. No text from Goethe's hand conforms exactly to this paradigm, however, and that means that scholars interested in Goethe's aesthetics have by necessity had to construct an ideal or hypothetical version of such a conceptual array by extracting from Goethe's scattered and extremely diverse writings on art, art works, and topical matters such as imitation or style or the ancients something that has the rough shape of an encompassing conceptualization. I do not mean to imply that such an enterprise is a fool's errand. On the contrary, I consider the research tradition represented, for example, by Ernst Cassirer's Goethe chapter in *Freiheit und Form* (1916), Mattijs Jolles's *Goethes Kunstanschauung* (1957), or, more recently, Waltraud Naumann-Beyer's article "Ästhetik" in the *Goethe Handbuch* (vol. 4.1, 1998) or Norbert Christian Wolf's *Streitbare Ästhetik* (2001) to be indispensable. Indeed, with every new development in philosophical aesthetics as practiced by philosophers, this tradition will be called upon to renew itself. Certainly, the upheaval in Hegel studies that has unfolded internationally since the publication of Robert Pippin's *Hegel's Idealism. The Satisfactions of Self-Consciousness* (1989) cries out for renewed inquiry into the conceptual foundations of Goethe's writings on art.

Despite its subtitle, Mattias Pirholt's interesting study does not conform to the pattern just described, and precisely herein resides its interest. His project is to solicit from areas of Goethe's writing the historically specific character of aesthetic experience that informs them. The theoretical points of reference that support Pirholt's line of inquiry are robustly unfashionable: Hans-Georg Gadamer's *Wahrheit und Methode* (1960) and Hans Robert Jauß's *Ästhetische Erfahrung und literarische Hermeneutik* (1982). The thought of Gadamer's that is crucial for Pirholt is that philosophical thought should be understood not as an array of timeless problems and proposed solutions, but as an experientially grounded labor of self-understanding that is intrinsically historical. Jauß applies this thought to aesthetic experience, conceptualizing the historical dynamic of such experience as the dialectical tension between *Wiedererkennen* and *Vorschein*. Such is the general conception that orients Pirholt's examination of Goethe's work. That examination unfolds as a study of five constitutive dimensions of aesthetic experience as it is articulated in Goethe's thought, his artistic politics, his literary writing, his reflections on meaning, and his strategies as a collector. The red thread that runs through the five studies is the notion of the border or limit and hence the notion of crossing or transgression. Aesthetic experience—this brings us back to the book's title—assumes its shape as a *Grenzerfahrung*.

The first chapter of Pirholt's study nicely highlights both the originality and the fecundity of his "studies on Goethe's aesthetic." The topic is the genesis

(*Entstehung*) of aesthetic experience, its emergence in the life of the subject as a specifically contoured experiential type. How might one investigate such a topic? Pirholt's approach is ingenious. He examines Goethe's own accounts of the moment of emergence across the *Theatralische Sendung*, the *Lehrjahre*, and *Dichtung und Wahrheit*. Although Pirholt does not make this connection, one might compare the approach taken to studies of the child's gradual acquisition of categories in the manner of Piaget, for Pirholt focuses centrally on fictional or remembered scenes of childhood in which a unique form of attention and a unique object of that attention comes into being. The preeminent example is the child's experience of the puppet theater and this chapter provides an excellent longitudinal reading of variants of this episode. The experiential structure elicited is centered on a border, a division (*Urtrennung*) that is at once spatial and ontological, and on repeated efforts to cross that border and to link, in some meaningful sense, the severed realms. This primordial experience develops across the works examined and extends into other domains (such as the discovery of poetic talent related in *Dichtung und Wahrheit*). In this way, Pirholt's interpretation brings to light what might be thought of as a genealogy of Goethe's self-understanding as an artist.

In his second chapter, Pirholt turns to what I will call the semantic dimension of aesthetic experience as it comes to expression in Goethe's letter to Schiller of August 17–18, 1797. That letter, needless to say, is the *locus classicus* for the formulation of Goethe's concept of the symbol, a well-trodden pathway of Goethe scholarship. Pirholt develops a highly original approach to the topic, emphasizing the temporal character of the symbol. The core of this interpretation is the contention that Goethe's notion of the symbol must be understood as influenced by Schiller's concept of the sentimental (*Über naive und sentimentalische Dichtung*). This thesis (for which the letter itself provides some evidence) will be regarded as controversial, but however that discussion turns out in the long run, it seems clear to me that the core thought regarding the temporal (I might rather say: processual or effective) aspect of the symbol takes us a step beyond the broadly held belief that the symbol is a case of the complete coincidence of particular empirical appearance and universal content. Indeed, alluding to Derrida, Pirholt identifies a structural moment of deferral in Goethe's thought, a contention that will heighten the controversies unleashed by this reading of the Goethean symbol.

In Pirholt's discussion of the symbol, the mediation between art and reality is an important theme, but that theme is fully exfoliated in the third chapter, which deals with the topic of ornament and arabesque. This chapter usefully lays out the full spectrum of Goethe's thinking on these topics, with a certain emphasis, appropriately enough, on the 1789 essay *Von Arabesken*. Two elements emerge into the foreground: Goethe's emphasis on the frugality that underlies the arabesque décor of the homes in Pompei and Herculaneum and his discrimination of a directive function of such wall décor, which was felt to lead the viewer to the apprehension of the essential matter, the exemplars of "higher art" centrally displayed. Here a major thesis of Pirholt's book, which was touched on in the first two chapters, comes to the fore: the contention that, contrary to a broad consensus in the research, Goethe's "aesthetics" does not rest on the notion of artistic autonomy. Indeed, the lesson of his treatment of ornament and arabesque, Pirholt argues, points rather to a notion of "*ästhetische Heteronomie*," which stresses mediation (e.g., economic, perceptual) between work and world. It is perhaps worth noting that this argument is directed against a notion of autonomy as the strict separation of art from actuality, of ideal from reality. At least to this reviewer, however, it is questionable whether *that* definition—as opposed, for example, to self-legislation—adequately captures what aesthetic autonomy means.

Local differences aside, I find the general tendency of Pirholt's analysis richly suggestive. His strategy is to excavate the experiential and material conditions that make specific modes of artistic achievement possible. This intention governs the fourth and fifth chapters as well. The fourth chapter introduces the concept of "semitechnical reproducibility" in order to characterize the means through which artworks were made accessible to Goethe and his contemporaries. From his early inspiring visit to Mannheim on, Goethe's experience of art would have been impossible without reproductive techniques: drawn copies, engravings, lithographs, plaster casts, and so forth. Dresden and Italy were the (staggeringly important) autoptic exceptions, of course, but the grand enterprise of *Kunst und Altertum* is unthinkable apart from a flourishing industry of imagistic reproduction and publication. Pirholt brings out the significance of this medial configuration with admirable breadth and clarity, documenting inter alia Goethe's highly developed and, to a degree, theoretically reflected "medientechnologisches Bewusstsein."

In the fifth chapter, Pirholt investigates one of the foundational conceptual structures of the age, the distinction between "ancient" and "modern" art. Approaches to this distinction on the conceptual level are, of course, well-known, but Pirholt's exploration of the issue—in line with the entire orientation of his study—turns to concrete cases, the prize competitions Goethe and Meier organized and the essay "Polygnots Gemälde," products from the cusp of the nineteenth century. Two distinct projects, one an effort to fix a set of classicist expectations as a norm for contemporary artistic production, the other the attempted "reconstruction" of lost or destroyed products of ancient works. It is in this chapter that Pirholt develops his own account of one of the central topics of research on Goethe's thought generally: his concept of *Anschauung*. Perhaps it is not an altogether inaccurate characterization of these highly compelling pages to say that the goal is to disclose what might be termed the anthropology of *Anschauung* as it is developed in Goethe's work. The center of that anthropological interpretation, as brought out in Pirholt's compelling account, is the "unwiderstehliche Begierde nach unmittelbarem Anschauen."

Professor Pirholt is known to readers of the *Goethe Yearbook* and to English-language scholarship on Goethe and his age. (See his *Metamimesis: Imitation in Goethe's "Wilhelm Meisters Lehrjahre" and Early German Romanticism*, 2012). His *Grenzerfahrungen*, the riches of which I could only adumbrate in this review, deserves an engaged response from a North American readership.

*University of Chicago*                                                    *David E. Wellbery*

Nora Ramtke. **Anonymität—Onymität. Autorname und Autorschaft in Wilhelm Meisters "doppelten Wanderjahren."** Heidelberg: Universitätsverlag Winter, 2016. 423 pp.

Friedrich Pustkuchen (1793–1834) is, at best, a footnote in the literary history of Germany. But Nora Ramtke commendably lifts the Westphalian pastor, pedagogue, and author to our attention in her engaging study of authorship.

Specifically, Ramtke uses Pustkuchen's scandalous 1821 continuation of Goethe's *Wilhelm Meisters Lehrjahre* (published the same year as Goethe's own) to explore the complex operations of anonymity and onymity in the creation of an author's name, the conception of work(s), and literary discourse more broadly. The term "onymity" is borrowed from Gérard Genette but here looks beyond the peritextual and juridical grounding of his definition, which designates when an author signs with a legal proper name, to include the discursive and poetological consequences of named authorship. Understanding the name of an author as a hermeneutically robust part of a text helps us understand not just how authors make a name for themselves, but also how a name is made for them. The droll incident of Pustkuchen and Goethe's doubled *Wanderjahre* makes for an enlightening case study thanks to Ramtke's careful readings and analysis.

Ramtke first explores the conditions and consequences of onymous authorship. She considers the various players involved in the construction of this name: the author who creates the work, the publisher who technically realizes the unity of the author's works through a typographically standardized product that guarantees the authenticity of the text, and the consumers who believe they are holding a piece of the author in their hand when they read the book. I especially admire Ramtke's consideration, throughout *Anonymität—Onymität*, of the original appearance, layout, and content of title pages as she builds her argument, showing that it is Goethe's name that binds together the *Wilhelm Meister* texts (and sets them in conversation with all of Goethe's works). An anonymously published work that explicitly refers to a text by another author, the argument goes, thus challenges the onymously organized understanding of what constitutes a work or set of works. It is, in Ramtke's words, a provocation.

In her construction of the concept of (onymous) authorship, Ramtke relies, like many before her, on the pioneering work of Heinrich Bosse to demonstrate the connection between the author as an individual and the creation of a work as a form of property. More recent scholarship, however, has complicated Bosse's narrative and the underpinnings of intellectual property purportedly based in this concept. Consequently, some of Ramtke's claims about the legal consequences assigned to this idea of the author are less nuanced and convincing than her other arguments. But this occurs to no great detriment since these claims are not at the heart of her text.

The monograph next turns to Pustkuchen's anonymously released *Wanderjahre*, which was published by Gottfried Basse in five parts from 1821 to 1828 along with several improved editions as well as Pustkuchen's *Wilhelm Meisters Tagebuch* (dated 1822) and *Gedanken einer frommen Gräfin* (1822), both of which were accompanied by the subtitle "Vom Verfasser der Wanderjahre." The most immediate effect of this allographic continuation was potential confusion with Goethe's own sequel, which the author and publisher may have hoped to exploit for financial reasons. At the start of the nineteenth century, the decision to list the author and/or the publisher on a book's title page influenced the legal obligations and liabilities attached to a text, and I wish Ramtke would have further explored this potential motivator. Regardless, the decision to publish the text anonymously was also inspired by aesthetic goals. After all, through the connection with its hypotext, Pustkuchen's novel insists on being read in conjunction with Goethe, and Ramtke analyzes how the anonymity (or performative anonymity in the case of the later-published parts of Pustkuchen's text) enables a criticism of Goethe. She makes interesting a text that few today will read, even if it caused a sensation at the time of its publication.

Nevertheless, contemporaries soon solved the problem of potential market confusion by labeling Pustkuchen's text as "falsch," a "literarische Blasphemie," and "unächt." Further, Goethe published his *Wilhelm Meisters Wanderjahre oder Die Entsagenden* with the subtitle "Ein Roman von Goethe," leaving no doubt about who wrote the text (and did not write the other). As a result, the utopian goals of the anonymously published text were shattered on Goethe's onymity.

Pustkuchen revealed his identity as the author of the *Wanderjahre* after Basse published another anonymous allographic text, *Wilhelm Meisters Meisterjahre* (1824), which was credited to Pustkuchen and with which the author wanted no affiliation. Paradoxically, then, the anonymous *Wanderjahre*, together with the *Tagebuch* and *Gedanken*, both of which were attributed to the author of the *Wanderjahre* (and not the *Wanderjahre oder Die Entsagenden*, or Goethe), made a name for Pustkuchen. Many readers, intrigued by the mystery of the doubled *Wanderjahre* had already identified Pustkuchen as the author, thanks to his practice of using pseudonyms elsewhere. Further, emerging bibliographic forces, which increasingly relied on alphabetization and authors' names as the organizing principle, put additional pressure on anonymity. In the end, Ramtke argues, only an unambiguous and constant designation can bind together a work and author as a canonical unity. And this name, as the case of Pustkuchen shows, can be made *for* the author.

In her final chapter, Ramtke reconstructs the discursive dialectic of anonymity and onymity, deftly analyzing the bizarre and humorous responses to the *Wanderjahre* texts and how they influenced each other. Here, Ramtke's insightful readings of poems, letters, illustrations, and other ephemera bring to life the potent productivity of the tension between the two modes of authorship. Goethe is a true onymous author, whose name is not just a mere factual peritextual presence but itself a discursive force with symbolic and hermeneutic capital. The name Pustkuchen, in contrast, exists only parasitically (as contemporaries noted) in relation to Goethe and Pustkuchen eventually comes to be seen as apostatic "anti-Goethe" who questions and perverts the holy name itself. Nonetheless, the name Pustkuchen is fused with Goethe's and becomes an integral part of its host. The discursive power of the onym thus allows the anonym to have an effect in the world. Thus, dialectally intertwined, they shape literary history. An author's name, in the end, has no inherent intrinsic value, but is part of a complex dynamic made up of readers, critics, rivals, and scholars.

Overall, the monograph is a great addition to work on literary production and book history around 1800 and paints a meticulously and theoretically rich picture of the role of anonymous and onymous authorship at the time. It is also an entertaining read that should compel us all to think more critically about the connections between names and works, including those we might relegate to footnotes.

Ohio State UniversityMatthew H. Birkhold

George Santayana. **Three Philosophical Poets: Lucretius, Dante, and Goethe.** Coedited by Kellie Dawson and David E. Spiech. Introduced by James Seaton. Cambridge: MIT, 2019. xxxvi + 239 pp.

Why might anyone turn now, more than a century after its publication, to Santayana's *Three Philosophical Poets* (1910)? Reading Santayana's essay is a bit like reading Erich Auerbach. It attunes one to concerns that, though fixed firmly in the field of philology, quite clearly hover in the spheres of philosophy. As with Auerbach, Santayana's preoccupations with nature and history result in an essay of daunting intellectual sweep and grand pretension: he aims to sketch—using the examples of Lucretius, Dante, and Goethe—tectonic shifts in the history of philosophy.

The essay, unfortunately, only recommends Santayana as a poor man's Auerbach. Driven by his commitment to naturalism, the history he traces is clichéd and undifferentiated. His insights are rarely original or even interesting. Whereas Auerbach could take up Dante and make a case for him as the first "poet of the secular world," Santayana—in a tired recapitulation of rationalist readings—views him as a talent *despite* his age, a supernaturalist who peddles a "mirage" while neglecting the evidence of nature. This, despite the fact that Santayana, in a significant anticipation of Auerbach's key arguments, regards Dante's afterlife as a "fulfillment" of an individual's life on earth (as opposed to a punishment or reward). Santayana's affections lie with Lucretius and Goethe, the two naturalists among the three poets. But here, too, certain clichés govern the lines of his inquiry: Goethe, whom he writes about with reference only to *Faust*, is above all the poet of "Romantic immediacy," in Santayana's view, and no poet of special philosophical or scientific competence. To get at the philosophical dynamics at play in *Faust*, Santayana leans on Spinoza, which is helpful, save for the degree to which it shunts from view any other portions of Goethe's philosophical diet.

Santayana treats Goethe's Romanticism as a historical affair, but ironically, we find in Santayana himself the traces of a lingering Romanticism. He may have been unaware of it, but his conjunction of precisely these three poets was an unusually Romantic gesture. Around 1800, Goethe and Schelling had planned a didactic poem of nature in the style of Lucretius's *De rerum natura*; when Goethe relinquished the project, Schelling planned to complete the poem in the style of Dante's *Commedia*. At the same time, Friedrich Schlegel, in his essay on changes in Goethe's poetic style, conceived of the Olympian in Weimar as a new Dante. Santayana's history of poetic philosophers, in other words, emerges from a peculiarly Romantic history of poetry. But whereas Romantics like Schelling and Schlegel located affinities across these texts, Santayana finds, by and large, differences. He is keen to summarize them as such: "Goethe is the poet of life; Lucretius the poet of nature; Dante the poet of salvation." In their differences they complement and complete each other; what conjoins the three poets, according to Santayana, is their status as representatives of a historical age.

Perhaps it is that status, widely intuited as such, that has led many self-professed "amateurs" to write about Dante and Goethe. Indeed, these sorts of texts may amount to a semischolarly genre unto itself, with predictably mixed results. Santayana's essay announces itself as the "impressions of an amateur," and Vittorio Hösle, citing Santayana, has defended his own "amateur" contributions to the scholarship of Dante and Goethe. But Hösle and other scholars of diverse backgrounds, e.g., Josef Pieper, have rendered meaningful contributions to the knowledge of such poets and their texts. I am not convinced Santayana has. But, to be clear, if Santayana's text is imperfect, it is rhetorically magnificent in its imperfection and, as such, a useful foil for budding scholars. The section on Goethe's *Faust*, for example, could easily serve as a usefully problematic commentary in an undergraduate seminar on Goethe. For the professor who wishes her students to see Goethe's prophetic comprehension of capitalism, colonialism, and environmental destruction, Santayana's text-immanent interpretations are a sharpening stone against which to hone one's arguments. His essay reminds us that literary criticism, to the extent that it constitutes a phenomenological exercise, rises and falls on the merits of its rhetoric. He may have little new to say to scholars of these poets, but he says it so well that the experience of reading him is its own pleasure. Santayana's essay appears in an MIT critical edition that comes equipped with an excellent introduction by James Seaton, as well as a set of useful appendices, including a chronology of Santayana's life, extensive notes and a bibliography, and textual commentary, variants, and an index.

*Worcester Polytechnic Institute*                                    *Daniel DiMassa*

Bettina Brandt and Daniel Leonhard Purdy, eds. **China in the German Enlightenment.** Toronto: University of Toronto Press, 2016. 224 pp.

Bettina Brandt and Daniel Purdy have composed a concise yet comprehensive volume about the shifting perceptions, both favorable and unfavorable but all textually mediated, of China in the seventeenth- and eighteenth-century German intellectual landscape. A much-needed, important resource for historians, philosophers, and literary scholars, this volume is especially timely in examining a historical moment that witnessed heated philosophical debates about concepts foundational for contemporary race theory. The contributions show how political conditions in Europe such as shifting stances on absolutism and Christianity were projected onto preconceptions of China and the Chinese people. China functioned as an emblem of scholarship, of static and stable systems in governance. Confucianism and Daoism were often considered philosophical ideals in early modern Europe. In much of the accumulated knowledge about China transmitted by Jesuit missionaries, China came to represent the kind of morality, ethics, and government that Europeans yearned for themselves.

As Brandt and Purdy clearly articulate in their introduction, writings on European relationships with the cultures of China and Asia have largely been influenced by Edward Said's *Orientalism*, resulting in an immense amount of scholarship devoted solely to the British empire. In German studies, from the 1990s onward, scholarship sought to work against the exclusion of Germany from discussions related to colonialism and orientalism during the Enlightenment; such work includes Suzanne Zantop's *Colonial Fantasies* (1997), Todd Kontje's *German Orientalism* (2004), and, more recently, Chunjie Zhang's *Transculturality and German Discourse in the Age of European Colonialism* (2017). Brandt and Purdy pinpoint a trend in eighteenth-century German studies to nonetheless remain "blissfully immune from the later evils of modernity." The scholars contributing to the volume question this tendency in their essays, as they do in their scholarship at large. Furthermore, the contributions succeed in fulfilling the editors' aim to "avoid generalizations that characterize the 18th century as a transition from the Sinophilia of Leibniz to the Sinophobia of Hegel."

The book opens with the historian Walter Demel's 1992 canonical historical survey "How the Chinese became Yellow," first appearing in English as a skillful translation by Brandt and Purdy. Demel's study compiles a comprehensive array of historical sources such as travel narratives by priests and merchants to recount the emergence of race theory in the late eighteenth century prior to Kant's two essays on race. With these sources, he evaluates the veracity of the narrative that identifies Kant as the inventor of skin-based racism. He situates the racial stereotypes toward Asians as "yellow" globally, exposing the connection between the discourse around slavery and late Enlightenment German thought which, as Brandt and Purdy aptly observe, is "an association that still suffers under the double burden of being both controversial and ignored."

Philosopher Franklin Perkins's essay then asks why Chinese philosophy such as Confucianism is rarely taught or researched in philosophy departments in the West and is not even categorized as philosophy as it should be. He begins his study with Leibniz's favorable view of Confucianism, which Perkins attributes to his universalistic conception of philosophy based on the belief that everybody has the ability to think reasonably. Confucianism was centered upon practical ethics, which, while initially appreciated by European philosophers such as Leibniz, was later devalued, once philosophy was conceived as abstract, theoretical reflection. Hegel introduced a new moment in philosophy, the "science [*Wissenschaft*] of philosophy," from which he excluded the Chinese, which, as Perkins argues, expressed racial hierarchies within philosophical discourse. The racial components of Hegel's philosophy are likewise taken up again in this volume by Robert Bernasconi.

We follow the thread of Leibniz with Michael Carhart's essay, which focuses on Leibniz as a Hanoverian courtier eager for knowledge on the "origins and migrations of the European nations." Carhart brings to life Leibniz's obsessive hunt for the letter of a Jesuit missionary in order to gather crucial information about Central Asian and Chinese linguistic history for his *Novissima Sinica*. He tells of the innumerable political and geographical obstacles Leibniz faced in trying to communicate with scholars, diplomats, and missionaries, and of the networks of correspondence between Jesuit missionaries in China and European intellectuals. Ultimately we learn that Leibniz aimed to show that northern Europeans had Asian origins. The juxtaposition between Perkins's and Carhart's essays reveals the multidimensionality of Leibniz's engagement with China.

Carl Niekerk's essay focuses on the role of China in eighteenth century Enlightenment anthropology by addressing debates between Buffon, de Paux, Herder, and Blumenbach. All of these figures sought to explain the origins of human diversity, with varying agendas, all generally agreeing that such diversity was due to differences in climate and geography rather than essential biological differences. While this might appear "emancipatory" and a defense of human rights (as for Blumenbach and Herder), Niekerk insightfully argues that these descriptive aims are, in fact, prescriptive, "introducing new forms of normativity" and introducing implicit hierarchical standards.

In lieu of focusing on canonical philosophers as in the rest of the essays in the volume, Birgit Tautz argues for the significance of what she describes as small, local, genres—for example, anonymous compilations such as encyclopedias, journals, tea poems, and anecdotes. None of these conveniently fit into the master narratives of literary history and idealist philosophy in representations of China. The easy narrative of a shift from positive assessments of China to negative ones over the course of the eighteenth-century does not hold up upon close examination of these minor yet widely circulated local publications that displayed knowledge of China just as effectively as Goethe's better-known late adaptations of Chinese poems. Tautz also addresses the crucial role of Chinese language texts in Goethe's concept of *Weltliteratur*, something that is surprisingly overlooked in scholarship on the topic.

In contrast, John K. Noyes focuses entirely on a canonical authorial figure as he conducts an original close reading of Goethe's cycle of poems in the 1829 *Chinesisch-deutsche Jahres- und Tageszeiten*. He argues that Goethe uses China as a cipher to critique Kantian aesthetics, thus innovatively showing Goethe's complex philosophical investments at play in the lyric cycle. By exploring the influence of Herder's thought on foreign literatures in the context of Goethe's poems, Noyes concludes that Goethe performs an encounter with foreignness in his poetry, while, in contrast to the Orientalists, presenting universal limits of understanding.

Robert Bernasconi then returns our focus back to Hegel, presenting research that shows how he manipulated sources for his later lectures on world history in order to develop a racist bias against Africans and Asians, including the Chinese. Based on the results of his investigation, Bernasconi argues that Hegel had no philosophical grounds for presenting them as lacking spirit, as static and outside history, and even as less than human.

The volume concludes with Jeffrey S. Librett's study of Martin Buber's employment of Daoism to critique the hermeneutic logic of the Pauline Christian tradition, notably the division between faith and law, letter and spirit, and supercession. Librett places Buber in conversation with the Enlightenment figure Moses Mendelssohn and makes intriguing connections between Jewish theology and Daoism, arguing that Buber undermines the "Pauline split between matter (or letter) and Orientalism at once."

Brandt and Purdy's well-researched volume is impressive in terms of the methodological diversity of its contributors, all of whom are engaged with Enlightenment intellectuals' fascination with and, for some (notably Hegel), repulsion toward China. While ordered chronologically, the contributions speak to each other in a variety of ways, depending on the reader's own agenda and interests. However, I would have liked to see contributions in the collection that made use of Chinese-language sources as well. This could have opened up new questions about their translations, reception, and transmission in Germany—for example, regarding Goethe's late lyric cycle addressed by Noyes.

Brandt and Purdy have produced an impressive volume with consistently high-quality contributions, resulting in an enjoyable read even for nonspecialists. The book will undoubtedly have an impact on a number of fields of inquiry beyond China and the German Enlightenment. It exposes intellectual historians, philosophers, and literary scholars to methodologies they may otherwise neglect in their usual research on the same shared primary sources, thereby enriching future research on related topics. They have achieved the clearly articulated aims they outlined in their introduction admirably.

*Yonsei University**Tanvi Solanki*

Michel Chaouli. **Thinking with Kant's *Critique of Judgment***. Cambridge, MA: Harvard University Press, 2017. xv + 312 pp.

What can a new book on Kant's *Critique of Judgment* tell us that we have not heard before? Considering that Kant's arguments have been examined and evaluated from the most varied angles, it may be time to leave behind established discussions and return to the third *Critique* with a fresh eye. This is the path Michel Chaouli has chosen in his beautiful book. Well versed in Kant scholarship, he wears his learnedness lightly, as if to deny knowledge to make room for an unobstructed encounter with Kant's text.

In an exposition that sets the stakes for his reading, Chaouli makes clear that Kant's distinction between the beautiful and the agreeable, although much disputed by contemporary theorists, is of fundamental importance. Without it, aesthetic pleasure would amount to "just another preference" that lacks emancipatory potential and is subject to the market and consumerism. If the agreeable is the effect of "something giving me pleasure," the beautiful emerges in "my taking pleasure in it." Such taking combines receptivity with "a kind of making." In fact, in Chaouli's reading of the third *Critique*, the receptivity involved in aesthetic experience is but an aspect of this peculiar *making*.

As if to illustrate the efficacy of such receptivity, Chaouli lets himself be surprised by the wording of Kant's text. Unlike many professional philosophers who treat Kant's third *Critique* as a repository of often obscure and convoluted arguments that beg to be reformulated as straightforward propositions, Chaouli adheres to more capacious hermeneutic principles. Perplexed by unexpected formulations that do not disclose their meaning at first sight, he takes a step back to reflect on the perceived strangeness and surprise us with intricate and frequently ingenious readings in the process. Thus, in his chapter on "community," which starts with a deft juxtaposition of Hume's and Kant's respective aesthetic theories, Chaouli offers an incisive analysis of the Kantian "grammar of claiming universal assent." Rather than simply assuming that Kant got himself into logical tangles or was unable to recognize how paradoxical some of his formulations were, Chaouli prefers to take him at his word. His meticulous readings even of seemingly inconsequential details—such as the precise meaning of *ansinnen*, the prevalence of derivatives of *Stimme/Stimmung* throughout the third *Critique*, and the metaphor of the *Gängelwagen*—handsomely repay the attention that Chaouli lavishes on them.

Chaouli divides his book into three parts on beauty, art, and nature, each of which comprises three chapters. Their sequence constitutes a developmental narrative of sorts. The first part offers an introduction that outlines the scope and structure of the entire project, followed by close readings mainly of Kant's "Analytic of the Beautiful." Of central importance is the possibility of a genuine aesthetic judgment, in opposition to cognitive judgments, moral judgments, and agreeable experiences. This distinct mode of experience permits us to find new relations to the world around us. Or, as Chaouli puts it, "in beauty I exceed myself," which is to say that the concomitant pleasure concerns a specific relation of our representations of a particular object to our feeling of pleasure and displeasure. This relation is *sui generis*—determined neither by laws of nature (as much as contemporary bioaesthetics would have it), nor by the moral law within.

The second part of Chaouli's study marks its physical as well as conceptual center. It consists of an elaborate argument regarding the status, production, and meaning of art in relation to aesthetic judgment. The link between beauty and art—and thus the first two parts of Chaouli's book—is provided by the notion of *making*. According to Chaouli, this connection has hitherto not been sufficiently recognized. "Making poetically," Chaouli writes, "is making unintentionally, even when all that is made is a certain form of experience." Thus, he takes the mere experience of beauty as a creative act, akin to the creation of a work of art. The stated homology between beauty and art is supported, as he is quick to point out, by the utterance ascribing beauty to an object: it does not belong to the language game of communication, but relies "on the poetic dimension of language."

Art must create its own rules in the making. It is not simply free from all restrictions, but bound by the requirement of internal coherence, which prevents it from becoming "original nonsense" (Kant, Ak 5:308). This is key, since art literally *makes sense*, unlike other things in the world. Strictly formalist interpretations of Kant's aesthetics fail, precisely because they cannot accommodate Kant's account of the role of genius and aesthetic ideas in this sensemaking that is art. In keeping with his overall attempt to treat aesthetics and art as coextensive domains, Chaouli goes on to claim—less convincingly—that "I know that I face [an artwork] when it engages me in an aesthetic experience." In contrast, the later sections of the aesthetic half of the third *Critique* make clear that the appreciation of art as the expression of aesthetic ideas involves much more than mere aesthetic experience. For Kant, it would seem, there are aesthetic experiences that differ significantly from those we have when faced with art. Furthermore, from the account that Kant gives of aesthetic ideas as well as from Chaouli's own interpretation of them, we may surmise that there must be art that exceeds and frees itself from the constraints of beauty altogether.

Addressing the first of these concerns, Chaouli points out that Kant's "anxious distinction of nature and art" is frequently undermined. He claims to have merely made explicit what the third *Critique* has been saying from the start, namely, that "in the aesthetic realm the structure of making and the structure of experience are homologous." In his view, the "Analytic" provides only the transcendental structure or "skeleton of aesthetic experience." The insights into the structure of pure judgments of beauty are merely the "grammar" of aesthetic experiences, which also require embodiment and engagement with the world. If this is so in the case of natural beauty, it applies all the more in the case of art, where aesthetic ideas—forms that exceed all conceptual determination—point "to what *in* beauty exceeds the beauty of artworks." Conceding that "a different logic" may be involved here, Chaouli nonetheless proposes a strong analogy between beauty in nature and art. As he sees it, both instances point to the hermeneutic urgency of the aesthetic, its occurrence "at the very cusp of meaning itself, on the indeterminate boundary between meaning and nonmeaning, sense and nonsense."

In short, Chaouli's conception of aesthetic experience (i.e., the conception he ascribes to Kant) strongly favors "meaning production" over "the production of presence" (to use Hans Ulrich Gumbrecht's handy terms). The nonhermeneutic aspect of beauty—so clearly discernible in Kant's "Analytic"—is colonized by culture when Chaouli reads beauty backward from art to nature, for "the mystery lodged in the making of beauty" is said to come clearly into view only in the former. Our aesthetic ecstasy in the face of nature is a response, then, to "the suggestion that nature's form of making parallels the purposefulness of art."

All types of reflective judgments are enlisted in our efforts to understand the world as "cognitively and affectively habitable to us." This is what Kant's teleology and aesthetics have in common. In a memorable passage, Chaouli describes our capacity for aesthetic and teleological judgments as "a physio-philosophical antenna for hints 'as it were given to us by nature.'" Thus, our pleasure in natural beauty indicates the *Faßlichkeit* of nature for the human power of judgment (Kant, Ak 5:359).

In a similar vein, the point of teleology, the topic of the concluding part of Chaouli's book, is not a different legislation that stands in opposition to causal natural laws. Rather, it indicates that *by our lights*, a mechanical account cannot sufficiently explain life. A particular form (of life) may appear contingent in relation to mechanical laws of nature, but we cannot fail to also see it as a coherent unity, a lawfully organized being. In fact, this very mode of seeing is, in a profound sense, of our own making: it is a matter of *judging when the idea of purpose applies*. Only by looking at organized beings as produced in a manner that is analogous to our own *making* of things, does the "technique of nature," as opposed to its mere "mechanism," come into view (Kant, Ak 20:219).

The most significant achievement of Chaouli's book is that it provides a powerful and provocative reading of the *Critique of Judgment* entirely in terms of *poiesis* or *making*. Naturally, some risks lurk in such single-mindedness, first and foremost among them the temptation to overinterpret. Although Chaouli is not prone to forced readings, there is one important exception: he may be making rather too much of Kant's contention that in aesthetic contemplation we "make for [ourselves] an object of pleasure out of whatever." The passage—frequently invoked and cited in full at least seven times by Chaouli—is assigned a prominence that reflects neither its marginal role in Kant's text, nor its limited potential for generalization beyond the negation within which it occurs. For Chaouli, the passage serves as a precept of sorts that yokes together aesthetic contemplation and the genius's aesthetic creation in the notion of *making*. In consequence, art is assigned the place of primary aesthetic paradigm, whereas the beauty of nature is relegated to a supporting role.

In summary, Chaouli's forceful and frequently brilliant reading that fully absorbs the aesthetic in art firmly places Kant at the origin of what Jean-Marie Schaeffer has called the "speculative theory of Art." If Schaeffer is at pains to unearth a Kantian alternative to the dominant post-Kantian identification of aesthetics with the philosophy of art, Chaouli's reading, in marked contrast, sees Kant's importance most of all in having inaugurated their close alignment.

Be that as it may, Michel Chaouli deserves much praise for his enormous erudition, his hermeneutic sensitivity, and, most of all, his profound and provocative *tour d'horizon* of a most challenging foundational text in the history of aesthetics. Whether one is persuaded by his thesis of *aesthetic experience as making*, of which art—and not, as the *opinio communis* would have it, nature—is considered Kant's paradigmatic example, ultimately matters less than the numerous thought-provoking insights and well-executed close readings offered along the way. The specialist as well as the novice who would like to learn more about Kant's aesthetic theory and the stakes of aesthetics in general will find much to ponder and savor in Chaouli's beautiful book.

*Cornell University*                                                                 *Peter Gilgen*

Laura Deiulio and John B. Lyon, eds. **Gender, Collaboration, and Authorship in German Culture: Literary Joint Ventures 1750–1850.** New Directions in German Studies, vol. 27. New York: Bloomsbury Academic, 2019. 332 pp.

This collection offers "collaboration" as a lens through which to scrutinize literary production in the long eighteenth century, in opposition to continued

scholarly insistence on single authorship, in particular by the concept of authorship as literature by "a single (male) genius." The editors remind their readers that
the model of single authorship is undergirded by capitalist conditions that created both copyright and literary ownership.

The editors and the twelve articles "demonstrate that cooperative work is
quite common in literary and artistic production" and the "modes of collaboration are as varied as the artist who practice them." Indeed, several of the articles
themselves are collaborations between academic authors. Yet, sadly, the volume
is theoretically underdeveloped as the editors acknowledge: no single theoretical
approach to the concept of collaboration emerges. Accordingly, collaboration is
defined broadly; for example, as joint creation within the confines of a marriage
with varying degrees of power differentials between husband and wife. Other
collaborations might more aptly be called mentorship or intertextuality or even
the "sharing of ideas." Some authors define collaboration as two authors working
together; others view plurivocality in texts as collaboration.

The messy theoretical underpinnings of collaboration are addressed explicitly only in the opening article. As the concept of the single author-genius was just
developing in the eighteenth century, Margaretmary Daly argues that the coau-
thored texts of Johann Christoph and Luise Adelgunde Victoria Gottsched elude
the theoretical models that describe single authorship. This model cannot
account for the lived creativity shared by the husband and wife team nor can it
account for the editing, rewording, and translating that happens between the first
draft and publication. Daly appropriately suggests that the work of literature
should be viewed as a function (just like the author function) and not an attribut-
able product.

Many of the authors grapple with the issue that voice in collaborative texts is
problematic. Does collaboration lend itself to a unified voice or does the ensuing
product retain its polyphonic structure? In her analysis of Bettina Brentano-von
Arnim's work *Die Günderode*, Karen R. Daubert traces the most innovative
model of collaboration presented in this volume. *Die Günderode* collapses historical authors and fictional characters in a plurivocal work that challenges nor-
mative views of authorship, documentary history, and literary transmission. Brian
Tucker applies the same concept to the collaborative diary written by Clara and
Robert Schumann. While Daly shows that it is impossible to tease apart the voices of the two Gottscheds, Tucker writes that the Schumanns retained their individual voices creating a dialogue rather than one unified voice. The article by
Rob McFarland and Michelle Stott James presents a third model of plurivocality,
which describes how the author Elise von der Recke created a virtual collaboration with her younger self in her book about Count Cagliostro.

Monika Nenon poses the question of how women developed their voices in
the eighteenth century. While many women nurtured male authors, she claims
that some of these relationships were mutual, as in the case of Sophie von La
Roche and Christoph Wieland. Collaboration in this instance led to the publication of La Roche's famous novel. With her network analysis, Nenon shows that
women could be powerful members of literary circles. Salons and sociability also
emerge as important loci of collaboration in Tom Spencer and Jennifer Jenson's
article about Sophie Mereau. Mereau viewed collaboration—defined as sociability—as necessary for the socialization process of her female characters.

Several of the essays are engaged in dissecting the works of male authors to
find the contributions of women. Adrian Daub and Eleanor ter Horst attempt to

recover the theoretical contributions of the lesser-known partner in a literary marriage. They both argue that the husbands' works were influenced by theoretical ideas developed by their wives. Daub recuperates Dorothea's contribution to Friedrich Schlegel's thinking and shows how she shaped not only Friedrich's ideas but contributed her own poetry to his collections. Ter Horst analyzes how Caroline de la Motte Fouqué's theoretical concept of hermaphroditism is reflected in Friedrich's novel *Undine*. Julie L. J. Koehler tackles the Grimm Brothers' network. She argues that the Grimms viewed their female informants as passive vessels supplying the raw material for their tales, and traces how several of these informants (Droste-Hülshoff, Brentano-von Arnim, Benedikte Naubert, and Adele Schopenhauer) wrote against the appropriation of their tales. Charlotte Lee investigates how Goethe's *West-östlicher Diwan* emerged from his friendship with Marianne von Willemer. A number of poems can be attributed to Willemer, while others might be Willemer's work, albeit edited by Goethe. Laura Deiulio uncovers the collaboration of siblings Rahel Varnhagen and Ludwig Robert. While collaboration is often oral and therefore ephemeral, the numerous letters going back and forth between the siblings allow Deiulio to pinpoint exactly how ideas were shaped and developed in tandem. Judith E. Martin shows that collaboration can also be one-sided: Therese Robinson responded to Goethe's call for a new American novel twenty years after his death.

The twelve essays in this collection are collectively well-researched and well-argued and show the breadth of female contributions to the literature of the age. The editors concede that the volume leaves out many other collaborative endeavors such as Friedrich Schiller's interaction with his female contributors to the *Horen* or collaborations among women. Particularly this lack of female collaborations makes the volume into a recuperative project with many of the authors excavating women's contributions to the literature of great men. As a gesture, this is commendable but it leaves the question unanswered how literary collaborations can be theorized so that all collaborators can be acknowledged.

University of Utah    Karin Baumgartner

Sara Munson Deats. **The Faust Legend: From Marlowe and Goethe to Contemporary Drama and Film.** Cambridge: Cambridge University Press, 2019, 275 pp.

In her 2019 book *The Faust Legend: From Marlowe and Goethe to Contemporary Drama and Film*, Sara Munson Deats chronicles the life of the Faust legend from its forerunners and early iterations through its contemporary musical theatre and film adaptations. Each chapter is dedicated to a different chronological period, beginning with the background and early origins of the Faust legend.

Her first chapter, "The Background of the Faust Legend" focuses on the origins of the Faust legend. It begins by looking at the Magus Legends, Simon Magus, St. Cyprian, and Theophilus, whose fantastic feats and superhuman powers align with many of the traits associated with Faust as the legend takes shape. Deats then discusses medieval biblical and morality plays as an important step in the development of the Faust legend because of their allegorical nature and their use of a devil or Antichrist figure that sets the stage, so to speak, for future Faust and Mephistopheles characters like those in the early literary version of the story. Then, the mysterious historic Faust is discussed. Deats outlines the issues of time and namesake that are associated with this person and speaks broadly on whether or not a true Faust existed. A discussion of the Faustbooks, both the English and German versions, with a more in-depth look at the English version of this text, completes the first chapter.

Her second chapter is dedicated solely to Christopher Marlowe's *Doctor Faustus*. Deats offers a complete look at the text, speaking on issues related to publication date and authorship, and also includes a brief synopsis of the performance history. She then offers two close readings of the text: one Christian reading and an alternative reading of the play. The inclusion of these close readings of the text makes this chapter great secondary source material for any Faust-focused course in English or in German, offering a means of making students aware of what the text itself presents to readers and suggesting methods that students could use to examine a text more closely.

Goethe's *Faust* is the focus of the third chapter, "From Hero to Harlequin." The chapter begins with a brief explanation of the time following Marlowe's success with *Doctor Faustus*, during which others turned Marlowe's *Doctor Faustus* into farces, harlequinades, or puppet shows. It was these farces and puppet shows that influenced German versions in the same style, which Deats posits are likely the first place that Goethe encountered the Faust material. She includes a brief discussion of the date of the play and she emphasizes the influence of the *Zeitgeist* of the sixty-year period during which Goethe wrote the text. She also briefly writes about *Faust*'s performance history, in which she mentions the difficulty, or rather intimidation, factor of producing a play of that length. It is here that she mentions Peter Stein's ambitious 2000 production of both *Faust I* and *Faust II* in their entirety, a feat not attempted by many. She then digs deeper into the content of Goethe's adaptation, pointing out some of the changes Goethe made, like his redemption of Faust from hell's flames. She also mentions Goethe's transformation of Marlowe's text and hero into "a magnificent drama that fits no category, a phantasmagoric epic with a biblical flame, numerous fantastic masques and pageants, an aspiring hero, and a surprise happy ending." In addition to her initial discussion of the play and its context within its literary tradition and within Goethe's time, she offers an alternative reading of the play as well, in which she discusses the political exploitation of the play and how different ideologies have used the text for their specific purposes. She finally offers a more traditional close reading of both *Faust I* and *Faust II*, in which she addresses some of the more traditional concerns associated with the work.

The fourth chapter marks a transition in the text as Deats shifts her focus from singular texts to "Post-Goethe Dramatic Versions of the Faust Legend." She mentions several versions of the story in dramatic form, including W. B. Yeat's *The Countess Cathleen*, George Sand's *Faust and the City*, and the obscure version *An Irish Faustus: A Morality in Nine Scenes* by Lawrence Durrell. Deats highlights the differences of each of these productions with regard to their relationship to Marlowe and Goethe while also emphasizing contributions of each of these versions to the Faust legend tradition in their own right. In doing so, she reveals their place within their respective philosophical and social epochs.

The final chapter "Cinematic Fausts" looks at the Faust legend on the big screen, a rather recent phenomenon for the story. She begins by looking at Faust in its earlier cinematic versions. For example, she gives a brief thumbnail sketch of F. W. Murnau's *Faust* as well as three other films where Faust is the focus. The second part of this chapter focuses on adaptations, or "appropriations" as Deats calls them, of the Faust legend, including titles like *The Devil and Daniel Webster*, *Alias Nick Beal*, *Damn Yankees*, *Bedazzled* and its subsequent sequel, *Oh, God! You Devil*, *Crossroads*, and *Angel Heart*. Her epilogue to the book mentions the media coverage of the 2016 presidential election in the US, which featured many allusions to the Faust legend, and speaks briefly about the durability of this text.

*The Faust Legend: From Marlowe and Goethe to Contemporary Drama and Film* would serve any BA- or MA-level course focused on the Faust Legend as an overview text to accompany an in-depth look at either Marlowe's or Goethe's text. Both its chronological focus and its inclusion of post-Goethe materials make this text accessible to students at these levels and it offers a thorough enough overview for an introductory course.

*University of Cincinnati*                                    *Katherine H. Paul*

Lorna Fitzsimmons and Charles McKnight, eds. ***The Oxford Handbook of Faust in Music.*** Oxford: Oxford University Press, 2019. xxxi + 581 pp.

*The Oxford Handbook of Faust in Music* will long serve as a primary reference on musical creations made for Goethe's *Faust*, as well as adaptations and reception of the poetic drama, constituting a standard for this rich artistic crossing between poetic and musical inventions.

The editors Lorna Fitzsimmons and Charles McKnight and Oxford University Press have invested in an exemplary apparatus for the volume's twenty-five contributions, allowing the reader to efficiently navigate and mine the essays. This apparatus includes a list of both images and musical excerpts—at least two of the latter appear in each chapter, with an average of four or five—while also providing extensive and well-outlined tables, from a list of symphonic, choral, chamber, and solo Faust compositions discussed in the essays, to tables that help readers delineate, for example, the complex process of a musical creation such as Robert Schumann's *Scenen aus Goethe's Faust* (1847–1853) or Helen Gifford's various text sources from Marlowe's play for her 1983 opera *Regarding Faustus*. The editors also maintain a welcome consistency in quotes from Goethe's play; they appear first in German—using the Frankfurter edition by Albrecht Schöne—and then in English, from Stuart Atkin's English translation. Each essay includes an extensive bibliography, and the volume as a whole is rounded out by a helpful index.

These user-friendly components indicate that Lisa Fitzsimmons, a highly regarded Faust scholar, and Philip McKnight, a musician and musical historian, meticulously prepared and curated their edition, clearly seeking to provide as comprehensive a handbook on Goethe's *Faust* in music as was feasible. And they certainly delivered, organizing the extensive scope of musical compositions into three parts: (1) the symphonic, choral, chamber, and solo *Faust* works; (2) operatic renditions of *Faust*; and (3) *Faust* in ballet and musical theater (with the latter the shortest of the three parts).

The usual suspects are notably covered, such as Franz Schubert's setting for *Faust I*, Liszt's various Faust compositions, and Mahler's magnanimous Eighth Symphony, one of the few compositions that draws the listener toward the last part of *Faust II*. Gounod's and Busoni's productions of *Faust* feature in the discussion on opera, as do Alfred Schnittke's life-long interest in the Faust complex, prompted by his reading of Thomas Mann's 1947 novel, and John Adams and Peter Sellars's *Doctor Atomic* (2005).

What makes this handbook stand out, however, is its inclusion of neglected, forgotten, and largely unknown or overlooked compositions related to Goethe's dramatic poem. Examples include Louis Spohr's *Faust* (1816), which Clive McClelland describes as an "unjustly neglected masterpiece," and Hanns Eisler's *Goethe-Rhapsodie*, written for Goethe's bicentennial in 1949 and including text from *Faust II*, which has remained "little known," as Joy H. Calico observes, much like the Czech composer Josef Berg's opera *Johannes Doctor Faust* (1963–69). Havergal Brian's long-forgotten Gothic opera *Faust* (1956), also discussed, was slated to be recorded for the first time only in 2019—but, as far as I can ascertain, it remains unrecorded. Goethe's influence on American musicals and rock music has also been generally ignored, as Elizabeth L. Wollman notes in her discussion of musicals such as Randy Newman's *Faust*, Tom Sankey's *The Golden Screw*, and the short-lived rock opera *Soon*, all of which are marked by rock music's "tensions between authenticity and commercialism." While it is possible to dig up other forgotten *Faust*-related works, such as Hermann Reutter's *Doktor Johannes Faust* (1936), in the major online encyclopedias *Musik in Geschichte und Gegenwart* and the *Grove Music Online*, this handbook is as rich in scope as it is reasonable.

In addition to the high degree of scholarly care evident in the book's apparatus and in the editors' introduction and conclusion, as well as the frankly astounding—and scrupulous—scope of included musical renditions of Goethe's tragedy, the quality of the twenty-five essays, though variable (as are the scholars' methodologies), is also quite impressive. I'd like to highlight in particular three essays—one from each of the book's three major sections—because of their innovative and rich hermeneutic approaches.

Thomas S. Grey's essay, entitled "Ideas of Redemption and the Total Artwork in Wagner's Encounters with *Faust*," is especially comprehensive. While Wagner's *Sieben Kompositionen zu Goethes Faust*, composed at the tender age of seventeen (1830–31), and his *Eine Faust-Ouvertüre* (1839–40), both included in Grey's discussion, are, at best, of historical interest about the composer's musical development, Grey's stimulating argument convincingly reads *Tristan und Isolde* as a response to Goethe's concept of the *Ewig-Weibliche* (eternal feminine), and, based on research by Hans Vaget, he views the ending of the *Götterdämmerung* as indicative of Wagner's interest in a redemptive catharsis that, in the composer's eyes, was central to Goethe's *Faust*.

If Wagner's ending of his tetralogy does not immediately lend itself to association with Goethe's *Faust*, Igor Stravinsky's *The Rake's Progress* (1947–51), with a libretto by W. H. Auden and Chester Kallman, is likewise not the most obvious opera to come to mind when thinking of *Faust*, since the musical drama was primarily inspired by a series of paintings and engravings by William Hogarth. Yet the devil's appearance immediately evokes the Faust legend, even if placed within a fairy tale structure, as Auden and Kallman do. Maureen A. Carr's article elucidates not only the multiple collaborations between Stravinsky and Auden but also those between the two librettists; above all, she shows in fascinating detail how Auden's talent for versification inspired the composer's process of composing.

Last but certainly not least, Raymond Knapp's intriguing essay "The American Musical and the Faustian Bargain" interprets the juxtaposition of the American musical as a genre and the Faust tradition as an antithesis to the genre of the musical itself because it easily aligns with the Mephistopheles character by promising pleasure, success, and sex, but cannot reconcile the Christian framework of redemption for Faust. Given that these are just three of the handbook's far-ranging twenty-five essays, I am positive that every serious scholar invested in the Faust legend and its intersection with the musical arts will find ample reason to consult and enjoy *The Oxford Handbook Faust in Music.*

*Emory University*                                                                *Peter Höyng*

Goldstein, Amanda Jo. **Sweet Science: Romantic Materialism and the New Logics of Life.** Chicago: University of Chicago Press, 2017. 336 pp.

An early nineteenth-century revival of interest in Lucretian materialism provides the lynchpin of this breathtaking work. Exhibiting a unique combination of historical acumen and theoretical bravado, *Sweet Science* draws from an array of scholarly and disciplinary traditions including science and literature, gender studies, new materialism, and radical pedagogy in an attempt to shed light on a Lucretius-inspired countertrend to the increasingly sharp disciplinary boundaries that were drawn between art and the sciences over the course of the nineteenth century. Taking its cue from Lucretius's insight that *figuration* presents "the basic action and passion of matter," *Sweet Science* pushes back against the conventional wisdom that Romantic challenges to Enlightenment rationality and nineteenth-century industrialism were driven solely by an understanding of life as a vital, self-organizing activity. Goldstein instead shifts focus to the ways in which a "material continuity between physical and poetic shapes" is assumed in *De rerum natura*, a work that provided an atomistic alternative for Goethe, Shelley, and a young Karl Marx to an understanding of life as vitalist *causa sui*. An equally important intervention made by the book is the case it makes for a more comparative approach to Romanticism, one defined by the influence of Lucretius in Germany and Great Britain instead of Kant.

The book is divided into five chapters, an introduction, and a coda on Karl Marx's early writings. The introduction presents a nuanced account of *Sweet Science*'s historical and theoretical stakes, while also serving to highlight the diverse contingent of figures brought into the conversation in the following chapters. Recruiting scholarly and poetic voices as divergent as Judith Butler and William Blake, Raymond Williams. and Bruno Latour, the introduction serves as a sort of primer for contemporary critical discourse on the body, science studies, and new materialisms, which the main chapters draw from. William Blake, whose *Four Zoas* provides *Sweet Science* its title, serves as a through-line from the introduction to the first chapter, which turns to eighteenth-century debate surrounding epigenesis and the nature of organic matter. Blake joins a chorus of figures including Jean-Baptiste Lamarck and Erasmus Darwin in casting "animal formation as a work of acute circumstantial dependence, rather than of autotelic power."

This idea of a "circumstantial dependence" in Blake between figurative language and natural forms sets the stage for a reexamination of Goethe's morphology and his notion of tender empiricism, which provide the subjects of the second and third chapters, respectively. The first of these two chapters draws from Goethe's microscopic experiments of the 1780s, his writings on Kant, as well as an overlooked essay from the *Zur Morphologie* journal titled "Verstäubung, Verdunstung, Vertropfung." Lying hidden in this essay, Goldstein shows, are a number of astounding affinities between *De rerum natura*'s imaginative display of

Brownian motion via dancing dust mites and Goethe's own gradual understanding of figuration as central to the project of thinking nature and poetry concomitantly. This understanding of figuration, as chapter three shows, is exceedingly important to keep in mind as a means of reconsidering a divide between signs and material things. A training in tender empiricism as described by nature, in fact, enables the observer to become more attuned to the semiotics at display in the figural activities of material nature.

The fourth and fifth chapters explore Percy Bysshe Shelley's engagements with similar figurative, material concerns, focusing on *Triumph of Life* and *The Mask of Anarchy*, respectively. The fourth chapter zeroes in on wrinkles and displays of aging in Shelley's *Triumph*, interpreting these figurations of mortality as experiments in a nonvitalist, vulnerable understanding of material life. Chapter five turns to *The Mask of Anarchy*, Shelley's poetic response to the 1819 slaughter of unarmed civilians by British militiamen in Manchester. This poem, in Goldstein's analysis, seems to pose the question:"How do tender empirical, materialist poetics accommodate the historical fact of vulnerability violated?" It is this question that then leads Goldstein, in the coda, to Karl Marx, whose early engagement with atomist materialism is seen as a continuation of rather than a turn away from a Romantic understanding of life as definitely material and figurative.

In sum, Amanda Jo Goldstein's *Sweet Science* provides a compellingly fresh account of Romantic materialism as refracted through the lens of Lucretian atomism. This book is one that will surely impact critical discourse for years to come. Scholars interested in science and literature during the *Goethezeit* as well as those with interests in the poetics and politics of new materialism will find this book incredibly engaging.

*University of Pennsylvania*                                    *Bryan Norton*

Claudia Häfner and Francesca Fabbri. **Adele Schopenhauer. Unbekanntes aus ihrem Nachlass in Weimar.** Weimar:Weimarer Verlagsgesellschaft, 2019. 96 pp.

The high-quality book to be introduced here is on the title page termed an "Ausstellungsbuch," an exhibition book. It accompanied the Fall 2019 exhibition on Adele Schopenhauer (1797–1849), "Weil ich so individuell bin," in the Goethe and Schiller Archive in Weimar, the first exhibit to be dedicated solely to this artist and writer. Francesca Fabbri, a fellow of the Weimar Klassik Stiftung, researched holdings in Weimar collections and identified more letters, manuscripts, and anonymous publications and artworks than previously established. The exhibition was curated by Fabbri in collaboration with Weimar Klassik researcher Claudia Häfner and accompanied by several lectures. To readers of the *Goethe Yearbook*, Adele Schopenhauer is known for her artistic cutouts and arabesques as well as her writings, among them poems, fairy tales, an autobiographical novel and diaries. During her lifetime and throughout the nineteenth century, she was overshadowed by her mother, the writer and salonnière Johanna Schopenhauer, and her brother, the philosopher Arthur.

Among the pictures are a miniature painting of Goethe's garden house on a phial, eminent examples of Adeles *Scherenschnitte*, illustrations of the gospel, drawings in her reading diary, an 1843 watercolor drawing attributed to Allwina Frommann of the Berlin house with Adele who visited Frommann, the female owner of the house, and the student Wolfgang Maximilian von Goethe, each in separate quarters, as well as letters and diaries. Also included are Walter von

Goethe's obituary in the *Allgemeine Zeitung* and a complete transcript of the 1852 gift agreement between Schopenhauer's heiress Sibylle Mertens-Schaaffhausen and the state of Weimar with a list of all items and their valuations. The latter documents her considerable library. The illustrations are predominantly in color and of the highest quality, making it a pleasure to explore the richness and detail of the miniatures, arabesques, and cutouts and of her precise handwriting.

The book is more than a richly illustrated catalogue of the exhibited objects and an overview of her estate in the Weimar archives. The chapters by coauthors Häfner and Fabbri provide an overview of her complex biography and creative efforts, survey research, and editions of her works, as well as Adele's representation in literary and filmic works, marking open research questions. Schopenhauer's correspondence with Goethe regarding his efforts of collecting art and antiquities, her collaboration with his grandson Walter on an opera, the editing of her mother's literary estate, and the collaborative and mentoring nature of her friendships with creative women such as Ottilie von Goethe and Annette von Droste-Hülshoff are just a few aspects of her interests and connections explored in this book. Throughout their essays, Häfner and Fabbri point out new discoveries such as Adele's "silent" contributions to works by her mother or her reviews of literary and artistic works published in German papers while she lived in Italy during the last years of her life. The book also contains a substantial bibliography and will be of interest to anyone studying and researching creative women in the nineteenth century.

*University of Iowa*	*Waltraud Maierhofer*

Rengenier C. Rittersma, **Mytho-Poetics at Work: A Study of the Figure of Egmont, the Dutch Revolt and its Influence in Europe.** Leiden: Brill, 2018. xiv + 416 pp.

Does or did Egmont—Lamoral, Count of Egmont—rise to the level of myth? And, assuming he did, what can we learn about the process of "mythogenesis" by carefully tracking the circulation of his name and narrative, beginning with eye-witness reports of his execution on June 5, 1568, moving on to historiographical representations by authors writing in at least five languages, and culminating in the occurrence of the mythical Egmont in well-known works by Goethe and Schiller, as well as the anonymously authored *Beytrag zur Lebensgeschichte des berühmten Grafen von Egmond* (1785) and the Brabant pamphlet *Éloge du Comte Egmont, dédié aux États de Brabant à l'occasion de la Journée Glorieuse du 30 Mai 1787*? These are the questions posed by Rengenier Rittersma's monograph.

Rittersma approaches the concept of myth from the perspective of a trio of theorists: André Jolles, Hans Blumenberg, and Roland Barthes—simple form, linkage to history, and semiotic function. In "remarks," either "preliminary" or "concluding," that frame the three main parts of the book and the book itself, Rittersma offers lively reflections on how mythogenesis works. According to him, the myth of Egmont amounts to Egmont's "afterlife." His mythic status depends on and begins with "the swoop of the blade," which both exalted him and fixed the components of his myth to a limited and consistent set. Nonetheless, Rittersma calls the insinuating power of Egmont's myth a "cultural fungus" in comparison to the process of "mycorrhiza," referring to the way myth organizes its representation within new cultural constellations. In an afterword to his final concluding remarks, Rittersma gets geological when he asserts that the Egmont myth "occasionally seems organic, like the course of a river, in which periods lacking the presence of 'Egmont' remain connected to the main stream via subterranean channels." Since Egmont's headwaters begin with his execution, unlike the "secrecy-laden beginnings of the [William] Tell and Joan of Arc myths," no matter where Egmont pops up from subterranean depths, there are limits to the myth's "capacity for variation and, while it permitted most reinterpretations and different points of emphasis, it provided no occasions for 'new constructs.'" If Egmont operates/operated as a myth, then only in a constrained and limited way.

Rittersma understands Egmont as belonging to a set of "mythical companions" who share the property of martyrdom: William Tell, Joan of Arc, Arminius, and Carlo Guiliani, the young protestor shot dead by police at a G8 summit in Genoa in 2001. It's interesting company. While William Tell and Joan of Arc may still have some global currency, Arminius has largely disappeared (and I wonder about his range, in the first, place outside of certain German traditions) and, with a film and a song, the martyred Carlo Guiliani is still in the infancy of his mythogenesis. None of these rises to the level of a Gilgamesh, Jesus, or Faust, to name some of the mythical figures productively analyzed in similar ways by scholars such as Theodore Ziolkowski. As for Egmont, what diminishing currency he still has, I would argue, depends almost entirely on Goethe's play. Rittersma doesn't disagree. Were it not for Goethe's and Schiller's contributions, Egmont would hardly have an afterlife of note.

For Rittersma, "the year 1787–1788 turned out to be the quintessential *Egmont* year"—five separate accounts of the count in a matter of merely seventeen months! And not geographically confined to Weimar-Jena. The myth of Egmont also surfaced in Rome, Naples, and the Austrian Netherlands (though all of them are linked to Goethe). Although these claims are inflationary, Rittersma is making an important point. Others such as Dieter Borchmeyer have noticed the connections between Goethe's *Egmont* and the political circumstances of the liberal reforms of Emperor Joseph II leading up to the Brabant Revolution of 1789–90. Rittersma makes extensive use of the archival record of Goethe's conversations in Naples and Rome with the Duke and Duchess d'Ursel, members of the nobility in the Austrian Netherlands, to argue that their embodied insights drove home for Goethe the vital connection between Egmont's struggle with Philipp II, on the one hand, and the Brabantians' opposition to Joseph II, on the other. Rittersma's argument is that it was a confluence of unique and fortuitous circumstances (including what the young Goethe found in his father's library) that congealed in 1787. What the eighteenth century contributed to the fleshing out of the simple myth of Egmont was an anthropological vision of what we know as "der ganze Mensch" in stark and violent contrast with the kind of political reality that disposed of him. I agree with Rittersma on this point. But I also wonder if we are still in the realm of mythogenesis or more likely operating within the paradigm of the history of ideas?

For scholars of Goethe and Schiller, Rittersma performs an invaluable service. He exhaustively surveys the sources—all of the eye-witness accounts and all the historiographies that Goethe and Schiller consulted, regardless of language: Latin, Dutch, English, French, German, and Italian. You knew that the accounts of Emanuel van Meteren and Famiano Strada, for example, were important, but your access was limited—no longer.

In a footnote to his introduction, Rittersma conjectures that "it is probably only a matter of time before Disney (similar to its Pochahontas film) brings this historical subject [Egmont] to the screen." I think we can safely regard that as highly unlikely. In decades past, Egmont might have had a shot at the Classics Illustrated comic book series—after all, Faust made it. For my money, the most compelling instantiation—and repudiation—of the Egmont myth is to be found in Nico Rost's *Goethe in Dachau* (2001). As allied troops and SS exchange fire in the night before liberation, Rost rereads Goethe's *Egmont.* "[Egmont ist] im Grunde stets der Edelmann geblieben und [hat] die Freiheit, für die das Bürgertum kämpfte, niemals zu seiner Freiheit gemacht, sondern den 'aufrührerischen' Bürgern [zugerufen]: 'Was an euch ist, Ruhe zu halten, Leute, das tut; ihr seid übel genug angeschrieben. . . .' Ähnliche Ratschläge haben wir in den letzten Jahren ja oft genug gehört! So viele Egmonts haben so zu denen gesprochen, die für die Freiheit kämpften." The timely untimeliness of Egmont in 1787 turned out to be fleeting. As a framework for unfolding the layers of semantic and narrative reorganization in the time between the beheading of Egmont and Goethe's play, Rittersma's mythogenesis has heuristic value. As for the mythical status of Egmont: I am not convinced.

*University of Pennsylvania*                                      *Simon Richter*

Steven Y. Wilkerson, **A Most Mysterious Union: The Role of Alchemy in Goethe's *Faust.*** Asheville, NC: Chiron, 2019. 386 pp.

This is a *very* introductory book. The author's choice to write an introduction has yielded a study with the predictable strengths and weaknesses. There is much to recommend this book to beginners, either with Goethe, with alchemy, with Jung, or with all three. It is for the most part intelligent and lucidly written. It begins with a capsule biography of Goethe, then proceeds logically to an introduction to alchemy, to a short biography of Jung, to the centrality of his alchemical studies, to an interpretation of *Faust*, and finally to brief considerations of other texts, Faustian and otherwise.

Alas, the book also displays the weaknesses of an introduction. It replicates information that is easily found elsewhere. Indeed, *A Most Mysterious Union* consists largely of citations and allusions to extant studies, chiefly Gray's *Goethe the Alchemist* (1952) and Raff's *Jung and the Alchemical Imagination* (2000). It is telling that the author closely follows Ronald Gray's nearly seventy-year-old book. (Alice Raphael's 1965 *Goethe and the Philosopher's Stone* is not mentioned, either in the body or in the bibliography: Could Wilkerson possibly be ignorant of it?) Seventy years is a long time, and there has been a flood of work on Goethe and alchemy since then. None of it finds its way into Wilkerson's bibliography. I fear that he greatly underestimates the widespread acceptance of the influence of alchemy on Goethe and the sophistication of the insights that have been generated in the interim.

Moreover, the biography of Goethe quotes several *nineteenth-century* studies, and is rather Victorian in simultaneously condemning Goethe's affairs and being titillated by them. Reading the biography, one might think that Goethe squeezed his writing into the little time left after his Byronesque adventures with women. Those of us who have lived through the sixties are not impressed by a 39-year-old virgin.

The most original section of the book is the end, where the author compares Goethe's *Faust* with Marlowe's, Mann's, Dante's *Divina Commedia*, and, oddly,

Bunyan's *Pilgrim's Progress*. These comparisons are, however, lamentably simplistic and wrongheaded. At multiple key points, Wilkerson demurs even recapitulating the central tenets of Gray's and Raff's studies. Why not simply skip this book and read them instead?

*University of Michigan*                                                    *Frederick Amrine*

W. Daniel Wilson. **Der faustische Pakt. Goethe und die Goethe-Gesellschaft im Dritten Reich.** Munich: dtv, 2018. 368 pp.

Daniel Wilson, now a professor emeritus in the Department of Languages, Literatures and Cultures at the Royal Holloway College at the University of London, has again opened up the Goethe industry to new insights, after his earlier works that have taken the author out of the cotton wool in which the notion of "Weimar classicism" had wrapped him. *Der faustische Pakt* turns our attention to the Goethe-Gesellschaft (Goethe Society), founded in 1885, to show how its claimed affinities to the humanism disguised a long-standing commitment to conservative nationalist views and an alignment with the Nazi regime—to creating a Goethe who would ultimately become commensurate with Nazi ideology and cultural imperatives.

Wilson adduces facts drawn from many archives to produce a well-researched and superbly written story of cultural opportunism that illuminates the many shades of grey in the cultural politics of the Nazi era, and how their legacies remain at play today. Most critically, he has filled in precise details about the post-May-1933 organization of the society, which have been vague since 1945 when its organizational files disappeared. Wilson found instead the correspondence of the leadership to tell an increasingly disturbing story of scholarly humanism.

The alignment of the Goethe Society with the Nazi cultural projects started slow. From its early years on, the Goethe Society had been an important cultural reference point for the *Bildungsbürgertum*, the educated population of Germany. Gustav Roethe, the society's president until 1926, worked toward establishing Goethe as an internationalist and moved to consolidate individual local author societies under the national organization. Receiving no state support, the society boasted a considerable membership as well as patronage by the ruling aristocracy.

As the Weimar Republic's financial crises led to declining memberships, reimaging Goethe as an antisemite made him a potential asset for Nazi cultural politics. The Nazi government had begun to intervene in organizations after 1933 in its move toward a kind of cultural *Gleichschaltung*; the Goethe Society was vulnerable initially to charges of liberalism because 8 percent of its members were Jewish and 20 percent international, with the result that after 1933 the society did not admit any new Jewish members (keeping many that they had for financial reasons until a 1938 general exclusion). "Jewish" themes like Goethe's interest in Spinoza were kept out of the society's journal; Roethe's cosmopolitan and tolerant Goethe was refigured as an antisemite, with skirmishes at both local and national levels of the organization. By the 1936 Olympics, new funding became possible as part of Germany's image building—and the society found its lifeline in ways effaced or denied after the war.

In the volume's first chapter, "Goethes Janusgesicht," Wilson draws out how these two possible readings of the author were crafted out of a body of work large enough to find support for both readings. The subsequent six chapters are organized chronologically to chart this course in detail; they are solidly documented, based on the private correspondence of important members of the society's leadership and internal records of the society's business and meetings. What emerges is the society's sense of dedication to its cultural mission under a pronounced sense of threat, leading to decision-making that prioritized the society's survival at all costs.

The prime mover in this preemptive decision-making was Hans Wahl, the vice president of the society and director of the National Goethe Museum, who became a party member in 1938 and an early member of the "Kampfbundes für deutsche Kultur," which put the organization under the patronage (but not direct control) of Joseph Goebbels and his *Reichsschrifttumskammer* and helped it to evade the total government takeovers that were becoming increasingly common and that often required wholesale surrender of archives and museum holdings. Instead, the Goethe Society preserved itself as it fell into a kind of codetermination and collaboration with government institutions. These decisions, however, created a questionable legacy of scholarship not adequately reassessed to this day.

Wilson's work is exquisitely argued and documented, a product of a clever researcher with much experience in Weimar cultural history and in telling uncomfortable stories hidden behind the *Klassiker-Mythos*. The result is a volume that reads almost like a novel, telling a morality fable about the politics of hegemonic cultures and how they can be used and abused. This book is a must for any Goethe scholar so that the persistent legacy of work by members of the Goethe Society can finally be confronted. They acted not only as productive academics but also as collaborators (based on various motivations, from resistance and self-preservation to full-throated approval of Nazi ideologies).

*University of Texas at Austin*                                          *Katherine Arens*

Paula Wojcik, Stefan Matuschek, Sophie Picard, and Monika Wolting, eds. **Klassik als Kulturelle Praxis. Funktional, Intermedial, Transkulturell.** Spectrum Literaturwissenschaft, vol. 62. Berlin: De Gruyter, 2019. 577 pp.

*What a classic!* What is the first thing you associate with the word classic? The classic in question could be a book, film, or even a play or design aesthetic. Classic can refer to so many things and, without context, one is left guessing as to what, precisely, the classic referent is. This edited volume strives to create several working definitions of the elusive term "classic." The term is especially tricky in the German-speaking context, where the term can be used to refer to a specific literary period: *Weimarer Klassik*. In both English and German, the classics can also refer to classical studies (i.e., the study of classical antiquity) and the ancient world in general. The volume does not focus on any literary period in particular but rather emphasizes the need to make the terms classic and classical contemporary rather than treating them as a fixed point in time. Classics are a ubiquitous aspect of everyday life, which Wojcik et al. note has lead to the semantic overloading (*Überfrachtung*) of the concept *Klassik*. Semantic ambiguity is primarily what hinders the creation of a single working definition. As the subtitle would suggest, the ultimate goal is a multitude of functional, medial, and transcultural definitions rather than one vague, imprecise one.

The volume's six subsections are a testament to its interdisciplinary and comparative focus. Section 1 considers the current state of the term "classic" and its contemporary uses. The transition of classic works to new forms of mass media such as radio and television are examined in section 2. The theme of section 3 is cultural icons as a form of classic. Section 4 focuses on intermediality as a means of mediation. The final two sections deal with cultural appropriation in both intermedial (section 5) and intertextual terms (section 6).

Canonical German authors most certainly make a good showing in the volume, but the forms in which internationally canonical texts such as Johann Wolfgang von Goethe's *Die Leiden des jungen Werthers* appear in are what make it a necessary addition to the Spectrum Literaturwissenschaft series. The explorations of how classics have evolved as they are adapted to radio, film, comic strips, graphic novels, and reimagined novels proves that classics do not inherently need to be boring or tired. On the example of Goethe's oeuvre alone, everything from mashup novels to rapped recitations of *Erlkönig* are cited as evidence of classical works having clearly moved beyond their static texts of origin to become a body of works centered around the aforementioned canonical point of origin.

Transnational interpretations and adaptations of classics is another focal point, which demonstrates the wide reaching, indeed global, impact of canonical classics and their expansion to different media. The currently popular forms of comics and graphic novels have proved a fruitful venue for modern interpretations of well-known classics. Comic adaptations discussed include Beckett's *Waiting for Godot*, Conscience's *Löwe von Flandern*, the profane comic anthology *Chopin New Romantic*, and a manga of Choderlos de Laclos's *Les Liasons Dangereuses*.

The increased representation of authors with multiple cultural identities (e.g., Turkish German, Iranian German) has also broadened transnational and transcultural perspectives within the German context. In the case of Ilse Nagelschmidt's essay "Vom Klassiker zum Kultbuch. Goethes *Werther* und Feridun Zaimoglus *Liebesmale, scharlachrot,*" intertextuality and transnationalism are simultaneously at play. Adaptations studies further show how transcultural and multilingual adaptations of classics bring these texts to broader audiences beyond the confines of the original's language of origin. Such works are not mere translations as can be seen in the examples of the comics mentioned in the previous paragraph. Parodies of classics are another form that transcends national and cultural boundaries.

Because of its comparative bent and interrogation of the specific brand of "classic literature" championed in school and university curricula, this volume will be of interest to literary scholars and students alike, although it is unlikely that many students would read these essays without the prompting of a teacher or professor. Debates on the literary canon have become a prominent fixture in classrooms and university seminars alike. Such discussions often emerge in public forums in connection to reading curricula and the banning or censorship of books in schools. In a broader sense, classics continue to influence and define so many facets of everyday life to the point that the term's ubiquity alone makes a compelling case for continued efforts to incorporate working definitions of it into academic settings as well.

*Vanderbilt University*                                    *Marissa Schoedel*